THE OXFORD HANDBOOK OF
MORAL REALISM

THE OXFORD HANDBOOK OF
MORAL REALISM

Edited by
PAUL BLOOMFIELD
and
DAVID COPP

Oxford University Press is a department of the University of Oxford. It furthers
the University's objective of excellence in research, scholarship, and education
by publishing worldwide. Oxford is a registered trade mark of Oxford University
Press in the UK and certain other countries.

Published in the United States of America by Oxford University Press
198 Madison Avenue, New York, NY 10016, United States of America.

© Oxford University Press 2023

All rights reserved. No part of this publication may be reproduced, stored in
a retrieval system, or transmitted, in any form or by any means, without the
prior permission in writing of Oxford University Press, or as expressly permitted
by law, by license, or under terms agreed with the appropriate reproduction
rights organization. Inquiries concerning reproduction outside the scope of the
above should be sent to the Rights Department, Oxford University Press, at the
address above.

You must not circulate this work in any other form
and you must impose this same condition on any acquirer.

Library of Congress Control Number: 20239443463
ISBN 978-0-19-006822-6

DOI: 10.1093/oxfordhb/9780190068226.001.0001

Printed by Marquis Book Printing, Canada

Contents

List of Contributors	ix
Introduction	xi

I. ABOUT MORAL REALISM AND ITS VARIETIES

1. Defining Moral Realism JENNIFER FOSTER AND MARK SCHROEDER	3
2. Metaphysical Structure for Moral Realists TRISTRAM MCPHERSON	18
3. Moral Realism and Objectivity SIGRÚN SVAVARSDÓTTIR	44
4. Epistemology for Realists SARAH MCGRATH	66
5. The Bearing of Moral Rationalism on Moral Realism MICHAEL SMITH	84
6. Does Anything We Care about Distinguish the Non-Natural from the Natural? MARK VAN ROOJEN	106
7. Ethical Naturalism, Non-Naturalism, and In-Between RALPH WEDGWOOD	131
8. Can a Moral Judgment Be Moorean? WILLIAM G. LYCAN	156
9. Real Ethics SIMON BLACKBURN	173

II. NATURALISM

10. Ethical Naturalism: Problems and Prospects — 193
    LOUISE ANTONY AND ERNESTO V. GARCIA

11. Ethical Realism and Robust Normativity — 220
    DAVID COPP

12. Moral Functionalism — 246
    FRANK JACKSON AND PHILIP PETTIT

13. Function, Fitness, Flourishing — 264
    PAUL BLOOMFIELD

14. Realism about the Good For Human Beings — 293
    L. NANDI THEUNISSEN

III. NON-NATURALISM

15. Moral Conceptual Truths — 317
    JOHN BENGSON, TERENCE CUNEO, AND RUSS SHAFER-LANDAU

16. Five Kinds of Epistemic Arguments against Robust Moral Realism — 345
    JOSHUA SCHECHTER

17. The Explanatory Roles of Moral Facts and the Case for Moral Realism — 370
    ROBERT AUDI

18. Derek Parfit's Non-Naturalist Cognitivism — 387
    ROGER CRISP

19. Ardent Moral Realism and the Value-Laden World — 414
    WILLIAM J. FITZPATRICK

20. Oh, All the Wrongs I Could Have Performed! Or: Why Care about Morality, Robustly Realistically Understood — 434
    DAVID ENOCH AND ITAMAR WEINSHTOCK SAADON

IV. NEITHER NATURALISM NOR NON-NATURALISM

21. Response-Dependent Realism 465
    MARK LeBAR

22. Deflationary Metaethics 484
    PAUL HORWICH

23. On the Properties of Quietism and Robustness 505
    MATTHEW H. KRAMER

24. Prospects for a Quietist Moral Realism 526
    MARK D. WARREN AND AMIE L. THOMASSON

25. Moral Anti-Exceptionalism 554
    TIMOTHY WILLIAMSON

Index 577

Contributors

Louise Antony, Professor Emerita, University of Massachusetts, Amherst

Robert Audi, John A. O'Brien Professor of Philosophy, University of Notre Dame

John Bengson, Associate Professor, University of Texas at Austin

Simon Blackburn, formerly Professor of Philosophy at the University of Cambridge, and Edna J. Koury Distinguished Professor of Philosophy at the University of North Carolina, Chapel Hill

Paul Bloomfield, Professor, University of Connecticut

David Copp, Distinguished Professor, Emeritus, University of California, Davis

Roger Crisp, Director, Oxford Uehiro Centre for Practical Ethics; Professor of Moral Philosophy, University of Oxford; Uehiro Fellow and Tutor in Philosophy, St. Anne's College, Oxford

Terence Cuneo, Professor and Marsh Chair of Intellectual and Moral Philosophy, University of Vermont

David Enoch, Professor, The Hebrew University of Jerusalem

William J. FitzPatrick, Gideon Webster Burbank Professor of Intellectual and Moral Philosophy, University of Rochester

Jennifer Foster, PhD Candidate, University of Southern California

Ernesto V. Garcia, Assistant Professor, University of Massachusetts Amherst

Paul Horwich, Professor, New York University

Frank Jackson, Emeritus Professor, Australian National University

Matthew H. Kramer, Professor of Legal and Political Philosophy, Cambridge University

Mark LeBar, Professor, Florida State University

William G. Lycan, William Rand Kenan, Jr. Professor Emeritus, University of North Carolina

Sarah McGrath, Professor, Princeton University

Tristram McPherson, Professor, The Ohio State University

Philip Pettit, L. S. Rockefeller University Professor of Human Values, Princeton University, and Distinguished Professor of Philosophy, Australian National University

Mark van Roojen, Professor, University of Nebraska-Lincoln

Joshua Schechter, Professor, Brown University

Mark Schroeder, Professor, University of Southern California

Russ Shafer-Landau, Professor, University of Wisconsin-Madison

Michael Smith, McCosh Professor of Philosophy, Princeton University

Sigrún Svavarsdóttir, Associate Professor, Tufts University

L. Nandi Theunissen, Associate Professor, University of Pittsburgh

Amie L. Thomasson, Daniel P. Stone Professor of Intellectual and Moral Philosophy, Dartmouth College

Mark D. Warren, Associate Professor, Daemen University

Ralph Wedgwood, Professor of Philosophy and Director of the School of Philosophy, University of Southern California

Itamar Weinshtock Saadon, PhD Candidate, Rutgers University

Timothy Williamson, Wykeham Professor of Logic, University of Oxford

Introduction

DAVID COPP AND PAUL BLOOMFIELD

WHAT is moral realism? And why does it matter whether moral realism is true? These are the questions we will address in this brief introduction. We will also explain the organization of the volume. We begin intuitively, with what we take to be the basic idea that underlies moral realism, and with several considerations that we think motivate it. The basic realist idea requires elaboration and articulation, and we will turn to this task later in the introduction. We conclude with a brief overview of the volume.

The fundamental thought underlying moral realism, we think, can be expressed as a *parity thesis*.[1] There are many kinds of facts, including physical, psychological, mathematical, temporal, and moral facts. *In that they are facts*, they have the same basic metaphysical status, *whatever that is*. There are many kinds of properties, including physical, psychological, mathematical, temporal, and moral properties. *In that they are properties*, they have the same basic metaphysical status, *whatever that is*. There are also many kinds of judgments, including moral judgments and judgments of the other kinds just listed. *In being judgments*, they have the same basic metaphysical status, *whatever that is*. These judgments are all beliefs, and some of our moral beliefs are true. *In that they are true*, they have the same basic metaphysical status as truths about other matters, *whatever that is*. The parity thesis does not rule out there being a variety of differences among facts and properties of different kinds. It only says that they are facts and properties, and that in this respect they are on a par.

Of course, there are obvious differences between a moral judgment and a judgment about ordinary non-moral matters. Moral judgments are normative and they have a bearing on what to do or what to choose or how to feel, whereas judgments about ordinary non-moral matters are non-normative. Furthermore, there are obvious differences between moral facts and properties and ordinary, non-moral ones. Many philosophers, including many who are moral realists, would claim in particular that moral facts and properties are too different from ordinary empirical or naturalistic ones for it to be possible that they *are* empirical or naturalistic ones (Enoch 2011: 4; also Parfit 2011, vol. 2: 325). These ideas and claims are, however, compatible with the realist's parity thesis. The parity thesis claims only a minimal parity. It says only that there are moral beliefs, just as there are beliefs about other subject matters, and moral facts, and properties, just as

---

[1] This idea is in Copp, forthcoming.

there are facts and properties in other domains, and it says that, *in being beliefs, facts, and properties*, these have the same basic metaphysical status. Realists agree with this, but why? Why would one accept the parity thesis?

There is a great deal that can be said, and that has been said, for and against moral realism. In this introduction, we will be content if we can at least motivate the realist position. We will not be able to consider objections to it in any serious way.

The first thing to be said in favor of the parity thesis is that, at first look, it seems obviously true, and it seems to be something that all of us with moral views are committed to accepting. Presumably all of us would agree that torture is at least pro tanto wrong. This is to say that we believe this, and that we take it to be true, just as we believe that torture is widespread, and we take that to be true. There is the obvious difference here that one of these beliefs is about a moral matter and the other is about an ordinary non-moral empirical matter, but on the face of things, there being this difference does not conflict with the parity thesis. It does not mean that the moral belief is different *qua belief* from the empirical one, or that the moral fact we are committed to is different (or would be different) *qua fact* from the empirical one that we are also committed to, or that the moral property of wrongness is different *qua property* from the empirical one. On the face of things, there is a parity of the minimal kind that the parity thesis claims. Why think otherwise? Why not accept that there is the parity that seems to be there, especially since accepting that there is this parity seems to be the simplest way to understand the appearance of parity?

A second point is closely related to the first. When people disagree about a moral issue, such as whether capital punishment is morally acceptable, each side thinks that the other side's belief is mistaken. This is on a par with how people think when they disagree about something in mathematics or astronomy. Each thinks that the other one has a mistaken belief. There is an apparent parity here. Indeed, it would be hard to make sense of disagreements in belief without the presumption that the disagreeing parties each assumed they believe the truth and that the other person believes falsely, and this is no less true in the case of moral disagreement than in the case of disagreement about other matters. The simplest way to explain the appearance of parity in the nature of disagreement is to think the parity is real.

The third point concerns moral error. We know that we disagree with other people about moral matters. And when we disagree, we think the other person is in error. Sometimes we change our minds, and when we do, we think that we used to be in error. So we think that moral error is possible. Indeed, we think that everyone can be wrong about some moral facts, and perhaps even that "global moral error" is possible. Women have always been the moral equals of men, even long ago when (practically) everyone believed otherwise. We can imagine an entire world of people committed to a "caste system" that erroneously denies the basic equality of people. We can each concede that we might even now have certain erroneous moral beliefs that we have never learned about and never will learn about. We can imagine moral errors that all of us are currently making that we have not yet discovered. So, we recognize that moral error is possible, and we think that there actually are cases of moral error, just as we recognize error in other fields. This supports the parity thesis. It seems that if moral error is possible, then morality is not "up to us," and the moral facts are "out there" to be discovered, just as in other fields of thought. The parity thesis captures this idea, as well as the idea that our moral judgments can either be, or fail to be, responsive to the moral facts, just in the way that other beliefs can either be, or fail to be, responsive to the facts.

The fourth thing to be said in favor of the parity thesis is that, unless it is true, it would be difficult to make sense of our taking morality as seriously as we do, in the way that we do. Those of us who take morality seriously believe that the moral facts appropriately regulate our behavior and our interpersonal relations in a way that mere matters of preference or taste do not. If our moral judgments were non-cognitive attitudes, preferences, or feelings, such as a feeling of abhorrence at the thought of torture, they would be akin to a taste for chocolate or an abhorrence of licorice. There would be no issue whether they are true in any robust sense, and it would be optional whether to take them into account in our decision-making. We do take our tastes seriously, of course. We aim to have a supply of chocolate on hand, and there is a worldwide trade in chocolate because so many people enjoy it. But the tastiness of the chocolate is basically a matter of our response to the chocolate, a response that might have been different, and we would not have been at fault in any way if we had not liked chocolate. But we take our moral beliefs seriously in a different manner. We take it that the wrongness of torture is a feature of torture that we would be *at fault* not to recognize and that we *ought* to take into account, when appropriate, in our thinking and in our decisions.

Fifth, in his argument about "objectivity's implications" (Enoch 2011: chap. 2), David Enoch contends that, although there is room for moral disagreement, there is no room for *negotiation* about what is morally required, or about what to do in light of what is required. But there is room to negotiate about what to do when people have different preferences or tastes. Should we have fish or beef for dinner? If the choice is merely a matter of preference or taste, we can negotiate, if we differ. But if it is a moral matter, and if it is wrong to eat meat, then if we take morality seriously, we will see that there is no room for negotiation about what we ought to do. (There might be a need to negotiate what we *will* do, but that's a different matter.) The truth of realism would explain this difference between moral facts and facts about preferences or taste.

A sixth point was made by Christine Korsgaard. She pointed out that morality can require us to make major sacrifices, and we need to explain why anyone would be willing to make such sacrifices (1996: 10–16).[2] This would be hard to explain if morality were simply a matter of preference or taste. If there weren't moral facts "out there"—facts that are not in one's control—and facts that purport to regulate our behavior in a way that is not optional, people would surely exercise the option not to make a major sacrifice even if morality required it.

A seventh point is that those of us who take morality seriously refer to what we take to be the moral facts, and treat them as facts, in deliberating about what to do and how

---

[2] She argues, however, that realism—which she called "substantive realism"—cannot provide an adequate account of the normativity of morality (Korsgaard 1996: 35–40). We won't go into her argument.

to live. It would be difficult to make sense of this if moral realism were not true. This idea is again due to Enoch, or, at least, it is one way to understand his argument about "deliberative indispensability" (Enoch 2011: chap. 3). Again, those who take morality seriously take it that the fundamental moral facts are "out there," out of one's control, and take it that these facts are such as to appropriately regulate our behavior in a way that is not optional. So, in deliberating about whether to have fish or beef for dinner, if we think it is a moral matter, we will refer, say, to the wrongness of eating meat and take this as a premise in our reasoning. But if the choice were merely a matter of preference or taste, we might or might not treat our preference in the same way. It would be optional whether to do this, whereas, if we take morality seriously, we do not think it is optional whether to treat our moral beliefs as setting constraints on our deliberation. Again, the truth of realism would explain this difference between moral facts and facts about preferences or taste.

To be clear, these are not by any means decisive arguments in favor of moral realism. For example, not every version of moral anti-realism construes morality as simply a matter of preference or taste. Nevertheless, we think that our arguments do make a strong prima facie case for realism. They are of the form: If one has moral beliefs, and if one takes morality seriously, then one is committed to certain further beliefs, and one will tend to have certain attitudes. And the *simplest* account of morality that entails the truth of these beliefs and the appropriateness of these attitudes is the moral realists' account. Other accounts might be available, however. And some moral skeptics would deny that it is appropriate to take morality seriously for one reason or another—that is, they would deny the appropriateness of the attitudes that we take to be involved in taking morality seriously, perhaps on the ground that, they think, morality is not authoritative in the way we take it to be. In any case, we hope we have made clear some of the reasons that might lead one to opt for a realist metaethics.

As we understand matters, moral realism involves certain doctrines that might not obviously follow from, or even be suggested by, the parity thesis. For this reason, and because it might be useful to spell out and emphasize certain aspects of the parity thesis, we will say more. We will first outline five main tenets of a minimal or "basic" moral realism. We will then consider the doctrine that distinguishes "mind-independent" realism from the basic form.[3]

The first doctrine characteristic of moral realism is the thesis that some *basic substantive* moral claims are *true*—with "true" understood literally, and in the sense in which an ordinary non-moral claim might be true. Geoff Sayre-McCord defined moral realism as the view that some moral claims, when construed literally, are literally true (1988: 5). But this is too weak to capture a disagreement between realists and anti-realists, because even anti-realists should agree that some moral claims are logical truths, some are analytic, and some are conceptual truths. For instance, it is true that any wrong action

---

[3] This approach to explicating the realist view was taken in Copp 2006. It is elaborated further in Copp, forthcoming.

is wrong. We describe such claims as "non-substantive," so we say that the realist holds that some *substantive* moral claims are true. But this also is too weak to capture a disagreement between realists and anti-realists, because there are some apparently substantive moral claims that even an anti-realist should agree to be true. Consider, for instance, the claim that either Davis is in California or lying is morally permissible. This is true since Davis is in California. Let us say that such claims are not "basic" moral claims, where a "basic" moral claim is a logically simple claim that ascribes (or at least purports to ascribe) a moral property to something. The claim that lying is wrong is basic, for example, and it is also substantive in our sense.[4] A realist holds that some such claims are true, with "true" understood literally, and in the sense in which an ordinary nonmoral claim might be true.

But even this is not enough to distinguish moral realism from every form of moral anti-realism. For some anti-realist "expressivists" have a deflationary theory of the meaning of "true," according to which some substantive basic moral claims can be true. Simon Blackburn's "quasi-realist expressivism" illustrates this idea (Blackburn 2006; see also his chapter in this volume). Blackburn and other anti-realists would, however, deny one or more of the following realist doctrines.

The second realist doctrine is that there are moral properties in the sense of "property" in which there are ordinary non-moral properties. There are many theories about the metaphysics of properties, and moral realists do not need to commit themselves on the question of which of these theories is preferable. But, as the parity thesis says, realists hold that, *in being properties*, moral properties have the same basic nature as non-moral properties. On one view, the "commonality view," to share a property is, roughly, to have something in common. On the commonality view, to claim that lying has the property of being widespread is to claim that it has something in common with other things that are widespread. To claim that lying has the property of being wrong, at least pro tanto, is to claim that lying has something in common with other actions that are pro tanto wrong. Accordingly, a realist might hold, actions that are wrong have something in common in virtue of which they are wrong. They share the property of being wrong. The second doctrine characteristic of moral realism is, then, that there are moral properties in whatever sense there are non-moral properties. Perhaps, for example, there are the properties of moral wrongness, of being a virtue, and so on.

Third, a moral realist holds that some moral properties are instantiated. Perhaps, for example, some kinds of action are wrong and some traits of character are virtues. The actual world includes persons, events, and states of affairs that have moral characteristics, such as that of being wrong or of being vicious or unjust.

Fourth, realists hold that the primary semantic role of moral predicates is to ascribe moral properties. The predicate "wrong" is used to ascribe wrongness; the predicate

---

[4] It is surprisingly difficult to define the idea of a "basic" moral claim. One issue is how to classify claims about permissibility. We think that permissibility consists in not being wrong. If this is right, then, on our definition, the claim that lying is permissible is not basic because it is logically complex, and it does not ascribe a moral property.

"just" is used to ascribe justice. And so on. Moral predicates ascribe moral properties just as ordinary non-moral predicates ascribe properties. On the commonality view, for instance, the sentence "Torture is wrong" ascribes to torture a similarity to other wrong kinds of action just as the sentence, "Torture is widespread," ascribes to torture a similarity to other kinds of action that are widespread. Moral language does not work in any special way that distinguishes its semantics fundamentally from the semantics of ordinary non-moral language.

Realists can take a hybrid view. They can hold, for example, that to call an action wrong is to express disapproval of the action, or of actions of its kind, *as well as* to ascribe wrongness. They can say that at least some moral predicates are used both to express non-cognitive states of mind and to ascribe moral properties. Slurs illustrate this idea. There are linguistic conventions governing the use of slurs, such as "frog," such that to call someone by such a term both categorizes her as belonging to a certain group and expresses contempt or some other pejorative attitude toward the person and others who belong to the group. A realist might think there are similar linguistic conventions governing the use of moral predicates. But, the realist insists, this does not gainsay the point that the primary semantic role of the moral predicates is to ascribe moral properties (see Copp 2007: chap. 5).

Fifth, moral assertions express *beliefs*—representational states that have propositional contents, and that are true just in case their propositional contents are true. For example, the assertion that certain kinds of action are wrong expresses the belief that certain kinds of action are wrong, and this belief is true just in case certain kinds of action are wrong. The fifth point is simply that moral assertions do not express states of mind that are different in any fundamental way from the states of mind expressed by ordinary assertions. Ordinary assertions express ordinary beliefs. And, the realist holds, if I assert that torture is wrong, I express the belief that torture is wrong, which is an ordinary belief even though it is normative. Moral realists hold that moral beliefs have the same basic metaphysical nature as other beliefs.

We can call the position that accepts the five doctrines we have been articulating, "basic moral realism" or "minimal realism."

There are additional distinctions that can be drawn among kinds of moral realism. Most important, perhaps, is the distinction between theories that accept and those that deny the thesis that moral facts and properties are "mind-independent." An example of a theory that denies this thesis, and views moral facts as *mind-dependent*, is the "caricaturized subjectivism" that Enoch criticizes (2011: 24–27). According to this view, "[m]oral judgments report simple preferences, ones that are exactly on a par with a preference for playing tennis or for catching a movie" (Enoch 2011: 25). On this view, the assertion that lying is wrong reports that the speaker prefers that people not lie. This view treats the moral facts (indexed to a particular person) as facts about the preferences of that person, so it treats the moral facts as mind-dependent. It perhaps qualifies as an example of basic moral realism, but, despite this, many and perhaps most philosophers would insist that it should not be considered to be genuinely realist.

The rationale for the idea that caricaturized subjectivism is not a form of moral realism can be made clear if we think back to the seven considerations that we used to motivate realism. Several of these considerations distinguished moral facts from facts about preferences or taste. A few of them relied on the idea that the moral facts are "out there," out of one's control, and that they are such as to appropriately regulate our behavior in a way that is not optional. But it is optional whether to regulate our behavior by our preferences. For example, I might prefer to see one movie but happily go to a different movie on a whim. In any event, caricaturized subjectivism is highly implausible, and, further, the seven-part case we made in support of moral realism rules it out, as not a form of realism. But it is one thing to hold that this theory is incompatible with the basic motivation for moral realism. It is another thing to claim that *any* theory that treats the moral facts as mind-dependent is incompatible with the basic motivation for moral realism. Part of the problem is that it is unclear what exactly is meant by "mind-dependence" when philosophers propose that a realist theory must not treat the moral facts as mind-dependent.

Roderick Firth proposed a theory, for example, according to which, very roughly, the nature of the moral facts is determined by the reactions of an "ideal observer," someone who has all the relevant non-moral facts clearly to mind, who makes no logical mistakes in reasoning, who is appropriately impartial, and so on (Firth 1952). A theory of this kind would seem to treat the moral facts as mind-dependent. Whether lying is wrong, on this theory, depends on the hypothetical state of mind of an hypothetical being who had all the relevant non-moral facts clearly to mind, made no logical mistakes, was appropriately impartial, and so on. But, on this theory, at least on a plausible interpretation, the moral facts are "out there," out of anyone's control. No-one controls how an ideal observer would react. Further, a simple divine command theory treats the moral facts as dependent on the commands of God, which are out of the control of any human being even though they are dependent on what God chooses to command. It is not clear that the motivation we offered for moral realism should be taken to rule out *all* theories that treat the moral facts as mind-dependent.

To avoid becoming embroiled in this issue here, in explicating moral realism, we will say that there are kinds of basic moral realism that *reject* the mind-independence thesis as well as kinds of basic moral realism that *accept* the mind-independence thesis. This volume includes chapters that defend basic moral realism—such as Michael Smith's chapter—as well as those that defend forms of mind-independent realism—such as David Enoch's chapter.

The final distinction that is relevant here is between naturalistic and non-naturalistic forms of moral realism. Moral naturalism holds, and non-naturalism denies, that the moral facts are *natural* ones. Further, the naturalist thinks, moral properties are natural ones; they have the same basic metaphysical status as ordinary natural properties such as solidity, deciduousness, and the property of being a railroad car. There is room to debate exactly what these claims come to, of course, and the issue is debated in some of the chapters in this volume. The volume includes chapters that are aimed at supporting moral naturalism—such as, again, Michael Smith's chapter—as well as those that aim to support non-naturalism—such as, again, David Enoch's chapter.

The volume is organized into four parts. The first, "About Moral Realism and Its Varieties," includes chapters that work at a meta-level. For example, an essay might discuss the distinctions we have drawn in this introduction, challenging them, or contending that they are not exhaustive. There is, for example, the article by Simon Blackburn contending that a kind of "quasi-realist expressivism" has all the intuitive advantages that we allege moral realism has. The second part of the volume includes chapters that develop one or another form of moral naturalism. The third includes expositions and defenses of moral non-naturalism. And the fourth, "Neither Naturalism nor Non-Naturalism," includes chapters that develop and argue for versions of moral realism that appear to be neither naturalistic nor non-naturalistic. Timothy Williamson argues vigorously against anti-realist positions, but without taking a position on the debate about naturalism. Also in the fourth section are chapters advocating or discussing so-called quietism and deflationary positions.

References

Blackburn, Simon. 2006. "Anti-Realist Expressivism and Quasi-Realism." In *The Oxford Handbook of Ethical Theory*, edited by David Copp, 146–162. New York: Oxford University Press.

Copp, David. 2006. "Introduction." In *The Oxford Handbook of Ethical Theory*, edited by David Copp, 3–35. New York: Oxford University Press.

Copp, David. 2007. *Morality in a Natural World*. Cambridge: Cambridge University Press.

Copp, David. Forthcoming. *Ethical Naturalism and the Problem of Normativity*. New York: Oxford University Press.

Enoch, David. 2011. *Taking Morality Seriously*. Oxford: Oxford University Press.

Firth, Roderick. 1952. "Ethical Absolutism and the Ideal Observer." *Philosophy and Phenomenological Research* 12: 317–345.

Korsgaard, Christine M. 1996. *The Sources of Normativity*. Cambridge: Cambridge University Press.

Parfit, Derek. 2011. *On What Matters*. Vols. 1 and 2. Oxford: Oxford University Press.

Sayre-McCord, Geoffrey, ed. 1988. *Essays on Moral Realism*. Ithaca: Cornell University Press.

I

ABOUT MORAL REALISM AND ITS VARIETIES

CHAPTER 1

DEFINING MORAL REALISM

JENNIFER FOSTER AND MARK SCHROEDER

And as imagination bodies forth
The forms of things unknown, the poet's pen
Turns them to shapes and gives to airy nothing
A local habitation and a name.

—William Shakespeare, A Midsummer Night's Dream

WHEREVER philosophers disagree, one of the things at issue is likely to be what they disagree about, itself. So also with moral realism, or metanormative realism more broadly. In addition to asking whether moral realism is true, and which forms of moral realism are more likely to be true than others, we can also ask what it would *mean* for some form of moral realism to be true—we can try to define "moral realism" and each of its standard variants, "naturalism," "non-naturalism," and so on. The usual aspiration of such inquiry is to find definitions that all can agree on, so that we can use terms in an unambiguous and uniform way. But we doubt that this aspiration is always possible, or even necessarily desirable. It will be our goal in this essay to sketch out some of our reasons for such skepticism, and to lay out a picture of what philosophical inquiry can look like in metaethics and beyond, even when it is impossible to reach uniform agreement on the terms of the debate.

1. FIXING VOCABULARY

We all know how important it is to fix the meanings of terms in order to have a clear topic for conversation. If we are having a conversation and Jen insists, "moral realism is not true," while Mark insists "moral realism is true," we may take ourselves to be in genuine disagreement — especially, say, if we have already agreed that "wrong" is synonymous with "fails to maximize happiness." But, in fact, we are having no disagreement at all, if Mark thinks that "wrong" being with synonymous with "fails to maximize happiness" is *sufficient* for realism being true, while Jen, following Nagel, Parfit, and others, prefers to use "realism" in a stingier way. Perhaps she thinks, along with Nagel, that

> If values are objective, they must be so in their own right, and not through reducibility to some other kind of objective fact. They have to be objective *values*, not objective anything else.[1]

So in order to fix what we are in disagreement about, we—Jen and Mark—need to fix our terms. In particular, we need to decide whether to use "moral realism" in a way that includes Benthamite analytic utilitarianism or not. So far, so trivial—all of this, we believe, should be uncontroversial.

But when philosophers look for the right definitions to use for classificatory terms like "moral realism," "reduction," "naturalism," "noncognitivism," "expressivism," "constructivism," "constitutivism," and many more, they are generalizing on this uncontroversial observation far beyond the purposes of one conversation or another. They are looking for definitions that will fix these terms *once and for all*—for all conversations that different people have about this topic, and for all conversations that we may come in the future to have about it. The metaphor of philosophical inquiry as a kind of ongoing conversation—a metaphor of which we are both fond, for many purposes—encourages the sense that this must be an important thing to do. After all, if it is important for Jen and Mark to fix *their* terms in debating moral realism, and their conversation is just a small part of a much bigger conversation, then surely that much bigger conversation can likewise only be productive if we can first fix terms for it, as well.

But we doubt that this is such a good idea. Indeed, we doubt that it is even possible. The core reason for our doubts is simple. It is that there is a key disanalogy between ordinary conversations, which have a limited number of participants and happen at a particular time and place, and the metaphorical "grand conversation" about philosophy to which we all aspire to contribute. The disanalogy is that precisely because ordinary conversations happen at a particular time and place, with a limited number of participants, the conversational participants can draw on features that they have in common in order to fix their terms adequately for the purposes of the conversation. The larger the conversation, however, and the less fixed in time and place, the less the conversational participants will have in common—and the harder it will be to adequately fix terms in a single meaningful way. We should expect, then, that in the "grand conversation" of philosophical inquiry as a whole, this task will be hardest of all: for such a (metaphorical) conversation is limited neither in time nor space, nor in who may join in, nor in which background assumptions those participants bring with them. For the purposes of *that* conversation, fixing terms once and for all in a single, meaningful way will be challenging, indeed.

---

[1] Nagel [1986, 138]. Contrast Schroeder [2005].

So how is it, in more ordinary cases, that the common features of the conversational participants make it easier to fix terms? The answer is that it gives them a *common ground*—both a set of assumptions that can be held fixed for the purposes of their conversation and a range of imaginative possibilities beyond which they do not need to plan in advance.[2] Assumptions can be held fixed for the purposes of a conversation either because they are taken for granted by all parties, or because they are accepted for the purposes of the conversation by the conversational parties in order to keep things simple. Or they can be held fixed even because *one* of the conversational participants takes the assumptions for granted and the others go along with it because disputing the assumptions would be a conversational distraction—as when an atheist engages in "God" talk to use the Euthyphro dilemma (the presuppositions of which she does not herself endorse) to challenge a theist interlocutor's unreflective endorsement of the divine command theory.

When conversational participants can avail themselves of a fixed set of background assumptions, they can have fruitful and meaningful engagements even if they have not fully fixed the meanings of their terms, and even if they would choose to fix them differently, were they to engage with interlocutors who accept a different set of background assumptions. It is possible to have meaningful engagements—even quite precise engagements—without converging on a single meaning, because sometimes different meanings *have the same conversational upshot*, holding the common ground fixed. Even when two definitions of a term are not equivalent, they can be *conditionally* equivalent, given some assumptions. And so when those assumptions are part of the common ground, it will not matter for the purposes of the conversation that the speakers have not converged on a single "once and for all" meaning for their terms. Likewise, it can make perfect sense for a single speaker to latch onto different definitions for different conversations—and to do so, even without equivocating in what they care about, because each of their definitions can each be conditionally equivalent to what they care about, conditional on what is held fixed as part of the common ground in each of their different conversations.

In addition to such various fixed assumptions, conversational participants also bring to the table a common set of *imagined possibilities*. *Pace* some naïve construals of the Stalnaker-Lewis picture of inquiry as "locating" ourselves in possible world space, we do not start with a fixed understanding of all of the possible ways that things can be and then gradually narrow down.[3] Rather, we start with some clear distinctions that make sense to us, sharpened against some clear foils that we want to deny. The *process* of inquiry then proceeds, dynamically, from there—and as it does, tends to reveal to us theoretical possibilities that we had not yet considered, yielding in turn the need for finer-grained distinctions. Conversational participants could get along very well

---

[2] Stalnaker [2002].
[3] Stalnaker [1984]; Lewis [1996].

without deciding, once and for all, whether a spork is a fork but not a spoon, or a spoon but not a fork, or both, or neither, so long as none of them have ever imagined a spork.

Finally, disagreement is pervasive in philosophy—both actual, and potential. Wherever we use a common vocabulary to define our terms, that vocabulary becomes an object of philosophical study, and its properties will become controversial. It is a consequence of this that sometimes what is at issue between two philosophers is in part a matter of what each of them is committed to in virtue of the theory that they accept. If these philosophers can appeal to at least *some* common ground assumptions that they both share (or are willing to countenance for the purposes of the conversation), then they can try to use those shared assumptions to triangulate on what is really at stake between them. Even philosophers who disagree on *a lot* can make progress this way, if they are sufficiently willing—for the time being—to grant, bracket, or otherwise "gloss over" orthogonal points of dispute. Triangulating via common ground thus requires a kind of *pro tem* flexibility or provisionality of framing: the more rigid we are at the outset of inquiry, and the more necessary we take it to be that our dispute be cast, *now*, in terms which will survive any controversy *later*, the less in common we will have to triangulate with in the meantime.

In the next three sections we will survey how each of these ways in which the common features of a limited number of conversational participants facilitates successful engagement with ideas have played out in debates—both substantive and terminological—about moral realism.

2. Conversational Common Ground

Moral realism seems like it *should* be easy to define. However we end up ironing out the details, surely the *gist* is clear enough: that some moral claims are *objectively* true, that there are moral properties *out there*, that those properties *ground* moral facts, and that those moral facts are true *independently* of what we think or feel about them. Indeed, this is essentially everyone's first pass—here are just a few representative examples:

- *Michael Rea*

    Moral realism is the view that there are objective moral facts. There are objective moral facts only if the following two conditions are met: (i) there are moral properties—e.g., properties like being a right action, being a wrong action, being praiseworthy, being depraved, and so on—at least some of which are exemplified by actual objects or events, and (ii) the exemplification of a moral property p does not entail that anyone has beliefs about what exemplifies p, about whether p is exemplified at all, or about the conditions under which p is exemplified. Condition (ii) is meant to express part, but only part, of what many philosophers aim to express by phrases like "moral properties are not mind-dependent" or "moral facts are not theory-dependent".[4]

- *David Enoch*

  Robust Realism is an objectivist, response-independence view of normativity. [. . .] Whether or not a given normative statement applies (for instance) to a given action does not depend on what attitudes regarding it—cognitive or otherwise—are entertained by those judging that it is (or is not) or by anyone in their environment, nor does it depend on the attitudes, desires, and the like of the agent whose action it is or of anyone in her environment.[5]

- *Schroeter and Schroeter*

  What is crucial to the realist position—whether Moorean or naturalist—is the claim that normative terms have a determinate reference and signify a specific property. [. . .] Call this the *Univocity thesis*. It's also distinctive of the realist position that speakers' opinions about what falls into the extension of normative terms are fallible. One's judging an action to be right does not make it so: there is an independent standard of correctness for normative judgments to which speakers are answerable. Call this the *Objectivity thesis*. Moorean and naturalist realists accept both the Univocity and Objectivity theses and take them to be constraints on an adequate realist account of the signification of normative terms.[6]

And why not start here? We have to start the conversation somewhere, after all, and this seems as natural and unproblematic a place as any—right?

As a sociological fact about philosophers, or at least the ones doing metaethics, "property-talk" seems indeed to come naturally to almost everyone. So *common* is the belief that properties exist at all that, for most metaethicists, it looms far in the conversational background, out of focus. But that something is even *widely* "common philosophical ground" does not, it's worth highlighting, actually make it *neutral* philosophical ground. Before most debates about moral realism even get off the ground, nominalists who deny the existence of any properties at all are bracketed out.

David Enoch, whose characterization above was the only one of our three not to use the word "property", makes this point explicit before going on to offer his more official characterization of realism in terms of properties:

---

[4] Rea [2006, 215–216].
[5] Enoch [2011, 3].
[6] Schroeter and Schroeter [2005, 5].

Let me say, then, that according to Robust Realism, *and general doubts about properties aside*, there are irreducibly normative properties; similarly, general doubts about facts aside, there are irreducibly normative facts; and so on.[7]

That he gets away with this is no surprise (and for the same reason, no big deal) given that, *for the purposes of most conversations about metaethics*, it *is* common ground among the conversational participants that nominalism is false, and that at least *some* properties exist—whatever else might be debated about "moral" ones. And . . . that's fine!! Indeed, it's precisely the point. What we wish to highlight, here, is not that philosophers like Enoch have *failed* in their metaethical theorizing because their definitions of "moral realism" are not sufficiently neutral between *every* participant in Philosophy's "grand conversation," but that our metaethical disputes can (and already do!) proceed perfectly fine *without* such a definition. We do not need to fix on a single, once and for all, meaning for metaethical inquiry to get off the ground.

So it is perfectly fair for people who agree that nominalism is false to characterize the terms of their disagreement in a way that presupposes the existence of at least some properties. They can do so without deciding whether one of them—the irrealist—would automatically win if nominalism is true and there are no properties at all, and they can even do so if they agree that their disagreement would survive the discovery that this presupposition is false, and nominalists could have essentially the same dispute as they are having, cast in slightly different terms. Since they each believe that this presupposition is true, however, they believe that there is no need for them to go down the route of having to work out how to recast the terms of their dispute until they actually begin having it with someone who rejects this presupposition.

But more: even if we know how to formulate what is at stake over whether moral realism is true in a way that is orthogonal to whether any properties exist at all, it is likely that whatever we build into this formulation in order to be sufficiently careful about this issue will only make our formulation more complicated. But complicated things are more difficult to think about, and so formulating the issue in these terms will only make it harder for us to decide whether moral realism is true. And if it is common ground among us that some properties do exist, then this is a cost that buys us no benefit that any of us think is worth having! So it is not only possible, but often advisable, to take advantage of what we accept as common ground in order to simplify the terms of our dispute.

3. Failures of Imagination

In the last section we argued that there is nothing wrong with characterizing the terms of your disagreement with someone in terms that presuppose something that is, or for

---

[7] Enoch [2011, 5 (italics added for emphasis)].

all that you are sure could be, orthogonal to what you are actually in disagreement about. This is a feature of ordinary conversation, and so it is no wonder that it should be a feature of philosophical conversations, which after all are just ordinary conversations that happen to be about philosophy. But in addition to knowingly presupposing things that you either actively agree about or are willing to grant for the purposes of conversation, conversational participants also frequently—indeed, we would argue, invariably—leave unresolved issues that they have not yet even imagined as possibilities that need to be distinguished.

It is so easy to fail to imagine even relatively obvious possibilities that this fact can be easily exploited for humorous effect:

Michael Bench-Capon
@MikeBenchCapon

People think that if two people are facing each other then one of them's left is the other one's right, but that's only true if neither or both of them are upside down

4:15 PM · May 8, 2021 · Twitter Web App

This works as a joke because (sorry, as philosophers we have to explain this) as you read it the words "facing each other" prime you to expect that indeed, one person's left is the other person's right, and so when the author describes people as "thinking" this, you think "of course they think it—it's true." And then the humor comes from obviousness in retrospect that this is not, in fact, generally true, but only true under the ordinary kind of circumstances that we imagine when we imagine two people facing one another.

The same thing, we know, has happened repeatedly in the recent history of metaethics. Before Mackie [1977], it was easy to define moral realism in contrast to noncognitivism or subjectivism, but after Mackie we needed to incorporate some specification that insists on whatever we take error theorists to deny—for example, that there really are moral properties, that some (positive) moral claims really are true, or the like. When we see Michael Rea [2006] explaining that some moral properties must actually be exemplified, we all understand that the error theory is what he is trying to rule out. And so we get on, pretty well, most of the time and for most purposes, by understanding that he is trying to rule out views that are relevantly similar to Mackie's from counting, without even needing to worry about whether his definition actually successfully rules out all such views.

And that is a good thing! For even once we have imagined the possibility of an error theory and decided that it is inconsistent with what we meant all along by "moral realism" or at least what we should have meant, much room remains to imagine different ways in which the moral error theory can be understood or developed. The differences between different sorts of views in this space and the grounds on which they get to count as sufficiently relevantly similar to Mackie's[8] to count as versions of the error theory are

---

[8] Or even whether Mackie's own view is determinate between various possible interpretations.

relatively diverse, and this diversity requires some finesse in formulating a single condition that does not just say "but nothing relevantly similar to Mackie's view is true."

For example, on the presuppositional version of the error theory formulated by Perl and Schroeder [2019], moral claims *do* attribute properties that actually exist and in many cases *are* actually exemplified—they just carry presuppositions *about* those properties that are false. Perl and Schroeder's presuppositional formulation of the error theory is not ruled out by Rea's formulation, but we conjecture that it is intended to be. Is that a problem? We say: no—it was not a problem while we didn't imagine the possibility of the presuppositional form of the error theory, and it isn't a problem after, so long as it is either common ground that the presuppositional error theory is false, or else that we should interpret Rea's formulation as successful at what it was obviously *trying* to do—to rule out views relevantly similar to Mackie's error theory.

The same pattern arises again with respect to metaethical contextualism. Both Rea's [2006] and Enoch's [2011] formulations of moral realism are consistent with Stephen Finlay's [2014] radically contextualist end-relational semantics, and on such grounds Finlay classifies his own view as realist. On Finlay's view, there *are* properties ascribed by moral terms in context, in context it is true to say that these are (as Rea put it) "properties like being a right action, being a wrong action, being praiseworthy, being depraved, and so on", and in the vast majority of contexts it is true to say that whether moral statements are true does not (à la Enoch) "depend on the attitudes, desires, and the like of the agent whose action it is or of anyone in her environment." Yet on Finlay's radical end-relational theory, these properties could be virtually any ordinary property, in the right sort of conversational context, and it *does* typically depend on our attitudes or desires which of these attitude-independent properties we happen to be talking about in each conversational context.

Rea and Enoch are not thinking about the possibility of a view like Finlay's. Both of them, we predict, would be happy to rule it out, but they are just not quite imagining why the things that they have said do not suffice to rule it out. In contrast, it is clear that Schroeter and Schroeter [2005] *do* intend to rule out views like Finlay's. That is why they require moral terms to be *univocal*. But the matter of how to rule out all such views without mistakenly committing moral realism to something obviously false is somewhat delicate. As Finlay points out, many words that we use to make moral claims are in fact *not* univocal, but on the contrary can make moral claims in one context while being used to make non-moral claims in another context. This is certainly true for "ought," "must," "may," and "reason," for example. So if moral realism is not to be inconsistent with the obvious observation that some words have both moral and nonmoral uses, then even more care is required, in order to say what kinds of context-dependence are and are not inconsistent with moral realism.

It is no doubt a worthwhile task, for some purposes, to try to finesse such refinements, to find the right formulation of moral realism that can rule out Finlay's end-relational semantics without saying anything obviously false. But for many purposes we can get on just fine by understanding that Schroeter and Schroeter intend to rule out similar views, and go from there, without worrying about whether they have succeeded at securing a precise definition that does the correct ruling out.

And more importantly, if it takes such care to carefully enough formulate moral realism to rule out the error theory and sophisticated forms of contextualism even after we do imagine them, we should not be very confident in our ability to successfully formulate conditions that will rule out the possibility of new creative views that exploit yet other possibilities that we have been so far unable to imagine. For example, the idea that a genuine form of relativism about truth might be coherent and applicable to metaethics was not taken seriously by many until the last twenty-five years. As a result, most philosophical defenses of "moral relativism" in the last three decades of the twentieth century precisified what they were defending as a kind of contextualism. Hence attempts to define moral realism to rule out relativism have often tried only to rule out contextualism, instead. But in the last twenty-five years, undeniably coherent forms of genuine relativism have been developed that have different commitments from contextualism, and *these* must now be ruled out by any formulation of realism that means to rule out relativism.[9]

Or consider the research program of dynamic semantics, according to which the meaning of a sentence is given by its potential to change the context. Dynamic semantics offers a more flexible semantic framework with some similarities and differences from both relativism and noncognitivism, but despite several decades of history in linguistics, it has only in the last ten or fifteen years begun to enter the consciousness of metaethical theorists,[10] and so it is no wonder that many attempts to rule out similar views from counting as "moral realism" do not yet rule it out. And of course there are many other possibilities we have not yet thought of. If it is hard enough to carefully rule out the things we know about, our confidence that we can successfully rule out the things that we don't even know about in advance should be very low.

And again, we say: that is okay. Indeed, it is more than okay. The kind of care and sophistication required in order to rule out sophisticated and creatively surprising views about moral talk, thought, and reality can only obscure what is really at stake. To the extent that our definition of what is at stake incorporates complexities that are there only for the purpose of ruling out possibilities that we are assuming are not true, these complexities can only get in the way of our thinking clearly about the issues. So it is better, really, to stick to simpler formulations. Until, that is, those complexities become relevant. But we can take that as it comes.

Sometimes, of course, once we imagine new possibilities—just as once we change our minds about things we had both taken for granted as part of the common ground—we find ourselves pushed in different directions about how to use classificatory terms like "moral realism." Finlay, for example, is moved to continue to use it in a way that includes his own view, while Schroeter and Schroeter are moved to try to count it out.

---

[9] See especially MacFarlane [2014].
[10] Compare Starr [2016].

That's fine—that just means that once this possibility is taken seriously they care about different things. It doesn't follow that they couldn't have been caring about the same thing so long as they were not taking this possibility seriously!

4. Irreconcilable Worldviews

And this brings us to the crux of the matter. We have seen in the last two sections not only that we *can* have substantive and precise disputes even without formulating them in terms that absolutely anyone could accept, but that it is often advisable to do so. First and foremost, relying on our common ground allows us to formulate what is at stake between us in ways that render it more tractable. This reason applies even when we are fully aware that there are other people who would reject the assumptions that we hold in common and even if we think that they could also, in principle, join in what would be recognizably the same dispute that we are having. But second and also important, our capacity to continually imagine new and creative possibilities for what philosophical views in some domain might look like means that it will likely be futile to even try, in advance, to iron out the wrinkles in a formulation that we might reasonably hope could stand the tests of both time and controversy.

This brings us to the problem that nearly everything is up for grabs in philosophy. Even if we wanted to formulate an issue in terms that could be accepted by everyone no matter what their other philosophical views, we would need some agreed-on terminology in which to formulate it. But since everything is ultimately up for grabs among philosophers, there is and can be no such agreed-on terminology.

For some purposes we might hope that little hangs on this. Surely, we might think, arcane questions in the metaphysics of properties and of propositions, the theory of grounding, the semantics of truth, the theory of explanation, and so on, must be independent of the central questions of metaethics, and there *must* be ways of reformulating our questions to get around whatever complications arise within the special concerns of each of these domains. But sadly, it turns out that we have excellent inductive evidence that this is not the case. Even where questions like these are *logically* independent of the concerns that animate us in metaethics, it frequently turns out that novel and initially surprising (to some of us, at least) views about fundamental topics in other areas of philosophy end up being key to defending the plausibility of metaethical theories. This is one of the central contributing factors to what makes philosophy *hard*, and for many of us, it is an essential part of why thinking about metaethics in particular, can be so rewarding.

In the last two sections we argued first that we *can* conduct perfectly respectable inquiry without fixing terms once and for all, and second that it is *advisable* to do so, even if we could work out the kinks in advance. But the fact that philosophers can disagree about everything has an even more striking consequence: it is *impossible* to define our terms in a way that can make our dispute proof against the development of future kinks.

For every dispute must be formulated in some way or other. And any way that we formulate it will use some words. But there are no words that constitute a privileged basic vocabulary in philosophy whose significance or connection to each other cannot be contested. So no matter which words we use to formulate moral realism, there will be possible views formulated in terms of these words that we have either not anticipated or whose defensibility we have not anticipated, which, if taken seriously, would undermine our attempt to use those words to formulate our original dispute in a way that is agreeable to all parties.

Many philosophers, of course, do work with a basic set of ideology within which to formulate their own sense of the issues. And some of these philosophers believe either that the ideology that they so use—or at least, some ideology which they hope is the one that they use—is privileged in some way that makes formulations of the issues couched within this privileged ideology to be privileged ways of understanding the issues.[11] We both have some healthy skepticism for this idea, however formulated or developed. But what is important for our purposes here is just that *even if* there is some privileged vocabulary in which disputes ought to be formulated in order for us to see perspicuously what is at stake, the fact that some parties to the dispute do not *themselves* accept this privileged way of formulating it means that it cannot be used as common ground in order to triangulate what is at stake between them. And yet, for all of that, there may still be something else—something nonprivileged, according to the proponent of the privileged vocabulary—that we *can* use to triangulate with both parties to the dispute, because it can be agreed on, or at least accepted for the purposes of the conversation, by both parties.

So we conclude that it is not only inadvisable, but in general impossible, to fully fix the terms of our disputes in advance. Philosophers who look like they are trying to do so should be charitably interpreted as just trying to fix them for a wide enough audience for the purposes at hand. And that, we say, is good enough—and often more than is strictly speaking needed.

5. Pro Tem Inquiry

So what, then, does it look like, to conduct philosophical inquiry in metaethics or about any other topic without being able to fix once and for all the terms that we are using to ask our questions and in which to express what is at stake between us? Our answer is that it looks, more or less, exactly like what we actually observe. Indeed it must, because as we have argued, there is no other way of doing things.

Since emotivism became widely visible in English-speaking philosophy in the 1930s, it has been common ground among many philosophers interested in the questions

---

[11] Compare Sider [2011].

of metaethics that whatever moral realism is, it isn't that. And so the question of what is at stake between views that fall in some sense into the same family as emotivism—noncognitivist views, for lack of a better name—came to be very closely associated with what is at stake over moral realism. That realism entails cognitivism, in the very loose sense where "cognitivism" is just the opposite of whatever Ogden and Richards [1926], Ayer [1936], Stevenson [1937], Hare [1952], Blackburn [1984], Gibbard [1990], Ridge [2014], and Charlow [2015] have in common, has become common ground in attempts to formulate the thesis of moral realism—all such attempts make some attempt that is believed or hoped to encompass a sufficient condition for noncognitivism, so understood, to be false.

Yet we know from experience that what this condition has been taken to be has varied over time, as it has become increasingly difficult to secure enough common ground in order to say what is at stake over noncognitivism itself.[12] In the early heady days of emotivism, of course, when the readily accepted definition of "noncognitivism" was that moral sentences cannot be true or false, people were taking for granted that the concerns of metaethics were sufficiently independent of philosophical theories of truth that we can use the vocabulary of truth in order to mark important distinctions. But once disagreements between correspondence and deflationary theorists about truth became prominent enough in metaethics, it became impossible to conduct this debate in terms of truth—too little was common ground.[13]

Those who accepted the correspondence theory of truth could still rationally believe that formulations in terms of truth were adequate to their ends, and they could still succeed at marking distinctions in ways that were communicatively successful in speaking to one another. But even if they are right that the correspondence theory of truth is true, speaking in this way simply came to exclude a larger and larger number of other people from the conversation. And so in order to include those people, new ways of characterizing what was at stake over noncognitivism had to be invented.[14]

It is our contention that this event in the recent history of metaethics was not a breakdown or failure of inquiry, but rather an example of inquiry going well. True, it took some struggle in the 1990s to recharacterize the issues about noncognitivism in ways that were independent of considerations about truth and still captured the disagreements that people had already been having. And true, much of this work is still ongoing. But the right time to do this work was when it became important in order for cognitivists and noncognitivists to still be able to talk to one another—not when this was a bare abstract possibility.

What we mean by this is that it was fine to bracket deflationism about truth—even for those of us who officially thought that deflationism was actually true—so long as it gave us a way of characterizing what was at stake that was not prejudicial to either

---

[12] Compare Schroeder [2010, chapters 2–4].
[13] See, in particular, how this issue played out in Boghossian [1990], Wright [1992], Horwich [1993], and Smith [1994a] (just to take a sample of the literature engaging with this topic at this time).
[14] Compare Smith [1994b].

side. But now that deflationism about truth has come to be commonly accepted by noncognitivists, and come to be used as a *defense* against some arguments against noncognitivism leveled by cognitivists, we need to use something else to triangulate in order to have a conversation to which both cognitivists and noncognitivists—and hence to which both moral realists and their opponents—can be parties.

6. MORALS

Some theorists seem to be genuinely troubled by the thought that if we're not *all* talking about *the very same thing* when we talk about, e.g., "normativity," or about "moral properties," then our disputes in metaethics about such topics are somehow "not real disputes"—that we are ultimately "talking past each other".[15] And it is this troubling thought, more than (just) an intrinsic desire for clarity and rigor, which we take to be drive recurrent ambitions in metaethics to define moral realism once and for all. And others, starting from the observation that we can't all be talking about just one thing, recommend that we simply distinguish between the many *different* things that we could talk about that are often run together, and recognize that each of these is, in its own right, an interesting thing to talk about.[16]

We do not claim that this ambition to fix terms once and for all is universal—indeed, many of the authors whose definitions of "moral realism" we cited in this chapter are very careful to steer clear of any such ambition. Nevertheless, it is an alluring pitfall that we see authors fall into again and again. And if we have any major takeaway to offer, here, it is that the troubling thought behind it may be safely put to rest: we do not need to fix on one meaning, or one universal definition, for our disputes about "moral realism" to be meaningful, or for us to make progress. Perhaps it should be the *aim* of our metaethical theorizing *eventually* to arrive at such a "clear and distinct" articulation. But we do not *need* to establish it before we get started; and more to the point, we should not *expect* ourselves to be able to.

The principal obstacle, after all, to getting things precise is that we often don't know *which things need refining* until their (relative) crudeness becomes salient to us. This has been the lesson of the previous sections: that in spite of even our most valiant efforts to precisify and preempt, we can—and usually do—have cognitive "blinders" to the deficiencies and excesses of our present definitions. We can fail to see where they are ambiguous, where they are overly general, and where they are underimaginative—and we can do so for utterly prosaic reasons. Perhaps it is because we share so *much* common ground with so *many* interlocutors that we mistake our background assumptions for universal givens. Or perhaps we share so *little* common ground with our perceived

---

[15] See, for example, Parfit [2011], Finlay [2019].
[16] See, for example, McPherson [this volume].

"opponents" that we have failed to imagine how they, on a worldview so different from our own, might accept the very definitions we proffered to exclude them. Perhaps *none* of us, yet, have thought to think about the relevant parts of logical space.

These are possibilities not just in conversations about moral realism, but about any topic on which philosophical inquiry has not yet been concluded. They are, however, especially *salient* in the context of moral realism, where the conversation about what "counts" as realist has evolved (and continues to evolve) in surprising and even dramatic ways, in part because the philosophical problems of metaethics are so challenging that they have served as a perpetual engine of innovation in what philosophical assumptions might be used to address them. We should not conclude from this, though, that we cannot successfully talk *about* "moral realism," or that the conversations we *are* having about it are somehow futile *unless and until* we can settle (for real this time!) *exactly* what we mean.

On the contrary, we should conclude that our conversations about "moral realism" are just like our conversations about anything else: that they are going to be only as productive as we are able to triangulate on the common ground between us and our conversational partners; and that the definitions we employ to *do* that triangulating are almost always going to be provisional at best. We ought to be wary, then, of being too high-minded or literal about the meanings of words like "realism," both in our own use but especially in our interpretations of others. Likewise, we should be modest as we offer characterizations which, even to us, may seem glaringly inadequate in only a few years' time.

References

Ayer, A.J. 1936. *Language, Truth, and Logic*. London: Gollanz.
Blackburn, Simon. 1984. *Spreading the Word*. Oxford: Oxford University Press.
Boghossian, Paul. 1990. "The Status of Content." *Philosophical Review* 99: 157–184.
Charlow, Nate. 2015. "Prospects for an Expressivist Theory of Meaning." *Philosophers' Imprint* 15: 1–43.
Enoch, David. 2011. *Taking Morality Seriously*. Oxford: Oxford University Press.
Finlay, Stephen. 2014. *A Confusion of Tongues*. Oxford: Oxford University Press.
Finlay, Stephen. 2019. "Defining Normativity." In *Dimensions of Normativity: New Essays on Metaethics and Jurisprudence*, edited by D. Plunkett, S. Shapiro, and K. Toh, 187–219. Oxford: Oxford University Press.
Gibbard, Allan. 1990. *Wise Choice, Apt Feelings*. Cambridge, MA: Harvard University Press.
Hare, R.M. 1952. *The Language of Morals*. Oxford: Oxford University Press.
Horwich, Paul. 1993. "Gibbard's Theory of Norms." *Philosophy and Public Affairs* 22: 67–78.
Lewis, David. 1996. "Elusive Knowledge." *Australasian Journal of Philosophy* 74(4): 549–567.
MacFarlane, John. 2014. *Assessment-Sensitivity: Relative Truth and Its Applications*. Oxford: Oxford University Press.
Mackie, J.L. 1977. *Ethics: Inventing Right and Wrong*. New York: Penguin.
Nagel, Thomas. 1986. *The View from Nowhere*. Oxford: Oxford University Press.
Ogden, C.K., and I.A. Richards. 1926. *The Meaning of Meaning*. New York: Harcourt Brace.

Parfit, Derek. 2011. *On What Matters*. Oxford: Oxford University Press.
Perl, Caleb, and Mark Schroeder. 2019. "Attributing Error without Taking a Stand." *Philosophical Studies* 176(6): 1453–1471.
Rea, Michael. 2006. "Naturalism and Moral Realism." In *Knowledge and Reality: Essays in Honor of Alvin Plantinga*, edited by Thomas Crisp, David VanderLaan, and Matthew Davidson, 215–242. Philosophical Studies Series. Dordrecht: Springer.
Ridge, Michael. 2014. *Impassioned Belief*. Oxford: Oxford University Press.
Schroeder, Mark. 2005. "Realism and Reduction: The Quest for Robustness." *Philosophers' Imprint* 5: 1–18.
Schroeder, Mark. 2010. *Noncognitivism in Ethics*. New York: Routledge.
Schroeter, Laura, and Francois Schroeter. 2005. "Is Gibbard a Realist?" *Journal of Ethics and Social Philosophy* 1(2): 1–18.
Sider, Ted. 2011. *Writing the Book of the World*. Oxford: Oxford University Press.
Smith, Michael. 1994a. "Why Expressivists about Value Should Love Minimalism about Truth." *Analysis* 54(1): 1–11.
Smith, Michael. 1994b. "Minimalism, Truth-Aptitude, and Belief." *Analysis* 54(1): 21–26.
Stalnaker, Robert. 1984. *Inquiry*. Cambridge: Cambridge University Press.
Stalnaker Robert. 2002. "Common Ground." *Linguistics and Philosophy* 25: 701–721.
Starr, William. 2016. "Dynamic Expressivism About Deontic Modality." In *Deontic Modality*, edited by Nate Charlow and Matthew Chrisman, 355–394. Oxford: Oxford University Press.
Stevenson, C.L. 1937. "The Emotive Meaning of Ethical Terms." *Mind* 46(1): 14–31.
Wright, Crispin. 1992. *Truth and Objectivity*. Cambridge, MA: Harvard University Press.

CHAPTER 2

METAPHYSICAL STRUCTURE FOR MORAL REALISTS

TRISTRAM MCPHERSON

Introduction

Debates about moral realism are nearly as old as philosophy. Over the past century, intramural debates among moral realists have proliferated, concerning whether theses like *moral naturalism, reductionism,* or *Moorean non-naturalism* are true. These debates about the metaphysics of morality are typically motivated by certain more or less intuitive ideas about morality. This chapter examines competing attempts to illuminate those intuitive ideas by drawing on resources from general metaphysics.[1]

The topic of this chapter is limited in several ways. First, realist views about morality are *motivated* in a variety of ways. I will sometimes mention those motivations, but I am primarily focused here on questions about how to *formulate* realist theses, rather than what can be said in favor of them.

Second, many moral realist research programs include commitments that are not, at least in the first instance, about the metaphysics of morality. These include, for example, that moral facts or judgments have some distinctive practical or normative significance, that the truth-conditions of certain sentences with moral words in them are invariant across contexts, or that we have some moral knowledge.[2] I will not discuss these hypotheses here.

---

[1] In keeping with the theme of this volume, my explicit focus in this chapter is on the metaphysics of morality. However, much of the discussion of this chapter can be smoothly adapted by readers more interested in realism about various types of nonmoral normativity, such as the epistemic, the prudential, or what "really matters."

[2] An especially extreme example is Dreier (2010), who argues for a nonmetaphysical characterization that (as he argues) classifies nihilistic moral error theory as a form of moral realism.

Third, some central debates in moral metaphysics concern certain ways that the moral facts might depend upon our psychologies. And some influential taxonomies treat the absence of such dependence as partially defining moral realism.[3] Due to space limitations, and the fact that these debates are to some extent independent of the ones I will discuss, I will not address these issues here.[4]

Fourth, some philosophers believe that much apparently metaphysical vocabulary ("true," "fact," "property," etc.) can be given so-called minimalist glosses, which entail that claims made using these terms are much less metaphysically informative than they might appear.[5] For example, on standard minimalist views, "it is a fact that racism is wrong" tells us nothing metaphysical not already stated by "racism is wrong." Here, I will generally assume for the sake of brevity that when we use words like "fact" and "property" we are thereby doing metaphysics. If you think that some other words are needed to do that work—perhaps some novel technical philosophical terms—I hope that much of what I say will be translatable into your preferred framework.

Finally, I assume without argument the controversial idea that it is possible to fruitfully engage in the metaphysics of morality.

Here is one motivation for the project of this chapter. Suppose that one wants to make an argument in the metaphysics of morality, for or against realism, reduction, or non-naturalism. One will probably have some intuitive idea in mind of what one's target thesis amounts to. However, as I will show, significantly different ways of sharpening those intuitive ideas will be plausible (or even visible) given different background assumptions about what general metaphysical structure there is, and what explanatory work that structure can do.

Because of this, understanding how the intuitive ideas intersect with theories of metaphysical structure can help us to make our arguments clearer and more careful. One reaction to this chapter is to use the resources it provides in seeking to identify the "correct" way to formulate theses like moral realism or moral non-naturalism.[6] Another reaction, however, is to grant that "competing" formulations may be useful for different purposes, and instead focus directly on what can be said in favor of accepting moral "realism" (e.g.) *given* one or another clear and useful formulation.

This chapter is organized into three sections. The first explores competing ways of understanding moral realism. The second section introduces the question of what makes a property *natural*. The third section builds on the first two, spelling out three contemporary frameworks for understanding variants of moral realism that appeal, respectively,

---

[3] Two examples among many: (Shafer-Landau 2003, 15; Street 2006, 110) (although Street is discussing *normative* realism).

[4] See Svavarsdóttir *this volume* for relevant discussion.

[5] For relevant discussion, see for example (Enoch and McPherson 2017; Horwich *this volume*; McPherson 2022; Thomasson and Warren *this volume*).

[6] I have argued for reasons to prefer certain formulations of some of the relevant theses in (McPherson 2015) and in (McPherson and Plunkett *forthcoming*).

to modal resources, to grounding and essentialist resources, and to the idea of objective similarity.

1. Moral Realism as a Metaphysical Thesis

I am interested in exploring ways of understanding moral realism as a *metaphysical* thesis. One way of seeing the bite of this condition is to consider a canonical formulation of moral realism:

Truth Realism Some moral sentences, when literally construed, are true[7]

Consider two points about Truth Realism, that also apply to many of the formulations I offer below. First, it is existentially quantified. That is, on this formulation, realism requires only that there are *some* moral truths. It is thus compatible (e.g.) with the hypothesis that what we believe about morality is a tissue of error. Second, Truth Realism may need to be amended so that only certain *types* of moral truths are sufficient for realism. For example, consider the sentence: "Nothing is morally required." One might think that the truth of *this* sentence does not entail moral realism. The question of how to formulate the relevant amendment to the scope of Truth Realism (and the other formulations I offer) is a complexity I set aside here.

I introduce Truth Realism primarily as a foil. This is because Truth Realism may not be a metaphysical thesis. This is because, on one prominent understanding, truth is a *semantic* relation: a certain relation between a sentence and a language.[8] If this is right, then Truth Realism is not a thesis about the metaphysics of morality at all, but rather a claim about moral semantics.

In this section, I consider four competing ways of characterizing moral realism as a *metaphysical* thesis and explain how these interact with certain general metaphysical commitments.

1.1 Truthmakers

Here is an intuitive thought about Truth Realism: even if Truth Realism is itself a semantic thesis, its being satisfied might *entail* something about extralinguistic reality.

---

[7] Compare the slightly more sophisticated formulation of realism in (Sayre-McCord 1988, 5).

[8] On some views of truth (notably correspondence theories), truth *is* a metaphysical relation. On such views, there will arguably not be much of a gap between Truth Realism and the Truthmaker Realism I discuss next.

Notably, one might think that if a sentence is true, then there must be something in reality that *makes* it true; that is, a *truthmaker* for that sentence.[9] For example, perhaps the fact that I am alive is the truthmaker for the sentence "Tristram is alive." Truthmaking appears to be a metaphysical relation. And the plausibility of Truth Realism as a formulation of realism might rest on the implicit assumption that truth entails truthmaker. These ideas motivate the following way of characterizing moral realism:

Truthmaker Realism   There is a truthmaker for at least one moral sentence

If one accepts the idea of truthmaking, Truthmaker Realism arguably expresses a recognizably realist kind of metaphysical commitment about morality.

However, some philosophers might think Truthmaker Realism is nonetheless too weak to capture the core idea of moral realism. The question once again rests on delicate issues. Here is the core question: would the satisfaction of Truthmaker Realism entail that there are *moral* entities, properties, or facts? On one way of thinking about the issue, the answer is "yes." Thus, you might think that if a fact makes a moral sentence true, that fact is *for that very reason* a moral fact.

On an alternative view, however, a sentence can be true despite appearing to make claims about entities that do not, in fact, exist. Let me explain via an example. Some metaphysicians deny that there are complex material objects such as tables. On this view, all that exist are *simple* material entities. Now, some of these entities are arranged into table-y shapes. And someone might say: the truthmaker for the sentence "There is a table in the living room" is simply the existence of a collection of simple entities in a relevant location. The point is that on this view, the truthmaker for this sentence does not include a table, because tables do not exist.[10]

On such a view, Truthmaker Realism is compatible both with there being moral *entities*, *properties*, or *facts*, and with there failing to be any of these.[11] The latter would be the case if the truthmakers for moral claims are *nonmoral* entities, facts or properties. If this is right, the satisfaction of Truthmaker Realism may be compatible with the absence of any *moral* reality. And this may motivate some philosophers to look for a stronger metaphysical claim to characterize moral realism.

---

[9] For an introduction to the complexities of truthmaker theory, see (MacBride 2019). Cameron (2008) offers a contemporary exposition of a truthmaker criterion of realism (it departs from the criterion in the text by including a mind-independence criterion).

[10] For one important way of developing such a view about metaphysics and ordinary talk, see (Sider 2011, 292–3).

[11] Sinhababu (2018, 38–9) explicitly defends the compatibility of moral realism with the lack of moral properties. Cuneo and Shafer-Landau (2014, 403) characterize a related possibility in their formulation of "minimal non-naturalism."

1.2 Existence and Objective Similarity

Such realists might begin with the intuitive thought that the real is what *exists*.[12] In light of this, some might think that moral realism requires that something *moral* exists:

> **Existence Realism** There exists at least one moral fact, individual, or instantiated moral property or relation

Existence Realism is disjunctive, and much of its significance comes from exploring its disjuncts.

First consider the mention of *facts* in Existence Realism. On an initially plausible picture, this is superfluous.[13] To see why, consider one example of a claim that, if it were a fact, would vindicate moral realism: *Cho's caring for their child is morally good*. One might think that this fact either consists in—or is parasitic upon—the instantiation of a moral property (moral goodness). Generalizing, one might think that wherever there is a moral fact, this will be explained by there being an instantiated moral property or relation. And if this is so, there being moral facts would not be a *distinct* way for moral realism to be true.

Next consider the classic metaphysical distinction between *individuals* which might be alleged to exist (e.g., me; the Armenian economy) and the *properties and relations* that those individuals might be alleged to have or stand in (*being a philosopher*; *experiencing economic growth*; *being larger than*). (For brevity, in what follows, I will use "property" expansively to include relations.)

At first blush, a realist about physics is likely to be committed both to the existence of physical individuals (e.g., electrons) and to the instantiation of physical properties (e.g., *negative charge*). By contrast, most moral realists do not appear to be committed to the existence of distinctive moral *individuals*. For example, it is absurd to suggest that there are fundamental moral particles alongside the familiar physical ones.[14]

An apparently especially plausible way to be an Existence Realist is thus to accept the existence of instantiated moral properties and relations. On this view, the truth of moral realism is secured by the fact that that some individuals are *virtuous*, some actions are *wrong*, some considerations are *moral reasons* for certain agents to perform certain actions, etc. As I now explain, this view interacts in an important way with the metaphysics of properties.

The idea that the correct metaphysics includes properties can be motivated by two linked ideas. First, reality appears to be at least partly *qualitative*. That is, a description

---

[12] This intuitive thought is reflected in Quine's (1948) famous account of *ontological commitment*. For useful introduction to theories of ontological commitment, see (Bricker 2014).

[13] The mention of facts in Existence Realism would not be superfluous given ontological *Tractarianism*: the view that *facts* are metaphysically fundamental. See (Turner 2016) for an important recent exposition. Tractarian moral realism is, to my knowledge, unexplored.

[14] As noted by Dworkin (1996, 104).

of reality which simply listed all of the individuals that had ever existed would be incomplete, because it would not say anything about what those individuals were *like*. A metaphysics that includes properties can characterize the qualitative nature of reality. Secondly, some distinct individuals appear to be *similar* to each other, in certain respects. For example, two spheres are similar to each other in respect of shape. Properties can be understood precisely as dimensions of similarity.

Some metaphysicians reject the idea that we need to vindicate these appearances. Consider a simple version of class nominalism.[15] According to this view, a property is just a collection of individuals. The fact that caring for one's child is good, for example, just amounts to the action *caring for one's child* being part of a certain collection of things. Supposing we do not introduce anything else qualitative into our metaphysics, reality contains nothing qualitative on the simple class nominalist view. This is because a collection is just a group of things, not a quality. Since similarity is naturally understood as qualitative, the simple class nominalist may abandon the idea that objects can be (in any metaphysically interesting sense) similar to each other.

We are now in a position to see an interesting implication of this view. Suppose that we accept the idea, suggested above, that if Existence Realism is to be true, it is in virtue of the instantiations of moral properties. And suppose that simple class nominalism is true, so that moral properties are just certain collections of individuals. There are no interesting "moral similarities" in the world. Arguably, on this combination of views, despite Existence Realism being true, there is again no *moral* reality to speak of. Compare the nihilist about tables mentioned in §1.1: as in that case, our talk of moral goodness can come out true, on simple class nominalism, but not in virtue of their being any goodness *in the world*. For example, suppose that it is true that Samir is virtuous. On simple class nominalism, all this amounts to is the idea that there is a set of individuals {Samir, ...} that we happen to pick out with the word "virtuous."[16] Of course, the simple class nominalist might also be able to find a truthmaker for sentences like "Samir and Zeta are morally similar." But again, the truthmakers for those sentences will not consist in similarities in the world. In order to mark a contrast with this sort of possibility, I will use the term "objective similarity" to pick out a kind of qualitative similarity in the world that is not captured by this sort of gloss.

I now discuss three competitors to simple class nominalism, each of which implies the possibility of objective similarity.

First consider trope theory.[17] The trope theorist takes reality to be characterized by *qualitative individuals*. So consider the goodness of Cho's caring for their child. That act is associated with a qualitative individual—a goodness trope. Suppose next that Ali's

---

[15] For a useful introduction to nominalism, see (Rodriguez-Pereyra 2015).

[16] The astute reader will notice that an analogous implication holds for every debate about realism that concerns qualitative features. For example, "property dualism" in the philosophy of mind might seem odd given simple class nominalism.

[17] For a useful introduction to trope theory, see (Maurin 2018). For an application of trope theory in the metaethical context, see, e.g., (Ridge 2007).

caring for their child is good in precisely the same way. What this amounts to, according to the trope theorist, is that Cho's act also has a certain trope, and this trope is exactly similar to the trope had by Ali's act. To be good, on this picture, is to have a trope in a certain objective similarity class—the "goodness class."

Assume again that Existence Realism will be true in virtue of the instantiation of moral properties. On the trope theorist's view, this can be glossed as follows: for Existence Realism to be true is for there to be at least one similarity class of moral tropes with an actual member. This seems like a commitment to the sort of *moral* reality that was absent from the simple class nominalist's picture.

Next consider the view that properties are *universals*.[18] As with trope theory, the proponent of universals takes entities to *instantiate* qualities. The trope theorist takes the quality instantiated by an individual to be particular and unsharable: the goodness of Ali's act is a *different thing* from the goodness of Cho's act, despite being perfectly similar. By contrast, the proponent of universals claims that perfect objective similarity in a respect just amounts to instantiating the very same qualitative entity: a universal. So, on this view, Ali's act and Cho's act instantiate the *very same* qualitative thing: the universal *goodness*. Assume again that Existence Realism will be true in virtue of the instantiation of moral properties. The universals theorist says that this is just for there to be a moral universal that is instantiated. This again seems like a commitment to a substantive moral reality.

Finally, consider the *similarity primitivist*. The trope theorist and universals theorist attempt to explain similarity by introducing their new qualitative entities. A metaphysician might be impressed by how parsimonious the simple class nominalist's ontology of collections of individuals was, but nonetheless want to find similarity in the world. One strategy is to retain class nominalism, but to claim that it is a primitive fact that comembership in certain classes of individuals amounts to objective similarity, while comembership in others does not.[19] We can label the similarity-making classes "elite."[20] This sort of account makes similarity a primitive relation, much as the trope theorist does. Unlike the trope theorist, however, the proponent of elite collections aims to do without anything qualitative in its fundamental metaphysics, beyond eliteness and similarity.

The similarity primitivist again seems to allow Existence Realism to vindicate a kind of moral realism not vindicated by the simple class nominalist. On the former view, for there to be a moral property instantiated is for there to exist an elite collection, which marks a genuine *moral* dimension of similarity in the world.

---

[18] (Armstrong 1989) is still an excellent introduction to the topic.

[19] In the text I ignore the subtle distinction between the view that the *resemblance* relation is wholly primitive, and the view most naturally associated with (e.g.) Lewis, that certain classes are primitively *resemblance-making*.

[20] I take the label from Lewis (1986, 161). Lewis famously hypothesized that eliteness (or as he more commonly dubbed it, "naturalness") united a host of interesting metaphysical features, of which here I am focusing only on similarity-making.

These examples suggest a useful contrast: between views on which reality contains *moral similarity*, and those which do not. This contrast motivates our next formulation of moral realism:

Similarity Realism   There are actually existing or instantiated moral facts, individuals, or properties, which make for a dimension of objective similarity

One way to motivate Similarity Realism is to consider contrast cases. For example, there is currently a glass of water to my left. That the water in the glass is *liquid* is arguably a respect in which those contents are objectively similar to other liquids. By contrast, consider the *being to the left of* relation. This relation is instantiated, but is *not* plausibly a way that things are objectively similar to each other. And on this basis, one might resist the thought that we should be realists about this relation.

Some metaethicists are at pains to flag their metaphysical commitments concerning the moral as "robust" or "relaxed."[21] The contrast between Truthmaker Realism and Similarity Realism suggest one way to make good on those metaphors. Accepting Truthmaker Realism while denying Similarity Realism is one way of characterizing what it is to be a "relaxed" realist: on this view, reality makes some moral claims true, but not in virtue of there being any objective moral similarities in the world.

1.3 Fundamentality

According to many philosophers, some facts are more *fundamental* than others. For example, consider the fact that I enjoy eating dosas. This fact is arguably explained by more fundamental facts about (e.g.) my dispositions to have certain experiences when eating dosas. (And these facts are in turn plausibly explained by yet more fundamental facts.)

On an influential recent gloss, to be real is to be *fundamental*.[22] This suggests another gloss on moral realism:

Fundamentality Realism   At least one moral fact is fundamental[23]

---

[21] See, e.g., Railton's allegiance to "stark, raving" moral realism (1986) and many contemporary realists labeling their views as "robustly" realist, e.g., Enoch (2011). I take the "relaxed" terminology from (McGrath 2014).

[22] The canonical statement of this view is in (Fine 2001). In the metaethical context, see (Dunaway 2017).

[23] This formulation reflects the common contemporary view that the relata of grounding relations are always facts. See (Bliss and Trogdon 2014, §3) for discussion. One might instead seek to spell out the idea of a fundamental individual or property. One could then formulate an alternative to Fundamentality Realism which was like Existence Realism in being officially agnostic concerning whether the relevant relata were facts, individuals, or properties.

On this gloss, my enjoyment of the dosas is not real; what is real are the fundamental facts that the fact of my enjoyment metaphysically depends on.

Fundamentality Realism seems plausible in some cases. For example, as we noted above, one might resist the thought that we should be realists about *to the left of* facts. Fundamentality realism can explain this: the fact that my water glass is to my left is plausibly not fundamental, being fully explained by facts about my location and orientation, and the location of my water glass. To use a common metaphor, we might think that *to the left of* facts are mere shadows of the more fundamental facts that underlie them.

In other cases, however, it seems less plausible that the nonfundamental is unreal. Consider natural kinds like *gold*, *water*, or *cell*. It is implausible, given what we currently know, that facts about the instantiation of any of these kinds are metaphysically fundamental. For example, the fact that there is water instantiated in my glass is presumably fully grounded in the fact that a certain complex subatomic structure is instantiated at that location. But facts about water do not appear on their face to be "mere shadows" of complex subatomic structures. They appear to be part of reality in a way that the *to the left of* facts arguably do not.[24]

One way to reply to this is to contrast *relative* and *absolute* fundamentality. For example, facts about molecular kinds like water are plausibly not *absolutely* fundamental, but they are arguably considerably *more fundamental* than (e.g.) facts about *to the left of* relations. One might retain the link between reality and fundamentality, and suggest that we should conclude from this that reality is itself a degreed notion.[25] On this picture, the water facts would be *more real* than the *to the left of* facts, but *less real* than the fundamental physical facts. On this picture, we could sensibly ask of the moral facts: *how* real are they?

2. The Natural

Thanks in part to the striking influence of G. E. Moore, questions about moral naturalism and non-naturalism are central topics in the metaphysics of morality (Moore 1993/1903). As with "realism," however, the word "naturalism" has been used by philosophers to pick out a wide variety of theses, some of them metaphysical, some of

---

[24] On a prominent approach to metaphysics associated with Lewis (e.g., 1983) and Sider (e.g., 2011), both fundamentality and maximal similarity-making are associated with a single notion—being "natural," "elite," or "structural." On this approach, there might not be much of a contrast between Similarity Realism and Fundamentality Realism. For doubts about this idea, see especially Dorr and Hawthorne (2013).

[25] See (Dunaway 2017) for this suggestion. One reason to take the degreed notion seriously is that there may be metaphysically possible worlds where *every* fact is grounded in further, more fundamental facts. See (Bohn 2018) for discussion. On the absolute fundamentality view, such worlds would, absurdly, count as having nothing real in them, even if they were more richly populated than the actual world by any other measure.

them not.[26] This section begins my discussion of moral naturalism as a metaphysical thesis.

Because of the complexity of the topic, the discussion of this section will be limited in three ways.

First, just as with the question of realism discussed in §1 we can frame questions about naturalism as concerning different sorts of ontological categories (facts, properties, individuals, etc.).[27] For simplicity, in this section I set aside important complexities that result from these possibilities, and focus on accounts of what it is to be a natural *property*.

Second, I am discussing the natural before I discuss reduction. (This is because the discussion of reduction introduces several metaphysical complexities that it makes sense to discuss separately.) This is important because one way a property might count as natural is in virtue of being *reducible* to natural properties (Dowell 2020, 1–2). Because I am ignoring reduction in this section, the accounts I discuss here are best understood as accounts of what it is for a property to be *basically* natural. That is: to be natural and not in virtue of being reducible to natural properties.

Third, this section will concern what it is for a moral property to be natural. This is not quite the same thing as the question of what it is for moral *naturalism* to be true. The next section will in part explore different views about how morality would need to be related to basic natural properties in order for (certain sorts of) moral naturalism to be true, most notably, so-called reductive and nonreductive naturalisms.

A final clarification before I turn to the first account of the natural. Many philosophers follow Moore in claiming that moral properties (or perhaps: normative properties) are "*sui generis*," that is: different in kind from all non-normative properties. Some of these philosophers go on to use the word "natural" to refer to any properties that are not "*sui generis*" moral or normative properties.[28] So, for example, the sorts of *supernatural* properties that might feature in theological discourse would be classified on this usage as "natural." Readers should track these distinctive uses where they occur. Here, however, I set them aside, assuming that supernatural properties are paradigmatically *not* natural.

2.1 Epistemic Characterizations of the Natural

Here is one way to get a grip on the significance of the question of moral naturalism. It is a striking fact that there is no mature science of morality, in the way that there is a mature

---

[26] The most prominent nonmetaphysical way of thinking about naturalism is methodological: on this approach, naturalism is, roughly an approach to inquiry that centrally applies scientific findings and methods to metaphysical questions. In metaethics, Gibbard (2003, 32) introduced an influential contrast between "naturalistic" and "non-naturalistic" *concepts* which is distinct from either the metaphysical or methodological theses.

[27] For example, (Cuneo and Shafer-Landau 2014) suggests a contrast between natural and non-natural *truths* that would fit naturally with Truthmaker Realism, discussed above.

[28] E.g., (Rosen 2017, 152). For worries about this tendency see, e.g., (Sturgeon 2009, 63–6).

science of chemistry or psychology. The moral realist might ask: does this mean that moral reality lies outside of the natural world that scientific investigation reveals, or can we nonetheless find a place for moral reality within this natural world? This is one way of understanding the intuitive heart of metaphysical debates about moral naturalism.

This way of understanding the question of naturalism suggested that the natural world is revealed by scientific investigation. One might think that what makes an investigation *scientific* is something about its epistemology: the sorts of evidence or methods that we can use to acquire scientific knowledge. This motivates an influential way of characterizing natural properties: to be natural, a property must have certain epistemic properties.

On the most prominent version of this sort of account, for a property to be natural is for its instantiation to be discoverable *empirically*, if it is discoverable at all. For a property to be empirically discoverable is, roughly, for us to be able to know about its instantiation only by appeal to evidence provided by our senses.[29]

This characterization of naturalism is vulnerable to three general sorts of worries. First, one might worry about the tenability of the distinction between "a priori" and "empirical" justification or knowledge.[30] Second, one might worry that this characterization *excludes* too much science. For example, much of mathematics appears to be discoverable a priori. This is a worry for two reasons. First, one might think that mathematics itself is a scientific discipline. Second, one might think that mathematical results play a central and indispensable role in epistemology of the natural sciences, suggesting that they too may have an important a priori component. Finally, one might worry that this account *includes* too much. For example, one might think that the existence of the God of traditional Judeo-Christian theology is paradigmatically inconsistent with naturalism. But some theists have argued that both the existence of such a being, and at least some of His supernatural properties, are discoverable only by empirical means.

One might seek to avoid these worries by withdrawing the substantive characterization of the relevant epistemology. This suggests the following formulation:

Epistemic Naturalness   What it is for a moral property M to be a basic natural property is for it to be the case that, in appropriate circumstances, instantiations of M are discoverable by epistemic means characteristic of scientific inquiry

The first thing to note in this formulation is the reference to *appropriate circumstances*. Some properties might be such that none of their actual instances are ever discoverable. For example, perhaps certain properties are instantiated only outside of the light cone of any intelligent life. Such a property could count as natural if it were such that, e.g., *were it to be instantiated around here*, we could discover this fact using scientific means.

---

[29] For detailed discussion and defense, see (Copp 2003).
[30] E.g., (Williamson 2013).

Epistemic Naturalness seeks to finesse at least the first two of the objections just considered by being less committal concerning the epistemology of science. The key point is that the proponent of Epistemic Naturalness can embrace either doubts about the distinction between the a priori and empirical, or the idea that scientific inquiry includes some a priori components.

What remains distinctive of Epistemic Naturalness is the assumption that there is something epistemically unified about scientific inquiry.[31] If Epistemic Naturalness is to be illuminating, it must be that the epistemic character of scientific inquiry amounts to more than *the methods that are good for learning about the world, whatever they are*. One worry about this is that scientists appear to make discoveries using all sorts of epistemic resources. For example, theoretical physics appears quite epistemically distinct from plant biology, and sociology appears different again.

2.2 Causal Characterizations of the Natural

A different worry about Epistemic Naturalness is that, even if it correctly classifies properties as natural or not, it might seem metaphysically superficial. That is, one might think that there must be a deeper fact about the natural properties, which *explains* why they are discoverable in distinctive ways.

One salient candidate for such a deeper fact is the idea that natural properties have (or are constituted by) *causal powers*. If a property has causal powers, it might seem unsurprising that we can often discover its instantiation using scientific inquiry.

As with the empirical discoverability account, a causal account of the natural might include too much. For example, standard theologies are shot through with alleged miraculous divine causation. And the instantiation of such causation appears to be paradigmatically inconsistent with naturalism.

In reply, one might introduce a contrast between causal powers which operate according to *laws of nature*, and "miraculous" causal powers, which do not. This suggests the following formulation:

Causal Naturalness For a property M to be a basic natural property is for it to be the case that M possesses, or is constituted by, causal powers that operate in accordance with laws of nature

This sort of account might suffice (e.g.) to rule out God's omnipotence from counting as a natural property.

---

[31] For sketches of the putatively unifying characteristics, see, e.g., (Boyd 1988, §3 and Dowell 2020).

One reason to take Causal Naturalness seriously as a characterization is that it appears to fit well with some extremely influential approaches to naturalistically minded metaphysics, both generally and with respect to the metaphysics of morality.[32]

Despite this, one might worry about Causal Naturalness on naturalistic methodological grounds. The worry is that causation might itself fail to be a deep feature of the natural world. For example, many candidate fundamental physical laws are symmetric with respect to time, where our ordinary notion of causation is often taken to be robustly asymmetric. If so, causation might fail to identify the metaphysically deep feature that unifies the natural properties. (One might reply in turn that even if this is so, Causal Naturalness might be a *sufficient* condition for naturalness.)

2.3 Objective Similarity Characterizations of the Natural

Very often, we can be reasonably confident *that* a collection of entities bears some objective similarity, without knowing *what* that similarity is. For example, we were arguably in a position to be reasonably confident that water was a natural kind long before we discovered its distinctive chemical constitution. It might be argued that we are in a similar situation with respect to the natural. It might be that we are reasonable to be confident that there is some objective similarity distinctive of the natural properties, without yet being in a position to know what it is.

Further, it might be claimed that the idea that the natural properties form an objective similarity class is the *minimal* commitment required to think that metaphysical debates over moral naturalism are substantive. For imagine that the natural did not form such a similarity class, instead comprising a gerrymandered mess. Then it is hard to see why the question of whether moral properties were natural would matter at all for our metaphysical inquiry.[33]

This suggests the following formulation:

> **Similarity Naturalness** For a property M to be a basic natural property is for M to be a member of the narrowest objective similarity class that is partially constituted by the properties correctly postulated by paradigmatic natural sciences (and that excludes paradigmatic supernatural properties)[34]

Similarity Naturalness attempts to capture the minimal commitment just mentioned. Let me briefly unpack it.

---

[32] In the moral case, a vast literature was launched by (Harman 1977) and (Sturgeon 1985), which precisely concerns whether moral properties can play a role in causal explanations. In the metaphysics of mind, a similarly central role has been played by the causal exclusion argument, e.g., (Kim 1989).

[33] Compare (McPherson 2015, 129).

[34] See (McPherson 2015, 130) for further discussion of this sort of view.

To begin, it focuses on *paradigmatic* natural sciences. These are the sciences most marked by the sorts of explanatory and epistemic success that largely motivates our interest in the question of naturalism. The idea is that our taxonomy should remain neutral on controversial questions concerning whether (e.g.) economics, psychology, or history are sciences.

Note next that some of the properties currently postulated by these sciences may turn out to fail to accurately describe reality. (Consider examples of properties posited by previous best theories that arguably fail to be instantiated, such as Newtonian mass.) So the formulation focuses on the properties *correctly* postulated by the paradigmatic natural sciences. These properties will fall into various objective similarity classes (for example, *property* may itself be an objective similarity class). The natural properties are the narrowest such similarity class that includes all the correctly scientifically postulated properties.

The formulation ends with a caveat: if this narrowest similarity class were to include paradigmatic supernatural properties, members of this class would not count as natural. This reflects the assumption that a contrast with the supernatural is partly definitive of naturalism.

It is worth noting that Causal Naturalness and Epistemic Naturalness might turn out to be *realizations* of Similarity Naturalness. For example, it might turn out that the similarity class mentioned in Similarity Naturalism *just is* the class of properties constituted by causal powers that operate in accordance with natural laws.

3. Reduction, Nonreduction, and Non-Naturalism

In the contemporary metaphysics of morality, pride of place is often given to the divisions among non-naturalism, nonreductive naturalism, and reductive naturalism. This section builds on the discussion of the previous section to explore competing ways of understanding these (and related) views in the metaphysics of ethics. The discussion is structured around three groups of metaphysical resources that one might use to characterize distinctions among these views: *modal* notions, *essentialist and grounding* notions, and *objective similarity* notions. As Ralph Wedgwood points out in his contribution to this volume, the range of views between Moorean non-naturalism and reductive naturalism is sometimes neglected in contemporary metaphysics of ethics.[35] One aim of this section is to make vivid just how varied that range can be, given a variety of background metaphysical assumptions.

As in §2, I will often simplify my discussion by focusing on understanding the relevant notions in terms of moral *properties* to the exclusion of alternatives. However,

---

[35] (Wedgwood *this volume*).

because it is standard to take facts to be the relata of grounding relations, I will sometimes frame the discussion in terms of moral facts.

3.1 Modal Accounts

One central idea associated with naturalism about a class of properties is that naturalism is true of such properties just in case their instantiation is *nothing over and above* the instantiation of natural properties. What "nothing over and above" means is a vexed issue. Many philosophers have thought that we can provide attractive regimentations of this and related ideas in the metaphysics of ethics using the idea of *metaphysical modality*.

The core idea of metaphysical modality is that there is a class of questions and facts about necessity and possibility that do not concern our epistemic circumstances or linguistic conventions, but rather concern reality itself. Metaphysical possibilities are extremely "broad". For example, given the laws of nature that govern the actual world I couldn't cast a spell that turns you into a frog. But many philosophers take those laws to be metaphysically *contingent*. That is, they think it is metaphysically possible that I turn you into a frog. As this example illustrates, the metaphysical possibilities are extremely expansive. They are not, however, unlimited. For example, consider the thesis that water consists of molecules made up of hydrogen and oxygen ions, appropriately bonded. This is *necessarily* true of water: something made up of other sorts of molecules *couldn't possibly* be water. According to proponents of metaphysical modality, this claim isn't epistemic, linguistic, or conceptual: it tells us something about *water itself*.[36]

For much of the past fifty years, many philosophers have sought to use metaphysical modality as a resource in explaining central metaphysical ideas and arguments. Such arguments often appeal to the idea of a *metaphysically possible world*. To get a handle on this notion, think of the actual world as encompassing all of space and time, and everything that has happened and will happen. The actual world so understood is one metaphysically possible world. Other possible worlds are equally determinate and encompassing. They just consist (at least in part) of things that could have happened, but did not.

We can begin to understand how a modal condition might seem to capture the "nothing over and above" idea by considering the idea that our mental properties are *modally independent* of our physical properties. For example, David Chalmers famously argued that there are possible worlds physically just like this one, where we have no qualitative mental states (like experiencing what it is like to see red or taste curry).[37] It is plausible that if these mental properties are modally independent of the physical properties in the way Chalmers imagines, then the mental is something "over and above" the physical, and so physicalism about the mental is false.

---

[36] The metaphysics of metaphysical modality is itself a vexed issue. See (Borghini 2016) for a useful introduction.

[37] (Chalmers 1996).

On this basis, one might propose a simple *supervenience* criterion for naturalism about a class of properties M: M-naturalism is true just in case there can be no M-difference between worlds without a difference between the basic natural properties in those worlds.

In the context of formulating physicalism, many philosophers have taken such a criterion to be too demanding. Here is an example of why.[38] Suppose that mental properties can be fully realized by both purely physical entities, and also by supernatural entities. Suppose next that in the actual world, there are no supernatural entities, but that there is a possible world that is just like ours in all natural and physical respects which also includes a supernatural mind. According to the supervenience formulation of naturalism, this possible world renders naturalism about the mental false. But for all that, it seems to many philosophers that even if this is possible, the *actually instantiated* mental properties are nothing over and above the physical. After all, nothing supernatural realizes *these* instantiations of mental properties. On this basis, it might be claimed that the mere possibility of supernatural minds is compatible with physicalism and naturalism about the mental.

This motivates modifying the simple supervenience criterion. Here I adapt a prominent proposal from the literature on physicalism.[39] This proposal involves a modal relation that I will call *duplication entailment*. To see the idea, imagine that we created a world that was a minimal naturalistic duplicate of the actual world: that is, we can imagine it being created by instantiating all and only the actual basic natural properties and relations that are instantiated in the actual world, and then stopping. Some nonbasic properties will be instantiated in that world as well. For example, if the hypothesis discussed in the previous paragraph is correct, all of the actual mental properties will be instantiated in this world. Call every property instantiated in that world a property that is *duplication entailed* by the complete natural way things are. We can use the relation of duplication entailment to formulate a modal characterization of moral naturalism:

Duplication Naturalism The complete moral way things are is duplication entailed by the complete basic natural way things are

Duplication Naturalism can be motivated as follows. First, if Duplication Naturalism is satisfied, then every actual instantiation of a moral property is (in one sense) modally secured by the instantiation of some natural properties. This is a promising attempt to make precise in modal terms the idea of "nothing over and above." Second, a generalization of this thesis initially seems to classify cases plausibly. On the one hand, it does not appear to be overdemanding in the way that the simple supervenience criterion is. On the other, consider a Chalmers-style hypothesis about morality: that a naturalistic

---

[38] Compare (Jackson 1998, 11–12), which draws on similar points by Terry Horgan and David Lewis.
[39] The text broadly follows (Jackson 1998, 12–13). There are several competing proposals to restrict the relevant modal relation, and there is continuing controversy about the ability of any of these formulations to avoid decisive counterexample. See (Stoljar 2010, Chs. 6–8) for helpful discussion.

duplicate of the actual world could completely lack moral properties. Duplication Naturalism plausibly treats this hypothesis as inconsistent with moral naturalism.

It is common to distinguish "reductive" from "nonreductive" forms of naturalism. However, if we combine the modal framework with the idea of a basic natural property introduced in the previous section, we can see that there are in fact a complicated range of distinctions among views that satisfy Duplication Naturalism. Here, I briefly discuss three broad classes of possibilities.

First, consider the idea that moral goodness is a basic natural property in the sense explored in the previous section. (Depending on which view in the preceding section one adopts: we can investigate it using scientific methods, or it is causally efficacious, or it is a member of the naturalistic similarity class.) There are two further possibilities here, which metaethicists have cared about. One possibility is that we also have a nonmoral word for this property. For example, perhaps moral goodness is just identical to pleasantness. Another possibility is that we do not have a nonmoral word for this property. Some metaethicists take the idea that goodness is identical to pleasantness to be the paradigm of a *reductive* form of moral naturalism.[40] Reduction, on this view, is just identity. Some also take the idea that moral goodness is a basic natural property, but we lack a nonmoral word for it, to be definitive of a *nonreductive* form of moral naturalism.[41] One worry about this way of understanding the cut between "reductive" and "nonreductive" versions of naturalism is that it seems to make this apparently metaphysical distinction hang on metaphysically uninteresting facts about which nonmoral words we happen to have in our lexicon. *Metaphysically* speaking, the two possibilities seem similar: on both possibilities, moral goodness is a basic natural property.

Second, suppose that Duplication Naturalism is satisfied, but goodness is not a basic natural property. For concreteness, consider the hypothesis that pleasantness and fairness are both basic natural properties, and that to be good is just to be either pleasant or fair. What we say about this case can depend upon further deep questions about the metaphysics of properties. On a *sparse* view of properties, only dimensions of objective similarity count as genuine properties. And disjunctive conditions paradigmatically fail to mark dimensions of objective similarity. On the sparse view, then, our hypothesis entails that there is no property of moral goodness: perhaps "moral goodness" sentences can be true, but their truthmakers are facts about the instantiation of pleasantness and fairness, because there is no property of moral goodness to be instantiated. (Compare §1: this is an example of a view on which Truthmaker Realism could be true without Similarity Realism being true.) On a *plenitudinous* way of thinking about properties, properties are simply *ways things can be*, and because disjunctive conditions are ways things can be, there are disjunctive properties. On the plenitudinous view, our hypothesis entails that there is a property of moral goodness. Since this property is just a simple disjunction of

---

[40] E.g., (Sinhababu 2018, 32).

[41] E.g., this seems to be suggested by (Darwall, Gibbard, and Railton 1997, 28) and structures the discussion in (Miller 2003).

basic natural properties, one might want to classify this as a reductive hypothesis: goodness, on this view, reduces to the disjunction of pleasantness and fairness.

Third, suppose that Duplication Naturalism is satisfied, but goodness is neither a basic natural property, nor a finitely describable logical function of basic natural properties (as on the preceding hypothesis). But suppose that a plenitudinous view of properties is true, so that there is a property of moral goodness. Here, the absence of a finite function leads many philosophers to conclude that we lack a reduction.[42] So we might call this view a form of nonreductive naturalism.

Finally, consider how the modalist construes the idea of non-naturalism. We can characterize a *broad* form of non-naturalism as simply the negation of Duplication Naturalism: for broad non-naturalism to be true is just for the natural character of the actual world to fail to duplication entail the moral character of the actual world.

As I mentioned in §2, the Moorean non-naturalist is committed to more than this broad form of non-naturalism. They insist that moral properties are distinct not just from the natural properties, but from supernatural properties, and from any other classes of non-normative properties as well. So the modalist non-naturalist may want to characterize a class of all of the *possibly instantiated* non-normative properties {the natural, the supernatural, . . .}, and insist that the moral character of the actual world is not duplication entailed by the collected properties in this class.

While the modalist can offer this gloss, it is worth emphasizing that most self-identified Moorean non-naturalists appear committed to rejecting it. This is because most such Mooreans appear to accept moral supervenience claims that entail that Duplication Naturalism is satisfied.[43] Indeed, a supervenience thesis that would entail the satisfaction of Duplication Naturalism has been described as "the least controversial thesis in metaethics."[44] This is because it can seem very hard to believe that a world could differ from the actual world *only* in some moral respect: that a world could be identical to this one in every way, except that genocide was OK, or that spitefulness was a virtue rather than a vice. Non-naturalists who find the supervenience of the moral compelling thus appear committed to denying that Duplication Naturalism is a correct gloss on naturalism.

3.2 Accounts That Appeal to Essence and Grounding

The sort of Moorean non-naturalist just mentioned can take comfort from the fact that their rejection of Duplication Naturalism would not be idiosyncratic. In recent years it has become common for philosophers to worry that modal notions are not adequate tools to perform the sort of central metaphysical work they have been called upon to do.

---

[42] See, e.g., (Brink 1989, 178). The classic statement of this sort of antireductive idea is (Fodor 1974).

[43] E.g., (Moore 1903/1993; Enoch 2011; Leary 2017). Contrast, e.g., (Rosen 2020), and see (McPherson 2019) for broader discussion of the significance of supervenience in ethics.

[44] By Rosen (2020), who goes on to reject it.

Consider the central modal notion discussed in the preceding section: duplication entailment. All that a duplication entailment claim strictly *says* is that certain properties covary in certain ways across certain parts of "modal space." One might think that, rather than being an illuminating way of characterizing what (e.g.) naturalism is, such covariation, if it holds, is a fact that calls out for further explanation.

If we make a certain controversial theological assumption, we can provide an especially clear example of modal relations calling out for explanation. The crucial assumption is:

God's Love   *Necessarily*, God loves a thing just in case it is good

If God's Love is true, it seems itself to call out for explanation. And famously, those who accept God's Love divide concerning how it is to be explained. On one explanation, God loves the good *because* of God's perfectly benevolent nature. A second explanation proceeds in the opposite direction: a thing is good *because* God loves it; that is, for something to be good *just is* for God to love it. The key point is that God's Love is a metaphysically necessary claim, which has competing metaphysical explanations.

The most influential contemporary way of regimenting metaphysical explanation appeals to the idea of *grounding*, an allegedly unified class of asymmetric metaphysical determination relations.[45] Grounding explanations are *constitutive*, not *causal*. Consider the fact that I am smiling. A (partial) causal explanation of this fact might be that I just heard a good joke. By contrast, a grounding explanation of the same fact might be that the matter that makes up my face is spatially configured in a certain way.

Grounding relations are generally assumed to necessitate. For example, if the spatial configuration of my face fully grounds the fact that I am smiling, then it is metaphysically necessary that: if my face is thus configured, then I am smiling. Because of this, grounding relations appear well-placed to *explain* modal relations, and thus to supply the explanatory asymmetry that it was natural to read into metaphysical entailment.

Many contemporary proponents of grounding relations in metaphysics connect grounding to another metaphysical idea: *essence*.[46] The idea here is that some facts characterize the *nature* of a thing; what it *is to be* that thing.[47] Those facts comprise the essence of that thing. For example, it is plausibly part of the essence of water to be partially constituted by hydrogen, and some people think that it is part of my essence that I am human. The key point is that not all necessary truths about a thing are essential truths about that thing. For example, it is necessarily true of me that I cannot know that 2 + 2 =

---

[45] It is controversial whether grounding facts are themselves explanatory, or whether they underlie metaphysical explanations. See (Bliss and Trogdon 2016, §4). It is also controversial whether there is in fact a unified "grounding relation" that can do metaphysical work. See, e.g., (Wilson 2014) for dissent.

[46] E.g., (Fine 1994, Rosen 2010).

[47] The astute reader will notice that the preceding subsection, dedicated to modal approaches, included some *what it is* talk. The ambitious modalist will attempt to offer a modal reduction of essence. The grounding and essentialist framework being discussed here is partly motivated by the thought that such reductions are implausible.

5. But this plausibly follows from the essence of *knowledge*, and the fact that 2 + 2 = 5 is necessarily false, not from anything about *my* essence.

How is essence so understood linked to grounding? One idea is that some essentialist fact(s) underlie every grounding fact. For example, why does the configuration of my face ground the fact that I am smiling? Because this follows from the essence of smiling: what it is for me to be smiling is just for my face to have this configuration.

We can use the resources of grounding and essence to develop a framework for thinking about naturalism, non-naturalism, and reduction.

To begin, consider a grounding-based formulation of moral naturalism:

Grounding Naturalism Every moral fact is either a basic natural fact, or is (immediately, or by transitivity) grounded in a collection of basic natural facts[48]

The basic idea of Grounding Naturalism is that the grounding relation is tailor-made to capture the core "nothing over and above" ideas associated with naturalism.

The grounding and essentialism framework also provides a very natural way of characterizing reduction. Suppose that we can give a complete account of the essence of something in independent terms. We could call that account a *real definition* of that thing. For example, perhaps the real definition of water is that what it is to be water is to be wholly composed of molecules which each consist of two hydrogen ions bonded to an oxygen ion. One might think that this sort of real definition provides a *reduction* of the defined entity.[49] Similarly, if *what it is* to be good is simply to be loved by God (as in the second explanation of God's Love), one might think this provides a supernaturalist reduction of goodness.

This suggests an essentialist formulation of reductive moral naturalism:

Essentialist Reduction For there to be a naturalistic reduction of a moral property M is for some natural condition to define M's essence[50]

For example, recall the hypothesis discussed in the previous section, that to be good *just is* to be pleasant or fair. If pleasantness and fairness are natural, then this hypothesis will count as a naturalistic reduction of goodness, given Essentialist Reduction.

We can characterize nonreductive naturalism by conjoining Grounding Naturalism with the denial of Essentialist Reduction. However, as in the parallel discussion within the modal framework, it is worth noting that this characterization really lumps together two very different hypotheses. On the first, (which we might call *basic moral naturalism*) some moral properties are among the basic natural properties. On the second, some moral properties are (i) not basic natural properties, and (ii) lacking a naturalistic definition, but nonetheless (iii) such that their instantiation is fully grounded in the natural

---

[48] Compare (Rosen 2017, 163).
[49] Compare (Schroeder 2005, 10).
[50] Compare (Rosen 2017, 163).

properties.⁵¹ These are two very different metaphysical hypotheses that should not be lumped together.

As we noted in the previous section, the Moorean non-naturalist is typically committed to a stronger claim than simply the rejection of moral naturalism. For example, they also want to reject reductive moral supernaturalism. One might think that the key idea is that some normative properties are metaphysically fundamental. This suggests the following formulation of Moorean non-naturalism:

> **Grounding Mooreanism** There is some moral property M such that some facts of the form Ma are not fully grounded in the non-normative facts⁵²

Grounding Mooreanism about goodness rules out reductive supernaturalism, for example, since on that view, every goodness fact *is* fully grounded in non-normative facts, namely facts about God's love. Notice that Grounding Mooreanism is compatible with every M-fact being fully grounded in some *other* normative fact. It is thus compatible with "internormative" reductions. But if we assume that grounding chains must "come to an end" with metaphysically fundamental facts, then Grounding Mooreanism entails that there are metaphysically fundamental normative facts.

3.3 Objective Similarity Accounts

We have seen that objective similarity can be used to characterize notions of realism and naturalness. Here I explain how it can be used to characterize notions like reduction and non-naturalism, and to identify metaphysically interesting distinctions that might otherwise remain invisible.

To begin, consider whether Grounding Mooreanism captures central Moorean commitments.⁵³ There are at least two worries here. First, in §3.1, I noted that many Moorean non-naturalists would reject the modal formulation of their view, because they embrace supervenience theses that entail Duplication Naturalism. Grounding Mooreanism faces similar worries, because many of the same non-naturalists seem to accept the idea that the moral is fully grounded in the non-normative.⁵⁴

---

⁵¹ Some essentialist philosophers will be suspicious that this second hypothesis is possible, e.g., (Rosen 2020). Others will deny it is a form of naturalism, e.g., (Leary 2017).

⁵² Compare (Rosen 2017, 167). I have made one noncosmetic change to Rosen's formulation: explicitly restricting the scope of the account to normative properties. Without that restriction, Rosen's account would entail, absurdly, that every fundamental natural property is a non-natural property.

⁵³ For related worries, see (van Roojen *this volume*).

⁵⁴ This is especially true of many 20th-century non-naturalist discussions of supervenience, which treated supervenience as either being or entailing something like a grounding relation. For this point, see (Berker 2018). A recently prominent response to this tension has been to deny that normative properties are fully metaphysically grounded in, or indeed supervene on, the non-normative properties. See, e.g., (Hattiangadi 2018) and (Rosen 2020). Rosen has attempted to make rigorous the alternative suggestion that the normative is only "normatively grounded" in the non-normative.

Second, the Moorean non-naturalist characteristically thinks that moral properties (or perhaps more broadly: normative properties) are *sui generis*, different in kind from all non-normative properties.[55] This appears on its face to be a matter of *objective similarity*, not a matter of *fundamentality*. And one might worry that Grounding Mooreanism fails to secure this idea. For example, consider an (admittedly implausible) hypothesis:

(i) painfulness is a metaphysically fundamental natural property
(ii) the normative property of badness is identical to painfulness

Because badness/painfulness is fundamental, the badness facts will all be ungrounded on this hypothesis. Because of this, Grounding Mooreanism classifies badness, on this hypothesis, as a non-natural property. But badness/painfulness is by stipulation, a fundamental *natural* property. It is thus not "sui generis" or "just too different" from natural properties.

The idea of objective similarity can be used to provide a formulation of Mooreanism that avoids these worries.[56] The core idea is this when we are thinking about similarity classes, we need to think about levels of taxonomy. For example, consider *cats* and *rabbits*: they are both members of the taxonomic class of *mammals*. But at the level of species, there is an important objective cut between them (assuming that these biological taxonomies reflect objective similarities).

Similarly, supernatural properties are like natural properties in that they are both *properties*. What we want to do is to isolate a specific taxonomic level where, e.g., the contrast between *the natural* and the *supernatural* similarity classes is relevant. We can then formulate Moorean non-naturalism this way:

Similarity Mooreanism   There is some moral property M such that M is a member of the objective similarity class: *the normative*, which is at the same taxonomic level as, and objectively dissimilar from, the natural and supernatural

Similarity Mooreanism mitigates both of the worries just mentioned for Grounding Mooreanism. First, it is tailored to capture the idea that the normative is "sui generis." Second, it makes no mention of either modal or grounding relations. It thus leaves it as a substantive question whether moral properties so understood supervene on, or are fully metaphysically grounded in, non-normative properties.

The objective similarity relation allows us to distinguish several interestingly distinct *naturalistic* hypotheses about morality. First, we can hold fixed the idea that the moral (or normative) properties form an objective similarity class, but imagine that it is

---

[55] Witness, e.g., Enoch's infectious "just too different" slogan in his (2011). For discussion, see (Paakunainen 2018).

[56] Both the motivating hypothesis, and the discussion of the similarity alternative in this section draw substantially on (McPherson and Plunkett *forthcoming*).

a taxonomic subclass of the natural, in the way that (e.g.) the biological is. Alternatively, some naturalists might think of moral properties as a subset of the social properties.[57] Both of these hypotheses suggest what we might think of as a kind of "robust" naturalistic realism about the moral: on these views, the moral forms a distinctive part of the structure of the natural world.

Finally, consider reduction. Here I will briefly note possibilities that arise when we combine the essentialist account of reduction with the idea of objective similarity. Recall that account:

> **Essentialist Reduction**   For naturalistic reduction of a moral property M to be true is for some natural condition to define M's essence

If we allow a plenitude of properties, there are two interesting variants of this sort of hypothesis: one on which M constitutes a dimension of objective similarity, and one on which it does not. For example, one might think that, despite water having a reductive real definition, *being made of water* is a dimension of objective similarity. By contrast, one might think that a mere disjunctive real definition, like *being pleasant or fair* does not make for a dimension of objective similarity.

Conclusions

It would easy to be overwhelmed by the taxonomic forest offered in this chapter. Given this, it may be useful to step back and explain two ways that I hope this chapter can be useful to students and practitioners of the metaphysics of morality.

First, I hope that it will empower the reader to better "keep score" of important arguments in the contemporary metaphysics of ethics. While space constraints prevent me from illustrating it here, many such arguments become significantly more or less forceful given contrasting ways of understanding the target theses that they are intended to defend or attack.[58]

Second, I hope it puts readers in a position to begin evaluating the competing formulations I discuss here. In doing so, readers can ask the following questions about the formulations introduced:

- Are the metaphysical assumptions packed into the formulation legitimate?
- Does the formulation successfully capture what we care about in using the relevant terms?

---

[57] E.g., (Copp 1995).

[58] van Roojen (*this volume*) illustrates this sort of possibility, arguing for a mismatch between contemporary arguments for and against non-naturalism and how that thesis is frequently characterized.

- Does the formulation provide a useful way to organize our inquiry into the metaphysics of morality?

Answering these questions will help the reader to develop a deeper grasp of the metaphysics of morality, one that is responsive both to our distinctive concerns about morality, and to the metaphysician's characteristic concern to understand deep facts about the nature of reality.

Acknowledgments

Many thanks to Paul Bloomfield, David Copp, David Faraci, Jamie Fritz, David Plunkett, Miles Tucker, and Evan Woods for helpful comments on this chapter.

References

Armstrong, David. 1989. *Universals: An Opinionated Introduction*. Boulder, CO: Westview Press.

Berker, Selim. 2018. "The Unity of Grounding." *Mind* 127(507): 729–777.

Bliss, Ricki, and Kelly Trogdon. 2014. "Metaphysical Grounding." In *The Stanford Encyclopedia of Philosophy*, edited by Edward N. Zalta (Winter 2016 Edition). https://plato.stanford.edu/archives/win2016/entries/grounding/.

Bohn, Einar Duenger. 2018. "Indefinitely Descending Ground." In *Reality and Its Structure: Essays in Fundamentality*, edited by Ricki Bliss and Graham Priest, 167–181. Oxford: Oxford University Press.

Borghini, Andrea. 2016. *A Critical Introduction to the Metaphysics of Modality*. London: Bloomsbury Academic.

Boyd, Richard. 1988. "How to Be a Moral Realist." In *Essays on Moral Realism*, edited by Geoff Sayre-McCord, 181–228. Ithaca: Cornell University Press.

Bricker, Phillip. 2014. "Ontological Commitment." In *The Stanford Encyclopedia of Philosophy*, edited by Edward N. Zalta (Winter 2016 Edition). https://plato.stanford.edu/entries/ontological-commitment/.

Brink, David. 1989. *Moral Realism and the Foundations of Ethics*. Cambridge: Cambridge University Press.

Cameron, Ross. 2008. "Truthmakers, Realism, and Ontology." In *Being: Contemporary Developments in Metaphysics*, edited by Robin LePoidevin, 107–128. Cambridge: Cambridge University Press.

Chalmers, David J. 1996. *The Conscious Mind: In Search of a Fundamental Theory*. Oxford: Oxford University Press.

Copp, David. 1995. *Morality, Normativity, and Society*. Oxford: Oxford University Press.

Copp, David. 2003. "Why Naturalism?" *Ethical Theory and Moral Practice* 6: 179–200.

Cuneo, Terrence, and Russ Shafer-Landau. 2014. "The Moral Fixed Points: New Directions for Normative Nonnaturalism." *Philosophical Studies* 171: 399–443.

Darwall, Stephen, Allan Gibbard, and Peter Railton. 1997. "Toward *Fin de siècle* Ethics: Some Trends." In *Moral Discourse and Practice*, edited by Stephen Darwall, Allan Gibbard, and Peter Railton, 3–50. Oxford: Oxford University Press.

Dorr, Cian, and John Hawthorne. 2013. "Naturalness." In *Oxford Studies in Metaphysics*, vol. 8, edited by Karen Bennett and Dean Zimmerman, 3–77. Oxford: Oxford University Press.

Dowell, Janice. 2020. "Naturalism, Ethical." In *International Encyclopedia of Ethics*, edited by Hugh LaFollette, 1–12. Hoboken, NJ: Wiley-Blackwell.

Dreier, Jamie. 2010. "Mackie's Realism: Queer Pigs and the Web of Belief." In *A World without Values: Essays on John Mackie's Moral Error Theory*, edited by Richard Joyce and Simon Kirchen, 71–86. Dordrecht: Springer.

Dunaway, Billy. 2017. "Realism and Objectivity." In *The Routledge Handbook of Metaethics*, edited by Tristram McPherson and David Plunkett, 135–150. New York: Routledge.

Dworkin, Ronald. 1996. "Objectivity and Truth: You'd Better Believe It." *Philosophy and Public Affairs* 25(2): 87–139.

Enoch, David. 2011. *Taking Morality Seriously: A Defense of Robust Realism*. Oxford: Oxford University Press.

Enoch, David, and Tristram McPherson. 2017. "What Do You Mean 'That Isn't the Question'?" *Canadian Journal of Philosophy* 47(6): 820–840.

Fine, Kit. 1994. "Essence and Modality." *Philosophical Perspectives* 8: 1–16.

Fine, Kit. 2001. "The Question of Realism." *Philosophers' Imprint* 1: 1–30.

Fodor, Jerry. 1974. "Special Sciences." *Synthese* 28(2): 97–115.

Gibbard, Allan. 2003. *Thinking How to Live*. Cambridge, MA: Cambridge University Press.

Harman, Gilbert. 1977. *The Nature of Morality: An Introduction to Ethics*. Oxford: Oxford University Press.

Hattiangadi, Anandi. 2018. "Moral Supervenience." *Canadian Journal of Philosophy* 48(3–4): 592–615.

Jackson, Frank. 1998. *From Metaphysics to Ethics: A Defense of Conceptual Analysis*. Oxford: Oxford University Press.

Kim, Jaegwon. 1989. "Mechanism, Purpose, and Explanatory Exclusion." *Philosophical Perspectives* 3: 77–108.

Leary, Stephanie. 2017. "Non-Naturalism and Normative Necessities." In *Oxford Studies in Metaethics*, vol. 12, edited by Russ Shafer-Landau, 76–105. Oxford: Oxford University Press.

Lewis, David. 1983. "New Work for a Theory of Universals." *Australasian Journal of Philosophy* 61(4): 343–377.

Lewis, David. 1986. *On the Plurality of Worlds*. Malden, MA: Blackwell Publishing.

MacBride, Fraser. 2019. "Truthmakers." In *The Stanford Encyclopedia of Philosophy*, edited by Edward N. Zalta (Spring 2020 Edition). https://plato.stanford.edu/archives/spr2020/entries/truthmakers/.

McGrath, Sarah. 2014. "Relax? Don't Do It! Why Moral Realism Won't Come Cheap." In *Oxford Studies in Metaphysics*, vol. 9, edited by Russ Shafer-Landau, 186–214. Oxford: Oxford University Press.

McPherson, Tristram. 2015. "What Is at Stake in Debates among Normative Realists?" *Noûs* 49(1): 123–146.

McPherson, Tristram. 2019. "Supervenience in Ethics." In *The Stanford Encyclopedia of Philosophy*, edited by Edward N. Zalta (Winter 2016 Edition). https://plato.stanford.edu/entries/supervenience-ethics/.

McPherson, Tristram. 2022. "Expressivism without Minimalism." In *Meaning, Decision, and Norms: Themes from the Work of Allan Gibbard*, edited by William Dunaway and David Plunkett, 147–169. Ann Arbor, MI: Maize Books.

McPherson, Tristram, and David Plunkett. ms. "Ground, Essence, and the Metaphysics of Metanormative Non-Naturalism."

Maurin, Anna-Sofia. 2018. "Tropes." In *The Stanford Encyclopedia of Philosophy*, edited by Edward N. Zalta (Winter 2016 Edition). https://plato.stanford.edu/entries/tropes/.

Miller, Alexander. 2003. *An Introduction to Contemporary Metaethics*. Cambridge: Polity Press.

Moore, G. E. [1903] 1993. *Principia Ethica*. Repr. Cambridge: Cambridge University Press.

Paakkunainen, Hille. 2018. "The 'Just Too Different' Objection to Normative Naturalism." *Philosophy Compass* 13(2): 1–13.

Quine, W. V. O. 1948. "On What There Is." *Review of Metaphysics* 2(5): 21–38.

Railton, Peter. 1986. "Moral Realism." *Philosophical Review* 95(2): 163–207.

Ridge, Michael. 2007. "Anti-Reductionism and Supervenience." *Journal of Moral Philosophy* 4(3): 330–348.

Rodriguez-Pereyra, Gonzalo. 2015. "Nominalism in Metaphysics." In *The Stanford Encyclopedia of Philosophy*, edited by Edward N. Zalta (Winter 2016 Edition). https://plato.stanford.edu/entries/nominalism-metaphysics/.

Rosen, Gideon. 2010. "Metaphysical Dependence: Reduction and Grounding." In *Modality: Metaphysics, Logic, and Epistemology*, edited by Bob Hale and Aviv Hoffman, 109–136. Oxford: Oxford University Press.

Rosen, Gideon. 2017. "Metaphysical Relations." In *The Routledge Handbook of Metaethics*, edited by Tristram McPherson and David Plunkett, 151–169. New York: Routledge.

Rosen, Gideon. 2020. "Normative Necessity." In *Metaphysics, Meaning, and Modality: Themes from Kit Fine*, edited by Mircea Dumitru, 205–233. Oxford: Oxford University Press.

Sayre-McCord, Geoffrey. 1988. "Introduction: The Many Moral Realisms." In *Essays in Moral Realism*, edited by Geoffrey Sayre-McCord, 1–26. Ithaca: Cornell University Press.

Schroeder, Mark. 2005. "Realism and Reduction: The Quest for Robustness." *Philosophers' Imprint* 5(1): 1–18.

Shafer-Landau, Russ. 2003. *Moral Realism: A Defence*. Oxford: Clarendon Press.

Sider, Theodore. 2011. *Writing the Book of the World*. Oxford: Oxford University Press.

Sinhababu, Neil. 2018. "Ethical Reductionism." *Journal of Ethics and Social Philosophy* 13(1): 32–52.

Stoljar, Daniel. 2010. *Physicalism*. New York: Routledge Press.

Street, Sharon. 2006. "A Darwinian Dilemma for Realist Theories of Value." *Philosophical Studies* 127(1): 109–166.

Sturgeon, Nicholas. 1985. "Moral Explanations." In *Morality, Reason, and Truth*, edited by David Copp and David Zimmerman, 49–78. Totowa, NJ: Rowman and Allanheld.

Sturgeon, Nicholas. 2009. "Doubts about the Supervenience of the Evaluative." In *Oxford Studies in Metaphysics*, vol. 4, edited by Russ Shafer-Landau, 53–92. Oxford: Oxford University Press.

Turner, Jason. 2016. *The Facts in Logical Space: A Tractarian Ontology*. Oxford: Oxford University Press.

Williamson, Timothy. 2013. "How Deep Is the Distinction between A Priori and A Posteriori Knowledge?" In *The A Priori in Philosophy*, edited by Albert Caullo and Joshua C. Thurow, 291–312. Oxford: Oxford University Press.

Wilson, Jessica. 2014. "No Work for a Theory of Universals." *Inquiry* 57(5–6): 535–579.

CHAPTER 3

MORAL REALISM AND OBJECTIVITY

SIGRÚN SVAVARSDÓTTIR

Is morality fundamentally about respecting the autonomy of rational agents as the Kantian claims or about maximizing the well-being of sentient creatures as the Utilitarian claims? Pondering this question, some may come to wonder whether it has an objective answer. I dare say that for those unschooled in metaethics, this is an example of how the issue between moral realists and moral antirealists surfaces in normative inquiry. But what exactly is the issue between the moral realist and the antirealist?

Looking to the metaethical literature, there is a wide agreement that moral realism minimally commits to the following two theses:

(i) The moral cognitivist thesis that sentences containing moral terms are truth-evaluable.
(ii) The thesis that at least some of these sentences are synthetically true, i.e., true not in virtue of meaning alone but also thanks to how reality is.[1]

There is a disagreement as to whether some kind of objectivity condition needs to be added[2] and, if so, to what exactly it amounts. Now, many metaethicists warn that there is no substantive issue here: "moral realism" is a term of art and different theoreticians make different terminological choices with respect to how to use this piece of jargon. Fair enough. However, it is a substantive question whether there is a philosophically interesting objectivity condition that meets the following two desiderata:

a) It goes beyond the two minimal realist theses asserted in (i) and (ii).

---

[1] Those who reject the traditional analytic/synthetic distinction are invited to read the second thesis as, "at least some of these sentences are true thanks to how reality is."
[2] There is also a disagreement as to whether to add an epistemological thesis to the effect that moral knowledge is within our ken, but I will set epistemological issues aside for the purposes of this chapter.

b) It speaks to the concern of moral inquirers who wonder whether there is an objective answer to moral questions like the one that opens this chapter.

This is the question pursued here.

The issue is elusive. So, to sharpen the focus of my inquiry, I approach it by way of the more specific question whether the relevant objectivity condition concerns the "response-independence" of moral discourse. Now, this jargon often surfaces in discussions of objectivity and of moral realism, but it is often used rather loosely. My strategy is to work with the technical notion of response-dependence that Mark Johnston introduced into the philosophical literature with an explicit definition (see next section). Thus, the issue raised with the more specific question will be relatively clear. Not that I am about to argue that response-independence in Johnston's sense is the condition of objectivity that meets the desiderata laid out above. However, it will be instructive, for identifying the appropriate objectivity condition, to see why a general response-independence condition does not fit the bill.

I argue that if we are to understand questions of objectivity that arise within and about moral discourse, we must pay attention to the fact that this discourse is embedded within a somewhat conventionally regimented practice that comprises attempts to guide attitude and action by way of justifying, criticizing, validating, or excusing them. The appropriate condition of objectivity rules out a specific narrow kind of response-dependence that would run counter to this kind of guiding role for moral verdicts.[3] Moral realism needs to incur a commitment to such an objectivity condition if it is to be a viable metaethical position, since otherwise it is open to the worry that it has not made sense of and vindicated the notion that moral verdicts can be called upon to guide action and attitude by way of justifying and criticizing them.

The first section sets the stage: it introduces Mark Johnston's notion of response-dependence and presents a challenge, due to Gideon Rosen, to the idea that realism about a discourse is committed to a condition of objectivity that rules out such response-dependence. I accept Rosen's crucial point but argue, in the sequel, that it is irrelevant to the concerns of objectivity circumscribed above. These concerns point to an objectivity condition that speaks not to the intrinsic metaphysical nature of the facts in the domain of moral discourse but, rather, to the relation of these facts to the discourse and to the wider practice that encompasses the discourse. This objectivity condition is dubbed "The DP-independence condition": a shortening for "The Discourse- and Practice-independence condition." While section two sets the stage and motivates

---

[3] I make no claim to the effect that the condition in question addresses every concern about morality that has been, or may reasonably be, characterized as a concern about objectivity. Arguably, there is more than one notion of objectivity. There is an epistemic notion of objectivity, applied inter alia to the method of moral inquiry. A concern about objectivity in morals may exclusively concern what kind of method is available to make headway in moral inquiry. Also, "objective" is sometimes used interchangeably with "impartial" in moral inquiry. A concern about objectivity in morals may be a concern about impartiality or even fairness.

this condition, the notion of *DP-independence* is explicitly introduced and the condition stated in the third section. The fourth section responds to the challenge that a dispositional theory that rejects DP-independence for the moral domain may, nevertheless, do justice to the guiding role of moral verdicts. Finally, the fifth section examines a challenge to the effect that the DP-independence condition does not go beyond the two minimal moral realist theses, provided that the first one (the moral cognitivist thesis) is adequately developed. In this context, we will see that the DP-independence condition does not obviously favor non-naturalist over naturalist moral realism, although it puts constraints on how the latter can be successfully developed.

1. A Prelude: Response-Dependence and Objectivity

Again, the credit goes to Mark Johnston for the jargon "response-dependent". Here is how he introduces the term:

> ... a concept is response-dependent just in case it is either a response-dispositional concept or a truth-functional or quantificational combination of concepts with at least one non-redundant element being a response-dispositional concept. (Johnston, 1993, 104)

while defining "a response-dispositional concept" as follows:

> (9) The concept F = the concept of the disposition to produce R in S under C,
> .... a concept F is a response-dispositional concept when something of the form of (9) is true and (i) the manifestation R is some response of subjects which essentially and intrinsically involves some mental process ... , (ii) the locus S of the manifestation is some subject or group of subjects, and (iii) the conditions C of manifestation are some specified conditions under which the specified subjects can respond to the specified manner. Moreover, we shall require (iv) that the relevant identity does not hold simply on trivializing 'whatever it takes' specifications of either R or S or C. (Johnston, 1993, 103)

In a nutshell, a response-dependent concept is either a concept of the disposition to produce a certain kind of mental response in a certain kind of subject under certain conditions or a complex concept that has such a dispositional concept as one of its nonredundant components.

It is worth highlighting that Johnston applies "response-dependent" to concepts rather than properties, when a *concept* is a theoretical postulate that helps to talk about how we conceive of the world, whereas a *property* is a theoretical postulate that helps to talk of something in the world (a feature of reality).[4] In other words, he introduces the

---

[4] This is my attempt to draw the relevant distinction between concept and property without taking a more substantive stand either on the nature of concepts or on the nature of properties.

jargon "response-dependent" to mark off a way of conceiving rather than a way of being: conceiving of something in terms of a mental disposition with respect to it. A relatively uncontroversial example of a response-dependent concept is the concept expressed by the predicate "is attractive." Conceiving of something as attractive comes to one and the same thing as conceiving of it as disposed to evoke the mental response of attraction (a feeling of attraction, if you wish) in experiencing subjects.[5,6]

I also emphasize that Johnston applies "response-dependent" to concepts rather than predicates, when "predicate" is used to talk about pieces of public language rather than about something at the level of thought. However, the two are related such that synonymous (or intertranslatable) predicates express one and the same concept. So, given that the predicate "is handsome" is synonymous with "is attractive" (in some of its uses), the former predicate expresses the same response-dependent concept as the latter (in the relevant uses), even if it is not lexically marked for doing so. This phenomenon is likely to be more widespread: i.e., predicates of the language that do not bear any obvious lexical connection to names for mental responses, may nevertheless express response-dependent concepts. While this is a mundane observation in the case of the predicate "is handsome," there may be more philosophically interesting cases. Popular candidates are color predicates and value predicates. However, the question that concerns us here is not whether any specific predicates of ordinary language, including those distinctive of moral language, express response-dependent concepts but, rather, whether that issue has any bearing on questions of objectivity.

Addressing that concern, Gideon Rosen argues that the response-dependence of a concept is not a reason per se for rethinking a commitment to the objectivity of the subject matter of a discourse that relies on that concept (Rosen 1994). His discussion of response-dependence and objectivity takes place in the context of a philosophical inquiry into what is at issue between realists about a discourse and putative antirealists who do not question that there are truths to be stated within that discourse but deny objectivity to the facts captured by these truths. His starting point is that the debate concerns a right to "the rhetoric of objectivity" with respect to the discourse in question:

> ... the right to say things like this: Our discourse about X concerns a domain of fact that is *out there*. These facts obtain *anyway*, regardless of what we may think. When all goes well, inquiry in the disputed area *discovers* what is *already* there, rather than *constituting* or *constructing* its object. Successful thought amounts to the *detection* of something real, as opposed to a *projection* onto the real of our own peculiar or subjective perspective.... (Rosen 1994, 278)

---

[5] What is it for *conceiving of something as F* to come to one and the same thing as *conceiving of it as G*? As I understand Johnston, he takes this to be roughly a matter of the same body of (*de dicto*) background beliefs being required for the competent application of the concept *F* and of the concept *G*.

[6] It may be asked whether "is attractive" is better understood as expressing the concept of being *worth* such a mental response. My sense is that at least in a prevalent usage, this English predicate expresses a response-dispositional concept as defined by Johnston.

So, when Rosen concludes that the response-dependence of the concept expressed by the predicate distinctive of a given discourse is "no reason to withhold the rhetoric of objectivity" with respect to that discourse, he is rejecting the proposal that one of the points at issue between realists and antirealists about a discourse is, or should be, the satisfaction of a condition that rules out response-dependence of its distinctive concepts.

Notice that the rhetoric of objectivity, as identified by Rosen, concerns the metaphysical status of the facts in the domain of the discourse in question: what is at issue is *a way of being* rather than a way of conceiving. By contrast, response-dependence, as defined by Johnston, concerns *a way of conceiving* rather than a way of being. However, conceiving of something as having the disposition to produce a certain kind of mental response in a certain kind of subject can capture truths only if there are facts to the effect that some things have that disposition. So, if a discourse relies on response-dependent concepts, then those who reject error theory about this discourse are committed to a certain way of being: namely, that of being related to the mental in such a way as to produce a certain kind of mental response in a certain kind of subject under certain conditions. Rosen's point is that such a way of being should not raise any metaphysical qualms, assuming realism about mental dispositions. A discourse that relies on a response-dependent concept expresses thoughts that truly or falsely relate one kind of perfectly real and, thus, appropriately objective phenomenon (that to which the concept is applied) to another perfectly real and, thus, appropriately objective phenomenon (the relevant kind of disposition to respond). In this respect, it is much like a discourse about what stimulates the secretion of saliva in a certain kind of subject. True, the response is mental in the former case while physical in the latter, but that does not have any antirealist upshot for realists about the mental (Rosen 1994, 293–4).

Rosen illustrates his point with the response-dependent concept of being annoying to fox terriers. With reference to that concept, his point seems trivial.[7] However, he is taking an aim at those who accept, say, that color discourse or value discourse rely on response-dependent concepts and conclude, on that basis, that color or value do not have the objectivity that realists claim for them, since truths about the color or the value of things concern mental responses and are, therefore, not quite "out there" or obtain regardless of how we mentally respond to them. Rosen is arguing that this conclusion is a muddle just like the comparable conclusion concerning a discourse about what is annoying to fox terriers.

Recall that my concern is whether there is a philosophically interesting objectivity condition that goes beyond what is asserted in the two minimal moral realist theses and, moreover, speaks to the concern of moral inquirers who wonder whether there is an objective answer to the opening question of this chapter. My more specific question is whether this condition would require response-independence in Johnston's sense. Now,

---

[7] If we had an entrenched predicate, say, "is fox terrier bombast," which arguably but not obviously expressed this concept, Rosen's point might sound slightly less trivial: namely, the response-dependence of the concept would be no ground for being an antirealist about the discourse about what is fox terrier bombast.

I accept Rosen's point that the response-dependence of the concepts distinctive of a discourse would not per se raise any metaphysical worries about its subject matter, assuming realism about the mental and about dispositions.[8] However, I argue below that there is a narrower kind of response-dependence that is of concern with respect to moral concepts. The concern does not so much have to do with metaphysical worries about the subject matter of moral discourse as with implications for the integrity of the justificatory framework that moral discourse offers. The appropriate condition of objectivity rules out a narrow kind of response-dependence that would undermine the role moral verdicts play in guiding action and attitude by way of justifying and criticizing them.

2. On Seeking Objective Grounds for Moral Evaluation

If two discourses share the same subject matter, then there can hardly be any metaphysical issue concerning the facts that fall within the domain of one of these discourses but not the other. However, there may be a concern about the relation between these facts and one of these discourses that does not extend to the other: a relation that affects speakers' right to "the rhetoric of objectivity" with respect to the discourse. To see this possibility, consider an oral tradition of communal storytelling. An ongoing story is spun within a community and stored in collective memory: what gets added today is part of the story as continued tomorrow. Scribes take turns listening to the storytellers and, aiming for accuracy, recording the story as it unfolds, but they never become part of the storytelling community. Now, pick an arbitrary time when the community is gathered to continue the story and consider an event in the story as it is recounted by a storyteller and accurately recorded by a scribe. It is one and the same (possible/fictional) event, described in the very same words, albeit orally by the storyteller, while in writing by the scribe. However, the relationship of the event to the two different speech acts is quite different, and it seems to affect the right of the authors of these speech acts to "the rhetoric of objectivity": the right to say things like, "Our discourse about X concerns a domain of fact that is *out there*. These facts obtain *anyway*, regardless of what we may think" (Rosen, 1994, 278). It is at least less controversial that the scribes have a right to this kind of rhetoric than that the storytellers have such a right.

Perhaps, it will be objected that the scribes have a right to this rhetoric with respect to facts as to how the storytellers' actual story unfolds but not to the fictional facts. Even if that were true, it would not undermine the main point that I want to make with this example. It serves to illustrate that the same spoken or written text can relate the same events or facts, yet be the vehicle of two very different discourses, embedded in

---

[8] Indeed, Rosen's point would hold equally well, were it *a posteriori* true that moral judgments ascribe a disposition to evoke mental responses of one kind or another.

very different practices. A discourse is something more than spoken or written words, combined in rule-governed ways to form syntactically and semantically well-formed sentences, imbued with meaning. It is a language-infused human activity, which is often embedded within a practice that has various other components to it. The storytellers and the scribes may, for all that matters, recount word by word the same story, yet they are not engaged in the same kind of discourse. It is not obvious that they have the same right to the rhetoric of objectivity that Rosen has identified as being at issue in debates between realists and antirealists about a discourse. So, even if we adopted Rosen's starting point as our own, we should consider the possibility that the relevant question of a right to the rhetoric of objectivity with respect to a discourse pertains neither to the semantics of the language characteristic of that discourse nor to the metaphysics of facts represented in that language, considered in abstraction from how those who thus discourse relate to the subject matter.

I submit that if we are to understand questions of objectivity that arise within and about moral discourse, we had better pay attention to the fact that moral discourse is something more than spoken or written words. It is a language-infused human activity, which is embedded within a wider practice, moral practice, which comprises attempts to guide attitude and action by way of justifying, criticizing, validating, or excusing them. It is a practice that is somewhat conventionally regimented. Not that actual moral practice is monolithic. Some who partake in the practice are quick to blame, while others are forgiving or resort to shaming instead of blaming. Some are quick to pass a moral judgment, while others are less judgmental. Some are apt to be guided by their moral evaluations, others are not. Some are extremely emotional about moral transgressions, while others remain calm even in the face of the gravest injustice. Moreover, all of these propensities come in degrees. It is, nevertheless, safe to say that moral practice does not merely amount to a discourse about good and evil, virtue and vice, right or wrong, social justice and injustice, rights and duties. Moral practice comprises at least (somewhat conventionalized) attempts to steer attitude and action toward what is deemed good, virtuous, right, or just and away from what is deemed bad, vicious, wrong, or unjust. This is done through means like praise, encouragement, exhortation, direction, criticism, condemnation, blame, shame, sanction, and punishment.

The observations in the last paragraph, general and vague as they are, should not be controversial. Notice that they do not introduce the contested doctrine of motivational internalism about moral judgments: the thesis that, necessarily, there is a specific connection between an individual's moral judgment and her motivational state. One can accept that moral discourse has its home within moral practice that comprises attempts to guide attitude and conduct, yet be skeptical of the motivational internalist take on the connection between moral judgment and motivation.[9] One may, moreover, be skeptical

---

[9] I am speaking here of traditional motivational internalism. However, my remark may seem friendly to communal internalism (Tresan 2009; Bedke 2009): (roughly) the thesis that, necessarily, an individual A tokens a moral judgment of a kind M only if A is part of a community in which tokens of M are typically related to a specific kind of motivation. I am not sure whether to accept this modal claim, and nothing in the text commits me to it. Thanks to Tristram McPherson for pressing me to make this clear.

of the idea that a motivational role is somehow writ into the semantic content of moral sentences, or the intentional content of the mental states expressed.[10] Of course, one of the challenges of metaethics is to illuminate the nature of the guiding role of moral judgments, but that project will not be undertaken in this chapter. The point to be made here is that this role, whatever its exact nature, bears on how to understand the nature and significance of questions of objectivity that arise within and about moral discourse.

Also, notice that the guiding role of moral discourse with respect to attitudes does not merely pertain to the kinds of attitude that are needed for moral judgments to motivate action. Within moral practice, a discourse about good and evil, virtue and vice, right and wrong, rights and duties, social justice and injustice plays a far more extensive role in guiding and shaping mental attitude. It has at least an indirect role in cultivating compassion, a sense of justice and fairness, respect for autonomy and rights, conscientiousness and responsibility toward others, etc. Our moral sentiments and other emotional responses are honed within moral practice such as to instill principles or values into the very fiber of our being, shaping not only how we act but, also, what we expect and demand of ourselves and of others. Judgments reached within moral discourse serve as a basis for criticizing or justifying not only motivations, decisions, intentions, and actions but also the sentiments, be they our own or those of others. Though motivational and emotional reform is not directly under our voluntary control, it is to some extent feasible to initiate changes in attitudes through means like praise, encouragement, exhortation, criticism, blame, shame, sanction, and punishment. At least, so our moral practice presumes.

It is open to question whether moral claims would provide a credible basis for justification or criticism of our attitudes were the subject matter of moral discourse our dispositions to have these very mental responses. This point is something that Jeremy Bentham was onto in his criticism of "the principle of sympathy and antipathy":

> By the principle of sympathy and antipathy, I mean that principle which approves or disapproves of certain actions, not on account of their tending to augment the happiness, nor yet on account of their tending to diminish the happiness of the party whose interest is in question, but merely *because a man finds himself disposed to approve or disapprove of them*: holding up that approbation or disapprobation as a sufficient reason for itself, and disclaiming the necessity of looking out for any extrinsic ground. . . . It is manifest, that this is rather a principle in name than in reality: it is not a positive principle of itself, so much as a term employed to signify the negation of all principle. *What one expects to find in a principle is something that points out some external consideration, as a means of warranting and guiding the internal sentiments of approbation and disapprobation*: this expectation is but ill fulfilled by a proposition, which does neither more nor less than hold up each of those sentiments as a ground and standard for itself. (Bentham, 1789, Chapter 2, §11–12—italics mine)

---

[10] For my skepticism of traditional motivational internalism, see Svavarsdóttir 1999 and 2006.

It was important to Bentham as a social and moral reformer that there be grounds for criticism of received moral opinions, intuitions, and sentiments. A principle that specifies our dispositions to approve and disapprove of things as a measure of what is right or wrong would not win favor with him. However, his point cuts deeper: this could not be the content of the fundamental moral principle (the most general claim about what makes for right or wrong) because a principle with such content does not provide a ground sufficiently independent of moral sentiments to serve to justify and guide them. True, he mentions only approval and disapproval but, surely, he intends these to encompass any kind of moral sentiment.[11]

Bentham hankers for "some external consideration, as a means of warranting and guiding the internal sentiments of approbation and disapprobation" (Bentham, 1789, Chapter 2, §11–12). Such talk of "external" considerations or grounds is part of the common rhetoric of objectivity: the discourse in question is about facts that are "out there" or part of "the external world." If such rhetoric were taken literally, it might be thought that objectivity is supposed to be a matter of the relevant facts existing at a spatial location different from those occupied by those who thus discourse. More plausibly the allusion to spatial location is treated metaphorically. One possibility is that these locutions be taken to refer to the part of reality that does not contain or essentially relate to anything mental. After all, "out there" and "external" form a triad with "mind-independent" in the rhetoric of objectivity.[12] However, since Bentham finds his "external consideration" in the disposition of actions and policies to produce pain and pleasure,[13] he is hardly using this locution to refer to something essentially unrelated to the mental realm. His worry has nothing to do with the metaphysical status of mental dispositions, and it would not arise simply on the grounds that the concepts of moral discourse display some form of response-dependence in Johnston's sense. Rosen's point is, therefore, irrelevant to Bentham's concern.

Bentham's worry pertains to the possibility that a disposition to produce *specific kinds of* mental response sets the standard of right and wrong: the very same kinds of mental response as are justified or criticized with reference to that standard. His worry concerns the integrity of the justificatory framework that relies on the standard of right and wrong if that standard is set by dispositions to produce specific kinds of mental response: namely, moral sentiments toward the object of assessment. Thus, "external consideration" refers, in his mouth, to the part of reality that is independent of the kinds of mental response that verdicts, reached on the basis of moral principles, are called upon

---

[11] There is a familiar strategy for responding to such a worry by arguing that the subject matter concerns idealized responses. The significance of this strategy for our inquiry into objectivity will be discussed in section 4.

[12] See my discussion of this triad in section V of Svavarsdóttir 2001, 161–66.

[13] I am alluding here to Bentham's utilitarian moral theory according to which the fact that an action is right or wrong concerns the balance of pleasure over pain that the action is disposed to produce as compared to the balance of pleasure over pain that its alternatives are disposed to produce.

to guide by way of justification or criticism. This may, however, be parts of mental or social reality.

Bentham is a normative ethicist in search of grounds in a moral principle for criticism of legal, political, and social institutions. It is tempting to see his quest for external grounds as an example of how the concern for objective grounds for moral evaluation may surface in normative inquiry. If that is so—if his quest for "external consideration" is reasonably seen as a yearning for the right to the rhetoric of objectivity with respect to moral discourse—then earning that right requires that the subject matter of moral discourse be proven to lie within the part of reality that is independent of the kinds of mental response that moral verdicts are called upon to guide by way of justification or criticism.

Moreover, a very similar worry to Bentham's faces the metaethicist in pursuit of an understanding of moral discourse: can the discourse be interpreted such as to make sense of and vindicate the idea that its verdicts can be called upon to guide action and attitude by way of justifying and criticizing them? This is a perfect niche for a question of objectivity regarding moral discourse: do these verdicts, if correct, provide an objective enough a ground for them to play such a guiding role? I will refer to this as "the Benthamite metaworry" from now on. The question of objectivity is not only whether such verdicts have correctness conditions and whether some of them are indeed correct. It also concerns whether their correctness conditions are independent of the kinds of attitude that are, by the conventions of moral practice, to be justified or criticized on their basis. At issue is not only the dependence relation between an actual moral verdict and an actual attitude (or attitude-disposition) that the moral verdict is, on a particular occasion, used to criticize or justify. The worry concerns whether the correctness conditions for a type of moral verdict is independent enough of actual and possible attitudes (or attitude-dispositions) of a certain kind for that type of verdict to play a role in an entrenched practice of basing criticism or justification of that kind of attitude on that type of moral verdict.[14] Rosen's point is irrelevant for addressing that concern. Like Bentham's own worry, the Benthamite metaworry is not rooted in antirealism about the mental realm. It concerns the integrity of the justificatory framework that moral discourse offers with respect to our attitude and conduct.

3. The Objectivity Condition Identified: DP-Independence

Recall that the first minimal realist thesis is that sentences containing moral terms are truth-evaluable, while the second minimal realist thesis is that some moral sentences

---

[14] Of course, the independence in question is not a sufficient condition for moral verdicts of that kind to provide a credible basis for criticism and justification of that type of attitude.

are true not in virtue of meaning alone but, also, thanks to how reality is. The main question of this chapter is whether there is a philosophically interesting objectivity condition that goes beyond the two minimal realist theses about moral discourse and that speaks to the concern of moral inquirers who wonder, say, whether any objective answer is to be found in the fundamental disagreement between Kantians and Utilitarians. The reflections of last section have, I submit, put us in a position to identify this condition.

The example of the storytellers and the scribes helped us to see that even if we adopted Rosen's starting point as our own, we should consider the possibility that the relevant question of a right to the rhetoric of objectivity with respect to a discourse pertains neither to the semantics of the language characteristic of that discourse nor to the metaphysics of facts represented in that language, at least not their metaphysical nature considered in abstraction from how those who thus discourse relate to the subject matter. Plausibly, the relevant question of objectivity probes, at least in part, whether the subject matter of the discourse is ontically dependent in any way on the area of thought, discourse, or inquiry *in question*. In other words, the issue is whether the existence and configuration of facts in the domain of the given discourse depend in any way on how people conceive of, talk about, or conduct inquiries about them *within that very discourse*. This is what I have called (somewhat inadequately) "observer-independence" in earlier work (Svavarsdóttir 2001). To highlight the discourse-relationality of such questions of objectivity, I shift now to the jargon "discourse-independence."

To see better what is at issue consider a toy example of a discourse about "cool outfits." Let's assume (for the purpose of illustration) that all that is being discussed within that discourse is whether one outfit, or another, is disposed to be admired in a city that is leading on the creative art scene at the time. Moreover, let's assume (also for the purpose of illustration) that we are realists about facts about the following: outfits; the mental disposition to admire; cities; creative art scenes; and leadership on the creative art scene at a time. Yet, which outfits are cool, at any given time, may depend on how people conceive of and talk about outfits within the "cool-outfits" discourse. For which outfits, people in the leading cities on the creative art scene currently admire may be partly determined[15] by how the discourse unfolds in the leading cities on the art scene. So, it makes perfect sense to wonder whether the subject matter of the discourse about cool outfits is *discourse-dependent*.[16] I venture that this is easily recognizable as a question regarding the objectivity of the discourse, although it may not raise any practical concern that this discourse, in particular, lacks this kind of objectivity.

---

[15] In a metaphysical rather than an epistemological sense of "determine."

[16] This requires neither that it be *a priori* that the discourse helps to determine which outfits are admired by the relevant people nor that it is *necessary* that what a group of humans admire is partly determined by how they communicate with each other. It suffices that, given the contingent as well as the necessary features of the actual world and given the semantics of the discourse, the discourse could not have "latched onto" any discourse-independent features of reality such as to be about them. The consequent in the last claim may, however, need to be understood as negating a metaphysical possibility.

The issue of discourse-independence can arise for any kind of discourse. The reflections on moral discourse and practice in last section suggest, I submit, that a certain kind of practice-relationality is also at issue in discussions of objectivity with respect to moral discourse. At least partly, they pertain to the relationship between the subject matter of the discourse and the kinds of mental response that the discourse is called upon to guide within an entrenched practice. The question is whether the existence and configuration of facts that lie in the domain of the discourse depend on *the very same kinds* of mental response that verdicts, reached within the discourse, are called upon to guide within a *somewhat conventionally regimented* practice of which the discourse is a proper part. If the answer is in the affirmative, I will say that the subject matter of the discourse is *practice-dependent*. It is my contention that the opposite, *practice-independence*, is needed for the objectivity condition that meets the desiderata laid out in the introduction. To clarify this condition, let me add a few words about the qualification "somewhat conventionally regimented" in the characterization of practice-dependence.

We humans are inventive in exploiting extant discourses for diverse purposes, including those of guiding attitude and conduct. Any kind of verdict from almost any kind of discourse can be creatively used to guide attitude or conduct in some context, or another. One or more individuals may even make it their practice or habit to exploit one particular discourse for that purpose, even in the absence of an entrenched social or linguistic convention to do so. However, often we use "practice" over more conventionally regimented patterns of linguistic as well as nonlinguistic behavior within a population. Talk of "moral practice" is a case in point. Of course, within such a conventionally regimented practice, individuals make many creative and idiosyncratic "moves" for diverse purposes. This may include the exact way they use its verdicts to guide attitude or conduct, their own or that of others. However, in doing so, they most likely rely on their understanding of how verdicts, reached within the discourse, are called upon to guide attitude and conduct in more conventionally regimented ways.[17] Practice-independence with respect to a discourse is a matter of its verdicts being suitably independent of *the kinds of* mental response that they are conventionally called upon to guide rather than of the mental response that they are actually called upon to guide on any given occasion. Some of the latter uses may be very unconventional and even highly creative.

To see better the significance of the qualification "somewhat conventionally regimented" in the characterization of practice-independence as well as, more generally, what the issue is, I turn again to the toy example of the "cool outfits" discourse. For

---

[17] For example, within moral practice creative uses of moral verdicts to guide attitude or conduct are most likely to rely on an understanding how verdicts, reached within moral discourse, are conventionally called upon to guide attitude and conduct. To take a simple example, verdicts couched in terms of "is good" and "is right" are, by and large, used to guide people toward what is thus described, whereas verdicts couched in terms of "is bad" and "is wrong" are, by and large, used to guide people away from what is thus described. Another example is that there is a significant difference between the conventional use of moral verdicts to guide an attitude such as guilt and to guide an attitude such as amusement (insofar as such attitudes can be guided).

the sake of illustration, one more assumption needs to be added: namely, that verdicts about cool outfits are conventionally called upon to guide the sentiment of admiration directed toward outfits within a practice that encompasses the discourse. Given our assumption regarding the subject matter of this discourse, what is, or is not, a cool outfit is a practice-dependent matter because what is, or is not, a cool outfit depends on *the very same kind* of response (admiration) that verdicts about what is a cool outfit are conventionally called upon to guide within an entrenched practice that encompasses this discourse. This does not mean that it is impossible to use these verdicts to guide sentiments of admiration. Indeed, it may make it quite easy when addressing those who aspire to admire outfits admired in cities leading on the creative art scene. Practice-dependence need not even bother anyone with respect to the "cool outfits" discourse.

I will call practice-independence in combination with discourse-independence with respect to the same discourse, "discourse-and-practice-independence"—or, "DP-independence" for short. I will not attempt to formulate counterfactually, or in a possible world speak, the dependence relation at stake, since such an approach to stating dependence relations precisely has not proved successful. The important thing to note is the characteristic relata that enter into the dependence relation at stake: on the one hand, the kinds of fact that lie within the domain of a discourse and, on the other hand, the kinds of verdict that are reached within that discourse (discourse-dependence) or the kinds of mental response that are somewhat conventionally guided by such verdicts (practice-dependence). My thesis is that the objectivity condition with respect to moral discourse, which meets the desiderata laid out in the introduction, is the condition of DP-independence: *The DP-independence condition*, from now on.[18]

It may be of limited philosophical or practical interest whether the toy discourse about "cool outfits" meets the DP-independence condition. Even if verdicts reached within that discourse were conventionally used to guide sentiments of admiration, practice-dependence may in no way undermine the discourse, especially insofar as the verdicts are addressed to those who aspire to admire outfits admired in cities leading on the creative art scene. The same hardly holds for moral discourse. If the reflections in last section have not yet made this amply clear, consider the concern of moral

---

[18] I am not aware of anyone having already identified this condition of objectivity.—David Enoch (Enoch 2011, 3) introduces an objectivity condition as one of the commitments of his robust moral realism and initially characterizes it as requiring what he loosely calls "response-independence" and, then, elaborates on that jargon such that the requirement is a combination of observer-independence, as characterized in my 2001 article, and what he calls "agent-independence." His notion of agent-independence is very different from my notion of practice-independence as it focuses on the attitudes of the person appraised. Enoch does not develop his notion of agent-independence, and I doubt that it is on the right track to identifying the appropriate kind of condition of objectivity.—A condition called "standpoint-independence" has figured into some of the recent literature on the distinction between moral realism and moral constructivism. As specified, this condition seems close to my condition of observer-independence although the connotations of "observer" are avoided, and it made explicit that the conceptions, of which the facts are independent, may be the content of practical attitudes like valuing or the kind of attitude that an individual or collective decision yields (Milo 1995; Shafer Landau 2003, 15; Street 2010, 271).

inquirers who wonder whether there is an objective answer in the fundamental disagreement between Kantians and Utilitarians. *Prima facie*, their concern would not be addressed by an answer whose correctness depends on whether the moral sentiments of one group of people, or another, are apt to comport better with the Kantian or the Utilitarian view.[19] For in moral practice, guidance is sought in a verdict that provides the basis for justification or criticism of sentiments *of that kind*. Moral verdicts guide by way of justification or criticism. Practice-dependence would presumably undermine this role of moral verdicts. It would, also, be *prima facie* troublesome for the guiding role of these verdicts, if they were discourse-dependent: that is, if there were nothing independent of how people conceive of, talk about, or conduct inquiries within moral discourse that determined whether verdicts reached within moral discourse were correct. The burden would at least be on the shoulders of those who embrace discourse- or practice-dependence of moral verdicts to show that this does not undermine their role in justifying or criticizing the moral sentiments.

The concern of moral inquirers who wonder whether there is an objective answer in the fundamental disagreement between Utilitarians and Kantians would, I submit, be addressed by showing that the DP-independence condition is met: (i) the correct answer is determined by facts that are independent of how people conceive of, talk about, or conduct inquiries within moral discourse; and (ii) the existence and configuration of these facts are independent of the kinds of mental response that verdicts, reached within moral discourse, are conventionally called upon to guide within moral practice. Notice that the DP-independence condition pertains to a metaphysical dependence relation between, on the one hand, the kinds of fact that lie within the domain of a discourse and, on the other hand, the kinds of verdict that are reached within that very discourse (discourse-dependence) or the kinds of mental response that such verdicts conventionally guide by way of justification or criticism (practice-dependence). So, after all, Rosen is right that the issue of objectivity is metaphysical, although it does not concern the intrinsic metaphysical nature of the facts in the domain of moral discourse, considered in abstraction from how those who thus discourse relate to the subject matter. Moreover, he is right that the response-dependence of moral concepts per se is not a problem. The DP-independence condition, nevertheless, rules out a narrow kind of response-dependence of moral concepts: a moral concept cannot be, or incorporate, a concept of the disposition to produce a mental response of a kind that moral verdicts conventionally guide by way of justifying or criticizing. This is the kind of response-dependence that would undermine the guiding-role of moral verdicts.

Should the DP-independence thesis be included among the commitments of moral realism? As noted in the introduction, one may worry that questions as to whether the commitments of moral realism extend beyond the two minimal realist theses merely

---

[19] What if the group of people were the morally wise or ideal agents with respect to the moral sentiments? This suggestion is of a piece with the suggestion that Bentham's worry does not arise if the subject matter of moral discourse concerns idealized instead of actual dispositions to approve or disapprove. Again, this suggestion will be addressed in section 4.

raise a philosophically uninteresting terminological issue as to how to use the jargon "realism" within metaethics. However, we are now in a position to appreciate that moral realism should incur a commitment to DP-independence. Assuming that moral realists are committed to meet the Benthamite metaworry, they are committed to give an account of moral discourse that vindicates the idea that the verdicts of moral discourse can be called upon to guide action and attitude by way of justifying and criticizing them.[20] Consequently, they should be committed to the DP-independence condition.

4. Moral Dispositionalism and DP-Independence

Perhaps, it will be objected that there is room to address the Benthamite metaworry within a dispositional theory that accepts the two minimal realist theses about moral discourse but rejects DP-independence for its subject matter. If that were correct, the reason that I have given for including DP-independence among the commitments of moral realism would be undercut. A case in point is a sophisticated version of the dispositional theory that identifies the subject matter of moral discourse as the moral sentiments that would be evoked in actual human beings under specific hypothetical conditions: conditions selected because they are recognizable as ideal for forming these sentiments. This development of the dispositional theory is, indeed, designed to accommodate the guiding as well as the justificatory role of moral judgments.

On this view, the judgment that the action is right (or wrong) is the judgment that some feature of the action would evoke, under such and such conditions, a certain kind of sentiment: a sentiment that is known to ground a disposition to take (or avoid) that kind of action. Presumably, the crucial idea is that *the understanding* of a moral judgment *as directing people toward (or away from) an action* is an abstraction from *the understanding* of the sentiment (that the action is judged to evoke) as *grounding a disposition to take (or avoid) that action*. Moreover, given that the specified conditions are *recognizable as ideal for forming such a sentiment*, the moral judgment can sensibly be understood as providing *good* guidance with respect to the action and as providing a basis for justifying (or criticizing) our actual moral sentiment toward the action. For our actual moral sentiments can be measured against what the moral judgment tells us: namely, how we would be disposed toward the action under such and such conditions (*recognizable as ideal for forming the kind of sentiment in question*). Needless to say, the understood directive, provided by a particular moral judgment, would not matter unless the judgment were true.

---

[20] Notably, Peter Railton is a reductive moral realist who acknowledges the need to give a vindicating account of moral discourse. See his distinction between vindicative and eliminative reduction in Railton 1989.

This response to the Benthamite metaworry requires that there be some standard for sentiments in light of which some conditions are recognizable as ideal for forming the relevant kind of moral sentiment. There are various approaches for developing the view that there is such a standard. One possibility is to argue that these sentiments have representational content—they represent the world as being a certain way—and forming them under certain conditions enhances the likelihood, or even guarantees, their accuracy. Another possibility is to argue that the standard in question is a norm of practical rationality that applies to such sentiments. The third possibility is that the standard has to do with prudence: forming such sentiments under such conditions is conducive to living one's life guided by sentiments that one will not later regret. A fourth possibility is that the standard has to do with some other ideal, say the ideal of leading an enlightened life rather than wallowing in ignorance. That is, the standard pertains to sentiments formed under full or the best available information.

As ingenious as this approach is, it would be overly hasty to conclude that a dispositional theory that rejects DP-independence for the subject matter of moral discourse can do justice to the guiding role of moral verdicts with respect to the sentiments and can, thus, successfully address the Benthamite metaworry. For the worry can be resurrected with respect to the proposed standard for sentiments. It may be questioned whether there is a standard for doing the requisite job in underwriting the justificatory and critical role of moral judgments: a standard that is independent of the workings of moral discourse and of the kinds of mental response that moral verdicts are conventionally called upon to guide in moral practice.

Assume that this worry can be met. That would amount to showing that it is possible to secure the appropriate kind of DP-independence within a theory that identifies an idealized disposition to evoke moral sentiments as the subject matter of moral discourse. If that can indeed be shown, it would not undermine my claim that moral realism should incur a commitment to DP-independence, presuming that it is committed to meet the Benthamite metaworry. Instead, it would show that *even if the DP-independence condition is included among the commitments of moral realism*, it is open to question that all versions of a dispositional theory that identifies the subject matter of moral discourse as dispositions to evoke moral sentiments count as antirealist positions. That would be no mean feat.[21]

---

[21] According to expressivists, dispositionalists, like other natural subjectivists, mistake the attitudes that moral language is semantically suited to express for the subject matter of moral discourse. At issue is the first minimal moral realist thesis, the moral cognitivist thesis. Now, as I have formulated the DP-independence thesis, it has teeth only if moral cognitivism is presupposed. For it is the cognitivist thesis that imports the idea that the discourse has a distinctive subject matter that may, or may not, be DP-dependent. However, we have seen that the objectivity worry is not so much a metaphysical worry as a worry about the integrity of the justificatory framework that relies on the standard of right and wrong, if that standard is set by dispositions to evoke the kinds of mental response that is subject to justification or criticism on the basis of moral verdicts. It makes no difference to this worry whether moral claims describe or express such mental responses. Thus, it is far from clear that expressivists can duck the question of objectivity identified and clarified here. In other words, expressivism is not at an obvious advantage to moral realism when it comes to the issue of objectivity with respect to moral discourse.

5. Moral Realism and DP-Independence

Once again, the first minimal realist thesis pertains to the semantics of the discourse (namely, the cognitivist thesis that sentences containing moral terms are truth-evaluable), while the second minimal realist thesis is about the relation between the discourse and the world (namely, some moral sentences are true thanks to how reality is). The main question of this chapter is whether there is a philosophically interesting objectivity condition that goes beyond the two minimal realist theses about moral discourse and that speaks to the concern of moral inquirers who wonder, say, whether any objective answer is to be found in the fundamental disagreement between Kantians and Utilitarians. I have proposed an answer to this question: a condition requiring that the subject matter of moral discourse be DP-independent fits the bill. In this section, I examine a final challenge to the effect that the DP-independence condition is superfluous because it does not go beyond the two minimal moral realist theses, provided that the moral cognitivist thesis is adequately developed.

This challenge may be developed with reference to the work of J. L. Mackie, the father of moral error theory (Mackie 1977). Mackie's queerness argument against moral realism rests on an analysis of moral concepts that supposedly reveals what the world would have to be like for synthetic moral judgments to be true.[22] According to Mackie's analysis, the objects of moral evaluation would literally have to *call for action* irrespective of the attitudes that any of us may have:

> The ordinary user of moral language means to say something about whatever it is that he characterizes morally, for example a possible action, as it is in itself, or would be if it were realized, and not about, or even simply expressive of, his, or anyone else's, attitude or relation to it. But the something he wants to say is . . . something that involves a call for action or for the refraining from action, and one that is absolute, not contingent upon any desire or preference or policy or choice, his own or anyone else's. (Mackie 1977, 33)

Mackie's analysis implies that the meaning of moral terms, or the content of moral concepts, is such that there would not be any (synthetic) moral truths unless there were DP-independent[23] features that ornate whatever is subject to moral evaluation and that call for action (or the refraining from action). If this were correct, the second minimal realist thesis would imply that there are such DP-independent but action-calling

---

[22] In analyzing moral concepts, Mackie does not use the method of thought experiments but, instead, scrutinizes general claims about rightness and goodness that philosophers have made on putative *a priori* grounds. See especially Mackie 1977, 30–35. He agrees with G. E. Moore that an analysis of moral concepts will not yield a naturalistic reduction. Nevertheless, he offers an analysis of the contribution of moral concepts to the truth-evaluable content of moral judgments.

[23] I take Mackie to be talking about independence from attitudes, inclusive of those kinds that are expressed or regulated by moral judgments. Or perhaps, these are the only attitudes that he has in mind.

features.[24] In other words, Mackie's analysis implies that DP-independence is writ into the conceptualization of the subject of any moral judgment, so that the DP-independence condition would be satisfied if there were true moral judgments as the second minimal realist thesis claims. So, the DP-independence condition seems superfluous, given Mackie's analysis of moral concepts.

I stand by the conclusion of section 3 and reject the claim that the DP-independence condition would be superfluous, were the moral cognitivist thesis adequately developed. First of all, note that the DP-independence condition is stronger (i.e., rules out more possibilities) when advanced as a self-standing thesis that goes beyond the two minimal realist theses rather than as a condition writ into the conceptualization of the object of moral evaluation. A self-standing DP-independence condition would be violated if the kinds of mental response open to moral criticism, though not the subject matter of moral discourse, figured into the reference (or extension) fixing mechanism for moral concepts.[25] In that case, which configurations of facts provide the truth-conditions for moral judgments would be at least partly dependent on the relevant kinds of mental response, or dispositions to have them, because *ex hypothesi* those helped to fix the reference (or the extension) of the moral concepts applied. By contrast, writ into the content of moral conceptualizations, the DP-independence condition only rules out that the contribution of moral concepts to truth-evaluable thought content is such that the object of evaluation *is represented as* disposed to evoke a moral sentiment (or some other kind of response that is subject to moral scrutiny). Thus, the DP-independence condition would not be superfluous even if an adequate development of the cognitivist thesis ruled out that such were the truth-evaluable content of moral thought.

It may be objected that I have failed to do justice to Mackie's crucial claim: to conceive of something in moral terms is to conceive of it as, irrespective of any attitude, calling for action. The conceived feature is *a DP-independent call for action*, something akin to *an attitude-independent demand* emanating from the object of evaluation. This is the mysterious feature that moral judgments supposedly ascribe. If, *per impossible*, some attitudes figured into the mechanism for fixing the reference of moral concepts to such a feature, their role in the reference fixing would in no way undermine the action-guiding role of moral judgments. Regardless of how the reference were fixed, it is the very nature of the feature—the attitude-independent call for action emanating from the object of evaluation—that would underwrite the action guiding role of moral judgments. Of course, Mackie believes that there is no such feature in reality and, hence, that no moral concept (or moral predicate) successfully designates such a feature. However, it is an implication of his conceptual thesis that if moral judgments were true, then the

---

[24] A denial of this thesis is the second premise in Mackie's argument from queerness. According to Mackie, it is "factual analysis" that reveals that the world is and could not be that way. Given his empiricism, it is clear that he has in mind an analysis of the results of empirical inquiry.

[25] If the reference or designation of a concept is essential to its nature, the point would have to be reformulated such as to be about the mechanism that fixes that *our* representations involve a concept that references or designates such and such a property.

DP-independent thesis would be satisfied. In other words, if Mackie were right about the contribution of moral concepts to the truth-evaluable content of moral judgments, then a separate DP-independence condition would be superfluous.

I take the point. However, I question its significance because I am skeptical of Mackie's analysis of the content of moral claims. Granted, Mackie captures something about our understanding of moral claims, at least many moral claims, when he characterizes them as *calls for action* (or the refraining from action) that are not supposed to be "contingent upon any desire or preference or policy or choice," neither the speaker's nor anyone else's (Mackie 1977, 33). However, such an understanding is best seen as relying on a metaphorical way of thinking and speaking. It is people who literally call for something, issue imperatives, make demands, or otherwise boss us around. We speak figuratively when we say that something about an action calls for it. It is people who call for this or that, but moral considerations are often cited as the justification for the call to action or for attitude. The real mystery about morality is not that to be right or good is to call for action or attitude. That way of speaking just reflects our tendency to anthropomorphize. Instead, the mystery is that being right or good grounds justification or criticism of attitude and action.[26]

One of the challenges of metaethics is to illuminate the nature of the guiding role of moral judgments, including their role in the criticism and justification of moral sentiments. However, it is not clear what implication this role has concerning the contributions of moral concepts to the truth-conditional content of moral judgments and, hence, concerning what reality would have to be like for at least some of them to be true. It is far from trivial to assume that for a judgment to provide a basis for justification or criticism irrespective of any actual or possible attitude toward its subject, its content must be such that it is true only if its subject has a metaphysically mysterious feature, at least, by the lights of naturalists. Certainly, it is a completely familiar thought that justification and criticism need to be grounded in judgments that are true thanks to the natural or social order of things, yet not thanks to anyone's attitude toward what is to be justified or criticized based on these judgments.

Perhaps, it will be objected that moral and other normative judgments are distinctive exactly in that they do not merely provide a basis in natural or social reality for justification and criticism of action and attitude. Rather, they purport to provide the ultimate normative grounds of justification and criticism: grounds based in *normative reality*, which is independent of non-normatively characterized attitudes. Moral and other normative judgments conceive of the grounds for justification and criticism in normative terms: i.e., whichever features moral judgments identify as the basis for justification or criticism, the judgments identify them by means of normative concepts (modes of presentation) that signal that these features provide grounds for justification or criticism.

---

[26] I borrow this remark, almost *ad verbatim*, from the introduction of Svavarsdóttir 2019. However, here I ignore the main conclusion of that paper regarding how to rethink moral cognitivism. Bringing together my conclusions as to how to construe the objectivity condition and as to how to develop the cognitivist condition will have to await another time.

I readily concede the last point. However, it does not trivially imply that the features identified are metaphysically different from any feature of the empirically accessible social or natural order. Recall the distinction drawn in the first section between *a way of conceiving* and *a way of being*. I readily concede that *a moral way of conceiving* of an object of evaluation is *a way of conceiving some of its features as grounding a justification or criticism of actions and attitudes*. Such a way of conceiving an object may come with a commitment to a certain way of being: namely, having features that *provide basis for justification or criticism* of a certain kind of mental response. However, I question that it is in any way obvious that conceiving of an object in this way comes with a commitment to *a way of being* that raises metaphysical mysteries about the object of evaluation, or its features, even for naturalists.

Sure, there are philosophical puzzles regarding the nature of justification and criticism, including the kind that draws upon moral judgments. However, the philosophical mystery we ponder when we try to understand what it is to *justify or criticize* actions and attitudes *based on their features* may solely lie at the level of mind rather than at the level of reality, except insofar as the mental is part of reality. It is, indeed, hard to illuminate what distinguishes the following three kinds of thought processes: free-associating about φ-ing in light of *that p*, explaining φ-ing with *that p*, and justifying φ-ing on the grounds *that p*. Nevertheless, it is questionable to assume that an illuminating account of these three kinds of thought process must postulate that whatever explains or justifies something else is a metaphysically mysterious feature over and above the empirically accessible features of the natural or social order that are referenced in the explanation or justification.[27] It is far from clear what implication the role of moral judgments in justification has for what to say about the contributions of moral concepts to the truth-conditional content of moral judgments and, hence, for what reality would have to be like for at least some of them to be true.

A self-standing DP-independence condition seems less controversial than Mackie's analysis of the contribution of moral concepts to the truth-evaluable content of moral judgments. So, I question an appeal to Mackie's analysis in defense of the claim that a self-standing DP-independence condition is superfluous. The reflections in section 2 set the stage for and motivated the DP-independence condition without making any assumption about the content of the concepts that figure into moral judgments. We saw that the significance of questions of objectivity that arise within and about moral discourse cannot be fully appreciated without understanding the role that moral claims play in a somewhat conventionally regimented practice of guiding action and attitude by way of criticizing, justifying, validating, or excusing them. This observation played a crucial role in motivating the DP-independence condition, and it seems less controversial than

---

[27] These remarks do not presuppose that a purely naturalized account can be given of the threefold distinction between free-associating, explaining, and justifying, be it in the theoretical or the practical domain. In particular, it might be impossible to give a fully naturalized account of what it is to justify something within moral practice, even if moral judgments (on which such justification is based) had truth conditions that naturalists would find unproblematic.

Mackie's conceptual analysis of the content of moral judgments. Hence, it seems questionable to reject DP-independence as a well-motivated self-standing condition on the grounds that it does not go beyond the two minimal moral realist theses given Mackie's analysis of moral concepts.

To summarize, my response to the Mackie-inspired challenge to the significance of adding the DP-independence condition to the commitments of moral realism is as follows: Admittedly, the condition would be superfluous, were Mackie's analysis of the contribution of moral concepts to the truth-evaluable content of moral judgments correct. For his analysis implies that DP-independence is writ into the conceptualization of the subject of any moral judgment, so that the DP-independence condition would be satisfied if there were true moral judgments as the second minimal realist thesis claims. However, due to other features of his analysis, the DP-independence condition is less controversial than his analysis. It is, therefore, questionable to appeal to Mackie's analysis in defense of the claim that a self-standing DP-independence condition is superfluous. This does not rule out the possibility of introducing DP-independence as integral to the moral cognitivist thesis rather than as a self-standing thesis. My reason for favoring the latter is that the DP-independence condition is appropriately stronger when advanced as a self-standing thesis than as writ into the content of moral judgments. Of course, as a self-standing thesis, the DP-independence condition provides a motivation to steer clear of accounts of the truth-evaluable content of moral claims that introduce DP-dependence and, hence, puts constraints on how naturalist moral realism can be successfully developed. However, that hardly weighs in favor of a challenge to the significance of adding a self-standing DP-independence condition to the commitments of moral realism.

6. Concluding Remarks

Although nothing approximating a proof has been offered, I hope to have convinced the reader that there is a philosophically interesting objectivity condition, going beyond the two minimal realist theses about moral discourse and speaking to the concern of moral inquirers who wonder, say, whether any objective answer is to be found in the fundamental disagreement between Kantians and Utilitarians. This is the DP-independence condition, which as applied to moral discourse requires (i) that the existence and configuration of facts in its domain do not depend on how people conceive of, talk about, or conduct inquiries about them within moral discourse, and (ii) that the existence and configuration of facts that lie in its domain do not somehow depend on the same kinds of mental response that moral verdicts are (conventionally) called upon to guide within moral practice. Insofar as moral realism is committed to make sense of and vindicate the notion that moral verdicts can be called upon to guide action and attitude by way of justifying and criticizing them, it should incur a commitment to the DP-independence condition. Finally, we have seen that the condition does not obviously favor non-naturalist over naturalist moral realism, although it puts constraints on how the latter can be successfully developed.[28]

References

Bedke, M. S. 2009. "Moral Judgment Purposivism: Saving Internalism from Amoralism." *Philosophical Studies* 144: 189–209.

Bentham, Jeremy. [1789] 1988. *Principles of Morals and Legislation*. Repr. New York: Prometheus Books.

Enoch, David. 2011. *Taking Morality Seriously: A Defense of Robust Realism*. Oxford: Oxford University Press.

Johnston, Mark. 1993. "Objectivity Refigured: Pragmatism without Verificationism." In *Reality, Representation, and Projection*, edited by John Haldane and Crispin Wright, 85–130. Oxford: Oxford University Press.

Mackie, J. L. 1977. *Ethics: Inventing Right and Wrong*. New York: Penguin Books Ltd.

Milo, Ronald. 1995. "Contractarian Constructivism." *Journal of Philosophy* 92(4): 181–204.

Railton, Peter. 1989. "Naturalism and Prescriptivity." *Social Philosophy and Policy* 7: 151–176.

Rosen, Gideon. 1994. "Objectivity and Modern Idealism: What Is the Question?" In *Philosophy in Mind*, edited by M. Michael and J. O'Leary-Hawthorne, 277–319. Dordrecht: Kluwer.

Russ Shafer-Landau. 2003. *Moral Realism: A Defence*. Oxford: Oxford University Press.

Street, Sharon. 2010. "What Is Constructivism in Ethics and Metaethics?" *Philosophy Compass* 5(5): 363–384.

Svavarsdóttir, Sigrún. 1999. "Moral Cognitivism and Motivation." *Philosophical Review* 108: 161–219.

Svavarsdóttir, Sigrún. 2001. "Objective Values: Does Metaethics Rest on a Mistake?" In *Objectivity in Law and Morals*, edited by Brian Leiter, 144–193. Cambridge: Cambridge University Press.

Svavarsdóttir, Sigrún. 2006. "How Do Moral Judgments Motivate?" In *Contemporary Debates in Moral Theory*, edited by J. Dreier, 163–181. Oxford: Blackwell.

Svavarsdóttir, Sigrún. 2019. "Value Ascriptions: Rethinking Cognitivism." *Philosophical Studies* 176: 1417–1438.

Tresan, Jon. 2009. "The Challenge of Communal Internalism." *Journal of Value Inquiry* 43: 179–199.

---

[28] Thanks are due to the editors of this volume, David Copp and Paul Bloomfield, for extremely helpful comments on an earlier version of this chapter. I also thank David Enoch and Tristram McPherson for comments on the penultimate version. Finally, I thank students in my 2020 seminar at Tufts University for helpful discussions of moral realism and objectivity.

CHAPTER 4

EPISTEMOLOGY FOR REALISTS

SARAH MCGRATH

1. INTRODUCTION

THE moral realist is a cognitivist: she thinks that moral judgments express truth-evaluable propositions. In contrast to the subjectivist or individual relativist, the moral realist holds that moral facts are objective: they hold independently of our moral opinions, and independent of which moral framework we accept. Moreover, although the moral realist will readily admit that at least some moral facts are unobvious, she is not a moral skeptic: she does not think that our best efforts to achieve genuine moral knowledge are doomed to fail. Rather, the moral realist holds that although the discovery of some moral facts might be an intellectually demanding task, we are capable of attaining, and in fact possess, substantial moral knowledge. Thus, she faces the question: how, exactly, is this substantial body of moral knowledge achieved?

In contemporary metaethics, it is sometimes assumed that it is harder for moral realists to answer this question than it is for theorists who occupy various kinds of antirealist, relativist, or nihilist positions. Many of these theorists will deny the presupposition of the question, namely that we have a substantial body of moral knowledge to explain. The nihilist thinks all claims to the effect that some moral property is instantiated are false, so she does not think we have substantive moral knowledge to explain. Antirealists who think that we do have moral knowledge tend to think that it is mind-*dependent*; they think that you can achieve moral knowledge by reflecting on your own attitudes. Similarly, relativists who think that moral truth is a function of personal values can think of moral knowledge as a special kind of self-knowledge. But since the realist thinks that our knowledge is of mind-independent moral reality, she faces the question of how that knowledge is achieved.

One might think that in order to address this epistemological question, a theorist must first offer answers to prior questions about the metaphysics of morality:

specifically, are moral facts natural, or non-natural facts? Suppose that moral facts are natural facts—facts that are part of the world as it is described by science. On this supposition, presumably we don't need a special story to explain where moral knowledge comes from. Ordinary empirical means would do. By contrast, a theorist who offers a non-naturalist account of moral reality might be expected to liken moral knowledge to a priori knowledge of mathematics or modality. More radically, moral knowledge might be thought to require "some special faculty of moral perception or intuition, utterly different from our ordinary ways of knowing everything else." (Mackie 1977/1990: 38) But although the expectation that epistemology will depend on metaphysics is to some extent borne out, contemporary moral realists who differ widely with respect to their metaphysical commitments agree to a surprising extent on the question of where moral knowledge comes from.

The leading view, embraced by naturalists and non-naturalists alike, is that it emerges from the application of *the method of reflective equilibrium*. In this chapter, I will first present two realist views on opposite ends of the spectrum with respect to moral epistemology—Millian Empiricism and Moorean Intuitionism—in order to illustrate the way in which a theorist's views about moral epistemology can shape her moral metaphysics, and vice versa. I will then explain what the method of reflective equilibrium is, and present some of the reasons why it has emerged as a method with such broad appeal. In sections 4 and 5 I will offer some reasons for thinking that, if moral realism is true, then the Method of Reflective Equilibrium is *not* a satisfying answer to the question of where mind-independent moral knowledge comes from. In section 6, I will discuss some alternatives.

2. Millian Empiricism and Moorean Intuitionism

According to John Stuart Mill, what it is for an action to be morally right is for it to be the option available to you that will bring about the most happiness (Mill 1861/2002). If the property of moral rightness can be defined in this way, then finding out what to do—assuming you want to do the morally right thing—is something that you could investigate, empirically. There might be various practical difficulties in finding this out: it can be hard to know what consequences your actions will have, or what will make which people happy. But in principle, it is the kind of question that could be answered by the natural and social sciences.

By contrast, consider G. E. Moore's view that the right action is the action that will bring about the most *good*, where "good" cannot be defined in terms of happiness or in terms of anything else (Moore 1903/2004).[1] If we put the idea that "good" is simple and

---

[1] Moore famously holds that any attempt to define goodness—in terms of happiness or anything else—is doomed to fail. The basic argument is that for any purported definition in terms of a natural

indefinable together with the idea that the right actions are the actions that produce the most good, it is not at all obvious how empirical methods could help us settle ethical questions. Moore's own positive epistemological story is complex, but it crucially involves the claim that we can find out which things are intrinsically good simply by thinking about them in the right way.[2] Because of the essential role that "thinking about things in the right way" plays in Moore's epistemology of value, the view is commonly referred to as "Moorean intuitionism."

Whereas Mill's definition of moral rightness makes moral epistemology seem tractable, this tractability might seem to come at the cost of changing the subject from goodness to happiness. By contrast, Moore's refusal to define goodness in terms of anything at all might seem to come at the cost of endorsing an epistemological picture that many found to be too mysterious to believe. As A. J. Ayer complained:

> it is notorious that what seems intuitively certain to one person may seem doubtful, or even false, to another. . . . Some moralists claim to settle the matter by saying that they 'know' that their own moral judgements are correct. But such an assertion is of purely psychological interest, and has not the slightest tendency to prove the validity of any moral judgement. For dissenting moralists may equally well 'know' that their ethical views are correct. And as far as subjective certainty goes, there will be nothing to choose between them. When such differences of opinion arise in connexion with an ordinary empirical proposition, one may attempt to resolve them by referring to, or actually carrying out, some relevant empirical test. But with regard to ethical statements, there is, on the . . . 'intuitionist' theory, no relevant empirical test. (1936/1952: 106)

For Ayer and many of his empirically minded contemporaries, the claim that there is a realm of objective, mind-independent facts for which there is no "empirical test" is an embarrassment to philosophy: they adamantly reject Moore's claim that there is a realm of moral facts for which no empirical evidence can be adduced. But since they agree with Moore that goodness can't be defined in naturalist terms, they conclude that there aren't any moral facts. If there aren't any moral facts, then what are we to make of moral judgments? The noncognitivist's simple and powerful answer is that when we make moral judgments we are not describing anything or expressing beliefs about matters of fact, but rather expressing our emotions, or attempting to persuade or influence one another by nonrational means (Ayer 1952; Stevenson 1937). Noncognitivists avoid making any implausible claims about the nature of moral facts and our epistemic access to them

---

property N, we could know of some object x that it had N, and the question of whether it was good would still have an "open feel." According to Moore, the fact that the question would have an "open feel" shows that goodness and happiness aren't the same thing. And you can repeat this test for any proposed definition of moral goodness. (Moore 1903/2004: 62–69).

[2] In particular, in order to determine whether something had intrinsic value, one was to use "the method of absolute isolation" which involved thinking of it existing in isolation from everything else. (*Principia Ethica* 1903/1993 Chapter VI section 112.)

by denying that there are any such facts. And noncognitivists also have a good explanation for why attempts to define goodness will always leave us with an "open question": to call something good is to express some kind of positive endorsement of it or attraction to it, not to describe it as having any particular feature or other.

Versions of noncognitivism dominated moral philosophy throughout the early twentieth century, focusing on how moral language is used, and on how to reconcile the descriptive-seeming surface features of moral language with the idea that moral judgments aren't in the business of trying to describe anything. So long as the predominant opinion is that there are no moral facts to be known, the obvious default would be that there isn't any moral epistemology to be done.[3]

3. The Method of Reflective Equilibrium

This section begins by presenting some of the developments in 20th century moral philosophy that help explain how the method of reflective equilibrium emerged. It goes on to offer a description of the method, together with some of the reasons why it has had such broad appeal.

If you were only paying attention to metaethics in the middle of the twentieth century, you might have gotten the impression that there is *no such thing* as moral epistemology: it might have seemed that there is no moral knowledge to explain. According to C. L. Stevenson, for example, since an ethical statement is essentially a "social instrument" or a "vehicle of suggestion",

> To the extent that ethics predicates the ethical terms of anything, rather than explains their meaning, it ceases to be a reflective study. (Stevenson 1937: 31)

Of course, few contemporary philosophers would agree with the idea that when philosophy takes on substantive moral questions it ceases to be a reflective study. Since at least the 1960's, philosophers have been publishing arguments for objective answers to controversial ethical questions.[4] And this enterprise of ethical theorizing may seem to

---

[3] Notable exceptions to the noncognitivist trend include the British moral philosophers C. D. Broad, A. C. Ewing, and W. D. Ross. For an overview of their contributions and in-depth discussion their views on moral epistemology see (Hurka 2015).

[4] This change in attitude toward the possibility of philosophically respectable moral theorizing may have occurred for reasons having as much to do with historical events and changes in public consciousness as philosophical arguments or insights. For example, Elizabeth Anscombe and Philippa Foot, two of the earliest influential ethicists of the twentieth century, both explain their hostility toward the noncognitivism prevalent at Oxford in the 1940s by reference to the events of World War II. In her pamphlet "Mr. Truman's Degree," Anscombe writes that the prevailing views about moral philosophy at Oxford (most predominantly, R. M. Hare's version of noncognitivism) "contain a repudiation of the

presuppose that there *are* objective answers to controversial ethical questions, and that we can find out what those answers are by doing philosophy.

Thus, the expansion of applied ethics can be seen as breathing new life into metaethics by reopening the traditional metaphysical and epistemological questions. The first chapter of Gilbert Harman's influential *The Nature of Morality* (1977) urges that the "basic" issue in moral philosophy is that of whether moral principles can "be tested and confirmed in the way that scientific principles can." (1977: 3). In the preface of the book, Harman expresses his dismay at the fact that philosophical interest was shifting to applied ethical questions, and skipping over the basic questions of moral epistemology. He writes:

> This book … differs from existing texts by focusing on a basic philosophical problem about morality, its apparent immunity from observational testing. Other texts either ignore this issue altogether, in order to concentrate on interesting but largely non-philosophical discussions of moral problems. … [T]his has often been interesting but has less often had much to do with philosophy, and philosophers have had little to say in recent years about the basic problem about morality, the seeming irrelevance of observational evidence. (1977: vi–vii)

Harman goes on to describe his view of the difference that this shift was making to the moral philosophy courses being offered to university students:

> Courses in ethics are more 'relevant' and students are more 'involved.' It may even be true that these courses are doing some good; perhaps students learn something; perhaps their powers of analysis are improved. (Probably not!) But students in such courses are not really studying philosophy. The basic philosophical issues are not being addressed. (1977: viii–ix)

It is natural to see J. L. Mackie (1977/1991) as similarly responding to the revival of ethical theorizing when argues that there is no plausible story to be told about how objective moral values could be within our cognitive grasp. Mackie argues that "the central thesis of intuitionism is one to which any objectivist view of values is in the end committed," and he argues from the implausibility of intuitionism to the claim that we have no knowledge of objective values. (1977/1991: 38)

---

idea that any class of actions, such as murder, may be absolutely excluded" (1956/1981: 71). She sees the rejection of moral absolutes as a commitment of noncognitivism, and thus sees the prevalence of noncognitivism as connected to her Oxford colleagues' willingness to award Truman an honorary degree, despite his role in the decision to use atomic weapons. Foot explicitly related her own rejection of Oxford moral philosophy to the scenes from concentration camps she saw on newsreels at the end of the war (Lipscomb 2021: 5). The social upheaval of the 1960s and 1970s (including the civil rights and women's liberation movements, and the Vietnam War) can also be seen as playing a role in the burgeoning subdiscipline of first-order moral philosophy: classic papers such as Judith Jarvis Thomson's "A Defense of Abortion" and Peter Singer's "Famine, Affluence, and Morality" appeared in the first issue of *Philosophy and Public Affairs* in 1972, and John Rawls' book *A Theory of Justice* (1971/1999) argued for a substantive theory of distributive justice.

Interestingly, the most compelling answer to the question of where moral justification and/or knowledge comes from didn't come from theorists who were explicitly responding to challenges such as those posed by Harman and Mackie. Rather, the answer came from within normative ethics itself. In *A Theory of Justice* (1971), Rawls not only argues for substantive claims about what justice requires, lending credibility to the idea that reasoning can extend our moral knowledge, he also coins the term "reflective equilibrium" for a dynamic theory of justification, or method of normative inquiry—one which seemed much more sensible and down-to-earth than the mysterious method Moore described.[5] Contrary to the idea that how a theorist answers epistemological questions about our access to moral facts will be bound up with how she answers metaphysical questions about the nature of moral facts, this account of where moral knowledge comes from lends itself to theories with widely varying metaphysical commitments. It has become by far the most popular view among naturalists and non-naturalists alike.

Proponents of the method of reflective equilibrium will spell out the details of the view in different ways, but the basic components are explained in Thomas Scanlon's summary, which is worth quoting at length:

> In broad outline, the method of reflective equilibrium can be described as follows. One begins by identifying a set of considered judgments, of any level of generality, about the subject in question. These are judgments that seem clearly to be correct and seem so under conditions that are conducive to making good judgments of the relevant kind about this subject matter. If the subject in question is morality, for example, they may be judgments about the rightness or wrongness of particular actions, general moral principles, or judgments about the kinds of considerations that are relevant to deter- mining the rightness of actions. . . . The method does not privilege judgments of any particular type—those about particular cases, for example—as having special justificatory standing.
>
>   The next step in the method is to formulate general principles that would "account for" these judgments. By this Rawls means principles such that, had one simply been trying to apply them, rather than trying directly to decide what is the case about the subject at hand, one would have been led to this same set of judgments. If, as is likely, this attempt to come up with such principles is not successful, one must decide how to respond to the divergence between these principles and considered judgments: whether to give up the judgments that the principles fail to account for, to modify the principles, in hopes of achieving a better fit, or to do some combination of these things. One is then to continue in this way, working back and forth between principles and judgments, until one reaches a set of principles and a set of judgments that "account for them." This state is what Rawls calls reflective equilibrium. (Scanlon 2016: 76–77)

---

[5] (Rawls 1971), (Rawls 1974). Although the term "reflective equilibrium" is due to Rawls, arguably, the first clear articulation of the method is in (Goodman 1953: 63–64). Goodman articulates the method as a story about how rules of deduction are justified and then applies it to the case of induction in order to "dissolve" Humean skepticism about induction.

This account of the method is broadly representative of the way in which it has been understood by its proponents. Different theorists might offer accounts of how exactly this search for a more coherent equilibrium should go that differ from Scanlon's in some respects. But the general picture is one on which justification arises out of this process of attempting to arrive at a more coherent overall moral view. The ideal endpoint of the process would be a stable equilibrium among one's judgments, judgments that stand in relations of mutual support to one another.

It is worth pausing to appreciate the popularity that the method of reflective equilibrium has enjoyed among theorists whose commitments are otherwise diverse. Friends of the view include naturalist realists, non-naturalist realists, and antirealists of many varieties. As if it were not striking enough that so many professional philosophers will say that the method of reflective equilibrium is the correct method for investigating the normative domain, some will go so far as to say that the method is not only the view to beat, but also, the only game in town. Thus, according to Michael Smith, it is among the "platitudes" about morality that properly conducted moral inquiry has "a certain characteristic coherentist form" of a kind that was given systematic articulation by John Rawls in his seminal discussion of the method (Smith 1994: 40–41). Similarly, Scanlon says:

> it seems to me that this method, properly understood, is in fact the best way of making up one's mind about moral matters and about many other subjects. Indeed, it is the only defensible method: apparent alternatives to it are illusory. (2002: 149)

DePaul (2006: 2016) argues that, when it comes to moral inquiry, "there is simply no reasonable alternative to reflective equilibrium." (Kagan 1998: 16, 306) suggests that, in practice, something very much like the method of reflective equilibrium is accepted by anyone doing normative ethics, whether they realize it or not. Harman argues that a fundamental division among moral philosophers is the division between philosophical naturalists and practitioners of "autonomous ethics," but claims that the method of reflective equilibrium is the shared method of both (Harman 2000: 79).

Why has the method seemed so appealing to so many as an answer to where moral knowledge comes from? At least part of the answer is that the method is, as Nelson Goodman put it, "refreshingly non-cosmic" (Goodman 1953/1983: 60). There are no appeals to moral intuition or self-evidence. The starting points for moral theorizing, according to the method, are the judgments that seem right to you in conditions for judging well. And applying the method does not require you to change the subject from an ethical question to an empirical one. Moreover, the method as it is standardly described resonates with the actual practice of moral philosophers working in applied ethics: they consider candidate moral principles and then consider whether there are counterexamples, or whether instead the principles are adequate to account for our judgments about particular cases.

4. THE WRONG EPISTEMOLOGY? NATURALIST REALISM AND THE METHOD

Offhand, it might seem strange that the naturalist realists of the 1980s such as Nicholas Sturgeon and Richard Boyd would embrace the method of reflective equilibrium as the method for investigating moral reality. After all, these theorists were at pains to emphasize that ethics is continuous with science:

> (a) ethical properties... are of the same general sort as properties investigated by the sciences, and... (b) they are to be investigated in the same general way as that we investigate those properties. (Sturgeon 2006)

If the method of reflective equilibrium is the method for investigating ethics, and the method for investigating ethics is the same as the method for investigating science, then it follows that the method of reflective equilibrium is the method for investigating science. But is it really true that biologists investigate viruses or zoologists investigate tigers by using the method of reflective equilibrium? Offhand, it might seem as though the answer is "no." Perhaps it is true that biologists and zoologists work back and forth between their judgments at different levels of generality, resolving conflicts as they go, not privileging any judgments in virtue of their level of generality. But that is not a *full* description of what they do. After all, in attempting to answer scientific questions, scientists rely very heavily on *perception*. Suppose, for example, that you are a scientist undertaking to develop a vaccine for a certain virus. You will not simply start with your considered judgments about viruses and work back and forth, seeking to bring them into a state of reflective equilibrium with one another. That is something that you could do from the armchair, without actually making any observations about any viruses at all! The fact that you will actually be observing samples of the virus seems to be a crucial part of the method you employ. So even if a search for reflective equilibrium is *part* of the story of why scientists end up with justified beliefs about the relevant subject matter, there is reason to doubt that it is the whole story, because it appears to leave out the key notion of perceptual observation.

In "How to Be a Moral Realist," (Boyd 1996) explicitly claims that the method of reflective equilibrium *is* the method for doing science: "the dialectical interplay of observations, theory, and methodology which... constitutes the discovery procedure for scientific inquiry just is the method of reflective equilibrium" (1996: 119). What should we make of this claim?

It may be useful to assess the claim that the discovery procedure for scientific inquiry just is the method of reflective equilibrium in light of the epistemological distinction between coherence vs. foundationalist theories of justification. *Coherence theories* are theories on which *any justification a belief enjoys derives from the relations of support that it stands in to other beliefs*. Having justified beliefs is a matter of having a set of beliefs that cohere sufficiently well with one another. The opposing view, foundationalism, is the view that there are some beliefs ("properly basic" or "foundational" ones) that have at least some measure of positive epistemic status apart from considerations of coherence. Foundationalists typically think that, if this were not so, then *no* beliefs would be justified, no matter how well-integrated they were within a coherent set. In contrast, it is characteristic of the coherentist to insist that an adequate level of coherence is *sufficient* for justification.

Foundationalists agree that some beliefs are justified by something other than the relations that they stand in to other beliefs, but they differ about which beliefs are basic, and what justifies the basic beliefs. According to *experiential foundationalism*, beliefs that are based on perceptual experience are candidates for being basic. Suppose, for example, you look out the window and come to believe *it is snowing*. The experiential foundationalist will say that your belief is justified, not by relations it stands in to other beliefs, but rather by the *visual experience* that you have when you look out the window.[6] Thus, on this view, perceptual beliefs—at least those formed in good lighting conditions, etc.—*already* enjoy a positive epistemic status, prior to the application of a process that would bring them into equilibrium with other beliefs. The experiential foundationalist will grant that certain other beliefs that you might hold could *defeat* the positive epistemic status conferred by your visual experience. For example, if you believe that you are on a movie set with an excellent snow machine that happens to be outside this very window, this can defeat the justification provided by your visual experience. But, absent such defeaters, your belief is justified by the experience itself.

With the distinction between coherentism and foundationalism in hand, let's consider the claim that the correct application of the method of reflective equilibrium is sufficient to render the resulting beliefs justified. Is this a coherentist, or a foundationalist view? The method has often been understood to be a dynamic coherence theory, on which justification arises as a result of the process of working back and forth among one's judgments, making them more coherent. But if it is a dynamic coherence theory, this casts doubt on the claim that it is the method of science. For it is plausible that the scientist's perceptual observations are justified, not by working back and forth between judgments at different levels of generality, but rather, directly, before the method is applied. If, as our example above suggests, scientists' methods for investigating the subject matters they investigate are anchored by at least some basic perceptual beliefs, then the epistemology of science is not coherentist. Thus, if the method of reflective equilibrium is coherentist, then the method of reflective equilibrium is the method of science.

There are substantive "if's" in the line of argument just presented: there is substantial room for debate at more than one premise of the reasoning. Perhaps we should

---

[6] The main alternative is *classical foundationalism*, on which one's basic beliefs are about one's own mental states, and what justifies them is something like the fact that they are certain, indubitable or incorrigible. For discussion, see (W. Alston 1971). This view is associated with Descartes. In what follows I will focus on experiential foundationalism, for simplicity.

think of the method as a foundationalist view, on which there are some moral beliefs that are justified, not by the process of being made to cohere with other beliefs, but instead by something else. I will consider this possibility in the final section. For now, I will offer some reasons that might help to explain why this option did not tempt the 1980s naturalists. Part of the explanation might be that these theorists were strongly influenced by the Quinean idea that no belief is immune to revision[7] (Quine 1951). At the time, foundationalism was associated with the Cartesian idea that for a belief to count as foundational, it would have to be indubitable, incorrigible, infallible, self-evident, or in some other way irrevisable. Foundational beliefs tended to be restricted to beliefs about one's own mental states. Moreover, during the time when Boyd and Sturgeon were writing, coherentism was receiving a good deal of attention as a general epistemological account of justification.[8] The landscape has changed in at least two ways that are significant for our purposes. First, foundationalists have generally dropped the idea that the foundational beliefs needed to be indubitable or self-evident or incorrigible or otherwise irrevisable. (Again, your belief that it is snowing could be basic even if it is revisable in light of information about the snow machine.) According to the "modest foundationalist," it is enough for a belief to count as basic that it is justified in a way that doesn't depend on other supporting beliefs.[9] Second, a certain kind of case in the literature has been taken to provide a decisive counterexample to coherentism. The recipe for constructing the relevant kind of case is this: take a subject and make his beliefs as coherent as they can possibly be. But make him such that he is entirely unresponsive to obvious changes in his immediate environment. Here is such a case, due to Richard Feldman:

> **The Strange Case of Magic Feldman**: Professor Feldman is a rather short philosophy professor with a keen interest in basketball. Magic Johnson was an outstanding professional basketball player. While playing a game, we may suppose, Magic Johnson had a perfectly coherent system of beliefs. Magic Feldman is an unusual character who is a combination of the professor and the basketball player. Magic Feldman has a remarkable imagination, so remarkable that while actually teaching a philosophy class, he thinks he is playing basketball. Indeed, he has exactly the beliefs Magic Johnson has. Because Magic Johnson's belief system was perfectly coherent, Magic Feldman's is also perfectly coherent. (Feldman 2002: 68)

The verdict that we are invited to draw is that while Magic Johnson's beliefs are justified, Magic Feldman's are not. The same kind of case appears in (Plantinga 1993: 80). The basic

---

[7] The related idea that "all observation is theory-laden" may also have played a role in antifoundationalist thinking. If what you observe depends, in some sense, on the background theory that you hold, this may seem to threaten some versions of foundationalism. For discussion, see (Koons 2017). For an argument that perception itself can be shaped by background theory, see (Siegel 2017).

[8] For an influential defense of coherentism, see (BonJour 1988).

[9] For discussion of this development, see the papers collected in (W. P. Alston 1989), and (Pryor 2001: 100–103).

point is that if epistemic justification depended entirely on how a subject's beliefs cohere with one another, then it would not depend at all on whether the subject's beliefs make contact with external reality. It wouldn't depend at all on whether a subject's beliefs are responsive to her experiences! Magic Johnson and Magic Feldman would have equally coherent sets of beliefs. But it seems absurd to say that their beliefs are equally justified, given that Magic Feldman's beliefs are entirely unresponsive to his experiences. For this reason, many theorists have concluded coherence alone is insufficient for justification.

5. A Better Fit? Non-Naturalist Realism and the Method

One might think that the method of reflective equilibrium is a better fit for *non-naturalist realism*. After all, a central commitment of non-naturalism is that morality and science are *really different*. There are objective moral facts, but these aren't part of the world as conceived by science. (In this way, new non-naturalists are in agreement with Moore.) Many contemporary non-naturalists hold that different domains have different standards of epistemic justification, and they deny that moral principles can be tested and confirmed in the way that scientific principles can be. (See, for example, (Dworkin 1996), (Dworkin 2013), (Enoch 2013), and (Scanlon 2016). But they think that this is not bad news for moral knowledge at all. And some new non-naturalists even share Moore's sense that to conceive of moral reality as part of the world is to commit some kind of obvious fallacy. Dworkin derides the idea that we could test moral principles in the same way we could test scientific principles by imagining that what we would be looking for would be moral particles—"morons"—that could "interact in some way with human nervous systems so as to make people aware of . . . morality or immorality or of . . . virtue or vice" (Dworkin 1996: 119).

Since non-naturalist realists think that the story about justification in the moral domain will obviously be very different from the story about justification in science, it is no objection to their view if it turns out that the method of reflective equilibrium is an underdescription of the way that scientists investigate their subject matter. That the whole enterprise could be carried out from the armchair might seem unproblematic when the subject matter is morality, which, after all, is naturally thought to be an a priori domain. Moreover, the kinds of cases that are often taken to be counterexamples to coherentism, such as the case of Magic Feldman discussed in the last section might seem to be beside the point. These examples always involve a subject who is insensitive to perceptible changes in her immediate environment. But at most, such examples show that there is a problem of taking coherentism to be a *general* story of epistemic justification, across the board: they might not tell against the view that the method of reflective equilibrium is the correct method for investigating *ethics*. The subject matter consists of a domain of necessary, a priori, causally inert, non-natural features and truths. Since our alleged knowledge of this domain is not underwritten by sense perception in the first place, perhaps Magic-Feldman-type counterexamples cannot arise.

But in fact, even assuming that morality is an a priori domain, and that moral facts are necessary, irreducible, and causally inert, there is still room to worry about whether the method of reflective equilibrium will be adequate for acquiring knowledge about moral reality, assuming that reality is mind-independent. Critics of the method have often complained that whether the method is sufficient for conferring knowledge or justification on the views that result depends on the quality of the views you began with. This is sometimes called the "garbage in, garbage out" objection. Friends of the method reply by pointing out that it already has a kind of built-in filter: the starting points for applying the method are not just any old judgments that you happen to find yourself with, but rather, your "considered judgments." Your considered judgments are judgments that seem true to you in conditions that are conducive to judging well. These conditions are spelled out differently by different theorists: within the broadly Rawlsian tradition, your considered judgments are judgments that you make when you are not distracted, frightened, self-interested, or upset.[10]

But although these conditions on considered judgments are substantive and will rule out quite a lot, we can still imagine someone who has horrific claims among her considered judgments. Consider:

We are morally required to occasionally kill randomly.[11]

In principle, that is something that a person could believe even if she is not distracted, frightened, self-interested, or upset. And it is far from clear that the conditions on considered judgments could be tweaked in such a way that they would successfully rule out that such perverse judgments. There is nothing in the reflective equilibrium picture to rule out that a person's having this, and many more absurd claims as among her considered judgments. Would a person who started with such perverse considered judgments and brought them all into equilibrium, following the method impeccably, at the end of the process, be justified in believing that we are morally required to occasionally kill randomly? Maybe the fact that she has managed to bring this perverse judgment into a state of equilibrium with the other things she believes *doesn't* make it any more reasonable for her to believe than does the fact that Magic Feldman's beliefs are perfectly coherent render them reasonable.

In a way, the worry here is just a more general version of the worry we raised for the naturalist realist's claim that the method of reflective equilibrium is the method of science. The complaint there was that scientists do not simply work back and forth between considered judgments at different levels of generality seeking coherence among them,

---

[10] Rawls himself uses "considered judgment" as a technical term, and its meaning evolves from work to work. For discussion, see (McGrath 2020: 30 n. 18).

[11] For further discussion of this objection, see (Kelly and McGrath 2010) and (McGrath 2020, Chapter 2).

so the description offered by the reflective equilibrium theorist leaves something out. To give a full description of justification in science, we would have to start the story "further back," and mention the role of perception. Even achieving a perfect equilibrium among your views about viruses would count for very little unless the views you started with already enjoyed some level of credibility—the kind of credibility that could be conferred on them by the fact that they issued from a reliable source, such as sense perception. And it wouldn't really help very much to say: well if you want to end up with justified beliefs about viruses, then start with your *considered* judgments them, and bring those into equilibrium. The example of the person who starts with perverse considered judgments suggests that the same is true when it comes to our moral views. Whether making them more coherent will land you in a place where you are justified in believing the things you believe depends on what you started with in the first place.

Thus, the worry is that the "garbage-in/garbage out" objection sticks even if the subject matter is morality, and even if the method of reflective equilibrium is understood as a kind of dynamic coherence theory, and even if we conceive of it as a kind of foundationalism on which considered judgments enjoy some level of positive justification independently of the relations that they stand in to other beliefs. At this point, it might seem as though the non-naturalist should say that the starting points for moral theorizing are not our considered judgments, but some subset of them: perhaps they are the subset of our considered judgments that are self-evident, or that are the deliverance of a faculty moral intuition that is conceived of as on a par with sense perception in that its deliverances are prima facie justified beliefs. Alternatively, she might offer a non-naturalist defense of moral perception. Depending on the details of the view, this might indeed be a non-naturalist solution to the garbage-in garbage out objection.

The problem with this move is that it shifts the epistemological heavy lifting to the epistemological story that justifies the starting points. Reflective Equilibrium was supposed to be an *alternative* to Moorean intuitionism, in that it was supposed to make the epistemology of value less mysterious. But if reflective equilibrium is characterized as a foundationalist view with starting points that have positive epistemic status in virtue of the fact that they are self-evident or intuitive, it is no longer this kind of alternative. Traditional, Ayer-type worries, about whether moral intuitions deserve the kind of respect that the Moorean intuitionist is willing to give them, reemerge.

Finally, there is a different reason why the method of reflective equilibrium may not be a good fit for realism. While on the one hand there is the worry that the method is, in the way just explained, too permissive, there is also a worry that it is in another way too strict. Again, realists think that moral knowledge is not esoteric knowledge: they think it is not only achievable but common. But offhand, it seems like many ethical claims that the ordinary person knows to be true she knows to be true independently of engaging in anything like reflective equilibrium reasoning. Consider the claims *slavery is unjust* and *rape is wrong*. If these claims are known by anyone, then they are known by most ordinary people. But it is not very plausible that every person who knows that these claims are true knows this on the basis of working back and forth between her judgments at different levels of generality in the ways described by the proponents of the method. To say that this is necessary may seem to overintellectualize ordinary moral knowledge: it makes it seem as though knowledge of these truths would be available only to relatively reflective individuals. To the extent that realists are committed to the view that moral knowledge is something that most people have plenty of, there is pressure to reject any view on which knowledge could only emerge as a result of application of an intellectually demanding method.[12]

6. Beyond the Method of Reflective Equilibrium

Realists think that the aim of moral inquiry is knowledge of mind-independent moral truth. Interestingly enough, Rawls himself did not think of the aim of moral inquiry in quite this way. Rawls provisionally characterizes moral philosophy as the attempt to describe our underlying "moral capacity" or "moral sensibility," or to investigate the "substantive moral conceptions" that people actually hold, and he describes the procedure is "a kind of psychology." In Rawls's explicitly methodological essay, "The Independence of Moral Theory" (Rawls 1974), it is only after he has set aside the possibility that there *are* any objective moral truths that he introduces the method of reflective equilibrium as the best method for pursuing the psychological task of uncovering our own substantive moral conceptions.

In the previous two sections I explained some challenges for moral realists who think that the method of reflective equilibrium is the method for investigating the moral domain. Even if Rawls is right that the method is well-suited for a psychological investigation into our own moral conceptions, there are worries about whether it is a suitable means of investigating mind-independent moral reality. At least as it is standardly characterized by its proponents, reflective equilibrium might be insufficiently tethered to the mind-independent subject matter that realists think is within our cognitive grasp. And while it is true that the standard kinds of counterexamples to pure coherence theories in epistemology involve subjects whose beliefs are coherent but who are insensitive to easily perceptible empirical features of their environment, this is not an essential part of the recipe for such cases. The charge has force even when the topic is not empirical justification but moral justification: provided that the moral truths are not of our own making, it will be possible to conceive of a subject who begins with perverse judgments which remain unreasonable for her to hold even when they are brought into coherence with one another by impeccably following the prescribed method. Moreover, the worry remains even if we are thinking of the method of reflective equilibrium not as a coherence theory, but rather, as a foundationalist theory in which "considered judgments" are playing the foundational role. That a subject's judgments are

---

[12] See (McGrath 2020) for further discussion of this point.

her *considered* judgments may be insufficient to give them the requisite epistemic heft, because it is perfectly possible to make terrible judgments in conditions that are generally conducive to judging well.

But if the method is an awkward fit for realism, then (i) why have so many realists embraced it, and (ii) what's a plausible alternative story? Perhaps the answers to these two questions are interrelated. Part of the reason that the method of reflective equilibrium has been so popular among realists is that it makes moral knowledge seem achievable: it tells us a down-to-earth story on which we start with our considered judgments and make them more coherent with one another. Moreover, it tells us where moral knowledge comes from using only plain mundane ingredients to which the most empirically minded philosophers won't object: there is no faculty of moral intuition, nothing is posited as self-evident or innate. Nor does the method require, as a Millian story would, a strong reduction of moral properties to empirical properties. Thus the realist who embraces Rawls's method avoids the main objections faced by both Moorean intuitionism and Millian empiricism, and she can say that it is no harder for moral realists to explain where moral knowledge comes from than it is for antirealists to explain this.

Some realists have seemed to take it that if moral properties can't be reduced to empirical properties, then the only alternative to a coherentist story about moral epistemology is a foundationalist story on which the foundationalist beliefs are moral intuitions. Thus, Sturgeon, in considering the question of whether "some . . . direct knowledge is already ethical", assumes that if there is direct ethical knowledge then it is "intuitive": "if assigning ethical knowledge to intuition is ruled out as too mysterious," then, he continues, the best remaining option is to reject foundationalism and endorse the method (2006: 105).

But perhaps there is a more expansive menu of options available to the realist. Think about our knowledge of *non*moral reality. There is not one answer to the question of where it comes from: we get it in a variety of different ways. Some of it is perceptual, some of it is testimonial, some of it is abductive, some of it is a priori. Thus if moral realists take knowledge of *non*moral reality as their model, they won't say that there is just one source of moral knowledge: they could say that our moral knowledge has a variety of sources, these sources are typically the *same* sources that are involved in our knowledge of nonmoral facts.

Bracketing for the moment the question of knowledge, it does seem like some of our moral *beliefs* are delivered in these ordinary ways. First, it seems like some of our moral beliefs are delivered by ordinary faculties of perception. For example: you believe that a visiting speaker was unkind to a student who asked a question. Why do you believe that? You because you *saw* her act unkindly. Second, taking appearances at face value, some moral beliefs are delivered by testimony. You believe that you can trust your landlord to deal with you honestly. Why do you believe that? Because other tenants have told you that he is honest. Similarly, some of our moral beliefs appear to be inferences to the best explanation: you believe that your congressman is no damned good because of the policies that he supports.

Now, of course, there are serious challenges to each of these as potential sources of moral knowledge. That is, there are serious challenges to the idea that one can acquire moral knowledge on the basis of perception, or on the basis of testimony, and to the idea that moral facts are ever the best explanation of anything. A full defense of *moral epistemological antiexceptionalism* would require meeting all of these challenges.[13] But from the realists' perspective, these challenges might be worth trying to meet: for if moral perception, or moral testimony, or inference to the best explanation, sometimes delivers moral knowledge (or belief that is justified in some relatively strong sense), then beliefs that have positive epistemic status in any of those ways can play this tethering role, in a way that the judgment that *we are morally required to occasionally kill randomly* cannot (even if the latter fulfills the conditions for being a Rawlsian considered judgment, for some given believer).

It might be thought that, whatever can be said for moral epistemological antiexceptionalism, the naturalist and the non-naturalist couldn't agree about it. Many non-naturalists explicitly deny that, for example, we could have observational moral knowledge. But consider the example of our mathematical beliefs. Even if we assume that mathematical properties are abstract, non-natural properties, nevertheless, I can perceive that the cookies on my children's plates are equinumerous—thus perceiving that a mathematical property, *equinumerosity*, is instantiated. Similarly, even if cruelty is a non-natural property, that doesn't show that I can't know on the basis of perception that my twelve-year-old just acted cruelly toward my seven-year old. By the same token, it might seem like naturalists couldn't agree with non-naturalists that much of our moral knowledge is a priori. After all, they think that moral knowledge is continuous with empirical knowledge, and that is, by definition, not available from the armchair! I think that in response to this unexceptionalists should say that while any source of empirical knowledge is a potential source of moral knowledge, the reverse does not hold. The thought is that, however it is that we achieve a priori moral knowledge, it's of a piece with the way we achieve armchair knowledge of other nonempirical subject matters that have nothing to do with morality, or even normativity.

I want to emphasize that some reflective equilibrium theorists will agree with the idea that moral knowledge is not delivered by a method that is specific to morality. For example, Scanlon thinks that the method of reflective equilibrium is not only the method that delivers knowledge of normative truths, but is also the method that puts set theorists in a position to know which axioms to accept in set theory. He, and many other reflective equilibrium theorists, think the method of reflective equilibrium is the correct method to use in exploring other subject matters as well. While I am skeptical that it's a good characterization of knowledge-delivering reasoning in any mind-independent domain, I am sympathetic to the unexceptionalist spirit: that methods for delivering moral knowledge deliver knowledge in other domains as well.

---

[13] I borrow this term from Williamson (this volume). I attempt to address some of these challenges in (McGrath 2019).

References

Alston, William. 1971. "Varieties of Privileged Access." *American Philosophical Quarterly* 8(3): 223–241.

Alston, William P. 1989. *Epistemic Justification: Essays in the Theory of Knowledge*. 1st ed. Ithaca: Cornell University Press.

Ayer, Alfred J. 1936/1952. *Language, Truth and Logic*. 2nd ed. New York, NY: Dover Publications.

BonJour, Laurence. 1988. *The Structure of Empirical Knowledge*. 2nd printing ed. Cambridge, MA: Harvard University Press.

Boyd, Richard. 1996. "How to Be a Moral Realist." In *Moral Discourse and Practice*, edited by Stephen Darwall, Allan Gibbard, and Peter Railton, 105–136. New York: Oxford University Press.

DePaul, Michael. 2006. "Intuitions in Moral Inquiry." In *The Oxford Handbook of Ethical Theory*, edited by David Copp, 595–623. Oxford: Oxford University Press.

Dworkin, Ronald. 1996. "Objectivity and Truth: You'd Better Believe It." *Philosophy and Public Affairs* 25(2): 87–139. https://doi.org/10.1111/j.1088-4963.1996.tb00036.x.

Dworkin, Ronald. 2013. *Justice for Hedgehogs*. Reprint edition. Cambridge, MA: Belknap Press.

Enoch, David. 2013. *Taking Morality Seriously: A Defense of Robust Realism*. Repr. Oxford: Oxford University Press.

Feldman, Richard. 2002. *Epistemology*. 1st ed. Upper Saddle River, NJ: Pearson.

Goodman, Nelson. 1953. *Fact, Fiction, and Forecast*. Cambridge, MA: Harvard University Press.

Harman, Gilbert. 2000. *Explaining Value*. Oxford: Oxford University Press. https://doi.org/10.1093/0198238045.001.0001.

Hurka, Thomas. 2015. *British Ethical Theorists from Sidgwick to Ewing*. 1st ed. Oxford: Oxford University Press.

Kagan, Shelly. 1998. *Normative Ethics*. 1st ed. Boulder, CO: Westview Press.

Kelly, Thomas, and Sarah McGrath. 2010. "Is Reflective Equilibrium Enough?" *Philosophical Perspectives* 24(1): 325–359. https://doi.org/10.1111/j.1520-8583.2010.00195.x.

Koons, Jeremy Randel. 2017. "A Myth Resurgent: Classical Foundationalism and the New Sellarsian Critique." *Synthese* 194(10): 4155–4169. https://doi.org/10.1007/s11229-016-1134-9.

Lipscomb, Benjamin J. B. 2021. *The Women Are Up to Something: How Elizabeth Anscombe, Philippa Foot, Mary Midgley, and Iris Murdoch Revolutionized Ethics*. New York: Oxford University Press.

Mackie, J. L. 1977/1990. *Ethics: Inventing Right and Wrong*. New York: Penguin Books.

McGrath, Sarah. 2019. *Moral Knowledge*. Oxford: Oxford University Press.

Mill, John Stuart. 2002. *Utilitarianism*. Edited by George Sher. 2nd ed. Indianapolis: Hackett.

Moore, G. E. 1903/2004. *Principia Ethica*. 1st ed. Mineola, NY: Dover Publications.

Plantinga, Alvin. 1993. *Warrant: The Current Debate*. 1st ed. New York: Oxford University Press.

Pryor, James. 2001. "Highlights of Recent Epistemology." *British Journal for the Philosophy of Science* 52(1): 95–124.

Quine, W. V. 1951. "Main Trends in Recent Philosophy: Two Dogmas of Empiricism." *Philosophical Review* 60(1): 20–43. https://doi.org/10.2307/2181906.

Rawls, John. 1971. *A Theory of Justice*. 2nd ed. Cambridge, MA: Belknap Press.

Rawls, John. 1974. "The Independence of Moral Theory." *Proceedings and Addresses of the American Philosophical Association* 48: 5–22. https://doi.org/10.2307/3129858.

Scanlon, T. M. 2016. *Being Realistic about Reasons*. Repr. Oxford: Oxford University Press.

Siegel, Susanna. 2017. "How Is Wishful Seeing Like Wishful Thinking?" *Philosophy and Phenomenological Research* 95(2): 408–435. https://doi.org/10.1111/phpr.12273.

Smith, Michael. 1994. *The Moral Problem*. 1st ed. Oxford, UK; Cambridge, MA: Wiley-Blackwell.

Stevenson, Charles Leslie. 1937. "The Emotive Meaning of Ethical Terms." *Mind* 46(181): 14–31.

Sturgeon, Nicholas L. 2006. "Ethical Naturalism." In *The Oxford Handbook of Ethical Theory*, edited by David Copp, 91–121. Oxford: Oxford University Press.

CHAPTER 5

THE BEARING OF MORAL RATIONALISM ON MORAL REALISM

MICHAEL SMITH

1. REALISM ABOUT MORALITY

In his "The Many Moral Realisms," Geoffrey Sayre-McCord helpfully spells out the commitments of weaker and stronger versions of *moral realism* (1988). The weakest version he considers holds that moral judgments are expressions of belief, rather than some nonbelief state like desire or approval, and that the world is the way that some such (perhaps merely possible) belief represents it as being. Moral realism, so understood, is thus the conjunction of *cognitivism* (the view that moral judgments express beliefs rather than desires) and what Sayre-McCord calls *success* (the view that certain such beliefs, if someone had them, would be true).

Note that what makes the weaker version of moral realism weak is the fact that it is noncommittal on the precise way in which a moral belief represents the world as being. Conversely, stronger versions are stronger because they take a stand on this further issue. For example, one of the most important debates among proponents of stronger versions of moral realism is that between *mind-dependence theorists*, who hold that moral beliefs represent the world as being some mind-dependent way (an example is *simple subjectivism*, which is the view that something's being morally good is its being approved of, where being approved of is one of the properties postulated by the natural science of psychology), and *mind-independence theorists*, who hold that moral beliefs represent the world as being some mind-independent way (an example is Moore's view that something's being morally good is its having a simple property that is not among those postulated by any of the natural sciences, and not a construction out of such properties either). But, as Sayre-McCord notes, these examples of mind-dependent versus mind-independent theories make it clear that there is another debate, orthogonal to this one, between *naturalists*, who think that moral beliefs represent the world as being some way among those postulated by the natural sciences, or among constructions from such ways, and *non-naturalists*, those who think that they represent the world as being some way that is neither among these ways nor a construction from them.

Though there are weaker and stronger versions of moral realism, and though there are multiple stronger versions, we should not suppose that we could argue for the weakest version Sayre-McCord considers without taking a stand on which of the stronger versions are correct. In order to see that this is so, remember that there are sophisticated versions of *moral antirealism* according to which moral judgments do express beliefs, but the beliefs they express are constituted by desires that the world is some nonmoral way (Blackburn 1993, Gibbard 2003, Dreier 2004). A view of this kind is not a version of cognitivism, as that doctrine is defined above, despite holding that moral judgments are expressions of belief. As defined above, cognitivism is the view that moral judgments express beliefs *rather than desires*.

A good question to ask is why we should restrict the definition of cognitivism in this way. The reason is simple. If there are two kinds of beliefs, some constituted by desires and some not, then there is a corresponding distinction to be drawn in the functional role of belief. In giving an account of the functional role of beliefs not constituted by desires, we will have to make an essential reference to way the world is represented as being, as the belief functions properly when the world is that way. If our explanatorily basic theory of world doesn't require us to suppose that the world is that way, either because that way fails to figure in the explanatorily basic theory of the world or to be a construction out of the ways that do figure, then we will have to combine our cognitivism with what Sayre-McCord calls *error*. The resultant view would be a version of *cognitivist antirealism* of the kind argued for by John Mackie (1977).

By contrast, if there are beliefs that are constituted by desires, then no such essential reference to the way the world is represented as being when we have that belief is required for us to give an account of its functional role. Because that role is fully captured by the role of the desires that constitute them, all we need refer to is the nonmoral way the world would be if the desires that constitute these beliefs were satisfied. The fact that our explanatorily basic theory of the world does not require us to suppose that the world is the way that the constituted moral belief represents it as being, in the case of these sophisticated versions of moral antirealism, would be no ground for supposing that there is an error in such beliefs. It would instead be a ground for supposing that the view is a version of *noncognitivist antirealism*, where some of the constituted moral beliefs may even be true in some deflationary sense. The restriction in the definition of cognitivism allows us to capture the distinction between these two kinds of antirealist view, both of which hold that moral judgments express beliefs, as one is a version of cognitivism and the other a version of noncognitivism.

In order to adjudicate the debate over the weakest version of moral realism Sayre-McCord discusses, we therefore need to take a stand on what our explanatorily basic theory of world tells us the world is like, and on whether moral beliefs represent the world as being some such way or construction from such ways. This in turn requires us to ask which of the stronger versions of moral realism is correct. But which of the stronger versions of moral realism do we need to take a stand on? My initial and most important suggestion is that we need to take a stand on a debate that hasn't yet been mentioned.

2. Traditional Moral Rationalism

In their introduction to *The Many Moral Rationalisms* (2018), Karen Jones and François Schroeter tell us that traditional moral rationalism is captured by four core commitments.

1. *The psychological thesis*: reason is the source of moral judgments.
2. *The metaphysical thesis*: moral requirements are grounded in the deliverances of practical reason.
3. *The epistemological thesis*: moral requirements are knowable a priori.
4. *The normative thesis*: moral requirements entail valid reasons for action.

(Jones and Schroeter 2018: 2)

If Jones and Schroeter are right, then there are two important consequences.

The first is that, if the epistemological thesis is true and moral requirements are knowable a priori, then moral judgments express beliefs, and some such (perhaps merely possible) beliefs are true. Is traditional moral rationalism thereby committed to the truth of Sayre-McCord's weakest version of moral realism? For reasons already given, it is not. The question of realism turns on whether the relevant beliefs are or are not constituted by desires. There are various ways in which we could establish that they are not so constituted, but in the case of beliefs that are a priori, the least controversial way is by demonstrating that the beliefs in question are beliefs about conceptual truths, or perhaps beliefs that we can reason ourselves to in some demonstrably a priori way from conceptual truths. If so, then traditional moral rationalism would be committed to the weakest version of moral realism discussed earlier, but it would be so committed because of these further commitments about the route by which we establish the a priori truths of morality.

Assuming that Jones and Schroeter are right about the commitments of traditional moral rationalism, there is a further commitment as well. If both the epistemological and normative theses are true, and the reasons for action that moral requirements entail are knowable a priori, then it follows that these reasons are not themselves conditional on the contingent desires that agents have, given that reasons for action that are conditional on such contingent facts could only be known a posteriori. Traditional moral rationalism is thus committed to the existence of *unconditional* reasons for action, as distinct from merely *conditional* reasons. Indeed, if the reasons entailed by moral requirements are the only unconditional reasons for action, then traditional moral rationalism would also be committed to a *content-free* way of making the distinction between moral and nonmoral reasons for action, as we could make this distinction without taking a stand on their content (compare Dorsey 2016).

Putting these two points together, a natural suggestion emerges. Traditional moral rationalism is committed to the view that moral beliefs are beliefs about unconditional reasons for action, where the truth of certain such beliefs is knowable a priori. If it turns out that such truths are themselves conceptual truths, or follow in some demonstrably a priori way from conceptual truths, then traditional moral rationalism will also be committed to the weakest version of moral realism discussed earlier. But it will be so committed because of its commitment to a stronger version of moral realism that takes a stand on the way in which moral beliefs represent the world as being. The question we must ask next is therefore whether traditional moral rationalism is plausible.

3. The Psychological Thesis

Focus on the psychological thesis. Talk of reason being the source of moral judgment is presumably talk of the causal origins of such judgment. Commonsense observations about the early acquisition of moral beliefs suggests that the thesis so understood is false (compare McGrath 2019).

Many parents train their children not just to be nice to each other, but also to label their being nice to each other "the right thing to do." Since this is the way in which many children acquire their initial moral belief that they're morally obliged to be nice to each other, it follows that their moral beliefs are the product of their parents' testimony, not their use of reason. Testimony is thus *a* source of many people's initial moral beliefs, and hence a source of the moral judgments they make when they express their beliefs. Moreover, some children who grow up in the bosom of a nurturing family, but then experience racism, sexism, classism, ableism, or prejudice of some other kind for the first time when they venture into the wider world, have no trouble recognizing such acts as wrong despite having had no idea that they existed beforehand. If we think of their moral education as having equipped them with excellent gut reactions to novel circumstances, then their acquisition of the belief that such acts are wrong is the result of experience and gut reactions, not their use of reason.

Commonsense observations like these suggest that moral judgments have multiple sources. The psychological thesis is therefore false, from which it follows that traditional moral rationalism is false as well. The question with which we're left is whether a view that shares some, but not all, of the core commitments of traditional moral rationalism is true and whether that view supports the truth of moral realism. For ease of discussion, let's stipulate that any view that entails at least one of the four core theses embraced by traditional moral rationalism is a form of moral rationalism, albeit a weak and nontraditional form. With this stipulation in mind, let's ask whether any form of weak and nontraditional moral rationalism is plausible (from here on I will drop the qualifiers, as only weak and nontraditional forms of moral rationalism will be discussed).

4. The Normative Thesis

To my mind, the normative thesis is immensely plausible, and provides us with an excellent reason for being a moral rationalist. It is a truism that when someone acts morally wrongly, they become an appropriate target for blame if they have neither an excuse nor an exemption (see also Wallace 1994). For these purposes, blame can be understood as including any or all of the following: keeping track of the wrongdoers actions with a view to diminishing the extent to which you trust them; verbally censuring the wrongdoer; demanding an apology from the wrongdoer or, if you are the wronged party, compensation from them; and engaging in a variety of responses aimed at preventing and deterring the wrongdoer from engaging in wrongdoing in the future for the sake of others. The question is why acting wrongly connects with the appropriateness of blame, so understood. As we will see, the answer lies in the connection between acting wrongly and doing something you have a reason not to do, and thus presupposes the truth of the normative thesis.

Let's get clearer about exemptions and excuses. When an agent acts wrongly, it is only appropriate to blame them if it is their fault. There are, in turn, two reasons why an agent's moral wrongdoing might not be their fault. The first is that they lack the capacity to recognize or respond to the fact that their action is morally wrong. Examples include global incapacities like being a toddler or being an adult who has no real understanding of their surroundings. In these cases, the agents in question are exempted from blame in all areas of conduct. But there are more local incapacities as well, and so more local exemptions. Adults who have been brainwashed into having some false moral view that they can't hold up for critical evaluation—acting in some specific way prescribed by a cult might be an example—and those who suffer from some sort of compulsion—they know that (say) shoplifting is morally wrong, but they lack the self-control required to get themselves to intend to refrain from shoplifting—are similarly exempted from blame, but only in the relevant domains.

The second reason that agents who perform actions that are morally wrong might not be at fault takes for granted that they have the capacity to recognize and respond to the fact that their actions are morally wrong, but then takes account of the fact that the exercise of such capacities is beholden to our fallibility, and that such capacities may also be more or less difficult to exercise. Perhaps the evidence available to the agent who acts morally wrongly was misleading—they wouldn't have acted wrongly if the world had been the way they reasonably believed it to be, given the evidence available to them—or perhaps the exercise of their powers of self-control would have required unusually demanding feats of attention and concentration. Even though such agents aren't exempted from blame, they have an excuse for doing what's morally wrong, so blaming them will turn out to be either less severe than it would have been, absent the excuse (the case of difficulty), or altogether inappropriate (the case of misleading evidence).

The flipside of exemptions and excuses, so understood, is that those who act morally wrongly and are at fault violate an expectation we have of them. Talk of an expectation here is both normative and empirical. The agents in question have the capacity to recognize and respond to the fact an act is morally wrong (this is the empirical part), so we expect them to exercise that capacity, absent an excuse (this is the normative part). The empirical part entails that, they have but fail to exercise either their capacity to access the evidence available to them in the formation of their beliefs about which actions are morally wrong, or their capacity for self-control, where the exercise of that capacity would have led them to form the intention to refrain from performing such actions. Or, to put the point another way, the empirical part entails that there are nearby no-fault worlds in which they both exercise their capacity to access the evidence available to them, and so know that their act is wrong, and exercise the self-control required to intend to refrain from acting wrongly, and so act permissibly. But there is evidently a lacuna here.

Suppose that someone breaks a rule and that they are neither in an evidentially impoverished state—they know that the rule applies to them—and they aren't suffering from a compulsion. Can we conclude that that rule-breaker had, but failed to exercise, self-control? The answer is that we cannot. But if we cannot then why can we conclude that someone who acts morally wrongly, and is neither in an evidentially impoverished state nor compelled, does have but fail to exercise self-control? What is so special about *moral* rules that tells us that there are nearby possible worlds in which rule-breakers act permissibly? The answer, which at this point may come as no surprise, lies in the truth of the normative thesis. To act wrongly, and so to violate a *moral* rule, is to act in a way that you have a reason not to act. Indeed, it is to act in a way that you have a decisive reason not to act. So, if you know your act is wrong, and you aren't compelled, then if you act in that way, you must have had but failed to exercise the self-control required to get yourself to do what you know you have a decisive reason to do: that is, to refrain from so acting. The possible worlds in which you act permissibly are therefore nearby, as compared to the case in which you act morally wrongly because you lack the capacity for self-control altogether.

Note that this isn't true of all rule-violators. There are rules we are bound by that we have decisive reasons to break. A striking example is discussed in the advice given to Canadian Forces on the NATO website about what to do if they are taken hostage.

> Unless you have clear reasons for doing otherwise, such as the violation of your personal dignity or security reasons, it is wise to consent to the demands made by your captors. Many observers believe that overt resistance is counterproductive in hostage situations. Be aware that some captors will play games by varying the rules in order to deliberately 'catch you out.' Of course, there may be rules, such as forbidding all communication with other hostages, which you may want to thwart and may be willing to pay the price for if detected. Be careful and be devious, and balance the likely payoffs of your behaviour with the possible consequences. (Murphy and Farley 2021: 6)

Strikingly, the advice takes it for granted that the rules apply to the hostages, and that in this sense they are bound by them, but it does so while also taking it for granted that their being bound is unjust and that compliance may therefore be unwilling. The analogue of the normative thesis in the case of the rules that captors impose on hostages is therefore false. Hostages will have decisive reasons to abide by certain rules imposed on them by their captors some of the time, but they will equally have decisive reasons to break certain of those rules some of the time. There is therefore no entailment from being bound by their captors' rules to reasons for action, and because there is no entailment, it is not the case that hostages who knowingly break the rules imposed on them by their captors, and who aren't suffering from compulsion, must have had but failed to exercise self-control in failing to have the intention to abide by the rules. Absent an exemption or an excuse, no one can be reasonably expected to do what they have decisive reasons not to do. Hostages who break rules imposed on them by their captors may therefore not be appropriate targets of blame, absent an excuse or an exemption.

With this case in mind, consider again the appropriateness of blame in the case of moral requirements. If moral requirements were like the rules imposed on hostages by their captors, then the mere absence of an exemption or an excuse would not suffice to make it appropriate to blame them. So moral requirements aren't like such rules. The appropriateness of blame presupposes that moral requirements differ from such rules in entailing valid reasons for action. Indeed, it presupposes that they entail decisive reasons for action. This explains why it is appropriate to blame those who violate the expectations we have of them.

5. Naturalism, Moral Relativism, Moral Rationalism, and Moral Realism

We are now in a position to describe a very weak form of moral rationalism and a correspondingly stronger form of moral realism. As we will see, this view faces a serious objection that isn't faced by stronger forms of moral rationalism. The ultimate question will be whether a stronger form is plausible.

Gilbert Harman makes a distinction between two kinds of moral judgment (Harman 1975). There are judgments about what agents morally ought to do, which he calls "inner moral judgements", and there are judgments about agents' moral character, like the claim that someone is evil, which he calls "outer" moral judgments. This distinction is important because Harman thinks that, by contrast with true outer moral judgments, true inner moral judgments entail corresponding reasons for action. Since a true inner moral judgment is a moral requirement, it follows that Harman is a weak moral rationalist about moral requirements.

In order to understand the motivation for Harman's view it is important that he simply assumes Humeanism about reasons for action. What makes it the case that someone has a reason to act in a certain way, according to Humeans, is that their so acting will realize some intrinsic desire they have, where intrinsic desires lead us to form the intentions we form. This assumed view about reasons and intentions leads Harman to give the following mind-dependent account of the truth-maker of inner moral judgments. Let's suppose that A judges that B morally ought to act in a certain way in certain circumstances, and that A's inner moral judgment is directed at conversational partners C, D, and E. In Harman's view, the truth of A's inner moral judgment requires that B's acting in that way in those circumstances accords with an intention A shares with B, C, D, and E to act in that way in those circumstances on condition that the others act in that way in those circumstances too. Since they each have reasons for their intentions, it follows that the truth of the inner moral judgment entails that they all have corresponding reasons to act, indeed, decisive reasons.

If we call those who share such conditional intentions a "community," then Harman thinks that the members of a community typically come to share these intentions as the result of an informal negotiation about what each community member is prepared to do for the others on condition that the others do the same for them, a negotiation whose outcome will inevitably reflect both what they intrinsically desire and their differential power relations when it comes to the realization of their intrinsic desires. Extremely powerful agents may be able to foist their will on those around them without any negotiation, so such agents will have no reason to form relevant conditional intentions, and will accordingly make no inner moral judgments. But those who are less powerful will have such a reason, and how much they will have a reason to do for others to get enough in return for it to be reasonable for them to form the corresponding conditional intentions will depend on how powerful they are vis a vis those others. The results of the informal negotiation will in this way set the expectations community members have of each other.

The upshot of all this is that Harman is a *naturalist*, a *weak moral realist*, a *moral relativist*, and a *weak moral rationalist*. He is a naturalist because he thinks that an inner moral judgment is an expression of a belief rather than a desire, about a way the world is where that way is a posit of a natural science. Indeed, his view is a version of what Sayre-McCord calls "*intersubjectivism*", so the way in question is a *mind-dependent* way the world is. Since he thinks that certain such beliefs are true, he is also a weak moral realist. But his weak moral realism is a version of moral relativism because he thinks that what makes inner moral judgments true is a relation that holds between those who make moral judgments and the members of their community. An inner judgment made by a community member is true if and only if and because community members share certain conditional intentions where it is contingent both whether this is so and, if it is so, what the content is of these intentions. To repeat, Harman thinks these contingencies are determined by power relations, and that they ensure that in all possible worlds in which inner moral judgments are true, community members have corresponding reasons for action. Harman is therefore a weak moral rationalist.

Initially, Harman's view seems to square well with the fact that it is appropriate to blame those who fail to do what they morally ought to do, as he holds that they fail to act on decisive reasons for action that they have. It is, however, worth making it explicit just how weak his moral rationalism is. Harman's commitment to a Humean account of reasons for action means that he rejects the view that moral reasons for action are unconditional. All reasons for action, both moral and nonmoral, are conditional. Moreover, as befits a Humean, though he holds that people may share conditional intentions for reasons, he places no constraints on the reasons they could have for doing so: that is, no constraints on the contents of the intrinsic desires that could be satisfied when they act on their shared conditional intentions. Agents in different communities might intrinsically desire very different things, and hence have conditional intentions to act in very different ways from those in another community, and even more radically, agents within a community may do so because they intrinsically desire very different things. Acting on their shared conditional intention might serve the self-interested intrinsic desires of some, the self-referentially altruistic intrinsic desires of others, and the impartial altruistic intrinsic desires of yet others. As a result, even though the members of a community all have the same instrumental reason to realize the contents of their shared conditional intentions, the reasons they have for having their shared conditional intentions might be correspondingly different.

The upshot is that Harman is committed to rejecting both the epistemological and metaphysical theses associated with traditional moral rationalism. If he is right, knowledge of moral requirements requires all kinds of a posteriori knowledge: knowledge of the contents of one's own intrinsic desires, causal knowledge of which options available to one will realize these intrinsic desires, knowledge of the conditional intentions one forms in the light of this knowledge, and, of course, knowledge of the contents of the conditional intentions of others in one's community. Moral requirements are thus not knowable a priori. Moreover, even though Harman thinks that moral requirements entail corresponding reasons for action, and so are grounded in part in facts about practical reason, he does not think that they are wholly grounded in such facts. On his view, moral requirements are also partially grounded in empirical facts, typically facts about differential power relations, that explain why community members have the specific conditional intentions they have. Harman thus rejects the metaphysical thesis associated with traditional moral rationalism too.

We saw earlier that Harman thinks that all reasons for action—moral reasons and nonmoral reasons alike—are conditional. This means he cannot distinguish between moral and nonmoral reasons in the content-free way we earlier suggested a traditional moral rationalist might distinguish them. Instead he thinks that what makes a reason for action a moral reason is its content: that is, the fact that it is a reason *to act on certain intentions on condition that others act in that way too*. By contrast, the distinctive feature of nonmoral reasons for action is that they are not reasons to act on intentions that are conditional in this way. Though this *content-committed* way of distinguishing moral from nonmoral reasons only partially specifies the content of moral reasons, as there are many things that someone could intend to do on condition that others act in that way too, the partial specification suffices for the distinction to be made.

I've explained at some length how very weak Harman's moral rationalism is because its weakness is the source of its main problem. Remember that Harman distinguishes between inner moral judgments and outer moral judgments, and that he thinks true inner moral judgments entail corresponding reasons for action whereas true outer moral judgments do not. Suppose someone causes us extreme harm. Have they done something morally wrong? According to Harman, their causing extreme harm to us is morally wrong only if they are members of our community, and only if causing extreme harm to us is something that members of our community have a conditional intention not to do, as in that case they do something that they have a decisive reason not to do. Those who cause us extreme harm who are not members of our community therefore may not do something that's morally wrong. Indeed, they may do something that they have every reason to do. But, Harman tells us, this doesn't mean that they escape our moral condemnation altogether. For even though we can't make an inner moral judgment about them, we may still make an outer moral judgment about them. Specifically, we may judge them to be (say) evil, where true claims to the effect that someone is evil do not entail corresponding reasons for action.

Harman doesn't say much about what it is for someone to be evil, but one thing he cannot say is that someone's being evil is a matter of their being disposed constantly to perform acts that are extremely morally wrong. In this respect, his account of what it is for someone to be evil, whatever it is, stands in stark contrast with the immensely plausible "fixed dispositional account of evil personhood" recently defended by Luke Russell in his independent study of evil (2020: 114). Russell defines evil people in terms of the evil actions they perform, where an evil action:

> ... is a wrong that is extremely harmful for at least one individual victim, where the wrongdoer is fully culpable for that harm in its extremity, or it is an action that is appropriately connected to an actual or possible extreme harm of this kind, and the agent is fully culpable for that action. (Russell 2020: 8–7)

But since in Harman's view only members of our community can be culpable for performing wrong actions, it follows that, for him, only members of our community can be evil in Russell's sense. If being Russell-evil is the only sense of evil in the offing, then for Harman the judgment that someone is evil would turn out to be an inner moral judgment after all, as its truth would entail that the evil person has a decisive reason not to do what he does. Noncommunity members would be exempted from moral evaluation altogether.

Russell's tying of evil to culpability in his independent study suggests that Harman's distinction between inner and outer moral evaluation is unmotivated. We should therefore ask what drives him to make this distinction. As we have seen, Harman thinks that the only thing anyone has reason to do is what will satisfy their intrinsic desires, and hence that all reasons for action are conditional. In this respect, he parts company with traditional moral rationalists. They think that even if some reasons are conditional, the reasons for action entailed by moral requirements are unconditional, and that this explains why any normal human adult who violates a moral requirement is culpable, including those who are evil. Moral reasons are in turn unconditional, they say, because they are wholly grounded in the capacity for practical reasoning. The question to which we must turn is whether there is an alternative to the Humean's account of reasons for action, an alternative that accepts the traditional moral rationalist's normative and metaphysical theses.

6. Two Ways to Reject the Humean's Account of Reasons for Action

There are at least two alternatives to a Humean account of reasons for action that accept the traditional moral rationalist's normative and metaphysical theses. But before describing these alternatives, it is worthwhile reminding ourselves why Humeanism is so appealing.

The Humean is a naturalist. He thinks the world is a spatio-temporally-causally ordered whole whose nature is contingent, and that among the objects in the world are objects like us who are equipped with perceptual capacities. He further thinks that reflection on the nature of our perceptual experiences can lead us to make and test reasonable hypotheses about the nature of the objects that caused them, and that we can in this way acquire knowledge of what the world is like. Given that the making and testing of such hypotheses is done most rigorously in the natural sciences, naturalists conclude that they provide us with our best understanding of the nature of the world in which we live. Every contingent way the world is must therefore be either a way among the ways the natural sciences tell us the world is, or a construction out of those ways.

The fact that people have beliefs and desires is a contingent way the world is, so Humeans think that these states must also either be ways that the natural sciences tell us it is, or constructions out of such ways. Because we can understand beliefs and desires in terms of their distinctive causes and effects, they opt for the latter. The role of belief is, they say, to represent the way the world is so that, in combination with our intrinsic desires about the way the world is to be, these two states can combine and cause a change in the ways our bodies are oriented, if a change is needed (from here-on I will omit this qualification), which will in turn cause the world to be that way. To play their complementary roles in a robust way, Humeans think that beliefs must therefore amount to knowledge of how to make these changes—for short, knowledge about means—as only knowledge about means can combine in a robust way with intrinsic desires to cause changes that amount to the realization of those intrinsic desires.

This functional conception of belief and intrinsic desire, and what it is for them to play their proper role, leads Humeans to think that there is a fundamental difference in the way that belief and desire relate to reasons. In keeping with their naturalism, they think of reasons as truth-supporting considerations, and so accept that there are reasons for beliefs. Indeed, given that beliefs can amount to knowledge, they think that it is crucial that there are reasons for beliefs. But since intrinsic desires are either satisfied or unsatisfied, not true or false, Humeans think that no sense can be made of there being reasons for or against them. Reasons for instrumental desires are, of course, different. Instrumental desires are composites of intrinsic desires and beliefs about means, so Humeans think that reasons for them reduce to reasons for the belief component. And they also think that reasons for action are different. Given that what makes an event an action is the fact that it was caused by an intrinsic desire and a belief about means, Humeans think that reasons for them are a construction out of the beliefs and desires that would cause them when these states play their proper role. An agent has a reason to act in a certain way, Humeans think, when there is some change in their bodily orientation they know how to bring about that would cause the content of some intrinsic desire they have to be realized.

With this reminder of the appeal of Humeanism about reasons for action before us, it should be clear that there are two ways to resist the view. One is to accept naturalism, but to take issue with the naturalistic account offered of the function of belief and desire that provides the basis for the Humean account of reasons for action. The second is to reject naturalism and provide instead a non-naturalistic account of reasons for action. Moreover, it should also be clear that, if we had to choose between these two ways of resisting the Humean view, then parsimony would tell in favor of the first. It would be unreasonable to reject the posits of the natural sciences as elements in our explanatorily basic theory of the world given all that they explain, but it would not be unreasonable to reject further posits if there is no explaining for them to do. We will consider these two ways of rejecting Humeanism in reverse order.

7. Reasons Primitivism, Non-Naturalism, Moral Absolutism, Moral Rationalism, and Moral Realism

There are many ways to pursue the second strategy (Enoch 2011, Parfit 2011, Shafer-Landau 2003), but here the focus will be on Scanlon's (1998, 2013). Though his view is complex, the basics are easy enough to explain, and the problems that his view ends up facing are problems that arise for the others as well.

According to Scanlon, reasons discourse is discourse about an array of necessary and a priori knowable four-place relational facts holding between considerations, attitudes, persons, and circumstances. In his view, this four-place relation, which is a primitive normative relation, is important for understanding a sub-class of psychological states, namely, the *judgment-sensitive attitudes*, where these are those...

.... that an ideally rational person would come to have whenever that person judged there to be sufficient reasons for them, and that would, in an ideally rational person, 'extinguish' when that person judged them not to be supported by reasons of the appropriate kind (Scanlon 1998: 20).

The reasons Scanlon speaks of in this passage are the *considerations* in the four-place reason relation, and what these considerations provide, at least when the judgments mentioned in the passage are true, are sufficient reasons in the standard normative sense for the relevant *attitudes* of the relevant *person* in the relevant *circumstances*.

Scanlon tells us that judgment-sensitive attitudes "constitute the class of things for which reasons in the standard normative sense can be asked or offered" (Scanlon 1998: 21). The paradigmatic example of such considerations are those that support the truth of our beliefs, as beliefs are by nature sensitive to the considerations that believers take to provide reasons for them. But Scanlon thinks that there are other judgment-sensitive attitudes as well. These include intention, intrinsic desire, fear, trust, and admiration, as in his view all these come and go in an ideally rational person depending on what that person takes to be reasons for acquiring or ridding themselves of them. If he is right about this, then that is significant, as it suggests that the fact that reasons are considerations that are truth-supporting in the case of beliefs does not generalize. Intentions, intrinsic desires, fear, trust, and admiration are not themselves states that are truth-assessable, so reasons for them, whatever they are, are not considerations that support their truth. But in that case, how are we to characterize the reason-relation? Scanlon thinks that we can't. The reason-relation is, he tells us, a primitive and mind-independent normative relation.

> Any attempt to explain what it is to be a reason for something seems to me to lead back to the same idea: a consideration that counts in favor of it. "Counts in favor how?" one might ask. "By providing a reason for it" seems to be the only answer. (Scanlon 1998: 17)

When we put this together with Scanlon's definition of the class of judgment-sensitive attitudes we get the following surprising result.

Certain psychological features, namely the judgment-sensitive attitudes, are themselves non-natural features of the world because our understanding of their nature depends on our positing mind-independent facts about reasons in the standard normative sense in the explanatorily basic theory of the world in terms of which these attitudes are understood. An ideally rational person is someone who is maximally sensitive to what they take such considerations to be in the formation of their judgment-sensitive attitudes, where that taking is itself either correct or incorrect depending on whether the mind-independent facts about reasons are the way that that person takes them to be. Crucially, however, these mind-independent facts about reasons are not themselves the posits of any natural science (compare Copp and Sobel 2002: 248).

The move from Scanlonian non-naturalism about judgment-sensitive attitudes to non-naturalistic moral realism and moral rationalism requires three further steps. The first, obviously enough, is an argument that Scanlon is right that there exists a non-natural reason relation. We will return to this step in the next section. The second step is a definition of reasons for action in terms of the primitive reason relation. Since actions are not attitudes, Scanlon holds that reasons for action are reasons in a different but related sense. As he puts it,

> ... 'reason for action' is not to be contrasted with 'reason for intending'. The connection to action, which is essential to intentions, determines the kinds of reasons that are appropriate for them, but it is the connection with judgment-sensitive attitudes that makes events actions, and hence the kind of things for which reasons can sensibly be asked for and offered at all. (1998: 21)

Reasons for actions count in favor of actions, according to Scanlon, by counting in favor of the intentions that produce those actions. But since intentions are the upshots of intrinsic desires and beliefs about means, he might just as well have said that they count in favor of actions by counting in favor of either the intrinsic desires or beliefs about means that give rise to intentions. Scanlon thus holds that reason for actions are *mind-dependent* features of the world in the following sense. Reasons *for action* exist in virtue of the fact that certain considerations stand in the mind-independent favoring relation to certain *mental features*, specifically, to intentions to perform those actions, or to intrinsic desires that those actions realize. In this respect, Scanlon's non-naturalism is very different from that of Moore who holds that reasons for action are mind-independent features of the world. This is because, as Moore sees things, reasons for actions exist in virtue of the fact that the actions for which there are reasons have outcomes with the simple non-natural property of being good. Mental features play no role in the characterization of reasons for action.

An example of a consideration that Scanlon thinks provides a reason for intentions includes the fact that performing an activity would be enjoyable, which he thinks provides a reason for intending to engage in that activity, and, in virtue of that, makes it the case that there is a reason to engage in that activity. Another example is the fact that an act would impose a burden on people, which he thinks provides a reason for an intention not to perform that act, and, in virtue of that, makes it the case that there is a reason not to perform that act. These examples are important because they show that Scanlon thinks that both agent-relative features—the fact that an act would be enjoyable for the agent himself—and agent-neutral features—the fact that an act would impose burdens on people without regard to who they are—provide reasons for action. An example of a consideration that Scanlon thinks never provides a reason for intending to perform an act in its own right is the fact that that act would satisfy some intrinsic desire the agent has. This is important for two reasons. First, it shows that Scanlon doesn't conceive of enjoyment as desire-satisfaction, and second, it entails that he thinks no reasons for action are conditional on the agent who has the reason having some desire that would be satisfied by acting on the reason. According to Scanlon, all reasons for action are unconditional.

This brings us to the third step in the move from Scanlonian non-naturalism about judgment-sensitive attitudes to non-naturalistic moral realism and moral rationalism. An account needs to be provided of what's distinctive about moral reasons for action, as opposed to nonmoral reasons. Though Scanlon is somewhat skeptical about this distinction, he thinks that there is fairly well-defined sub-class of reasons for action having to do with what he calls "morality in the narrow sense". Of course, given that he thinks that all reasons for action are unconditional, he cannot draw this distinction in the content-free way that is available to some traditional moral rationalists. Instead he provides a *content-committed* way of drawing this distinction. When our actions impose burdens on other people, then in some such cases there are considerations to which we could appeal that would allow us to justify our actions to them, where these considerations would do that by showing that what we did was not an instance of our failing to do what we owe it to others to do for them. These considerations having to do with what we owe to others are distinctively moral-in-the-narrow-sense reasons. The justification for imposing burdens on people would then consist in showing that there was no decisive moral-in-the-narrow-sense reason for us to intend not to do exactly what we did, as this would entail that there was no decisive moral-in-the-narrow-sense reason for us not to do what we did. In other words, what we did was morally-in-the-narrow-sense permissible.

Suppose we take these three steps. The upshot would then be a view that is a version of *non-naturalism*, *moral realism*, *moral absolutism*, and *moral rationalism*. The view would be a version of non-naturalism because moral facts would turn out to be facts about reasons for action which are in turn facts about the non-natural mind-independent reason relation holding between considerations, judgment-sensitive attitudes, people, and circumstances, but it would be a version of non-naturalism according to which moral facts themselves, being facts about reasons for action, are mind-dependent. The view would be a form of moral realism because moral judgments would turn out to be expressions of beliefs, as opposed to desires, about these reasons for action, and—at least if Scanlon is right that there exists a non-natural reason relation, and right that the relata of that relation include considerations of what-we-owe-to-others kind and intentions to act accordingly—some of these beliefs would turn out to be true. The view would be a stronger form of moral rationalism than that embraced by Harman because it would take on board three of the commitments of traditional moral rationalism, and so be a version of moral absolutism. Moral requirements would entail reasons for action; moral requirements would be a priori knowable; and moral requirements would be grounded in facts about practical reason, assuming that facts about practical reason on this view would be facts about the mind-independent and non-natural reason relation holding between considerations, intentions, people, and circumstances.

Because Scanlon's view embraces these three commitments of traditional moral rationalism, it avoids the problem faced by Harman's view. There is no need for a distinction between inner and outer moral judgments because all moral judgments would turn out to be judgments about a domain of facts grounded in facts about practical reason that are a priori knowable and entail the same unconditional reasons for action for everyone who is in the same circumstances. Every rational being who does what there is a decisive moral-in-the-narrow-sense reason for them not to do in their circumstances with neither an exemption nor an excuse would therefore be liable to blame for violating a moral requirement. But Scanlon's view embraces these three commitments at a considerable conceptual and metaphysical cost. The reason relation that holds between considerations and judgment-sensitive attitudes is a conceptual primitive, so it cannot be understood in terms of truth-supportingness, and non-naturalism about this relation, together with the role that that relation plays in understanding the judgment-sensitive attitudes, means that that this aspect of psychology cannot be understood in wholly naturalistic terms either.

Those who find Scanlon's arguments otherwise compelling, but who are unwilling to pay these costs, will therefore find themselves having to combine his cognitivism with error, rather than success, and embrace a form of *cognitivist antirealism*. This makes it sensible to ask whether it is necessary to pay these costs. Is it necessary to posit a non-natural reason relation?

8. Constitutivism, Naturalism, Moral Absolutism, Moral Rationalism, and Moral Realism

We saw earlier that there are two ways to take issue with the Humean account of reasons for action. The one just considered requires the rejection of naturalism. The other accepts naturalism, but takes issue with the Humean's account of what it is for beliefs and intrinsic desires to function properly. This strategy is pursued by some constitutivists. Though there are many versions of constitutivism (Katsanafas 2018), here the focus will be on the version that seems to me to be most promising (Smith 2013, 2020).

Let's begin with points of agreement. Constitutivists think that Humeans are right that beliefs and intrinsic desires are distinctive feature of agents, where agents are objects in the world with the capacity to both know what the world is like and satisfy their intrinsic desires in it. Note that there are therefore both human and nonhuman agents, and note as well that nonhuman agents may include beings from other planets. Given that an agent may have the capacity to know some aspects of the world but not others, and to satisfy some of their intrinsic desires but not others, and given that they may have but fail to exercise such capacities as they have, constitutivists point out that the kind *agent* is therefore what Judith Jarvis Thomson calls a *goodness-fixing kind* (Thomson 2008). These are kinds that generate an ordering of objects falling under the kind depending on how well these objects meet a standard internal to the kind itself.

The point of disagreement with Humeans lies in the constitutivist's conviction that we need to go beyond Humeanism in order to fully explain the ordering internal to the kind *agent*.

Humeans will presumably agree that at the top of this ordering we find those agents who robustly have and exercise maximal capacities for knowledge acquisition and desire satisfaction, and that at the bottom we find agents who have as few such capacities as possible and who exercise them as infrequently as possible. In slightly more detail, *ideal agents*—those at the top—have and exercise the capacity to know what the world is like no matter what it is like, to the extent that the world is knowable; they have and exercise the capacity to satisfy their intrinsic desires no matter what their content, to the extent that they are satisfiable; and their possession and exercise of these capacities is a robust fact about them: it not a total fluke that they possess and exercise them. This more detailed characterization of ideal agents entails that though an inability to know (say) what's happening beyond the light cone does not disqualify an agent from being ideal, and an inability to satisfy an intrinsic desire that the world be some impossible way does not similarly disqualify them from being ideal, the fact that an agent's possession and exercise of their agential capacities is a modally fragile fact about them—that it turns on some fluke about their circumstances—does disqualify them from being ideal. As we will see, though there is nothing non-naturalistic about ideal agents, so understood, the modal robustness of their agency does seem to require that their intrinsic desires play roles beyond those posited by Humeans.

Since agents are temporally extended, the robust possession and exercise of agential capacities must itself be temporally extended. Agents who possess and exercise their agential capacities robustly must therefore have the wherewithal within themselves, or the worlds in which they exist must contain the wherewithal, to overcome two kinds of vulnerability to which they would otherwise be subject. The first is the vulnerability of an agent's later self to their earlier self. Imagine an agent at a certain time who exercises the capacity to know what the world is like and satisfy their intrinsic desires at that time. For their possession and exercise of this capacity to be robust, that exercise cannot be dependent on the fact that, at some earlier time, they just so happened not to have and act on an intrinsic desire to deceive themselves at the later time, or that at the earlier time, they just so happened not to have and act on an intrinsic desire to undermine their satisfaction of their intrinsic desires at the later time. Moreover, if their possession of those capacities is itself the product of their efforts to develop and maintain their capacities at some earlier time, then it cannot be dependent on the fact that, at that earlier time, they just so happened to help make sure that they develop and maintain such capacities at the later time. They must instead have some feature, in virtue of being an agent who robustly has and exercises maximal agential capacities at each moment they exist, that explains why at the earlier time they helped develop and maintain their having their agential capacities, and why at the earlier time they didn't interfere with their later exercise of these capacities.

One obvious feature to imagine them having, given our understanding of what it is to be an agent, is a pair of intrinsic desires at the earlier time, constitutive of what it is to be an agent whose possession and exercise of their agential capacities is robust. The ideal agent must have an intrinsic desire to help ensure that that they have agential capacities to exercise, and an intrinsic desire not to interfere with their exercise once they have them (on condition that their exercise won't itself constitute interference—from here-on this qualification will be omitted). Another obvious feature to imagine them having is the self-control required to make sure that they act in accordance with these intrinsic desires in nearby worlds in which, via apathy or weakness of will, they would otherwise be instrumentally irrational absent that exercise. Agents who lack these two intrinsic desires, or who lack the capacity for self-control, would for that very reason be less than ideal. Note that this requires us to go beyond the Humean's account of the role played by intrinsic desires. According to constitutivists, in addition to playing the role of contributing to their own satisfaction, certain intrinsic desires play the role of minimizing an ideal agent's vulnerability to intrapersonal conflict, a role they play by ensuring that such conflicts are at worst a distant possibility for them.

A second kind of vulnerability that agents who robustly possess and exercise maximal agential capacities must overcome is the interpersonal analogue of the intrapersonal vulnerability just described. Imagine an agent at a certain time who exercises the capacity to know what the world is like and satisfy their desires in it at that time. For their exercise of this capacity to be robust, it cannot be the case that that exercise is dependent on the fact that, at that time, it just so happens that there are no other agents, or that there are other agents, but they just so happen not to deceive them or undermine their satisfaction of their intrinsic desires. Moreover, if their possession of those capacities at that time is the product of the efforts of other agents to help them develop and maintain their capacities, then the robust possession and exercise of their agential capacities cannot be dependent on the fact that those other agents just so happen to exist and want to help them develop and maintain their capacities. Those other agents must instead have a feature that explains why they are there and why they help but don't interfere in a robust way.

This suggests an even more demanding conception of what it is for an agent to be ideal. For an agent's possession and exercise of their agential capacities to be maximal and robust, it seems that they must be in the company of other agents who also robustly have and exercise maximal agential capacities—ideal agents are social, not isolated— and they must all intrinsically desire to help develop and maintain the agential capacities of every agent, and intrinsically desire not to interfere with the exercise of the agential capacities of any agent. Moreover, all those who robustly possess and exercise maximal agential capacities must also have the capacity for self-control required to ensure that, in nearby worlds in which they suffer from apathy or weakness of will, they act in accordance with such intrinsic desires anyway. Agents who are alone, or who lack fully general intrinsic desires to help but not interfere, or who are surrounded by agents who lack these two intrinsic desires, or who lack the capacity for self-control or are surrounded by agents who lack self-control, are less than ideal because of the resultant modal fragility in their possession and exercise of their maximal agential capacities.

Though the differences between this constitutivist conception of the ideal agent and the Humean conception are manifest, note that constitutivism shares with Humeanism a commitment to naturalism. In characterizing an ideal agent, neither constitutivists nor Humeans posit any properties beyond those that are posited by, or those that are constructions from those posited by, the natural sciences. The contrast between the constitutivist's view of the ideal agent and that of Scanlon's reasons primitivism is thus stark indeed. Reasons primitivism is committed to characterizing ideal agents as those whose intentions and intrinsic desires are sensitive to the considerations that favor having them, where the favoring relation is non-naturalistic. Assuming that the constitutivist's naturalistic conception of the ideal agent is on the right track, the move to moral realism and moral rationalism requires just two further steps.

The first is an account of what agents have reasons to do in terms of facts about ideal agents. Constitutivists think, in the spirit of Humeanism, that what an agent in certain circumstances has reason to do is whatever their ideal counterpart would want them to do in those circumstances. Reason for action facts thus turn out to be *naturalistic* and *mind-dependent* for constitutivists, just as they are for Humeans. Facts about the reasons for action ideal agents have are fixed by the ideal agent's own desires, and facts about the reasons of nonideal agents are fixed by the desires of their ideal counterparts. Since in virtue of being their counterparts, the ideal agents in question will have all the same intrinsic desires concerning the nonideal agents' circumstances as the nonideal agents themselves have concerning those circumstances, assuming that their intrinsic desires all survive the process of idealization, it follows that constitutivists think that all agents have *conditional* reasons to do whatever they intrinsically desire to do. But since the ideal agents in question will also have intrinsic desires to help but not interfere, as these are constitutive of their being ideal, constitutivists think that all agents also have *unconditional* reasons to help but not interfere. The intuitive idea can be put this way. Ideal agents have and act on reasons for action by definition, but they also have contingency action plans for every circumstance. Nonideal agents, to the extent that they do what they have reason to do, simply act out these contingency plans of their ideal counterparts, where this is a matter of balancing reasons to do whatever they want against their reasons to help but not interfere.

The second step is to provide an account of the distinction between moral and nonmoral reasons for action. As should now be clear, constitutivists can explain this distinction in the *content-free* way available to some traditional moral rationalists. Moral reasons for action, they can say, are unconditional reasons, whereas nonmoral reasons for action are conditional. Armed with this distinction, they can then spell out what it is for an action to be morally wrong in terms of moral reasons. An action is morally wrong, they can say, when there is a decisive moral reason not to perform it, and there is a decisive moral reason not to perform an action, they can say, when the reasons to help but not interfere tell in favor of not performing the action, and when these moral reasons outweigh any nonmoral reasons to perform the action that there might be given the agent's other intrinsic desires. Facts about the relative strengths of moral and nonmoral reasons in various circumstances can in turn be understood as fixed, they can say, by how strong an ideal agent's corresponding intrinsic desires are concerning those circumstances, facts that must exist given that ideal agents have contingency plans for every circumstance.

Constitutivism is thus committed to *moral realism*, as it entails that moral judgments are expressions of beliefs, where these beliefs are not constituted by desires, and it further entails that certain such beliefs are true. The version of moral realism it entails is, however, stronger than the weakest version Sayre-McCord describes. For one thing, is a version of moral realism that is *naturalistic, mind-dependent,* and *moral absolutist*. Moral beliefs turn out to be true in virtue of facts about the psychology of ideal agents, where ideal agents are themselves entirely natural objects, and where all ideal agents share intrinsic desires to help but not interfere. For another, the version of moral realism it entails is a form of *moral rationalism* that is like Scanlon's reasons primitivism in embracing three of the core commitments of traditional moral rationalism: moral requirements entail corresponding reasons for action because they reduce to facts about reasons for action; moral requirements are knowable a priori because they follow from conceptual truths about the nature of moral requirements and reasons for action; and moral requirements are grounded in facts about practical reason because facts about reasons for action reduce to facts about the psychology of ideal agents.

Because the view embraces these three commitments of traditional moral rationalism it is also like Scanlon's reasons primitivism in avoiding the problem faced by Harman's view. Since every rational being has moral reasons to help but not interfere, those who fail to help or interfere when there are decisive moral reasons to do otherwise are, absent an exemption or an excuse, blameworthy for violating a moral requirement. But unlike Scanlon's reasons primitivism, it secures this result without incurring any conceptual or metaphysical costs. On the metaphysical side, constitutivism is consistent with the view that all contingent matters of fact can be understood naturalistically, so it is more parsimonious. On the conceptual front, though constitutivism holds with Humeans, and against Scanlon, that what makes a consideration a reason for having some judgment-sensitive attitude is the fact that that consideration is truth-supporting, it holds with Scanlon, and against Humeans, that there are reasons for both beliefs and intrinsic desires.

The crucial point on this matter was made by Thomson (2008). Reasons for attitudes with correctness conditions are, she points out, considerations that support the truth of the propositions that are those attitudes' correctness conditions. Given that the class of judgment-sensitive attitudes and the class of attitudes with correctness conditions are one and the same, it follows that the explanation of there being reasons for belief is exactly what Humeans say it is, namely, the existence of considerations that support the truth of the proposition believed, as the proposition believed is the correctness condition of belief. But, since intrinsic desires, and hence the intentions that derive from them, also have correctness conditions, it follows that there are reasons for them too. To focus on intrinsic desires, reasons for them are considerations that support the truth of propositions to the effect that the objects of intrinsic desires are intrinsically desirable. Given that constitutivism suggests that the intrinsic desirability of a state of affairs is a matter of that state of affairs' being the object of an ideal agent's intrinsic desires, it follows that considerations that support the truth of claims giving the contents of an ideal agent's intrinsic desires are, in virtue of that fact, reasons for having intrinsic desires with those contents. The arguments for constitutivism thus turn out to be reasons we all have to intrinsically desire to help but not interfere.

9. Conclusion

Moral realism is simply the combination of *cognitivism* and *success*. As such, it is a relatively weak doctrine. Though it turns out that moral realism is true, we have seen that the arguments for this conclusion require us to take a stand on which stronger form of moral realism is true. The stronger form that seems best supported is a version of constitutivism. This view combines *moral realism* with *naturalism*, *mind-dependence*, *moral absolutism*, a *content-free* way of making the distinction between the moral and the nonmoral, and, most importantly, a fairly strong version of *moral rationalism*. Facts about the moral wrongness of actions are facts about the existence of actions that there are decisive unconditional reasons not to perform.

References

Blackburn, Simon. 1993. *Essays in Quasi-Realism*. Oxford: Oxford University Press.
Copp, David, and David Sobel. 2002. "Desires, Motives, and Reasons: Scanlon's Rationalistic Moral Psychology." *Social Theory and Practice* 28: 243–276.
Gibbard, Allan. 2003. *Thinking How to Live*. Cambridge, MA: Harvard University Press.
Dorsey, Dale. 2016."Moral Distinctiveness and Moral Inquiry." *Ethics* 126: 747–773.
Dreier, James. 2004. "Meta-Ethics and the Problem of Creeping Minimalism." *Philosophical Perspectives* 18: 23–44.
Enoch, David. 2011. *Taking Morality Seriously*. Oxford: Oxford University Press.
Harman, Gilbert. 1975. "Moral Relativism Defended." *Philosophical Review* 84: 3–22.
Katsanafas, Paul. 2018. "Constitutivism about Practical Reasons." In *The Oxford Handbook of Reasons and Normativity*, edited by Daniel Star, 367–394. Oxford: Oxford University Press.
Mackie, J. L. 1977. *Ethics: Inventing Right and Wrong*. Harmondsworth, UK: Penguin.
McGrath, Sarah. 2019. *Moral Knowledge*. Oxford: Oxford University Press.
Murphy, P. J., and K. M. J. Farley. 2021. *Hostage Survival Skills for CF Personnel*. Accessed November 8, 2021. https://www.nato.int/docu/colloq/w970707/p6.pdf.
Parfit, Derek. 2011. *On What Matters*. Oxford: Oxford University Press.
Russell, Luke. 2020. *Being Evil: A Philosophical Perspective*. Oxford: Oxford University Press.
Sayre-McCord, Geoffrey. 1988. "The Many Moral Realisms." In *Essays on Moral Realism*, edited by Geoffrey Sayre-McCord, 1–26. Ithaca: Cornell University Press.
Scanlon, Thomas. 1998. *What We Owe to Each Other*. Cambridge, MA: Harvard University Press.
Scanlon, Thomas. 2013. *Being Realistic about Reasons*. Oxford: Oxford University Press.

Shafer-Landau, Russ 2003: *Moral Realism: A Defense*. Oxford: Clarendon Press.
Smith, Michael. 2013. "A Constitutivist Theory of Reasons: Its Promise and Parts." *LEAP: Law, Ethics, and Philosophy* 1: 9–30.
Smith, Michael. 2020. "The Modal Conception of Ideal Rational Agents: Objectively Ideal Not Merely Subjectively Ideal, Advisors Not Exemplars, Agentially Concerned Not Agentially Indifferent, Social Not Solitary, Self-and-Other Regarding Not Wholly Self-Regarding." In *Explorations in Ethics*, edited by David Kaspar, 59–79. New York: Palgrave Macmillan.
Thomson, Judith Jarvis. 2008. *Normativity*. Chicago: Open Court.
Wallace, R. Jay 1994. *Responsibility and the Moral Sentiments*. Cambridge, MA: Harvard University Press.

CHAPTER 6

DOES ANYTHING WE CARE ABOUT DISTINGUISH THE NON-NATURAL FROM THE NATURAL?

MARK VAN ROOJEN

I used to be a non-naturalist, or at least I used to think I was. But I no longer think I know what the debate between naturalists and non-naturalists is about. My reason for saying this is that I don't see how some of the arguments that people make line up with what strike me as the main motivations for wanting to be either a naturalist or a non-naturalist. As I see it, there are two basic motivations in play, one for each "side" of the debate. For non-naturalists, the "just too different" idea looms large. That is they think that there is some fundamental difference between moral and normative properties on the one hand, and properties standardly thought of as natural, such as the properties that are the proper object of scientific inquiry, on the other. The friends of naturalism are motivated by the thought that the world, along with everything in it, is natural.[1] Even if there could have been gods and ghosts and things beyond our ability to understand via the tools of natural science, our world is not like that. Both of these, it seems to me, are perfectly respectable motivations. In fact I think I endorse both of them, though I worry a bit about the right way to formulate each of the underlying thoughts.

Yet the most prominent current argument that purports to determine which of the competing views—naturalism or non-naturalism—is correct does not seem relevant to

---

[1] Some naturalists also have an epistemic motivation—skepticism about substantive a priori knowledge—which I'll only discuss somewhat briefly since I'm not convinced it really favors naturalism over non-naturalism.

capturing either of these ideas. That argument is about grounding and about the possible extension of moral and normative properties. Are there distant but possible worlds non-normatively just like ours, where the normative facts differ from those in our world? According to many of the partisans, for non-naturalism to be true the answer must be yes.[2] I can't really see why. As I will argue, neither answer seems to bear very directly on the two motivations for either the naturalist or non-naturalist position. Supposing that the extension of normative properties cannot vary as the proposal suggests, this tells us little about the nature of the properties in question and about whether they are in some way significantly different from paradigm natural properties. And supposing that the answer, which is about distant possible worlds, turns out to be that yes the extensions of moral properties do vary at these worlds, it is not at all obvious what this tells us about the nature of our world.

That, anyway, is what I will argue.

1. The Plan

To make that argument well I will need to explain what I think would be needed for the dispute to be genuine and substantive. I will also need to get as clear as I can on the motivations, commitments and resources of each naturalism and non-naturalism. Having done all that I will be in a position to address the current debate which focusses on grounding. It will become clear to the reader that this debate only deepens a puzzlement that begins elsewhere—namely about what sorts of differences from other paradigm natural properties would make normative properties other than natural.

Section 2 sets up my favored way of thinking about what is at stake in the debate. Section 3 considers two motivations for naturalism partly in hope of discovering what unifies the natural as natural. Section 4 considers a problem for normative naturalism and several possible strategies to solve it. Some of these will be a bit peripheral to the main line of argument insofar as they concern reductive rather than non-reductive naturalism, but they are worth considering in their own right and also for understanding the motivations for naturalism. Section 5 looks at the motivations for non-naturalism, again in hope of discovering what constitutes naturalness, this time by getting a sense for what non-naturalists think distinguishes the non-natural from the natural. Section 6 explains my puzzlement about the newfangled grounding arguments for and against non-naturalism, and Section 7 wraps the discussion up in a not very tidy package.

---

[2] Rosen (2010, 2020), Fine (2002), Bader (2017), Leary (2017).

2. One Way the Debate Between Naturalism and Non-Naturalism Might Have Substance

Before there were vocal non-reductive naturalists, it was easy to think of the naturalism/non-naturalism debate as being about whether the normative properties could be reduced to the natural properties. That made it easy to think that the issue turned on whether normative properties could be identified with simple uncontroversially natural properties or complexes of such properties, and on whether relations short of identity such as constitution and composition were sufficient for reduction. But non-reductive naturalists opened up the possibility that properties which could not be explicitly identified with natural properties or complexes of natural properties via obviously naturalistic definitions might still be natural even while constitution or composition by themselves are not sufficient for a naturalistic reduction. Nick Sturgeon very nicely highlighted the possibility that normative properties aren't sufficiently different from the properties postulated by natural sciences other than physics—which themselves supervene on and hence are constituted by physical properties while remaining distinct from them—to be considered non-natural (Sturgeon, 2006, 92–99). If the relations between these higher-level scientific properties and the lower-level properties on which they supervene is similar to the relation of moral properties to lower-level natural properties, and if each of these higher-level properties also has something to distinguish it as a level making up its own science, that might make them not really much different from the normative properties.

With that possibility opened up, it makes sense to ask what the debate between naturalists and non-naturalists is really about. Both views deny identity; both views typically allow some sort of composition or relation of asymmetric dependence; both views deny there is any good way to pick out the normative properties with non-normative vocabulary. So what do they disagree about?

I think that the best way to think of the root disagreement is as a debate about natural or, less confusingly in this context, elite kinds of kinds and properties.[3] If naturalists are right, there is some real similarity shared by all and only the natural properties and kinds. This similarity would be shared by the normative properties so that they too count as natural by this criterion. If non-naturalists are right, there is also a real similarity shared by all and only the natural properties and kinds but the normative properties do not share it (Sturgeon, 2003, 92; Suikkanen 2010, McPherson, 2015, 129; van Roojen, 2015, 222). In both cases the relevant similarity would have to be other than accidental;

---

[3] I'm following Dunaway and McPherson (2016) in using "elite" to pick out what David Lewis (1983) called "natural properties"—the subset of the abundant properties that involve real similarities which are not "Cambridge properties" or gruesome, and which might be thought of as genuine universals.

the real similarity shared by all and only the natural properties would be essential to explaining why the normative properties are either natural or not. As McPherson (2018, 197, fn 14) puts it, "the natural properties form an elite similarity class among properties, and naturalistic moral realism is the thesis that the moral properties are part of that class." Furthermore, for the actual debate between naturalists and non-naturalists to be about naturalness so construed the relevant similarity would have to connect up with the arguments people make for or against their respective positions.

That a given property shares in this real similarity, in other words that it has the higher order property of being natural (or, for that matter, non-natural or supernatural),[4] should be a property the relevant properties have as a matter of metaphysical necessity. If metaphysical necessities are those secured by the essences of the relevant entities the fact that the property instantiates the higher order property would be of that sort. If metaphysical necessities are secured by the natures of the relevant entities plus metaphysical laws they will be of that sort. But whether the properties in question are natural or not will not necessarily be a conceptual truth. The metaphysical possibilities are a proper subset of the conceptual possibilities and we may therefore coherently think something metaphysically possible while being wrong about that. Thus we can without conceptual confusion make mistakes when classifying a property as natural or not.

Furthermore, if there are supernatural properties[5] these must not share in the real similarity that makes the natural properties natural.[6] And presumable they will share some real similarity that makes them supernatural. You might think that all it would take to be supernatural on this picture is not to share in the real similarity that unifies the natural. But if there is to be a possibility that a property could be neither natural nor supernatural we had better not say that. G. E. Moore (1903) noticed this a long time ago. Thus he defined non-natural properties as neither natural nor "metaphysical"—his term for a class of properties that included the supernatural.

---

[4] FWIW, it isn't clear that this list is exhaustive at least at the level of possible properties.

[5] There may not be, since—for all I think I'm in a position to know, not having knowingly encountered one—they could turn out to be metaphysically impossible.

I might as well flag my assumption that uninstantiated properties can exist, so long as they are metaphysically possible. You can think of them as possibilities for how (parts of) the world might be. Insofar as the actual world might not contain instances of all the properties that might have been instantiated, it is likely better to say that no instances exist at the actual world than to say the property doesn't exist at the actual world. Still things get complicated. There are or could be uninstantiated properties that essentially involve what would be individuals. I don't have a daughter, but I could have. If I had a daughter there would be properties to which she—that very person would be essential. For example being her favorite toy. But it isn't clear what to say about that property here and now in the actual world. For there is no particular individual who is or would be my nonactual but possible daughter. So properties instantiable and even instantiated in a counterfactual but possible world that essentially involve such individuals who don't actually exist can't be singled out from here. Should we think they exist uninstantiated?

[6] Though I suppose it could turn out that the supernatural properties (if there are any) and the natural properties share some other higher order similarity that distinguishes them from non-natural properties.

We should probably think this anyway. Let's assume that the properties postulated by physics astronomy and geology are all perfectly natural. Then it seems there could be a sparsely populated and purely natural possible world or universe containing just two galaxies each of which was a mirror of the other. Such a universe would instantiate equinumerosity since the two galaxies would have the same number of planets. But, on the assumption that supernatural properties are metaphysically possible and independent of physical properties, we could also imagine a purely supernatural world with two ghost families with the same number of members. It too would instantiate equinumerosity. Is equinumerosity a natural or supernatural property? If we put it in either category we seem to create difficulties for the idea of either a purely natural world or a purely supernatural world. Probably the best thing to say is that some properties are neutral—their instantiation does not make a world either natural or supernatural or non-natural in some other way (van Roojen 2006, 190, McPherson 2015). Surely mathematical and geometric as well as structural properties of certain sorts could be instantiated in either purely natural or purely supernatural worlds. And their instantiation in an otherwise natural world is completely consistent with a scientific and naturalistic world view. So such properties should not falsify the kind of naturalism that stands opposed to supernaturalism. For this to be plausible to say about any given property, we may need to think of that property as more unified than just a big disjunction of distinct properties some natural others not. We should be able to think of the property instances as sharing a real similarity that makes them instances of something that is multiply instantiable (see Suikkanen, 2010). How many such properties there are is an interesting question.[7]

If there are such "neutral" properties there is an interesting issue for both naturalists and non-naturalists. It could be that normative properties are natural in the same way that the properties of physics, etc. are natural. It could also be that the normative properties are more like equinumerosity—one of the neutral properties the instantiation of which does not change the basic character of the world with respect to naturalness. Or it could be that the normative properties were non-natural (but not supernatural) in some more robust sense. If it turned out that they were such neutral properties it would be an interesting question whether naturalists or non-naturalists were right.

It is well worth investigating these options further. But first I think it will be useful to get some sense of what naturalists (and perhaps also some non-naturalists) think unifies the natural. To do that I am going to look into two motivating ideas that seem to me to stand behind naturalistic characterizations of the natural. The hope would be that we can use the motivations for naturalism to figure out what makes a property

---

[7] There is some pressure to think it works the other way around as well. The fact that a property can have instances in a perfectly natural world like ours also would not make an otherwise supernatural world in which it is instanced suddenly mixed. But it may be that naturalists should want to resist a general symmetry claim for properties of this sort.

natural. Unfortunately, that hope will only be somewhat fulfilled—we can get a rough idea of what many naturalists take naturalness to be but nothing like a full account. Even so it will be useful to have a rough idea since we will want however we implement naturalism to be consistent with it. I will then come back in Section 4 to examine how normative properties could be fully natural consistent with the possibility that they could be instantiated by non-natural beings perhaps even in otherwise fully non-natural worlds.

3. Motivating Naturalism: Making the World Safe for a Scientific View of Reality

One thing the natural properties might have in common with one another is that they are all the proper objects of some science or other. This idea is often suggested when either naturalists or non-naturalists gesture at the properties they mean when they speak of the natural properties. For example, Peter Railton describes naturalism of the sort he favors as holding that, "all bona fide fundamental entities, properties, relations, or facts are, or are reducible to or grounded in, entities, properties, relations or facts of the kind posited in the natural sciences." (Railton, 2017, 47) And Michael Smith characterizes non-naturalism in the following way: "Non-naturalists want to enrich our ontology with an extra property over and above those which earn their credentials in a natural or social science, neither constituted by nor analyzable in terms of such properties." (Smith, 1994, 25) Russ Shafer-Landau, no naturalist himself, says that "Naturalism, understood as a metaphysical thesis about the nature of properties, claims that all the real properties are those that would figure ineliminably in the perfected version of the natural and social sciences," (2003, 59) though he thinks that this idea does not involve thinking of the natural properties as having something in common.

Letting the sciences tell us which properties are natural fits well with one of the primary motivations for philosophical naturalism—the thought that we live in a world governed by scientific laws and discoverable through the methods of empirical science (McPherson, 2015, 130). On this way of thinking there is no magic and there are no gods and ghosts. This general motivation has both metaphysical and epistemological aspects. On the metaphysical side, a basically naturalistic picture of our world and the concrete particulars in it does a pretty good job of explaining the world we experience. There was a time when it seemed to people that gods and ghosts were needed to explain various phenomena. That time is over. The various things for which we might once have thought we needed supernatural explanations have for the most part been explained by various forms of scientific theorizing. There is reason to think that similar explanations will be forthcoming for other phenomena of this sort or at least that in principle such explanations exist whether we find them or not. Given this way of looking at things we want to find a place for normative and moral phenomena in a perfectly natural world.[8]

Epistemology comes in here as well. Non-naturalists believe that the world contains extra properties over and above those postulated by naturalists and that these extra properties exist alongside the natural properties. It is thus a fair question to ask how we come to know about them, given that naturalists and non-naturalists alike think we do know about the distribution of moral properties. A flat-footed perceptual model seems unpromising since perception is a causal process and already fully explained by the natural properties that undergird our perceptual abilities (Smith, 1994, 21–25; but see McGrath, 2004 for a more sophisticated story). And insofar as the world of our experience is fully explained by the natural sciences, no inference to the best explanation of the events in our world will seem to require supplementation with extra non-natural posits. Non-naturalists have things to say in response to these worries but it is fair to note they have work to do that naturalists can seemingly avoid.

These are perfectly respectable motivations for those of us who don't think the actual world is in any way supernatural. If you can explain everything you need to explain without having to posit anything actual over and above the natural and if you can avoid making your epistemology more difficult by adding to the things you have to be in a position to know about, that is something to aim for.

There is a further epistemic payoff that motivates many naturalists—a general aversion to the synthetic a priori. If the natural properties are all the proper object of some natural science and the methodologies of the natural sciences are all empirical, bringing the normative into the naturalistic fold will allow us to argue that moral knowledge requires no special a priori ability to find out the nature of the normative truths. Since it looks like many moral claims are substantive truths, and since many of us find substantive or synthetic a priori knowledge mysterious, we might be able to avoid the mystery if moral truths just turn out to be ordinary empirical truths.[9]

I can see the attraction of this motivation even while I doubt it works out this neatly. One worry I have is just that we can only do without substantive a priori knowledge in a domain if it is *completely* empirical in its method for reaching substantive conclusions. Even in the sciences it looks as though substantive assumptions are sometimes used to decide between equally empirically adequate hypotheses. I'm pretty sure that phenomenalism and constructive empiricism are empirically adequate but I buy the explanations of our experience offered up by physics rather than these more austere theories. Furthermore, too much of our actual moral thinking seems underdetermined by empirical evidence. So even if the subject matter is natural, and even if we could find out

---

[8] It is worth noting that being the proper object of a science might not be the most fundamental thing natural properties have in common but rather something to be explained by some more fundamental similarity.

[9] David Copp's forthcoming *Ethical Naturalism: The Challenge to Explain Normativity* is motivated by such empiricist goals.

the relevant truths via purely empirical methods, we don't seem actually to be using such methods when we draw moral and normative conclusions.

In any case, these motivations for naturalism leave us in roughly the same place—the natural properties are all apt for investigation by some natural science or other. This doesn't look very much like the sort of elite similarity we were looking for as a way of saying what the natural properties all have in common. But perhaps it does give us this—the sought for similarity is something that explains why the natural properties are all knowable by empirical scientific investigation.

4. Can One be a Naturalist Consistent with the Supervenience of the Normative on Properties That Aren't Natural?

At one time it was a popular move for naturalists to note that the supervenience of the normative on the non-normative guaranteed that there was a (possibly highly disjunctive) property describable in non-moral terms that was coextensive with each normative property across all metaphysically possible worlds (Jackson and Pettit, 1995). Furthermore, it was sometime argued, the criteria of property identity are such that necessarily coextensive properties are identical (Jackson, 1998). On this basis, normative properties could be identified with the properties on which they supervene. One can worry about this coarse-grained way of identifying properties. And I'll pause later to consider whether just any disjunctive property can do the work needed here. However the more basic worry is that this argument doesn't get us all the way to an identity of the normative with the natural, since the supervenience claim only holds with respect to the non-normative. At least it doesn't get us all the way to naturalism if we are going to use "natural" not in Moore's way (including metaphysical properties) but rather in such a way as to exclude supernatural properties, as the motivation for naturalism that I think most proper would require. Perhaps there are metaphysical constraints that rule out gods and ghosts and magic even as possibilities. But supposing there are no such constraints, supernatural facts will be in the cross-world supervenience base of some normative properties. In counterfactual situations where ghosts exist, it will be wrong to treat them in certain ways; if gods were to exist we might be required to treat certain gods in particular ways; if magic were to exist it would be advisable to avoid certain sorts of magic, and so on. If there are worlds entirely composed of otherwise supernatural stuff there might be moral properties instantiated there in virtue of how the creatures in them treat one another. And this means that the disjunctive property guaranteed to be coextensive with any normative property will have supernatural disjuncts. Hence we can't rely on the principle that properties constructed from disjuncts of natural properties are themselves natural in order to identify the normative with the natural (van Roojen, 1996, Jackson & Pettit 1996, McPherson 2015).

This really shouldn't be a problem for the naturalist who is moved by the thought that our world is contingently a natural place. There are several strategies, each of which allow such naturalists to admit the presence of normative properties in otherwise supernatural worlds and it might be worth taking a quick tour of the options. Let's start with of *reductive*[10] naturalists about normativity. As I see it they have two different strategies available to them consistent with thinking normative properties identical with natural properties, even those natural properties specifiable in non-normative terms.

Reductive naturalists could adopt what we might call "relational normative naturalism". Such naturalists identify normative properties with relations between actual natural agents and the objects that can possess the relevant property. These will include various possibilia, be they possible actions, possible characters, possible worlds, or possible states of affairs. (Similar to Schroeder, 2008, Hume (Enquiry), or less obviously Smith, 1994.) Such views have the virtue of placing few limits on what can stand in the relevant relation while being able to characterize the relation itself entirely naturalistically. So, for example, if the relational property is being approved of by a certain sort of naturally specifiable agent, there seems to be no limit to what could have that property so long as the agent can think of the relevant item that has the normative property. This means that the possibility that there might be ghosts of good character is consistent with the complete naturalness of the property of having a good character. For an actual person might approve of a merely fictional or counterfactual ghost. Since the objects of the attitudes can be merely counterfactual and not actual, the view is totally compatible with the underlying naturalist thought that this world is perfectly natural. There is no need for such a view to think of the property of being of good character as involving anything supernatural even if its counterfactual extension could include the supernatural. Everything that makes up the property (the relation plus the actual natural relatum) is natural and its instances in this world are all natural as well. So it seems like it just is a natural property. Interestingly, this relational property does not seem quite to be of the same sort as properties such as equinumerosity which I mentioned earlier as be good candidates for genuine neutrality. The present relational property is natural because all of the property's components are perfectly natural. Thus if something in a seemingly purely supernatural world comes to stand in that relation to some actual natural thing and thus to instantiate the relational natural property it looks like the formerly supernatural world now contains an instance of a natural property and that world would therefore now be impure. This is in contrast with what we said about properties such as equinumerosity.

This brings up a further complication. Does the mere possibility of a supernatural world make our world impure in the same way? The fact that you are such that a

---

[10] Some theorists treat reduction as an identity relation (Smart, 1959; Feigle, 1967; Jackson, 2002); others as an asymmetric relation in the ballpark of composition (Schroeder, 2007). For present purposes I don't need to choose.

benevolent god would approve of you would seem by parity of reason to make this world also into a mixed world. And that would be bad for naturalism of the antisupernatural variety. Actualist naturalists will want to resist any symmetry. Probably an actualist naturalist should deny in general that properties consisting of relations to merely counterfactual entities change the status of a world as purely natural or purely supernatural when that world is considered as actual. But I'm not fully confident that this is right.

The other strategy for reductive naturalists to allow that moral properties could be instantiated in purely supernatural possibilities is to identify normative properties with some construction out of natural properties central to a natural science whose properties might themselves be multiply realizable. I'm thinking here of theorists like Neil Sinhababu in his non-eliminativist mode (2018, 48). Such a theorist can identify certain normative properties with happiness or health or constructions out of conjunctions or disjunctions of such properties. And they can define further normative properties out of these properties. If these properties, which are multiply realizable in the actual world, have enough flexibility to be realizable even in otherwise supernatural worlds by happy gods or ghosts, our world will remain perfectly natural for including normative properties so-reduced. What makes these properties natural is not the nature of their supervenience base but rather their role in the natural science of which they are a part. This suggests that naturalness must be determined by the nature of the property or kind itself and not by how it can or can't be realized. That might be all to the good but it puts more pressure on identifying what the natural properties (or natural sciences) have in common such that they are in the class of natural properties.

This brings us to non-reductive naturalists about normativity. Their views are incredibly similar to old-fashioned non-naturalism. Non-naturalists can agree with naturalists that the actual world is devoid of supernatural entities, properties and relations.[11] The class of non-naturalist theories will include relational variants akin to the relational reductive naturalism discussed above but now deploying normative terms in the specification of the relational property in question. Since some non-naturalist theories will be relational in similar ways, this will constitute another parallel between non-reductive naturalism and non-naturalism. Furthermore the best versions of both non-naturalism and nonreductive rationalism share a levels model on which a new level with its own regularities, objects, and modes of explanation emerges from a lower level, the entities of which constitute the higher level. On both views, the higher level entities, facts and regularities are grounded in the lower level. And neither view can rely on an identity claim to explain why the normative supervenes on the non-normative.[12] For both views are committed to the distinctness of the emergent property from the lower level

---

[11] Except perhaps tricky philosopher's constructions such as the property of being blue or loved by God.

[12] Leary (2017, 81) suggests that naturalists are better off in this regard because normative properties just are natural properties. It is important to keep in mind that those of us who think there is a metaphysically necessary supervenience claim it is about the relationship between normative properties and the rest whereas identity is about the relation of normative properties to itself.

on which it supervenes. The difference between them is just that naturalists insist that emergent higher order normative properties are perfectly natural, whereas the non-naturalists deny just this.

Tristram McPherson (2012, §5 & §6) has forcefully argued that this puts the naturalist at an advantage. Necessary connections between distinct things are in need of explanations and these will be harder to generate when the distinct things are also of distinct and discontinuous kinds. I think this is correct. But it now seems to me that this is a problem for every realist about moral properties given the most plausible version of the supervenience thesis—that the moral supervenes on everything else. This means that if there are (or can be) properties other than the natural properties, these too will be among the properties that generate the instantiation of normative properties, at least in some circumstances.[13] If the real similarity that defines the natural excludes, for instance, the supernatural and we think that supernatural properties could make a moral difference if there were any instances of them, naturalists as well as non-naturalists will need to postulate necessitation relations across discontinuous kinds. I suppose it could still be true that natural and supernatural properties are more similar to one another than either will be to the normative as non-naturalists conceive of it. In that case naturalists will have less trouble from discontinuity than non-naturalists. But this will depend on what the difference between the normative and the nonnormative is supposed to be and how much more discontinuity there is supposed to be between those two classes of property compared to the discontinuity between the natural and the supernatural. Relatedly, if supernatural properties were metaphysically impossible the naturalist would retain the alleged advantage over non-naturalism.

One last point before I return to searching for a substantial characterization of the alleged difference between the natural and the normative. The similarities between nonreductive naturalism and non-naturalism seem to me to make each view compatible with the main motivation for naturalism—the conviction that the actual world is natural. It contains no gods or ghosts or contingent spooky stuff that is not apt for investigation by some science on a broad conception of science.[14] Nor is it obvious that either view better realizes the epistemic goal of eliminating reliance on a priori knowledge than the other. For each view, insofar as it accepts a levels conception of the properties and relations instantiated in our world and treats these as irreducible to the levels below, is going to have to let the epistemology of a level be relatively autonomous of the levels below. To be sure, each level will be constrained by the underlying physics. But since the entities, properties and relations of the next level are not wholly definable

---

[13] Something that does no work in realizing the supervenient property can harmlessly be included in the supervenience base of that property. But we cannot rule out that further properties beyond the natural——such as supernatural properties if there are any——could be morally relevant.

[14] I realize that some naturalists want to get rid of more than others, so that *abstracta* and math don't find a home in the world as conceived of by some naturalists. But naturalism need not involve such nominalism, and the motivations for ordinary naturalism that I endorse (the actual world does not include gods and ghosts) don't seem to me to extend to abstractions and math.

in terms of what is going on at the level below, knowledge of these will require us to accept substantive conclusions about how the higher level properties can be realized by the level below.

5. Motivating Non-naturalism: The "Just Too Different" Intuition

If there is to be an important difference either between the normative and the natural or between the normative and the rest perhaps we can find it in what non-naturalists have to say about it. Non-naturalists famously insist that moral and normative properties are "just too different" from other natural properties to be natural themselves (Enoch 2011, 4, Chapter 5). If we knew more about *how* they are too different perhaps we could make some progress.

It is sometimes a bit hard to know what to make of this thought or to know exactly what non-naturalists mean when they say that moral and normative properties are "just too different" from the natural properties to be natural properties themselves. It is part and parcel of the levels picture that both nonreductive naturalists and non-naturalists accept that each level has some features to distinguish it from the rest. Biology is not physics partly because the kinds of explanations it offers and the properties and relations it postulates in the course of offering these explanations are not of the same sort as those offered by fundamental physics. Such differences are insufficient to place any of the special sciences beyond the realm of the natural. Even though biological properties are distinct from physical properties because of features they share only with other biological properties, and geometric properties are distinct from economic properties, these differences are not sufficient to exclude any of these properties from the realm of the natural. That our target properties are different insofar as they are all normative doesn't differ in form from the claim that the biological properties differ from the (rest of the) biological properties in being biological.

David Enoch—the most eloquent advocate of the "just too different" argument—treats the claim as an intuition to be explained or explained away (2011, 97). This strikes me as too quick, since the claim is a conclusion—that the intuitive differences between normative properties and properties that are natural are so great that they can't be natural. It would be better, I think, to start from the suspicion that normative properties are very different from the properties we are confident are natural. Non-naturalists should then try to get as clear as they can on the nature of the relevant difference. Only once we have a clear idea of what the difference is can we figure out whether this difference makes them too different from the other natural properties to fall within the same similarity class. Enoch says a little more about the kind of difference—he suggests that it is the normativity of normative properties that distinguishes them from the rest (2011, 80 and 100). But it would be helpful to know what that normativity consisted in in some more detail. What feature of the normative realm is potentially such as to exclude it from the natural?

Here's a hypothesis. Ethics and normativity generally seem autonomous in some significant way from the rest of what we know. It seems that, whenever we have reached an end to our empirical reasoning it is still a further step to any moral or normative conclusion we would wish to draw from these empirical judgments. Enoch (2011, 80) notes that non-normative answers don't answer the question he is asking when he deliberates. Only a normative answer will do.

This leads naturally to a new question—Why does the answer need to be normative? When I used to be a non-naturalist I might have said something like the following: Normative properties have different functional roles than scientifically delimited natural properties and as such their criteria of application are going to be limited only by their practical role and they will thus not be answerable to the same constraints. That the properties in question have to be apt for guiding the actions of agents places different constraints on what it takes to be in the extension of a normative property than what it takes to be in the extension of a non-normative property. This leads to different criteria for cutting reality at its normative joints than the usual causal explanatory criteria deployed by the sciences.[15]

Relatedly, natural science often seems to aim for causal explanations. Many non-naturalists think that normative properties are not causally efficacious (Shafer-Landau 2003, 98 ff.; Enoch 2011, 159).[16] Worries about the autonomy of ethics might partially explain why. If one thought that cutting nature at its natural joints requires dividing things up so that the elite properties—the genuine universals—track and unify causality, one might then reject any ethical distinction that cut across these metaphysical joints. Accepting that normative properties have causal powers might then render

---

[15] I'm not sure whether this concern animates the thoughts of contemporary non-naturalists. It fits decently with Scanlon's (2014) insistence that so long as a moral view does not contradict something we know about another domain, whether or not a view is correct depends on standards and practices internal to the discipline. But Scanlon's non-naturalism doesn't seem best captured by any claim about the nature of moral properties other than nonidentity with ordinary scientific properties proper to other disciplines. On the other hand, Parfit's (2011) motivations seem to fit with the "just too different" slogan, even while his views are expressed in ways that sound antimetaphysical. Shafer-Landau's (2003, 111) strongly denies that we individuate moral properties by their causal properties on the basis of considerations similar to those I suggest in the main text. And many of FitzPatrick's (2014) objections to naturalism turn on the extensional adequacy of various naturalist accounts, along with arguments to the effect that we have more reason to hang onto our moral convictions than we do to accept naturalism. Those concerns fit better with worries about the autonomy of ethics, though FitzPatrick's (2014) argument also raise issues about categorical normative authority.

[16] Though some have hedged their bets here (Shafer-Landau 2007). It is worth noting that the arguments on this issue are at least somewhat confusing. That goodness is a universal "in platonic heaven" (Enoch 2011, 219) is neither here nor there. If that's where universals reside, so does solidity, and no one worries about solids having causal powers. Furthermore, as Shafer-Landau notes, even if one thinks that causation is not emergent, we normally credit the causal powers of the things that constitute emergent entities to the entities so-constituted. So even if bulldozers do no more causal work than the matter that constitutes them, we don't worry about whether our bulldozer can move earth.

them subject to constraints irrelevant from the normative point of view. If investigation of some putative fundamental normative property suggests that it has boundaries that don't line up with our judgements about what we have most reason to do or what we owe to other people, we might find our independently arrived at moral judgements threatened by naturalism.

As I said, I used to be bothered by this kind of thing when I thought I was a non-naturalist, but I think I was mistaken to worry. It is part and parcel of the kind of levels picture postulated by nonreductive naturalists like Sturgeon that each level corresponding to a discipline has a certain amount of autonomy vis-à-vis the rest. Competent ethical investigation may determine that some distinction is needed to capture what is practically relevant. And this could be true even though that division does not line up with a simple division as characterized in physical, biological or chemical terms. Still, that will be no reason to relinquish its normative legitimacy given that the normative constitutes its own subject matter. We will want some story about how properties at these levels constitute the ethical properties delineated as the practical purposes of normative and moral enquiry require. But that will be a story about how the lower-level properties can realize the roles needed by the higher-level discipline. If our need for normative thought and normative guidance generates a need for a certain way of cutting up the world, there won't be anything with which the other sciences can constrain the upshot of investigation.

This line of thought also seems to be an adequate response to worries about the categorical authority of normative properties (FitzPatrick 2014, 575–576). If the distinctive emergent commitments of normative thinking that lead us to think that the normative constitutes a natural level over and above the levels of the other special sciences include reason to believe there are categorical demands, so be it. The fact that we think the relevant demands natural won't in any way constrain us from including categorical demands in our conception of the normative domain. The nonreductive naturalist just does not think that the natural excludes the normative conceived of as a relatively autonomous domain of inquiry. There will of course be some constraints—moral theory can't build in assumptions that violate the laws of the other special sciences. But its autonomy makes it unlikely to do so. The hostages it gives to empirical fortune are just those needed to allow that instances of the normative properties can be constituted out of the physical, chemical, biological, and other properties that the natural sciences tell us are the basic constituents of the world as we know it.

In a way this is unfortunate, since we were looking for a basic difference between natural properties and normative properties sufficient to explain and understand the "just too different" refrain of some non-naturalists. The nonreductive naturalist way of conceiving of the relationship between the special sciences including ethics sounds very much like Scanlon's (2014) story about how ethics relates to other domains—so long as it does not contradict the claims of one of the other scientific domains, the adequacy of a moral or normative claim will have to be assessed from within the normative. And Scanlon mostly eschews metaphysics even if you might think his non-naturalism does entail something about the properties in question. Still we may have gleaned a little bit from the excursion into non-naturalism. Non-naturalists think that the contours of moral theorizing are constrained by different explanatory demands than other, putatively natural, properties. And they think that those demands are dissimilar enough from those of the other sciences to render them of another kind.

6. Grounding Normativity?

But if that's the point, I am entirely puzzled by the recent direction of non-naturalist theorists, when they characterize the commitments of non-naturalism in terms of grounding. It has long been a vexing question for non-naturalists how they should explain the (formerly uncontroversial) supervenience of the normative on the non-normative given that they don't want to identify the normative with the natural. Until recently it was largely taken for granted that normative properties supervene on other properties as a matter of metaphysical necessity. And this claim in turn entails that there is a true principle giving non-normative conditions for being in the extension of any given normative property and that this principle holds of metaphysical necessity. The argument was over how to explain this (Blackburn 1971, Dreier 1992, McPherson 2012, 2015, Elliott 2014). That's no longer so. For it has come to be widely agreed that only naturalism is compatible with metaphysically necessary supervenience of the normative on the non-normative. I can't see why that is. I would have thought that as long as the non-naturalist had some explanation of metaphysical supervenience she was on safe ground. But that no longer seems to be the dominant view.

Perhaps surprisingly, it is the non-naturalists themselves who have saddled the view with denying metaphysically necessary supervenience (Rosen 2020, Fine 2002, Bader 2017). These innovators dispense with the metaphysical necessity of the supervenience claim and replace it with a weaker notion of moral supervenience where this is defined in such a way that it is more restrictive than metaphysical necessity. Their views combine two thoughts. (1) That supervenience on the non-normative determined by the essential natures of the normative properties would tie them too closely to those properties to be themselves non-natural. And (2) metaphysical necessity is grounded in the essences of the things involved. Other somewhat sympathetic non-naturalists, following Leary (2017), try to hang on to the idea that supervenience of the normative on the non-normative is metaphysically necessary,[17] but go on to offer what they take to be an adequate explanation of supervenience that posits intervening entities whose essences do the explanatory work. In this way they avoid having the essences of the normative specify the extension in naturalistic terms.

---

[17] I take it that is what they mean given the prior discussion, though they sometimes phrase their acceptance in terms of the normative on the descriptive (Leary 2017, 91).

Between the two camps there is disagreement over whether the relevant explanatory work is to be done by laws or essences. Leary, who favors essences, registers this complaint against those who let metaphysically necessary moral laws do the relevant explanatory work:

> ... [I]t is unclear whether this metaphysical picture provides a genuinely non-naturalist view of the normative. This is because the view implies that normative properties metaphysically relate to paradigmatic scientific properties in exactly the same way as certain derivative natural properties do. . . . according to the Wilschian metaphysics that Lawfully Grounded Non-naturalism relies upon, what explains why the fact that Ellie's being a mammal grounds that Ellie is a mammal or a truck is the fact that it is a metaphysical law that if x is F, then x is F or G, for any G.
>
> According to Lawfully Grounded Non-naturalism, then, the normative facts relate to paradigmatic scientific facts in exactly the same way that mammal-or-truck facts do: both the particular contingent normative facts and the particular contingent mammal-or-truck facts are numerically distinct from, but fully grounded in, paradigmatic scientific facts, and facts about which scientific facts ground which normative or mammal-or-truck facts are grounded in the metaphysical laws. But then it's not clear why normative properties are nonetheless significantly different in kind from paradigmatic scientific properties and why countenancing them is incompatible with a scientific worldview. (Leary, 2017, 91–2)

What is striking to me is that this objection locates the difference between naturalists and non-naturalists in the relationship between the supervening normative facts (or properties) and the base facts (or properties).[18] That might be one place you could find a difference but it is surely not the only place. If, as the target view suggests, there are metaphysically necessary laws connecting the normative with the rest, just as there might be such laws connecting biology and physical systems which compose biological kinds, the thing that makes them uniquely non-natural might be found elsewhere. Also, it is worth noting just how slight this difference might be. So far as I know, those non-naturalists who think that supervenience isn't metaphysically necessary want to say that it is metaphysically possible that the important substantive truths about morality aren't metaphysically necessary. Grave injustices here will remain grave injustices in all metaphysically possible worlds. So that leaves just the unimportant (or to be fair

---

[18] It is worth noting that Leary has defined non-naturalism as incompatible with a scientific worldview, something that strikes me as too strong for reasons I've already explained.

We might take note of a point already made here as well——to the extent that there is an a priori knowable metaphysically necessary supervenience constraint, it is about supervenience on the non-normative and not necessarily on the natural. So it isn't even obvious that the relation here is genuinely the same as the relationship of natural properties constructed out of other natural properties. Not every concatenation of non-normative properties is obviously natural or even compatible with a scientific worldview.

Lest it seem I'm picking on Leary, I think she's written an interesting and important paper, and one that reflects some common assumptions that I'm trying to highlight.

less important) stuff about morality metaphysically up for grabs in distant worlds. How could anything fundamental turn on this?

Leary goes on to specify her favored strategy for formulating non-naturalism in essentialist terms and as part of doing that specifies a sufficient condition for a property to be non-natural.

> For any property F:
> (i) If the essence of F cannot be specified entirely in non-normative terms and does not specify non-normative sufficient conditions for its instantiation, then F is a (sui generis) non-natural normative property.
> (ii) If the essence of F involves a non-natural normative property N, then F is a non-natural normative property. (Leary, 2017, 97–8)

If this is the right way to define non-naturalism, there may no longer be any room for non-reductive naturalism. Principle (i) consists of two conditions. Non reductive naturalists accept the first since they think normative kinds are irreducible kinds and hence not to be captured without using normative terms. The second sufficient condition—that the essence not specify sufficient natural conditions for being in the extension of a moral predicate—is not obviously incompatible with naturalism. For all such non-reductive naturalists have said there can be intervening links of the sort Leary herself postulates between the essences of some normative properties and their extensions. Perhaps more importantly, an antireductionist about some normative property might be antireductionist precisely because they thought that the property constitutes a real similarity that one could not capture just by listing its extension in some disjunctive way. So the essence of a normative property N (picked out by a term "N")—which captures the real nature of the property in question—would be the essence of the only feature that all the things that are N have in common such that they are in the extension of N. The only way to genuinely explain why the extension of N is what it is would presumably then have to cite this feature. A non-reductive naturalist who thinks that should also, therefore, endorse the second condition in (i). Here it looks like the most plausible versions of non-reductive naturalism have been stipulated out of existence and this makes me worry that, some of the parties to the disagreement are just talking past one another. I hope not.

While I think Leary is wrong to think that law-based explanations are incompatible with non-naturalism, I don't think that law-based explanations are *better* suited for non-naturalist explanations of supervenience than essence-based explanations. One could, it seems, translate law-based explanations into essence talk and vice versa. For any explanation of the metaphysically necessary features of a property that deploys an essence it seems you could create a parallel account of the using laws rather than essences. The relevant laws would be those that determined the nature of the things that exist with those essential features and those laws would obtain in all the metaphysically possible worlds. Wherever the standard essentialist metaphysician postulates an essence such a theory could postulate a law to do the work previously done by the essences. If, like Bader (2017), you think it plausible that laws explain the supervenience of the normative on the nonnormative, you would of course include laws ensuring such supervenience into the account. On this way of going, this supervenience would plausibly now count as metaphysically necessary (contrary to Bader's intention). But I don't see why that should be a big deal, nor do I see how we can adjudicate between theories on which the metaphysical necessities depend on laws and those on which the depend on essences.[19] And furthermore, I don't see why the metaphysical necessity of the supervenience claim should be more attractive if we keep our books one way than if we keep them the other way.[20]

Those like Bader, who think laws do essential work in securing the supervenience constraint, think that much turns on this difference so that non-naturalists must supplement essential truths and logic which are by themselves sufficient to secure the metaphysical necessities, with laws to get moral necessities such as the supervenience of the moral on the nonmoral. Suppose that as it turns out, the only things that determine what it takes to be a particular kind of thing are metaphysical laws, each governing a particular kind of thing. I have no idea how we would ever be in a position to find that out, but suppose it were true. Would that mean there were no metaphysical necessities? I don't think so. It would be more reasonable to conclude that such laws determined the metaphysical necessities. This makes it hard for me to see how anything about the debate between naturalists and non-naturalists could turn on such an issue.

Still my point is not merely negative. It seems like an essentialist non-naturalist could think there was more work for an essence to do than just to determine the extension of the property of which it is an essence. If that work involved some normative aspect of the properties in question beyond their extension, any reason to think that natural properties could not play normative roles would also be reason to accept non-naturalism. Of course any case that natural properties could not play such a role would still need to be made. I've spent a good bit of this chapter looking for reasons to decide one way or the other.

Still the abstract point remains and I will pursue it using Rosen's (2020) explication of non-naturalism as he conceives of it. That treatment shares many features with that of Fine (2002), who is responsible for the general framework of explaining metaphysical necessity using essences. As I understand the framework, the metaphysical necessities

---

[19] Wilsch (2015) in fact uses laws to explain metaphysical necessities, though I think his emphasis on the general nature of laws would prevent his version from making the relevant supervenience relation metaphysically necessary.

[20] I will confess to being confused by the importance of the distinction between essences and laws. When I was first introduced to metaphysical necessity I was told that metaphysical necessities are those ensured by the natures of the things involved plus logic and perhaps also some metaphysical principles that go beyond logic. Advocates of the present view, such as Bader, seem to think it important that laws rather than essential natures explain why the moral supervenes on the nonmoral and that this explains why the moral necessities go beyond the metaphysical necessities. If I thought that moral laws required supervenience I would be inclined to think that being governed by the relevant laws was of the essence of morality.

are specified by taking all the essential truths about things and then using logic to generate all the necessary truths which follow from them. Non-naturalism is then taken to require that this much is not sufficient to generate the complete extension of normative properties. The metaphysical necessities must be supplemented with a further necessary truths that are necessary in some weaker sense, call it moral or normative necessity. It is necessary only in this weaker sense that the moral facts supervene on the non-moral facts. Thus it must be metaphysically possible for there to be acts just like those that are wrong in the actual world, which are not in fact wrong. Those would be distant possibilities but not impossibilities. Otherwise (on the Rosen/Fine view) naturalism would be true since fully grounding the normative facts in the natural facts is sufficient for naturalism.

Again, there is a worry about the possibility of supernatural things mucking this up, but put that aside. I'll come back to it later. And there is also a worry about moral epistemology—how do we know the alternative extensions are only distant possibilities?[21] Put that aside as well. Why can't a moral realist who may or may not be a naturalist just think that it is the nature of morality that at least the basic moral/non-moral connections are simply built into the nature of moral properties.[22] Rosen thinks not. He writes:

> To a good first approximation, ethical naturalism is the thesis that every normative item (property, relation, etc.) admits of real definition in wholly non-normative terms. I emphasize *real* definition to make the familiar point that naturalism is not, in the first instance, a thesis about moral language or moral thought. Present-day naturalists mostly concede the Hume/Moore point that no non-normative predicate can have the same linguistic meaning or cognitive significance as a normative predicate, while maintaining that every moral predicate "picks out a natural property" But a natural property is a property that can be defined in wholly non-normative terms. . . .
>
> . . . The nonnaturalist's distinctive claim is that even if there are true propositions that specify naturalistic necessary and sufficient conditions for each moral feature —as there must be, given supervenience, if we allow infinitary conditions—these principles do not tell us what it is for an action to be, say, right. They are rather metaphysically synthetic moral laws that connect a normative feature, moral rightness, with utterly distinct nonnormative features, the so-called "right-making" features. The naturalist' distinctive claim must therefore be that not only do such principles exist: they tell us *what it is* for an action to be right. (Rosen 2020, 211–12)[23]

---

[21] Rosen (2020) has quite a bit to say about this at the end of the paper.

[22] There will still be plenty of room for contingency if it is in the nature of morality that kind acts are, other things equal, to be done. For what kindness consists in is very circumstance dependent. In one relationship it might find expression in kind words, in another it might be expressed with gruff teasing.

[23] I'm not completely sure I understand metaphysical syntheticity. I read Rosen here as attributing to non-naturalists the view that the basic principles which explain why particular configurations of non-normative stuff generate particular facts about the distribution of normative properties are not telling us anything about the essential nature of these normative properties.

I'm very sympathetic to the idea that naturalism can be captured by talking about real definitions. But I doubt that every biconditional of the form he suggests would be such as to tell us *the whole* essence of normative properties. Essences of properties can do work other than to specify an extension for the property. Let me use a toy moral theory to illustrate my point. Suppose actions are right when they generate as much chocolate as any other action that could have been chosen. And now suppose when asked why such actions are right, our theorist says it is in the nature of rightness that this is so. Does this mean that we understand the whole nature of rightness? I am in a position to judge which actions are in the extension of rightness and which aren't across a wide range of counterfactual scenarios. But suppose I don't have any sense of the connections we normally think rightness has with action. I see no connection with an action being right and any reason to do it. Do I know what it is to be right? My tentative reaction is that I know *part* of what it is to be right—it is to be chocolate maximizing. But that isn't the whole essence of rightness. To be right is also to be the sort of thing we should choose. Rightness has a practical upshot. It seems we don't know the whole essence of rightness if we don't know that. And knowing the extension of rightness even across all possibilities won't tell us that unless we already see some connection between maximizing chocolate and choice.

Rosen's paper has a lot of further complication to handle cases where the natures of yet further normative properties (such as being favored by reasons or being what we should do) are part of the explanations of the connections between a given normative property and its natural ground. Those complications might be relevant here. The issue is related to similar issues for network analyses of normative terms—as in Jackson and Pettit's (1995) moral functionalism—where a number of normative terms are interdefined. Some of what seems central to our normative concepts (as Jackson and Pettit conceive of them) relate normative kinds to each other. And it is only via these interconnections that some normative concepts get their connections to non-normative stuff. Jackson and Pettit's general strategy is to construct a Ramsey sentence which treats all the normative terms as variables and to hope that this sufficiently restricts the candidates for filling the roles that there is a unique natural realizer for each. Rosen's added complication is similar insofar as it allows that we might need to know about the essences of related normative properties or kinds to understand the essence of a property or kind of interest. If it were to turn out that the normative essences as a bunch explained why the natural facts determined the all of the normative facts, we'd still have naturalism.

But the worry remains. If part of the essence of one normative property is something about how it relates to another normative property, something about that essence might well be unreducedly normative, even if each of the properties can be uniquely picked out as coextensive with some nonnormative property. The normative-normative connection might be essential to either or both of them even when it might be also essential to each that they were necessitated by certain non-normative properties. Furthermore, if the functional role of these properties is to guide action, and if this is part of their essence, knowing the extension in whatever detail you like won't be sufficient for knowing the essential nature of these properties.

Here's an analogy that might help. I've made clear that I think the most attractive non-naturalist picture seems to me to be a levels picture, akin to one way of thinking about the relations between properties and entities postulated by various special sciences, for example the relationship between biology and physics. One point of thinking in terms of levels is that there are regularities or patterns at the upper level that are (1) explanatorily important and (2) more general than anything you could state using just physical vocabulary. Perhaps that would be because they involve certain roles which, given our universe, are physically realized but which might also be realized differently in some alternative possible universe with a different physics, or even be realized by some kinds of nonphysical things. And you might just think, for example, that it is essential to the biological kinds postulated by biological theory that they are governed by the principles which relate them to other biological kinds, perhaps because they are functional kinds. This might be true even while there are true principles explaining why biological properties and kinds are grounded in physical stuff in our world and in all physically possible worlds.[24] Here is one way that this might go. Suppose the higher level biological properties are role properties, and the roles are such as to include certain necessary connections to other such role properties. So what it is to have one of these properties will include a certain connection to the other property or properties. At the same time, it is in the nature of each of the natural properties or objects that ground instantiations of the role that items with that property are capable of playing that role in suitable conditions. Telling just the physical necessitation story would not then be enough to fully unpack the essence of these biological kinds. It wouldn't unpack the most important feature of these biological essences.

No one is going to want to argue that biological kinds are not natural. But we can use the analogy to see an important point. A biological non-reductionist might think that biological properties are different enough from physical properties to constitute a distinct kind because they do not share the real similarity that the physical properties share with one another. They might still agree that the biological supervenes on and in the actual world is constituted by physical stuff. The disagreement just is not about the extension of the determination relation. It is about the nature of the properties as relatively elite kinds. On a levels picture, normative properties stand in the same sort of relation to the set of natural properties that the biological stands to the physical. Non-naturalists who think the set of normative properties is "just too different" from the plainly natural properties to be of the same higher order kind will likely think that the distinguishing difference is an emergent property at the higher level. But you can't capture that disagreement by talking about the supervenience base. Finding out that we can give naturalistic necessary and sufficient conditions for being in the extension of each normative property should not change your mind about whether there is a difference since the thought about the difference was not about the extension.

---

[24] And grounded in physical stuff in physically possible worlds and in some nonphysical alternative stuff in nonphysical but metaphysically possible worlds where they are instantiated, if there are any such worlds.

7. So Where Are We?

It has been a theme of this chapter that we should think of the difference between naturalists and non-naturalists as being about the nature of the real similarity, if any, between sets of properties which hopefully themselves capture real similarities. As McPherson suggests, this is to think of the issue in terms of elite as opposed to gruesome or Cambridge properties. Even if you think eliteness might be a matter of degree, and even if it is sometimes hard to figure out whether a property is elite or gerrymandered, part of the point of properties is to capture what instances have in common. If the relevant similarity tying some emergent level together is higher order and also emergent, there will be something missing from any characterization of the essences of the properties at this level if we just track their extensions. And here the possibility that non-actual but possible properties might affect the distribution of normative properties comes back in to tell us something. Those who think the naturalism/non-naturalism debate turns on whether supervenience is metaphysically necessary all seem committed to the thought that a property which supervenes as a matter of metaphysical necessity on natural properties must itself be natural. In other words, they must think that such a supervening property shares in the real similarity that unites the properties which characterize the circumstances that matter to the possible extension of the supervening property. But we seem to have a disjunctive supervenience base made up of both supernatural and natural properties. I see no reason to think that the real similarity shared by each disjunct of the property underlying the relevant normative property (some natural some supernatural) must turn out to be natural. Certainly that similarity can't simply inherit naturalness from the properties in the not completely natural Supervenience base.

More importantly, many people think they have some idea of the real similarity that normative properties share in common—that they all have a distinctively action and thought-guiding role to play. That similarity is not going to be well-captured by even the most fine-grained mapping of their modal extension. At least I don't see how you could get that information from such a mapping. Nor do I see how one would get it from the network of relations between the various properties at the higher level unless one already grasped the nature of one of the normative properties in the network. The thing many want to say is essential, is that one *should do* the honest or kind thing in these circumstances, and that not to do so would be *wrong*. But unless one already knew that wrongness was to be avoided, that the extensions of rightness and wrongness exclude one another, doesn't really tell us the crucial thing about what we should do.

Of course on a levels picture, every level will have its own unifying characterization of what makes for the level, and also what distinguishes that level from the rest. So to say that the normative is action-guiding and that one doesn't really understand the essence of normativity unless you grasp that doesn't immediately entail non-naturalism. We need to know whether this difference from phenomena at other levels is different enough that it is too different to allow the level to be thought of as natural. Both nonreductive naturalists and non-naturalists can agree on everything that leads up to this question while disagreeing on how it should be answered. I've tried to clarify what that remaining disagreement might be about, but I think I have come up short. Absent a better idea of what unifies the natural and what could distinguish normative properties from the rest I don't have a view on whether that difference is sufficient to exclude the normative from the natural.[25]

REFERENCES

Armstrong, David. M. 1978. *Nominalism and Realism: Vol. 1: Universals and Scientific Realism.* Cambridge: Cambridge University Press.

Bader, Ralph. 2017. "The Grounding Argument against Non-Reductive Moral Realism." In *Oxford Studies in Metaethics*, vol. 12, edited by Russ Shafer-Landau, 106–134. New York: Oxford University Press.

Blackburn, Simon. 1971. "Moral Realism." In *Morality and Moral Reasoning*, edited by John Casey, 101–124. London: Methuen.

Copp, David. Forthcoming. *Ethical Naturalism: The Challenge to Explain Normativity.* New York: Oxford University Press.

Dancy, Jonathan. 2006. "Nonnaturalism." In *The Oxford Handbook of Ethical Theory*, edited by David Copp, 91–121. Oxford: Oxford University Press.

Dreier, James. 1992. "The Supervenience Argument against Moral Realism." *Southern Journal of Philosophy* 30: 13–38.

Dunaway, Billy, and Tristram McPherson. 2016. "Reference Magnetism as a Solution to the Moral Twin Earth Problem." *Ergo: An Open Access Journal of Philosophy* 3(25): 639–679.

Elliot, Aaron. 2014. "Can Moral Principles Explain Supervenience?" *Res Philosophica, Special Issue: Moral Nonnaturalism* 91(4): 629–659.

Enoch, D. 2011. *Taking Morality Seriously: A Defense of Robust Realism.* Oxford: Oxford University Press.

Feigl, Herbert. 1967. *The "Mental" and the "Physical": The Essay and a Postscript.* Minneapolis: University of Minnesota Press.

Fine, Kit. 2002. "The Varieties of Necessity." In *Conceivability and Possibility*, edited by T. Gendler and J. Hawthorne, 253–281. Oxford: Oxford University Press.

FitzPatrick, W. 2014. "Skepticism about Naturalizing Normativity: In Defense of Ethical Nonnaturalism." *Res Philosophica* 91: 559–588.

Jackson, Frank. 1998. *From Metaphysics to Ethics: A Defense of Conceptual Analysis.* New York: Oxford University Press.

---

[25] Thanks to Trevor Adams, Paul Bloomfield, John Brunero, David Copp, Aaron Elliot, Bjorn Flanagan Guillermo Gonzalez, Janelle Gormley, Jennifer Haley, Frank Jackson, Robert Johnson, Eunhong Lee, Tristram McPherson, Joe Mendola, Justin Morton, Talhah Mustafa, Phillip Pettit, Gideon Rosen, Michael Smith, Mark Schroeder, Anand Varkey, Quinn White, Seungchul Yang, and Lyle Zynda for conversations (in person or virtual) on these topics. Special Thanks to Paul Bloomfield, David Copp, Jennifer Haley, and Tristram McPherson for reading drafts of this chapter and providing detailed comments.

Jackson, Frank. 2002. "From Reduction to Type-Identity." *Philosophy and Phenomenological Research* 65(3): 644–647.

Jackson, F., and Phillip Pettit. 1995. "Moral Functionalism and Moral Motivation." *Philosophical Quarterly* 45(178): 20–40.

Jackson, F., and Phillip Pettit. 1996. "Moral Functionalism, Supervenience and Reductionism." *Philosophical Quarterly* 46(182): 82–86.

Leary, Stephanie. 2017. "Non-Naturalism and Normative Necessities." In *Oxford Studies in Metaethics*, vol. 12, edited by Russ Shafer-Landau, 76–105. New York: Oxford University Press.

Lewis, David. 1983. "New Work for a Theory of Universals." *Australasian Journal of Philosophy* 61(4): 343–377.

McGrath, Sarah. 2004. "Moral Knowledge by Perception." *Philosophical Perspectives* 18(1): 209–228.

McPherson, T. 2012. "Ethical Non-Naturalism and the Metaphysics of Supervenience." In *Oxford Studies in Metaethics* vol. 7, edited by Russ Shafer-Landau, 205–234. Oxford: Oxford University Press.

McPherson, T. 2015. "What Is at Stake in Debates among Normative Realists?" *Noûs* 49(1): 123–146.

McPherson, T. 2018. "Naturalistic Moral Realism, Rationalism, and Non-Fundamental Epistemology," in *The Many Moral Rationalisms*, edited by Karen Jones and Francois Schroeter, 107–209. Oxford: Oxford University Press.

McPherson, Tristram, and David Plunkett. 2022. "Ground, Essence, and the Metaphysics of Metanormative Non-Naturalism." manuscript.

Moore, George E. 1903. *Principia Ethica*. Cambridge: Cambridge University Press.

Paakkunainen, Hille. 2018. "The 'Just Too Different' Objection to Normative Naturalism." *Philosophy Compass* 13(2): 1–13.

Parfit, Derek. 2011. *On What Matters*. Oxford: Oxford University Press.

Railton, Peter. 2017. "Naturalistic Realism in Metaethics." In *The Routledge Handbook of Metaethics*, edited by Tristram McPherson and David Plunkett, 151–169. New York: Routledge.

Rosen, Gideon. 2010. "Metaphysical Dependence: Grounding and Reduction." In *Modality: Metaphysics, Logic, and Epistemology*, edited by B. Hale and A. Hoffmann, 109–136. New York: Oxford University Press.

Rosen, Gideon. 2020. "What Is Normative Necessity?" In *Metaphysics, Meaning and Modality: Themes from Kit Fine*, edited by M. Dumitru, 205–233. Oxford: Oxford University Press.

Scanlon, T. M. 2014. *Being Realistic about Reasons*. Oxford: Oxford University Press.

Schroeder, Mark. 2007. *Slaves of the Passions*. Oxford: Oxford University Press.

Shafer-Landau, Russ. 2003. *Moral Realism: A Defense*. New York: Oxford University Press.

Shafer-Landau, Russ. 2007. "Moral and Theological Realism: The Explanatory Argument." *Journal of Moral Philosophy* 4(3): 311–329.

Sinhababu, Neil. 2018. "Ethical Reductionism." *Journal of Ethics and Social Philosophy* 13(1): 32–52.

Smart, J. 1959. "Sensations and Brain Processes." *Philosophical Review* 68: 141–156.

Smith, Michael. 1994. *The Moral Problem*. Oxford: Blackwell Publishers.

Sturgeon, N. 2006. "Ethical Naturalism." In *The Oxford Handbook of Ethical Theory*, edited by D. Copp, 91–121. Oxford: Oxford University Press.

Suikkanen, Jussi. 2010. "Non-Naturalism: The Jackson Challenge." In *Oxford Studies in Metaethics* 5, edited by Russ Shafer-Landau, 87–110. New York: Oxford University Press.

van Roojen, Mark. 1996. "Moral Functionalism and Moral Reductionism." *Philosophical Quarterly* 46(182): 77–81.

van Roojen, Mark. 2006. "Knowing Enough to Disagree: A New Response to the Moral Twin Earth Argument." In *Oxford Studies in Metaethics*, vol. 1, edited by Russ Shafer-Landau, 161–193. Oxford: Oxford University Press.

van Roojen, Mark. 2015. *Metaethics: A Contemporary Introduction*. New York: Routledge.

Wilsch, T. 2015. "The Nomological Account of Ground." *Philosophical Studies* 72(12): 293–312.

CHAPTER 7

ETHICAL NATURALISM, NON-NATURALISM, AND IN-BETWEEN

RALPH WEDGWOOD

The central questions of metaethics are not the questions that are characteristic of ethical thought and discourse itself; instead, they are questions *about* ethical thought and discourse. Specifically, the questions of metaethics include the following.

a. There are questions belonging to both metaethics and the philosophy of mind, about the nature of ethical thought—the questions of *moral psychology*.
b. There are questions belonging to both metaethics and the philosophy of language, about the meaning of ethical statements—the questions of *moral semantics*.
c. There are questions belonging to both metaethics and the theory of knowledge, about the nature of ethical knowledge and rational ethical belief—the questions of *moral epistemology*.

In addition to these three kinds of questions, many metaethicists hold that there is also (d) a *fourth* group of questions. These are the questions belonging both to metaethics and to *metaphysics*, concerning how ethical thought and talk fit into reality as a whole.

In Section 1 below, I will give a brief introductory survey of these metaphysical questions. As I shall explain, the contemporary debate on the metaphysical side of metaethics is dominated by two paradigms—as I shall call them, *reductive naturalism* and *primitivist non-naturalism*. As I shall argue, these are both extreme views. In principle, it should be possible for there to be a host of intermediate views between these two extremes.

Section 2 will explore some of the views that were taken on these metaphysical questions by philosophers of ancient and medieval times. As we shall see, most of these views differed from both the two paradigms that dominate the contemporary debate—that is, these views differed from both reductive naturalism and primitivist non-naturalism. However, as I shall also explain, the metaphysical views of these past philosophers cannot easily be endorsed today. This is because our conception of the natural world has changed from that of these premodern thinkers, because of the development of modern natural science.

Nonetheless, in Section 3, I shall try to explain how it is still possible to make sense of intermediate positions, lying between the two extremes of reductive naturalism and primitivist non-naturalism. Finally, in Section 4, I shall close by arguing that these intermediate positions are *prima facie* promising, and deserve careful consideration from contemporary metaethicists.

1. Moral Metaphysics

Metaphysics is the branch of philosophy that seeks to develop a general conception of the nature of reality. The most important problem for our purposes seems to arise in the following way. Our thoughts concern many different kinds of phenomena—covering fields as diverse as astronomy and legal theory, zoology and social history, pharmacology and musicology, to name just a few. This raises the question: How can thoughts of all these different kinds be ways of representing a single world? How do the features of the world that these different kinds of thoughts concern themselves with fit together to constitute a single intelligible reality?

In this chapter, I shall restrict my attention to questions that only arise once certain assumptions are in place. These assumptions are the following: first, for a statement to count as an ethical or moral statement, it must contain an expression—such as a predicate like " ... is good" or " ... is better than ..."—that, in the context of that statement, expresses a moral concept; secondly, each of these moral concepts has a straightforwardly truth-conditional semantics.[1] To fix ideas, I shall assume that any truth-conditional semantics for a concept that is expressed by a predicate implies that there is some *property* or *relation* that is determined by the nature of this concept as the *semantic value* of this concept—that is, as the contribution that this concept makes to the truth conditions of any proposition in which it appears. As we may put it, this property or relation is fixed by the nature of the concept as the property or relation that the concept *stands for*.

These properties and relations that are fixed by the nature of the moral concepts as the properties and relations that those concepts stand for may be called *moral properties and relations*. Thus, the assumptions that I am relying on imply that there are indeed, in this sense, moral properties and relations. For example, there are properties that can be picked out by terms like "goodness" and "rightness"; for every way in which one thing can be said to be "better than" another, there is a relation that holds between two

---

[1] For a discussion of these assumptions, see Chaps. 9 and 22 in this volume.

items x and y if and only if x is better than y in that way. To keep things simple, however, from now on I shall mostly stop referring to relations: I shall simply assume that "moral properties" include both moral properties and moral relations. Finally, I shall also assume that these ethical or moral properties and relations are instantiated or exemplified in the actual world: that is, some propositions of the form "x is good" or "x is right" are true in the actual world. In other words, I shall assume this minimal version of *moral realism*.

I shall not distinguish here between "ethical" and "moral" properties. In many contexts, these two terms can be used so that they differ in sense; but here I shall use them interchangeably. Indeed, I shall understand the class of moral properties as broadly as possible. The goal is to include *all* properties that are, in their metaphysical character, of the same fundamental kind. According to many views, this category of properties does not just include "moral" properties in a narrow sense of the term, but also includes all evaluative and normative properties and relations of any kind.

For example, consider the relation of *being a good reason for*, which holds between a fact and an agent's having an attitude, whenever the fact is a good reason for the agent to have the attitude. It seems that this relation holds, not only in cases that seem paradigmatically "moral" (as when your having made a promise is a good reason for you to intend to keep your promise), but also in cases that seem paradigmatically *epistemic* (as when your having certain evidence is a good reason for you to believe a certain conclusion). Admittedly, some philosophers might try to argue that the expression "is a good reason for" is used in different senses in these two contexts; but it seems preferable to avoid postulating hidden ambiguities if we can. If the term is used univocally in these two contexts, this makes it plausible that the relation that it stands for is a broadly normative or evaluative relation; and it seems that these normative or evaluative relations are, in their metaphysical character, of the same fundamental kind as the ethical or moral properties that we are concerned with here.[2] If that is right, then this relation is itself, in the broad sense that I intend here, an ethical or moral property.

If there are moral properties of this kind, then we face a version of the central metaphysical problem. Consider the properties that are correctly posited in the domains of thought that I listed above—in astronomy and legal theory, zoology and social history, pharmacology and musicology. How exactly do moral properties fit into a single intelligible reality that also includes these astrophysical, legal, zoological, social, pharmaceutical, and musical properties?

The contemporary debates on the metaphysical side of metaethics often invoke the notion of a *natural property*. With this notion in hand, we can ask about the metaphysical relations that hold between moral properties and natural properties. However, if we formulate these questions in terms of "natural properties," we need to ensure that we understand what exactly the phrase "natural property" means in this context.

---

[2] For an extended defense of the parallel between moral and epistemic properties, see Cuneo (2007, Chap. 2).

Some philosophers may be tempted to explain this distinction between the "natural" and the "non-natural" by giving a *list*: such things as stars and planets, plants and animals, are quintessentially "natural," while God is "supernatural," and abstract mathematical entities like numbers and the empty set are "non-natural."

On further reflection, however, it is not clear that a list of this sort can provide an adequate understanding of this distinction. Stars, planets, plants, and animals are all *particular objects*—and so too, at least on most views, are God, numbers, and the empty set. What we need here is a distinction between two kinds of *properties*—not between two kinds of particular objects. Of course, if these particulars exist, they have various distinctive or characteristic properties, including properties that are essential to them—such as biological properties, like the property of *being alive*, or mathematical properties, like the property of *being a set that has exactly one member*, or theological properties, like the property of *being omniscient*. However, it is not clear what exactly it would mean to label any of these properties as "non-natural." The property of *being a set that has exactly one member* is undeniably capable of playing an extensive role in explanations of phenomena involving animals, plants, and minerals, of the kind that are given by the natural sciences. (For example, biology might explain why a species died out at a particular point in time by appealing to the fact that the species reached a point where it had exactly one member.[3]) It is also unclear what it means to say that the property of *being omniscient* is non-natural, since it seems definable in terms of the paradigmatically psychological relation of *knowing*. If *knowing all truths* is a non-natural property, how could *knowing some truths* be a natural property?

Moreover, this list clearly cannot define a coherent distinction unless some substantive assumptions are presupposed. For example, the property of *being God* clearly could not be accepted as paradigmatic of the "non-natural" by anyone who accepted Spinoza's pantheistic view that the whole physical universe is a single divine being, aptly referred to by the term "*God-or-Nature*." But simply giving this list cannot by itself make it clear exactly what substantive assumptions are being presupposed here.

It is more promising, I believe, to start by inquiring into the relations between *ethics* and the *natural sciences*—above all, physics, chemistry, and biology. In particular, we can inquire into the following metaphysical question: What metaphysical relations hold between the properties that are centrally and characteristically discussed in ethics and those that are correctly posited by the natural sciences?[4] This question can be raised in terms of "natural properties" if we define natural properties as follows: a property is a natural property if and only if it is either (a) a *paradigmatic* natural property—that is,

---

[3] Even the property of *being a prime number* seems capable of playing an explanatory role in biology. The periodical cicadas have a developmental cycle of either thirteen or seventeen years— apparently because living underground for a prime number of years makes it easier for them to evade predators.

[4] As I understand it, this question does not presuppose an *epistemological* conception of the natural sciences: it presupposes an understanding of the natural sciences as defined by their *subject-matter* (not by the methods that can be used to investigate that subject-matter). Thus, on this understanding, there is no difficulty in supposing that some physical or biological facts may be wholly unknowable.

one of the properties that are correctly posited by the natural sciences, such as physics, chemistry, and biology, or (b) a property that is, in its metaphysical character, of the same fundamental kind as these paradigmatic natural properties.

This definition of "natural properties" involves the idea of a property that is, "in its metaphysical character, of the same fundamental kind as" the paradigmatic natural properties (that is, those that are correctly posited by the natural sciences). This idea can be clarified by invoking a proposal that is due to Tristram McPherson (2015). According to this proposal, we can make sense of objective similarity relations *between* properties. Some properties are more similar to each other, while others are more dissimilar. For example, *redness* and *orangeness* are more similar to each other than are redness and the property of *being unconstitutional in the United States*; *being a square number* and *being a cubic number* are more similar to each other than are being a square number and the property of *being a talented movie actor*; and so on.

Invoking this idea of real similarities between properties, we may reformulate our definition of "natural properties" as follows: the *natural properties* include (a) the paradigmatic natural properties that are correctly posited by the paradigmatic natural sciences (such as physics, chemistry, and biology), and (b) any other properties that are, in the most important respects, at least as similar to these paradigmatic natural properties as these paradigmatic properties are to each other.[5]

This definition of "natural properties" has two important corollaries. First, natural properties are defined in terms of their similarity to each other; but non-natural properties are *not* defined in terms of their similarity to each other—they are simply defined as properties that are not natural. Thus, this approach implies that, while all natural properties have a certain deep similarity to each other, non-natural properties may have virtually nothing in common, except for the fact that they are all non-natural. Secondly, in a way this approach allows us to make sense of the idea that among the non-natural properties, some may be "more non-natural" than others—in other words, non-naturalness is a matter of *degree*. Some non-natural properties may be more similar or more closely related to the natural properties than others.

The questions that concern us, then, focus on the "metaphysical relations" between moral properties and natural properties. What sort of "metaphysical relations" are in question here?

The simplest metaphysical relation of all is *identity*. What I shall call "full-blooded naturalism" is the view that moral properties simply *are* natural properties. If this full-blooded naturalism is combined with my definition of natural properties, it has the following implication. Take any moral property—for example, the property of moral goodness; and take two paradigmatically natural properties that are as dissimilar to each other as any two such properties are—for example, a property that is correctly posited by quantum mechanics (like the property of *being a charm quark*) and a property that

---

[5] Compare how McPherson (2015, 130) suggests defining a "basic natural property" as "a property that is a member of the narrowest real similarity class that is partially constituted by the real properties correctly postulated by paradigmatic natural sciences".

is correctly posited by evolutionary biology (like the property of *evolutionary fitness*). Then full-blooded naturalism entails that there is *no* natural property P such that the property of moral goodness is more dissimilar to P than these maximally dissimilar paradigmatically natural properties are to each other.[6] As I shall argue in the following section, this kind of full-blooded naturalism faces a serious problem.

A second crucial metaphysical relation is the relation of *being reducible to*. According to what I shall call *reductive ethical naturalism*, all moral properties are reducible to natural properties. What is it for a property to be "reducible" in this way? A property is reducible just in case there is a true reductive account of it. Some reductive accounts of some properties may be conceptual analyses or analytic truths, but there may also reductive accounts that are not conceptual or analytic truths.[7]

The crucial point is that any such a reductive account is in effect a "real definition" of the property.[8] For example, a real definition of what is *good* would give an account of *what it is* for something to be good. Such an account would take the form: "To be good is to be G"—where, at least if this is a nontrivial real definition, it articulates an *essential* or *constitutive* feature of what it is to be good. Admittedly, there may be true nontrivial statements of the form "To be F is to be G" that do not count as real definitions; there seems to be a true reading of the sentence "To be red is to not be green." A nontrivial statement of this form counts as a real definition only if it in some sense identifies *being F* with *being G*.[9] Moreover, not every true identity statement counts as a real definition. The identity statement "The property of being good = what was actually Plato's favorite property" might be true, but it is not a real definition of being good. Plausibly, it is not a real definition because it does not articulate an *essential* or *constitutive* truth about this property.

Crucially, however, not all real definitions are reductive. Reductions must be in a strong sense *noncircular*; real definitions, by contrast, do not have to be noncircular in this way. For example, consider the following proposed definition: "To be red = to be disposed to look red under normal conditions." This proposed definition is certainly nontrivial: it is clearly not a logical truth. However, it also appears to be circular: the

---

[6] One philosopher who seems aware of this implication of the view, and still takes the view seriously, is McPherson (2015, 131).

[7] For an example of a naturalistic reduction of moral properties that is presented as an analytic or semantic thesis, see Finlay (2014); for a naturalistic reduction that is presented as a synthetic nonconceptual thesis, see Schroeder (2007).

[8] I have argued elsewhere that reductive accounts must be real definitions, and that these real definitions are also what are sometimes called "constitutive accounts" of properties (see Wedgwood 2007, Chap. 6).

[9] The interpretation of these real definitions as "identifications" is developed in Dorr (2016); for a rival view, see Rosen (2015). One interesting account of these "identifications" is given by Elgin (2021), who argues that it is true that to be F is to be G just in case the states of affairs that *make it the case* that something is F are identical to the states of affairs that make it the case that it is G; according to Elgin, a proposition of the form "To be F is to be G" counts as a real definition just in case the complex predicate "G" reveals the mereological structure of the states of affairs that make an object F in a way that the predicate "F" does not.

term "red" appears, in the very same sense, on the right-hand side of this definition. Still, this might be a correct real definition of the property of being red, even if its circularity prevents it from being a genuine reduction.

What exactly does this kind of "circularity" amount to? If the real definition "To be F is to be G" counts as a *reduction*, then "G" must be a complex predicate such that all the simple predicates appearing inside this complex predicate "G" pick out properties that are *metaphysically more fundamental* than the property of being F that is being reduced. These properties would be "metaphysically more fundamental" in the sense that neither the property of being F nor any other property of essentially the same kind need be mentioned in any real definition of what it is for anything to have any of these "more fundamental" properties.[10] For example, suppose that the following is a correct real definition of the property of being admirable: "For x to be admirable = for it to be correct to admire x." This would fail to be a reductive account of what it is for something to be admirable if the property of *being correct* is not metaphysically more fundamental than the property of *being admirable*.

On the other hand, suppose that it is possible to give a wholly nonethical, nonevaluative, and non-normative account of what it is for you to have a *higher balance of pleasure over pain* in one world than in another. Then the following real definition, if true, would be reductive: "For a world w_1 to be better for you than a world w_2 = for you to have a higher balance of pleasure over pain in w_1 than in w_2." This hedonistic definition would succeed in giving an account of what it is for one world to be *better for you* than another in metaphysically more fundamental terms.

As this example makes clear, a correct reductive definition of this kind would be a powerful explanatory principle. This principle would make it possible in principle to give an explanation of every truth concerning the property that it reductively defines. For example, the hedonistic definition that I have just considered implies that, whenever one world is better for you than another, its being better for you can be explained by its being a world in which you have a higher balance of pleasure over pain, and whenever one world is not better for you than another, its not being better can be explained by its not being a world in which you have such a higher balance of pleasure over pain. If this is a genuine reductive account, then in each of these explanations, a fact about whether or not one world is better for you than another is explained by a fact that is metaphysically more fundamental—in the sense that this more fundamental fact can be explained in wholly nonethical, nonevaluative, and non-normative terms.

These, then, are two forms that ethical naturalism can take: full-blooded naturalism, which claims that moral properties are themselves natural properties; and reductive naturalism, which claims that moral properties are reducible to natural properties. With

---

[10] Strictly, we can allow that the right-hand side of this reductive definition may contain *complex* expressions that refer to the property that it reductively defines. However, the *simple* terms that these complex expressions are built up out of must *not* refer to this reduced property, and the real definitions of the properties that these simple terms refer to must also be able to avoid referring to this reduced property or to any other property of essentially the same kind.

the interpretation of "natural properties" that I have proposed here, this gives us two clear and interesting versions of naturalism for us to discuss.

There are admittedly other views that have been called "ethical naturalism" in recent philosophical literature. For example, Nicholas Sturgeon (1998, Section 1) explains "ethical naturalism" in the following way. First, he states that a "naturalistic worldview" is "one that takes the emerging scientific picture of the world as approximately accurate and that rejects belief in the supernatural." Then he gives the following definitions of ethical nihilism and ethical naturalism: "Ethical nihilists deny that real values can fit into such a picture. Cognitivist naturalists reply that they can, and that we can learn about them by methods similar to those by which we learn of other natural facts."

Unfortunately, however, it is doubtful whether Sturgeon's explanation of ethical naturalism gives us a position that is clear enough to warrant extensive discussion. This is because it is not clear what Sturgeon means by his asking whether real values "fit into" the "emerging scientific picture of the world". If the only facts that "fit into" this scientific picture are those that *logically follow* from this picture, then it seems doubtful whether "real values" can possibly "fit into" this picture. If all facts that are *logically consistent* with this picture "fit into" this picture, then real values clearly will "fit into" the picture—but so too would any domain of abstract mathematical entities, no matter how ontologically extravagant it may be. Thus, it seems that Sturgeon has in mind some condition that is *stronger* than being logically consistent with the scientific picture, but *weaker* than logically following from the scientific picture. But he never explains exactly what this condition is.[11] For this reason, it is perhaps not surprising that the most prominent versions of ethical naturalism in the contemporary metaethical debate are what I have called full-blooded naturalism and reductive naturalism.

The most prominent alternative to this kind of reductive ethical naturalism is known as *non-naturalism*. On this view, moral properties are not themselves natural properties, and cannot be reduced to natural properties. However, the best-known form of non-naturalism goes beyond simply denying the two forms of naturalism that I have identified above. Instead, it adds a number of additional claims as well:

a. They typically add that moral properties are just "*too different*" from natural properties for it to be even conceivable that reductive naturalism is true.[12]

---

[11] Another interesting conception of naturalism is David Copp's (2007, 39) proposal that "a property is natural if and only if any synthetic proposition about its instantiation that can be known could only be known empirically." My concern about this is that it makes ethical naturalism into an *epistemological* doctrine—effectively, a doctrine to the effect that no synthetic ethical proposition can be known a priori. But on the face of it, both this doctrine and its negation are compatible with a very wide range of different views about the metaphysical character of moral properties. Since our concern here is with the metaphysical side of metaethics, it is doubtful whether Copp's proposal is suitable for our purposes.

[12] For example, Derek Parfit (1997, 121) writes, in discussing reductive views on which normative facts are reducible to natural facts, that "These two kinds of fact are as different as . . . chairs and propositions . . . "; Michael Huemer (2005, 94) claims that "value properties are radically different from natural properties"; David Enoch (2011, 4) writes that "Normative facts are just too different from natural ones to be a subset thereof."

b. In particular, they often add that moral properties differ from natural properties in the following crucial respect: unlike natural properties, moral properties are *causally inefficacious*.
c. They typically also add that the most fundamental moral properties are not only irreducible to natural properties, but also have no nontrivial real definition of any kind.

According to this third claim (c), the most fundamental moral properties are utterly *primitive* and *unanalyzable*. As G. E. Moore (1903, 6) put it:

> If I am asked 'What is good?' my answer is that good is good, and that is the end of the matter. Or if I am asked 'How is good to be defined?' my answer is that it cannot be defined, and that is all I have to say about it.

In other words, even if some nonfundamental moral properties may be defined in terms of other more fundamental moral properties, there is no nontrivial real definition of the most fundamental moral properties. For this reason, we may characterize this view as "*primitivist*" non-naturalism." It is important to see that this kind of "primitivism" does not follow from the mere claim that moral properties are not reducible. According to primitivism, the fundamental moral properties are not just irreducible, but have no nontrivial real definition at all (not even a circular nonreductive definition).

These three claims—(a), (b), and (c)—seem to cohere tightly with each other. Arguably, if there were any essential connections between the fundamental moral properties and any nonmoral properties, these essential connections would be reflected in the real definition of each fundamental moral property, making the definition nontrivial. So, it seems that the primitivist non-naturalist who accepts (c) must also accept that there are no essential connections between the fundamental moral properties and any nonmoral properties. This makes it seem plausible that (a) is also true: the fundamental moral properties form a special class of properties, completely unlike and distinct from all nonmoral properties (which in their view include all natural properties). On this view, in effect, these fundamental moral properties stand in a kind of splendid isolation from all other properties whatsoever.[13]

---

[13] Some primitivist non-naturalists—such as T. M. Scanlon (2014, 72–6)—appear to compare moral properties with *mathematical* properties. On the face of it, however, moral properties and mathematical properties are strikingly dissimilar. Moral properties are instantiated or exemplified by such items as agents, actions, and choices, and by states of affairs that can be the outcomes of actions and the like—but they are not instantiated by purely abstract items (like the empty set), or by sets of inanimate natural objects (like specks of interstellar dust). Mathematical properties are primarily instantiated by abstract objects like pure sets and numbers, and derivatively by any set of objects whatever. A charitable reading of Scanlon would interpret him as claiming, not that ethical and mathematical properties are intrinsically similar in their role in the world, but that they are similar merely to the extent of both being knowable non-natural properties.

Adherents of this sort of primitivist non-naturalism may also have a reason to accept the second claim (b), that moral properties are *causally inefficacious*. There are a number of reasons why this might be thought to follow from the doctrine that the fundamental moral properties lack nontrivial real definitions. First, if these properties were causally efficacious, there would be nomological regularities—in a sense, laws of nature—explaining the way in which they were causally efficacious; and it is arguable that these nomological regularities would somehow follow from, or be implicit in, the real definitions of these properties.[14] But if the only real definitions that the fundamental moral properties have are trivial, then no such nomological regularities could follow them—since any real definitions from which such nomological regularities followed would clearly be nontrivial. Secondly, it may be thought that the natural facts form a causally complete domain of facts, so that nothing outside the domain of natural facts could ever causally explain any natural fact.[15] Thirdly, some philosophers have thought that it was just obvious that moral properties must be causally inefficacious. Thus, R. M. Dworkin (1996, 104) has no compunction about mocking the view that moral properties are causally efficacious as the absurd claim that physics needs to postulate special moral particles—"morons"—even though he never offers any argument for interpreting the view as committed to anything so absurd.

Among those who accept that moral properties exist and are exemplified in the actual world, this kind of primitivist non-naturalism is widely viewed as the leading theoretical alternative to the two forms of naturalism that I have discussed above.[16] However, it should be clear that primitivist non-naturalism is far from being the only possible alternative to these two forms of naturalism. There could in principle be *intermediate* positions, between the extremes of reductive naturalism and primitivist non-naturalism that dominate the contemporary debate.

First, even if moral properties are reducible, they might not be reducible to *natural* properties. For example, some views in the philosophy of mind might deny that mental properties are strictly natural properties—that is, these views might insist that mental properties are different in kind from the distinctive properties of physics, chemistry, and biology—while it could be true that moral properties are reducible to *mental* properties (for example, the reductive form of hedonism mentioned above might be true).

In general, moral properties might not be primitive, in the way that primitivist non-naturalists believe, even if they are also not naturalistically reducible, in the way that reductive naturalists believe. As I have characterized it, for a property to be primitive is for it to have no nontrivial real definition; and as I have argued, a real definition does not have to be reductive in order to be nontrivial.

---

[14] For this view that a property's causal role is essential to it, see Shoemaker (2003, Essay 11), and Bird (2007).

[15] For a discussion of the analogous idea of the causal completeness of physics, see Papineau (2001).

[16] Thus, for example, Parfit (2011, Chap. 31) seems to hold that something like primitivist non-naturalism is the only realist alternative to reductive naturalism; something similar seems to be true of Enoch (2011).

If a property has a nontrivial real definition, this definition should be capable of providing explanations of many of the property's metaphysical features. For example, as I have already mentioned, a nontrivial real definition of a moral property should provide an account of the causal or cosmological role that the property plays in the world.[17] But it also seems plausible that these real definitions—even if they are nonreductive—can provide explanations of many other metaphysical phenomena as well.

For example, another set of metaphysical questions that a real definition of moral properties should illuminate concerns the degree to which moral properties "carve" the world "at its joints," as Plato put it (*Phaedrus* 265e). Properties that "carve at the joints" mark real objective similarities among the objects that exemplify them, and in that respect differ from more gruesomely disjunctive or gerrymandered properties.[18] Moreover, as we have seen, Tristram McPherson (2015) has argued that we can also make sense of real objective similarity relations *between* properties: some properties are more similar to each other, while others are more dissimilar. Thus, a further set of questions concern which properties the moral properties are more similar to, and which they are less similar to. If properties can be located on a map of their proximity and distance from each other in a real similarity space, these questions concern where the moral properties are located on this map. The answers to these questions would also be illuminated by correct real definitions of these properties.

A final group of questions concern the application to moral properties of a range of broadly *modal* notions. Are fundamental moral principles metaphysically necessary, or necessary in some other way, and if so, why? What explains why moral properties supervene on other properties in the way that they do?[19] Are moral facts "grounded" in facts of some other kind, and what is the relation between this kind of "grounding" and notions such as supervenience and the like? Answers to these questions too could be provided—or at least constrained—by correct real definitions of the moral properties.

These reflections already indicate the broad outlines of an argument for such an intermediate position on the metaphysics of moral properties. On the one hand, primitivist non-naturalists are incapable of providing explanations for the answers that they give to these metaphysical questions. On the other hand, the naturalist is committed to making an extremely bold claim about every moral property—specifically, that the moral property is either itself a natural property or else reducible to natural properties. By contrast, the intermediate positions can provide these metaphysical explanations without making any such bold claims. I shall develop this sort of argument for an intermediate position in Sections 3 and 4 below. In the next section, however, I shall comment on the historical background of this debate. An understanding of this historical background will enhance our understanding of what exactly is at stake.

---

[17] On the idea of a property's cosmological role, see Wright (1992, 191–99).
[18] The idea of properties that "carve the world at its joints" was famously explored by Lewis (1983).
[19] I have explored this question in more detail elsewhere (Wedgwood 2007, Chap. 9).

2. Moral Metaphysics in the History of Philosophy

Most of the ancient Greek philosophers—including the Platonists, Aristotelians, and Stoics—accepted a *teleological* conception of the world. According to such teleological conceptions, the events of the natural world normally happen for the sake of some end or purpose; and according to many versions of this teleological conception, this is interpreted as meaning that these natural events occur precisely because it is *good* for them to occur.[20]

Plato gives us a striking idea of what a teleological conception of the universe would be like (*Phaedo* 97d–98a, my translation):

> [The ideal natural philosopher] would tell us first whether the earth was flat or round, and, when he had done so, would also explain the cause that necessitated it, saying what was better about it—better, that is, that the earth should be like this. And if he said that it was in the center of the universe, he would also explain how it was better that it should be in the center....

This passage makes it clear that according to Plato, a complete explanation of *why* the earth is at the center of the universe will imply that the earth has to be at the center because it is *better* for it to be so. In general, it is a basic tendency of the natural world for states of affairs to obtain in the natural world precisely when and because it is better for them to obtain.[21] It is presumably for this reason that Plato seems to describe the Form of the Good as the "unhypothetical first principle of everything" (*Republic* 511b5). In some way, the Form of the Good is an essential part of the ultimate explanation of everything whatsoever.

Aristotle rejects Plato's idea of the Form of the Good (*Nicomachean Ethics* I.6, 1096a11–1097a14)—in some way, Aristotle believes that it is a mistake to "separate" universals from the world of particular things—but Aristotle's conception of the world is also teleological, in a way that has some crucial similarities to Plato's. Admittedly, there are many interpretative controversies about what exactly Aristotle's teleology amounts to; but, on at least one defensible interpretation, for Aristotle too, there are conditions that obtain in the natural world precisely *because* it is in the relevant way "*best*" for these conditions to obtain.[22] The difference between Plato and Aristotle may come down to

---

[20] The Stoics would deny that it is always strictly speaking "good" when natural events fulfill their natural purposes (in their view, only the virtue of a rational agent is genuinely good)—but they do believe that these natural purposes are intended by the divine world-mind, which is supremely good and rational. Unfortunately, however, it will not be possible to discuss the Stoics in more detail here.

[21] Compare the interpretation of teleological explanation that is given by Bedau (1992).

[22] See Aristotle's account of what it is for something to be the "final cause" of a phenomenon (*Physics* 195b4), and his defense of such "final causes"—which seems to involve arguing that animals develop

this: according to Plato, the kind of goodness that explains natural phenomena is an *absolute* and nonrelative kind of goodness, while for Aristotle, the kind of goodness that explains natural phenomena is a *relative* kind of goodness—what is *good for* the natural organism in question. Still, for both Plato and Aristotle, it appears that broadly ethical or evaluative properties—properties of being good in some way or other—play a crucial role in explaining the phenomena of the natural world.

This ancient idea of the explanatory role of goodness within the cosmos seems to lie behind the notorious claim of Thomas Aquinas that "being and goodness are really the same" (*Summa Theologica*, Ia, 5.1). Aquinas concedes that the *idea* of "goodness" and the *idea* of "being" are distinct ideas: these two ideas present the property that they stand for under different aspects or guises. However, he argues that goodness and being both fundamentally consist in what he calls "perfection." For something to be "actualized" is for it to have made at least some progress towards perfection—that is, fulfilling its natural purpose; as Aquinas argues, "everything is perfect so far as it is actual," and "it is being that makes all things actual".

In this way, many ancient and medieval philosophers give an utterly central explanatory role within the whole cosmos to certain moral properties—specifically, to certain varieties of goodness. In their view, these properties appear in explanations of a huge range of natural phenomena. This is not because these properties are reducible to any metaphysically more fundamental properties. On the contrary, they constitute an utterly irreducible family of properties, which play a fundamental role in the natural world.

It is clear that this ancient view of moral properties differs sharply from the view of the reductive naturalists. On this ancient view, goodness is not reducible to any more fundamental properties of any kind—and so, *a fortiori*, it is not reducible to natural properties. On reflection, it is also clear that this traditional view differs from contemporary primitivist non-naturalism as well. First, this view is as far removed as possible from the idea that moral properties are causally inefficacious. On the contrary, on this view, moral properties like goodness are involved in the causal explanation of countless different natural phenomena. Secondly, in this way this traditional view does not conceive of moral properties as existing in splendid isolation from the natural world, but as properties that play a profound and pervasive role throughout the natural world. Finally, this traditional view does at least implicitly point towards an illuminating real definition of at least some moral properties. Roughly, it is implicit within most versions of this traditional view that the real definition of goodness is precisely that it is the property that plays this fundamental cosmological role in the world.

Thus, this traditional view of the metaphysics of goodness seems to be a version of what in the previous section I called "full-blooded naturalism." This is because, on this view, moral properties like goodness are an inextricable part of nature. They are among

---

the kinds of teeth that they have precisely because it is *good* for them to have such teeth (*Physics* II.8, 198b29–32).

the properties that must be appealed to in any adequate version of the natural sciences: specifically, these moral properties must be appealed to in either physics or biology or both.

As I shall now argue, however, it is quite doubtful whether this premodern conception of the metaphysics of goodness is still available to us. Many contemporary metaphysicians and philosophers of science would view this premodern conception as having been swept away by the development of modern natural science. Even in ancient times, there was an alternative conception of nature—the fundamentally *nonteleological* conception that was articulated by the Atomists and by their followers the Epicureans. One way to sum up the scientific developments that are of most importance for us here is to state that modern science has shown that the nonteleological conception of the Epicureans and Atomists is fundamentally correct, while the rival teleological conception is mistaken.[23]

These crucial scientific developments took place in two stages—which I shall call the "Galilean" and the "Darwinian" revolutions respectively. First, the new science that was pioneered by Galileo and his contemporaries transformed the study of physics. According to the Aristotelian conception of the motion of material bodies, each of the different forms of matter had a fundamental tendency towards its natural place in the universe. This conception was replaced by a mathematically precise account of the forces that act on bodies, and of the laws that describe the operation of those forces. The teleological notion of the end or purpose for the sake of which natural events occur ceased to play any role.[24]

Even though Galileo revolutionized physics in this way, it was not obvious to all thinkers at that time that teleological explanations had to be banished from nature altogether. In particular, it was not obvious that the new physics described absolutely all the motions of bodies. Many thinkers thought that biological phenomena, in particular, might involve distinctive "vital forces," and that in consequence teleological explanations would still have a safe home in biology.[25] Thus, a number of moral philosophers of the early modern period were still happy to appeal to the idea of natural purposes.[26]

Moreover, in the early modern period, moral properties were often viewed as having great explanatory relevance within the natural world—though this view was widely interpreted as having a theistic basis. It was still widely held, for example, that animals normally have eyes precisely because it is good for them to have eyes. But this is explained, not by appealing directly to the ancient idea that natural events tend to happen precisely because it is good for them to happen, but rather because the universe

---

[23] For an account of the early modern period's revival of interest in the Epicureans' atomistic conception of the world, see Greenblatt (2011).

[24] On Galileo, see Machamer (2017).

[25] This aspect of the historical picture is well described by Papineau (2001).

[26] For example, there are unmistakable appeals to natural teleology in the ethical writings of Lord Shaftesbury and Bishop Butler; see Raphael (1969, §197 and §376).

is rationally designed by God, who is supremely good. Nonetheless, it is still supposed that the goodness of some state of affairs is causally efficacious in explaining why the state of affairs obtains, because the will of an omnipotent Creator lies behind all natural phenomena, and if the Creator wills a state of affairs this is always because the state of affairs is good in some way.[27]

Following the Galilean revolution, the Darwinian revolution transformed our understanding of *biological* phenomena. Admittedly, there are many philosophical controversies about the best interpretation of Darwinian biology. Some philosophers argue that the great discovery of Darwin (1859) was to show how all teleological notions invoked in biology can be reduced to the theory of natural selection, which can ultimately be understood without any appeal to natural purposes. Others argue that irreducible teleological notions are indispensable in biology. However, virtually all philosophers would agree that, whatever else is true of the kind of teleology that is consistent with contemporary biology, it does not give a central explanatory role in biology to the moral properties that are most centrally discussed in ethical theory. In this way, Darwinism seems to leave no room for the kind of biological teleology that could serve as a foundation for ethics. Bernard Williams (1995, 110) gives voice to this interpretation of Darwinian biology when he says: "The first and hardest lesson of Darwinism" is "that there is no such teleology at all".[28]

Thus, it is doubtful whether the contemporary natural sciences need to make any appeal either to natural purposes or to the purposes of a divine Creator. For this reason, it is also doubtful whether there is any need for these natural sciences to make any explanatory appeal to goodness or any other moral property whatsoever. Indeed, it is widely held that the explanations of contemporary physics, chemistry, and biology—and of all the contemporary special natural sciences, such as astrophysics and biochemistry and ethology—are all couched in austerely secular and value-neutral terms.

Suppose that this view is correct—that is, suppose that it is true that contemporary natural science makes absolutely no appeal to any moral properties (even in the broad sense of "moral properties" that I am using here). Then it follows that moral properties are not among the paradigmatic natural properties—they are not themselves among the properties that are correctly posited by the natural sciences, such as physics and biology. Moreover, unless these moral properties are naturalistically reducible, it also seems doubtful whether they can belong to the set of properties that are *most objectively similar* to these paradigmatic natural properties that are correctly posited by the natural sciences. If they did belong to this set of properties, then they would be objectively at least as similar to each of these paradigmatic properties as any two paradigmatic

---

[27] See, for example, William Paley (1802, Chap. 1).
[28] For the contemporary debates about teleological notions in biology, see Allen and Neal (2020). The only contemporary philosophers who seem to think that some kind of biology could serve as a foundation for ethical theory are those who follow the theory of "natural goodness" that was devised in the late works of Philippa Foot (2001). In my judgment, these ethical theorists are attempting to swim against an overwhelmingly powerful tide in contemporary biology.

properties are to each other. But consider a moral property, and two paradigmatic natural properties that are objectively as dissimilar from each other as possible—for example, a property that is posited by quantum mechanics and a property that is posited by evolutionary biology. As dissimilar as these two paradigmatic natural properties are from each other, it seems plausible that the moral property will be even more dissimilar from the quantum-physical property than the evolutionary biological property is.

If this is correct, then our post-Darwinian worldview makes it hard for contemporary philosophers to accept any nonreductive form of the full-blooded naturalist view that moral properties are themselves natural properties (at least given the strict interpretation of "natural properties" that I am working with here). The most promising option for any metaethicists who believe in the existence of moral properties, but also wish to defend an austerely naturalistic worldview, seems to be some form of reductive naturalism.

3. Between Naturalism and Non-Naturalism

As I claimed at the end of Section 1, there is room for a range of metaphysical accounts of moral properties that occupy intermediate positions, between the extremes of reductive naturalism and primitivist non-naturalism that dominate the contemporary debate. In Section 2, we saw that many premodern thinkers embraced a kind of nonreductive naturalism; but we also saw that it is doubtful whether the position of these premodern thinkers is still a live option, in light of the development of modern natural science.

As I characterized it, primitivist non-naturalism, of the kind that is prominent in contemporary metaethical discussions, claims that the basic moral properties are wholly primitive and unanalyzable, lacking any illuminating real definition. So, to find such intermediate positions, between primitivist non-naturalism and reductive naturalism, we will need to identify ways of giving such an illuminating real definition of moral properties, without relapsing into either reductive naturalism or into the premodern nonreductive naturalism that has arguably been superseded by modern science.

Suppose that there is an illuminating real definition of a moral property—say, a real definition of the form "To be good is to be G." If this is an illuminating nontrivial definition, then it seems plausible that some nonmoral property—say, the property of being F—will be mentioned somehow with this complex predicate "G." In this way, this definition posits an essential *link* between the property of goodness that is being defined and the nonmoral property of being F. For most philosophers, the most plausible essential link of this kind between moral and nonmoral properties would be some connection between moral properties and the properties of *psychology* and *social science*.[29]

---

[29] Another such link that some philosophers would be drawn to would be a connection between moral properties and the broadly divine or theistic properties of God. For this sort of approach, see Adams (1999).

These intermediate positions that I propose to consider in this section all understand moral properties in terms of their relations to the properties of psychology and social science—as I shall call them, mental and social properties.

Now, given certain widely held assumptions, an account of moral properties in terms of their connections to mental and social properties would count as a naturalistic reduction of the moral properties. The relevant assumptions are: (a) that mental and social properties are themselves entirely natural properties, and (b) the simple predicates that appear in this account of moral properties all refer either to mental and social properties, or to metaphysically fundamental natural properties.

This is in fact the commonest kind of naturalistic reduction that philosophers have tried to devise. For example, David Lewis (1989) offers a reductive account of what it is for a property or a state of affairs to be "a value" in terms of what we are disposed to desire to desire under ideal conditions. Then, in the philosophy of mind, Lewis (1980) develops a reductive form of functionalism that explains how mental properties are reducible to metaphysically more fundamental natural properties.

Lewis's version of reductive naturalism incorporates both a reduction of moral properties to mental properties, and also a reduction of mental properties to more fundamental natural properties. Some philosophers will be tempted to claim that, even if mental properties are irreducible, they are nonetheless fully natural properties. Given the way in which I am using the term "natural property" here, this claim can be explained in terms the *paradigmatic* natural properties—the properties correctly posited by physics, chemistry, and biology. Specifically, the claim is equivalent to the thesis that mental properties are objectively no more dissimilar from any of these paradigmatic properties than these paradigmatic properties are from each other. For example, according to this interpretation of the claim, mental properties are no more dissimilar from quantum-physical properties than biological properties are. (In the previous section, I argued that it would be implausible to claim that irreducible *moral* properties are natural properties in this way, but perhaps it is less implausible to make this claim about *mental* properties.) If it can be argued that mental properties are natural in this way, then a reduction of moral properties to mental properties would count as a naturalistic reduction.

By contrast, if it cannot be argued that mental properties are themselves natural properties in this way, and if mental properties are also not reducible to more fundamental natural properties, then mental properties are not fully natural properties. On this view, psychology and the social sciences belong to a significantly different branch of rational inquiry from the natural sciences. On this view of mental properties, the thesis that moral properties are reducible to mental properties would not count as a form of reductive ethical naturalism, as I am using the term. (For example, the reductive form of ethical hedonism considered in Section 1 would not be a form of reductive naturalism if *pleasure* and *pain* are not themselves strictly natural properties.) In general, to give an account of how moral properties fit into the world that is revealed by the natural sciences, it would be not enough just to explain how moral properties reduce to mental properties; one would also have to explain how *mental* properties fit into the world that is revealed by the natural sciences.

At all events, if there are any illuminating real definitions of moral properties, it seems plausible that these real definitions will imply that there are certain essential connections between moral properties and mental properties. The reason for thinking that there is an intimate link between moral and mental properties arises from the primary roles that moral properties seem to play in the world. First, some moral properties seem to be primarily instantiated by distinctively mental phenomena—such as by attitudes like choices or decisions, or by voluntary or intentional actions, or the like. Secondly, some other moral properties are exemplified by other items—such as states of affairs that could be the outcomes of actions, or the objects of attitudes—but in a way that has immediate *implications* for the evaluation of mental phenomena like actions or attitudes. (For example, the *admirableness* of a person's achieving something has the immediate implication that it is *appropriate or fitting* to have an attitude of admiration towards that person's achievement, and so on.)

In this way, it is plausible that, unless moral properties are wholly primitive and unanalyzable, their metaphysical fate is intimately tied to that of mental properties. A full metaphysical account of moral properties will have to address the following two questions. First, what are the moral properties' relations to mental properties? Secondly, what is the correct account of the metaphysics of these mental properties themselves?

On the first question, as we have seen, one possibility is that moral properties are reducible in some way to mental properties. If moral properties are *not* reducible, there are two ways in which this could be the case. One way is that it might be that, for some moral property, it is simply impossible to give necessary and sufficient conditions for the instantiation of the moral property using simple predicates that stand only for mental and nonmoral properties.

However, there is a reason for thinking that it must be possible, at least in principle, to give such necessary and sufficient conditions. This reason arises from the plausible principle that moral properties *strongly supervene* on mental and nonmoral properties. Given certain plausible assumptions, it can be proved that every strongly supervening property is necessarily coextensive with the disjunction of the subvening properties that necessitate that supervening property. The significance of this proof is open to question, but it at least raises a problem that will have to be surmounted somehow by any philosopher who denies that it is possible, even in principle, to give necessary and sufficient conditions for the instantiation of any moral property in entirely mental and nonmoral terms.[30]

Even if it is possible to give such necessary and sufficient conditions for the instantiation of a moral property, using no simple predicates except for those that stand for mental and nonmoral properties, this statement of necessary and sufficient conditions need not count as a *reduction*. In particular, such a statement will fail to count as a reduction if it mentions certain *mental properties* that are *not themselves metaphysically more*

---

[30] This argument seems to be originally due to Kim (1993, 151–52), but it was redeployed by Jackson (1998, 122–3). Strictly speaking, as I have pointed out (Wedgwood 2007, Chap. 9), the argument requires S5 modal logic—or at least the truth of all the relevant instances of the S5 axiom. But this is something that most philosophers are willing to grant.

fundamental than that moral property. This is the second way in which a moral property might fail to be reducible to mental and other nonmoral properties—if the relevant mental properties are not metaphysically more fundamental than the moral property.

The relevant mental properties—I shall assume—are those that are ascribed and appealed to in folk psychology, the kind of psychology that we all have at least some intuitive grasp of. Why might these mental properties fail to be metaphysically more fundamental than the moral properties? This would be the case if a certain view of these properties were correct: specifically, the view that moral properties—or some closely related properties, such as normative or evaluative properties—have to be mentioned in any adequate real definition of these mental properties.

This is the view that is sometimes called "normativism" about the mental—the view that the essential nature of each of these folk-psychological properties is given, at least in part, by certain normative principles that apply to them. On one version of this view, for example, part of what it is for a state to be the mental state of *belief* is that it is a state that (a) counts as *correct* if and only if its propositional content is true, and (b) counts as *rational* at a given time if and only if it is adequately supported by the evidence that the thinker has at that time.

According to this sort of normativism about the mental, then, the mental properties distinctive of folk psychology are not located at a metaphysically more fundamental level than normative and evaluative properties. On the contrary, these two families of properties are metaphysically on a par—essentially interconnected with each other, and neither of them more fundamental than the other. As I noted in Section 1, I am using the term "moral property" broadly, so that it includes all normative and evaluative properties as well as the more narrowly moral properties. This is why this kind of normativism about the mental entails that no specification of necessary and sufficient conditions for the instantiation of a moral property that employs simple predicates that stand for these mental properties can count as a reductive account of the moral property.

One example of this sort of normativism about the mental is the kind of philosophy of mind that was developed by Donald Davidson. According to Davidson (1980, 222), we must have some disposition for "believing the truth and loving the good", if we are to be correctly interpretable as having the attitudes of belief or desire at all.[31] According to a philosophy of mind of this sort, it is essential to each of the relevant types of mental state that there is a correct or proper role that this type of mental state should play in our thinking and reasoning, and in every thinking agent, these mental states must have at least some disposition to play this correct or proper role, if the agent is to be capable of mental states of that type at all.[32]

---

[31] This view need not imply that every desire that we ever have arises from this disposition for "loving the good"—there can be irrational desires on this view—but it implies that a being who wholly lacked this disposition to "love the good" would not count as having desires at all.

[32] I have offered a defense of this approach to the philosophy of mind elsewhere (see Wedgwood 2007, Chap. 7).

In effect, this kind of philosophy of mind adopts a *restricted* kind of teleology—a teleological conception of the *mind*. The various types of mental states are defined, at least in part, by some of the good or right or proper ways for them to function; and a thinker's states must have some disposition to function in these ways if they are to count as instances of these types at all. Unlike the kind of teleology that was undermined by the Galilean and Darwinian revolutions, however, this kind of teleology is restricted to a narrow range of phenomena—just to the realm of mental states of the kind that is distinctive of folk psychology. There is no claim to a more general teleological conception of the natural world. (Indeed, arguably the central error of premodern natural teleology was that it involved taking a kind of explanation that is only applicable within the sphere of folk psychology and applying it generally to the natural world as a whole.)

Strictly speaking, this kind of normativism about the mental is consistent with claiming that both moral properties and mental properties are reducible. Even if normativism about the mental is true, there could still be a simultaneous reduction of the whole family of mental, normative, and moral properties to some metaphysically more fundamental set of properties. Presumably the most plausible version of such a grand simultaneous reduction of this big family of properties would be some kind of functionalism—or perhaps the kind of biological or "teleofunctional" reduction that is advocated by philosophers like Ruth Millikan (1984). Nonetheless, it may be that the problems that philosophers have raised for such functionalist or teleofunctional reductions of the mind would reappear in an even more acute form for a functionalist or teleofunctional attempt to give a grand simultaneous reduction of both the mental and the normative properties.

Moreover, even if this kind of normativism about the mental is consistent with claiming that mental, normative, and moral properties are reducible, it also seems consistent with the view that they are irreducible. If these properties are not naturalistically reducible, this raises a question about what form a correct real definition of these properties would take. The answer may be that these normativist principles linking these mental properties with various normative and evaluative properties may form the core of the real definitions of both kinds of properties. We are not left without any way of explaining the nature of these properties, even though our account of these properties does not involve reducing them to any more metaphysically fundamental level.

The fact that this sort of normativism is a limited kind of teleology makes it clear that it is controversial. It seems to imply that psychology—or at least the kind of psychology that is continuous with everyday folk psychology—differs from the paradigmatic natural sciences in some important ways. For example, whereas our knowledge of the real definitions of the paradigmatic properties of physics, chemistry, and biology is empirical through-and-through, on this approach our knowledge of the real definitions of the mental properties that are characteristically appealed to in folk psychology is at least in part a priori, since these real definitions consist at least in part in normative principles that apply to these mental properties.

Nonetheless, this sort of normativism about the mental still allows for many sorts of empirical psychology. One good question is whether it can be reconciled with everything that we have learned from empirical psychology over the last century or so. If not, then this kind of normativism about the mental should be discarded, just as the more general premodern teleology about the natural world was discarded as a result of the Galilean and Darwinian revolutions. But if it can be reconciled with what we have learned in empirical psychology, then this sort of normativism may be great significance to the metaphysical side of metaethics.

4. The Virtues of Moderation

These intermediate positions on the metaphysics of moral properties have certain advantages over both of the more extreme positions. They can provide explanations of puzzling metaphysical phenomena, which primitivist non-naturalism cannot explain; but they are not open to the objections that have been raised against the reductive forms of naturalism.

A number of objections can be raised against the reductive form of ethical naturalism. Reductive naturalism is committed to the claim that there is a reductive account of every moral property; it is also committed to the claim that every simple predicate that appears in this reductive account stands for a genuinely natural property—or at least for a property that is ultimately reducible in terms that stand only for such natural properties. No one has ever produced such a reductive account that has commanded the assent of more than a small minority of philosophers. For this reason, many reductive naturalists have not in fact offered any such account, but contented themselves with providing grounds for optimism that such an account can in principle be found.

Many of these grounds for optimism rely on the assumption that only a reductive account can explain all the phenomena that need to be explained. However, this assumption is undercut by the arguments that I shall now give about the explanatory virtues of the intermediate positions. If my arguments are sound, then these intermediate positions can also explain all the phenomena that clearly need to be explained—and it is debatable whether there are any further phenomena that these intermediate positions cannot explain. For this reason, these grounds for optimism are not strong arguments for the conclusion that some true reductive account can in principle be found.

On the other hand, the reasons against primitivist non-naturalism are clear. This non-naturalist position provides no explanation for a host of phenomena that seem to call for explanation. In the remainder of this discussion, I shall canvas a range of these phenomena, and I shall argue that whereas they cannot be explained by the primitivist non-naturalist, the intermediate positions sketched in the previous section should be able to explain them.

First, if there is a nontrivial real definition of moral properties, it will be able to explain the causal role that these properties play in the world. Of course, if—as many primitivist non-naturalists believe—moral properties play no causal role in the world, then this could be explained by the primitivist approach. However, it seems plausible that moral properties do play some nontrivial causal role. Rational agents often make the choices that they make precisely *because* they have *good reasons* for those choices. Indeed, arguably this is precisely what it is to choose rationally, or in a rational manner. We cannot capture this point by saying that rational agents make the choices that they do because they *believe* that they have good reasons for doing so. Making a choice merely because you believe that you have good reasons for making it is not sufficient for choosing rationally—since even if you believe that you have good reasons, you might in fact not have any such good reasons at all. Moreover, making a choice because you believe that you have good reasons for doing so is also not *necessary* for choosing rationally—since an agent can often make a quick and unreflective choice, in an entirely rational manner, without having any higher-order attitudes towards the proposition that they have good reasons for this particular choice.

On the other hand, the causal role of moral properties certainly appears to be restricted to explaining events, like choices, that involve mental properties. As modern physics has shown, Plato was wrong to think that the sun moves through space as it does because it is "best" for it to do so. A real definition of moral properties would be able to explain why moral properties have this restricted kind of cosmological role—causally efficacious in relation to mental events, but inefficacious in relation to the motions of the stars.[33]

At the end of Section 1, I gestured towards the idea of real objective similarities between properties, and the idea of a similarity space in which different properties can be located, depending on how similar or dissimilar they are to each other. Primitivist nonnaturalists view moral properties as maximally dissimilar from the natural properties—as we might picture it, in a region of this similarity space that is as far as possible from the region that contains the natural properties. Full-blooded naturalists and reductive naturalists locate moral properties as squarely within the same region as the natural properties. But as explained in Section 1 above, the definition of "natural properties" that I have proposed here allows that some non-natural properties are more similar to the natural properties than others. In this way, it is open to these intermediate positions to locate the moral properties as occupying a region that is outside that of the strictly natural properties, but still relatively *close* to the natural properties—and presumably especially close to the region that contains the mental and social properties. In this way, these intermediate positions are capable of giving a more nuanced account of where the moral properties are located in this similarity space.

A further set of questions where an explanation seems to be called for concerns supervenience. It seems plausible that moral properties supervene on other nonmoral properties. But if this is so, it seems that it should be explicable why it is so. Moreover, if moral properties "strongly supervene" on other properties, then it follows that there will be principles to the effect that certain nonmoral properties *necessitate* certain moral

---

[33] The view that evaluative and normative properties are causally efficacious in relation to mental events of these kinds is defended by Oddie (2005) and by me (Wedgwood 2007, Chap. 8).

properties. For example, if wrongness strongly supervenes on nonmoral properties, then for every actual instance of wrongness, it is not just true but *necessary* that anything that has exactly the same nonmoral properties as that instance of wrongness has in the actual world is likewise an instance of wrongness. But if this is necessary, why is it necessary? Is there simply an infinite assortment of such nonmoral-to-moral necessitations, or is there some way of unifying and explaining them?

The primitivist seems to have no way of giving any explanation here. The primitivist may resort to stating that the truth about wrongness must be capable of being captured by a set of such necessary principles; but this is simply to restate the phenomenon that needs to be explained, not to offer any explanation of it.[34] By contrast, a constraint that any real definition of a moral property must meet is that it must be capable of explaining these phenomena. It seems that a real definition would not have to be reductive in order to provide these explanations. So, it looks as if a nonreductive real definition—unlike primitivist non-naturalism—should be able to provide the needed explanations here.

Finally, another range of phenomena that seem to call for explanation are the facts about what *grounds* the truth of propositions involving moral properties. It seems that moral truths—or at least, contingent moral truths, such as the true proposition that Socrates was wise, or that the Athenian jury committed a grave injustice in convicting him—seem to be *grounded* in other truths about the world.[35] But why are moral truths grounded in just this way (rather than being wholly ungrounded, or grounded in other different facts about the world)? Again, an illuminating real definition of moral properties should be able to provide an explanation.

This notion of grounding can be used to formulate a sense in which, even if reductive naturalism is rejected, intermediate positions of the kind that I have been exploring here are consistent with a kind of *moderate* naturalism. Even if moral properties are not themselves natural properties, and are irreducible, it could still be that natural facts are fundamental in a different way. Specifically, it could still be that all contingent truths about the world whatsoever are *grounded* in facts that can be stated using no simple predicates other than those that stand for natural properties. This idea—of irreducible moral facts that are nonetheless wholly grounded in these wholly natural facts—could be one way of making sense of the idea that moral facts are "emergent" features of the world, emerging from the world's natural features without being reducible to them.

To conclude: if moral realism is true, then a series of metaphysical questions arise about the nature of moral properties. There are more questions here than just the one that has dominated the attention of metaethicists for the last few decades—the question of whether moral properties are naturalistically reducible or not. If moral properties are naturalistically reducible, then the correct reductive account of these moral properties would provide an answer to these metaphysical questions; but as I have argued, it is not the only way of answering these questions. The primitivist non-naturalists seem not

---

[34] This, as I read it, is the approach taken by Scanlon (2014, 41).
[35] For an argument for the centrality of grounding to normative theorizing, see Berker (2018).

to have any clear way of addressing these questions, but the intermediate metaphysical views—between the two extremes of reductive naturalism and primitivist non-naturalism—seem more likely to be able to address these questions. Finally, it seems plausible that any attempt to tackle these metaphysical questions about moral properties will also have to come to grips with the parallel questions about mental properties. As Aristotle said (*Nicomachean Ethics* I.13, 1102a23), "The student of politics must study the soul."

References

Adams, R. M. 1999. *Finite and Infinite Goods*. Oxford: Oxford University Press.
Allen, Colin, and Neal, Jacob. 2020. "Teleological Notions in Biology." *The Stanford Encyclopedia of Philosophy*, Spring 2020 Edition, edited by Edward N. Zalta. https://plato.stanford.edu/archives/spr2020/entries/teleology-biology/.
Bedau, M. A. 1992. "Where's the Good in Teleology?." *Philosophy and Phenomenological Research* 52: 781–806.
Berker, Selim. 2018. "The Unity of Grounding." *Mind* 127: 729–777.
Bird, Alexander. 2007. *Nature's Metaphysics: Laws and Properties*. Oxford: Oxford University Press.
Copp, David. 2007. *Morality in a Natural World*. Cambridge: Cambridge University Press.
Cuneo, Terence. 2007. *The Normative Web*. Oxford: Oxford University Press.
Darwin, Charles. 1859. *On the Origin of Species by Means of Natural Selection*. London: John Murray.
Dorr, Cian. 2016. "To Be F Is to Be G." *Philosophical Perspectives* 30(1): 39–134.
Davidson, Donald. 1980. *Essays on Actions and Events*. Oxford: Oxford University Press.
Dworkin, R. M. 1996. "Objectivity and Truth: You'd Better Believe It." *Philosophy and Public Affairs* 25(2): 87–139.
Elgin, Samuel Z. 2021. "The Semantic Foundations of Philosophical Analysis." *Review of Symbolic Logic*, First View: 1–21. https://doi.org/10.1017/S1755020321000046.
Enoch, David. 2011. *Taking Morality Seriously: A Defense of Robust Realism*. Oxford: Oxford University Press.
Finlay, Stephen. 2014. *Confusion of Tongues: A Theory of Normative Language*. Oxford: Oxford University Press.
Foot, Philippa. 2001. *Natural Goodness*. Oxford: Oxford University Press.
Greenblatt, Stephen. 2011. *The Swerve: How the World Became Modern*. New York: W. W. Norton.
Huemer, Michael. 2005. *Ethical Intuitionism*. New York: Palgrave Macmillan.
Jackson, Frank. 1998. *From Metaphysics to Ethics: A Defence of Conceptual Analysis*. Oxford: Clarendon Press.
Kim, Jaegwon. 1993. *Supervenience and Mind*. Cambridge: Cambridge University Press.
Lewis, David. 1980. "Mad Pain and Martian Pain." In *Readings in the Philosophy of Psychology*, vol. 1, edited by Ned Block, 216–222. Cambridge, MA: Harvard University Press.
Lewis, David. 1983. "New Work for a Theory of Universals." *Australasian Journal of Philosophy* 61: 343–377.

Lewis, David. 1989. "Dispositional Theories of Value." *Proceedings of the Aristotelian Society* 63: 113–137.

Machamer, Peter. 2017. "Galileo Galilei." *The Stanford Encyclopedia of Philosophy*, Summer 2017 Edition, edited by Edward N. Zalta. https://plato.stanford.edu/archives/sum2017/entries/galileo/.

McPherson, Tristram. 2015. "What Is at Stake in Debates among Normative Realists?." *Noûs* 49(1): 123–146. https://doi.org/10.1111/nous.12055.

Millikan, Ruth G. 1984. *Language, Thought, and Other Biological Categories*. Cambridge, MA: MIT Press.

Moore, G. E. 1903. *Principia Ethica*. Cambridge: Cambridge University Press.

Oddie, Graham. 2005. *Value, Reality, and Desire*. Oxford: Oxford University Press.

Paley, William. 1802. *Natural Theology*. London: R. Faulder.

Papineau, David. 2001. "The Rise of Physicalism." In *Physicalism and Its Discontents*, edited by Carl Gillett and Barry Loewer, 3–36. Cambridge: Cambridge University Press.

Parfit, Derek. 1997. "Reasons and Motivation." *Proceedings of the Aristotelian Society* 71: 99–130.

Parfit, Derek. 2011. *On What Matters*, vol. 2. Oxford: Oxford University Press.

Raphael, D. D. 1969. *The British Moralists: 1650–1800*. Oxford: Oxford University Press.

Rosen, Gideon. 2015. "Real Definition." *Analytic Philosophy* 56(3):189–209.

Scanlon, T. M. 2014. *Being Realistic about Reasons*. Oxford: Oxford University Press.

Schroeder, Mark. 2007. *Slaves of the Passions*. Oxford: Oxford University Press.

Shoemaker, Sydney. 2003. *Identity, Cause, and Mind*. Exp. ed. Oxford: Oxford University Press.

Sturgeon, Nicholas L. 1998. "Naturalism in Ethics." In *Routledge Encyclopedia of Philosophy*, edited by Edward Craig. Abingdon, UK: Taylor and Francis. https://doi.org/10.4324/9780415249126-L067-1, https://www.rep.routledge.com/articles/thematic/naturalism-in-ethics/v-1/ .

Wedgwood, Ralph. 2007. *The Nature of Normativity*. Oxford: Oxford University Press.

Williams, Bernard. 1995. *Making Sense of Humanity*. Cambridge: Cambridge University Press.

Wright, Crispin. 1992. *Truth and Objectivity*. Cambridge, MA: Harvard University Press.

CHAPTER 8

CAN A MORAL JUDGMENT BE MOOREAN?

WILLIAM G. LYCAN

The recent resurgence of interest in Moore's method of "common sense" and his claimed refutations of idealism and skepticism is overdue and very welcome. A few of us have been defending him for years.[1]

The humble, David-sized propositions he used against the Goliaths are familiar: "I had breakfast before I had lunch," "This is a pencil," "Here is one hand, and here is another," "I know that I am standing up."[2] Those are unpretentious truths of fact, not what would ordinarily be called matters of opinion, though of course some philosophical idealists and skeptics have denied at least by implication that they do really obtain.

In previous works I have argued that although several versions of Moore's strategy fail, there is one that, once carefully teased out, is immune to all the standard objections and succeeds against its targets. I shall not repeat its details or much of its defense here, though I shall list its key elements in Section II below. Rather, in this chapter my question is: *Assuming* some version of Moore's strategy succeeds against traditional idealists, can a parallel strategy work against some contemporary moral antirealists?[3] In particular, does some class of moral antirealisms stand or fall with eliminative idealism of Bradley's and McTaggart's sort, as attacked by Moore?

An obvious reason why that question has not attracted much attention is that unlike temporal relations and the existence of your hands, moral realism is genuinely controversial, even among nonphilosophers.

It may be thought that the question presupposes or in some looser way *waits upon* moral realism. I cannot see that it does. But even if it did, it remains a good question:

---

[1] E.g., Lycan (2001, 2007, 2019); Greco (2002); Pryor (2004); Lemos (2004); Kelly (2005); Baumann (2009).

[2] All from Moore's famous papers, collected in Moore (1953/1962), (1959/1962), (1968).

[3] Thus, my project is the same as that of McPherson (2009); but the Moorean argument he considers differs from mine. I shall comment on his discussion in Section IV below.

assuming that Moore's strategy works against idealisms, would that strategy, in particular, work against moral antirealisms? And whether or not moral realism is true, we can just start with moral *beliefs* and see if they have, or do not have, the Moorean kind of epistemological trumping power.

I

It is important to identify the appropriate original opponent(s). Bradley and McTaggart were eliminative idealists: they maintained that physical objects, physical space and the passage of time were illusory, and that all assertions like "I have hands" and "I started writing this paragraph two minutes ago" are in the end false.[4] But Moore's strategy would have had no force at all against *Berkeleyan* idealism, for Berkeley emphatically did not deny either the truth of any first-order commonsense judgment or the reality of hands and pencils, but only the existence of what he called "matter." And there is a sort of skeptic who is unfazed by Moore: one who grants a perfectly good contextual/pragmatist sense of "know" and the truth of everyday knowledge claims but insists that there is a genuine and important sense in which no one *really* knows anything.[5]

Which moral antirealists, then, might be vulnerable to Moorean attack? Not all, indeed far from all. The obvious *in*vulnerables would be (1) a metaethical Berkeley, who grants all commonsense truths about morality and agrees that there are perfectly real moral facts but offers a metaphysically deflationary analysis of them, e.g., in contractarian terms;[6] (2) a Carnapian (or Sellarsian) "framework" theorist who

---

[4] Each of the British Idealists' works has been interpreted otherwise. Here and in what follows I simply assume my Moorean's exegeses. If Moore committed an ignoratio elenchi, then substitute a more accurate example.

[5] On such a skeptic, see 34–36 of Lycan (2019). But in the rest of this chapter, I will not address the question of moral knowledge, because it would take us into general epistemological issues that would require at least an article to themselves. For the record, I am sympathetic to the Moorean views of both Lemos (2004) and Baumann (2009), but only against a background of explanatory coherentism as a theory of justification, as well as contextualism about knowing.

[6] Obviously a contractarian may be a moral realist, but some contractarians regard their view as an eliminative replacement for moral facts and truths; others fall somewhere in between (see Milo 1995). One desideratum among others is the Euthyphro question of whether the relevant contracts arrive at the moral facts because they are rational and well conceived, or whether the moral facts are constituted merely by having arisen from some practically rational set of contracts.

A degenerate case of Moore-proof deflationism would be "subjectivism" as defined by Ayer, the view that moral judgments are factual claims about the speaker's own attitudes.

Relativisms also divide, depending on the interpretation of the theorist's favored relational predicate and on the size of the reference class. For example, there is a realist interpretation of Harman's (1977) contractarian relativism (Harman 2015). For another example, suppose one is a *species* relativist, maintaining that there are moral judgments that are, in light of human nature, true for all humans, but would not be true for differently constituted Venusians if any (cf. Lukes 2008, 27–28); I would be loath to classify such a view as antirealist. But a relativism modeled on the obviously true *legal* relativism should, I think, be counted as an eliminativist theory, as its predicate "moral-for" or "moral-in" means only

distinguishes between "internal" and "external" questions;[7] and (3) a "quasi-realist" such as Blackburn (1993), who like the Berkeleyan does not dispute first-order moral truths and is happy to speak of moral facts but who maintains that in some sense moral judgments' appearances of factuality have to be "earned" and do not reflect the fundamental nature of moral judgments.

The obvious targets of a Moorean attack would be eliminative, nihilist, and error theories such as Mackie's (1977), according to which, moral judgments are perfectly factual in nature but are all false. The arguments for such a position identify implications allegedly shared by moral judgments, e.g., that the facts the judgments state would have to be intrinsically motivating (Mackie) or "objectively prescriptive" (Garner 1990, 1994; Olson 2014), which properties are incompatible with a naturalistic worldview or are otherwise metaphysically unacceptable.

II

How, exactly, would a confrontation go, between a moral Moorean and an error theorist? Much in the way that Moore attacked instances of eliminative idealism. The key points are these: (1) Every known deductive argument for idealism has a premise that is an abstract philosophical principle, typically one that is contentious even among philosophers. (2) Any deductive argument on any topic whatever can be turned on its head; in the assessing of any deductive argument there must be a judgment of comparative credibility as between, piecemeal, each of its premises and the denial of the argument's conclusion. (3) In every case I have ever heard of, when an abstract and contentious philosophical principle is forced into a credibility faceoff with a Moorean fact, it loses (by any standard). Moreover, (4) the Moorean fact, itself or in conjunction with undisputed assumptions, entails the falsity of the idealist doctrine.

Consider one of McTaggart's arguments against the reality of time. Since the existence of a temporal relation is directly entailed by something Moore finds tediously obvious and undeniable, that he did have his breakfast before he had lunch that day, he must look at the premises of McTaggart's argument and see whether each and every one of them is more credible than that he had breakfast before he had lunch. But when he does that, he finds that at least one premise is, though perfectly intelligible, distinctively abstract and somewhat arbitrary. For example, one of McTaggart's assumptions was that temporal modes such as pastness and futurity are monadic properties of events (1908, 459–60). The validity of McTaggart's argument forces a piecemeal choice between that premise and what the conclusion denies. And now, how could it possibly be more reasonable

---

something like "is customary in" (compare a naïf who thought that legality is a property that an action has regardless of institutional jurisdictions).

[7] Ditto Chrisman's (2016) inferentialism.

to believe that pastness and futurity are monadic properties of events, than to believe that we had breakfast before we had lunch?[8] (N.b., the assumption was a *bare* assumption, not itself defended; had McTaggart defended it in turn, Moore's strategy would not apply to it.)

A more relevant contemporary example would be the Moorean refutation of Churchland's (1981) eliminativism regarding the propositional attitudes, the claim that no one has ever had a belief or a desire. Lycan (2005) argued predictably as follows: Numerous common-sense mental ascriptions, such as that Granny wants a beer and believes there is one in the cellar, are individually more credible than are the a priori philosophical premises of any known eliminativist argument designed to convince us to the contrary. (The eliminativist may protest that her/his case is not purely philosophical, but rests on scientific considerations of cognitive psychology, neuroscience, dynamic systems modelling, and the like. But the Moorean point is that each eliminativist argument also contains at least one nonscientific, purely philosophical premise. In order to reach the staggering conclusion that there has never been a belief, a desire, or any other propositional attitude, every argument for eliminativism rests on one or more a priori principles connecting scientific truths and methodology to nonexistence. And if we look at them piecemeal, we find no such principle that is more credible for us than that Granny wants beer.) And as always, Moore's technique deliberately leaves open the underlying ontology: Propositional attitudes need not be brain states, or representations, or states of Cartesian egos; perhaps Analytical Behaviorism is true, or Dennettian interpretive instrumentalism.

I must quickly run through standard objections to Moore and point out that my particular version of his technique is not subject to any of them.

(1) *Moore is just begging the question.* No; on my interpretation Moore is only inviting a credibility comparison, between, e.g., (a) "I had my breakfast before I had lunch" and (b) McTaggart's philosophical assumption that pastness and futurity are monadic properties of events. Even if some strange reader were sincerely to report finding (b) more credible than (a), Moore has in no way begged the question.

(2) *Moore has arbitrarily privileged a category of "common sense" propositions.* No; Moore has not singled out any particular class of propositions, much less proposed that "common sense" propositions per se have any particular credibility-making property. Moore never employs any *premise about* either commonsensical propositions as such or philosophical propositions as such, far less even suggested that any proposition is known in virtue of being commonsensical.[9]

---

[8] For that matter, why would anyone accept that assumption at all? For one thing, it conflicts with the fourth-dimensional view of time. But that is not to the present point, which is only that the assumption is metaphysically daring, and pales in credibility beside "I had breakfast before I had lunch"—or "I sat down five minutes ago," "A thought occurred to me just now," and on and on. And notice that the very concept of memory presupposes the passage of time.

[9] Nor, on my interpretation, does Moore employ any *premise about* certainty or degrees of certainty, as he is reconstructed by, e.g., Rowland (2013), 16.

Streumer (2013) understands the Moorean strategy as comparing the credibility of the commonsense proposition to that of the *theory* under attack. For the case of metaethical error theory he ingeniously

(3) *Moore is being dogmatic, cleaving to commonsense beliefs come what may.* No; Moore is happy to grant both that commonsense beliefs may be overturned by scientific discovery and that everyday beliefs held with great confidence sometimes prove to be mistaken.

(4) *Moore is at least being dogmatically antiphilosophy, maintaining that philosophy alone cannot overturn commonsense beliefs.* If Moore himself accepted any such generalization, I do not. I appeal only to the piecemeal credibility comparisons, one at a time.[10]

Expanding that last point, I must emphasize also that Moorean refutations are fallible. It remains theoretically possible that a large and comprehensive theory, unrivalled in its degree of explanatory coherence, might justify an eliminative idealism. What Moore made us safe from is any *short road* to idealism, such as a deductive argument based on one or more undefended purely philosophical assumptions.[11] There might be a longer and elegantly curved boulevard, or plaza. An explanatory wide reflective equilibrium incorporating a future interpretation of quantum mechanics or the like, based on strong and widely shared intuitive principles of some kind, *might* vindicate Hegel instead of Moore. (But I am not holding my breath; it seems very unlikely.)

III

What, then, would be good examples of Moorean moral facts? Here are a few: (i) Alan having firmly promised Betty that he will look after her children tomorrow while she is called away on an emergency, Alan is obligated to show up and do that. (ii) It was morally hideous of Hitler and Eichmann to round up and murder millions of people simply because of the victims' ethnicity. (iii) It is wrong to torture a helpless cat just for fun (Harman's 1977 favorite). (The obvious nonmoral facts are assumed in each case: Alan's and Betty's circumstances do not relevantly change; there were no even faintly extenuating reasons for the Nazis' extermination program; cats do suffer and are not mindless machines as Descartes supposed.)

The rest is straightforward: Mackie's eliminativist argument rests on the premise that a moral fact would have to be intrinsically motivating. That premise is highly controversial and indeed (as is argued in Lycan 1986) confused; even the far more plausible assumption that moral *beliefs* intrinsically motivate is vigorously contested.[12] Garner's

---

but unconvincingly argues that the theory cannot be believed at all, and so cannot be put to credibility comparison. For critique, see Rowland (2013) and Olson (2014).

[10] Contemporary Mooreans are split as between those who think that idealist and skeptical arguments need to be rebutted one at a time, and those who do take the more general position that an eliminative idealist must in principle succumb to Moore and so is doomed. On the latter and why I reject it, see 18–20 and especially 34–35 of Lycan (2019).

[11] And I endorse this carefully narrowed generalization: "If an undefended premise is controversial even among philosophers, it cannot, standing alone, win in a credibility faceoff against a Moorean fact" (Lycan 2019, 34).

[12] Bloomfield (2001), Ch. 4; Shafer-Landau (2003), Ch. 6.

premise, that moral facts would have to be "objectively prescriptive," has more to recommend it but can easily be resisted on the basis of standard and non-question-begging views about a posteriori property identity (Lycan 2018).[13] Joyce (2003) interprets objective prescriptivity as a matter of affording reasons for action that obtain regardless of the agent's desires or interests, and he rejects it on the basis of a complex and controversial view of reasons. Neither Mackie's nor Garner's premise is as rationally compelling as any of (i)–(iii).[14]

(There are other arguments for error theories. For example, a simple one that combines Karamazovian Divine Command theory with atheism—and so much the worse for Divine Command theories. To make my realist case conclusively, I would have to look at every eliminativist argument there has ever been and find in it a premise that is less credible than one of (i)–(iii). I am personally confident that I could do that, just as I am confident that I could do the same for idealist arguments, but it remains a prediction.)

Moral facts and properties are sometimes compared, à la Churchland on propositional attitudes, to supernatural entities such as witches or evil spirits, relics of a prescientific age. Of course we have come to reject the existence of such things as science advances (more recently we have rejected chemically anomalous characteristics of living creatures, such as *élan vital*). We do not want Moore's technique to block sound "error theories" of that kind. What, then, of arguments like this one?:

(a) If there are witches, then there is magic.
(b) There is no such thing as magic.
∴ (c) There are no witches.

(Which seems clearly sound.) Garner's argument is exactly parallel:

---

[13] The general idea is that when identity of properties is not a priori but empirically discovered or theoretically posited, the terms designating the properties are not synonymous. (Standard examples of the type supplied by Smart 1959 include the identity of water with H_2O and that of lightning with electrical discharge in the sky.) Since the terms may have quite different meanings, they also have different logical and conceptual implications; "Here's a glass of water" semantically entails nothing about hydrogen, and "There was a big electrical discharge in the sky" entails nothing about a flash of light. On that model it would be no objection to a theory that identifies moral obligatoriness with a natural property, say with that of reducing unhappiness in the world, to point out that "X is now obligatory for S" entails "S now ought to do X" (and possibly "S, do X!") while "X would reduce unhappiness in the world" has no such implication. On at least the obvious interpretation of "prescriptivity," whether a fact or property is prescriptive depends on how it is described; it is the description uttered, not the chunky fact described, that semantically entails the prescription.

[14] A compressed version of this argument is given by Michael Huemer (2005), 115–17. Enoch (2011, 117–19) expresses sympathy with the Moorean objection to error theory but thinks the realist should do better; Kulp (2017, 3–7) agrees that Moorean arguments have merit.

The earliest Moorean moral realist argument known to me is that of Ewing (1947), 30. I owe the reference to Olson (2014).

(Ga) If there are moral facts, then there is objective prescriptivity.
(Gb) There is no such thing as objective prescriptivity.
∴ (Gc) There are no moral facts.

Assuming (Gc) is taken to entail that it was not in the least wrong for Hitler to exterminate 6 million people, the Moorean will simply, and correctly, reject either (Ga) or (Gb), depending on what is meant by the technical term "objective prescriptivity" (and possibly on some substantive philosophical disagreement). But what if we were to travel 500 years back in time and try, in the same way, to convince people that there are no witches?[15] Would our hearers not simply turn (a)–(c) on its head—or, less drastically, just refuse to grant (b), since "There is magic" had considerable credibility for them?

To offer a (proto-)Moorean argument in support of magic via witches, one would have to have and deploy a common, everyday belief entailing the existence of a witch. The fact would have to be as obvious/credible and as universally generalizable all over the world as "Here is a hand" or "I had lunch five minutes ago." Could anyone really and legitimately have found "That woman there is a witch" (where again being a witch requires magic powers) as credible as one of those? I doubt it, but it might have happened, even on a large scale. If it did, then, yes, at that time it would have been just as reasonable to believe in magic. (In the sixteenth century, it may actually have been anyway, and empirically so.)

IV

Tristram McPherson (2009) directly addresses moral Mooreanism and my main question in particular; indeed the project of his paper is the same as mine in this one, except that it considers only error theories. His conclusion is contrary to mine: that whether or not Moore's strategy ultimately works against idealists and skeptics, it is at best significantly less effective against metaethical eliminativists and error theorists.

He begins by focusing on what I have been calling a credibility comparison, and, cued by a quote from Moore's "Four Forms of Scepticism,"[16] he construes that notion in terms of degrees of certainty. He understands "certainty" psychologically, as a degree of confidence. Since psychological confidence does not perfectly track normative epistemic status, McPherson understands confidence as "defeasible *indirect* evidence of the truth of a claim" (5, italics original). Indeed he says it is one of five "*generic indicators of epistemic quality*[,] ... features the presence or absence of which would, other things being equal, reasonably lead us to raise or lower our estimation of how well supported that

---

[15] Thanks to Paul Bloomfield for enforcing the comparison in this way.
[16] "I cannot help answering: It seems to me *more* certain that I *do* know that this is a pencil and that you are conscious, than that any single one of these four assumptions is true, let alone all four. . . " (1959/1962, 222).

proposition is" (6). (These include such factors as how drastic it would be to eliminate the proposition from our belief systems, and the availability of "debunking" or deflationary explanations of our holding the belief.) He then goes on to evaluate a belief with respect to a given indicator in terms of traditional epistemic criteria such as reliability (8) and coherence (5).

This is a novel, ingenious and useful interpretation of Moore, but it is not my interpretation, and so McPherson is not addressing Moorean refutation as I conceive it. (N.b., that is not per se an objection.[17] Nor am I faulting McPherson's argument against the particular Moorean he has constructed.) The main differences between his Moorean and mine are (a) that what I call "credibility" is not a psychological magnitude like confidence, but a normative epistemic property of propositions, and (b) that for me "credibility" is an internalist notion, not externalist in any way at all. Under forced choice, *should* I believe that I have hands or, instead, that every existent thing has proper parts that are substances (McTaggart 1921, with the implication that everything is infinitely divisible)? I submit that I (normatively) should prefer the former.[18] The *explanation of why* I should prefer that is a task for epistemological theory and will be controversial, but it is no part of the argument. Now, it is theoretically possible that hordes of people will not share my normative intuition, and will exclaim," *Of course* every existent thing has proper parts that are substances—gosh, too bad for hands"; but I think that is terminally unlikely.

Each of the features I have mentioned, (a) and (b), needs further explanation.[19] (a): A degree of credibility is a property of a proposition (in a context; obviously we can make up scenarios in which the same proposition would have had a very different credibility rating). The proposition epistemically-should, to degree n, be believed. For McPherson, the corresponding property is: *being* believed with n degree of confidence. As we have seen, he goes on to treat that psychological property as a sign or *indicator of* "epistemic quality," a feature which would "reasonably lead us to raise or lower" our epistemic esteem for the proposition. And so, naturally, he considers the property alongside and in conjunction with other signs and indicators, and assesses each in terms of reliability as well as coherence. Which brings us to difference (b).

By "internalist" I mean what epistemologists standardly do: roughly, that a justification does not depend on worldly factors external to the subject, and (normally) the subject can tell from the inside that it obtains. McPherson's notion of credibility is unequivocally and necessarily externalist; he has to *assess* degrees-of-confidence considered as merely signs of epistemic value, in terms of reliability and such properties that are

---

[17] Moore himself offered no single coherent version of his technique, and many of its instances are, as written, ineffective for one reason or another; I could never say that McPherson or any other commentator has misinterpreted Moore. And there are other externalist interpretations, most notably Sosa's (1999).

[18] Immediately following the passage McPherson has quoted, reproduced here in fn 16, Moore adds, "Nay more: I do not think it is *rational* to be as certain of any one of these four propositions, as of the proposition that I do know that this is a pencil. . . ." (1959/1962, 222, italics original).

[19] Each of the volume editors has gently assured me of this.

external to them. I do not. A normative epistemic intuition is what it is, regardless of considerations that would have to be investigated from the external viewpoint.

(Now, some philosophers are skeptical about intuitions considered as evidence or as otherwise justifying epistemological judgments; indeed, some are skeptical even of logical and syntactic intuitions. But that is a different issue, and a much larger one. I have addressed it at length elsewhere.[20] And, n.b., we are talking about epistemological intuitions, not moral intuitions.)

Even assuming you respect epistemological intuitions generally, you may naturally feel that a bare normative intuition of my comparative sort, involving beliefs with specific, substantive contents, has little weight, and hold that more support of some sort is called for. But remember, what is easy to forget: Credibility comparisons of exactly that sort are *presupposed* by every deductive argument put forward on any topic whatever. To accept a deductive argument is at least tacitly to *have judged* that each of its premises is more credible than is the denial of its conclusion. Credibility comparison in my sense is epistemologically more fundamental than deductive argumentation itself.

(Lest that claim seem extravagant: It falls directly out of stage (2) of Moore's technique as expounded in Section II, the familiar point that "one person's Modus Ponens is another's Modus Tollens."[21] In fact, I believe it is nearly tautologous. Consider an "argument" just as a list of propositions, that starts with one or more suppositions and validly deduces a particular logical consequence. Nothing yet tells us whether that list is a proof of the consequence or a reductio of one of the assumptions. In fact, even if its author tells us it will be used as a reductio, that does not yet tell us which assumption is refuted if there are two or more.

The "argument" considered just as an unadorned list does not presuppose a credibility comparison; the propositions are just sitting there. By "argument*ation*" in my claim of presupposition I meant a *use* of the list either to justify the consequence taken as a proven conclusion, or to be an indirect proof of the falsity of one of the premises. One cannot be justified in accepting all the premises and the conclusion unless that is more reasonable than denying the conclusion and at least one of the premises. It is in that sense of "argumentation" that argumentation presupposes a credibility comparison.)

Olson (2014) addresses the Moorean strategy, and like McPherson he grants that Moore's point is credibility-comparative. Moreover, he seems to join me in understanding credibility as a normative property of propositions, so his version of Moore includes (a) above. But either he departs in the matter of (b), and assumes his Moorean opponent is an externalist rather than internalist, or he makes an illicit move.

---

[20] Lycan (2019), Chs. 7 and 8. I defend the epistemic value of intuitions generally and normative intuitions in particular. Further, I argue for internalism as regards their justificatory force, concluding: "I have no rational or dialectical obligation to show that any of my [intuitions or spontaneous] beliefs is externally connected to truth, or that they are probable in the Kolmogorov and/or Bayesian sense, or that I have any extraneous special entitlement to hold them" (125). (To insist that I do have such an obligation is simply to beg the question in favor of a competing epistemological theory.)

[21] I.e., again, that any deductive argument can be turned on its head. I do not know who first put it in "Ponens/Tollens" terms; I believe I first heard that slogan from the late John Haugeland.

His objection to the Moorean argument is based on the availability of debunking explanations: for reasons pointed out by many,[22] there is strong evolutionary pressure for human beings to hold moral beliefs. Of course there is, and the moral realist will hardly deny that; but the fact is in itself neutral as between the beliefs' truth and falsity. How does it actually debunk, i.e., reduce the credibility of our judgments about Alan, Hitler, and the hoodlums? Olson moves toward addressing that on 146–48, but he gives no explicit answer, because at this point his target seems to be the non-naturalist ("irreducibly normative properties and facts").[23] He observes that if there is a plausible evolutionary explanation, we should not draw "ontological conclusions" *from* our confident moral judgments, and he appeals to Occam's Razor vs. non-natural properties; but neither of those points affects our simple credibility comparisons.

At one point he mentions truth-tracking, though only in regard to the epistemological value of parsimony and not directly as applying to moral beliefs. Other debunkers, notably Street (2006), have suggested that an evolutionary explanation of our holding strong moral beliefs diminishes the likelihood that those beliefs (even naturalistically understood) track truth. Which may be so, but is a reliabilist consideration. So far as Olson's target Moorean is an internalist regarding the credibility that figures in deductive argumentation, this kind of externalist debunking objection would beg the question.[24]

V

It surely will be objected that in putting forward my moral bromides (i)–(iii) as obvious truths, I have simply begged the question against expressivist and other views that deny that moral judgments have a fact-stating function at all. But remember that my present argument is directed solely against error theorists who grant, indeed insist, that moral judgments are factual in nature and ascribe putatively real properties to actions and states of affairs. I have not begged the question against the error theorist. Of course s/he has the option of challenging my factualist/descriptivist/cognitivist

---

[22] Hauser (2006), Street (2006), Joyce (2006), Churchland (2011), among others.

[23] He has argued in his Ch. 6 that non-naturalist moral beliefs would be evolutionarily more advantageous than ontologically neutral ones.

[24] As in the concluding paragraph of Section II above, my Moorean strategy is decisive only against direct, deductive antirealist arguments such as (here) Mackie's or Garner's. I cannot rule out the possibility of a very wide reflective equilibrium, incorporating facts about human nature and human psychology along with strong and widely shared intuitions of one or more kinds, that by superior explanatory coherence would trump moral realism and justify the view that everything is morally permitted. And there is where debunking explanations properly come in: All philosophy rests ultimately on intuitive judgments. And every intuition is fallible. For purposes of explanatory coherence, we cannot just reject an intuition without explaining it away; but even the strongest intuition on any topic (including formal logic) could, in principle, be explained away.

presupposition. But that would be to abandon error theory and switch to a different species of moral antirealism.

Well, then: Allowing such a change of subject, how does the Moorean fare against out-and-out, naïve Emotivism such as Ayer's (as opposed to a fictionalism or quasi-realism that is expressivist or otherwise nonfactualist at bottom)?

Ayer's position was that a moral judgment merely evinces or expresses the speaker's normative attitude and does nothing else. If I were to say to him that Alan ought to keep his promise, Hitler committed monstrous acts, and the hoodlums were very wrong to torture the kitty, he would presumably agree in the sense of verbally assenting and sincerely so, but that would do nothing to embarrass his Emotivism. Were I to persist and insist that it is a *fact*, dammit, that Alan ought to keep his promise, just as it is a fact that Alan made the promise, I would then be begging the question. So far as I can see, the Moorean strategy has no force against the pure noncognitivist.

The same point supports the prescriptivist (Hare 1952), who agrees that moral judgments are not statements of fact but maintains that they are more like imperatives or directives than like mere expressions of attitude.

VI

There are further antirealisms, which are variously intermediate in that they grant truth-values to moral judgments but only in variously deflationary or scare-quoted or backhanded ways. I shall consider intermediate views of three types: truth-pluralist views according to which moral judgments are true but not in the same correspondence or otherwise robust sense of "true" as are ordinary factual statements; fictionalisms based on error theories; and fictionalisms based neither on error theories nor on antecedent noncognitivisms.

There are many truth-pluralist views, depending on what less-than-robust notion of truth gets assigned to moral judgments: Michael Lynch's (2009) "super-coherence," and any of a number of "deflationary" or "minimalist" types of truth. (Of course, many proponents of coherence conceptions and various deflationary notions have offered those as theories of *all* truth, truth per se; the pluralist I have in mind selectively distinguishes moral judgments from straightforwardly factual nonmoral statements by assigning *them* a debased sort of truth-value.) The antirealists of this broad category are multifarious, and to discuss all or even one of them would require a digression into the contested nature of truth. For purposes of this chapter I shall simply concede that a Moorean argument is unlikely to succeed against any truth-pluralist view, for much the same reason as it will not against the pure noncognitivist: the truth pluralist will agree not only that Alan ought to show up, etc., but that it is true that Alan ought to show up. For me to protest "No, I don't mean just 'true,' I mean *really true*," or "There are real obligation properties in the world," would beg the question. It would also be philosophical rather than Moorean.

Let us turn to fictionalisms.

VII

There are many kinds of fictionalism, especially if they are not distinguished from pretense theories. I shall not enforce the finer distinctions here.

Sainsbury (2010) makes the fairly obvious point that "the starting point for fictionalism is some kind of ontological scruple" (2). No one goes fictionalist about a subject-matter unless s/he sees some fairly heavy obstacle to realism about that domain. (Though of course one could maintain a watching *at-least*-fictionalism, pending resolution of the ontological scruple.) So as a Moorean I can expect some surface camaraderie though with a mental reservation behind it.

On the face of things, the fictionalist's rebuttal of the Moorean attack will be like the noncognitivist's and the truth-pluralist's: I insist that Hitler's actions were hideously wrong, and the fictionalist enthusiastically agrees. To prosecute the objection, I would have to say, "No, I'm making a genuine and literal factual assertion," or "No, I don't mean just according to the 'morality' script, I mean really," and I would thereby both beg the question against the antirealist and start talking philosophy instead of stiffarming philosophy.[25] That is especially clear if my opponent's fictionalism is based on an underlying expressivism rather than on an error theory, for that opponent will never grant that my Moorean judgment is a genuine and nonfictional assertion.

But what of the error-theoretic fictionalist, who agrees that moral judgments are factual and truth-valued, maintaining that they are factually false but fictionally true? At this point we must respect one of the main taxonomic boundaries, that between "revolutionary" or revisionary and "hermeneutic" or descriptive.[26] The revisionary fictionalist (Joyce 2005) is a forthright error theorist, but for obvious social and practical reasons recommends making moral judgments, to others and to oneself, respecting them as if

---

[25] David Copp has reminded me that there could still be a useful credibility faceoff, so we should not be too quick to plead guilty to question-begging. (As I said in presenting my own version of Moore's strategy, there is no special sacred category of "commonsense" propositions, alone available for credibility comparison.) Suppose I do confront the fictionalist with "Torturing helpless cats is wrong *and not in any stupid fictional sense either*." Now, some linguistic claims can have huge credibility, with Moorean trumping power: "Glory" does not mean *a nice knockdown argument*; "So foul and fair a day I have not seen" has ten words. (Suppose Alan later explains "I'm a fictionalist about 'watching.' When I said 'I'll watch your children for you,' in my speech that means that I was going to lie in my own bed at home drinking gin and spend two seconds trying to remember your children's names."—No, no. "Watch" does not mean lying in bed . . .) So I continue my pronouncement to the fictionalist: "'Wrong' does not mean just 'disapproved of by my mother' or 'bad manners in our society' or 'would make most people feel guilty' or whatever deflationary thing you're using it to mean, it means *wrong*." Whether or not that response succeeds in refuting the fictionalist—I do not think it is strong—it does not beg the question.

[26] The "hermeneutic"/"revolutionary" terminology as applied to fictionalism comes from Stanley (2001), but goes back to Burgess (1983).

they were true, and living accordingly. Joyce concedes that this will take some deliberate self-deception or at least self-management. So when I make my judgment about Alan, or Hitler or the hoodlums, to that fictionalist, say to Joyce himself, he will agree, but only to the extent that his self-management is holding on that particular day. And if we are in the philosophy seminar room (Joyce 2003 speaks of "critical contexts"), he will not, because what he really believes is that my judgments are factually false.

It does not follow that revisionary fictionalism is refuted by the Moorean strategy, for so long as Joyce's will is strong, he will stoutly agree with my rock-solid moral judgments, and he may be quite sincere at the time. But the strategy does undercut the revisionist's motivation: there is no longer any reason to be a fictionalist. If you were an error theorist to begin with, you are refuted in the philosophy room, and so (unless you quickly switch to a different species of antirealism) you can join in the moral judgments with a whole heart.

VIII

Hermeneutic or descriptive moral fictionalism is a little hard to pin down. I know of only one professed hermeneutic fictionalist, Kalderon (2005), and he is a pretense theorist.[27]

At least as I use the term, pretense theories are illocutionary, not semantic.[28] The idea is that the speaker who utters a declarative sentence of the type at issue is not really making an assertion but only seems to be, and (normally) does not believe what the sentence literally means. That is Kalderon's view of moral judgments. Out-loud verbal judgments, that is; though he takes moral sentences as "representational," factual and truth-valued, he is noncognitivist about the mental states from which they arise, for he argues at length against the existence of moral beliefs. The speaker is only pretending to believe what s/he says.

Kalderon's view faces a dilemma. As I have described it so far, nothing distinguishes Kalderon from the revisionary fictionalist. The utterer of a moral judgment does not believe what s/he is saying but is only pretending to. (Why, then, is the speech act only a quasi-assertion, rather than an insincere assertion?) That is the dilemma's first horn. And on it, Kalderon would be refuted, or rather undercut, by Moore.

---

[27] That may be why van Roojen (2015), a textbook, considers *only* Kalderon's pretense theory under the section heading "Hermeneutic Fictionalism..." (177–90).

[28] See, e.g., Kripke (1972/2012) on fictional names. To my knowledge, Kripke's view is the first contemporary pretense theory of a subject-matter, though later, Walton (1990) set off a vogue for such theories of various linguistic phenomena, such as irony and metaphor.

Van Roojen (2015) unfortunately makes it true by definition that a hermeneutic fictionalism is not semantic (178). Since there are many semantic fictionalisms in philosophy, let us not follow him in that. (And by contrast, Olson seems to regard pretense theories as eo ipso revisionary fictionalisms (2014), 182.)

So, wherein is Kalderon's fictionalism hermeneutic, as he insists it is? The idea seems to be that speakers have internalized the fiction, and the pretending has become so automatic that they do not realize they are engaged in pretense. It is "an unwitting pretense" (152). We are "not always fully transparent" to ourselves (154).

As has been remarked by many (e.g., Joyce 2012, van Roojen 2015), the claim of *unwitting* pretense is very hard to swallow.[29] But that is not our concern here. Plausible or not, Kalderon's view as he intends it is unscathed by Moore.

Let us move on to types of fiction that are semantic: (1) Logicogrammatical "fictions" in the Russellian sense. E.g., superficially definite descriptions that are obviously not singular referring terms, the classic example of such being "the average homeowner": competent users do not ask "What is his name? Could you introduce me to him?" Likewise, "The student who can prove Smullyan's conjecture would be a better logician than anyone I know." But such do not merit an "-alism." (2) Iconic references to fictional characters, the classic example being Santa Claus as in "What did Santa bring you this year?," are understood as fictional and fictionalism is true of them. (Here too it would sound a bit funny to say, "I am a fictionalist about Santa Claus," though only because adult realists regarding that Christmas figure are rare.) (3) In science there are fictions of various sorts, in the form of ideal entities such as frictionless planes, idealizing assumptions as in the reduction of thermodynamics to statistical mechanics, and the propounding of laws known to be only approximations. (4) Linguistic relics of old commonsensical views long discredited by science, such as talk of the sun's rising and traveling across the sky, or for that matter of the sky as a canopy that turns various colors.

But in each of these cases, only people ignorant of the relevant subject-matter take the fictional assertions strictly and literally. Consider a Lewis-Carroll-style naïf who really does take a known fiction literally. Could that person launch a Moorean attack? Agatha says: "For every parent P, the number of P's children is an integer." Buddy responds, "Haha, you're wrong, because the average American homeowner is a parent and has exactly 2.37 children!" Buddy has not refuted Agatha, because Buddy has misunderstood his own sentence, apparently just not knowing what "average" means.

A better comparison might be with a descriptive fictionalism about mathematics. I am uncertain whether anyone holds such a view; the best-known broadly-speaking fictionalists about mathematics, e.g., Field (1980), are revisionaries, though perhaps Yablo (1998, 2001) is a descriptivist. In any case, even if apparent quantifications over numbers are fictions and really do not semantically entail objectual quantification over

---

[29] There may be such a thing, either a kind of self-deception or a strange introspective blindness, but the idea that it is universal or at least the norm borders on fantasy. Ordinary people engaged in moral dispute or just moral pronouncement would never doubt that they believe what they are saying.

Moreover, to adapt a nice point of Joshua Gert's (2002): If a whole generation of unwitting pretenders brings up its children to use moral language in the ordinary way we all do, and (of course) do not tell the children that the seeming assertions are only pretend, that next generation and succeeding ones will certainly just *make* the assertions and fall into factual error.

numbers, mathematicians, who do know the subject-matter!, do not know that, and would be in the position of Buddy above, misunderstanding their own utterances.

Hermeneutical or descriptive fictionalists are not refuted by Moore. The real question is whether there really are any hermeneutical semantic moral fictionalists. I can make up a halfway plausible descriptive-fictionalist view: It would be a sort of ossified Divine Command theory. We speak of moral "laws" and of what morality "demands." Occasionally we hear "God'll get you for that." Moral language (as is, not just treated that way) is the language of laws and a lawgiver.[30] Over centuries, the literal usage just leached out and is gone. But it is now still metaphorical rather than literal, so harmlessly fictional and not subject to factual error as alleged by atheists.[31] This fictionalist of course endorses our judgments about Alan, Hitler, and the hoodlums, and so Moore's technique is ineffective.

IX

Conclusion: Moore's technique works against error theories and antirealisms based on underlying error theories, but only against those. At least it does not seem to work against any other moral antirealism.

You may not agree that Moore succeeds even against error theories. I do not know how many philosophers today side with Moore against Bradley and McTaggart, though certainly more do than in the 1970s. If your quarrel is with Moore generally, I respectfully refer you to Chs. 1 and 2 of Lycan (2019). If you agree that Moore refuted the idealists but balk at my argument against error theories in metaethics, then I would like to hear what you take to be the key difference.[32]

References

Anscombe, G. E. M. 1958. "Modern Moral Philosophy." *Philosophy* 33(124): 1–19.
Baumann, Peter. 2009. "Was Moore a Moorean? On Moore and Scepticism." *European Journal of Philosophy* 17(2): 181–200.
Blackburn, Simon. 1993. *Essays in Quasi-Realism*. Oxford: Oxford University Press.
Bloomfield, Paul. 2001. *Moral Reality*. Oxford: Oxford University Press.

---

[30] Anscombe (1958) argued specifically against claims of obligation on the ground that they presuppose a lawgiver.

[31] That last, of course, is grievously implausible; because even if at some stage the moral language had turned metaphorical, more recently the metaphor has itself gradually died, and now has its altered meaning literally.

[32] This chapter has been greatly improved by extensive discussion with the volume editors. I am more than usually grateful to each of them for his time, effort, and insight.

Burgess, John, 1983. "Why I Am Not a Nominalist." *Notre Dame Journal of Formal Logic* 24(1): 93–105.
Chrisman, Matthew. 2016. *The Meaning of "Ought": Beyond Descriptivism and Expressivism in Metaethics*. Oxford: Oxford University Press.
Churchland, Paul M. 1981. "Eliminative Materialism and the Propositional Attitudes." *Journal of Philosophy* 78(2): 67–90.
Churchland, Patricia S. 2011. *Braintrust*. Princeton: Princeton University Press.
Enoch, David. 2011. *Taking Morality Seriously*. Oxford: Oxford University Press.
Ewing, A.C. 1947. *The Definition of Good*. London: Routledge and Kegan Paul.
Field, Hartry. 1980. *Science without Numbers*. Princeton: Princeton University Press.
Garner, Richard T. 1990. "On the Genuine Queerness of Moral Properties and Facts." *Australasian Journal of Philosophy* 68(2): 137–146.
Garner, Richard T. 1994. *Beyond Morality*. Philadelphia: Temple University Press.
Gert, Joshua. 2002. "Expressivism and Language Learning." *Ethics* 112(2): 292–314.
Greco, John. 2002. "How to Reid Moore." *Philosophical Quarterly* 52(209): 544–563.
Hare, Richard M. 1952. *The Language of Morals*. Oxford: Oxford University Press.
Harman, Gilbert. 1977. *The Nature of Morality*. New York: Oxford University Press.
Harman, Gilbert. 2015. "Moral Relativism Is Moral Realism." *Philosophical Studies* 172(4): 855–863.
Hauser, Marc D. 2006. *Moral Minds: How Nature Designed Our Universal Sense of Right and Wrong*. New York: Harper Collins.
Huemer, Michael. 2005. *Ethical Intuitionism*. Basingstoke: Palgrave Macmillan.
Joyce, Richard. 2003. *The Myth of Morality*. Cambridge: Cambridge University Press.
Joyce, Richard. 2005. "Moral Fictionalism." In *Fictionalism in Metaphysics*, edited by Mark Eli Kalderon, 287–313. Oxford: Clarendon Press.
Joyce, Richard. 2006. *The Evolution of Morality*. Cambridge, MA: MIT Press.
Joyce, Richard. 2012. "Review of Kalderon, M.E., *Moral Fictionalism*." *Philosophy and Phenomenological Research* 85(1): 161–173.
Kalderon, Mark Eli. 2005. *Moral Fictionalism*. Oxford: Oxford University Press.
Kelly, Thomas. 2005. "Moorean Facts and Belief Revision, or Can the Sceptic Win?" *Philosophical Perspectives* 19: 179–209.
Kripke, Saul A. 1972/2012. "Vacuous Names and Fictional Entities." In *Philosophical Troubles: Collected Papers*, vol. 1, 52–74. Oxford: Oxford University Press. (Originally delivered at the 1972 Oberlin Colloquium in Philosophy under the title "Vacuous Names and Mythical Kinds.")
Kulp, Christopher. 2017. *Knowing Moral Truth*. Lanham, MD: Lexington Books.
Lemos, Noah. 2004. *Common Sense: A Contemporary Defense*. Cambridge: Cambridge University Press.
Lukes, Steven. 2008. *Moral Relativism*. London: Profile Books.
Lycan, William G. 1986. "Moral Facts and Moral Knowledge." *Southern Journal of Philosophy* 2(Suppl.): 79–94.
Lycan, William G. 2001. "Moore against the New Skeptics." *Philosophical Studies* 103(1): 35–53.
Lycan, William G. 2005. "A Particularly Compelling Refutation of Eliminative Materialism." In *Mind as a Scientific Object: Between Brain and Culture*, edited by D. M. Johnson and C. E. Erneling, 197–205. Oxford: Oxford University Press.
Lycan, William G. 2007. "Moore's Antiskeptical Strategies." In *Themes from G.E. Moore: New Essays in Epistemology and Ethics*, edited by S. Nuccetelli and G. Seay, 84–99. Oxford: Oxford University Press.

Lycan, William G. 2018. "Garner and Objective Prescriptivity." MS, University of Connecticut.
Lycan, William G. 2019. *On Evidence in Philosophy*. Oxford: Oxford University Press.
Lynch, Michael Patrick. 2009. *Truth as One and Many*. Oxford: Oxford University Press.
Mackie, John L. 1977. *Ethics: Inventing Right and Wrong*. New York: Penguin Books.
McPherson, Tristram. 2009. "Moorean Arguments and Moral Revisionism." *Journal of Ethics and Social Philosophy* 3(2): 1–24.
McTaggart, J. M. E. 1908. "The Unreality of Time." *Mind* 68(4): 457–474.
McTaggart, J. M. E. 1921. *The Nature of Existence*. Vol. 1. Cambridge: Cambridge University Press.
Milo, Ronald. 1995. "Contractarian Constructivism." *Journal of Philosophy* 92(4): 181–204.
Moore, G. E. 1953/1962. *Some Main Problems of Philosophy*. New York: Collier Books. Originally published in London by George Allen & Unwin.
Moore, G. E. 1959/1962. *Philosophical Papers*. New York: Collier Books. Originally published in London by George Allen & Unwin.
Moore, G. E. 1968. *Philosophical Studies*. Totowa, NJ: Littlefield, Adams & Co.
Olson, Jonas. 2014. *Moral Error Theory: History, Critique, Defence*. Oxford: Oxford University Press.
Pryor, James. 2004. "What's Wrong with Moore's Argument?" *Philosophical Issues* 14: 349–378.
Rowland, Richard. 2013. "Moral Error Theory and the Argument from Epistemic Reasons." *Journal of Ethics and Social Philosophy* 7(1): 1–24.
Sainsbury, R. M. 2010. *Fiction and Fictionalism*. London: Routledge.
Shafer-Landau, Russ. 2003. *Moral Realism: A Defence*. Oxford: Oxford University Press.
Smart, J. J. C. 1959. "Sensations and Brain Processes." *Philosophical Review* 68(2): 141–156.
Sosa, Ernest. 1999. "How to Defeat Opposition to Moore." *Philosophical Perspectives* 13: 141–153.
Stanley, Jason. 2001. "Hermeneutic Fictionalism." In *Midwest Studies in Philosophy*, vol. 25: *Figurative Language*, edited by Peter French and Howard Wettstein, 36–71. Oxford: Basil Blackwell.
Street, Sharon. 2006. "A Darwinian Dilemma for Realist Theories of Value." *Philosophical Studies* 127(1): 109–166.
Streumer, Bart. 2013. "Can We Believe the Error Theory?" *Journal of Philosophy* 110(4): 194–212.
Van Roojen, Mark. 2015. *Metaethics: A Contemporary Introduction*. New York: Routledge.
Walton, Kendall. 1990. *Mimesis as Make-Believe*. Cambridge, MA: Harvard University Press.
Yablo, Stephen. 1998. "Does Ontology Rest on a Mistake?" *Proceedings of the Aristotelian Society* Suppl. 72: 229–261.
Yablo, Stephen. 2001. "Go Figure: A Path through Fictionalism." In *Midwest Studies in Philosophy*, vol. 25: *Figurative Language*, edited by Peter French and Howard Wettstein, 72–102. Oxford: Basil Blackwell.

CHAPTER 9

REAL ETHICS

SIMON BLACKBURN

> We remain unconscious of the prodigious diversity of all the everyday language-games because the clothing of our language makes everything alike.
> —Wittgenstein 1953 Pt. II, XI, p. 224

1. GLIMMERINGS

My engagement with issues about realism predated my real introduction to philosophy, which only started when I went up to Cambridge. For while I was still at school, wrapped up in Mathematics, Physics, and Chemistry, a master gave me G. E. Moore's *Principia Ethica* to read, hoping no doubt to create a veneer of culture that might deceive Cambridge's interviewers. I there read Moore's argument that beauty cannot lie in the eye of the beholder, for we can readily imagine a beautiful scene to which nobody is a witness, or equally imagine an unseen ugly wasteland. I immediately felt, and tried to convince anyone who would listen, that although Moore was right that we do not suppose the beauty or ugliness of a scene to vary with whether we also suppose there to be any actual observer of it, this was nevertheless a rotten argument. For as I observed we do not escape the deliverances of our own aesthetic sensibilities as we perform these acts of imagination, and this is surely enough to support the idea that beauty is, as it were, down to us, lying in the eye or at any rate the imagination of the beholder. It was only much later that I learned that Berkeley's spokesman Philonous makes the identical reply to Hylas, in the service of a more wide-ranging idealism.

I suppose that two traits that have stayed with me were already visible here in embryonic form, perhaps vindicating William James's view that often our philosophies are a matter of temperament as much as argument. One was a scientist's ambition to explain things, and a belief that we wouldn't properly understand aesthetics without paying attention to human psychology and its variations. The second trait was a lurking sympathy with the antirealist side of things, at least in this case, where attention to our psychology seemed to offer more in the way of explanatory promise than Moore could. I later hoped to reconcile this with what was right in Moore, in the character of the quasi-realist, who tried to help antirealism, in the forms that it had principally taken in discussions of ethics, modals, probability and conditionals. I now somewhat regret the term "quasi-realism," largely because I now think that "realism" has diversified, diluted, and dissipated enough to lose any utility as a landmark, and I shall try to explain why in what follows.

2. Flavors of Realism

For the first twenty years or so of my life in professional philosophy, I thought it was reasonably clear what was meant by realism in ethics. The essential point was that realism was to be a theory *about* ethics. It purported to clarify or explain some salient feature of ethical discourse. It seized on features of our thought and talk that apparently demanded this metatheory to explain them. It was only later that this became doubtful, for reasons I shall go on to describe. But let us first explore this starting point.

The leading image behind realism, in connection with ethics, mathematics, possible worlds, probabilities, and other contested areas is simple enough. It is that what we say or believe is made true, when it is, by the way the world is. Realism is the idea that there is something that needs to exist to make up or constitute this. As we describe this something we can be right or wrong about it, just as we can be right or wrong as we talk about chairs and rocks. We are right or wrong according to whether this part of reality answers to our descriptions of it. It is often added that this reality is independent of us, in the sense that how we think about it does not affect it (this does not imply that our ethical judgments about a situation are independent of the states of mind of persons in that situation). The independence in question can be put by insisting that discussion and thought is aimed at discovery rather than invention. Or it is sometimes insisted that there are objective moral reasons that bear on people whether or not they take any notice of them. Their subjective states are one thing, but the objective reasons another. It might be thought that it is this objective correlate that puts beef or biff or backbone into our subjective states. A major task of philosophy, indeed its fundamental task, is to understand the nature of these realities, and then the nature of our knowledge of them.

What was right in Moore was his distinction between two directions such an investigation might take. It might classify the reality in question as just some part of the familiar natural world—the world that is open to us through empirical observation and scientific theory. If we know everything about the natural world, then our knowledge also embraces ethics. This has the advantage that ethical reality is nothing but a part of the natural world. Unfortunately, Moore argued, it does this by failing to recognize that however full our description of the natural world might be, there is always a residual question, an open question. Is the natural reality we describe actually good or not? Is the behavior we describe right or not? The fact that these are always open questions suggests strongly that we have to go beyond mere descriptions of how things are in their natural respects, in order to settle questions of value. A comprehensive description of a situation might suggest an ethical verdict—what else could do so? But it does not itself contain any such verdict, for it is never contradictory to admit the description but dissent from the verdict.

Sticking with the realistic starting point, this drove Moore to supposing that morality must instead answer to something else, a different way the world is, made by the "non-natural" properties of things.[1] Having established this to his satisfaction Moore unfortunately had to remain embarrassingly silent about what these non-natural properties were. He suggested they would be known by "intuition," but couldn't fill the term with any detail, for since they lie outside the causal networks of the natural world, they lie beyond sense experience as well. And he also couldn't explain why on earth we would care about them. His problem was in effect one that beset Plato. Plato offered the famous Myth of the Cave to suggest how the person who is to know the Good has to struggle from the darkness of the cave up to the light, where eventually he or she can look directly at the sun itself, the giver of light and warmth and life. The vision has a celestial, otherworldly object, but Plato offers no way of connecting the metaphor of the sun as an object of sight with mundane problems and their moral solutions. Nor does he offer any help in understanding how the heroes who achieve the vision do any better than anyone else when they return to the cave to communicate with and perhaps help the benighted souls who were unable to journey to the light.

So the dilemma Moore bequeathed to realism in ethics was to choose between naturalism, mundane, familiar, but wrong, and non-naturalism, strange, spooky, inviting more questions than it answered, yet apparently compulsory.

Both these views, naturalism and non-naturalism or "intuitionism," share the realism, supposing that there is some part of reality—the ethical part—that it is the task of good ethics to describe truly. As we think about simple descriptions of our sensory environments, we are familiar with, and happy with, the chairs and tables and rocks of which we speak. If there were no such things, there would be no facts about them, and no truths about them to voice. If we are to be similarly content speaking of moral properties, or referring to such things as rights, duties, or values, we must stand by the analogy to physical space and its denizens. It is just that we may have to expand our conception of the environment we inhabit. In connection with ethics, we either need moral properties as well as natural ones, as intuitionism holds, or a reduction of moral properties to natural ones, finding a way past Moore's challenge.

The task I have pursued has been to uproot this realist analogy. It is the task of explaining and justifying the features of language and thought that wrongly tempted people to this view. I could never for a moment believe that confidence that it is wrong to stamp on babies for fun, or that a child's grief is a reason for sympathy, is only defensible

---

[1] For the purpose of this paper I talk of morality, ethics, and normativity interchangeably. Any differences between them do not matter to the points I hope to make.

if we acknowledge some spooky metaphysical reality lying outside and beyond the natural events of pain and grief. I feel about the choice between intuitionism and naturalism as the literary critic F. R. Leavis did in a different connection, remarking, "When people line up so promptly one suspects . . . that the differences are not of a kind that has much to do with thinking" (Leavis 1968, p. 171).

3. A Way Out

The approach I adopted, as had many writers discontent with Moore's view, was a descendant of Scottish sentimentalist theories of the eighteenth century. It was once unhappily called emotivism, and unhappily too called prescriptivism, projectivism, or noncognitivism. In its contemporary form it has dropped many of its older, misleading, connotations, and is probably best known as expressivism, although for reasons I shall come to, it might be better if that name also follows its predecessors to the grave. In any case it is primarily a theory about the nature of normative commitment. Like its Scottish ancestors it concentrates on what is done by communicating normative and evaluative judgments, and says that their function is drawn from the enormous reservoir of preferences, desires, concerns, attitudes, policies, recommendations, commitments, agreements, demands, allowances, prohibitions, and other practical stances that altogether make up our social lives. The function of ethical language and thought is to discuss, defend, and perhaps improve these building blocks of human life. Without these practical concerns, there would be no ethics, just as without the pleasures that beauty and form give, there would be no aesthetics.

Realists will complain that the sentimentalist tradition is all very well, but that it doesn't tell us what moral states of affairs *consist in*. It tells us what we do by saying that stamping on babies for fun is wrong, but it leaves us no sense of what the state of affairs, or the fact, of stamping on babies being wrong actually *is*. What is its truth-maker, the aspect of the way the world is that is responsible for this fact? What is the fact that it describes? People have similarly worried that Hume's theory of causation told us when a causal interpretation of happenings strikes us, but it did not tell us what *constituted* the relationship whereby one event necessitates another. Ramsey thought that with the language of probability and chance we discuss and refine the degrees of confidence to hold in forthcoming events, but this does not tell us what probabilities and chances *actually are*. Ryle thought that with conditionals we offer "inference tickets" licensing the move from antecedent to conclusion, but this does not give us the constitution of hypothetical *facts* (Ryle 1950). All these theories proceed instead by describing what we do as we think and speak in such terms, without getting involved in constitutive questions. This is their strength, but realists will complain that the strength is only gained by leaving out what they regard as the most important part of any adequate theory. My Moorean Cambridge teacher Casimir Lewy used to declaim against Ryle's theory that conditionals function as inference tickets, asking passionately "*Yes, but what issued these inference tickets?*". The same question, especially in connection with counterfactuals, was the major weapon deployed by realists such as David Armstrong (1983) and C. B. Martin (2008). But although it silenced his students at the time, Lewy's question has a simple enough answer. It is we who issue the inference tickets, as we observe the pattern of events, and in the light of them monitor each other's inferential movements.

Realists about ethics may feel that they alone give this constitutive task its proper place. But they will find it hard to articulate what would count as its successful execution. The Moorean alternatives are either to stay within a normative vocabulary, perhaps offering lame visual analogies like Plato, or to attempt naturalistic reductions, perhaps offering, not analyses falling foul of the Open Question argument, but rather clusters of natural properties containing such things as happiness, opportunities, freedom, health, and others, which are indeed held to be good. My problem with that is not what it gives us, but what it leaves out. What it gives us is pleasantly natural—pleasantly realistic one might say. Suppose we ask some question such as this: is the attraction of liberalism as a political theory explained by it being the *right* theory? The only possible approach is surely to list some of its natural virtues: it does better than other theories in maximizing personal safety, welfare, opportunities and freedoms. If anyone is dissatisfied in Moore's way, thinking that this still leaves it an open question whether it is right or not, it is hard to imagine anywhere else to look for an answer.

This is correct. All we can do is give as complete a list of its natural benefits as we can muster. But it is wrong to conclude that this is all there is to the matter. For it leaves us flatly referring to this cluster of natural properties that may indeed be the marks of the best political theory. But the normative guise or mode of presentation of any such cluster is left out. What is left out is the crucial implication that such-and-such a cluster is the one of which to approve, or the one that ought to be chosen or protected. Without this, ethics goes missing. The missing element is precisely that which expressivists put in the forefront (I discuss this at more length in connection with "Cornell" realism, in Blackburn 2015).

Expressivists think that the metaphysical hankering is a mistake, akin to that of hunting the Snark without any conception of what it might be, and using a map to guide you that has no points of reference but is instead a "perfect and absolute blank" (Carroll 1876, p. 16). However, we faced what has often seemed to be a formidable obstacle, and this is where quasi-realism came in. The obstacle is that the things we say in discussing ethical matters are clothed in the vocabulary of truth and falsehood, objectivity and reason. We say, for instance, that it is true, or a fact, and certainly not just a matter of opinion that it is wrong to stamp on babies for fun. And where there are truths and facts isn't it compulsory to have a view about what they consist in, or what constitutes them?

4. Creeping Minimalism?

In the good old days people knew that expressivists about ethics were supposed to evade Moore by saying that there were no moral properties, and no moral facts, so sentences expressing moral commitments did not describe or represent anything and were not even candidates for truth or falsity.

Quasi-realism was the project of showing that expressivists need not be so self-denying. It set out to show that it should be no surprise that an ethics that exists in order for us to monitor our own attitudes and those of others should take on a propositional form identical with that of other mundane commitments. The root of ethics would be as the sentimentalists had said, and the justification of our propensity for a propositional mode of expression would be the way in which it facilitates inference and reasoning. This form enabled reasoning and inference to function in normative matters as in others, and it could perfectly well end up with us saying that it is true, or a fact that, say, it is wrong to stamp on babies for fun. Or it could end up with our saying that such an activity would be deplorable or vile, and having said that we could be said to be attributing the property of deplorability or vileness to it.

A nice parallel is the way in which talking in terms of probabilities and chances facilitates discussion of appropriate betting rates or degrees of confidence in the occurrence of events. It is a pity that this approach, pioneered by Frank Ramsey and Bruno de Finetti, got tarred with the brush of "subjectivism," since while it is indeed subjects (we ourselves) who have degrees of confidence, direct evidence from frequencies and indirect evidence from scientific theories can make chances as objective as anything else. For instance, there are no two things to think about the chance of a Carbon 14 isotope decaying in approximately 5,700 years. It is very close to .5. And the chance of any one particle decaying is the same as that of any other. Any other opinion in physics is just wrong. It could not be part of a useful theory with which to meet the future (Ramsey 1929, p. 149).

Toward the end of the twentieth century the quasi-realist enterprise was aided immeasurably by the increasing popularity of deflationist or minimalist views in the philosophy of truth, and in semantic theory in general. Such views had a distinguished lineage, beginning with Frege, and common to Ramsey, Wittgenstein, and Quine. The details differ but the shared element is that if we start with an assertoric sentence, say "ducks quack" and we assent to it, it then makes no difference if we add further affirmations of truth. Thus "I believe that ducks quack" can transform into "I believe that it is true that ducks quack," "I believe that it is a fact that ducks quack," and "I believe that it is true that it is a fact that ducks quack," and so on forever, without actually affecting the content of what was said at the beginning. There is no increased depth or change of subject matter, and in fact no difference at all between the content of the first remark and the content of the last. There could at most be a difference of emphasis, as if you said "ducks quack" while shaking your fist or thumping the table.

This simple observation has profound consequences. I said in the last section that realism purports to be a theory *about* ethics and its nature—a metaethical theory, in the jargon. And it uses features of our thought and talk to motivate that theory. But now we can ask: which features? Primarily, as already mentioned, the way in which we think in terms of normative truth, or normative facts, or the ways in which these are supposed to be independent of us and in that sense objective. Now if "it is true that p" or "it is a fact that *p*" were likewise themselves remarks *about* a moral proposition, we could see the appeal of such an argument. But if, as deflationism holds, they are not such remarks, but merely ways of staying within the moral and the normative, then there is a serious mismatch between the evidence and the conclusion. According to the deflationist "It is true that *p*" or "It is a fact that *p*" are neither of them metaethical remarks, comments on the status or metaphysical make-up of the fact that *p*. So they shouldn't be taken as evidence for one theory or another attempting to tell us something about that, such as realism is.

One line, probably most prominent in the voluminous writings of the legal theorist Ronald Dworkin, was to keep the label "realist" but jettison the idea that this was a view *about* the nature of normative commitment. All that was necessary, according to Dworkin, was that you hold some normative view. If you hold that it is wrong to stamp on babies for fun, then you are a normative realist. Since all right-thinking people do think this, all right-thinking people are normative realists (Dworkin 1996). Curiously, although all expressivists have shared this first-order thought—all of us disapprove of stamping on babies for fun—Dworkin nevertheless fulminated against expressivism, identifying it with skepticism or perhaps nihilism, this being the view that there are actually no obligations, duties, rights, or values. But the sentimentalist tradition has had few nihilists in its ranks (Ayer 1936, Chapter 6, being the embarrassing exception). In fact nihilism is much more likely to be a consequence of a metaethical realism when that takes one of the Moorean or Platonic forms, and then honestly confronting the unfortunate fact that the quest for a credible metaphysics collapses, subsides into error theory and skepticism (Mackie 1977).

It is now over thirty years since I began to worry whether the triumphant quasi-realist would better be called a queasy realist, for if Dworkin were right the label of realism is there for free, for all of us (Blackburn 1986, 1993). In the years following, the idea has gained considerable momentum. As soon as you say, for instance, that you ought not to stamp on babies for fun you are committed to there being moral truths and moral facts, for by deflationism or minimalism "it is true that *p*" and "it is a fact that *p*" are simple implications of *p* itself. And similarly for moral properties, and, as the minimalist tide rises, the claim that we describe them, represent them, and believe in them. However this would scarcely be a victory for realists in the old debate, since in that debate realism was a theory *about* the nature of ethics. But under the deflationist dispensation such prized sayings as "there are real moral facts and truths" amount to no more than elementary implications of first-order theses that nobody except perhaps fictionalists, error theorists, or nihilists queried. There was therefore no real ". . . ism" left in "realism"—no theory about normativity and its epistemology and no successful search for something that normative relations "consist in." Any trophies realists won this way are made of tin rather than silver.

As the deflationist tide rose, the negative theses that characterized expressivism in the good old days were to be jettisoned, and, as Jamie Dreier noticed in a landmark paper, the good old days mostly went with them (Dreier 2004). According to Dworkin this was not to be regretted, since there were never really any metaethical issues at stake. According to others we might be able to cling on to some kind of litmus test, such as a thick, theory-laden conception of real belief, whereby moral commitments could be said not to be real beliefs (Jackson, Oppy, and Smith 1994). But no such suggestion caught on, for after all, "beliefs" in any ordinary sense were as wide ranging as other propositional attitudes, covering conditionals, necessities, probability statements, or moral commitments without evident strain.

I was flattered that in his paper Dreier talked of Blackburn's "famous slogan" that it's not what you say at the end of the day, but how you got there that matters. I did not know that the slogan was famous, but it did and still does encapsulate my belief that there are contrasting ways of justifying and explaining the propositional forms and inferential powers of evaluative, modal, and conditional commitments, and that a route taking us through expressivism has virtues of economy, simplicity, and explanatory power that blunter realisms lack. More on this in the final section.

The arrival of deflationism was certainly useful to quasi-realism. But it did not solve all the problems. It is not entirely plain sailing to explain why our propensity for propositional clothing goes as far as it does, and no further. Why, a critic might ask, should we give ourselves moral propositions, and their truth and falsity, if we do not think of commands, or desires and policies, as themselves true or false? If moral commitments have a close affinity with these things, is it not surprising that we go as far as we do? As I have indicated, the answer must be that it is necessary, or at least useful, for us to have a grammar that enables us to map out the inferential moves that normative commitments have. Precisely because they are going to be insisted upon, they are going to be discussed as acceptable or not.

It is also worth noticing that similar transformations (into a propositional form) are naturally made with commands. If the President instructs the Defense Chief to put troops on the streets, he might meet the pained question "if we are to do that, are we also to shoot into the crowds?" Latin has the gerundive case to enable inferences of this kind: in "Carthago delenda est" the gerundive has become an adjective, and the imperative to destroy Carthage as it were crosses the boundary into being a proposition, and debatable.

In one of his last books Nietzsche noticed the transformation and saw it as a sinister result of the "protracted and domineering fundamental feeling on the part of a ruling order ... they say 'this *is* this and this', they seal everything and every event with a sound, and, as it were, take possession of it" (Nietzsche 1887, Essay 1, §2). It is certainly true that Cato could exert more influence by transplanting his plan to destroy Carthage from being "let's destroy Carthage" into "Carthage must be destroyed," as if Carthage were itself calling out for destruction. Nietzsche had a low opinion of the move, imagining that it involves us in a delusion, the error we make according to Mackie's "error theory." But I offer a more generous account of the function. I share Nietzsche's desire for an evolutionary or genealogical story, and I see it as pointing us to a Darwinian adaptation, rather than a delusion.

However, I also think Nietzsche's insight needs embracing. The hankering after moral realities can indeed be interpreted as the hankering after words. After the full scale of Nazi atrocities came to light, at the end of the second World War many intellectuals, including for example Iris Murdoch and Jurgen Habermas, supposed that the depth of horror they felt was uncomfortably inadequate to the enormity of what had occurred. They needed more to say, needed some words for something that could be presented as an "objective" correlate in the reality of the evil. This prompted a flight from any kind of subjective or expressivist theory, such as existentialism was supposed to be, to Platonism, in Murdoch's case, and rationalism in that of Habermas. The expressivist response to such an event is complete sympathy with the aching desire to find more words. But the words that we need would best be penned by poets and sung in mourning, despair, or rage, rather than lying inert in the parched deserts of moral metaphysics.

5. The Neo-Pragmatist Alliance

In recent years expressivism has also gained a new lease of life from its association with the wider movement of neo-pragmatism. The alliance has been welcome, for who would not feel fortified by finding themselves standing alongside a tradition boasting such philosophers as Ramsey, Wittgenstein, and Sellars? I feel embarrassed to say that while I had always recognized the first pair as major pioneers, I was ignorant of the extent to which Sellars also had foreseen the shape that expressivist insights should take. In Huw Price (2015) reminds us of this, quoting a salient passage demonstrating Sellars's affinity with quasi-realism:

> We have learned the hard way that the core truth of 'emotivism' is not only compatible with, but absurd without, ungrudging recognition of the fact, so properly stressed (if mis-assimilated to the model of describing) by 'ethical rationalists,' that ethical discourse as ethical discourse is a mode of rational discourse. It is my purpose to argue that the core truth of Hume's philosophy of causation is not only compatible with, but absurd without, ungrudging recognition of those features of causal discourse as a mode of rational discourse on which the 'metaphysical rationalists' laid such stress but also mis-assimilated to describing. (Sellars 1958, p. 285)

We should note that Sellars was happy to use a negative or contrastive characterization of his position, as indeed were Ramsey and Wittgenstein, for whom the core function of many indicative sentences needed to be contrasted with that of describing things. It is still a live issue within the church of pragmatism whether this contrast should remain, or whether a general deflationism removes it along with other landmarks (Kraut 1990, pp. 157–83).

In the case of causal modalities, although Sellars starts by following Hume and Ryle, the end point is rather different. He imagines a diachronic process, whereby causal and counterfactual inferences become cemented into descriptive content that, confined to registering uniformities, would originally have been innocent of them. A later passage in the same paper expands this point. Talking of ramifications of causal vocabulary and ideas he says that

> It is therefore important to realize that the presence in the object language of the causal modalities (and of the logical modalities and of the deontic modalities) serves not only to express existing commitments, but also to provide the framework for the thinking by which we reason our way (in a manner appropriate to the specific subject matter) into the making of new commitments and the abandonment of old . . . (1958 p. 303)

He gives as examples the kinds of sentence that rationalists and realists like to showcase, such as "There are causal connections which have not yet been discovered," and we can add "There are obligations which have not yet been recognized," or "There are qualities which no one has yet experienced." Sellars argued that these quantifications need not describe hidden abstract objects, and should not excite metaphysical or "realist" imaginings. They too are expressive, simply showing that we are open to the possibilities of inquiry and discovery in their respective areas. In a similar vein someone thinking of the half-lives of undiscovered radioactive isotopes will think that there are probabilities that are yet unknown. Such quantifications arise from what Sellars called "language militant", a nice metaphor showing that we countenance the possibility of future changes and improvements in meanings themselves, which we might be marched towards by new reasonings or experiences. A rather different tack is taken here by one of Sellars's most loyal followers, Robert Brandom, who has no qualms about supposing that his "analytic pragmatism" ends up with full-scale realism, even about morals, modals, or conditionals (Brandom 2008, pp. 201–36, queried in Price 2017, pp. 157–8). Although I applaud Brandom's linkage of pragmatism with "algebraic" inferential clarity, which was also the goal of quasi-realism, my reaction is still that it is how you get there that counts, so that the label "realism" is best avoided.

Pragmatists, with their interest in genealogy as opposed to analysis, are happy to emphasize Sellars's diachronic change. In spite of his supposed skepticism a salient example would be the genealogy Nietzsche himself sketched, whereby a notion of justice, originally deriving as Hume described from conventions governing transactions between roughly equal parties, becomes ever more extensive through time, eventually applying in circumstances and ways that quite disguise its origins (Nietzsche 1880, 92; Queloz 2017, pp. 1–23).

The ungrudging recognition that Sellars recommends gives us the right way of dealing with the Frege-Geach problem. This is in effect to invert it. Far from being a sticking point, the inferential functions of sentences that express the propositional reflections of attitudes, plans or policies are exactly what explain the fact that they are in our lexicon. This is why we have "lying is wrong," as opposed to: "boo to lying!," just as we have "Carthage is to be destroyed" as well as "Destroy Carthage!" In other words, rather than it being a problem that we seamlessly use such sentences in complex and indirect contexts, happily negating them or putting them in the antecedents of conditionals, it is precisely the inferential power that this transformation unlocks that explains why we have predicates that enable us to go in for propositional expression of the commitments in the first place. If we did not want to locate attitudes and practical policies within complex webs, subject to constraints of coherence and consistency, we would not need propositional expression, but could rest content with atomic expressions, such as ejaculations, imperatives, or optatives. But since we do want coherence and consistency, we want an inferential ("algebraic") discipline, and this is what the indicative form gives us.

So are Sellars and Wittgenstein right that it remains useful to contrast the function of normative language with description, or would they do better to succumb to the deflationist tide? One motivation for keeping the contrast emerges in a paper in which Michael Williams identifies three elements in any pragmatist explanation of the meaning of a sentence in terms of its use: an inferential component, an epistemological component, and a functional description explaining what this bit of the language does for us (Williams 2010). These clauses give the essential contrast between normative vocabularies and empirical vocabularies, in that the latter are tied to "language entry" rules, requiring that a report be made as the result of a reliable disposition to a differential response to some feature, whereas the former, while free from language-entry rules, are tied to language-exit rules, in the way they guide and grade policies, preferences, and actions. It is of course, the detachment from language entry rules that underlies the point of Moore's Open Question Argument that there is no *semantic* obstacle to querying and rejecting any particular standard for a normative judgment. Moore failed to realize that this is precisely because its use is anchored at the other end, so to speak, in the practical direction in which it seeks to steer us. Indeed much later Moore candidly admitted that the bare possibility of positions like emotivism had not occurred to him at the time of *Principia Ethica* or his later book *Ethics* (Moore 1952, p. 546). It is also, one might add, an excuse for the negative theses of the good old days, for if the rules governing moral and evaluative (and modal and conditional) language make no use of any notion of reliable response to a feature, it is not stretching things very far to suggest that they are not describing or representing any feature either. Some may think that the minimalist tide has obliterated that landmark, but it was certainly useful to Ramsey, Wittgenstein, Austin, and Sellars in its day. And just as it was negative about the idea that normative and modal languages describe anything, so it was firmly negative about the need for a metaphysics of what it is that they describe. The urge to leave metaphysics and receptivity to metaphysical facts out from our understanding of normativity and modality was always the principal driver of antirealism in its various forms (Thomasson 2020).

6. Semantics and Metasemantics

With truth deflated, a lot of other points of reference can get the air taken out of them with it: facts, reference, representation, description, and properties are among them. So as soon as we commit ourselves to any normative judgment, we might hear ourselves admitting that the judgment is true, that there is a fact of the matter, that the attribution of a normative property is correct, and it seems anything else that used to be part of the negative content of antirealism.

One line of thought that opens up here is exploited in many papers by Huw Price. Price is a dyed-in-the-wool semantic minimalist, but nevertheless recognizes that there is a pull toward a notion that he calls e-representation, which can obtain between terms and features of the environment to which they are tied by causal relations. The terms that e-represent will be ones that directly or indirectly require the reliable dispositions to differential responses for a user to be able to use them in reports of environmental features. It is this language-entry requirement that marks them out. Price holds that e-representation is a niche area within the much wider field of i-representation, this being certified for terms by the inferential relations of sentences within which they occur. So although causal responsiveness may play a large role in deciding, for instance, that Wittgenstein's builders refer to their slabs and beams, it is the inferential power associated with names and descriptions that allows us to say that we equally refer to fictional characters, abstract objects, and for that matter possible worlds, causal powers, or rights and obligations.

Although it is not central to issues surrounding normativity, it may be worth pausing briefly to offer one helping hand to neo-pragmatism in general. I believe that this movement took a wrong turn in the hands of Richard Rorty. Rorty seems to have thought of himself as following Dewey in having a general suspicion of semantic terms, notably reference, representation, and truth, across the board. I do not know if there is evidence of Dewey sharing that suspicion. It is more certain that he disliked a particular *theory* of how semantic or intentional powers come about. Dewey wrote that:

> The basic fallacy in representative realism is that while it actually depends upon the inferential phase of enquiry, it fails to interpret the immediate quality and the related idea in terms of their functions in inquiry. On the contrary it views representative power as an inherent property of sensations and ideas as such, treating them as "representations" in and of themselves. Dualism or bifurcation of mental and physical existence is a necessary result, presented, however, not as a result but as a given fact . . . psychological or mental existences which are then endowed with the miraculous power of standing for and pointing to existences of a different order. (Dewey 1968, p. 514–5)

The complaint is that by making representative power an intrinsic self-standing property of ideas or concepts or any "thing" we simply generate mystery. For, since physical things like inscriptions and sounds evidently do not have these intrinsic powers, we add the false idea of a dualism of mind, where there must reside things such as ideas or concepts that do have such powers, and the inert external world where nothing does. It is the idea that semantic properties are intrinsic to some *thing* or other that is the target, not the propriety of semantic terminology itself. It is interesting to note how this point is echoed in Wittgenstein's attack on the idea of a rule as a presence in the mind with the power to determine applications and non-applications across an indefinitely large, or even infinite, range of cases, and also in his attack on the notion that to understand the command to bring a red flower, you must first conjure up an image in the mind for your flower to match.

As far as this goes, neither Dewey nor Wittgenstein are enemies of reference or representation, or indeed intentional powers in general (how could one be?). It is just that the false theory forgets to embed semantic notions in the overall uses of terms, or what Dewey calls the "inferential phases of inquiry". Even Wittgenstein's builders have practices made possible by their single-word communications, and going beyond them we know when we are talking of slabs rather than beams, hammers rather than screwdrivers, and shapes rather than sizes because we have an indefinite range of such practices whose success is only explicable by this knowledge. Among those practices are those of communicating what is to be fetched, and what is not, and understanding that communication. We can then see how reference and representation fall into place as a summary description of these practical abilities.

Because these explanations of meaning in terms of use are substantial metalinguistic descriptions of pieces of vocabulary, it is potentially misleading to talk in Price's terms of a generalized semantic minimalism. The Oxford dictionary tells us that "semantic" means relating to meaning in logic or language. It does not insist that you have to be talking about meaning in any particular way in order to be involved in semantics, but you are to talk about signs and how they mean what they do. Semantic descriptions are substantial, in the sense both that they are contingent—it is not necessary that any particular expression should mean what it does—and that they put real conditions of use on any population of which they are true. Those conditions clearly employ, but go beyond, mere causal relations with elements of the environment, for those might not by themselves bring about the shared attention and shared dispositions that sameness of reference and representation require.

It was always bizarre of Rorty to put a total embargo on reference, representation, and truth, as if we cannot be said to pay attention to the things in our environment and their properties, nor use language to induce other people to share this attention. But with this much semantics on the table we do not have to creep all the way with minimalism. We can see a substantive use for the idea of representing and describing things in our sensed environment or parts of our physical environment causally connected with those things, and reinstate a contrast between our sayings answering to the world, and those being injunctions or expressions of preferences or plans that the world be made to conform to them. In this way a background of pragmatism, explaining meaning in terms of use, can coincide with fine-grained distinctions of function. It also implies that like the pragmatists of the good old days we can maintain negative theses, for as well as saying what a semantic account of words such as "ought" would be, we can insist on what it is not. It is nothing like such an account for terms whose use is partly defined by language entry rules, and this is enough to reinstate functional, and semantic, diversity. This is compatible with deflationism about truth, since that is not a contribution to the semantics of sentences—the functions that enable them to express propositions about which truth is claimed. It is notable that at the same time as he introduced the deflationist view of truth Ramsey suggested exactly the same division of labor (Ramsey 1927, pp. 38–9).

However, I do not want to overstress the way the bifurcation, or multifurcation, of function implies semantic divisions. In my view it is the division of function that is itself important, and that must not be occluded by the end result that "the clothing of language makes everything look the same". Price himself not only recognizes but stresses and insists upon differences of function, but I interpret him as thinking that these give us different things to say *about* the semantics of different terms, but do not, as it were, trickle down to make the semantics themselves different. They remain at a metasemantic level. I do not say that this usage is wrong, but I do think it is optional, both because there is nothing forced or unnatural about wrapping the functional differences into the semantic description of terms, and because it suggests that theorists in the good old days were wholly wrong in employing negative semantic bearings as a way of identifying their insights. I think it is more charitable to give them a perfectly good excuse for having done so.

7. Perspicuous Explanations

As already mentioned above, the difficulty of making "realism" into a significant ". . . ism", can be brushed off by denying that there is in fact space for metaethical theory at all. So it is necessary to repeat that there are many issues where expressivism coupled with quasi-realism provides a satisfying, economical source of explanations of facets of our thinking and our language where not only substantive realisms, but both the hollow realism of Dworkin and Derek Parfit's "non-metaphysical, non-natural normative cognitivism" offer nothing at all, or just mystery (Dworkin 2011; Parfit 2011).

Consider first the case of two persons with very different ideas, say about a moral feature such as the justice of some social arrangement. Why do we want to say that they disagree, rather than that they are simply talking past each other? Not because they are both responding to the same features of the arrangement, for if they have different standards they may well not do so. Perhaps because they cognize the same non-natural property? But why think that? Even if we free reference from confinement to causally related things, we don't thereby justify ideas of our cognition of, or reference to, non-natural normative properties and relations. For reference surely requires an ability to identify and count and reidentify the objects of reference, and there is no non-naturalist realist, or Parfitian cognitivist, account on offer of how that is achieved. Parfit liked to compare his own acquaintance with reasons to a mathematician's acquaintance with abstract structures. But if one mathematician decided to treat set theory in terms including the Axiom of Choice, and another decides to avoid it, and if all the consequences remain outside any impact on applied mathematics, we may well suppose that they have two different structures in their minds, but no disagreement. Similarly we have no method for counting non-natural properties. If there is one, there may be many. If we ask why we suppose that two people talking about, say, good traits of character are talking about the same thing, there is no empirically certain mark of them having in mind the same non-natural property or concept, save the practical upshots they associate with it. But once those practical upshots are doing all the work, the metaphysics and the cognitions equally drop away as irrelevant, and there will be no litmus test for a shared topic that does not eventually join forces with the language exit consequences, or in other words, with expressivism. The right answer stares us in the face. It is that they disagree because they share a practical topic: namely, trying to establish in which defensible direction social policy should move. They need not actually be planning to do anything to further social justice. But feelings prime one for action, even when one does not intend to light the touch paper. Practical attitudes of preference, encouragement, and hope are implicated by the vocabulary, and the shared concern.

Second, what explains the analytic nature of the supervenience of the normative on the natural? Not some particular topology of modal and normative space, but the simple requirement that whether we are assessing and grading apples, or courses of action, or anything else, the rule is that we do so in the light of the subjacent, natural or empirical features these things present. You simply do not understand the practice of grading examination papers unless you realize that it is to be done in the light of what the candidate has written (an immaculate account of this argument is in Mitchell 2017, pp. 2903–25).

Third, what explains the fact that we care as we do about duties, rights, obligations, and values? If they introduce a separate object of concern, not found in the natural world, it should seem very odd, even before we ask for an epistemology. Why should they worm their way into our motivations? The expressivist answer is instantaneous: normative terms constitute the language in which we talk of whatever it is that we care about. Any other object of care, such as "normative reason" would threaten actually to compete with the objects of care that naturally fill our humane views, such as welfare, happiness, and the absence of misery (Hayward 2019; Lenman 2014).

Fourth, realism encourages mystification and eventually skepticism about normative epistemology, as John Mackie supposed, and as has been argued at length more recently by Sharon Street (2006) and Richard Joyce (2016). Street's argument is basically that there is no Darwinian reason why getting moral propositions *right* would have any adaptive benefits, for we succeed or not in the natural world and our successes and failures have only natural explanations. Hence there is no reason to suppose that we have evolved to get them right. We do just as well, in the natural world, by being completely off-track about them. The argument assumes of course that moral properties are completely different to natural properties, and it disappears if realism takes a naturalistic form.

Although Street has tried to extend this argument to cast doubt on moral epistemology as the expressivist might conceive of it, her argument depends on saddling the expressivist with hospitality to a conception of moral truth that invites wholesale Cartesian skepticism (Street 2011). The only alternative, she appears to think, is her own kind of constructivism that exempts people from moral assessment if there is nothing in their own practical stance that entails such assessment. She says of a hideous villain that "If Caligula is aware of all the non-normative facts and has recognized every normative conclusion that follows from his own values in combination with those facts, then there is nothing he is failing to see" (2011, p. 371). This is reminiscent of Bernard Williams's problem with so-called external and internal reasons, except that even Williams allowed that we could say, of his confirmed wife-beater who has no resources enabling him to see that what he is doing is wrong, that he was dreadful, insensitive, cruel, and so forth. Williams only drew the line, unnecessarily, at our saying in our own voice that there is good reason for this character to change his ways. I can see no justification for this self-denial, and similarly an expressivist should find Street's attitude to Caligula highly regrettable. Caligula failed to see the disgusting impropriety of delighting in causing distress and pain, and like the wife-beater failed to see that the distress and pain of other people were good reasons for him to change his ways. It was his acting in the light of this moral defect that made him the monster that he was. Saying this, of course, we stay within *our own* moral and practical points of view, as we have to do, since we are voicing our own detestation of him. But we open no door to an unknowable view from nowhere, inviting Cartesian skepticism.

For expressivism the epistemological problem is whether we know how to run our lives, and the answer has to be that with a birthright of decent sentiments, moulded by upbringing, socialization, respect for a common point of view with others, and benefiting from experience of how things turn out, then often enough we do. We know to prefer happiness to misery, truth to lies, promise-keeping to arbitrary promise-breaking, law to chaos, and so on. We do indeed become puzzled and face intractable choices and dilemmas, but there is no question of being wrong across the board. We also know how to choose means to ends, so in countless particular ways, we know how to make things better, or how to avoid them getting worse. There is no other general problem of practical moral epistemology.

We should note that minimalism does not creep over these explanatory benefits. If realism in its transcendental form were correct about what we need in order to underwrite normative reasonings—unidentifiable properties, sui generis supervenience relations, bizarre objects of concern, and unknowable principles—it would either offer us nothing, as in Dworkin or Parfit, or simply serve to drag us down to the skepticism of Mackie, Street, and Joyce. Fortunately it is not.

References

Armstrong, D. M. 1983. *What Is a Law of Nature?* Cambridge: Cambridge University Press.
Ayer, A. J. 1936. *Language, Truth, and Logic*. London: Gollancz.
Blackburn S. 1986. "How Can We Tell Whether a Commitment Has a Truth Condition? In *Meaning and Interpretation*, edited by C. Travis, 201–232. Oxford: Blackwell.

Blackburn S. 1993. "Realism: Quasi or Queasy?" In *Reality, Representation and Projection*, edited by J. Haldane and C. Wright, 365–383. New York: Oxford University Press.
Blackburn, S. 2015. "Blessed Are the Peacemakers." *Philosophical Studies* 172(4): 843–853.
Blackburn, S. 2019. "Wittgenstein and Brandom: Affinities and Divergences." *Disputatio* 8(9).
Brandom, R. 2008. *Between Saying and Doing*. Oxford: Oxford University Press.
Carroll, L. 1876. *The Hunting of the Snark: An Agony in Eight Fits*. London: Macmillan.
Dewey J. 1968. *Logic: The Theory of Inquiry*. In *Last Works*, edited by Jo Ann Boydston, Carbondale: Southern Illinois University Press.
Dreier, J. 2004. "Meta-Ethics and the Problem of Creeping Minimalism." *Philosophical Perspectives* 18: 3–44.
Dworkin, R. 1996. "Objectivity and Truth: You'd Better Believe It." *Philosophy and Public Affairs* 2: 87–139.
Dworkin, R. 2011. *Justice for Hedgehogs*. Cambridge, MA: Harvard University Press.
Hayward, M. 2019. "Immoral Realism." *Philosophical Studies* 176(4): 897–914.
Jackson F., G. Oppy, and M. Smith. 1994. "Minimalism and Truth-Aptness." *Mind* 103: 287–302.
Joyce, R. 2016. *Essays in Moral Skepticism*. Oxford: Oxford University Press.
Kraut, R. 1990. "Varieties of Pragmatism." *Mind* 99: 157–183
Leavis, F. R. 1968 "Under Which King, Bezonian?" In *Readings from Scrutiny*, vol. 1, 166–175. Cambridge: Cambridge University Press
Lenman, J. 2014. "Deliberation, Schmeliberation: Enoch's Indispensability Argument." *Philosophical Studies* 168: 835–842.
Mackie, J. L. 1977. *Ethics: Inventing Right and Wrong*. Harmondsworth: Penguin Books.
Martin, C. B. 2008. *The Mind in Nature*. Oxford: Oxford University Press.
Mitchell, C. 2017. "Mixed Up about Mixed Worlds: Understanding Blackburn's Supervenience Argument." *Philosophical Studies* 174: 2903–2925.
Moore, G. E. 1952. "Reply to My Critics." In *The Philosophy of G. E. Moore*, edited by Arthur Schilpp, 535–554. New York: Tudor Publishing Company.
Nietzsche F. [1880] 1986. *The Wanderer and His Shadow*. In *Human, All Too Human*, part 2, edited by Richard Schacht, translated by R. J. Hollingdale, 181–366. Cambridge: Cambridge University Press.
Nietzsche, F. 1887. *On the Genealogy of Morals*. Translated by M. Clark and A. Swensen. Indianapolis: Hackett.
Parfit, D. 2011. *On What Matters*. Vol. 2. Oxford: Oxford University Press.
Price, H. 2015. "From Quasi-Realism to Global Expressivism—and Back Again?" In *Passions and Projections: Themes from the Philosophy of Simon Blackburn*, edited by R. Johnson and M. Smith, 134–152. Oxford: Oxford University Press.
Price, H. 2017. "Epilogue: Ramsey's Ubiquitous Pragmatism." In *The Practical Turn*, edited by C. Misak and H. Price, 149–162. Oxford: Oxford University Press.
Queloz, M. 2017. "Nietzsche's Pragmatic Genealogy of Justice." *British Journal for the History of Philosophy* 25: 727–749.
Ramsey, F. P. 1927. "Facts and Propositions." In *Philosophical Papers*, edited by D. H. Mellor, 34–51. Cambridge: Cambridge University Press.
Ramsey, F. P. 1929. "General Propositions and Causality." In *Philosophical Papers*, edited by D. H. Mellor, 145–163. Cambridge: Cambridge University Press.
Ryle, G. 1950. "*If*," "*So*," and "*Because*." In *Philosophical Analysis, A Collection of Essays*, edited by Max Black, 323–340. Ithaca: Cornell University Press.

Sellars W. 1958 "Counterfactuals, Dispositions, Causal Modalities." In *Minnesota Studies in the Philosophy of Science*, vol. 2, edited by Herbert Feigl, Michael Scriven, and Grover Maxwell, 225–308. Minneapolis: University of Minnesota Press.

Street, S. 2006. "A Darwinian Dilemma for Realist Theories of Value." *Philosophical Studies* 127: 109–166.

Street, S. 2010. "What Is Constructivism in Ethics and Metaethics?" *Philosophy Compass* 5: 363–384.

Street. S. 2011. "Mind-Independence without the Mystery: Why Quasi-Realists Can't Have It Both Ways." *Oxford Studies in Metaethics*, vol. 6, edited by Russ Shafer-Landau, 1–32. Oxford: Oxford University Press.

Thomasson, Amie 2020. *Norms and Necessity*. Oxford: Oxford University Press.

Williams, M. 2010. "Pragmatism, Minimalism, Expressivism." *International Journal of Philosophical Studies* 18: 317–330.

Wittgenstein, L. 1953 *Philosophical Investigations*. Oxford: Basil Blackwell.

11
NATURALISM

CHAPTER 10

ETHICAL NATURALISM
Problems and Prospects

LOUISE ANTONY AND ERNESTO V. GARCIA

Introduction

ETHICAL naturalism has a long and distinguished philosophical history. Its defenders include Aristotle, Aquinas, Hobbes, Butler, Shaftesbury, Hutcheson, Hume, Adam Smith, Bentham, Mill, Nietzsche, and John Dewey. It's an attractive position for two reasons. First, *contra* metaethical views like noncognitivism, error theory, and moral fictionalism, it upholds the commonsense idea that when we engage in ethical reflection, we're in the business of forming and evaluating moral beliefs that certain actions (e.g., beneficence, stealing, lying), character traits (e.g., courage, honesty, ingratitude), and states of affairs (e.g., experiences of pleasure or pain) have the moral properties of being right or wrong, virtuous or vicious, and good or bad, and that at least some of these beliefs are true. Second, *contra* non-naturalistic substantive or robust ethical realism, it locates moral properties in the natural domain rather than appealing to any metaphysically mysterious or suspect non-natural moral facts.

In this chapter, we discuss fundamental problems and prospects for ethical naturalism. Our plan is as follows. In Section 1, we explain what we mean by "ethical naturalism" and survey different versions of the view. In Section 2, we discuss the central philosophical challenge to ethical naturalism, viz., the "Normativity Objection." This objection has been raised in different ways by thinkers such as Jonathan Dancy, David Enoch, William Fitzpatrick, David McNaughton, Piers Rawling, and Derek Parfit. In Section 3, we offer a battery of responses to it on behalf of the ethical naturalist. In Section 4, we explore what we take to be a promising and novel approach to ethical naturalism, viz., a moral nativist theory that that combines a Chomskian approach to moral competence with a structuralist metaphysics. Lastly, we offer some concluding remarks.

1. What Is Ethical Naturalism?

In this section, we provide a general lay of the land. The main question is: What is "ethical naturalism," or more fully unpacked, "naturalistic moral realism"?[1] To answer this question, we need to explain what we mean by two things: (1) "naturalism" and (2) "moral realism."

1.1 Naturalism

First, what do we mean by "naturalism"? The term "naturalism" is used to denote different doctrines by different philosophers. Here, we'll mention the three of these we take to be most pertinent to debates about ethical naturalism:

1) *Scientism*—this doctrine asserts that empirical science is the arbiter of the real. (To avoid complications irrelevant to our topic, we will assume that "science" here refers to an ideal completed science.) Naturalism so construed would be incompatible with moral realism. But we see no reason to adopt naturalism in this form. There are a great many truths that science will not cover, partly because there are a great many truths about which science is silent. This is not because such facts fall outside the realm of the natural, but because science doesn't (and shouldn't) *care*. That there is an orange barn in Leverett, Massachusetts, is a fact, but one that hardly demands scientific explanation. That there are *orange* things is a proper topic for vision science; and that there are *things like barns* is a good topic for research in metaphysics.

2) *Reductionism*—this is a two-part doctrine: reductionists hold that (a) reality is organized hierarchically, and (b) our descriptions (scientific or otherwise) of reality at each level are semantically reducible to descriptions at the next lower level.[2] This is the essence of the "unity of science" hypothesis, famously articulated and defended by Paul Oppenheim and Hilary Putnam.[3] But with the emergence of a general critique of logical positivism, spearheaded by Carl Hempel, W. v. O. Quine, and Putnam himself, this view of empirical science fell into disfavor.[4] Part of the critique involved

---

[1] This qualification is necessary in order to distinguish ethical naturalism from naturalistic approaches in metaethics more generally, where the latter can include, e.g., Blackburn's and Gibbard's noncognitivist views. For a different approach, see Suikkanen 2016, who groups all these different views under the general heading "naturalism in metaethics". Suikkanen categorizes Blackburn and Gibbard in particular as defending "semantic forms of naturalism in metaethics".

[2] Reductionism per se is not committed to there being a *fundamental* level, although it is often assumed by reductionists that this is so.

[3] Paul Oppenheim and Hilary Putnam (1958).

[4] See C. G. Hempel, "The Theoretician's Dilemma" (1958); W. v. O. Quine, "Two Dogmas of Empiricism" (1951) and "Epistemology Naturalized" (1969); Hilary Putnam, "What Theories Are Not" (1975a) and "Logical Positivism and the Philosophy of Mind" (1975b).

a general challenge to the possibility of distinguishing "definitions" from other sorts of widely accepted truths linking theoretical terms from different domains, and part of it stemmed from the recognition of the ubiquity of *functional* properties in characterizations of the natural world. The notion of "valence," for example, from chemistry, cannot be defined in the proprietary vocabulary of physics, because valence is a matter of structure that is only "visible" at the molecular level. This point was emphasized by Putnam, but also, importantly, by Jerry Fodor. Fodor pointed out that all the so-called special sciences—including, prominently, psychology, invoke properties that are "multiply realizable"; and hence indefinable in terms of any specific underlying physical natures. As we'll see shortly, the "normativity" argument against ethical naturalism is often stated in a way that presumes the truth of reductionism; the argument at its heart relies on claims about the indefinability of normative claims in terms of non-normative claims; thus the "open-question" argument depends on the premise that "good" cannot be defined in terms of "good-making" properties. But once we recognize that terms in higher-level, but paradigmatically naturalistic theories are also indefinable in terms of lower-level sciences, the indefinability of normative terms in non-normative language cannot be used as an argument against the naturalness of the normative.

However, one could give up the semantic part of the reductionist thesis, and still maintain the ontological part—that nature is organized hierarchically. But we contend that, even if this claim is true, it does not provide an adequate characterization of the natural. One natural way to interpret this claim is as a statement of mereology. Understood that way, it says that everything that is part of the natural order is composed, ultimately, of the same stuff. There are technical issues that would need to be addressed, in light of contemporary physics, in order to defend this claim, but even leaving those difficulties aside, this doctrine is importantly incomplete—it addresses the ontology of reality, but not what Quine calls the "ideology"—it doesn't tell what it is for a *property* to be natural.[5] This is especially important in considering matters involving *minds*. Cartesian dualists hold that mind and body are different substantially—this clearly contravenes the doctrine we are now considering. But many property dualists—such as Joseph Levine and David Chalmers—accept that sentient things beings are composed entirely of matter, while also maintaining that such beings exhibit properties that are of a completely different type from the properties stemming from their physical composition. Are such

---

[5] We are here alluding to Quine's distinction between the set of things which the theory takes to be the values of its bound variables ("ontology"), and the primitive predicates of the theory ("ideology"). Quine, who disparaged the intensional, did not say want to say that the correspondents of these predicates are *properties* (as opposed to classes), but it has become common in contemporary philosophy of mind to think of the ideology of a theory as the set of properties it attributes to objects in its domain. For details of Quine's view, see Quine (1951), "Ontology and Ideology," *Philosophical Studies* 2(1):11–15.

philosophers *naturalists* or not? Our truncated reductionism has nothing to say on this point.

This version of reductionism is also silent about the status of logic and mathematics. These lacunae are particularly pertinent to our main topic—the prospects for naturalizing normativity—because, as we'll argue below, we can learn from philosophers who have proposed naturalistic accounts of these domains.

3) *Confirmational-Holistic Naturalism*—this is the version of naturalism that we accept. We begin with what we'll call an "anchoring" truth: some paradigmatically naturalistic truth that could be a truth of fundamental physics, or some perfectly mundane truth like "dogs exist." We then add the condition that *every* truth is evidentially relevant to every other truth (confirmational holism), and hence to our anchoring truth. This version, like *scientism*, derives from the work of Quine, but foregrounds his rejection of reductionism over his praise of science. In "Epistemology Naturalized," Quine (1969) argued that philosophers ought to approach the study of knowledge in the way that scientists approached the study of nature generally—by orienting themselves to the *explanations* of apparent phenomena. In the case of epistemology, that meant taking the existence of certain kinds of knowledge—perceptual knowledge, for example—and studying the processes and circumstances that give rise to it.[6] Although some philosophers criticized Quine, alleging that he was abandoning the normative goals of epistemology, we maintain that a naturalized study of knowledge instead makes room for the normative by proposing an empirical investigation and assessment of epistemological norms.

There are two aspects of this version of naturalism that are especially important for defenders of ethical naturalism. The first has to do with our understanding of natural laws and natural kinds. A crucial element of the "scientific realism" that replaced the instrumentalism of logical positivism was a new view of natural kinds, coordinated with a new view of the reference of scientific terms. Putnam, together with Saul Kripke, argued that natural kind terms could not be defined in terms of the characteristic properties of members of the kind; rather, what made a group of individuals members of the same kind was their sharing an objective essence that explained (among other things) their observable similarities. Reference to such kinds was secured by (a) an initial act of ostension and (b) an intention on the part of the initiator and subsequent users of the term for it to refer to all things that bore a relevant resemblance to the original ostended object. Richard Boyd generalized this picture of kinds, arguing that a natural kind needn't have an essence (like an atomic number, molecular structure or genotype) but could be, instead, a "homeostatic property cluster." Kinds, in this sense, are groups of individuals which share an important set of projectible properties, where the coherence of this group is "disciplined" in some way. This view offers a useful way of thinking

---

[6] See also Quine, "Two Dogmas of Empiricism"

about functional kinds as well as social kinds, and has promise, we believe in developing a naturalistic account of morality. Boyd himself used his view to defend a version of moral realism (discussed below). While we reject his specific approach, we agree that his liberalization of the notion of a "natural" kind is vital to the conception of normative naturalism that we espouse.

The second important aspect of post-positivist realism is that it allows for—indeed, calls for—realism about the mental. Mentality, like normativity, has been thought to be a problem for naturalism, but largely because of the apparent irreducibility of properties thought to be essential to the characterization of minds, such as representation. But scientific realism takes semantic reducibility off the table, and requires only that mental phenomena be integrated into an overall explanatory framework of the workings of nature. Granted, there remains philosophical controversy about whether representation can be so integrated, but our conception of naturalism offers no barrier to doing so. We'll make free appeal to psychological facts—in particular, to empirically supported theories of native mental structure—in what follows.

In sum, we make two contentions: first, that confirmational holism is a fully adequate statement of naturalism, and second, that the prospects for naturalizing ethics according to this standard are excellent.

1.2 Moral Realism

On to our second question: What do we mean by "moral realism"? Just like with "naturalism," "moral realism" also comes in many varieties. What all versions of moral realism share are two basic theses:

1. Our moral beliefs/claims which ascribe moral properties of rightness/wrongness, virtuousness/viciousness, goodness/badness, etc. to actions, character traits, states of affairs, etc. are truth-apt—that is, capable of being true or false—in a nondeflationary sense [cognitivism]
2. At least some of our moral beliefs/claims are true in a non-deflationary sense [success theory]

Noncognitivist views like emotivism (Ayer), prescriptivism (Stevenson/Hare), quasi-realism (Blackburn), and norm expressivism (Gibbard) all reject (1). Metaethical views like error theory (Mackie) and moral fictionalism (Joyce), while accepting (1), reject (2). Call the conjunction of (1) and (2) *minimal moral realism* (cf. Sayre-McCord 1988, 2008; Rosen 1994; and Enoch 2011).[7] This view is "minimal" because it remains strictly speaking neutral in debates over whether morality is objective, subjective, or some

---

[7] Cf. Copp and van Roojen, who defend very similar though more expansive accounts of a minimal moral realist view. Copp, who labels the view "moral realism" (2006:7–8), and later, "basic realism"

combination thereof; mind-, response- or stance-independent or -dependent; incompatible or compatible with relativism, etc.[8]

Where moral realists part company is in terms of how they understand the nature of moral properties. The most fundamental divide is between moral realists who think that moral properties are (1) non-natural properties—either supernaturalistic (e.g., *divine command theory*) or *sui generis* non-naturalistic properties (e.g., *substantive or robust moral realism*)—versus (2) natural properties (e.g., *ethical naturalism*).

Focusing specifically on (2), ethical naturalists defend the combination of (i) minimal moral realism and (ii) the explicit naturalist claim that moral properties are natural properties. (We'll call (ii) "the naturalist thesis.") This allows for further distinctions depending on how different ethical naturalists answer the question: *Which* natural properties do our moral predicates pick out? There are three main options here. Following Geoffrey Sayre-McCord, we'll refer to these as "subjectivist," "intersubjectivist," and "objectivist" approaches to ethical naturalism.[9]

For "subjectivist" approaches, moral truths are constituted by the responses of individual agents, actual or hypothetical/idealized. Some notable examples of subjectivist ethical naturalism include:

- *moral subjectivism*, where what's morally "good" and "evil" just consists, say, in what an individual desires or seeks to avoid (Hobbes 1996 [1651])
- *ideal observer theory*, where moral truths are based upon the hypothetical approval or disapproval of an ideal observer (Firth 1951)
- *"reforming naturalism," full information, and/or full rationality accounts*, where moral values are grounded in what a person would rationally desire after full confrontation with facts and logic (Brandt 1979), or in what we would be disposed, in idealized conditions, to desire to desire (Lewis 1988), or in "what [a person] would want himself to want, or to pursue, were he to contemplate his present situation from a standpoint fully and vividly informed about himself and his circumstances, and entirely free of cognitive error or lapses of instrumental rationality" (Railton

---

(2013:120–1), identifies five doctrines related to minimal moral realism, while van Roojen (2015:13), who refers to the view as "minimal realism about morality", identifies eight different claims.

[8] For some instructive discussions of why we shouldn't require that moral realism as such be committed to some of these more substantive criteria e.g., being objective, mind-independent, nonrelativistic, etc. see Connie Rosati (2018) on realism and mind-independence and Michael Smith (1993) on realism and absolutism vs. relativism. For contrary views, see Shafer-Landau 2003 and Fitzpatrick 2008.

[9] Technically, Sayre-McCord's taxonomy covers *moral realism in general*. We demonstrate here how his taxonomy applies equally well to one specific subcategory of moral realism, viz., ethical naturalism. Notice that these categories are not always clear cut. For one example, while full information accounts are broadly subjectivist in nature, they nevertheless have objectivist elements, too cf. Railton's talk of "objectified subjective interests" (Railton 1986: 173). For another example, while McDowell's view is listed under subjectivism, there are clearly objectivist features in their accounts, too. Nothing hangs on this taxonomy, which is offered merely as a convenient heuristic device for thinking about the overall territory.

1986:16), or in an agent's "having a desire to act in that way in those circumstances if she were fully rational" (Smith 1994 and 1995)

For "intersubjectivist" approaches, there are two main variations. On what we'll call nonproceduralist models, moral truths are fixed by whatever specific historical communities take to be morally right or wrong. This is typically seen as "derived from certain human needs, desires, and purposes," where both the nature of such needs and how best to meet them "will have a culturally variable component" (Flanagan, Sarkissian and Wong 2016: 24). Some examples include *moral relativism* (Harman 2000, 2012) and *Duke naturalism or pluralistic relativism* (Flanagan 1995 and Wong 1984, 1996, and 2006). And on what we'll call proceduralist models like, for example, *contractarianism*, moral truths are instead constituted by, say, what rational self-interested parties would hypothetically agree with one another about so as to help them achieve their own particular ends (Gauthier 1987).[10]

Lastly, there are many different "objectivist" approaches. On one end of the spectrum are *neo-Aristotelian or neofunctionalist naturalistic ethics* (Nussbaum 1995; Hursthouse 1999; Foot 2001; Bloomfield 2001 Thomson 2008). On this view, normativity is grounded upon a thing's function. Just as there are natural norms for biological organisms—such as nourishment, growth, survival, reproduction, etc.—based on the end of self-maintenance, so there are ethical norms for *being a good person* based on ends related to our distinctive human nature: e.g., our practical rationality, freedom, and capacities for society, culture, and morality (cf. Foot 2001). And on the other end of the spectrum are more explicitly scientific approaches like, for example, *Cornell Realism* (Boyd 1988; Sturgeon 1988; and Brink 1989). What underlies Cornell Realism is a basic commitment to what Peter Railton describes as "the generic stratagem of naturalistic realism": viz., "to postulate a realm of facts in virtue of the contribution they would make to the *a posteriori* explanation of certain features of our experience" (Railton 2003:9). Nicholas Sturgeon argues that moral facts and properties figure into our best causal explanations of moral actions. And Richard Boyd models moral inquiry—especially with respect to what he sees as the natural property of "moral goodness"—upon a scientific realist methodology. The overall aim is to show how moral phenomena can comprise an empirically respectable part of our naturalistic account of the world.

To summarize our discussion so far, we've seen that ethical naturalism—which comes in many varieties—involves the following trio of claims:

1. **Cognitivism:** Our moral beliefs/claims which ascribe moral properties of rightness/wrongness, virtuousness/viciousness, goodness/badness, etc., to actions, character traits, states of affairs, etc. are truth-apt—that is, capable of being true or false—in a nondeflationary sense

---

[10] For a helpful naturalistic reading of Gauthier's contractarianism, see Susan Dimock (2003).

2. **Success theory:** At least some of our moral beliefs/claims are true in a nondeflationary sense
3. **Naturalist thesis:** Moral properties are natural properties

In addition, we've seen that what distinguishes the many varieties of ethical naturalism lies in their differing views about (3). With this broad overview, we're now in a position to discuss what is generally taken to be the most important challenge to ethical naturalism, viz., the "Normativity Objection."

2. The Normativity Objection to Ethical Naturalism

There are many different objections to ethical naturalism in the literature, including worries about moral semantics,[11] moral metaphysics,[12] moral epistemology,[13] and moral explanation.[14] What philosophers typically regard as the most fundamental challenge to ethical naturalism, however, is the so-called Normativity Objection. This objection states that ethical naturalism—which claims that moral facts are in some sense natural facts—is unable to explain or account for the normativity of morality. We can formulate this challenge as follows:

The Normativity Objection

1. Any adequate moral theory must be able to account for the normativity of morality
2. Ethical naturalism cannot account for such normativity
3. Therefore, ethical naturalism is not an adequate moral theory

Three qualifications are in order here. First, by "normativity," we mean to include both prescriptive judgments of the form "S ought to Ø," related to deontic notions such as "ought," "should," "must," "required," "obligatory," or "is permitted," as well as evaluative judgments of the form "x is F" where "F" is some evaluative predicate, related to axiological notions such as "good," "bad," "valuable," "disvaluable," etc.

---

[11] See Moore 1994 and Horgan.
[12] Rawling/McNaughton.
[13] Schafer Landau and Kant.
[14] Harman and Sturgeon.

Second, even the staunchest critics of ethical naturalism accept that at least some aspects of morality can be naturalistically accounted for, either wholly or in part: e.g., its evolutionary history; the psychological development of our basic moral capacities for empathy, altruism, and practical reasoning; etc. What they maintain cannot be naturalistically accounted for is morality's normative bindingness upon us.

Third and lastly, many critics of ethical naturalism argue that we need to distinguish between two fundamentally different types of normativity. Derek Parfit contrasts "rule-implying" and "reason-giving" normativity. Similarly, David Enoch and Tristram McPherson distinguish between "formal" and "full-blooded" normativity.[15] "Rule implying" or "formal" normativity merely presupposes that there exist some standards of correctness which we can meet or fail to meet. Examples of "formal" or "rule-implying" normativity can be found is social practices like game-playing, etiquette, and legal and political systems (e.g., that one ought not to move one's bishop vertically, that one should wait to eat until everybody at the table is served, or that one is legally required to stop at red lights) or in functional evaluations (e.g., "seaworthiness"). Notably, as we'll see below, many ethical non-naturalists accept that this type of normativity *can* be accounted for naturalistically.

By contrast, ethical non-naturalists argue that "reason-giving" or "full-blooded" normativity resists naturalistic explanation. This type of normativity not only involves there being standards of correctness, but also that some of these normative standards are *objectively correct*: that is, normative standards that we cannot escape simply by opting out or refusing to play (Enoch 2018). Some proposed examples of "reason-giving" or "full-blooded" normativity include epistemic norms (e.g., that one should proportion one's belief to the evidence), prudential norms (e.g., that one should jump from burning buildings),[16] and most relevant for our purposes, moral norms (e.g., that one should not torture babies for fun).

Why think that ethical naturalism cannot account for the normativity of morality? Ethical non-naturalists raise two different but related lines of attack, both of which fall under the label "the Normativity Objection." On the one hand, Jonathan Dancy (2008), David McNaughton and Piers Rawling (2004), and William Fitzpatrick (2008 and 2011) defend what we'll call the "Irreducible Metafacts Objection." On the other hand, Derek Parfit (2011) and David Enoch (2011 and 2018) defend what we'll call the "Just Too Different Objection." In the rest of this section, we discuss both objections in turn. In the next section, we offer several responses that ethical naturalists can make against them.

---

[15] Enoch (2018) and McPherson (2011).
[16] While Parfit uses this example, it's unclear whether he thinks of it as an objective moral or prudential norm.

2.1 The Irreducible Metafacts Objection

According to the Irreducible Metafacts Objection, all naturalistic attempts to explain the normativity of morality fail insofar they cannot account for certain *sui generis* or irreducible second-order normative facts, or what Jonathan Dancy calls "metafacts." William Fitzpatrick focuses on evaluative judgments. First, consider the evaluative claim "*A* is a good automobile." How should we account for such normativity? Fitzpatrick argues that it's not enough just to point to (1a) various natural features XYZ that *A* possesses: e.g., that it's reliable, gets good gas mileage, has numerous safety features, etc. Rather, we also need appeal to the (1b) *the further normative fact or "metafact" that, in virtue of (1a) obtaining, A thereby satisfies the standards of goodness for automobiles in general*. Nonetheless, Fitzpatrick claims that for this specific type of evaluative judgment, we can "plausibly give a naturalistic reduction for standards of goodness [. . .] in terms of their proper functions, understood in terms of such things as the intentions of the designers, social conventions, and so on" (Fitzpatrick 2008:187).

It's quite a different story for moral normativity. Take the case of Iago from Shakespeare's *Othello*. His vicious character is displayed in many ways: through his jealousy, treachery, deception, and his willingness to bring about innocent people's downfall and even their deaths. In keeping with his earlier analysis, Fitzpatrick argues that in addition to (2a) natural features XYZ—e.g., Iago's lying, betrayal, scheming to destroy innocent people's lives, etc.—we must also appeal to (2b) the further normative fact or "metafact" that, *in virtue of (2a) obtaining, Iago thereby satisfies the standards of moral badness for human actions in general*. In this case, however, Fitzpatrick argues that such evaluative judgments resist naturalistic explanation insofar as they presuppose objectively correct standards of moral rightness and wrongness that hold independently of any particular social conventions, intentions, aims, or standpoints we might happen to occupy.

Jonathan Dancy, David McNaughton, and Piers Rawling defend a parallel view for prescriptive judgments. Dancy distinguishes between what he calls (3a) "facts of normative significance", that is, "a fact that is of practical relevance" and (3b) "normative facts" or "metafacts", that is, the second-order "fact that another fact is of practical relevance" (Dancy 2008, 137, 139). McNaughton and Rawling defend a similar contrast between (4a) "the reason itself", which is the descriptive circumstance in question and (4b) the *sui generis* or non-naturalistic normative fact that, in light of this fact, we should act in a certain way in this case (McNaughton and Rawling 2004). To borrow a concrete example from Simon Blackburn, (3a/4a) a "fact of normative significance" or "the reason itself" is the fact that, say, bear-baiting causes bears pain, where this can be understood in fully naturalistic terms. By contrast, it's (3b/4b) *a sui generis* non-naturalistic "normative fact" or "metafact" *that* the fact that bearbaiting causes bears pain is "of practical relevance" for how we should think, feel, and act.

2.2 The "Just Too Different Objection"

The "Irreducible Metafacts Objection" claims that ethical naturalism overlooks a subtle and easily ignored distinction between (i) the fact that x has certain natural features and (ii) the second-order normative fact that, *in virtue of* having such natural features, x thereby satisfies certain normative standards such that we can judge x to be good/bad, right/wrong, etc. By contrast, the "Just Too Different Objection" asserts that ethical naturalism commits an obvious blunder: viz., the basic category mistake of thinking that normative facts can be natural facts.

What's the problem here? Derek Parfit insists that "natural and normative facts are in two quite different, non-overlapping categories" (Parfit 2011: 324). To understand Parfit's claim, we need to distinguish between three different types of cases. First, there are things, events, or facts which (1) undeniably belong to different categories (e.g., "[r]ivers could not be sonnets, experiences could not be stones, and justice could not be ... the number 4"). Second, although Parfit himself never explicitly mentions this, there are things, events, or facts which (2) undeniably belong to the same category (e.g., physical objects like rocks and trees; my spouse's mind and my mind; and necessary truths like that $2 + 2 = 4$ or that " 'If A, then B' & A, therefore B"). Third, there are things, events, or facts (3) where we presently are—or at one time were—uncertain whether they belong to the same or to different categories (e.g., the vitalist belief that life is *sui generis* and thus distinct from merely physical phenomena).

Given this taxonomy, where should we locate the relationship between normative facts and natural facts? Do they undeniably belong (1) to different categories, (2) to the same category, or are they (3) something about which we're still undecided? With regard to clear-cut examples of purely normative concepts,[17] Parfit argues:

> ... for naturalism to succeed, even the claims that are purely normative must, if they are true, state purely natural facts. *These purely normative claims could not, I believe, state such facts.* ... If, as I believe, reason-involving normative facts are in a separate, distinctive category, there is no close analogy to their irreducibility to natural facts. These normative facts are in some ways like certain other kinds of necessary truths.... [The empiricist view of mathematics] misunderstands arithmetic, and the ways in which mathematical claims can be true. Nor could logical truths be natural facts about the ways in which people think. *In the same way, I believe, normative and natural facts differ too deeply for any form of Normative Naturalism to succeed* (Parfit 2011:326, emphases added)

---

[17] In answering this question, Parfit importantly sets aside the case of thick ethical concepts, such as being "treacherous" or "chaste," which are partly normative and partly naturalistic. Nonetheless, Parfit argues that even in these cases, we can "distinguish between the normative and naturalistic parts of such concepts".

David Enoch defends a very similar view. He claims that "[n]ormative facts and properties ... are just too different from natural ones to be a subset of them" (Enoch 2011:100). The basic problem with any naturalistic reduction, he argues, is that "they lose the normativity of the normative and indeed moral facts—the very features they were supposed to capture" (Enoch 2011:105).

Why should we accept that normative facts are "just too different" from natural facts such that they can't possibly belong to the same category? Notably, Parfit never offers any positive argument in support of his just-too-different intuition. He just explains the intuition, asserts that normative truths are non-naturalistic necessary truths like mathematical and logical truths, and then proceeds to treat this assertion as obvious or self-evident. By contrast, Enoch is more forthright in this regard. He admits:

> Is there anything that can be said here, anything more general, and that does not constitute merely insisting on the just-too-different intuition ... ? Any positive argument that can be offered, supporting the irreducibility claim? *I do not have such an argument up my sleeve ....*" (Enoch 2011: 105, emphasis added)

At the end of the day, the Just Too Different Objection does not serve as a dialectically effective tool for convincing those who altogether lack this intuition, much less those with the contrary intuition. Rather, it's just a statement of what ethical non-naturalists take to be a self-evident or obvious truth, one that they insist best accords with our ordinary or commonsense views about these matters.[18] To adopt Humean terminology here, the overall idea is that normative facts—that is, "oughts"—are *just too different* from natural facts—that is, mere "is-es"—for these two types of facts to ever belong to one and the same category.

3. Replies to the Normativity Objection

The main debate is whether it's possible to offer a naturalistic account of moral normativity. As we saw in Section 2, ethical non-naturalists deny this, either (1) by defending the existence of *sui generis* or non-naturalistic second-order normative facts or "metafacts" (Fitzpatrick/Dancy/McNaughton/Rawling) and (2) by insisting that normative facts (that is, "oughts") are "just too different" from natural facts (that is, "mere is-es") for them to ever belong to the same category (Parfit/Enoch). How should the ethical naturalist reply? In what follows, we address each objection, starting with the Just Too Different Objection.

---

[18] For the idea that this the commonsense or default view, see Enoch 2018.

3.1 Critique of the Just Too Different Objection

How should ethical naturalists reply to the Just Too Different Objection? First, as we've already discussed in §2.2, some prominent ethical non-naturalists like Enoch are quite upfront about the fact that they have no positive argument in support of the Just Too Different Objection. More often than not, the Just-Too-Different intuition is simply presented as something that readers should recognize as *obviously true*. Or in the case of Parfit, it's just asserted that normative facts are in the same category as non-naturalistic facts like, say, logical or mathematical truths, without giving any non-question-begging arguments for why we should accept this claim. As Enoch observes:

> [A]ny argumentative move here will likely start either with accepting or with rejecting the just-too-different intuition, thus in a way begging the question. We may not be able to do here much more than just stare at the just-too-different intuition and see how plausible it seems to us ... (Enoch 2011:108)

Put differently, the Just Too Different Objection amounts to a kind of "incredulous stare" leveled against ethical naturalists, querying: "How can you possibly think that normative facts, or 'oughts', are in the exact same category as natural facts, or 'mere is-es?'" (cf. Lewis 1986:133.) Notably, Enoch admits that ethical non-naturalists face their own incredulous stare from critics who challenge: "Are you seriously suggesting that moral truths are *sui generis* facts inhabiting some Platonic heaven like numbers and sets?" (Enoch 2016)[19] As David Lewis informs us, when dealing with incredulous stares—in this case, two competing ones—it's hard to know how to respond.[20] We seem to be at a dialectical standoff. In general, incredulous stares do not amount to decisive objections. Further, ethical naturalists and ethical non-naturalists seem to be in the same boat, at least with respect to both embracing counterintuitive views about morality that go against at least some of our commonsense beliefs.

Second, we've also seen that at least some normative facts turn out to be *not so different* from natural facts after all. That is, many prominent ethical non-naturalists like Fitzpatrick, Enoch, and Parfit admit that some normative facts *do* in fact belong to the same category as natural facts. While they maintain that "reason-giving" or "full-blooded" normativity cannot be naturalistically explained, they all accept that "rule-implying" or "formal" normativity *can* be fully naturalistically accounted for. Recall Fitzpatrick's claim that, in the case of *A*'s being a good automobile, the evaluative normative fact in question—viz., that in virtue of *A*'s having natural features XYZ, *A* thereby satisfies the appropriate standards for automobiles such that we rightly judge *A* to be a

---

[19] This account somewhat modifies Enoch's discussion of the puzzlement related to ethical non-naturalism.

[20] Cf. Lewis 1986, pp. 133–5.

good automobile—can be given a plausible naturalistic reduction by appealing to the "proper function" of automobiles, which just consists in various naturalistic facts: e.g., the makers' intentions, social practices, etc.

Enoch defends a parallel claim about what he calls "formal normativity". Take the example of a game like chess. By inventing a rule—e.g., that bishops can only move diagonally—we've created normative standards such that certain moves are now correct (e.g., moving our bishop diagonally) and others incorrect (e.g., moving our bishop horizontally or vertically). Enoch fully accepts that this normative demand—e.g., that one ought not to move one's bishop vertically—can be accounted for naturalistically. As he writes:

> Notice that facts that are normative or evaluative in this formal sense don't seem too far from the natural facts mentioned above [in relation to human artifacts] [...]—the thought that, say, the incorrectness of a certain move in a game is entirely grounded in facts about us and our practices seems quite natural, as is arguably the fact that a motorcycle's being good-as-a-motorcycle is reducible to facts about the nature of motorcycles, or perhaps their function (itself understood in naturalistically respectable terms). (Enoch 2018: 32–33)

Finally, consider Parfit's account of "rule-implying normativity." In the case of legal normativity—e.g., that Ø-ing is illegal—Parfit argues that this can also be fully naturalistically accounted for in terms of, e.g., the founding of a political community, the creation of a legislature and passing of laws, intentions of legislators, various social agreements, etc. As he writes:

> The property of being illegal might thus be truly claimed to be a natural property, and facts about which acts are illegal would then be natural facts. This use of 'natural' is in part intended to imply that, from a scientific point of view, some property or fact needs no further explanation. There is nothing puzzling, or needing further explanation, in the fact that certain acts are illegal. (Parfit 2011: 308)

Allowing this, however, significantly narrows the scope of the Normativity Objection. It shows that "oughts" and "is-es" *understood as general classes* are not as radically distinct as we might have initially thought. Put differently, the alleged stark divide between normative facts ("oughts") and natural facts ("mere is-es") only seems daunting or even unbridgeable given the following type of taxonomy defended by Parfit:

Normative facts (oughts)	Natural facts (mere is-es)
Setting cats on fire for fun is morally wrong	This is a river
Other things being equal, it's morally required to refrain from lying	Shakespeare wrote sonnets
	Stones are physical objects
We ought to jump from burning buildings	Water is H_2O
Torturing babies is intrinsically bad	Heat is mean kinetic energy

However, drawing upon the claims made by Fitzpatrick, Enoch, and Parfit himself, we should revise Parfit's taxonomy to instead look something like this:

Normative facts (non-naturalistic *oughts*)	Normative/natural facts (naturalistic *oughts*)	Natural facts (naturalistic *mere is-es*)
Setting cats on fire for fun is morally wrong	Other things being equal, one ought not to shout in public	This is a river
Other things being equal, it's morally required to refrain from lying	When playing chess, you are required to move your bishop diagonally	Shakespeare wrote sonnets
		Stones are physical objects
		Water is H_2O
We ought to jump from burning buildings	It is legally forbidden to run red lights	Heat is mean kinetic energy
Torturing babies is intrinsically bad	This artifact (e.g., motorcycle/computer/car/etc.) is good	

Thus, the gap between normative facts and natural facts is indeed bridgeable for at least *some* normative claims. Put differently, as Fitzpatrick, Enoch, and Parfit all accept, there do exist some genuine naturalistic oughts.

To counter this worry, the ethical non-naturalist might qualify their view and insist that, strictly speaking, the type of alleged normativity involved with naturalistic oughts—that is, with merely "formal normativity" (Enoch/McPherson) or "rule implying normativity" (Parfit)—is in some sense not genuine normativity.[21] That is, the term "normative" should be reserved only for those requirements that are nonoptional or categorically binding in nature, where this includes, for example, moral, prudential, and epistemic norms. While it's true that, according to the merely arbitrary rules of chess, one "ought" or "is required to" only move one's bishop diagonally, this is altogether different from the type of genuine or robust—or what Enoch and McPherson call "full-blooded"—normativity involved with prudential, epistemic, or moral requirements.

In response, the ethical naturalist has three basic options. First, they might seek to accommodate robust normativity within a naturalistic framework—something we aim to do in Section 4. Second, they might just deny that moral demands are robustly normative. As Philippa Foot famously argues, moral requirements should be seen not as categorically binding but instead as merely "a system of hypothetical imperatives". This approach, however, won't be attractive to ethical naturalists who want to retain the commonsense moral belief that it's not merely optional, say, to refrain from torturing babies for fun.

Third and lastly, the ethical naturalist might directly challenge the view that *all* genuine normativity must be categorically binding or nonoptional in nature. In doing so, they can take a page from the ethical non-naturalist's own playbook (cf. Enoch 2016). Following David Enoch's well-known "shmagency objection" to moral constitutivism,

---

[21] Thanks very much to David Copp for pointing this out.

the ethical naturalist can argue as follows: For the sake of discussion, we grant that "normativity" applies solely to categorically binding requirements. When we talk about normativity, however—or more precisely, what we'll call "shnormativity"—we mean to include any type of prescriptive and/or evaluative judgments, whether categorically binding or not. "Shnormative requirements" still function as genuine oughts—or is it "shmoughts" (?)—for us, directing us how to think, feel, and act, even if at least some of them fall short of so-called normative requirements.

At the end of the day, the ethical non-naturalist move to restrict the term "normative" only to "full-blooded normativity"—as opposed to "formal" or "rule-implying" normativity—seems to amount to a mere terminological debate. More significantly, it obscures the fact that in order to avoid the objection raised above, the ethical non-naturalist has to importantly revise the overall worry. If we grant that "formal" or "rule-implying" normativity is—as Enoch's, McPherson's and Parfit's labels themselves all seem to imply—indeed a genuine form of normativity, then the Just Too Different Objection no longer turns on whether (1a) normative oughts and (1b) non-normative mere is-es as general classes are just too different to belong to the same category. Rather, it only focuses on whether (2a) a particular subset of normative claims—viz., categorically binding or non-optional oughts—are too different from *both* (2b) noncategorically binding normative oughts and (2c) non-normative mere is-es such that they cannot be put into the same category. However, given that ethical non-naturalists like Fitzpatrick, Enoch, and Parfit allow that at least some oughts can be purely naturalistically understood, this can be seen as at least getting the foot in the door, where the task now facing the ethical naturalist is to somehow extend this same analysis to the narrow subset of normative judgments that the ethical non-naturalists claim ultimately resists naturalization.

3.2 Critique of the Irreducible Metafacts Objection

Can an ethical naturalist accept metafacts? That is, can metafacts be accounted for naturalistically? As we've already seen, Fitzpatrick allows that at least some second-order normative facts—in particular, those involving evaluative judgments related to the proper functions of artifacts—can be naturalized. By contrast, Dancy, McNaughton, and Rawling all answer "no" to these questions.[22] They argue that second-order normative facts are irreducible and so can't be reduced to, identical with, or constituted by merely natural facts. The general idea is that while reasons themselves are natural facts, the metafact—that is, what we might call the "reason-relation" which relates natural facts that are reasons to relevant agents, sets of circumstances, etc.—is itself non-naturalistic and irreducible.

---

[22] For a more metaphysical defense of metafacts as non-naturalistic, see Cuneo 2016.

At this point, the ethical naturalist will most likely raise two objections: (1) How does this alleged non-natural metafact or reason-relation help to explain normativity, and (2) Why can't such metafacts be accounted for naturalistically? *Prima facie*, it's hard to see how exactly non-natural metafacts do any real explanatory work. One initial worry is similar to a complaint raised against another non-naturalistic metaethical view, viz., divine command theory. In explaining why a specific action, say, murder, is morally wrong, the divine command theorist claims: "It's wrong because God forbids it." But the standard reply is: "What's so special—normatively speaking—about the fact that God commanded us not to commit murder? That is, how does the fact that it's a *supernaturalistic property* help in any way to explain or account for the normative wrongness of murder?"[23] The same worry appears to apply here. Against non-naturalistic metaethical views in general, we can ask: "How exactly does the fact that the moral property in question—whether the concrete property of moral wrongness or the more abstract metafact or reason-relation—is a *non-natural property* help in any way to explain or account for the normative wrongness of setting cats on fire?" As Connie Rosati expresses this general type of worry:

> It is unclear why the fact that an act has the unanalyzable nonnatural property of, say, rightness gives us a reason to perform this act. What is it about the presence of such a property that would give us a reason to act? (Rosati 2018:367)

However, this worry is arguably misplaced. The ethical non-naturalist has a two-pronged response.[24] First, *contra* Rosati, they would most likely object that they aren't claiming that non-natural moral properties explain normativity *in virtue of their being non-natural*. Rather, following Moore's lead, they're simply appealing to an argument by elimination. If we accept that there are normative facts, and if such facts resist all attempts at naturalization, then we must conclude that they are non-natural facts. Understood this way, identifying metafacts as non-naturalistic isn't an attempt to explain normativity as much as it is to locate normativity, as it were, within the non-natural as opposed to natural domain. Second, ethical non-naturalists have a deeper story to tell about how normative requirements are generated. It's not so much the fact that the various facts in question are non-natural that explains why they're normative. Instead, normativity is explained in terms of reasons. And what ultimately explains reasons themselves is that a reason-relation obtains in this case, where the normativity of this relation is itself simply brute or primitive.[25]

Our main challenge to this line of argument is: In what sense are so-called metafacts actually doing any explanatory work in this overall picture? Recall our example of bear-baiting. In response to the first-order normative question, "Why is bear-baiting wrong?," it seems clear that appealing to a reason—in this case, the natural fact that bear-baiting

---

[23] For further discussion, see Louise Antony, "Atheism, Naturalism, and Morality" 2012.
[24] Thanks to the editors, Paul Bloomfield and David Copp, for raising the following criticisms.
[25] This paragraph borrows heavily from correspondence with the editors.

inflicts pain upon bears—helps to explain why one should not engage in bear-baiting. But what about the related second-order normative question: "And what explains this normative fact? That is, what explains why this reason has the practical relevance it does in these particular circumstances in the first place?" The ethical non-naturalist reply is: "This is explained by the existence of a metafact, that is, a reason-relation which holds between, on the one hand, the reason (viz., that bear-baiting causes bears pain), and on the other hand, the agent and her specific circumstances, such that the reason has practical relevance in this case."

But this doesn't seem like an actual explanation so much as merely putting a label on the very phenomenon that needs to be explained. In this way, it seems not so different from the notorious Scholastic appeal to "dormitivity." Consider the typical exchange: Q1: Why does opium cause people to sleep? A: Because of its dormitive virtue, that is, its tendency to cause people to sleep. In a similar vein, we can ask: Q2: Why is a reason, i.e., some natural fact, of practical relevance for how, normatively speaking, an agent should act in a given situation? A: Because of the existence of a "metafact," that is, a relation which makes the reason, on the one hand, practically relevant to the agent and her given situation, on the other hand. This sounds like simply asserting that such a relation exists, without any actual explanation of the normative fact in question. And to claim that we must simply accept that this reason-relation is "brute" or "primitive" doesn't help, either. It just seems to beg off offering any explanation, by simply insisting that such a relation obtains as a brute normative fact.

This leaves us in an interesting position. In terms of first-order normative questions—e.g., *Why* is bear-baiting wrong?—these are best explained by appealing to natural facts taken as reasons—e.g., because bear-baiting causes bears pain. But in terms of the second-order normative question—e.g., What explains *why* this is a normative fact in the first place?—we arguably should accept that such facts are brute or primitive full stop. Making an appeal to non-natural metafacts as allegedly normatively explanatory is a useless detour, insofar as this involves just putting a label upon and positing the existence of—rather than in any way actually serving to *explain*—the brute normative fact in question. At the end of the day, it seems that both ethical non-naturalists and ethical naturalists must simply accept—rather than in any way successfully explain—the existence of certain brute normative facts. Thus, the real issue becomes whether ethical naturalists are able to accommodate such brute normative facts within a generally naturalistic framework, a task to which we now turn.

4. Ethical Structuralism and Moral Nativism

We have surveyed the standard objections to ethical naturalism, and argued that none of them pose an insurmountable challenge. However, there is a version of the "Just

Too Different" objection that we need to respond to, given our particular construal of "naturalism."

We earlier endorsed the view that naturalism fundamentally involved a commitment to *confirmational holism*, the view that every truth of nature is evidentially relevant to every other. But this commitment may, ironically, provide the non-naturalist with a way of fleshing out the "difference" that is supposed to divide the natural from the non-natural facts in a way that poses a particular challenge to us. The non-naturalist might now claim—citing our own criterion of "the natural"—that the difference between natural and non-natural facts is that the former are subject to empirical confirmation, while the latter are not.

Perhaps it now seems that the only response we could make to this version of the "Just Too Different" objection would be to assert that normative facts *are* subject to empirical confirmation. And indeed, this is a claim that some normative naturalists—e.g., Richard Boyd—want to make. Boyd argues that we can confirm empirically that some ethical systems are better than others. Some, he argues, do a better job of disciplining the homeostatic property cluster that constitutes the good for human beings; this fact provides empirical warrant for those ethical systems. But Boyd's approach seems to us to depend for its plausibility on the meta-ethical assumption that some form of consequentialism is correct. Despite Boyd's assertion that his approach will work with any ethical metatheory, we do not see how to adapt it so as to apply to a deontological theory. And this is a problem not so much because we are more sympathetic to deontology than to consequentialism (although that's true); it's rather that we hold that an adequate moral naturalism should not, on its own, commit one to consequentialism.

What we propose to do instead, is to *embrace* the premise of this newly envisioned version of the "Just Too Different" objection. In fact, we want to enlarge it, and in so doing, introduce a new approach to naturalizing morality. We contend that the problem with naturalizing *ethics* is really the problem of naturalizing *normativity in general*. This "enlarged" problem of "difference" arises in connection with *logical*, and hence with *rational* normativity as well.

Our basic contention is that the natural world possesses *normative structure*, and that the truths of morality, rationality, logic, and mathematics are truths about that structure. We also contend that human psychology enables us to *apprehend* such structure.[26] Such apprehension, however, does not require our being able to formulate or even recognize as true statements that explicitly and correctly describe that structure. The apprehension of normative structure is, rather, reflected in our appreciation of the *normative force* of certain relations: in logic, the relation between the premises and conclusion of a valid inference, in mathematics, the relations between certain particular facts and their generalizations, and in morality, the relation between the wrongness of certain actions and our duty to refrain from performing them.

---

[26] Notably, Parfit (2011) argues that normativity need not involve any sense of psychological force or necessitation. However, we wish to emphasize that we regard the normative connections involved in morality, logic, and mathematics to be part of the objective normative structure we are positing. There is,

This new strategy, we believe, comports well with our final, summary criticism of non-naturalist accounts of morality, viz., that the mere labeling of moral truths as "non-natural" does nothing to explain the normative force of such truths. The account that we offer purports to explain normative force, whether that is the normative force of morality, or the normative force of rationality. Our approach, furthermore, is in line with the naturalistic approach of the Cornell realists, as we'll explain below.

Let us look at the normative force of logic. First, note that Hume's notorious insistence that one cannot derive an "ought" from an "is" applies as surely to logic as it does to morality. That is the lesson of Lewis Carroll's 1895 essay "What the Tortoise Said to Achilles."[27] The reader may recall that, in Carroll's fable, Achilles was trying to convince a tortoise of an elementary result in geometry by arguing that a certain proposition, Z, followed logically from two others, A, and B. The tortoise concedes that the *hypothetical* proposition "if A and B, then Z" is true, and concedes further that A is true and B is true. But he then avers that he does not see why those concessions put him under any *obligation* to accept Z. Achilles cheerfully amends his argument by adding the premise that, "If [(if A and B are true, then Z is true) and A is true, and B is true] then Z is true." The tortoise accepts this new premise readily, but still wants to know why he *ought* to accept Z. This goes through many iterations before the exhausted Achilles finally gives up.

Carroll's Achilles has been made to confront the fact that accepting some statement (or statements) as true is not *fungible* with feeling the "force" of logical entailment. Enriching a valid argument with a statement of a logical principle does not make any difference to the validity of the argument, *even if the principle is one that describes the valid form of that very argument.* In terms of contemporary cognitive science, adding a premise is a matter of adding to the stock of representations that are stored in one's "belief box," whereas the performance of an inference is a matter of how those representations are manipulated by the cognitive "machine." Thus it is one thing to believe that that the rule of *modus ponens* (or rather, some sentence expressing the rule) is *true* and another thing to be subject to the normative "feeling"—what Christopher Peacocke calls (in another context) a "primitive compulsion"—that one *must* accept certain statements if one accepts certain others. The moral of Carroll's story, as we wish to apply it, is that the acceptance of a logical principle does not, in itself, explain the normative force that the principle is meant to describe.[28]

This point is relevant to ethical naturalism in two ways: 1) it shows that *normativity* is not limited to the moral domain. The normativity of logic is every bit as puzzling as the normativity of morality. What needs explanation is the "ought-ness" of *both* logical and moral principles; 2) this point shows that principles, in order to be true, need not be

---

nonetheless, the question of what it is for a creature such as a human being to *apprehend* such normative structure. *That* is a matter of psychology and epistemology.

[27] *Mind* (New Series), Vol. 4, No. 14 (Apr., 1895), pp. 278–280.

[28] For a more detailed discussion of this point, see Louise Antony, "A Naturalized Approach to the A Priori" (2004).

statements that stand in the same confirmational relations as statements that do not express normative obligation. We do not explain the normative force of logical principles in terms of the truth of those principles; rather, the truth of the principles stems from their accurate characterization of the objective logical structure of reality. Similarly, we want to say that the truth of ethical principles reflects the objective normative structure of reality.

But more needs to be said about this "objective structure." For that, we turn to a promising account of the ontology of mathematics: structuralism. Structuralism in mathematics is the view that the "objects" of mathematics, such as numbers or sets, can be fruitfully considered to be positions within complex and abstractly characterized patterns, or sets of isomorphic patterns.[29] There are many forms of structuralism, beginning with early suggestions by Hilary Putnam, and subsequently views articulated and defended by Paul Benacerraf, Michael Resnick, Geoffrey Hellman, Stewart Shapiro, and others. While these theorists disagree about the reification of either the patterns or the positions within them, they all agree that it is a matter of objective fact whether or not a certain region of reality instantiates the patterns in question. Shapiro is the most realist of these thinkers, and is willing to reify not only the patterns, but the positions within the patterns; he is also committed to the view that the structures exist independently of and prior to instantiations of them. Most pertinently to our purposes, Shapiro holds that mathematical statements are truth-apt, and that their truth or falsity depends on objective mathematical structure.

One challenge (one of four "basic challenges," according to Reck and Schiemer) for structuralist realists in mathematics is the matter of "how we can have 'access' to structures seen as abstract objects."[30] As it happens, however, there is a substantial body of work coming from developmental cognitive psychology theorizing the nature and emergence of mathematical competence in human beings. Psychologists such as Stanislas Dahaene, Susan Carey, and Rochel Gelman,[31] have done outstanding work that makes clear that this competence is the unfolding of a specialized native ability. It is thus a contingent fact that, in at least one possible world (this one!), there emerged creatures with cognitive capacities that enabled them to notice and articulate mathematical structure, and to reason about and discover arcane facts about it.

We thus find a convergence between a plausible ontological account of the nature of mathematical reality and the psychological account of a specialized native competence in the terrestrial creatures capable of comprehending it. The structuralist proposal about

---

[29] See Erich Reck and Georg Schiemer, "Structuralism in the Philosophy of Mathematics," *Stanford Encyclopedia of Philosophy* (Spring 2020 Edition), edited by Edward N. Zalta (https://plato.stanford.edu/archives/spr2020/entries/structuralism-mathematics/).

[30] Ibid.

[31] Stanislas Dahaene, *The Number Sense: How the Mind Creates Mathematics*, Revised and Updated Edition (Oxford University Press, 2011); Susan Carey, *The Origin of Concepts* (Oxford University Press: 2011); R. Gelman (2006), "Young Natural-Number Arithmeticians," *Current Directions in Psychological Science* 15(4): 193–197.

the nature of mathematical reality is thus bolstered by the epistemological story. Not only does this story answer one of the "basic challenges" a realist structuralist account of mathematics must face, but it provides evidence that there is a reality "out there" that is being cognized by human beings.

We hold, then, that the existence of a compelling account of moral *knowledge*—of its etiology and its nature—can contribute to a structuralist account of moral reality. As with mathematical cognition, a naturalistic story of our apprehension of normative structure both responds to an important question about moral structuralism—"how do we know about such structure?"—and provides evidence that our moral intuitions are about something *objective*.

And indeed, such an account of moral knowledge has been proposed. John Mikhail, following a suggestion made by John Rawls, and drawing on the substance and methodology of Noam Chomsky's theory of language acquisition, has hypothesized the existence of a "Universal Moral Grammar" (UMG), offering what is to our minds a promising possibility for explaining human access to the structural facts of ethical normativity.[32,33]

Mikhail begins with certain data the explanation of which constitute desiderata on any adequate theory of human moral reasoning: (1) very young children (3–4 yrs. old) possess a complex "intuitive jurisprudence" evident in patterns of judgments involving, fundamentally, concepts *permissible, obligatory, and forbidden*; (2) these concepts are lexicalized in (as far as we know) every human language; (3) prohibitions against physical aggression, and legal distinctions involving causation, intention, and voluntariness appear to be universal, and correspond to the fundamental elements of explanatory codifications of jurisprudence proposed by some legal theorists; (4) there appears

---

[32] John Mikhail, "Universal Moral Grammar: Theory, Evidence and the Future," *TRENDS in Cognitive Sciences* 11(4).

[33] There is an important difference between Chomsky's UG and Mikhail's UMG. Chomsky's UG specifies only the linguistic universals in humanly acquirable languages, but provides for variation among languages with respect to certain parameters, such as whether or not the fundamental word order in a language is SUBJECT-VERB-OBJECT (as in English) or SOV (as in Turkish). See Dryer 2005. This provision is necessary because of the observed variation among human spoken languages. Mikhail's model, on the other hand, does not need to allow for any parametric variation, since, on Mikhail's reading of the evidence, there is no variation with respect to the fundamental moral principles he posits. One could, of course, dispute Mikhail's claims about universality, but the current point is that *if* the moral principles that constitute moral competence *are* universal, there is no empirical pressure to posit parameters of variation, as there is in the linguistic case.

Similarly, from the fact that we can imagine aliens who speak languages that are not acquirable by humans under conditions of casual exposure, it doesn't follow that there must, or even can be, aliens with different moral grammars. However, we are positing normative structure as part of the *necessary* structure of reality, just like logical and mathematical structure. Now of course it is *conceivable*, on a weak understanding of "conceivable," that we are wrong on this point. But we emphasize that this is an *epistemic* risk, and one that simply comes along with our commitment to naturalism. Naturalistic theories are subject to empirical disconfirmation; thus if we were to discover aliens with different moral principles, we would have to say that our theory was wrong in positing the necessity of this particular normative structure. But in such a case we would certainly be no worse off than the non-naturalist.

Thanks to Paul Bloomfield for raising questions about these points.

to be significant neurological localization of moral cognition.[34] All together, Mikhail argues, this picture resembles the evidential picture behind Noam Chomsky's posit of a Universal Grammar (UG) for humanly natural languages. The early emergence of complex moral reasoning in the absence of instruction parallels Chomsky's "poverty-of-the-stimulus" argument for native linguistic structure. The universality of the features of this competency suggest a native, species-wide cognitive structure, analogous to Chomsky's "universal grammar," and the neurological localization of moral reasoning suggest, as with the neurological localization of the language faculty, a degree of specificity and informational encapsulation not characteristic of general cognitive functions. Accordingly, Mikhail posits the existence of an innate capacity for moral judgment.

An important part of Mikhail's picture, again in analogy with Chomsky's picture of language acquisition, is that this native, internal moral competence involves principles that are not accessible to direct introspection. Mikhail emphasizes that part of the task of moral judgement involves translating the epistemically accessible aspects of a moral situation into a "structural description" of the situation—a description in terms of the primitive elements of the moral grammar. This translation occurs at a subpersonal, and hence subconscious, level, analogous to the apprehension of grammatical structure. (Just to illustrate, consider the following sentence: "Visiting relatives can be tedious." You are likely to recognize that this sentence is ambiguous before you are able to articulate the two different grammatical structures corresponding to each of the two readings.)

This aspect of Mikhail's theory offers an explanation of certain cases of "moral dumbfounding." Consider, for example, the puzzling patterns of judgment surrounding what are now known as "trolley problems." In the fundamental case, there is an out-of-control trolley headed for a group of five people on its track. You are to imagine that you can throw a switch that will divert the trolley to a different track, where there is only one person on the track. Should you do it? Most people say that one should divert the trolley, or at least that it would be morally permissible to divert the trolley. In the second case, there is an out-of-control trolley headed for five people, but the only way to prevent the trolley's killing them involves your pushing a very large person in front of the trolley to stop it before it reaches the five. Here, people generally judge that it would be morally wrong to push the large person into the path of the trolley. The cost/benefit ratio of the choices in both cases is, of course, the same—five persons dead vs. one person dead. When this is pointed out to subjects, they are "dumbfounded"—they cannot explain their own apparent inconsistency.[35] Mikhail, however, points out that there are

---

[34] Mikhail acknowledges that the evidence here is not conclusive.

[35] Joshua Greene (2007) has argued that the hesitation reflects cognitive dissonance between the (consequentialist) moral judgment that one ought to push the large person, and the emotional distaste for the "up-close-and-personal" contact that such pushing would entail. But work by Katharine Saunders (Saunders 2014) shows that young children display the same pattern of judgments as adults in analogous thought-experiments that do not involve any up-close-and-personal contact, nor indeed, any harm to any sentient creature.

two different moral principles involved in each case: there is the doctrine of double-effect, and there is the prohibition against battery, and these principles are ordered in the moral grammar. In the first case, the instance of double-effect (the death of the one person on the alternative track is foreseen, but not intended) precedes the instance of battery, whereas in the second case the battery (pushing the person into the path of the trolley) precedes the instance of double-effect. The subpersonal operation of the moral grammar produces the resulting judgments, but not in a way that is transparent to the subject.

Accordingly, Mikhail hypothesizes that our moral "competence" must be abducted from subjects' intuitions and behavior, together with other known psychological factors (like memory limitations and emotional disturbance.) In cases where it appears that a subject is not acting "in accordance" with hypothesized native principles, it is legitimate for the theorist to treat the "behavior" as the result of interaction effects. This is not the blank check that it may appear to be. Just like the linguist, the moral theorist is constrained, in building their overall model, to appeal only to factors for which there is independent evidence, and to offer psychologically plausible mechanisms to describe the interactions. Moral nativism, thus understood, offers insight into problems and complexities that have occasioned disagreement among moral theorists.

In sum: there is an empirically plausible nativist account of the human capacity for moral judgment that, if correct, explains how human beings could be in epistemic contact with an objective morally normative structure. If it seems like a cosmic accident that such a "preordained harmony" should exist, it is no less likely, a priori, than that there should be beings with our capacity for apprehension of an objective mathematically normative structure. The existence of this specialized native capacity coheres with and supports independent evidence that we possess the general cognitive and affective prerequisites for moral life: a recognition of the sensible and psychological natures of other creatures (especially human beings), and a sympathy for them in virtue of their possessing such natures.

How would this kind of objective structure explain normativity? In contrast with the non-naturalist's positing of a non- or extra-natural realm, our posit puts normative relations on a par with logical and mathematical relations, all of which are taken to be formal features of the natural world. As part of a confirmationally holistic theory of the natural world, the existence of ethically normative relations would be confirmed alongside the other posits of natural science and commonsense. We therefore see our project as fully consonant with the projects of the Cornell realists insofar as we show normative claims to be part of an empirically adequate theory of the world. It would then achieve what David Copp calls the "compatibilist" goal, viz., "to reconcile the existence of [normativity] with what science tells us to be true about the world around us."[36]

---

[36] Copp (2015).

5. CONCLUSION

In this article, we've undertaken four tasks. First, we've provided a general overview of ethical naturalism, identifying its core commitments and surveying its many varieties. Second, we've discussed the central challenge to ethical naturalism, viz., the Normativity Objection. Third, we've presented a number of responses to it, including:

1. attempting to muddy the waters by demonstrating that, even according to some prominent ethical non-naturalists, the general categories of normative facts ("oughts") and natural facts ("is-es") aren't as radically far apart as we might have initially thought in many cases
2. arguing that the ethical non-naturalist appeal to irreducible or non-natural metafacts fails to provide any advantage over ethical naturalism with respect to explaining or accounting for normativity

Fourth and lastly, we've argued that the challenge of naturalizing normativity is one that arises for logic and mathematics as well as for ethics. And we have outlined a proposal for naturalizing normativity in general that draws on structuralism in mathematics and moral nativism in psychology.

We conclude that ethical naturalism is an attractive philosophical view, with the resources to respond to all the main objections to it, including, most significantly, the Normativity Objection.

REFERENCES

Antony, Louise. 2004. "A Naturalistic Approach to the A Priori." *Philosophical Issues* 14(1): 1–17.
Antony, Louise. 2020. "Atheism, Naturalism, and Morality." In *Contemporary Debates in Philosophy of Religion*, 2nd ed., edited by Raymond Arragon and Michael Peterson, 66–78. Hoboken, NJ: John Wiley & Sons.
Bloomfield, Paul. 2001. *Moral Reality*. Oxford: Oxford University Press.
Boyd, Richard. 1988. "How to Be a Moral Realist." In *Essays on Moral Realism*, edited by Sayre-McCord, 181–228. Ithaca: Cornell University Press.
Brandt, Richard. 1979. *A Theory of the Good and the Right*. Oxford: Oxford University Press.
Brink, David. 1989. *Moral Realism and the Foundations of Ethics*. Cambridge: Cambridge University Press.
Copp, David. 2012. "Normativity and Reasons: Five Arguments from Parfit against Normative Naturalism." In *Ethical Naturalism: Current Debates*, edited by Susana Nuccetelli and Gary Seay, 24–57. Cambridge: Cambridge University Press.
Copp, David. 2015. "Explaining Normativity" *Proceedings and Addresses of the American Philosophical Association* 89: 48–73.
Cuneo, Terence. 2016. "What's to Be Said for Moral Non-Naturalism?" In *The Blackwell Companion to Naturalism*, edited by Kelly James Clark, 401–415. Oxford: Wiley Blackwell.

Dancy, Jonathan. 2008. "Nonnaturalism." In *The Oxford Handbook of Ethical Theory*, edited by David Copp, 122–145. New York: Oxford University Press.

Dimock, Susan. 2003. "Two Virtues of Contractarianism." *Journal of Value Inquiry* 37: 395–414.

Dryer, M. S. (2005). "The Order of Subject, Object and Verb." In *The World Atlas of Language Structures*, edited by M. Haspelmath, M. S. Dryer, D. Gil, and B. Comrie, 330–333. Oxford: Oxford University Press.

Enoch, David. 2011. *Taking Morality Seriously*. New York: Oxford University Press.

Enoch, David. 2016. "Agency, Schmagency: Why Normativity Won't Come from What Is Constitutive of Action." *Philosophical Review* 115(2): 169–198.

Enoch, David. 2018. "Non-Naturalistic Realism in Metaethics." In *The Routledge Handbook of Metaethics*, edited by Tristram McPherson and David Plunkett, 29–42. New York: Routledge.

Firth, Roderick. 1951. "Ethical Absolutism and the Ideal Observer." *Philosophy and Phenomenological Research* 12: 317–345.

Fitzpatrick, William. 2008. "Robust Ethical Realism, Non-Naturalism, and Normativity." In *Oxford Studies in Metaethics*, vol. 3, edited by Russ Shafer-Landau, 159–206. New York: Oxford University Press.

Fitzpatrick, William. 2011. "Ethical Naturalism and Normative Properties." In *New Waves in Metaethics*, edited by Michael Brady. New York: Palgrave MacMillan.

Flanagan, Owen. 1995. "Ethics Naturalized: Ethics as Human Ecology." In *Mind and Morals*, edited by Larry May, Marilyn Friedman, and Andy Clark, 19–44. Cambridge, MA: MIT Press.

Flanagan, Owen, and Hagop Sarkissian, and David Wong. 2016. "Naturalizing Ethics." In *The Blackwell Companion to Naturalism*, edited by Kelly James Clark, 16–33. Oxford: Wiley Blackwell.

Foot, Philippa. 2001. *Natural Goodness*. Oxford: Clarendon Press.

Greene, Joshua (2007). "The secret joke of Kant's soul." In *Moral Psychology*, edited by W. Sinnott-Armstrong, vol. 3. MIT Press.

Gauthier, David. 1987. *Morals by Agreement*. Oxford: Clarendon Press.

Harman, Gilbert. 2012. "Naturalism in Moral Philosophy." In *Ethical Naturalism: Current Debates*, edited by Susana Nuccetelli and Gary Seay, 8–23. Cambridge: Cambridge University Press.

Harman, Gilbert. 2000. *Explaining Value and Other Essays in Moral Philosophy*. Oxford: Clarendon Press.

Hempel, C. G. 1958. "The Theoretician's Dilemma." *Concepts, Theories, and the Mind-Body Problem*, edited by Michael Scriven Feigl and Grover Maxwell, 37–98. Minnesota Studies in the Philosophy of Science, vol. 2. Herbert, Minneapolis: University of Minnesota Press.

Hobbes, Thomas. [1651] 2009. *Leviathan*. Oxford: Oxford University Press.

Hursthouse, Rosalind. 1999. *On Virtue Ethics*. Oxford: Oxford University Press.

Joyce, Richard. 2016. "Evolution and Moral Naturalism." In *The Blackwell Companion to Naturalism*, edited by Kelly James Clark, 369–385. Oxford: Wiley Blackwell.

Lewis, David. 1988. "Desire as belief." *Mind* 97(418): 323–332.

Lewis, David. 1986. *On the Plurality of Worlds*. Oxford: Basil Blackwell.

McNaughton, David, and Piers Rawling. 2004. "Naturalism and Normativity." *Proceedings of the Aristotelian Society* 104: 187–203.

McPherson, Tristram. 2011. "Against Quietist Normative Realism," *Philosophical Studies* 154 (2): 223–240.

McPherson, Tristram, and David Plunkett, eds. 2018. *The Routledge Handbook of Metaethics*. New York: Routledge.

Moore, G. E. 1994. *Principia Ethica*. Cambridge: Cambridge University Press.
Nussbaum, Martha. 1995. "Aristotle on Human Nature and the Foundations of Ethics." In *World, Mind, and Ethics: Essays on the Ethical Philosophy of Bernard Williams*, edited by J. E. J. Altham and Ross Harrison, 86–131. Cambridge: Cambridge University Press.
Oppenheim, Paul, and Hilary Putnam. 1958. "The Unity of Science as a Working Hypothesis." Minnesota Studies in the Philosophy of Science 2: 3–36.
Parfit, Derek. 2011. *On What Matters*, vol. 2. New York: Oxford University Press.
Putnam, Hilary. 1975a. "What Theories Are Not." In *Mathematics, Matter and Method*, Philosophical Papers, vol. 1, 215–227. Cambridge: Cambridge University Press:
Putnam, Hilary. 1975b. "Logical Positivism and the Philosophy of Mind." In *Mind, Language and Reality*, Philosophical Papers, vol. 2, 441–451. Cambridge: Cambridge University Press.
Quine, W. v. O. 1951. "Two Dogmas of Empiricism." *Philosophical Review* 60(1): 20–43.
Quine, W. v. O. 1969. "Epistemology Naturalized." In *Ontological Relativity and Other Essays*. New York: Columbia University Press.
Railton, Peter. 1986. "Facts and Values." *Philosophical Topics* 14: 5–31.
Railton, Peter. 2003. *Facts, Values and Norms*. Cambridge: Cambridge University Press.
Rosati, Connie. 2018. "Mind-Dependence and Moral Realism." In *The Routledge Handbook of Metaethics*, edited by Tristram McPherson and David Plunkett, 355–371. New York: Routledge.
Rosen, Gideon. 1994. "Objectivity and Modern Idealism: What Is the Question?" In *Philosophy in Mind: The Place of Philosophy in the Study of Mind*, edited by Murray Michael, and John O'Leary-Hawthorne, 277–314. Dordrecht: Kluwer Academic.
Saunders, Katharine. 2014. *Investigating the Psychological Foundations of Moral Judgment*. Dissertation, Graduate School, Rutgers University New Brunswick.
Sayre-McCord, Geoffrey ed. 1988. *Essays on Moral Realism*. Ithaca: Cornell University Press.
Sayre-McCord, Geoffrey 1988. "Introduction." In *Essays on Moral Realism*, edited by Sayre-McCord, 1–23. Ithaca: Cornell University Press.
Sayre-McCord, Geoffrey. 2008. "Moral Realism." In *The Oxford Handbook of Ethical Theory*, edited by David Copp, 39–62. New York: Oxford University Press.
Shafer-Landau, Russ. 2003. *Moral Realism: A Defense*. New York: Oxford University Press.
Michael Smith. 1993. "Realism." In *A Companion to Ethics*, edited by Peter Singer, 399–410. Oxford: Blackwell Publishers.
Smith, Michael. 1994. The Moral Problem. Oxford: Wiley Blackwell.
Smith, Michael. 1995. "Internal Reasons." *Philosophy and Phenomenological Research* 55(1): 109–131.
Sturgeon, Nicholas. 1998. "Moral Explanations." In *Essays on Moral Realism*, edited by Sayre-McCord, 229–256. Ithaca: Cornell University Press.
Sturgeon, Nicholas. 2008. "Ethical Naturalism." In *The Oxford Handbook of Ethical Theory*, edited by David Copp, 91–121. New York: Oxford University Press.
Suikkanen, Jussi. 2016. "Naturalism in Metaethics." In *The Blackwell Companion to Naturalism*, edited by Kelly James Clark, 351–368. Oxford: Wiley Blackwell.
Thomson, Judith. 2008. *Normativity*. Peru, IL: Open Court Publishing Company.
van Roojen, Mark. 2015. *Metaethics: A Contemporary Introduction*. New York: Routledge.
Wong, David. 1984. Moral Relativity. Berkeley: University of California Press.
Wong, David. 1996. "Pluralistic Relativism." *Midwest Studies in Philosophy* 20: 378–400.
Wong, David. 2006. Natural Moralities. Cambridge: Cambridge University Press.

CHAPTER 11

ETHICAL REALISM AND ROBUST NORMATIVITY

DAVID COPP

To my mind, the most important objection to ethical realism is its purported inability to account for the "normativity" of the ethical facts that it postulates.[1] As I understand it, ethical realism postulates facts—broadly "ethical facts," such as the fact that it is rational to seek the things that one needs, and, more narrowly, "moral facts," such as the facts that torture is wrong, that kindness is a virtue, and so on. It takes these facts to be states of affairs partly constituted by ethical properties, such as the property of wrongness and the property of being rationally required. The normativity objection is that ethical realism, so understood, is unable to explain what the normativity of these facts consists in. In this chapter, I explore various strategies realists might follow to avoid the objection or answer it, and I argue that it is important to respond directly to it, by facing up to the challenge to explain normativity. I set out criteria of adequacy for such an explanation.

The normativity objection might seem to pose an especially acute challenge to the naturalistic variety of ethical realism.[2] According to ethical naturalism, the ethical properties and facts are "natural" ones, in a philosophically important sense. Intuitively, the natural world is the world we are immersed in; the world we learn about directly or

---

I presented this chapter in February 2021 to the Centre for Aesthetic, Moral, and Political Philosophy, at the University of Leeds, and in April 2022 to the Notre Dame and Australian Catholic University International Ethics Conference at the University of Notre Dame. I benefited from very helpful discussions on both occasions. Declan Smithies was the commentator on my paper at Notre Dame. I am especially grateful to him and to Robert Audi, Selim Berker, Paul Bloomfield, Steve Finlay, Tom Hurka, Pekka Väyrynen, Ralph Wedgwood, and two anonymous referees for Oxford University Press for their valuable comments and suggestions.

[1] Versions of the objection have been raised by Korsgaard (1996: 28–47), Gibbard (1990: 10), Mackie (1977: 35–42), etc.

[2] Versions of the objection might underlie Parfit's "normativity objection" (Parfit 2011: II, 310–325), Enoch's argument from the "just too different" intuition (Enoch 2011: 4, 80–81, 100, 108), and, perhaps, Moore's open question argument (Moore 1993: ss. 13). For responses, see Copp 2012; 2017; 2018; 2020.

indirectly through observation. Say, then, roughly, that natural properties and facts are "empirical." This idea can be formulated in a more technical way, but this rough formulation should be adequate for our purposes.[3] Examples of natural properties and facts are biological, psychological, and physical ones. Ethical naturalism holds that ethical properties and "basic" ethical facts are also natural ones.[4] I will argue, surprisingly, that ethical naturalism is better positioned than non-naturalism to answer the normativity objection.

To address the objection, I distinguish two ways in which an account of normativity can be deflationary. And I distinguish three relevantly different views that an ethical realist might have about the normativity of ethics: "normative formalism," "normative conceptualism," and "normative objectualism." I argue that the first two are actually kinds of antirealism. Normative objectualism is the best candidate for a realist theory of normativity, but it is the most vulnerable to the normativity objection.

1. Ethical Realism and the Normativity Objection

The normativity objection can seem easy to defuse. Realists hold, as I said, that there are ethical facts, such as the fact that lying is wrong. Basic ethical facts are paradigmatic examples of normative facts. If there are any such facts, they are normative. So, to ethical realists, the challenge to explain how an ethical fact could be normative can seem confused, for ethical realism entails that there are basic ethical facts, and, if there are any such facts, they are normative. It follows, realists might think, that the normativity objection does not pose a genuine challenge to ethical realism. I will return to attempts of this kind to defuse the objection.

Proponents of the objection—the Proponents—have a telling response. They can agree that ethical realism entails that there are normative facts. It follows that if it is not possible for a fact to be normative, then ethical realism is not correct. And if ethical

---

[3] In Copp 2007, I say that a "natural property" is such that no synthetic proposition about its instantiation is "strongly a priori" (chap 1, p. 43, also p. 39, note 22; see Field 2000: 117). There are two relevant views about what facts are. On the view that facts are true propositions, "natural facts" are true synthetic propositions that are not strongly a priori. On the view that facts are worldly states of affairs, a "natural" fact is a state of affairs that is the truth condition of a true synthetic proposition that is not strongly a priori.

[4] A "basic" ethical *claim* is a logically simple claim that ascribes (or at least purports to ascribe) an ethical property to something. The claim that lying is pro tanto wrong is basic, for example. A "basic" ethical *fact* is the truth condition of the proposition expressed by a true basic ethical claim. For example, the fact that lying is pro tanto wrong is basic. An example of a nonbasic ethical claim is the disjunctive claim that either lying is wrong or Truckee is in California. Another example is the claim that lying is permissible, assuming that permissibility consists in not being wrong. These claims are not basic because they are logically complex, and they do not ascribe a moral property.

realists cannot explain what the normativity of a fact would consist in, they cannot adequately support the truth of ethical realism. Proponents can then argue that realists are not entitled to claim that there are any basic ethical facts unless they can explain how it could be that a fact is normative. This is the challenge.

Ethical realists might demand an argument that undermines their view that there are normative facts. But this response misconstrues the objection. It is not (or need not be) intended as part of an argument for ethical antirealism. It rather poses a challenge to realism. It expresses a philosophical puzzlement about the idea that a fact—a state of affairs—a way that entities and properties are arranged in reality—could in itself "call for" action or decision. The challenge is to explain how this could be the case. Proponents can agree that some basic ethical claims are true—at least in a deflationary sense whereby to call a claim true is simply to affirm it—and they can agree that these truths are normative.[5] They challenge what they take to be the realist's construal of such truths, which is that they are true in virtue of the obtaining of ethical facts or states of affairs that they represent.

As I understand it, then, ethical realism has metaphysical implications, and the normativity objection questions these implications. Unfortunately, the terminology can be confusing.

First, consider the term "fact." There is a "deflationary" account whereby a "fact" is simply a truth—a true sentence or a true proposition—where "true" is also used in a deflationary sense. Antirealists of many kinds can agree that there are ethical facts on *this* account of how the term "fact" is used (e.g., Blackburn 2006). But realists think that there are ethical *states of affairs* that are partly constituted by ethical properties, such as the state of affairs that lying is wrong. Realists do not view such states of affairs as sentences or propositions, but rather think of them as the "truth-makers" of sentences and propositions (Armstrong 2004). These states of affairs are "facts" in a "robust" or "objective" sense rather than in any deflationary sense. Say that, in the realist view, there are "objective" or "robust" ethical "facts."

Second, realists think that there are ethical "properties," including both deontic properties, such as the property of wrongness, and evaluative properties, such as the properties of being a virtue, being rational, and being good. Here I use the term "property" to refer to characteristics of things that underwrite genuine similarities (Jackson 1998: 15–16; Wedgwood 2007: 141; McPherson 2023: 22-23). Realists distinguish properties, so understood, from the concepts we have of them. Ethical realists hold that there are *ethical* characteristics that underwrite genuine *ethical* similarities among things. We can speak of these characteristics as "objective" or "robust" ethical "properties." Metaphysical disputes about the nature of such properties are beside the point. Ethical realists hold that, in that they are properties, ethical properties have the

---

[5] A "basic" ethical claim is a logically simple claim that ascribes (or at least purports to ascribe) an ethical property to something. See the preceding note.

same metaphysical standing as ordinary worldly characteristics of things that underwrite genuine similarities.

The normativity objection challenges the thesis that basic ethical truths represent objective ethical states of affairs or facts which are their truth conditions—and that ethical properties, or characteristics that underwrite genuine similarities, are constituents of such facts. On this thesis, for instance, the claim that torture is wrong is true exactly on condition that there is a state of affairs whereby wrongness is a property of torture. The objection is that there is no plausible explanation of what the normativity of such facts would consist in, taking facts to be objective states of affairs; that is, there is no plausible "constitutive explanation" of the normativity of such facts. Further, there is no plausible "constitutive explanation" of what the normativity of a property would consist in, taking a property to be a characteristic that underwrites genuine similarities.

The normativity objection rests on two presuppositions. First, it presupposes that the basic ethical truths are normative. Second, it presupposes that, for a realist, the basic ethical truths are normative in virtue of the normativity of the robust ethical facts that they represent. Accordingly, it takes ethical realism to be committed to there being robust normative facts or states of affairs. This is what triggers the objection. Since the objection rests on these presuppositions, however, an obvious strategy for avoiding it is to deny one of the presuppositions. I will assess this strategy in what follows.

2. NORMATIVITY

Before we go further, we need an initial characterization of normativity. What we need here is not a theory or analysis of normativity. What we need is a way to identify or characterize the object of such a theory or analysis, the *explanandum*. The normativity objection asks realists to provide a constitutive explanation of normativity. What we need here is a way to characterize the explanandum, and to do so without begging any questions, prejudging the nature of the explanans, prejudging controversial issues, or building a contested theory into our characterization. For this reason, I start with the following vague characterization:

> *For a belief, concept, property, or fact to be normative is for it to have a characteristic essential relation to decisions, choices, intentions, or attitudes. It would have this relation in virtue of its semantics, content, or nature.*

Call this the "essential relation characterization." It is meant to point to the property of interest, rather than to provide an analysis of its nature. Let me explain its five main features—its breadth; the idea that a normative entity stands in a characteristic relation to *decisions, choices, intentions, or attitudes*; the idea that a normative entity stands in *a characteristic relation* to decisions, choices, etc.; the idea that this is *essential* to the entity; and the idea that the relation holds in virtue of the *semantics, content, or nature* of the entity.

First, the characterization leaves room for a variety of views about the kinds of entity that are normative. Ethical realists hold that ethical *facts* and *properties* are normative. At least the normativity objection presupposes that realists hold this. One might instead hold that only ethical *beliefs* and *concepts* are normative. There is also the view that only a subset of ethical beliefs are normative. Perhaps it is only first-person, present-tense, all things considered, *ought* judgments that are normative since only such judgments have a relevant normative role in decision-making. Our initial characterization does not rule out any of these views.

Further, our characterization is broad enough to allow both deontic facts and evaluative ones to count as normative. As I understand it, the normativity objection challenges the ability of ethical realism to account for evaluation as much as its ability to account for deontic normativity. It would be overly narrow, then, to characterize normative facts as *prescriptive*, or *action-guiding*, since these characterizations seem to exclude evaluative facts. For example, the fact that kindness is a virtue seems to be neither action-guiding nor prescriptive.

Second, I speak of a characteristic relation *to decisions, choices, intentions,* or *attitudes*. In this chapter, I am concerned with the normativity of "ethics," which I intend to include the normative domains that are standardly taken to fall within the realm of practical reason, including morality and prudence. Normative ethical facts stand in a characteristic relation to decisions, choices, intentions, or attitudes—such as counting in their favor. But thoroughgoing realists about the normative would hold that there are also normative epistemic facts, such as the fact that such and such belief is justified, and facts of this kind, if there are any, stand in a characteristic relation to other beliefs, such as the relation of counting in favor of them. To include the epistemic case, I will count belief as a kind of attitude—a propositional attitude. In any event, I will mainly ignore epistemic normativity in what follows.

Third, I speak vaguely of *a characteristic relation* to decisions, choices, intentions, or attitudes. There are various ways that one might try to precisify this, but I do not see how to do so without prejudging important issues. Four proposals can illustrate my worry.

To begin, one might think we could precisify the idea of a "characteristic relation" by using a generalization of motivational judgment internalism (MJI). MJI is intended in the first instance to account for the "practicality property" of first-person, present-tense all things considered *ought* judgments, such as someone's judgment that she ought to do such-and-such. MJI says, roughly, that, necessarily, anyone who judges that she ought to do such-and-such is motivated, at least to some degree, to do that thing. MJI is problematic, however, because, arguably, it is possible to be completely unmoved by a first-person, present-tense *ought* judgement (Brink 1989). A variety of attempts have been made to avoid this objection, by redefining the practicality property (e.g., Smith 1994), but the success of these attempts is debatable (e.g., Copp 2007, chap. 8). In any case, since first-person, present-tense all things considered *ought* judgments are not the only normative judgments, MJI would need to be generalized. Our characterization of normativity should accommodate, *inter alia*, the ideas that third person and past tense deontic judgments are normative as well as first-person present-tense ones, that evaluative and epistemic judgments are also normative, and that there are normative properties as well as normative judgments. Yet it seems possible to judge, for instance, that Caesar was wrong to cross the Rubicon, and that Caesar was vicious, without thereby being motivated to do anything, and without any failure of practical rationality. So it is unclear that any generalization of MJI would provide a suitable precisification of the essential relation characterization.

Next, Matti Eklund and others have introduced the concept of a "normative role" and proposed that normative concepts are those with normative roles, where a normative role might be a role in ethical motivation, or a role in practical reasoning, or both (Eklund 2017; Wedgwood 2018). On reflection, it might seem that the idea of a normative role is a generalization of the idea of a practicality property, since the practicality property of a concept is, roughly, its having a role in ethical motivation, whereas the normative role of a concept might include a role in reasoning as well as a role in motivation. Eklund considers the proposal that normative concepts are those that have normative roles, that their normative roles determine their reference, and that normative properties are those that are referred to by normative concepts (Eklund 2017: passim, 10–11, 16–17; see Wedgwood 2018: 28). This, however, is a sketch of a theory of normativity rather than a characterization of what such a theory must explain. Furthermore, it is an example of normative conceptualism, since it treats the normativity of properties as derivative from the normativity of the concepts that refer to them. Normative conceptualism is controversial, as I will explain. Furthermore, Eklund's suggestion that normative properties are those that are referred to by normative concepts is problematic since it is unclear why there couldn't be a normative property of which we have no concept. In any case, the idea of normative role is not significantly more precise than the idea of a "characteristic relation" to decisions or choices.

A familiar proposal, which is currently widely favored, is "reasons fundamentalism." This is the view that the fundamental normative notion is that of a reason, and that all other normative notions can be analyzed in terms of the notion of a reason (Scanlon 2014: 2; also Parfit 2011, vol. 2: 267–269). Reasons fundamentalism can be understood as offering an account of the "characteristic relation" since it analyzes reasons in terms of the "reason-relation," the relation that a fact has to an agent and an action, decision, intention, or belief when that fact is a reason for that agent to do, decide, intend, or believe as indicated (Scanlon 2014: 30–31). But, as I use the term, the fact that honesty is morally good is normative, and I don't want to build into the initial characterization of normativity a commitment to analyzing goodness in terms of reasons. Further, as I use the term, the fact that an action would be rational qualifies as normative, since, roughly, this fact would count in favor of the action in virtue of the nature of rationality. But it is not clear that there is generally a reason to act rationally, so it is not clear that reasons fundamentalism can accommodate the idea that facts about rational action are normative (Kolodny 2005, Broome 2007).

Finally, one might think that the relevant "characteristic relation" is that of *counting in favor (or against)*, given that the rationality and the goodness of an action both count in its favor. But there arguably are normative facts that do not count in favor of, or against, decisions, choices, intentions, or attitudes, except perhaps trivially. The fact that kindness is a virtue counts in favor of being kind, but this seems trivial. More important, there are non-normative facts that count in favor of, or against, decisions and choices. The fact that you are thirsty counts in favor of drinking some water, but it is not a normative fact. Our characterization needs to distinguish between *normatively relevant* facts, such as the fact that you are thirsty, and *normative* facts, such as the fact that you have reason to drink.

In short, I do not see how to precisify the essential relation characterization while avoiding the drawbacks I have mentioned. Some proposals would exclude evaluative facts from the class of normative facts. Some would make it problematic whether a property and a fact, as opposed to a concept and a belief, can qualify as normative. Other proposals are better viewed as controversial theories of normativity rather than as characterizations of our explanandum.

Let me turn, then, to the fourth main feature of the essential relation characterization, the idea that an entity's being normative is its having a characteristic *essential* relation to decisions, choices, intentions, or attitudes. That is, its standing in this characteristic relation to decisions, choices, intentions, or attitudes is an *essential* property it has. This distinguishes normative entities from entities that are merely normatively relevant. For example, it is of the nature of the normative fact *that you have a reason to drink* that it counts in favor of your drinking. It is essential to this fact that it stands in a relevant characteristic relation to your drinking. But although the fact *that you are thirsty* is normatively relevant, since it might be a reason for you to drink, this is not essential to it. It is not of the nature of this fact that it is a reason for anything. So the fact that you are thirsty is not a normative fact. It is of the nature of normative facts to have a relevant characteristic relation to decisions, choices, intentions, or attitudes.

Note, however, that it will facilitate discussing normative formalism and normative conceptualism later in this chapter to allow a looser usage according to which a property can be counted as "normative" even if its having a relevant relation to decisions, etc., is not essential to it. On the looser usage, such a property can count as "normative" even though it is not "essentially normative," or normative as a matter of its essential nature. I will indicate where I shift to the looser usage.

Fifth is an idea about what is essential to beliefs, concepts, properties, or facts. For beliefs or concepts, their semantics or content is essential to them. So, in the case of a normative belief or concept, there would be a characteristic relation to decisions, etc., in virtue of the semantics or content of this belief or concept. For properties or facts, the properties they have in every possible world where they exist are essential to them. For any normative property or fact, it is essential to it that it have a relevant characteristic relation to decisions, etc.; that it stands in such a relation is an essential property. To explain the normativity of ethical properties and facts, a theory would need to offer accounts of their essential nature.

I now need to introduce a complexity that I have so far been ignoring. This is the distinction between a merely "formal normativity," such as the "normativity" of certain facts about games, and the "robust" or "authoritative normativity" that is the object of our concern. Once I have explained this distinction, I will need to amend the essential relation characterization. Let me explain.

There can be situations in a game of chess where a player ought to castle. This is simply a truth about the player's strategic situation, given the rules of the game (Tiffany 2007; Parfit 2011, vol. 2: 308–309). Yet this truth is normative in a "formal" sense. That is, it, and relevantly similar truths, have the semantic marks of normativity, since they involve the concepts of *ought* and of a reason. They "call for" a response. The fact that, in chess, one ought to castle early "calls for" players to castle early. Basic ethical truths are also normative in this formal sense. The fact that one ought to be truthful "calls for" people to be truthful. But there is a crucial difference between the normativity of games and ethical normativity. The perspective of a game is *normatively arbitrary*, and it is *normatively optional* whether to take into account the reasons and oughts of a game—unless the context is such that, say, one has a moral or prudential reason to do so. The rules of any arbitrary imagined game would ground an equally arbitrary set of *oughts* for situations in which the game might be played. Consider, Calvinball, from the comic, "Calvin and Hobbes," which has a rule requiring that masks be worn at all times. In Calvinball, players ought to wear masks, but this *ought*, like the reasons and *oughts* of all games, has no normative significance in itself. It is optional whether to take it into account. A person playing chess who pays no attention to what she ought "chesswise" to do is not *thereby* making a mistake of any normative significance. Of course, someone might have a moral reason or a prudential reason to play a game well, in which case, for example, the fact that there is a chess reason to castle might be a prudential or a moral reason to do so. Intuitively, however, the normativity of morality and prudence are significantly different, for the ethical perspective is not arbitrary, and it is non-optional. A person who pays no attention to her *ethical* reasons is *thereby* making a mistake of normative significance. Ethical reasons and *oughts* seem in this way to be *robustly* normative, or *authoritative*, I will say.

One familiar view equates robustly normative reasons and requirements with "categorical" ones, where a categorical reason or requirement for an agent to do something obtains regardless of whether the agent has any contingent ends to which the action is a means. A "hypothetical" reason or requirement obtains only if the relevant agent has an end to which the relevant action is a means. The reasons and requirements of morality are taken to be categorical since, plausibly, whether one has a moral reason to do something, or whether one is morally required to do it, is independent of one's contingent ends. Self-interested reasons typically are categorized as hypothetical, since, it would seem, whether one has a self-interested reason to do something depends on one's ends. Unfortunately, however, it would be a mistake for our purposes to equate robustness with categoricity. First, at least some non-robust reasons appear to be categorical. For instance, the reason in chess to castle early is independent of one's ends. Second, there is the view that only self-interested reasons are robustly normative in themselves even though they are hypothetical rather than categorical. On this view, the robust normativity of moral reasons depends on whether morality can be grounded somehow in self-interest (e.g., Gauthier 1986). Again, I do not want to build any specific controversial theory about normativity into my characterization of it, so I don't equate robust normativity with categoricity.[6]

Some would deny that there is such a thing as robust normativity. I will discuss this view in the next section of the chapter. But several additional issues about robust normativity are not important for my purposes here, so I will set them aside. First, there is disagreement about *which* kinds of considerations are robustly normative. As we saw, one view is that only self-interested reasons and *oughts* are robustly normative in themselves. Another view is that moral reasons and *oughts* are also robustly normative in themselves (e.g., Darwall 2006). There is also disagreement as to whether etiquette and law are robustly normative or whether, instead, they are merely formally normative (Copp 2019a). Second, there is room to disagree about the "stringency" of robust normativity. Agents are making a normatively significant mistake if they ignore their robustly normative reasons, but realists can disagree about how serious such mistakes might be. Third, there can be disagreement as to whether robustness is a matter of degree.[7] Some might think that etiquette and law are robustly normative but not as stringently normative as morality. I want my characterization of robust normativity to be neutral on these points of disagreement.

Given all of this, it is difficult to characterize robust normativity. We can use the reasons and *oughts* of games to illustrate mere formal normativity, and we can then point to robust normativity by contrasting it with the formal normativity of games. We can also use the idea of a mistake of normative significance. A person who pays no attention to her *robustly* normative reasons is *thereby* making a mistake of normative significance. *Robustly* normative ethical reasons and oughts are in this way *authoritative*.

Since some philosophers maintain that robust normativity is unanalyzable, it perhaps unsurprising that the best we seem able to do here is to offer a rather vague characterization. As I said before, it is important at this stage to avoid characterizing robust normativity in a way that begs important questions or builds controversial views into its characterization.

In any case, the lack of a fully adequate characterization of robust normativity needn't be a problem since, again, what we need is a way to understand what the normativity objection aims to challenge. Accordingly, I will amend the essential relation characterization as follows:

> *For a belief, concept, property, or fact to be* robustly *normative, is for it to have a characteristic essential* authoritative *relation to decisions, choices, intentions, or attitudes. It would have this relation in virtue of its semantics, content, or nature.*

---

[6] This is at least a terminological change from what I wrote in Copp 2015.
[7] I thank Paul Bloomfield and Pekka Väyrynen for proposing this.

The normativity objection challenges ethical realists to explain what the robust normativity of an ethical fact or property could consist in.

To avoid controversies about the robustness of, for instance, aesthetics, law, and etiquette, I will narrow attention to moral properties and facts, and the properties and facts of prudential reason. In what follows, I will refer to these as "ethical" properties and facts. The normativity objection challenges realists to explain the robust normativity of ethical facts and properties, so understood.

3. Normative Formalism

To avoid the normativity objection, an ethical realist might deny one or more of its presuppositions. The first of these is that basic ethical truths are robustly normative. It is open to a realist to claim, on the contrary, that there is no such thing as robust normativity. I call realists who take up this strategy "normative formalists" because they hold that there is only formal normativity of the kind found in games. Truths about ethical reasons and *oughts* are like truths about what one ought (chesswise) to do and truths about reasons (chesswise) to do things in that they have the semantic marks of normativity. Such truths are normative in the "formal" sense that they "call for" a response. Formalists maintain that the normativity of ethical truths is *merely* formal, and they deny that ethical truths are *robustly* normative. Normative formalists therefore are antirealist about robust normativity. They can nevertheless qualify as *ethical realists* since they can hold that there are objective, robust, ethical facts or states of affairs that are partly constituted by ethical properties.

Parfit briefly discusses a view, much like formalism, according to which normativity is a matter of what is required by rules, such as rules of etiquette, spelling, or chess. He calls this the "rule-involving" conception of normativity (Parfit 2011, vol. 2: 267–268, 308–9). The "deflationary pluralism" proposed by Tiffany also appears to be an example of formalism (Tiffany 2007). Tiffany holds that reasons are generated by a "standpoint" or "standard" provided there are facts about which actions are favored or disfavored from that standpoint (251, 255). The moral standpoint generates moral reasons. The standpoint of etiquette generates reasons of politeness. Presumably too, the rules of chess generate chess-reasons. As a matter of psychology, someone might be guided by one of these standpoints and not by others, but, Tiffany contends, no such standpoint has "genuine deliberative weight" (251) or "intrinsic ultimate authority" (260). Hubin's "groundless normativity" appears to be another example (Hubin 2001). Hubin remarks that there are many perspectives from which to evaluate an agent's actions (468), including the perspective of her intrinsic values (466), the perspective of law (464), and perhaps also the perspective of chess. The perspective of the agent's intrinsic values has psychological salience for her (468), but aside from this, Hubin seems to view the different perspectives as being on a par. For Hubin, it seems, there is a reason from a certain perspective to perform an action just in case this action is favored from that perspective (466).

On one interpretation of formalism, facts about the reasons and *oughts* of games are not *genuinely* normative. They are empirical facts that can be completely explained by reference to the rules of a game and the strategic situations of players (Tiffany 2007; Parfit 2011, vol. 2: 308–309). They are not importantly different from facts that lack the formal marks of normativity, such as the fact that maple trees are deciduous. On this interpretation, formalism entails that ethical reasons and *oughts* are not genuinely normative. On a second, perhaps less radical interpretation, these reasons and *oughts* are genuinely normative but not *robustly* normative. Of course the difference between these interpretations might be merely terminological. The important point is that formalism is deflationary on both interpretations, for it rejects the intuitive view that ethical reasons and *oughts* are *robustly* normative.

Formalism is able to avoid the normativity objection because it is deflationary in this way. The normativity objection challenges the ability of ethical realism to account for the robust normativity of ethical considerations, but formalism denies that there is any such thing to account for. Of course, this response will not satisfy Proponents of the objection, for they hold that ethical considerations *do* (or would) have a robust normativity—an authoritative non-optional normativity that cannot be explained in the way that the formal normativity of games can be explained, by reference to the rules of a "practice" and the situations of participants in the practice.

It is hard to agree with formalists that ethical facts and properties are merely formally normative. That is, it is hard to agree that *moral* properties and facts, and the properties and facts of *prudential rationality*, are merely formally normative. It is hard to believe that the wrongness of torture is not different in kind, in itself, with respect to the "authoritativeness" of the restriction it places on our behavior, from the "wrongness" of failing to follow rules of Calvinball. Hence, I think, the strategy of avoiding the normativity objection by denying the presupposition that ethical truths are robustly normative is not promising. The presupposition is surely plausible.

4. Normative Conceptualism

Realists might instead deny the second presupposition of the objection, the claim that if ethical realism is true, the ethical truths are robustly normative in virtue of the robust normativity of the objective ethical facts that they represent. A realist might contend, against this, that normativity is found fundamentally in the province of thought rather than in the province of what our thought is about. Here I will shift to the looser usage of "normative." According to "normative conceptualism," it is the ethical concepts that are essentially normative, not the properties that these concepts represent or refer to.[8]

---

[8] Eklund calls this position "presentationalism" (2017: chap 6). I thank Väyrynen for bringing Eklund's work to my attention. I use "refers" in a wide sense that allows me to speak of concepts and predicates as referring to properties.

Further, ethical truths are robustly normative because the ethical concepts are essentially robustly normative, not because the properties they refer to are. If this position is combined with ethical realism, the resulting view is that there are robust or objective states of affairs that are partly constituted by ethical properties, yet these properties are not normative. Or rather, if they are normative, their normativity is derivative from that of the ethical concepts. In short, normative conceptualism aims to vindicate the proposition that ethical truths are robustly normative on the basis that the ethical concepts are robustly normative. (In what follows, I will often delete "robustly.")

Proponents of the normativity objection challenge realists to explain how a fact or property could be essentially robustly normative, presupposing that realists would need to explain this in order to explain the normativity of ethical truths. But normative conceptualism denies that ethical facts and properties are essentially robustly normative. It aims to explain the normativity of ethical truths in a different way, by invoking the normativity of ethical concepts. And this allows it to avoid the normativity objection, for Proponents of the objection should agree that there are normative *concepts*. Proponents and realists alike need an account of what distinguishes normative concepts from non-normative ones. Explaining this does not appear to be a special challenge for ethical realists.[9] Normative conceptualism eliminates the problem of explaining how objective properties could be essentially robustly normative and replaces it with a problem faced by everyone working in metaethics, the problem of explaining the nature of normative concepts.

Normative conceptualism is an attractive position both for ethical non-naturalists and ethical naturalists.[10] Naturalists who take up normative conceptualism can hold that ethical properties are garden-variety natural properties, which are not essentially robustly normative, although we have normative concepts that refer to them. For example, assume a version of utilitarian naturalism according to which the concept of wrongness refers to the property of failing to maximize expected general welfare. On this view, there are two concepts of this property, the concept [wrongness] and the concept [failing to maximize expected general welfare]. This property presumably is not *essentially* robustly normative, but on certain versions of normative conceptualism, it is *derivatively* normative.

We need, then, to distinguish between different versions of normative conceptualism (NC). On one version, which I will call the *non-derivationist* version, the properties referred to by the normative concepts are not normative at all. On a *derivationist* version, the properties referred to by the normative concepts are normative, but only *derivatively*.[11] According to a *simple* derivationist view, this is merely the verbal point

---

[9] Eklund holds that normative concepts are those that have "normative roles" (Eklund 2017: passim, 10–11, 16–17). Wedgwood contends that normative concepts are those that have a "reasoning guiding" conceptual role (Wedgwood 2018). Compare my account of the "fundamental role" of moral judgment (Copp 2019b). Eklund offers an overview (2017: chap. 4).

[10] Railton (2003) seems to be an example. It is not clear to me how Brink (1998) and Sturgeon (2006) should be classified.

[11] Väyrynen brought the derivationist version to my attention.

that the properties referred to by the normative concepts can properly be *called* "normative" or *classified* as "normative." These properties might have nothing in common besides membership in the set of properties referred to by a normative concept. This view is not different in any interesting way from the non-derivationist view. But there is a more interesting derivationist position, which I will call the *grounded derivationist view*.[12] According to this position, the properties referred to by normative concepts are normative in virtue of being referred to by a normative concept, but there is also *something else* that they have in common, over and above the fact that they belong to the set of properties referred to by a normative concept. There could be a variety of proposals about this "something else." For example, one might propose that all normative properties engender an ordering of objects of a relevant kind, along a relevant dimension; hence, the property of being a truth-teller engenders an ordering of people according to the degree to which they tell the truth; similarly, on the utilitarian naturalist view, the property of wrongness engenders an ordering of actions on the basis of how close they come to maximizing expected general welfare. The important point is that, since it is a version of NC, grounded derivationism denies that the normative properties are *essentially* robustly normative. Their normativity is *derivative* from the normativity of the normative concepts that refer to them.

NC faces the objection that there could be normative properties of which we have no concept. Plausibly kindness would have been a virtue even if we had had no concept of kindness. This objection raises an issue about the metaphysics of concepts that goes beyond what I can deal with here. One might think that concepts exist necessarily. On this view, derivationist versions of NC could answer the objection by saying that the normative properties are those that are referred to by the normative concepts *that exist*, not merely by the normative concepts *that we have*.

One might wonder, next, whether there is a plenitude of normative concepts even if we only have a limited number of them. Or, are there limits to the properties of which there could be a normative concept? Are there any properties of which there could not be a normative concept even in principle? Consider, for example, the property tallness. I think there actually is a normative concept of tallness and that some people evaluate other people in light of this concept. Call this the concept of tallness-plus. It orders people on the basis of how tall they are, and assigns priority to treating taller people better than shorter ones. Of course it is completely implausible that tallness is a normative property, but the problem is that, according to derivationism, tallness *is* a normative property if, as I think, there is a concept of tallness-plus. This is not an objection to non-derivationism since it denies that there are any normative properties at all, and if simple derivationism is not interestingly different from non-derivationism, then this also is not an objection to simple derivationism. But it *is* an objection to *grounded* derivationism.

---

[12] I thank Ralph Wedgwood for a very helpful correspondence about the difference between derivationist and non-derivationist versions. Wedgwood writes as if he has a derivationist view (Wedgwood 2018: 28), but in the end I suspect that his theory is actually a kind of normative objectualism.

It appears that there are some normative concepts that are reprehensible or repugnant in one way or another. Tallness-plus is an example. Another example is the concept of "whiteness" held by white supremacists. It is a normative concept, I take it, since it implicates a positive evaluation of "white" people by comparison with those who are not "white," and it is repugnant because of the attitude toward people that would be involved in using this concept in evaluating people and in deciding what treatment they deserve. A third example is the concept of feminine chastity, which is repugnant because of the attitude toward women that would be involved in using this concept in evaluating women (see Eklund 2017: 13–14, 73–74). In these cases, the concepts in question seem to refer to a property, but not to one that is normative, and this is a problem for grounded derivationism.

These examples point to the fundamental problem with *grounded* derivationism, which is that it is implausible that a property inherits normativity from the normativity of a concept that refers to it. The property of being tall is not normative, and it would not be normative even if there were a normative concept that referred to it. The property of feminine sexual modesty is not normative even if it is referred to by a normative concept of chastity. So derivationism is not plausible if it is read as proposing that properties inherit the second-order property of being normative from normative concepts that refer to them.

These examples also raise a problem for NC quite generally, however, including non-derivationism and simple derivationism. NC needs to distinguish between repugnant normative concepts and "respectable" normative concepts. It is not clear where NC could find the resources to draw this distinction and to argue that only the respectable ones merit being taken into account in reasoning. As I will explain, normative *objectualism* can argue that the key difference between the repugnant normative concepts and the respectable ones is that only the respectable ones are *veridical*—only they refer to a property that is itself normative. This strategy is not available to normative conceptualism, however, since it holds that the normativity of properties is at best derivative from the normativity of concepts.

Since at least some of these worries do not arise with respect to non-derivationism, I will set aside derivationism in what follows.

Turn, now, to the idea of a concept. I take it that concepts are ways of representing things in thought, and I think there can be more than one concept of a given thing. For instance, there are both the folk concept of heat and the thermodynamical concept. The possibility of there being more than one concept of a thing raises the question whether, in such cases, one of these concepts is privileged as "the" concept of the thing. I will set aside this difficult issue.

An important question for our purposes is whether concepts are necessarily accurate to their objects. Some views about color hold that folk color concepts misrepresent colors by representing them as inhering in the surfaces of things although colors are actually relational between things and our mental representations. So we need to be open to the idea that a concept can misrepresent the thing of which it is a way of thinking.

This is relevant to our concerns because, on a non-derivationist version of NC, if we assume the utilitarian naturalist view, for example, the concept of wrongness refers to the property of failing to maximize expected general welfare, which is not normative (not even derivatively). So if NC holds that this property is *represented* as normative by the concept of wrongness (assuming we have combined NC with utilitarian naturalism), the upshot is that the concept of wrongness misrepresents the nature of this property, since it represents it as normative even though it is not normative. There is, however, a distinction we can draw between "representationalist" versions of NC, according to which the normative ethical concepts represent ethical properties as normative, and "non-representationalist" versions, which deny this. I shall argue that the representationalist version is preferable.

The problem with non-representationalism is that ethical concepts do at least seem to represent the properties they refer to—or that ethical realists take them to refer to—as normative, and as authoritatively normative in a way that reasons and *oughts* of games are not. The concept of wrongness plausibly represents the property of wrongness as being such that actions with this property are *to be avoided* because they have this property. The concept of chastity plausibly represents the property of being chaste—that is the property of sexual modesty—as something *to be commended*. So non-representationalism seems to be implausible.

Furthermore, non-representationalism makes it hard to see why we think of the properties referred to by the ethical concepts as normative. Our ethical concepts are our ways of thinking of the ethical properties, and, according to non-representationalism, they do not represent these properties as normative. On the non-representationalist view, therefore, it is odd that we think of the properties as normative. Representationalism can at least explain this by drawing on its claim that the ethical concepts *represent* ethical properties *as* normative. Let us therefore set aside non-representationalism.

Since I have previously set aside derivationism, we are left with the version of NC that combines non-derivationism with representationalism. The problem is that this version must say that the ethical concepts *misrepresent* the nature of the ethical properties by representing them as normative even though they are not normative. We take it that there are properties the nature of which is that they authoritatively call for certain responses from us, but according to non-derivationism, no property is like this. In short, on the reading that combines non-derivationism with representationalism, NC is a kind of error theory. It views a mistake about normativity as infecting our ethical concepts.

An error theory of this kind, about normativity, is not a comfortable position for ethical realists. Normative conceptualism is intended to allow realists to vindicate the normativity of ethics. So it should be troubled by the objection that, on what seems to be the best version of it, the non-derivationist and representationalist version, it is committed to holding that mistaken ways of thinking are built into our ethical concepts.

In any case, I claim it is a *necessary truth* that, if there are any ethical properties—moral properties or properties of prudential rationality—they are essentially robustly normative. That is, if there are any such properties, it is of their nature that they are normative, and their normativity has a significance that is different in nature from the merely formal normativity of failures to castle early in chess. The problems we saw with derivationism support the necessity of the thesis that the ethical properties are essentially normative, if they are normative at all. And the problems we saw with normative formalism support the necessity of the thesis that these properties, if there are any, are robustly normative.

Now, according to NC, ethical concepts, such as the concept of moral wrongness, refer to ethical properties. According to NC, however, no such property is *essentially* normative. So, if it is a necessary truth that wrongness is essentially normative, NC must say that the property referred to by the concept of wrongness—such as, on one view, the property of failing to maximize expected general welfare—is not identical to the property of wrongness. Nor is it an ethical property, if it is a necessary truth that the ethical properties are essentially normative. Accordingly, NC seems forced to the conclusion that there are no ethical properties. But if there are no such properties, there are no robust ethical states of affairs partly constituted by ethical properties. Hence, on this showing, NC seems committed to a kind of ethical antirealism.

It might seem question-begging to claim in this context that it is a necessary truth that the ethical properties, if there are any, are essentially robustly normative, since normative conceptualism denies this. Recall, however, that my project here is to explore whether ethical realism has an adequate response to the normativity objection. If I am right, NC is not an option for ethical realists.

To avoid contradiction, NC needs to reject at least one of the following propositions: (1) The concept of wrongness refers to a property. (2) The property referred to by the concept of wrongness is not essentially normative. (3) The property referred to by the concept of wrongness is the property of wrongness. (4) The property of wrongness is essentially normative. The line of least resistance for ethical realists would be to reject (2), but, unfortunately, NC *entails* (2). It also entails (1). If it were to deny (1), it would become a kind of ethical antirealism—perhaps a relative of Parfit's irrealist cognitivism (Parfit 2017: 59), or perhaps a kind of noncognitivist expressivism (e.g., Gibbard 1990). If it were to deny (2), it would become a version of "normative objectualism," the position I will discuss in the rest of the chapter. So it is forced to deny either (3) or (4). If I am correct that (4) is a necessary truth, the best option would be to deny (3). But if the property referred to by the concept of wrongness is not the property of wrongness, there presumably is no such property.

The underlying problem, I think, is that NC involves a "conceptual deflationism" according to which normativity is fundamentally a feature of our concepts. NC wants to say that there are wrongful actions but that the *normativity* of this is external to the wrongness itself. Some actions have the property of being wrong, but this property in itself is not anything normative. I think this is necessarily false, but, at any rate, it is not intuitively plausible. Intuitively, the wrongness of lying is a feature of lying, not simply a feature of our thinking. And the normative significance of this is an essential feature of wrongness, not merely a feature of our thinking. NC flies in the face of this.

I conclude that the strategy of avoiding the normativity objection by denying either of its presuppositions is not promising. Normative formalism denies that ethical truths are robustly normative, but at the cost of assimilating the normativity of ethics to the normativity of games. Normative conceptualism denies that there are objective ethical facts that are essentially robustly normative, but at the cost of taking normativity to be fundamentally a feature of ways we think. Both of these views seem forced to choose between denying the necessary truth that the ethical properties are essentially robustly normative and denying that there are any ethical properties. They are not attractive positions for realists.

5. Normative Objectualism

To recapitulate, the normativity objection challenges the thesis that ethical truths represent essentially robustly normative, objective states of affairs that are their truth conditions, and that involve essentially robustly normative, objective ethical properties. The objection—shifting back to my preferred usage of "normative"—is that there is no plausible constitutive explanation of what the robust normativity of these facts and properties would consist in. I have contended that it is not promising to seek to avoid the objection by denying either of its two presuppositions. The remaining option—unless we are to ignore the objection, or claim it is not worth attention—is to offer a direct response, to provide an explanation of the robust normativity of objective ethical facts and properties.

Consider, then, a version of ethical realism according to which the ethical properties are robustly normative and the ethical facts are robustly normative in virtue of the robust normativity of the ethical properties that partly constitute them. Call this position "normative objectualism." Normative objectualism combines a realist view of the ethical facts with the objectualist view that these facts are partly constituted by properties that, as a matter of their essential nature, have the second-order property of being robustly normative. We can call this view "hardball" ethical realism.

Hardball realists think there are normative properties, but they do not deny that there are normative ethical concepts. Accordingly, hardball realists need to explain what distinguishes normative concepts from non-normative ones, but this is not a special problem for them. The special problem is to explain what distinguishes the putatively robustly normative properties and facts from non-normative ones.

There are two relevant camps of hardball realists, *primitivists* and *explainers*. By and large, the primitivists are non-naturalists and the explainers are naturalists. But I want to allow for the possibility of a philosophically interesting non-naturalist account of normativity,[13] and logical space also leaves room for naturalists who are primitivists.

What the explainers seek is an account of the essential nature of the second-order property of being robustly normative—a constitutive explanation. Explanations of this

---

[13] Wedgwood's position is perhaps an example (Wedgwood 2007: 4–6).

kind have been described as "real definitions," by Gideon Rosen (Rosen 2010), and as "metaphysical analyses," by Jeff King (1998).[14] An example is the "reduction" of the property of being an acid to the property of being a proton donor (Rosen 2010: 124). This analysis is metaphysical rather than conceptual, for it is meant as an account of the essential nature of the property of being an acid, which is different from an analysis of a concept.

As I understand matters, constitutive explanations or metaphysical analyses of the kind at issue would be propositions of the form, [To be F is to be X, Y, Z]. For instance, to be an acid is to be a proton donor. In this example, the explanandum or analysandum is the property of being an acid, and the proposed explanans or analysans is the property of being a proton donor. In successful metaphysical analyses, the clause that refers to the analysans sets out a complex condition, such as [being a proton donor], that describes the essential nature of the analysandum property, and is satisfied by everything that has this property. Everything that is an acid is a proton donor, and this is the essential nature of acids. Typically, moreover, a satisfactory analysis will be *reductive*. That is, none of the "elements" that are proper parts of the analysans clause refers to the analysandum, and none of them refers to something that has the analysandum property.[15] In the example, the analysans sets out the complex condition, [being a proton donor], of which the proper elements are [being a proton] and [being a donor of X], and neither of these elements itself refers to the property of being an acid, or to something that has the property of being an acid. For instance, protons are not acids.

Consider, however, the property of *being thought of by a human*. Selim Berker pointed out that any analysis of this property would have to refer to properties that have this very property, since they will have to have been thought of by humans.[16] So it appears that there could be successful metaphysical analyses that are not reductive in the sense sketched in the preceding paragraph. Notice, however, that although each of the properties referred to in the analysis of the property of *being thought of by a human* will have the property of being thought of by a human, they won't have this property as a matter of their essential nature. The proposition stating the analysis will have existed, and will have referred to these properties, regardless of whether any humans had yet thought of them. But I do need to add a qualification to what I said in the preceding paragraph. Say that, in a reductive analysis, if any of the elements that are proper parts of the analysans clause refers to something that has the analysandum property, it does not have this property as a matter of its essential nature. It seems to me that where the analysandum property is philosophically puzzling, a philosophically satisfactory analysis would need to be reductive in this sense. That is, a philosophically satisfactory analysis of such a property would need to be such that none of the elements that are proper

---

[14] This idea is also developed and used by Schroeder (2005 2007), Wedgwood (2007: 136–147), Fine (2012), and McPherson (2023: 36-38), among others.

[15] At least, none has the analysandum property *essentially*, or as a matter of its essential nature. See the next paragraph.

[16] He made this point in discussion of my paper at the Notre Dame conference.

parts of the analysans clause refers to the property, and none of them refers to something that has the property as a matter of its essential nature. It would be philosophically unsatisfying or disappointing to fail to achieve this.

Returning to hardball realism, the explainers are, or should be, seeking a constitutive explanation, or metaphysical analysis, of *the property of being robustly normative*. A philosophically satisfactory analysis, furthermore, would be *reductive*. That is, in the proposition stating the analysis, the analysans would be a complex "condition" that specifies the essential nature of the property of being robustly normative, where no proper element of this condition refers to the property of robust normativity or to anything that is itself robustly normative as a matter of its essential nature.[17] In a *naturalistic* analysis, the elements of the analysans would refer only to natural properties and relations, or to things that are themselves analyzable by reference only to natural properties and relations.

Primitivists deny that it is possible to provide a reductive metaphysical analysis of robust normativity, and deny also that it is possible to provide metaphysical analyses of the ethical properties. In principle, primitivism is compatible with ethical naturalism; a primitivist naturalist might contend, for example, that the property of failing to maximize the general welfare has the primitive unanalyzable natural property of being robustly normative. But although primitivism is compatible *in principle* with ethical naturalism, primitivism is the *standard* position of non-naturalist theories.[18] Non-naturalist theories reject all reductive naturalistic analyses of robust normativity, and, because of this, they typically describe robust normativity, or the normative ethical properties, as primitive, inexplicable, *sui generis*, or irreducible. To be sure, some non-naturalists aim to explain normativity in terms of a fundamental normative concept, property, or relation, such as the reason-relation, but if they take the normativity of their fundamental normative element as primitive, and not open to further explanation, they also qualify as primitivists.

To illustrate, let me briefly return to reasons fundamentalism. This is the view that the fundamental normative notion is that of a reason (Scanlon 2014: 2; also Parfit 2011, vol. 2: 267–269), and that all other normative notions can be analyzed in terms of the notion of a reason.[19] On a standard account, a fact is a reason for something if and only if it stands in the reason-relation to that thing, where the reason-relation relates (1) the fact that is the reason to (2) the action (or other reason-responsive thing) for which it is a reason, (3) the agent for whom it is a reason, (4) the circumstances in which it is a reason, and perhaps some additional relata (Scanlon 2014: 30–31). The reason-relation is the relation

---

[17] Recall that the property of being thirsty is perhaps normatively relevant, but it is not normative as a matter of its essential nature. Note, if an element does refer to something that is essentially robustly normative, then this thing can in turn be analyzed by a complex condition, no proper element of which refers to the property of robust normativity or to anything that is essentially robustly normative. And so on.

[18] Again, however, I do want to allow for the possibility of a non-naturalist reductive analysis of normativity.

[19] For subtleties, see Scanlon 2014: 2.

of "counting in favor" (Scanlon 2014: 30). The key point is that the reason-relation itself is normative, and primitivists would hold that the normativity of the reason-relation is primitive and unanalyzable. Reasons fundamentalism does not by itself avoid primitivism because it does not tell us what the robust normativity of the reason-relation consists in (Scanlon 2014: 101).

I do not find reasons fundamentalism plausible. For one thing, as I have pointd out, there are reasons of various kinds that are not normative in the philosophically most interesting and puzzling sense, such as reasons in games. We could try saying that reasons in games are not "genuine," but the key point is that they are not robustly normative. Most important for present purposes, even if we set aside the worry that some reasons are merely formally normative, reasons fundamentalism does not avoid primitivism.

Primitivism is philosophically unsatisfying or disappointing. The normativity objection is motivated by a philosophical puzzlement about what objective normativity can consist in, and primitivism simply allows that, when all is said and done, this puzzlement cannot be answered. If we are puzzled about what it could be for a state of affairs or property to be normative, we will not be satisfied by the answer that certain properties and states of affairs simply have the unanalyzable property of being normative. Primitivism plainly does not answer the puzzle about what objective normativity can consist in.

Perhaps, however, primitivism can deflect the normativity objection, or show that it is unreasonable. So let us ask whether primitivists can support the claim that the objection fails to raise a problem for ethical realism.

Scanlon would contend, I think, that the objection is "without merit" (2014: 87, 14). We have the concept of a robust reason, and we can deploy this concept effectively. Normative deliberation of an ordinary sort justifies our views about reasons. In many ordinary circumstances, we have no trouble identifying robust reasons for acting. We have no trouble distinguishing robust reasons such as moral reasons from the reasons of games. And in thinking about these matters, there is no need to engage in metaphysical investigations (Scanlon 2014: 85–87). So there is no need to go beyond reasons fundamentalism. There is no philosophical objection here to ethical realism.

This response misses the point. Proponents of the objection are challenging ethical realism, not the idea that there are reasons for action or that we can know what reasons we have. They should simply concede that we can deliberate about normative matters without engaging in metaphysical investigations. Mathematicians do not need to worry about issues raised in philosophy of mathematics about the nature of numbers. We can tell the time without worrying about the philosophy of time. Similarly, ethicists can theorize about the reasons we have without worrying about the normativity objection. But this does not show that the objection lacks merit.

Enoch would agree with Scanlon, I think, that the normativity objection is misguided. He holds that there are irreducible objective normative moral properties, such as, perhaps, the property of being morally required (Enoch 2011: 5). According to reasons fundamentalism, the issue whether the property of being morally required is normative boils down to the question whether there are reasons to do what is morally required (242). Enoch suggests that this is a "first-order" question for theories about what we have reason to do and about what we are morally required to do (243). It does not pose a metaethical challenge. But, Enoch contends, a challenge to "the normativity of the whole normative domain" would be neither coherent nor substantive. Certainly the question why we have reason to do what we have reason to do is neither coherent nor substantive. It is not to the discredit of ethical realism that it lacks a substantive answer to this question (244).

Properly understood, however, the normativity objection is not a challenge to explain why we have reason to do what we have reason to do. It rather challenges realists to explain what the normativity of ethical properties or relations can consist in, on the assumption that ethical realism is true. There are many relations among facts, persons, circumstances, and so on, most of which are not normative. The challenge is, *inter alia*, to explain what the normativity of the reason-relation consists in. Suppose that I am playing Calvinball. Call this the "Calvinball fact." Given the rules of Calvinball, the Calvinball fact stands in the Calvinball-reason-relation to my wearing a mask. Suppose now that some people are nervous to see me behaving strangely while wearing a mask. Their nervousness stands in the reason-relation to my reassuring them that I am only playing Calvinball. The latter fact about the reason-relation has "authority" over me whereas the fact about the Calvinball-reason-relation does not, but what does this authority consist in?[20]

Enoch seems to answer that it would be question-begging to deny that the reasons and *oughts* implied by a normative theory are "authoritative" since this would amount simply to denying the theory (Enoch 2011: 242–247; see Scanlon 2014: 14, 68). Suppose a theory says that my reassuring people stands in the reason-relation to me in my present circumstances, and suppose it says on this basis that I ought to reassure people. It would be question-begging to deny that these facts are "authoritative" or "robustly normative." For if the theory is correct, it follows that these facts are robustly normative.

This response again side-steps the normativity objection without addressing it. Proponents of the objection are challenging ethical realism, not the idea that there are reasons for action. They should concede that I have a reason to reassure people. They are asking for an explanation of the robust normativity of this—on the objectualist assumption that this fact is a state of affairs consisting in there being a relation among me, the Calvinball fact, people's nervousness, and my reassuring them. For objectualists, the normativity of this state of affairs is essential to it. The claim is that ethical realism cannot explain this essential robust normativity. Primitivism essentially agrees. It concedes, in effect, that philosophical puzzlement about what normativity amounts to or consists in cannot be answered. It claims in addition that this is no objection to ethical realism.

I do not think that an inability to answer the normativity objection would be fatal. But there is genuine philosophical puzzlement about the nature of normativity, and I think it is no less warranted than philosophical puzzlement about the nature of consciousness, about the nature of time, about numbers, and about any of the many other issues that

---

[20] Compare Dasgupta 2017. I thank Väyrynen for this reference.

perplex philosophers. Of course, one person's philosophical problem might be another person's irrelevant annoyance. Yet if we turn our backs to these issues, our position will be philosophically unsatisfying.

For these reasons, then, I think that the best position for an ethical realist is the position of the *explainers*. We have seen the problems faced by views that combine realism with normative formalism and normative conceptualism. This is why I think realists ought to favor normative objectualism. And primitivism is philosophically unsatisfying. This leaves us with the position of the explainers. All of the explainers I am aware of are ethical naturalists.[21] The main point, however, is that we are left favoring versions of ethical realism that accept objectualism about normativity and that attempt to provide an analysis of what this normativity comes to.

6. Desiderata for a Realist Theory of Normativity

I have been arguing that the best position for ethical realists to take about normativity is the objectualist position. The question I consider in this section is, What features would a realist theory need to have in order to provide a philosophically satisfying response to the normativity objection? What are the desiderata for a realist theory of normativity, or for an adequate realist response to the objection? There are at least the following four.

The first is to develop a theory of *robust* ethical normativity, and thereby to avoid the "formalist deflationism" inherent in treating ethical normativity as no different in kind from the normativity of games. I have tried to characterize robust normativity by contrasting it with the merely formal normativity of games and by using the idea of a mistake of normative significance. A person who pays no attention to her *ethical* reasons is *thereby* making a mistake of normative significance. Robustly normative properties and facts have a kind of authority over agents. But this is merely a vague characterization. The normativity objection challenges hardball realists to provide a metaphysical analysis of robust normativity.

The second desideratum is to develop a theory of *objectual* normativity—a theory of the normativity of ethical facts and properties—and thereby to avoid the "conceptual deflationism" involved in treating normativity as fundamentally merely a property of certain concepts. Normative objectualism holds that some objective properties and states of affairs are robustly normative. It holds that it is of the essence of wrongness, and of other ethical properties, that they are robustly normative. The challenge is to explain how this could be so by providing metaphysical analyses, first, of the normative ethical properties, and second, of the property of robust normativity itself.

---

[21] With the possible exception of Wedgwood (2007: 4–6).

The third desideratum, then, is to provide *constitutive explanations* or *metaphysical analyses of the ethical properties* (or a schema thereof) that shows them to be robustly normative as a matter of their essences. Such an analysis would reveal that their normative is essential to them.

The fourth desideratum is to provide a constitutive explanation, or metaphysical analysis, of *the property of being robustly normative*. This is the primary desideratum. A satisfactory analysis, furthermore, would need to be reductive. That is, in the proposition stating the analysis, the analysans would be a complex condition, no element of which refers to the property of robust normativity or to anything that is itself robustly normative as a matter of its essential nature,[22] but which as a whole specifies the essential nature of the property of being robustly normative. So the final desideratum is to provide a *reductive metaphysical analysis* of the property of being robustly normative.

Given that the analyses that are needed would be substantive and metaphysical rather than conceptual, it will be possible coherently to reject them. That is, any answer of this kind to the normativity objection could coherently be denied. But this is not a problem. It is similarly coherent to deny that an acid is a proton donor. Indeed, I think that the most compelling philosophical problems are similar in that plausible answers cannot be grounded merely in conceptual analysis, and this means that they could coherently be denied.

Successful analyses would most likely be naturalistic. For, to provide a satisfactory answer to the normativity objection, the analysis of normativity must refer only to properties that are not (or that are analyzable in terms of elements that are not) themselves essentially normative. The most obvious candidates are natural properties. The elements of the analysans must not themselves be normative, but they must compound into, or constitute, the property of being normative. This notion of constitution is perhaps obscure, but we have an example that illustrates the notion since, plausibly, to be an acid is to have a complex property constituted by the relation of [being a donor of] and the property of [being a proton]. That is, to be an acid is to be a proton donor. Similarly, in a naturalistic metaphysical analysis of the property of being robustly normative, the explanans would be a complex naturalistic condition referring to a complex property.

A naturalistic theory of normativity would, accordingly, satisfy a fifth desideratum. It would provide a reductive constitutive naturalistic explanation or metaphysical analysis of the property of being robustly normativity. That is, it would set out a complex condition and contend that this condition specifies the essential nature of the property of being robustly normative, where the proper elements of this condition refer only to natural properties and relations (or to things that are themselves analyzable by reference only to natural properties and relations).[23]

---

[22] Or, if an element does refer to something normative as a matter of its essential nature, then that thing can in turn be analyzed by a complex condition, no element of which refers the property of robust normativity or to anything robustly normative as a matter of its essential nature. And so on.

[23] Such a condition could be highly complex; the naturalistic properties and relations it refers to might stand to one another in a complex relation.

7. Conclusion

I have contended that ethical realists ought to be realists and objectualists about robust normativity. They ought to hold that the objective ethical properties that they postulate have the essential second-order property of being robustly normative. And they ought to hold that the objective ethical facts that they postulate are robustly normative because the ethical properties that partly constitute them are robustly normative. That is, they ought to contend that, roughly, ethical properties and facts have a characteristic essential authoritative relation to decisions, choices, intentions or attitudes in virtue of their essential nature.

I discussed two deflationary views about normativity, normative formalism and normative conceptualism. Both of these views deny that ethical properties, if there are any, are essentially robustly normative. If I am right, however, it is a necessary truth that the ethical properties, if there are any, are essentially robustly normative, and it follows that conceptualism and formalism are not tenable for ethical realists. Normative objectualism is the remaining option for ethical realists, but it faces the objection that it is unable to explain what the essential normativity of an ethical property or fact could consist in. I contend that a philosophically satisfying response to the objection would have to satisfy the following desiderata. It would have to be a theory of the robust normativity of objective ethical properties, provide a reductive analysis of robust normativity, and provide an analysis of the essential nature of ethical properties that shows them to be robustly normative.

There are several varieties of ethical naturalism that aim to provide a theory of normativity satisfying these desiderata. The most promising, in my view, are Subjectivist Neo-Humean Naturalism (e.g., Schroeder 2007), a kind of Neo-Aristotelian or Eudaimonist Naturalism (e.g., Bloomfield 2001), and my own Pluralist Teleology (Copp 2009, 2015). I discuss these theories and compare them systematically in another work (Copp forthcoming).

References

Armstrong, David. 2004. *Truth and Truthmakers*. Cambridge: Cambridge University Press.
Blackburn, Simon. 2006. "Anti-Realist Expressivism and Quasi-Realism." In *The Oxford Handbook of Ethical Theory*, edited by David Copp, 146–162. New York: Oxford University Press,
Bloomfield, Paul. 2001. *Moral Reality*. Oxford: Oxford University Press.
Brink, David O. 1989. *Moral Realism and the Foundations of Ethics*. Cambridge: Cambridge University Press.
Broome, John. 2007. "Is Rationality Normative?" *Disputatio* 2: 161–178.
Copp, David. 2007. *Morality in a Natural World*. Cambridge: Cambridge University Press.
Copp, David. 2009. "Toward a Pluralist and Teleological Theory of Normativity." *Philosophical Issues* 19: 21–37.

Copp, David. 2012. "Normativity and Reasons: Five Arguments from Parfit against Normative Naturalism." In *Ethical Naturalism: Current Debates*, edited by Susan Nuccetelli and Gary Seay, 24–57. Cambridge: Cambridge University Press.

Copp, David. 2015. "Explaining Normativity." *Proceedings and Addresses of the American Philosophical Association* 89: 48–73.

Copp, David. 2017. "Normative Naturalism and Normative Nihilism: Parfit's Dilemma for Naturalism." In *Reading Parfit On What Matters*, edited by Simon Kirchin, 28–53. London: Routledge.

Copp, David. 2018. "A Semantic Challenge to Non-Realist Cognitivism." *Canadian Journal of Philosophy* 48: 569–591.

Copp, David. 2019a. "Legal Teleology: A Naturalist Account of the Normativity of Law." In *Dimensions of Normativity: New Essays on Metaethics and Jurisprudence*, edited by David Plunkett, Scott Shapiro, and Kevin Toh, 45–64. New York: Oxford University Press.

Copp, David. 2019b. "Realist Expressivism and the Fundamental Role of Normative Belief." *Philosophical Studies* 175: 1333–1356.

Copp, David. 2020. "Just Too Different: Normative Properties and Natural Properties." *Philosophical Studies* 177: 263–286.

Copp, David. Forthcoming. *Ethical Naturalism and the Problem of Normativity*. New York: Oxford University Press.

Darwall, Stephen. 2006. "Morality and Practical Reason: A Kantian Approach." In *The Oxford Handbook of Ethical Theory*, edited by David Copp, 282–320. New York: Oxford University Press.

Dasgupta, Shamik. 2017. "Normative Non-Naturalism and the Problem of Authority." *Proceedings of the Aristotelian Society* 117: 297–319.

Eklund, Matti. 2017. *Choosing Normative Concepts*. Oxford: Oxford University Press.

Enoch, David. 2011. *Taking Morality Seriously*. Oxford: Oxford University Press.

Field, Hartry. 2000. "Apriority as an Evaluative Notion." In *New Essays on the A Priori*, edited by Paul Boghossian and Christopher Peacocke, 117–149. Oxford: Clarendon Press.

Fine, Kit. 2012. "Guide to Ground." In *Metaphysical Grounding: Understanding the Structure of Reality*, edited by Fabrice Correia and Benjamin Schneider, 37–80. Cambridge: Cambridge University Press.

Gauthier, David. 1986. *Morals by Agreement*. Oxford: Oxford University Press.

Gibbard, Allan. 1990. *Wise Choices, Apt Feelings*. Cambridge, MA: Harvard University Press.

Hubin, Donald. 2001. "The Groundless Normativity of Instrumental Rationality." *Journal of Philosophy* 98: 445–468.

Jackson, Frank. 1998. *From Metaphysics to Ethics: A Defence of Conceptual Analysis*. Oxford: Oxford University Press.

King, Jeffrey C. 1998. "What Is a Philosophical Analysis?" *Philosophical Studies* 90: 155–179.

Kolodny, Niko. 2005. "Why Be Rational?" *Mind* 114: 509–563.

Korsgaard, Christine. 1996. *The Sources of Normativity*. Cambridge: Cambridge University Press.

Mackie, J. L. 1977. *Morality: Inventing Right and Wrong*. Harmondsworth, UK: Penguin.

McPherson, Tristram. 2023. "Metaphysical Structure for Moral Realists." In *The Oxford Handbook of Moral Realism*, edited by Paul Bloomfield and David Copp, 18–43. New York: Oxford University Press.

Moore, G. E. 1993. *Principia Ethica*. Edited by Thomas Baldwin. Cambridge: Cambridge University Press. Originally published in 1903.

Parfit, Derek. 2011. *On What Matters*. Vols. 1 and 2. Oxford: Oxford University Press.
Parfit, Derek. 2017. *On What Matters*. Vol. 3. Oxford: Oxford University Press.
Railton, Peter. 2003. *Facts, Values and Norms: Essays Toward a Morality of Consequence*. Cambridge: Cambridge University Press.
Rosen, Gideon. 2010. "Metaphysical Dependence: Grounding and Reduction." In *Modality: Metaphysics, Logic, and Epistemology*, edited by Bob Hale and Haviv Hoffman, 109–135. Oxford: Oxford University Press.
Scanlon, Thomas M. 2014. *Being Realistic about Reasons*. Oxford: Oxford University Press.
Schroeder, Mark. 2005. "Realism and Reduction: The Quest for Robustness." *Philosophers Imprint* 5: 1–18.
Schroeder, Mark. 2007. *Slaves of the Passions*. Oxford: Oxford University Press.
Smith, Michael. 1994. *The Moral Problem*. Oxford: Blackwell.
Sturgeon, Nicholas. 2006. "Ethical Naturalism." In *The Oxford Handbook of Ethical Theory*, edited by David Copp, 91–121. New York: Oxford University Press.
Tiffany, Evan. 2007. "Deflationary Normative Pluralism." *Canadian Journal of Philosophy* 37 Supplement [vol. 33]: 231–262.
Wedgwood, Ralph. 2007. *The Nature of Normativity*. Oxford: Oxford University Press.
Wedgwood, Ralph. 2018. "The Unity of Normativity." In *The Oxford Handbook of Reasons and Normativity*, edited by Daniel Star, 23–45. New York: Oxford University Press.

CHAPTER 12

MORAL FUNCTIONALISM

FRANK JACKSON AND PHILIP PETTIT

1. Moral Functionalism: The Basic Idea and a Reason to Believe It

Moral functionalism is a thesis about the meanings of moral terms, originally inspired by analytical functionalism about mental state terms. According to analytical functionalism, terms for mental states get their meanings from their roles in a theory, the theory known as folk psychology. According to moral functionalism, ethical terms get their meanings from their roles in a theory, a theory we might call folk morality (see, e.g., Jackson 1992 and Jackson and Pettit 1995). "Is morally right," for example, is true of X just if X has the property that plays the "is morally right" role in folk morality. We spell out what this comes to shortly.

Folk morality has a tripartite structure. It has *input clauses*, clauses that go from matters described in nonmoral terms to matters described in moral terms; they concern what kinds of actions, motivations, policies, etc., are morally right and wrong, and what kinds of results are morally good and bad. Killing is typically wrong. Inflicting suffering is bad. Telling the truth is very often what ought to be done. Folk morality also has *internal role clauses*, clauses concerning the interconnections between matters described in moral terms. Illustrations are inevitably controversial, but many find plausible a clause like: what is morally best out of the options available to an agent settles what the agent ought to do, the morally right action for the agent. Others object that agents are not always obliged to do what is best—the objectors often have in mind cases where what is best is very demanding. However, although they are objecting to the example just given, they aren't objecting to the very existence of internal role clauses. For example, our objectors likely allow that what is best is always morally permissible. Finally, there are the *output clauses* of folk morality. They concern the connections between what agents believe about what they ought or ought not to do and what's good and bad, on the one hand, and what they in fact do, on the other. A simple example is: agents who believe that they ought to cease eating meat tend to become vegetarians. Some insist that there is some kind of conceptual connection between believing that something is what one ought to do and being at least inclined to do it. Others maintain that all that's true is that often (and maybe not often enough) agents tend to do what they believe they ought to do.[1]

We take it as obvious that there is such a thing as folk morality. It isn't controversial that people have beliefs about what kinds of actions are right and which are wrong, about how to reason using ethical terms and concepts, and about the influence of a person's moral opinions on their behavior. What's contentious are the details. The illustrations of input, internal role and output clauses given above are sketches, subject to one or another qualification by one or another theorist, but the picture in the broad is not. But why think, as moral functionalism maintains, that folk morality—or some suitable descendent of it (more on what this means below)—delivers an account of the meanings of moral terms?

One reason comes from reflecting on the nature of debates over the merits of one or another ethical theory. Consider, for example, what happens when philosophers (and nonphilosophers, if it comes to that) attack classical utilitarianism. Sometimes they point to the counterintuitive verdicts utilitarianism gives concerning what we ought to do in various cases described in nonmoral terms. They observe, for example, that utilitarianism tells us there is nothing wrong *as such* with punishing those we know to be innocent, and that the special place we give to the interests of those closest to us cannot be justified. Here the critics are targeting what utilitarianism says about input clauses. Sometimes critics of utilitarianism point out that it requires an agent to do that which is best out of the options available to them, no matter how demanding this might be, but surely, say the critics, sometimes it is morally permissible to do less than the best when doing the best is unduly onerous. Here the critics are targeting the implications of utilitarianism for an internal role clause. Sometimes critics of utilitarianism argue that no one could possibly live up to the demands of a theory that requires them to do what they believe is best, impartially considered (i.e., in a way that gives no special status to their own concerns). Here the critics are targeting the implications of utilitarianism for an output clause.

We all know how utilitarians respond. They grant what's common ground, namely that there is, prima facie, a clash between utilitarianism and what is often tagged "commonsense morality" (which is in effect another name for folk morality) but, they argue, careful reflection tells a different story. After reflection, it becomes clear that the implications of utilitarianism are ones we should embrace.

What matters for our purposes here is not who wins the familiar debate over utilitarianism that we have just reminded you of. What matters is that it is the debate that needs to be had.[2] Experiments in the sense meant in the social and physical sciences are not

---

[1] See, e.g., Brink (1989, ch. 3) for a detailed account of this debate.
[2] And is had in, e.g., Smart and Williams (1973), with Williams as the opponent and Smart the supporter of utilitarianism; for attempts to defang one or another objection from commonsense morality to consequentialist theories, see, e.g., Kagan (1982), Jackson (1991), and Pettit (2015, ch. 7).

going to decide whether or not utilitarianism is true, though they may tell us, for example, how popular it is. What is required—and what is in fact done—is to marshal the implications of utilitarianism for input clauses, internal role clauses and output clauses, and then to ask whether or not the implications are, after careful reflection, intuitively acceptable.

We grant that some utilitarian writings read as if what's on offer is in part a revisionary stipulation. But when it comes to defending the stipulation, what happens is the process we have just described. The stipulation is defended by supporting its implications for input clauses, internal roles clauses, and output clauses, often combined with suggestions about how to explain away the prima facie clashes with folk intuitions in one way or another, including in evolutionary terms. And, as those who offer the stipulation are well aware, its reception is precisely a function of how plausible their audiences find the defence being offered.

Much the same goes for debates over Kantian theories, virtue theories, reasons-first theories, modifications of utilitarianism that seek to ameliorate the putative clash with commonsense morality, and so on. The parties to the debates survey the verdicts of each theory for certain sorts of cases (i.e., for input clauses), the implications of each for which transitions between matters described in ethical terms are valid (i.e., for internal role clauses), and what each theory implies about the motivational force of the judgments we express in moral terms (i.e., for output clauses). They then perform a "compare and contrast" exercise, urging that it is their favorite theory that wins out in the end. The protagonists may not describe what they are doing in quite the way we have but, we submit, this is in fact what is going on. The simplest argument for moral functionalism is that it explains why this is what happens. The debate is all about finding the theory that delivers the best fit with our considered judgments—understood so as to include the 'explainings away' we mention above—concerning input clauses, internal role clauses, and output clauses.

One way to highlight our message is to imagine that utilitarians succeed in defusing all the famous objections. They convince us, for instance, that when we think matters through carefully, it is clear that sometimes, though not usually, it is right to punish the innocent, and that we always ought to do what's best, and that the belief that an action maximizes expected happiness has the exactly the right kind of connection to motivation. If that happened, it would be, as they say, game over. What more could one ask for by way of vindicating utilitarianism? Moral functionalism explains why this would be the case. What would have been established is that utilitarianism makes true the clauses that give moral terms their meaning. No wonder that it would be game over.

We can make essentially the same point from the other side of the fence, so to speak. Surely many who are certain that utilitarianism is false are certain precisely because they are convinced that utilitarians cannot explain away the prima facie clashes with commonsense or folk morality. Moral functionalism explains the relevance of this conviction: if correct, it means that the meanings of the moral terms imply that utilitarianism is false.

In what follows, we survey the implications of moral functionalism for a number of live issues in ethics (in one case, the issue is perhaps better described as one that should be more alive than it is) including, of course, for moral realism. It is an interested survey. We will be suggesting that the implications are plausible ones. In what follows, we use "moral" and "ethical" interchangeably.

2. The Supervenience of the Ethical on the Nonethical

The supervenience of the ethical on the nonethical differs from the supervenience of the mental on the physical in two important ways. First, it is far less contentious. Although many affirm that the mental supervenes on the physical, it is far from common ground among philosophers of mind. It is, however, rare to come across someone who denies that the moral supervenes on the nonmoral. Nearly everyone grants that if two actions, states of affairs, policies, etc., are exactly alike in nonethical ways—ways we can specify without using ethical terms—they are exactly alike ethically. Or, to say it the other way around, a difference in ethical nature demands a difference in nonethical nature: for example, if one action ought to be punished and another ought not, the actions must differ in some respect we can specify in nonethical terms. Second, it is necessary and a priori that the ethical supervenes on the nonethical, whereas the supervenience of the mental on the physical is, at best, an a posteriori truth, and (many would add) at best a contingent truth.[3]

Moral functionalism can explain the necessary a priori supervenience of the ethical on the nonethical because it makes possible a reductive analysis of the ethical in terms of the nonethical. It allows us to exploit the Ramsey–Carnap–Lewis way of defining theoretical terms (see Lewis 1970) in a way which makes it transparent how the nonmoral a priori entails the moral, so explaining the necessary a priori supervenience of the moral on the nonmoral. Here is how the account runs, in outline. We can think of folk morality as a longish conjunction of the input clauses, internal role clauses and output clauses that give the meanings of moral terms according to moral functionalism. Let $T(M_1, \ldots, M_n)$ be the sentence that gives the theory, where the M_is are all the moral terms. Folk morality will be satisfied just if there are properties standing in the required relations, if, that is, $(Ex_1) \ldots (Ex_n) T(x_1, \ldots, x_n)$, where each x_j is in M_j's place in T. (This is the "Ramsey sentence" for folk morality.) But if, as moral functionalism holds, each M_i is defined by its place in T, then we can specify what it is to be M_i, in terms of that very place. Here is how it looks for the case of being right

---

[3] See, e.g., Lewis (1994, p. 52).

(A) y is right if and only if $(Ex_1)\ldots(Ex_n) [y$ has x_i & $T(x_1, \ldots, x_n)]$

where x_i replaced "rightness" in T. To say it without symbols: to be right is to have the property that fills the "rightness" place in folk morality. *Mutatis mutandis* for being what ought not to be done, being morally permissible, being good, and so on.

The important point, in the current context, is that (A) specifies what it is to be right in nonmoral terms; there are no "M_i"s to the right of the "if and only if" in (A). It thus explains how the nonmoral can a priori entail the moral for the case of being right. *Mutatis mutandis* for the other moral properties. This is how moral functionalism explains the necessary a priori supervenience of the moral on the nonmoral.

Have we given a naturalistic account of the moral properties? The nonmoral terms that appear on the right-hand side of (A) presumably count as naturalistic. They contain no ethical expressions. (A) can, therefore, be regarded as a naturalistic reduction of being right. However, (A) says nothing about the property that fills the "rightness" place—that is, that plays the rightness role, and the same goes for the other properties that make the Ramsey sentence true. This suggests that a "Moorean" could insist that *these* properties, the ones that play the roles, cannot be captured without using ethical terms. In this context, our Moorean might draw attention to the familiar point that analytical functionalism is not, as it stands, a version of materialism or physicalism about the mind. It becomes a version of materialism when combined with a thesis about the kind of properties that stand in the relationships definitive of being in one or another mental state.

This would, however, be a mistake. (A)—and the corresponding accounts for the other ethical terms—imply that there are *no* properties that can only be captured using ethical terms; this is because they are reductive analyses of ethical language. What might be true, for all that (A) and its partners say, is that the properties that make the Ramsey sentence true are not natural properties in another sense; they may not be the kinds of properties that figure in one or another account of what our world is like to be found in the natural sciences. How likely this is, and further issues raised by Mooreanism, are discussed in the next section.

3. How We Learn the Meanings of Moral Terms

An account of what a word in a public language means should explain how it can come to have that meaning and how that meaning can come to be a shared meaning, at least in many cases. That's required if we are to use words to express agreement and disagreement. People don't agree or disagree merely by uttering the same or different words. Well not quite. Perhaps I hear the sentence "John Doe lost on a TKO." I may have only a rough idea what a TKO is. I may, nevertheless, accept what I hear and agree with it in the sense that I am confident that John Doe lost on what those more knowledgeable about boxing than I am mean by a TKO. That's the message of Hilary Putnam's division of linguistic labor (Putnam 1975), or so it seems to us. This does not, however, mean that I give "TKO" the same meaning as the knowledgeable. If it did, there'd be no point in proceeding to ask what a TKO is, which is of course what one typically does, after which one says that *now* one knows what the phrase means.

It is important that the key ethical terms have shared meanings. Agreements and disagreements over the morality of abortion, mercy killing, and our moral obligations to future generations are among the most important agreements and disagreements we have. What is more and obviously, we want more than agreement and disagreement about words; we want our agreements and disagreements to be substantive (agreement in the sense illustrated by the TKO example is not what we want).

It follows that an important desideratum for any account of the meaning of ethical terms is that it can give an account of how we came to acquire them that explains how it is possible for them to have shared meanings, and this needs to be an account that is consistent with the fact that the meanings we give our words is a contingent a posteriori matter. The importance of this desideratum can be overlooked. The reason may be the assumption that intending to mean what others mean is in itself enough to create a strong presumption that one does in fact mean what others mean—some seem to read Putnam as saying this—but intending to do so and so is one thing and in fact doing it is quite another. Intending to mean what others mean is not special among intentions in being presumptively successful.[4] Moreover, we want it to be the case, at least sometimes, that English speakers and, say, Croatian speakers can agree and disagree over moral questions, and for this to be revealed by the words that come from their respective mouths, pens, and keyboards, despite the fact that English and Croatian speakers use different words to express their opinions. This requires that the words in their different languages have the same meanings. But a typical speaker of English and a typical speaker of Croatian do not intend to mean the same by, for example, "morally good" and "moralno dobro." That's an intention they will *acquire* if and when they become competent in both languages.

According to moral functionalism, learning the meanings of moral terms is acquiring a mastery of the input, internal role and output clauses we talked about earlier. We learn which actions, policies, etc., receive which ethical labels (the input side of the story). We learn how to reason using the ethical labels (the internal role side of the story), and we learn what kinds of reactions are appropriate and are to be expected from those who

---

[4] Incidentally, intending to mean what others mean by a term isn't necessary for meaning what they mean. R is, we may suppose, a mathematical genius living in a poor village. As a result of limited access to texts, he wrongly believes that mathematicians use "prime number" for any positive integer divisible by itself and one alone. He resolves, however, that in his work he will use "prime number" for any positive integer divisible by itself and one alone with the exception of one, realizing that this is the theoretically better notion. Unwittingly, he is using "prime number" with the meaning mathematicians give it despite intending not to.

apply various ethical labels to actions available to them (the output side of the story). We trust that these remarks will resonate with parents who seek to introduce their children to ethical ways of thinking and talking. Don't we parents point to examples of what's morally good, wrong, etc., highlighting the features that make them so? Don't we indicate the kind of behavior called for by judgments of what's right and wrong? Don't we seek to give our children a sense of how to reason about ethical issues using ethical terms?

How can this story be a story about shared meanings, given how much disagreement there is over ethical issues; how, that is, can we find enough agreement over input, internal role and output clauses to allow this story to be one about shared meanings? There are two ways to respond to this fair question. The optimistic one is implicit in our earlier discussion of the debate over utilitarianism. There we pointed out what it would take for utilitarians to win; they would need to defuse the famous problem cases for utilitarianism. They would need to show that what looks bad on the face of it—"how can you possibly hold that the interests of my children have no special claim when I ask myself what I ought to do!"—isn't when one thinks the issues through. We made the same observation about, e.g., Kantian views. Suppose it is the Kantians who find themselves in the happy position of being able reconcile what their view says with folk morality. By the time the big books have been written and all the t's crossed and i's dotted, it becomes clear that a Kantian style ethical theory delivers the intuitively satisfying answers for the input, internal role and output clauses. In that case, the Kantians would be the winners. As we argued earlier, what is going on when theorists defend their favorite position in ethics is, in effect, an exercise in reconciling the answers their position delivers on the key input, internal role and output clauses with our preanalytic but considered intuitions (beliefs). So, the first response to the fair question is that, at the end of the day—and in this context we might talk of reflective equilibrium—we will find very substantial agreement over the key input, output, and internal role clauses. Our problem, as philosophers seeking the one true theory in ethics, is to find the crucial insights and ways of framing matters that tell us which overarching theory—utilitarianism, Kantianism, virtue theory, contract ethics, idealized desire ethics, ...—delivers the goods.

This view about what it takes to find the one true theory might sensibly be combined with an awareness that, in the process of searching for a way to make best sense of the famously abundant and far from uniform intuitions on display in books and papers on ethics, we will find it important to distinguish folk morality from what we might call *mature folk morality* (as in Jackson 1998, p. 133), where mature folk morality is the result of facing up to the fact that parts of extant folk morality may embody attitudes we rightly realize need to be jettisoned and may contain internal inconsistencies (think, e.g., of the way harvesting subjects' first up responses to variations on the trolley problem often deliver responses that are at war with each other). Our task then becomes that of finding the best theory that makes overarching sense of mature folk morality, and the moral functionalist account of the meanings of moral terms will need to be framed in terms of mature folk morality—the theory we will end up converging on—whatever that turns out to be, precisely. In discussion, some have expressed skepticism about the possibility of convergence. That's understandable perhaps, but we note that those who work in ethics must include a large number of optimists. For surely very many of those who give talks and write books and papers on ethics are doing so because they think they have some chance of convincing people—their audiences and their readers—that their claims about what's right and wrong are correct, or that what they say about moral reasoning is correct, or that what they say about the behavior of those with one or another moral opinion is correct. They must, that is, believe that there is some chance of agreement on input clauses, internal role clauses and output clauses (and of course on the relevant empirical considerations in the background). Here they may well have recourse to the 'explainings away' we mentioned earlier. For isn't this belief a major rationale for publishing those books and papers, and for giving those talks?

The more pessimistic response is to grasp the nettle and allow that we don't all give the key ethical terms the very same meanings, and this isn't going to change as time passes; the talk above of converging over time on an agreed theory, call it mature folk morality if you like, may be a hope that explains the publishing and advocacy behavior of many who work in ethics but it is a vain hope all the same. We insist that, as we say early on, there is such a thing as folk morality and there will be such a thing as mature folk morality—surely we are improving—but grant that, at the end of the day, what may become clear is that there is no *single* theory to call "mature folk morality." What we have, it may turn out, are a number of different, internally consistent theories that agree about a lot in the sense of having input clauses, internal role clauses and output clauses that are similar in many ways, but there may not be enough uniformity between the theories to imply that the ethical terms as defined by one of the theories have the very same meanings as those defined by another of the theories. There will be enough similarity to allow for substantive, and not merely nominal, agreement and disagreement on many issues as expressed using the terms as defined by the different theories, but this will not be true for all issues. Given what we say early on in this section about the importance of shared meanings for ethical terms, grasping the nettle will have a significant cost—sometimes what appears to be substantial agreement or disagreement will be merely nominal—but perhaps it will turn out that this is a cost we have to pay. Philosophers sometimes seem gripped by the idea that there is one true ethical theory, perhaps the one they have devoted their life to first finding and later defending. Maybe there is, but maybe there isn't, or maybe there is a degree of indeterminacy.

We close this section by addressing two further worries that regularly come up in discussion, which, as we will see, connect with the issues lately canvassed. The first worry might be expressed in the following words:

> It cannot be the case that the meanings of ethical terms are given by the kind of network account you have offered. The meanings of central moral terms like "morally right," "morally impermissible," "morally evil," etc. remain *fixed* as we debate the input, internal role and output clauses you regard as meaning-giving. For example, when we argue over a candidate input condition like that intentional killing not in self-defense is always morally impermissible, the meaning of "morally

impermissible" remains a constant. It isn't a function of where we end up on the question. The same goes for any other input condition that might be nominated, and the same goes for the internal role and output clauses that might be nominated as part of the network account of the meaning of moral terms. The meanings of moral terms are one thing; the verdicts we frame in moral terms are quite another.

We grant the initial appeal of this line of thought, as is evinced by the fact that it often comes up, in one way or another, but insist that it does not withstand scrutiny. To start with, it is a general point about meaning that the meanings of expressions and the verdicts we deliver using those expressions are intimately linked, as, e.g., Locke (1689/1975, Book III), says. We use words to express how we *take* things to be. For example, physicists use "Electrons exist" to make a claim about how they believe things to be (the verdict they have come to), and the claim they make is a function of the meaning they give the word "electron." Or think of what happens when we go to a philosophy talk. We recover what the speaker believes—their verdicts about this or that issue—to the extent that we *understand* the words that come from their mouth or appear on their slides. It isn't true that the verdicts we express using words float free of the meanings of those words.[5] A verdict on whether a certain action is right or wrong, for example, will be a function of the meaning of those moral terms and of the ascertained empirical facts about the action.

In any case, if the meanings of ethical terms float free of input, internal role, and output clauses, we need to ask what, in that case, does fix the meanings of the ethical terms? We saw earlier the problems attendant on relying on intentions to use the words as one's fellow language users use them to fix meaning—having an intention is one thing, fulfilling it is quite another. Moreover, intentions to mean what others mean, even when successful, radically underdetermine meaning: samenesses and differences underdetermine what the samenesses and differences hold between.

We suspect that what lies behind the line of thought in question is a view in metaphysics, the one we called "Moorean" earlier; the view that there are irreducibly non-natural properties, where to be irreducibly non-natural is to be a property that can only be picked out using ethical terms. We can then see, runs the thought, how the meanings of ethical terms can be independent of input, internal role and output clauses. Their meanings are fixed by being connected to these non-natural properties. But there are well known problems for any account of this sort. One is that it rests on an implausible view about the nature of our world. There is no reason to believe that the posited properties are instantiated. A second problem is that, even if they are instantiated and we somehow come to know this, how could we come to have justified beliefs about their distribution, and how could we explain how ethical terms come to pick them out in a

---

[5] "Can't competent speakers of English differ in their verdicts concerning which substances are poisonous without thereby giving 'poisonous' different meanings, consistently, that is, with their being in real disagreement?" Well, no. For they need to agree on what it takes to be poisonous; their disagreement needs to be limited to which substances have what it takes.

way that ensures that one person's use of "is morally required" picks out the same property as another's use of "is morally required," or picks out the same property as some phrase in Croatian. A third problem comes from the earlier noted supervenience of the ethical on the nonethical. The ethical *depends* (in the sense of Broad 1968) on the nonethical, in addition to supervening on it. It is impossible to have an ethical nature without having a relevant nonethical nature (a nature we can describe without using ethical terms). Good acts must also be acts that increase happiness, honor a promise or whatever. The upshot is that the ethical and the nonethical are locked together in a way that makes it very hard to believe that they are distinct in the way Mooreans hold that they are.[6]

The second of our two further worries relates to our observation that moral functionalism does not offer a guarantee that we all mean the same by moral terms; in consequence, we may have to allow that some (not all) agreements and differences over ethical questions are merely verbal. The worry is that this is a special, and undesirable, feature of moral functionalism. Our reply is that it is a feature of any and every account of moral language, be it expressivist, Moorean, causal, etc. What our words mean is a contingent, a posteriori matter, as we say above; that should be granted independently of whether one is a moral functionalist, an expressivist, a Moorean, a causal theorist, etc. All theorists in ethics must allow that it is an open question whether or not what one person means by, say, "morally right" is the same as what another means by "morally right," where an open question means one that has to be investigated empirically and one that may receive an affirmative or a negative answer. The same is true for whether or not what one English speaker means by "morally good" is the same as what some given speaker of another language, Croatian, say, means by "moralno dobro." In this case, the key point is especially obvious: compiling English–Foreign Language dictionaries is an exercise in linguistic fieldwork.

How one thinks the investigation should go will depend on one's views about moral language. Perhaps an English-speaking expressivist will approach the issue somewhat as follows: "Reflection on my use of 'is morally good' tells me that I use it to express a certain pro-attitude. Having this attitude manifests itself in various ways and I note that these manifestations are to be found in those around me, and also in those who speak one or another language other than English when they utter . . . ." An English-speaking Moorean will be concerned instead with how they can be confident that the properties they hold are picked out by their use of "is morally good," "is wrong," etc., are the same properties as are picked out by those terms by their fellow English speakers, and will want assurance that their English words pick out the same properties as do various terms in other languages. Arguably, as we suggest two paragraphs back, the special nature of the properties a Moorean holds are picked out by their own usage makes finding good reasons to hold that others pick out the same properties especially challenging.

---

[6] For more on this and related points, see Jackson (1998, ch. 5) and Streumer (2017, ch. 2).

But we are speculating. It is really for supporters of those views to explain how they can be confident that the meanings of moral terms (as they take them to be) are the same—or enough alike—across a language community and between different language communities to ensure that agreements and disputes framed in moral terms are genuine and not merely verbal. We have given the answer we like, and are discussing the issue as it arises more generally to make the point that there is no special problem here for moral functionalism.

4. The Utility of Moral Language

Why is the historical-causal theory of reference for proper names so plausible? The answer is that it explains why proper names are so useful, and, thereby, why language evolved so as to contain them. The platforms at Penn Station get assigned different numbers to avoid confusing one platform with another, and the numbers are then used to pass on information about where and when a train is arriving. That's common knowledge. In the broad, the same goes for proper names. People, cities, streets, buildings, etc., get assigned names to assist in distinguishing one from another. These distinguishing marks help us avoid confusing different people, cites, streets, etc., and are available to assist in passing on information about people, cities, streets, etc. This is as much common knowledge as our remarks about Penn Station's platform numbers. Philosophers of language debate whether this common knowledge should be viewed as a version of causal descriptivism, or as a version of a causal theory of reference for proper names, viewed as importantly different from a description theory. That debate is by the way here. What is important for our concerns is that it is clear what purpose is served by having names in our languages, and that this allows us to explain why they evolved so as to contain them.[7]

We should expect the same of an account of ethical terms. It should make it clear why they are useful—what purpose or purposes they serve—and thus of why our languages (English, Croatian, Chinese, etc.) evolved so as to contain them. Arguably, this desideratum has of late not received the attention it deserves (but see Sterelny and Fraser 2017). It has, however, a history in writings that go under the banner of evolutionary ethics. Here is a simplified version of a style of evolutionary ethics to be found in Alexander (1891–2). The feeling of pain is useful because it has two properties: it draws attention to bodily damage, and it tends to cause behavior that minimizes the damage. In similar vein, runs the theory, the feeling of obligation is useful because it has two properties: it is caused by the availability of possible actions of a kind such that performing them would have great utility in certain circumstances (typically, ones where cooperation and coordination between agents with different interests is important now or in

---

[7] The theory is due to Kripke (1980); we are not suggesting he would agree with the way we present it. Our presentation draws on Kroon (1987) and Jackson (2010).

the future—Alexander talks of the importance of an "equilibrium" in society between competing interests), and it tends to cause the performance of these actions. The fact that it has these two properties together explains why we evolved to experience it. And, of course, once we evolved to have the feeling of obligation, it was useful to have words for the kinds of actions that provoke it, and to grasp the category or categories to which the actions that provoke it belong. We have, accordingly, an evolutionary explanation of how we came to have words like "morally required" in our language, and to have the concept of the morally required, for we have an explanation of why ethical terms (and concepts) are useful.

This is the merest sketch of the theory Alexander outlines, but even so the problem with it is obvious. There is no feeling of obligation akin to the feeling of pain. What we do have are *beliefs* that certain actions available to us are ones we ought to perform. If we fail to act on them, we sometimes have "pangs of conscience" but often we do not, and, in any case, the pangs do not motivate in the way that pain does. What is more, beliefs that certain actions are ones we ought to perform are not typically caused in the way that feelings are. How hot a chilli tastes is a function of its chemistry, whereas our moral judgments are responses to how we take something to be—that it is an infliction of needless pain, that it is the keeping of a promise, etc.

Nevertheless, Alexander gives us an item on the agenda for any account of the meanings of moral terms: explain why, on the account in question, it would be useful to have moral terms and why we might have evolved to have them. Now there are a number of extant, interesting accounts of how moral concepts and terms evolved, directed precisely to the question of what makes them—the concepts and the words—useful. What is important for what follows are not the details of one or another account but what is in common between them: ethical terms, concepts and ways of thinking evolved through the need to adjudicate between competing interests, something that became especially pressing when we formed communities in ways that enhanced our chances of survival by encouraging cooperation.[8] Hermits can do what they like. They do not have to balance what they want against what others want. The downsides are that if bad things happen, they have no one to turn to for help, and that projects that require many hands to the wheel are beyond them. But, once we started to live in communities, a pressing issue became how to balance what one person or group wants against what another person or group wants, and how to regulate our behavior as members of a community in ways that promote the interests of the community as a whole and, thereby, at least sometimes, our own individual interests. We needed to find acceptable ways of adjudicating between competing interests in ways that enhance cooperation and lead to positive outcomes. When this started to happen was when we started to think ethically.

Although this lightning sketch prescinds from the details of how the evolution of thinking in ethical terms helps resolve disputes and aids co-operation, we can say this

---

[8] Thus Sterelny and Fraser (2017, p. 1003) talk of "principles of action and interaction that support forms of cooperation."

much in the broad. Three things must be true if an account anything like this is to explain the evolution of morality. The first is that there need to be properties with the following feature: acting so as to promote their instantiation has good effects for those who belong to communities. (What about properties whose *suppression* has good effects? We can think of these in terms of promoting the instantiation of their nonoccurrence.) The second concerns thinking in terms of these properties. It had better be possible to do so. Human agents are thinking agents. The third concerns motivation. It had better be the case that the belief that some course of action has one or another of these properties has, as a rule, some tendency to cause behavior that leads to their instantiation. One question is which properties are such that their instantiation *would* have good effects; a second and distinct question is the mechanism by which these properties might come to be instantiated. For intentional agents like us, the mechanism will often involve the tendency of beliefs about these properties to cause actions that realize them.

Suppose that all three requirements obtain. How could this be an account of the evolution of ethical ways of thinking? There is no mention of ethics as such in any of the three conditions. But if moral functionalism is true, there is mention of ethics—implicitly. The first condition was in effect that we need input clauses—they specify the actions, policies, etc., that have the properties whose instantiation would have utility; the second condition tells us in effect that we need internal role clauses—they tell us how to reason in terms of these properties; the third condition tells us in effect that we need output clauses—they tell us how the needed properties might come to be instantiated through the actions of intentional agents. The upshot is that the existence of properties that satisfy the input, internal role and output clauses of moral functionalism is exactly what would be required for some kind of evolutionary account of the emergence of moral ways of thinking to make sense. And the utility of ethical terms will then lie in the utility of having terms for the properties in question.

We started this section by noting that any account of ethical language should explain its utility. Talk of utility naturally invites evolutionary reflections, and we have seen how moral functionalism makes good sense from an evolutionary perspective. But, for those unimpressed by evolutionary ways of thinking about ethics, we note that the key point about how moral functionalism explains the utility of moral language can be made independently. It is a matter of record that describing matters in ethical terms makes things go better, especially when dealing with problems that arise from the fact that we live in communities and need to adjudicate between competing claims for a share of limited resources. It is very hard to believe that this is an accident. But if it isn't an accident, there must be a story to tell about the properties our ethical terms are picking out which explains this happy result. The situation is akin to that with names. It is a matter of record that assigned names—to cities, streets, people, etc.—are very useful. This fact calls for explanation and, as we say above, the explanation will advert to some version or other of a historical-causal theory. What's the right story in the case of ethical terms? First, they need to pick out properties whose promotion would make things go better, and properties that do the opposite. Second, they need to pick out properties we can reason about. (A feature of the way using ethical terms makes things go better is their role in facilitating deliberations about what ought to be done.) Finally, they need to pick out properties we tend to promote, and properties whose instantiation we have some tendency to suppress. The story will, therefore, have input clauses—clauses that tell us where the properties in question are to be found; internal role clauses—clauses that tell us how to reason about the properties; and output clauses—clauses that tell us about their motivational properties, both pro and con. All three are essential if moral terms are to be of use to us in negotiating our interactions with others in our communities in the ways distinctive of debates framed in moral terms. This is how moral functionalism can explain the utility of ethical language, independently of the question of how it evolved.

We close this section by noting that a focus on making sense of how ethical terms and ways of thinking did evolve—or would have evolved the way things might well have been—allows us to reshape the way we presented moral functionalism earlier. We presented it as a reductive analysis of moral terms, one that allows us to find a place for moral properties—the properties the moral terms pick out—within a naturalistic picture, and we noted why this would be a good thing to do. Our focus, however, wasn't on strict fidelity to our current moral concepts—that was the point of the distinction between folk morality and mature folk morality, and our suggestion that it would be best to analyze moral terms via their place in mature folk morality. There is, though, another way of thinking of moral functionalism. We can view it as what we would end up with if we asked after the *genealogy* of ethics. The key idea can be explained using the example of money.

No one, we take it, thinks that the concept of money is *sui generis*. There will be a reductive analysis of the following form

(B) X is money if and only if X is . . .

where the words after "if and only if" do not contain "money" or its equivalent. (When we say that there will be such an analysis, we are not suggesting that writing it down will be an easy task.) But, of course, there is a story to be told about how money came into existence, a story that will advert to its utility in assisting with the exchange of goods, etc. An (idealized) account of this kind is to be found in Menger (1892). This means that a good question to ask is, What would X need to be like in order for it have evolved in the way that money did, and for it to play the kind of role that money plays in society? And we should expect an answer to this question to deliver something like what appears after "if and only if" in (B), and a plausible thought is that a fruitful way of thinking about (B) is as an answer to the genealogy question, in the sense that it tells us what is required of money in order for it to have evolved in the way that it did, or for it to be such that it would have evolved in any society much like ours.

Likewise, as we emphasize above, there is a story to be told about how ethical ways of thinking and talking evolved. And, as we said, we can say this much in the broad. It will be a story about (i) there being properties whose instantiation promotes survival in the kinds of situations in which ethical ways of thinking in fact evolved, and properties that do the opposite; (ii) our being able to reason about these properties; and (iii) our coming to be such that beliefs about these properties have at least some motivational force, pro or con. Clauses (i), (ii) and (iii) correspond, respectively, to the input, internal role and output clauses of moral functionalism. The upshot is that asking after the genealogy of ethical terms and ways of thinking—how they came into existence the way things were or would have come into existence the way things might well have been—will deliver biconditionals like (A), and the corresponding ones for the other ethical terms.[9]

5. What It Takes to Be a Moral Realist

We take the *cognitivist* part of moral realism to be the thesis that there are moral properties, understood as the claim that predicates like "is morally wrong" and "is morally good" ascribe properties. The *realist* part of moral realism adds that the properties in question are, on occasion, actually possessed; being morally wrong is in fact a property of, say, needless killing, and being morally good is in fact often a property of, say, donating to charity.

How substantive is the cognitivist part of moral realism? We have the predicate "is morally wrong" in English, and can form the expressions "being morally wrong" and "the property of being morally wrong" from that predicate. Given that, it might be asked how could anyone doubt the existence of moral properties? Our answer to this good question is that the debate isn't about words and isn't about the constructions our language allows us to make from words. It is about whether or not certain words and phrases are good for telling us about how things are. Take, for example, the word "house." Imagine we have divided all the objects there are into those in the extension of "house" and those not in its extension. Is there a difference between the items in the two sets over and above the difference with regard to whether or not they are in the extension of "house"? Of course there is. There is a way something has to be for "house" to apply to it, and this way is over and above belonging to the extension of "house" and is the information about how things are that the word is good for delivering. If that were not true, the information the use of the word makes available would be limited to a fact about word usage, and it isn't. Cognitivism in ethics affirms, as we understand it here, that the same goes for ethical terms. There is, for example, a difference between actions in the extension of "is morally wrong" and those not in the extension of "is morally wrong," *over and above* the difference in whether or not they belong to the extension of "is morally wrong." The debate over the nature of the property of being morally wrong is, we urge, to be understood as the debate over this difference, and in particular the nature of the acts inside the extension of "is morally wrong."

We mentioned earlier Moorean views about the metaphysics of morals. If they are correct, the only words we have for the moral properties are expressions containing

---

[9] For more on the genealogical way of thinking in the case of ethics, see Pettit (2018).

moral terms. Any attempt to pick out moral properties in nonmoral terms is bound to fail. This is the sense in which Mooreanism is inconsistent with naturalism in ethics, on one understanding of naturalism. All the same, actions in the extension of one or another moral term will have something in common that outruns their falling under the extension of the term in question, namely, the very properties Mooreans hold we can only talk about by using ethical terms. In this sense, on Moorean views moral terms mark real and not merely nominal divisions among, for example, actions, and Moorean views are a species of cognitivism.

Moral functionalism likewise is a species of cognitivism. To fall under such and such a moral predicate is to have the property that plays the relevant role in the input, internal role and output clauses. Earlier, in §2, we spelt out what this comes to for "is right." Is moral functionalism a species of realism? Not as such. Realism about some given moral property will be the claim that there is a property, in the sense of an *instantiated* property, that fills the role definitive of that property. Is there, for example, a property that some actions in fact possess that fills the bill for being right that we gave in §2? As we note in that section, this question comes down to the question as to whether or not the Ramsey sentence for mature folk morality is true.

This means that one might embrace moral functionalism and proceed to use it as a platform for the denial of realism concerning, for example, the property of being right. One might, for example, insist that the only plausible version of an output clause for being right is that an action is right just if it has a property which is such that believing an action has that property *entails* desiring that the action be done, and proceed to argue that, as there is no such property instantiated in our world (and maybe, for Humean reasons, there could not be), nothing has the property of being right.

We favor a less hard-line approach. We have already commented on the manifest utility of moral language and how understanding its utility goes hand in hand with understanding how we came to acquire moral concepts. This makes it hard to believe that moral terms mark out empty categories. The situation is akin to that which obtains with analytical functionalism about the mind. The manifest usefulness of its folk psychological categories makes it hard to believe that they are empty. Advances in neuroscience may suggest important refinements and extensions, but elimination is very unlikely. We talked earlier of the nature of debates in ethics. They are, we suggested, best seen as attempts to find occupants for the roles we moral functionalists talk about. There is plenty of give and take, perhaps some explaining away, and sometimes a certain amount of bullet biting, but it is a matter of record that there is plenty of constructive engagement. We think the message is that, somewhere or other, somehow or other, there are instantiated properties to be found that near enough fill the roles that moral functionalism says need to be filled (while granting the possibility, noted earlier, that there may be irresolvable differences). Even Mackie, who argued that the roles were not filled—his error theory (1977) is in part based on insisting on demanding specifications of the roles of folk morality and mature folk morality, with the addition of the claim that nothing fills these demandingly specified roles—felt free to write a book with two apparently inconsistent parts. The first lays out his argument for an error theory. The second part is an essay on various topics in ethics. How could he have thought that this was a sensible enterprise? (We are not alone in asking this question.) He took it for granted that there were near enough occupants of the roles to allow the second half of the book to be worth writing. At any rate that is, we urge, the way to make good sense of what Mackie is doing in the second part of the book given the thesis he argues for in the first part.

In a number of places earlier in this chapter, we highlight the fact that what our words mean is a contingent a posteriori fact. Here we are suggesting that we might, if it is needed, make adjustments—sensible ones—to what ethical terms mean according to moral functionalism to ensure that realism comes out true. This is really no different from what happened when it was discovered that atoms could be split. The sensible semantic decision was to relax the clause that insisted that atoms had to be more than just very hard to split, so allowing us to avoid going eliminativist about atoms.[10]

REFERENCES

Alexander, S. 1891–2. "Is the Distinction between 'I' and 'Ought' Ultimate and Irreducible?" *Proc. Aristotelian Society* 2(1): 100–107.

Brink, David O. 1989. *Moral Realism and the Foundations of Ethics*. Cambridge: Cambridge University Press.

Broad, C. D. 1968. "Certain Features in Moore's Ethical Doctrines." In *The Philosophy of G. E. Moore*, edited by P. A. Schilpp, 43–67. La Salle, IL: Open Court.

Jackson, Frank. 1991. "Decision-Theoretic Consequentialism and the Nearest and Dearest Objection." *Ethics* 101(3): 461–482.

Jackson, Frank. 1992. "Critical Notice of Susan Hurley, *Natural Reasons*, Oxford University Press, 1989." *Australasian Journal of Philosophy* 70(4): 475–487.

Jackson, Frank. 1998. *From Metaphysics to Ethics: A Defence of Conceptual Analysis*. Oxford: Clarendon Press.

Jackson, Frank. 2010. *Language, Names, and Information*, Oxford: Wiley-Blackwell.

Jackson, Frank, and Philip Pettit. 1995. "Moral Functionalism and Moral Motivation." *Philosophical Quarterly* 46: 82–86.

Kagan, Shelly. 1982. *The Limits of Morality*. Oxford: Oxford University Press.

Kripke, Saul. 1980. *Naming and Necessity*. Cambridge, MA: Harvard University Press.

Kroon, Fred. 1987. "Causal Descriptivism." *Australasian Journal of Philosophy* 65(1): 1–17.

Lewis, David K. 1970. "How to Define Theoretical Terms." *Journal of Philosophy* 67: 427–446.

Lewis, David K. 1994. "Reduction of Mind." In *Companion to the Philosophy of Mind*, edited by Samuel Guttenplan, 412–431. Oxford: Blackwell.

Locke, John. [1689] 1975. *An Essay Concerning Human Understanding*, edited by Peter H. Nidditch. Oxford: Clarendon Press.

Mackie, J. L. 1977. *Ethics: Inventing Right and Wrong*. Harmondsworth: Penguin.

Menger, C. 1892. "On the Origin of Money." *Economic Journal* 2: 239–255.

---

[10] We have discussed moral functionalism with colleagues and friends over many years. Some have been sympathetic, some less so; thanks are due to them all, especially Michael Smith and David Lewis. We are also indebted to the editors for convincing us of the need to add to §3.

Pettit, Philip. 2015. *The Robust Demands of the Good: Ethics with Attachment, Virtue and Respect*. Oxford: Oxford University Press.

Pettit, Philip. 2018. *The Birth of Ethics: Reconstructing the Role and Nature of Morality*. New York: Oxford University Press.

Putnam, Hilary. 1975. "The Meaning of 'Meaning.'" In *Mind, Language and Reality*, 215–271. Cambridge, UK: Cambridge University Press.

Smart, J. J. C., and Bernard Williams. 1973. *Utilitarianism: For and Against*. Cambridge: Cambridge University Press.

Sterelny, Kim, and Ben Fraser. 2017. "Evolution and Moral Realism." *British Journal for the Philosophy of Science* 68: 981–1006.

Streumer, Bart 2017. *Unbelievable Errors: An Error Theory about All Normative Judgements*. Oxford: Oxford University Press.

CHAPTER 13

FUNCTION, FITNESS, FLOURISHING

PAUL BLOOMFIELD

We are moral apes...
— Kim Sterelny and Ben Fraser

THE relationship of morality to biology has long been fraught, reaching a nadir in 1903, when G. E. Moore skewered Herbert Spencer's (1879–1893) "evolutionistic ethics" with the naturalistic fallacy for equating what is "better" with what is "more evolved". Regardless of the merits of either Moore's open question argument or Spencer's Lamarkian utilitarianism, since *Principia Ethica*, most defenders of naturalistic moral realism have steered clear of trying to show direct links between biology and evolutionary theory, on the one hand, and morality on the other. There are notable exceptions to the rule, two being Richard Boyd's (1988) discussion of "homeostatic cluster properties" and Kim Sterelny and Ben Fraser's (2016) argument that moral facts can be understood, at least in part, in terms of evolved facts about social cooperation. As welcome as these discussions are, there are arguably deeper connections to be explored between evolutionary theory and a descendent of the ancient Greek concept of *eudaimonia*. Both Plato (1993, 352d–354c) and Aristotle (2000, 1097b21–1098a20) rested their understanding of virtue (*aretê*), including moral virtue, on an excellence (*aretê*) in functioning (*ergon*) by relying on biological analogies. Of course, our understanding of biological function has evolved (as it were) over the millennia, but this ancient insight can inform a contemporary theory of naturalistic moral realism in which eudaimonia, or the flourishing or happiness of a person, can be comprehended by terms derived from evolutionary theory while also grounding normative moral theory.

There are two basic moves to set up the position. The first claims that all genuine normativity found within human life can be grounded in human biology and psychology through the biological distinction between proper function and dysfunction or malfunction. "A function" is the nominalization of the verb "to function" which is a success term, as "it functions" entails "it is not malfunctioning". Degrees of functioning are required to express how qualitatively well an item is functioning, as functioning can be excellent or merely adequate, while dysfunction can be more or less severe, and malfunction implies failure. The fundamental claim is that when a trait or organ is functioning, it is doing what it ought to do, and when it is malfunctioning it is failing to do what it ought to do, or failing to do what it is there to do.[1]

Examples are:

1. A heart in myocardial infarction is not doing what hearts ought to do.
2. When belief-forming mechanisms of people form beliefs based on desires and wishes instead of evidence, people are not believing what they ought to believe.
3. When people say "right" when they mean "left", they are not speaking as they ought to speak.
4. When parents abuse or neglect their children, they are not behaving the way parents ought to behave.

Only one kind of normativity is required to explain these varied phenomena. Despite ontological protest from non-naturalistic moral realists and moral non-realists (including error theorists), the distinction between (1) a healthy heartbeat and a heart attack—which is as real as the difference between life and death—is sufficient to explain (4) the "ought" of morality (or the "ought" of human action), just as it is sufficient for (2) epistemology (the "ought" of human belief-formation) and (3) semantics (the "ought" of human communication).

Naturalism assumes that nature is sufficient to explain all the facts of biological life, including human life. Moral normativity, epistemic normativity, and semantic normativity can all be naturalized by grounding them in the distinction between proper functioning and malfunctioning, though here our focus will be moral normativity.

The second basic move also starts within biology and evolutionary theory. It involves the relationship of *function* to *fitness*, and yields a definition of "eudaimonia" in terms derived from "fitness". Eudaimonia is "species relative" such that each biological species will have its own form of eudaimonia based on shared characteristics of the conspecifics. The view is fairly though not completely neutral about which theory of biological function is correct, but it is not so ecumenical about theories of fitness: the view requires the "propensity theory" of fitness, as developed by Susan Mills and John Beatty (1979). Happily, this is the leading, extant theory of fitness.

The structure of what is to come is based on these two moves. §1 contains some background assumptions of the view. In §2, the concepts of *biological function* and *individual fitness* are introduced, and their relations described. In §3, "eudaimonia" is

---

[1] Judith Jarvis Thomson (2003) develops a theory of normativity that is in many ways similar to the present one, but in her discussion of *function*, she does not distinguish natural or biological functions from the functions of artifacts.

defined by way of "individual fitness" and this is followed by a discussion of the cardinal moral virtues, as these traits have been historically seen as, in some sense, required for eudaimonia. Finally, in §4, some prominent objections are addressed.

1. Systems, Reduction, Teleology, and Continuity

We begin with the question of whether or not naturalism requires reduction, as many assume that non-reduction entails non-naturalism. Biological systems are physical systems, and as such are bound by the laws of physics and in particular, the laws of thermodynamics. There is some debate about whether the second law of thermodynamics, involving the ineluctable increase of entropy over time, can be reduced to statistical mechanics. A stock philosophical example of "successful intertheoretic reduction" is that heat reduces to mean kinetic energy, but this reduction is in fact problematic because the second law of thermodynamics is asymmetric while all the laws of statistical mechanics are symmetric (Sklar 1993). There is at least some reason to think that neither heat nor physical systems in general reduce to the movements of particles alone, and this is true for biological systems as well. All systems, including biological ones, resist reduction. Even Moore (1903), our modern progenitor of moral non-naturalism, acknowledged that organic wholes are more than the sum of their parts, so they are naturalistic yet non-reductionistic. While reductions of life to chemistry and physics have been attempted (Schrödinger 1944), life resists being reduced to the movements of particles (Benardete, 1976); life is self-organizing (Kauffman, 1993).

None of this is meant to imply that the version of naturalistic moral realism defended below requires either reduction or non-reduction; it is neutral on this score. Either thermodynamics reduces to statistical mechanics or it does not, either biology reduces to physics and chemistry or it does not, either mental states reduce to brain states or they do not.[2] If we follow W. V. O. Quine (1953, 1960, 1963) and understand by "naturalism" roughly that there is a continuity among theories of empirical nature, then there is no reason to think that naturalism, by itself, requires reduction: for example, non-reductive materialism (Baker 2009), including some functionalist theories of mind, is an up-and-running research program in the philosophy of mind without contravening the principles of naturalism, whatever they may turn out to be. Naturalistic emergentism is a metaphysical possibility that does not entail non-naturalism, so reduction is neither required by it nor is reduction disallowed. Therefore, naturalistic moral realism can reject non-naturalism while maintaining neutrality between reduction and non-reduction.

---

[2] There are many precedents of using this kind of *tu quo que* arguments to defend moral realism. For discussion, see Lillehammer 2007 and Cowie and Rowland 2019.

Applying this general skepticism about reduction to evolutionary theory, a further assumption is that natural selection involves more than what is required for replicating genes, and as such Richard Dawkins's (1976) "selfish gene" theory of evolution is at best incomplete. In particular, there are more "units of selection" than merely the gene, so for example, selection can occur at the level of groups (Sober and Wilson 1998; Okasha 2006; Lloyd 2020). Something like "multilevel selection theory" is being assumed.

Another sticking point for reduction has been the ancient concept of *teleology*, the infamous early modern bugbear of biology and moral naturalism, when theories of "mechanics" seemed to rule it out. It is still common to think that evolutionary theory was final nail in the coffin of teleology. Nevertheless, teleology stubbornly remains in one form or another as long as the concept of *purpose* or *goal-directedness* is analytically built-into the concept of *biological function*, as it seems to be (Wimsatt 1972, more on this below). Indeed, recent developments in evolutionary theory make some form of teleology scientifically and philosophically respectable (Walsh 2008, 2012). In the past twenty years, there has been a refocusing of attention within evolutionary theory around the importance of the individual organism and ontogenesis as these affect our understanding of evolutionary processes as a whole. This subfield has come to be known as "evo-devo" (Müller 2007; Laubichler 2009). Again, the view of moral realism defended below can take its lead from other naturalized disciplines: if biology can do without teleology, then so can naturalistic moral realism, but if biology requires it, then it is not a metaethical problem.

The final assumption does not concern reduction but rather a form of non-exceptionalism about human beings. The most prominent form of moral realism closest to the position developed below is that of Philippa Foot (2001), Rosalind Hursthouse (1999), and Michael Thompson (1995, 2008), all of whom accept a form of "neo-Aristotelianism" in which "goodness" is understood in terms of an organism's flourishing and "badness" is understood in terms of "defect". G. E. M. Anscombe (1957) inspired Thompson, who argues that "Aristotelian categoricals" determine the conditions for flourishing. These are "natural-historical" judgments about how creatures of a kind live. So, for example, the lioness that fails to teach her cubs how to hunt is defective in this regard. But, on this view, the biological sciences drop out of the picture; the theoretical turn is Wittgensteinian (Mac Cumhaill and Wiseman, 2022). These philosophers do not speak of "species", understood empirically, but rather of "life-forms", and they see the flourishing of human beings as discontinuous with the flourishing of every other life-form. While the flourishing of plants and non-human animals can be comprehended by empirical science, humans are supposed to be exceptional by virtue of our practical rationality. Crucially, as human beings, we can question our "natural desires" in a manner that seems to set us apart from other animals (Lawrence 2011). For example, Foot (2001, 42) correctly points to the undeniable truth that human beings can flourish despite choosing to not reproduce (a claim to which we return below), and this kind of fact has led these philosophers to conclude that we cannot understand human flourishing on evolutionary principles, where only survival and reproduction reign. Because of this, they conclude there is a discontinuity between Homo sapiens and everything else alive.

Unsurprisingly, this rejection of biological science has brought strong criticism.[3] Contra Wittgensteinianism: the assumption henceforth is that, as different as humans may be from other species, there is nothing about us which requires thinking of ourselves as anything other than a species of animal, subject to the same natural laws and/or ethological principles that apply to other animals (Midgley, 1978). A helpful comparison is to the debate over the differences between animal communication and human language (Hurley and Nudds 2006; Lurz 2009; Bar-On 2013). Here, roughly, the empiricists argue for a continuity between non-human and human communication and the rationalists argue for discontinuity. The difference, however, is that, unlike Foot and her followers, the rationalists in this debate are not trying to take human communication out of the realm of science or claim that biology does not have the capacity to account for human language. The difference between non-human and human communication might be as great as the difference between flightless reptiles and birds, but no one suggests that this shows either avian flight or recursive grammar to be exceptions to empirical science, as Foot et al. claim about human flourishing. Evolution proceeds by way of punctuated equilibria (Eldredge and Gould 1972), and so whatever great leap humans beings represent past chimpanzees, it is nevertheless no more than punctuation. However wonderful and special human beings might be, a guiding assumption here is that we are nothing more than *Homo sapiens*, a species of mammal, phylogenetically continuous with other apes, period. The view assumes that nothing supernatural or non-natural is needed to explain human life.

Metaphysically, naturalism leaves aside theological posits of immaterial souls and entails a rejection of substance dualism in the philosophy of mind. It is inconsistent with libertarian free will and miracles if these imply breaking the laws of nature. Kantian noumenal rationality is out of the picture and Hegelian absolute idealism has no more place than backward causation. This form of naturalism is consistent with the existence of abstract objects or "universals" such as sets, numbers, properties, and propositions. The scope of "naturalism" here does not entail the claim that nature exhausts reality, nor that humans cannot comprehend X if X is non-natural, but rather that all human life and thought, including morality, is nothing other or more than what is comprehended by empirical science—physics (including thermodynamics), chemistry, biology, and psychology—all of which describe purely naturalistic phenomena.

---

[3] Philip Kitcher (2006) writes regarding Foot's view as well as Thomas Hurka's (1993) perfectionism, "Both these accounts, while often original and insightful, founder, I believe, because of the failure to take the details of current biological understanding sufficiently seriously" (164–5). See also FitzPatrick (2000) for a sustained critique of Foot et al., based on a selfish gene view of evolution.

2. From Function to Fitness

There are many theories of biological function. There are backward-looking, etiological theories and forward-looking, propensity theories (keeping the latter distinct from the propensity theory of fitness to which we soon turn).[4] There are learning theories focusing on the development of functions beginning with trial and error, and so-called Cummins functions which are instrumentalist and arguably antirealist.[5] And more recently, there are organizational theories of function.[6] Aside from the antirealist Cummins functions, the present view is consistent with all of them, though it would work differently for organizational theories than for the others (cf. footnote 10 below). What binds them together is the logical structure of function statements, as laid out by William Wimsatt (1972):

$$F\,[B(i), S, E, P, T] = C$$

This is to be read as follows: "A theorem of background theory T is that a function of behavior B of item i in system S, in environment E relative to purpose P is to do C" (32). For example, "According to biological theory, a function of the beating of the heart in a human in normal conditions and environments, relative to the purpose of exchanging O_2 for CO_2, is to circulate the blood." What makes this fit to ground normativity is the way *purposes* or *goals* are analytically built-in. Since attaining a goal is the purpose of a function, and goals can be successfully attained or there can be failure in that regard, the difference between function and malfunction can ground a distinction between how things "ought to be" and how they "ought not to be": items with functions ought to function and not malfunction.[7] (Whether or not this is sufficient to explain moral normativity will come out in the discussion below.)

---

[4] For etiological theories of function, see Wright 1973 and 1976; Boorse 1976; Millikan 1984; Neander 1991. For propensity theories, see Godfrey-Smith 1984; Bigelow and Pargetter 1987.

[5] For learning theories, see Mace 1949; Scheffler 1958; Campbell 1960; Wimsatt 1972; Enç and Adams 1992. For Cummins functions, see Cummins 1975.

[6] Schlosser 1998; McLaughlin 2001; Christensen and Bickhard 2002; Weber 2005; Mossio et al. 2009; Moreno and Mossio 2015.

[7] Kantians might worry about this based on Kant's claim that moral prescriptions are categorical and so do not rely on purposes or goals, while the present view does just that. But the distinction between categorical and hypothetical imperatives is valid only if the purposes involved are contingently possessed by agents, and the distinction becomes purely formal or notational for purposes which all agents have necessarily. One can see the distinction arising for Kant because he assumed happiness or prudence, which he recognized as a goal that all people seek, is different than morality which is contingent upon having a noumenal good will. If morality is understood in terms of eudaimonia, the hypothetical/categorical distinction loses its theoretical force. We can only imagine what Kant's philosophy would have looked like had he known about evolution. For further discussion of these claims see Bloomfield (2013).

Both epistemology and semantics have normative components and, in both fields, theories based on biological function have been developed. In the former, naturalistic descendants of Alvin Plantinga's (1993) functional theory of warrant have been developed by Tyler Burge (2009, 2010) and Peter J. Graham (2012), and bear strong resemblance to the virtue epistemology of Ernest Sosa (1980, 2007), John Greco (2010), and Bloomfield (2000, 2001). Regarding semantics, Ruth Millikan's (1984, 1990) influential teleosemantic theory is based on her etiological account of "proper function".[8] The plausibility of these epistemic and semantic views blunts one of the most prominent objections to naturalistic moral realism, which has been helpfully dubbed by David Enoch (2011), the "just too different" objection. The worry is that natural facts tell us how things are while moral facts tell us how they ought to be and these two kinds of facts are *just too different* from each other to see how normativity could be derived from nature. But what exactly is the bar to seeing normative moral facts as a subset of natural facts? If epistemic normativity (how we ought to form beliefs) and semantic normativity (how we ought to use words) can be grounded in biological function, then there can be no a priori reason why moral normativity (how we ought to act) cannot be grounded in the same way. The "just too different" objection is either the result of an unfamiliarity with the resources of biological science or a failure of imagination.

What about Hume's famous dictum (1739) that we can never derive an "ought" from an "is"? Here too, the concept of *function* can bridge the gap. While A. N. Prior's (1949, 1960) work on inferring an "ought" from an "is" has come under scrutiny from various philosophers (Pigden 2010), his most plausible counterexample to Hume is obscurely placed and has not received any attention at all. Alastair MacIntyre (1981, 57) quotes Prior claiming that from the premise "he is a sea captain" we can infer that "he ought to do whatever a sea captain ought to do".[9] Notice here that "sea captain" is operating strictly as a functional term and so has goals and purposes analytically built-in: a sea captain getting lost at sea is analogous to a heart in myocardial infarction. A better example than sea captains, because it comes directly from evolutionary theory, was used above: across all times and cultures, parents who abuse or neglect their children are not doing what they ought to do. Two paragraphs above, it was claimed that "items with functions ought to function" and this itself yields an "ought" from an "is": from the claim

---

[8] Drew Johnson (2021) has developed a compelling semantic framework for moral terms based on Millikan's teleosemantics that is overall consistent with the present picture. For more on moral language in this regard, see Bloomfield (1998, 2001, 2003) and Dowell (2016).

[9] In personal communication, MacIntyre confirmed that this example of Prior's was one that came up in conversation between the two of them. In Prior (1960), he explores a similar inference to the one above involving sea captains, but uses "Church officers" as an example. Bringing in religious conventions makes the chosen example problematic. Sea captains are better, as the functions of a sea captain are not as contingent upon convention as the functions of Church officers. As noted, the moral normativity of parenting is the best example as parenting is a purely natural phenomenon.

Another counterexample to Hume not discussed at all in the literature is an idea that seems platitudinous: namely, "treat like cases alike," which is elliptical for "when cases *are* alike, they *ought* to be treated alike".

that an item has a function, it follows that there is something it ought to do; and when an item is malfunctioning, something has gone wrong. We could use Prior's inference as a model for strict biological functions: from the premise "this is a heart" we can infer that "it ought to do whatever a heart ought to do".

The biological functions of traits are understood within evolutionary theory as "contributions to an organism's fitness" (Walsh and Ariew 1996). And population geneticists studying the fitness of traits per se require some understanding of the fitness of individual organisms, for the fitness of a trait is defined in terms of the average fitness of the organisms having that trait (Sober 2013). Fitness is most commonly understood as a propensity, given the dispositional quality of the concept of *fitness* (Mills and Beatty 1979). The crucial element of the propensity theory of fitness is that fitness should not be understood in terms of actual, categorical success at survival and reproduction, but rather in terms of propensities to survive and reproduce. As Elliott Sober explains the standard view (of which he is somewhat skeptical, see Sober 2020):

> there is the important insight that individuals of identical fitness can differ in how successful they are at surviving and reproducing. The individuals have the same abilities, but good luck for some and bad luck for others can lead to unequal outcomes. (2013, 336)

The key example was first discussed by Michael Scriven in 1959 and involves twins who are assumed to have equal fitness up to the point where one is struck by lightning and the other is not.

Now, while talk of the fitness of particular traits is not problematic, when it comes to discussing the fitness of individuals, taken as whole organisms, epistemic problems with experimental measurement arise. (Recall that "eudaimonia" will be defined below in terms derived from "individual fitness".) Whether or not having a larger dorsal fin enhances the survival and reproductive rates of a species of fish can be determined by measuring sizes of those fins of actual members of the species and analyzing the data to see if those with a bigger fin do better. The problem with measuring the fitness of an individual organism is that it cannot be derived from measuring its survival and reproductive rates from a single set of circumstances. As Sober (2013) suggests, we would need "carbon copies" of the organism to be placed in a variety of situations to analyze how it (they) would fare overall. But as Sober (2013) has eloquently put it, organisms "taste of life but once", and as Karl Popper (1959) has pointed out, unrepeatable events "cannot be decided by science". Because our lives are unrepeatable events, individual fitnesses cannot be measured by empirical science. Nevertheless, individual fitnesses need to be quantified over by evolutionary theory, as the value of a bound variable, for the reason given above: the fitness of a trait, which is measurable, is understood statistically as the average fitness of the organisms having that trait.[10]

---

[10] There is a theory of population genetics, called "statisticalism", which attempts to calculate the particular fitness of traits without appealing to individual fitnesses (Matthen and Ariew 2002; Walsh,

As for establishing realist credentials, crucially, this worry over individual fitness is epistemic not metaphysical: as a quantity, an individual's fitness cannot be empirically measured, even if this measurement is theoretically possible (as Sober suggests). An individual's fitness is like the number of stars, real but unknowable; it is unlike phlogiston, which is unknowable because it does not exist. The present version of moral realism is trying to demonstrate how moral properties are grounded by the biological properties of *having a function* and *individual fitness*. So, despite the epistemic difficulty, given how population geneticists rely on a metaphysically realist view of individual fitness, the present ontology of moral properties is not bothered by the fact that these fitnesses can neither be directly observed nor measured by scientists (contra Harman 1977). It is sufficient that we have good reason to think that natural facts exist determining which individuals are fit and which are not: however problematic an individual's fitness may be to measure, the denial that some members of a species are, in fact, more fit than others would make natural selection and thereby evolution impossible.

Before turning to eudaimonia, there is one measurement of individual fitness which evolutionary biologists have stipulated and which bears on the position of Foot and her cohort. Every theory of fitness, including the propensity theory, yields the result that sterile organisms have an individual fitness of zero, as it is impossible for them to reproduce. We will return to sterility below in its relation to eudaimonia, but the present point involves the fitnesses of individuals who are not sterile but nevertheless fail to reproduce for other reasons.

There have been (and perhaps still are) parts of Mexican culture in which the youngest daughter of a family was expected to never marry but rather to remain in her parent's house and take care of them as they age while her older sisters marry and raise their own children. On average, there is no reason to think these youngest daughters were any less capable of successfully reproducing than their child-bearing sisters. On the propensity theory of fitness, these youngest daughters were, on average, just as fit as their sisters despite failing to reproduce, assuming that siblings have, on average, the same or similar propensities. As an analogy, imagine a single, healthy acorn planted in an ideal

---

Ariew, and Matthen 2017). If these views can obviate the need to posit individual fitness, then a biologically grounded theory of moral realism will have to advert a different strategy to remain viable. One option would be to adopt the "organizational theory" of functions mentioned above, which holds that individual "self-maintenance" can be understood in a manner which is orthogonal to standard evolutionary theory. Such a view might be very close to Foot's and it has been impressively developed by Parisa Moosavi (2018, 2019, 2022). If this fails as well, there are at least two other options for the realist eudaimonist. One is to understand eudaimonia by way of a developed analogy between morality and language, using a roughly Chomsky-ian view of grammar as a constraint on human language as a model for how morality constrains eudaimonia. John Mikhail (2011) has developed one form of this argument. A second option would be to define "eudaimonia" in terms of "positive psychological health". The viability of this kind of view would depend on the future outcomes of the nascent subfield of "positive psychology," which might yield an empirically informed picture of human flourishing based on virtue (e.g., Seligman and Csikszentmihalyi 2000; Peterson and Seligman 2004). For extended general discussions of how to realistically model *moral goodness* on *physical healthiness*, see Bloomfield (1997, 2001).

environment for oaks. Because of its ideal niche, this acorn will grow into an oak whose traits have developed to a high degree relative to other oaks, it is strong and thriving. For whatever reason, however, imagine the acorn for this oak had been transported and planted too far from any other oak tree to successfully reproduce. The propensity theory of fitness would say the oak tree's individual fitness is not zero, despite its actual failure to reproduce. The same reasoning works for people who are kept from having children by social forces or those who simply *choose* to not have children: these non-reproducing people can still have an individual fitness greater than zero, they can still flourish.

One reason Foot (2001) defends human exceptionalism is because she thinks only it can accommodate the idea that humans can flourish despite choosing to be childless:

> Lack of capacity to reproduce is a defect in a human being. But choice of childlessness and even celibacy is not thereby shown to be defective choice, because human good is not the same as plant or animal good. The bearing and rearing of children is not an ultimate good in human life, because other elements of good such as the demands of work to be done may give a man or woman reason to renounce family life. And the great (if often troubling) good of having children has to do with the love and ambition of parents for children, the special role of grandparents, and many other things that simply do not belong to animal life. (42)

On the propensity theory of fitness, which was first published in 1979, it is not the case that being childless by choice entails having a fitness of zero, so Foot's (2001) drastic move to human exceptionalism was not warranted, at least for this reason.

(A note on "the special role of grandparents" that Foot mentions, which supposedly does not "belong to animal life": Darwin explains the sterile nature of female worker bees explicitly in terms of the relation between a Queen bee and her grand-offspring (Sober 2011). For the same sort of reason, in the parts of Mexican culture referred to above, the children of the older daughters might well get a selective advantage from their mothers not having to care for their grandparents.)

3. From Fitness to Eudaimonia

The present theory of *eudaimonia* does not equate it to *individual fitness*. For one thing, since fitness is a propensity, it is a dispositional property, whereas eudaimonia must be categorical. Rather, the goal is to construct the meaning of "eudaimonia" from a subset of all the functions of the organism which, when aggregated, yield the individual's fitness. So, which functions are those that are essential to an organism's flourishing or eudaimonia? A hypothesis can be drawn from Burge's (2009, 2010) discussions of perception, agency, and action theory. From the field of zoology, Burge imports into his account the concept of *whole animal function* or *organismic function*. The concept distinguishes those biological functions carried out by particular organs or sub-systems within an organism from those functions of organisms when these are considered only as whole individuals. Burge argues that organismic functions are the grounds of agency and action in general. Examples are sleeping, eating, navigating, predating, mating, parenting, etc.

So, each species will have evolved its own repertoire of traits to solve those particular evolutionary challenges (i.e., finding shelter, obtaining food, returning home, etc.) which must be managed by the entire organism. Call these challenges "life problems". Given these ideas, "eudaimonia" can be defined as follows:

> *Eudaimonia*: for any species X, a member of that species, x, is a eudaimon [is flourishing] if and only if x has developed to a high or excellent degree the propensities for carrying out the organismic functions characteristic of X, which solve, in normal environments, the life problems characteristic of X.

The "species relative" aspect of eudaimonia, adverted to above, is made plain in the definition.

"Normal environments" are those within which a species evolved, employing its characteristic traits or those traits distinguishing it as a species. In normal environments, birds build their nests and bees their hives. Species reproduce and generations come and go as the environment fluctuates within a normal range. Take members of a species out of their natural environment, take fish out of water, put dinosaurs in an ice age, and there may be no way to survive much less flourish. Mutatis mutandis, humans are no different. We live in societies which also give out and die, but our species continues (at least so far). Normal conditions are those in which human societies have arisen and declined. But there are also, at times, conditions in which the environment causes a partial extinction of the species, say severe famine, and these conditions are obviously not normal for the species, as survival in them is impossible, much less eudaimonia.

The hard normative question is whether there are environments in which survival is possible but eudaimonia is impossible even for the most excellently functioning members of the species.[11] This is an open empirical question, but there is something to be said for a creature doing as well as possible even in the worst of circumstances. Exhibiting grace under fire, whatever that amounts to for any species capable of it, might count as the height of flourishing for those creatures. ("It is a far, far better thing that I do . . .".) However hopeless our circumstances may be, no one can ask for more than the ability to live up to their best potential in the most difficult times. If more is necessary for eudaimonia, including Aristotelian "external goods", having them is pure moral luck and so out of our control, and as such outside the purview of moral theory. There is no reason to theorize morally about what is not under our control, and so there is also no reason to think that flourishing guarantees a trouble-free or even long life. All lives face

---

[11] This is a contemporary and generalized form of the ancient debate over whether the virtues are sufficient for eudaimonia. For more on this, see Annas 1993; Bloomfield 2014a.

rough seas at some point. It is most plausible to think that flourishing is doing the best we can wherever we may be.

In applying the definition of "eudaimonia" above to Homo sapiens, the relevant life problems, as situated in normal environments, have been baptized colloquially as "the human condition," and human flourishing is therefore the result of managing the human condition in an excellent fashion. Unsurprisingly, the obvious next question is: which traits allow Homo sapiens to flourish, given the human condition? Or, given the characteristic ways in which human beings navigate through the world, acquire and consume food, perform our rites of passage and mating rituals, parent our offspring, etc., which traits determine whether or not we meet these challenges excellently or poorly?

Up to this point, the account has been normatively neutral. We could adopt Kantianism, consequentialism, virtue theory, or some other option depending on which does best at making human life flourish. It is still an open question as to which normative ethical theory gives the best answers to the life problems we face. Refreshingly, one virtue of naturalistic moral realism is that, ultimately, it makes this question be an empirical one, however hard the relevant data might be to obtain: having a complete and true moral theory is as likely as having a complete and true medical theory (Becker 1998, 2012; Bloomfield 2001).

These normative questions about which lives do or do not flourish will have to be answered by the moral philosophers, psychologists, and ethologists who work on these issues. But one plausible answer comes straight from ancient Greek eudaimonism: the moral virtues. These are the "excellences" which make human life go well. While Socrates (as portrayed in *Gorgias*) and the Stoics argued that virtue is sufficient for eudaimonia, this claim is highly contentious. Still, it seems as if Socrates, Plato, Aristotle, the Stoics, even Epicurus, and much of commonsense (*endoxia*) agree that virtue is at least important to (if not necessary for or partly constitutive of) a flourishing life or eudaimonia. This may be wrong, but an attempt to ground eudaimonia at least partly in virtue is prima facie justified. Obviously, what follows is a mere sketch, but will suffice to demonstrate how the formal structure of eudaimonia, given in the definition above, could be normatively filled out for human beings.

We begin with the widely accepted claim, also rooted in Greek philosophy, that virtues are character traits. Character traits themselves are understood by psychologists nowadays as a subset of personality traits, where such a trait is defined as "a disposition to behave expressing itself in consistent patterns of functioning across a range of situations" (Pervin 1994, 108). According to Christian Miller (2014), what distinguishes the subset of character traits is that they are the traits over which we can exercise some amount of voluntary control and which open a person to normative assessment.

Crucial for understanding virtues is to attend to the "range of situations" in which character traits may express themselves. This thought too can be traced back to ancient eudaimonism; an extended quote from Martha Nussbaum (1988) is most indicative:

> What [Aristotle] does, in each case [of discussing a particular virtue], is to isolate a sphere of human experience that figures in more or less any human life, and in

> which more or less any human being will have to make some choices rather than others, and act in some way rather than some other. The introductory chapter enumerating the virtues and vices begins from an enumeration of these spheres (EN II.7); and each chapter on a virtue in the more detailed account that follows begins with "Concerning X . . .", or words to this effect, where "X" names a sphere of life with which all human beings regularly and more or less necessarily have dealings. Aristotle then asks, what is it to choose and respond well within that sphere? What is it, on the other hand, to choose defectively? The "thin account" of each virtue is that it is whatever it is to be stably disposed to act appropriately in that sphere. There may be, and usually are, various competing specifications of what acting well, in each case, in fact comes to. Aristotle goes on to defend in each case some concrete specification, producing, at the end, a full or "thick" definition of the virtue. (35)

This idea is familiar from contemporary virtue ethics: e.g., Christine Swanton (2003, 20–1) also appeals to the idea of "the field of a virtue" in her discussion of "The Anatomy of Virtue" while constructing her "pluralist view" of virtue.

The word "cardinal" derives from the Latin "*cardo*" that translates as "hinge" or "axis", conveying the idea of "that upon which something turns or depends". Terrence Irwin (2005) cites early Greek literary figures such as Aeschylus, Pindar, Xenophon, and Demosthenes grouping the cardinals more or less together and, citing Plato's *Laches* 197e10–198a6 and 199d4–e5; he writes that *courage, temperance, justice,* and *wisdom* were taken by Socrates as the "primary virtues to be collectively sufficient for being a good person . . . for he expects his interlocutors to agree that a person who has all the primary [cardinal] virtues thereby has the whole of virtue" (2005, p. 91). The basic structure of Stoic ethics is based on these virtues (Long and Sedley, 1987, §61) and Aquinas quotes Gregory saying, "The entire structure of good works is built on [these] four virtues" (1947, I. II. Q. 61, article 2). The basic idea is that the cardinal virtues are the axes upon which eudaimonia swings, where each virtue manages a "range of situation" or a "sphere of human experience" endemic to the human condition.

A brief gloss of these four virtues should demonstrate the scope of the theory and their relations with eudaimonia, as defined above. We may begin with courage, as it often but not always concerns survival. The world is dangerous, and we are mortal. In particular, Homo sapiens inherited the "fight, flight, or freeze" mechanism as a phylogenetically old adaptation for managing dangerous circumstances. *Courage* is the character trait by which we can gain control, to one degree or another, over this mechanism, such that we do not simply respond instinctually to danger and fear but rather respond in a controlled and excellent fashion, regardless of the circumstance. If we adopt Aristotle's hypothesis that each virtue is flanked by opposing vices (2000, 1106a26–b28), courage can be seen as flanked by the traits of cowardice and recklessness.

Also inherited from older species, human beings have a variety of appetites, desires (including aversions), and passions (including emotions), and *temperance* is the character trait which allows us to excellently self-regulate these non-cognitive or affective capacities. Temperate people have trained themselves to not be tempted by what ought not to be tempting. They do not struggle with continence, much less weakness of will:

they only succumb at will. Their emotional responses are appropriate or fitting to the circumstance; they are "well-tempered". Aside from learning to regulate appetites and desires, but by similar means, we may learn to regulate passions and emotions. One aspect of temperance comprises the psychological subfield of "emotional self-regulation" (Gross 2014; Vohs and Baumeister 2016). Temperate people celebrate joyous occasions, indulge salubrious passions in the right way and at the right times, and they mourn lost loved ones in a manner that allows them to heal and recover from the loss. Resilience and flexibility are the result of being well-tempered in both metallurgy and character development; these are different than grit (Duckworth 2007; Morton and Paul 2019), which is more closely related to diachronic perseverance (Battaly 2017), though these are still aspects of temperance. Being well-tempered in these ways becomes especially important to understanding whether or to what degree virtue is sufficient for eudaimonia. If, e.g., part of being well-tempered is withstanding and rebounding from hardship, then this will guard a temperate person's eudaimonia from all but the most tragic of circumstances. The vices opposing temperance are, on the one hand, gluttony, including emotional indulgences such as being envious, unduly worrisome, or being quick to anger or "losing one's temper". On the other hand, some people allow their desire for control to be too controlling and traits like teetotaling abstemiousness or being overly disciplined, rigid or dour, or just being a "stick-in-the-mud" are possible results.

The virtue of *justice*, understood as a personal character trait and not a trait of social institutions, was understood broadly by the Greeks to include all social behavior (Vlastos 1968; Annas 1999), and so the "range" of justice is found not merely in the courtroom or in relations between fellow citizens or strangers but includes familial and friendly relations as well (Hampton 1993, Bloomfield 2021). While not fully appreciated, central to justice is the concept of *respect*, where the proper respect of others is inextricably bound to proper self-respect (Bloomfield 2011, 2014a, 2017). Thus, we may follow Aristotle (2000, 1133b30), who says that "justice is a mean between committing injustice and suffering it, since the one is having more than one's share, while the other is having less". If we accept this, then we may see justice as the virtue flanked by the vices of arrogance (*pleonexia* or those who arrogate more respect than they are due) and servility (those who willingly accept less respect than their due).

The final cardinal virtue is *wisdom* or rationality, and it is a special case. This is because the solutions to all the life-problems of the human condition require practical rationality. If there is an "ur-virtue" or one informing, governing, or even binding the others together, it is wisdom. Indeed, Plutarch interprets Zeno of Citium, the founder of Stoicism, as thinking that there is only one virtue, namely wisdom, and it manifests as the others in different spheres of experience (Long and Sedley 1987, 377–78). To begin with, one function of wisdom is to veridically discern naturalistic value in the world, and given the moral realism presently on offer, there are facts about what is good and bad in the world and what is not. Wisdom ought to guide axiology. But on top of informing our values, wisdom or rationality ought to guide our deliberations and actions based on those values. So, rational choice theory is part of the *logos* of wisdom. There are also empirically informed theories of wisdom on offer, coming from psychology. One of the first contemporary theories of wisdom was Robert Sternberg's (1998) view, understanding it in terms of *balance*, while more recently the San Diego Wisdom Scale (SD-WISE) was developed with explicitly neurobiological underpinnings, and its developers claim that "results support the reliability and validity of SD-WISE scores" (Thomas et al. 2019). More philosophically informed than SD-WISE, the Berlin Wisdom Paradigm was developed by Paul Baltes and Ursala Staudinger (2000 and Baltes 2005). On this view, wisdom is a "metaheuristic" or an "expert system", the function of which is to help people navigate through the "fundamental pragmatics of life", which are understood as follows:

> knowledge and judgment about the essence of the human condition and the ways and means of planning, managing, and understanding a good life. Included in the fundamental pragmatics of life are, for example, knowledge about the conditions, variability, ontogenetic changes, and historicity of life development as well as knowledge of life's obligations and life goals; understanding of the socially and contextually intertwined nature of human life, including its finitude, cultural conditioning, and incompleteness; and knowledge about oneself and the limits of one's own knowledge and the translation of knowledge into overt behavior. (2000, 124)

Similar philosophical theories of wisdom have recently been developed which conceive of wisdom as a skill or expertise (Swartwood 2013; Stichter 2016, 2021; Tsai 2019). Note the themes running through Baltes's "fundamental pragmatics of life" are found in Nussbaum's "sphere[s] of life with which all human beings regularly and more or less necessarily have dealings" and how these are tied to the discussions above of "organismic function," "life problems," and the "human condition".

We expect wise people to be capable of navigating through the human condition in an excellent and fine way, as well as the vicissitudes of life allow. How do they do it? They must be finely attuned to the difference between appearance and reality and thus capable of seeing "below" the surface features of a situation, having genuine insight and perspicacity. Problems are rooted out. The desire to see through appearances and into the nature of reality is why philosophers study metaphysics and, in general, why *philosophy* is literally "love of wisdom". With wisdom in hand, the other virtues bring in specialized knowledge and experience which guides virtuous people to do the right thing, at the right time, in the right way, and for the right reasons. The overarching goal of virtuous action is "the noble" or "the fine", or *to kalon* (Crisp 2014). While the exact relation of the virtues to each other is complex and vexed, involving the "unity of virtues" thesis, one minimal and defensible claim is that possessing wisdom, including a generalized and veridic axiology, is necessary but not sufficient for the other virtues (Bloomfield 2014b).

Three final points may be helpful before turning to objections. First, the claim that virtues are grounded in evolutionary processes entails that the virtues are traits, not that they are adaptations. Human beings are neither moral nor immoral by nature. The idea can be understood on the model of language (cf. footnote 10): we inherit genetically the capacity for language which develops into a particular language in normal environments. Recursive grammar is an adaptation, speaking English is a trait. On this model, Aristotle got it right when he wrote, "The virtues arise in us neither by nature nor contrary to nature, but nature gives us the capacity to acquire them, and completion comes through habituation" (2000, 1103a24–5). The relevant "capacities" are the adaptations or mechanisms enabling human beings to have at least some long range, voluntary control over our characters.[12] E.g., courage was glossed above as the trait by which we may excellently manage our instincts to "fight, flight, or freeze". We can only excellently regulate our orectic and emotional instincts by temperance, our social lives by justice. Like the degree to which we become literate, the work to establish these forms of self-mastery, by developing these capacities is, ultimately, up to each of us alone.

The second and third points involve successful reproduction. Second, on this view, an organism can have a fitness of zero and still flourish. A sterile drone bee will flourish if it develops to an excellent degree its characteristic organismic functions, those solving the life problems of a drone bee. Sterile hybrids, like mules, can also flourish. Therefore, sterile members of Homo sapiens can still flourish. The flexibility of the view stretches beyond accommodating childlessness, as one can see how being a human eudaimon— being courageous, temperate, just, and wise—is compatible with a variety of lifestyles and vocations. Humans are multi-talented, highly adaptive creatures, and this flexibility allows our flourishing to take many forms. Whether or not it can accommodate being a gangster or being a slave will be discussed below.

The final point involves parenting. For evolutionary reasons, it is worth emphasizing the importance of the virtues for solving all the life-problems associated with being a good parent. There is more to successfully reproducing than conception and birth, as offspring must survive through adolescence to be capable of themselves reproducing.[13] Thus, parenting skills are essential to the evolutionary goals of survival and reproduction, and there is commonsense plausibility to the hypothesis that courageous, well-tempered, fair, and wise parents will be the best parents.[14] The following seems guaranteed by natural selection: were the traits constituting an individual's own eudaimonia to diverge too greatly from the traits that would make the individual be a good parent, this would amount to a recipe for the extinction of the species to which the individual belongs. So, the relation of eudaimonia to parenting is derived from the

---

[12] The term "long range, voluntary control" comes from William Alston (1988). See also Miller 2014.

[13] Ornithologists have coined the term "aggressive neglect" to refer to the way that some male birds are so busy defending their territories against interlopers that they neglect their paternal duties to feed their young, who end up malnourished and sometimes dying as a result (Dillon Ripley 1959, 1961; Hutchinson and MacArthur 1959).

[14] In personal communication (June 16, 2018), the anthropologist Sarah Hrdy writes, "Relevant to your thesis that the 'best human parents will be brave, well-tempered, fair, and wise, and the children of these parents will be most likely to survive and flourish themselves' is the recent interest by anthropologists in child-rearing among African and other people still living as hunter-gatherers. . . . In general, these findings are consistent with your thesis though I would add 'tolerant' [to the list of virtues]". A traditional virtue theoretic perspective would understand tolerance as an aspect of temperance. Hrdy cited the following in support: Hewlett and Lamb 2005; Konner 2010; Meehan and Crittenden 2016.

propensity view of fitness: what is necessary for an individual's flourishing is not actually being a parent, but rather having the propensities for being an excellent or virtuous parent.

4. Objections

There is a veritable plethora of objections to the present view. Here is a partial, chronological list, and only some of these have been touched upon above: Hume's (1739) gap between "is" and "ought", Moore's (1903) open question argument, Harman's (1977) worries about observation and explanation, Watson's (1990) gangster problem, Horgan and Timmons's (1991, 1993) Moral Twin Earth, Hursthouse's (1999) and Foot's (2001) human exceptionalism, Copp and Sobel's (2004) worry about relativism, Street's (2006) Darwinian dilemma, Millgram's (2009) Pollyanna objection, and Enoch's (2011) "just too different" argument. Obviously, addressing all these is too large a task for the closing section of an essay.[15] But there is a thread running through the objections of Millgram, Copp and Sobel, and Watson, as each worries in different ways about the normative implications of the view, and grouping them in this way helps show the resiliency of eudaimonistic moral realism.

Elijah Millgram (2009), along with Chrisoula Andreou (2006), object to the Pollyannish attitude toward the nature of Homo sapiens which they claim is on the table. In particular, in addressing Thompson's discussion of "Aristotelian categoricals" in *Life and Action* (2008) (with Foot's view (2001) in the background), Millgram writes that "it is pollyannish to suppose that justice is part of the human species form" (561). Citing empirical research in anthropology and evolutionary psychology, Millgram argues that natural selection has left us with behavioral tendencies to engage, in certain circumstances, in infanticide, rape, and domination all inconsistent with justice. We may add cross-cultural tendencies toward racism (Kurzban, Tooby, and Cosmides 2001) and sexism. And the problem seems compounded if we recall Foot's (1958) early claim, derived from Plato, that "if justice is not a good to the just man, moralists who recommend it as a virtue are perpetrating a fraud" (100). (We return to this claim below.) When we look closely at the facts about human life, it appears far too "red in tooth and claw" to be the source of morality.[16]

While there might be concerns about the evolutionary psychology behind the cited examples, let us set them aside for another time. To focus on infanticide first, Sarah

---

[15] For my response to Hume, see Bloomfield (1998, 2001) and to Moore, see Bloomfield (2006). For responses to Harman see Bloomfield (2001), to Horgan and Timmons, see Bloomfield (2001, 2003). This chapter as a whole constitutes a response to Street's dilemma as applied to naturalistic moral realism. Similar discussions of Millgram, Copp and Sobel, and Watson can be found in Bloomfield (2018).

[16] Midgely (1978) argues persuasively that, in fact, animal life is far more "humane" than we typically presume.

Hrdy (2000) acknowledges that under circumstances in which mothers are unable to care for their newborns, mothers often abandon them (passively letting them die) and in direst circumstances will commit infanticide. Now, as Millgram rightly argues, we cannot just squint and ignore such behavior when considering what kind of creatures Homo sapiens are. Natural selection has left mothers with these tendencies because it is selectively more advantageous for mothers to have them than not. If we consider the mothers who acted in these ways over the millennia, we clearly have a tragic picture on our hands and justice does not seem to be part of it. Perhaps one could try to argue that, in those circumstances, the mothers really had no choice: they faced a tragic dilemma and had to choose the lesser of evils, and thus preserve some notion of "justice", but this alone would be only a partial answer.

The proper response begins by looking beyond the prehistorical roots of such traits to how human beings, over the ages, have changed their behaviors despite the existence of such "unjust" tendencies. While it is true that we have been outfitted by natural selection to be violently unjust to our offspring in certain circumstances, we can look at the environments in which those circumstances arose and appreciate that now, given our different environment, most people do not follow their prehistoric tendencies. Prehistoric environments for human beings were radically different than our environment is today. For example, society is now structured so that child abandonment and infanticide is less prevalent than in the distant past (Hrdy 2000). We happily act on some instincts but have learned to resist others: jealousy is almost always frowned upon. Some actions we take go against all instinct, but generally only when the circumstances leave no better option. Some traits might be necessary to survive the worst of circumstances but might work against flourishing if they are engaged in situations where survival is not at issue. If so, then engaging these traits in safe circumstances should be seen as instances of malfunctioning, or that which ought not to occur.

It may be just a just-so story but assume that anger evolved as a response to danger, because the behaviors that demonstrate anger (fists, bared teeth, and loud noises) are effective in warding off danger. As far as this is concerned, humans are on par with other animals (Lorenz 1966). The difference for humans is that many of us use our fists and make loud noises when there is no danger present and, ceteris paribus, this makes anger wrong. Worst, perhaps, is when people have a hard day at work, continently holding their tempers, and then "take it out on" or get angry at their spouses or children back home. Folk morality excuses anger when it is in self-defense but not when someone becomes aggressively angry over a trivial matter. Exactly which circumstances justify anger, if any, is a matter of normative theory, and this knowledge is part of the difference between being temperate and intemperate. So is the basic folk knowledge holding that rape is always wrong under all circumstances. No other conclusion is acceptable.

There is no reason to deny selective pressures that made us susceptible to infanticide, rape, and all sorts of unjust practices. These tendencies, under certain circumstances, may have allowed for survival and reproduction, but this does not imply that they were ever unproblematic. With regard to infanticide, it seems likely that at least some (or most) women from ancient times who were compelled by circumstances to perform it felt dreadful remorse afterward. Men who engage in rape and leave progeny behind during war are, to say the very least, absent fathers whose children suffer for that reason (see footnote 13 above on "aggressive neglect"). Well-adjusted progeny are more likely to survive, turning their parents into grandparents, and evolution alone can give that result.

Slavery and torture used to be ubiquitous practices and thankfully are no longer, though they tragically and criminally still exist. The best explanation for the (sadly recent) repudiation of slavery and torture across much of humanity is that, aside from the obvious harms these practices inflict on their victims, we have also learned over the millennia that it is not good for humans to exercise these kinds of power over others. Tyranny and despotism are self-corrupting and to that degree self-defeating. Undeniably, we are more or less social creatures, so we should not be surprised to find hidden costs to angry, sexist, and racist forms of antisocial behavior. Of course, slavery is harmful to slaves but, as Frederick Douglass (1845/2016) notes, it is also harmful to slave owners. The argument for this kind of social learning is to look empirically, for example, at the modern downfall of slavery's acceptability, or at the behavior of mothers today who face circumstances which, in ancient times, would have led them to infanticide. In the presence of non-violent options, non-pathological mothers do not choose infanticide. The choices of mothers today, in our contemporary environment, are just as relevant to the argument about how violent human begins are as the tendencies to which we might have succumbed in the distant past due to contingent social or environmental pressure: what is needed for flourishing is not similarly contingent. What makes creatures like us flourish does not change with the environment we find ourselves in. Rather, as noted above, some environments make flourishing easier than others.

Ultimately, the response to Millgram's Pollyanna problem is to appeal to the claim above about why the virtues should not count as adaptations: nature has left us equipped to flourish but does not require flourishing for mere survival and reproduction. The definition of "eudaimonia" requires propensities to be developed to a "high or excellent" degree, where survival and reproduction are more like a minimum. We are capable of doing better than that. The instinct to "fight, flight, or freeze" is phylogenetically quite old and still has a proper function, but it is unreliable enough that we evolved the ability to manage it which is part of courage. Human traits which evolved when life was "nasty, brutish, and short" were naturally selected for, back then, to aid in survival and reproduction and to some degree they may remain despite now being more harmful than beneficial. What the ethologist Irenäus Eibl-Eibesfeldt (1972) says about the trait of aggression generalizes; in arguing that aggression aided in the survival of the species at early stages of our evolutionary history, she writes:

> Nevertheless, in order to make clear that I intend no justification of aggression, let me emphasize once again that not everything that was once adaptive will retain this species-preserving function necessarily forever. Thanks to environmental changes, it is not all that uncommon for an adaptation to reverse itself, for it to be retained as a historical vestige, while it has become in effect a selective hindrance. (p. 75)

Only some of the ancient tendencies we have inherited lead to human flourishing in our contemporary environment. It is the task of an empirically informed normative moral theory to sort which of our traits lead toward and which lead away from our flourishing.[17]

And this sorting problem leads to Copp and Sobel's (2004) review essay on virtue ethics, where a relativistic worry is discussed concerning the way in which virtue is supposed to engender a flourishing life. The worry is that if we do not make virtues, like justice, relative to culture then, in certain cultural circumstances, being virtuous might impose significant costs on the individual. For simplicity's sake, let's assume that Aristotle's view of eudaimonism is correct and that flourishing is the result of having both the virtues and some amount of "external goods".[18] Copp and Sobel write:

> [I]n rougher times, being fully virtuous might be more costly than it seems here today. Imagine a time and place in which a person who goes along with a vicious aspect of society, say slavery, has full opportunities for a long life of privilege, enjoyment, love, and achievement, whereas speaking up against the viciousness in society promises hostility from the powers that be and worse. (p. 528)

To make a case plausible, it would have to be that the privileged person is not some thoroughly vicious or sadistic slave-owner who enjoys beating and raping slaves, but rather an otherwise virtuous person who reluctantly "goes along" with these vicious yet parochially endemic practices.

Let us take Thomas Jefferson and slavery as our example. Like Douglass, who saw these issues from the other side, infamously, Jefferson had hypocritical attitudes toward race, slavery, and freedom and clearly saw the evil effects of slavery on both slaves and masters (Gordon-Reed and Onuf 2016, 57–65). He called slavery a "school for despotism" and sought to ameliorate the negative effects of slavery on his slaves as much as possible. He never beat slaves (though he did once have someone else beat a slave), and he established a factory on his plantation to make nails so that it could be run by his 10- to 16-year-old males slaves for the purpose of helping them learn a skill. Whatever vices Jefferson had, and he surely had many, he thought it was possible to be a "good slave master". Again, for the sake of simplicity, let us assume that Jefferson was as just and as good he knew how to be, given the unjust cultural environment in which he was raised.

By way of response, we may begin by acknowledging the force of Copp and Sobel's concern. Still, notwithstanding this force, it is not hard to imagine how Jefferson's life would have gone better had he been born into a just society in which slavery did not exist. It is far from unreasonable to think that humans on average live better lives in less

---

[17] For a different response to the Pollyanna problem, see Kim 2018.

[18] The problem discussed here would not arise for Stoics who think virtue is sufficient for eudaimonism. Of course, Stoics would use such examples to argue against the Aristotelian claim about "external goods" being necessary for eudaimonia, and Annas (1993) calls Aristotle's view "unstable" for this sort of reason.

violent and oppressive societies than in more violent and oppressive societies. Short of voluntary ostracism or emigration, there is often little way to escape unjust yet prevalent social practices; if leaving is not an option, then those who are immorally empowered do not choose the society in which they live. So, the real challenge has to be those cases where people do have a choice about where and how to live.

Given this, we should bite Copp and Sobel's bullet. Biting the bullet here means insisting that Jefferson's life would have been better had he the integrity to be true to his principles regarding human freedom and liberty. Had he that integrity, he could have freed his slaves, sold Monticello, and made his living some other way which did not involve owning slaves, even if he would not have ended up as prosperous and materially successful as he actually did. Compare the actual Jefferson to our hypothetical alternative who sells Monticello. Of course, the latter could have taken his prodigious intellect and talents (his individual fitness) with him wherever he went, so there is little reason to think Jefferson would have ended up starving or destitute. The point is that even if Jefferson had he grown old in, say, Boston, in circumstances not as luxurious as they actually were in Virginia, he also would not have been burdened by being a living embodiment of "a house divided against itself": writing his most famous and important words into the Declaration of Independence, "All Men are Created Equal", *while owning slaves* is staggering hypocrisy of mind-numbing proportion. The normative claim is that Jefferson's hypocrisies harmed his flourishing, and he would have been better off without them despite the lessening of "external goods" which may have accompanied these changes. If, on the other hand, Jefferson decided to abandon his political principles to avoid the hypocrisy, his life would have gone worse for the loss of the justice he actually possessed.

The reason behind this is that, if we accept the hypothesis of moral realism, then there are facts about which lives are good and which are bad, which acts are right and which are wrong; there are facts in general about what has value and what does not, given what is required for human eudaimonia. The normative claim is that speaking the moral truth while living in accord with immoral values is bad for a person: assuming a person knows the difference between right and wrong and good and bad, that person's flourishing requires them to value and honor what is good and scorn and disown what is bad. Failing this is a form of moral schizophrenia (Stocker 1976) which the actual Jefferson clearly manifested.

But, for the sake of argument assume this claim is false. Its denial is still equally in accordance with moral realism: all realism per se demands, is the truth of the claim that there are facts about which lives go better. If this were not the case, Sobel and Copp's argument would not have the force it does. For the moment, while staying normatively neutral about what is in fact good and bad, moral realism entails that, to whatever degree possible, it is good for human beings to value, honor, and respect what is truly valuable and good in the world, and that it is bad for them to value, honor, and respect what is in fact bad while mistaking it for what is good. (The triviality of this idea, given moral realism, is something no other metaethic can claim.)

And this leads directly into Gary Watson's important gangster example. In his (1990) paper, "On the Primacy of Character," Watson writes:

> Even if we grant that we can derive determinate appraisals of conduct from an objective description of what is characteristic of the species, why should we care about those appraisals? Why should we care about living distinctively human lives rather than living like pigs or gangsters? Why is it worthwhile for us to have those particular virtues at the cost of alternative lives they preclude? (469)

The worry about humans living porcine lives cannot be serious, at least, if taken literally: a human could not survive living in a literal pigpen among the pigs. But a gangster's life is different, and while we may presume the average gangster lives a shorter life than normal (or an incarcerated life), "gangster life" is one which has certainly allowed many to survive and reproduce. But can gangsters flourish too? While Foot gives her own response to Watson's example in *Natural Goodness* (2001, 53ff), we can finally return to an earlier thought of hers which also bears on interpreting Watson's challenge.

As referenced above, in "Moral Beliefs" (1958), Foot presents a version of a direct challenge to morality, the original of which is quite old, going back to at least Plato's time, if not Homer's. Again, Foot's Platonic claim is that "if justice is not a good to the just man, moralists who recommend it as a virtue a perpetrating a fraud" (100). Let's understand "justice" in a roughly conventional way and not, e.g., as "might makes right". So, the gangster is unjust. Given the way justice seems to require sacrifices to self-interest, why should we think that being just partly constitutes eudaimonia, rather than injustice which seems to require no such sacrifices? We should expect morality in general and justice in particular to be justifiable when challenged by immorality and injustice. There ought to be a principled answer to the question, "Why be moral?"

While various contemporary answers have been given at the level of normative theory (Brink 1990; Bloomfield, 2011, 2014a, 2017; Badhwar 2014), the moral realist's response to Watson, like the responses to Millgram and Copp and Sobel, begins by acknowledging the legitimacy of the challenge. Here too, the final response is to bite the bullet. The answer to the question "What kind of life is best for a human being?" is the point at which the metaphysical requirements of moral realism meet the normative task of answering that very question: what *is* required for human life to flourish? Is the life of a gangster compatible with eudaimonia? Many, from Thrasymachus and Callicles to Machiavelli (1995) and Nietzsche (1892/1954) seem to answer in the affirmative, at least for kings and Übermenschen. Plato answered in the negative: in *Republic*, he argued to hardly anyone's satisfaction that injustice and tyranny lead to "psychic disharmony". While it may be hard to imagine, biting the bullet here implies that if the gangster's life really is the best life humans can hope for, then the moral realist should conclude that Al Capone and Bugsy Siegel should replace Socrates and the Buddha as moral exemplars.

Given how our values are expressed in our actions and, therefore, given the central roles morality and immorality may play in our most important decisions, it seems incredible to think that eudaimonia is *equally* compatible with being just and unjust.

If realism is accepted, then both views cannot be correct. One can imagine a "tie" between deontologists and consequentialists insofar as both are equally good at producing eudaimonia. But one cannot imagine a similar tie between the normative theories of Socrates and Thrasymachus. Smart money would be on the saint and not the gangster, on justice and not injustice, but biting this bullet implies that we should let the chips fall where they may and if our best normative and psychological theory concludes that the gangster's life is really the best a human can hope for, then so be it.

Eudaimonist moral realism is the view that there are natural facts about moral values, about what is right and wrong, natural facts about which lives go well and which do not. But how much doubt can there really be over whether it is better, all things considered, for human beings, *regardless of their circumstances*, to have characters which are courageous, well-tempered, fair-minded, and wise or, alternatively, for their characters to be reckless, gluttonous, arrogant, and foolish? Even without assuming the answer is as obvious as it seems, eudaimonist realism is only committed to the claim that there is a factual, correct answer to this question.[19]

References

Alston, William. 1988. "The Deontological Conception of Epistemic Justification". *Philosophical Perspectives* 2: 257–299.
Andreou, Chrisoula. 2006. "Getting On in a Varied World". *Social Theory and Practice* 32(1): 61–73.
Annas, Julia. 1993. *The Morality of Happiness*. Oxford: Oxford University Press.
Annas, Julia. 1999. *Platonic Ethics, Old and New*. Ithaca: Cornell University Press.
Anscombe, G. E. M. 1957. *Intention*. Cambridge: Harvard University Press.
Aquinas, Thomas. (1947). *Summa Theologica*. Translated by Fathers of the English Dominican Province. New York: Benziger Bros.
Aristotle. 2000. *Nicomachean Ethics*. Translated by Roger Crisp. Cambridge: Cambridge University Press.
Badhwar, Neera K. 2014. *Well-Being: Happiness in a Worthwhile Life*. New York: Oxford University Press.
Baker, Lynne Rudder. 2009. "Non-Reductive Materialism". In *The Oxford Handbook of Philosophy of Mind*, edited by Brian McLaughlin, Ansgar Beckermann, and Sven Walter, 109–127. Oxford: Oxford University Press.
Baltes, Paul B. 2005. "Wisdom: Its Structure and Function in Regulating Successful Life Span Development". In *Handbook of Positive Psychology*, edited by C. R. Snyder and S. J. Lopez, 327–349. Oxford: Oxford University Press.
Baltes, Paul B., and Ursula M. Staudinger. 2000. "Wisdom: A Metaheuristic (Pragmatic) to Orchestrate Mind and Virtue toward Excellence". *American Psychologist* 55(1): 122–136.

---

[19] I would like to thank the following for their generous and helpful comments and/or conversations on earlier drafts of this essay: André Ariew, Dorit Bar-On, Matthew Bedke, Tyler Burge, David Copp, Dew Johnson, Tristan de Liège, David Enoch, Jennifer Lockhart, Micah Lott, Sonia Michel, Elijah Millgram, Parisa Moosavi, Elliott Sober, and Denis Walsh.

Bar-On, Dorit. 2013. "Expressive Communication and Continuity Skepticism". *Journal of Philosophy* 110(6): 293–330.
Battaly, Heather. 2017. "Intellectual Perseverance". *Journal of Moral Philosophy* 4(6): 669–698.
Becker, Lawrence. 1998. *A New Stoicism*. Princeton: Princeton University Press.
Becker, Lawrence. 2012. *Habilitation, Health, and Agency*. Oxford: Oxford University Press.
Bendardete, José. 1976. "Mechanism and the Good". *Philosophical Forum* 7(3–4): 294–315.
Bigelow, John, and Robert Pargetter. 1987. "Functions". *Journal of Philosophy* 84(4): 181–196.
Bloomfield, Paul. 1997. "Of Goodness and Healthiness: A Viable Moral Ontology". *Philosophical Studies* 87(3): 309–332.
Bloomfield, Paul. 1998. "Prescriptions Are Assertions: An Essay on Moral Syntax". *American Philosophical Quarterly* 35(1): 1–20.
Bloomfield, Paul. 2000. "Virtue Epistemology and the Epistemology of Virtue". *Philosophy and Phenomenological Research* 60(1): 23–43.
Bloomfield, Paul. 2001. *Moral Reality*. New York: Oxford University Press.
Bloomfield, Paul. 2011. "Justice as a Self-Regarding Virtue". *Philosophy and Phenomenological Research* 82(1): 46–64.
Bloomfield, Paul. 2013. "Error Theory and the Concept of Morality". *Metaphilosophy* 44(4): 451–469.
Bloomfield, Paul. 2014a. *The Virtues of Happiness: A Theory of the Good Life*. New York: Oxford University Press.
Bloomfield, Paul. 2014b. "Some Intellectual Aspects of the Moral Virtues". In *Oxford Studies in Normative Ethics*, vol. 3, edited by Mark Timmons, 287–313. New York: Oxford University Press.
Bloomfield, Paul. 2017. "Morality Is Necessary for Happiness". *Philosophical Studies* 174(10): 2613–2628.
Bloomfield, Paul. 2018b. "Tracking Eudaimonia". *Philosophy, Theory, and Practice in Biology* 10(2): 1–24. http://dx.doi.org/10.3998/ptpbio.16039257.0010.002.
Bloomfield, Paul. 2021. "Skills of Justice". In *The Routledge Handbook of Skill and Expertise*, edited by E. Fridland and C. Pavese, 460–475. London: Routledge.
Boorse, Christopher. 1976. "Wright on Functions". *Philosophical Review* 85(1): 70–86.
Boyd, Richard. 1988. "How to Be a Moral Realist". In *Essays on Moral Realism*, edited by G. Sayre-McCord, 181–228. Ithaca: Cornell University Press.
Brink, David. 1990. "Rational Egoism, Self, and Others". In *Identity, Character, and Morality*, edited by O. J. Flanagan and A. O. Rorty, 339–378. Cambridge: MIT Press.
Burge, Tyler. 2009. "Primitive Agency and Natural Norms". *Philosophy and Phenomenological Research* 79(2): 251–278.
Burge, Tyler. 2010. *Origins of Objectivity*. Oxford: Oxford University Press.
Campbell, Donald T. 1960. "Blind Variation and Selective Retentions in Creative Thought as in Other Knowledge Processes". *Psychological Review* 67(6): 380–400.
Christensen, Wayne David, and Mark H. Bickhard. 2002. "The Process Dynamics of Normative Function". *The Monist* 85(1): 3–28.
Copp, David, and David Sobel. 2004. "Morality and Virtue: An Assessment of Some Recent Work in Virtue Ethics". *Ethics* 114(3): 514–554.
Cowie, Christopher, and Richard Rowland, eds. 2019. *Companions in Guilt Arguments in Metaethics*. London: Routledge.
Crisp, Roger. 2014. "Nobility in the Nicomachean Ethics". *Phronesis* 59(3): 231–245.
Cummins, Robert. 1975. "Functional Analysis". *Journal of Philosophy* 72: 741–764.

Dawkins, Richard. 1976. *The Selfish Gene*. Oxford: Oxford University Press.
Douglass, Frederick. [1845] 2016. *Narrative of the Life of Frederick Douglass, An American Slave: Written by Himself*. New Haven: Yale University Press.
Dowell, Janice. 2016. "The Metaethical Insignificance of Moral Twin Earth". In *Oxford Studies in Metaethics*, vol. 11, 1–27. New York: Oxford University Press.
Duckworth, Angela. 2007. "Grit: Perseverance and Passion for Long-Term Goals". *Journal of Personality and Social Psychology* 92(6): 1087–1101.
Eibl-Eibesfeldt, Irenäus. 1972. *Love and Hate: The Natural History of Behavior Patterns*. New York: Holt, Rinehart and Winston.
Eldredge, N, and S. J. Gould. 1972. "Punctuated Equilibria: An Alternative to Phyletic Gradualism". In *Models in Paleobiology*, edited by T. J. M. Schopf, 82–115. San Francisco: Freeman, Cooper & Co.
Enç, Berent, and Fred Adams. 1992. "Functions and Goal Directedness". *Philosophy of Science* 59(4): 635–654.
Enoch, David. 2011. *Taking Morality Seriously: A Defense of Robust Realism*. Oxford: Oxford University Press.
FitzPatrick, William. 2000. *Teleology and the Norms of Nature*. New York: Garland Press.
Foot, Philippa. 1958. "Moral Beliefs". *Proceedings of the Aristotelian Society* 59(1): 83–104.
Foot, Philippa. 2001. *Natural Goodness*. Oxford: Oxford University Press.
Godfrey-Smith, Peter. 1994. "A Modern History Theory of Functions". *Noûs* 28(3): 344–362.
Gordon-Reed, Annette, and Peter S. Onuf. 2016. *"Most Blessed of the Patriarchs": Thomas Jefferson and the Empire of the Imagination*. New York: W. W. Norton & Company.
Graham, Peter J. 2012. "Epistemic Entitlement". *Noûs* 46(3): 449–482.
Greco, John. 2010. *Achieving Knowledge: A Virtue-Theoretic Account of Epistemic Normativity*. Cambridge: Cambridge University Press.
Gross, James J. 2014. *Handbook of Emotion Regulation*. 2nd ed. New York: Guilford Publications.
Hampton, Jean. 1993. "Feminist Contractarianism". In *A Mind of One's Own*, edited by Louise Antony and Charlotte Witt, 337–368. Boulder, CO: Westview Press.
Harman, Gilbert. 1977. *The Nature of Morality: An Introduction to Ethics*. New York: Oxford University Press.
Hewlett, Barry S. 2005. *Hunter-Gatherer Childhoods*. New Brunswick, NJ: Routledge.
Horgan, Terence, and Mark Timmons. 1991. "New Wave Moral Realism Meets Moral Twin Earth". *Journal of Philosophical Research* 16: 447–465.
Horgan, Terence, and Mark Timmons. 1993. "New Wave Moral Realism Meets Moral Twin Earth". In *Rationality, Morality, and Self-Interest*, edited by J. Heil, 115–133. Lanham, MD: Rowman & Littlefield Publishers.
Hrdy, Sarah Blaffer. 2000. *Mother Nature: Maternal Instincts and How They Shape the Human Species*. New York: Ballantine Books.
Hume, David. [1739] 1978. *A Treatise of Human Nature*. 2nd ed. Edited by L. A. Selby Bigge and P. H. Nidditch. New York: Oxford University Press.
Hurka, Thomas. 1993. *Perfectionism*. Oxford: Oxford University Press.
Hurley, Susan, and Matthew Nudds. 2006. *Rational Animals?* Oxford: Oxford University Press.
Hursthouse, Rosalind. 1999. *On Virtue Ethics*. Oxford: Oxford University Press.
Hutchinson, G. E., and Robert H. MacArthur. 1959. "Appendix on the Theoretical Significance of Aggressive Neglect in Interspecific Competition". *American Naturalist* 93(869): 133–134.

Irwin, Terrence. 2005. "The Parts of the Soul and the Cardinal Virtues (Book IV 427d–448e)". In *Platon: Politeia*, edited by O. Höffe, 119–135. Berlin: Akademie Verlag.
Johnson, Drew. 2021. "Proper Function and Ethical Judgment: Towards a Biosemantic Theory of Ethical Thought and Discourse". *Erkenntnis*. https://doi.org/10.1007/s10670-021-00481-y.
Kaufmann, Stuart. 1993. *The Origins of Order: Self-Organization and Selection in Evolution*. New York: Oxford University Press.
Kim, Richard T. 2018. "Human Nature and Moral Sprouts: Mencius on the Pollyanna Problem". *Pacific Philosophical Quarterly* 99(1): 140–162.
Kitcher, Philip. 2006. "Ethics and Biology". In *The Oxford Handbook of Ethical Theory*, edited by David Copp, 163–185. New York: Oxford University Press.
Konner, Melvin. 2010. *The Evolution of Childhood: Relationships, Emotion, Mind*. 1st ed. Cambridge, MA: Belknap Press.
Kurzban, Robert, John Tooby, and Leda Cosmides. 2001. "Can Race Be Erased? Coalitional Computation and Social Categorization". *Proceedings of the National Academy of Sciences* 98(26): 15387–15392.
Laubichler, Manfred D. 2009. "Form and Function in Evo Devo: Historical and Conceptual Reflections". In *Form and Function in Developmental Evolution*, edited by Manfred Laubichler and Jane Maienschein, 10–46. Cambridge: Cambridge University Press.
Lawrence, Gavin. 2011. "Acquiring Character". In *Moral Psychology and Human Action in Aristotle*, edited by M. Pakaluk and G. Pearson, 233–284. Oxford: Oxford University Press.
Lillehammer, H. 2007. *Companions in Guilt: Arguments for Ethical Objectivity*. New York: Springer.
Lloyd, Elisabeth. 2020. "Units and Levels of Selection". In *The Stanford Encyclopedia of Philosophy*, edited by Edward N. Zalta. https://plato.stanford.edu/archives/spr2020/entries/selection-units/ (April 26, 2020).
Long, A. A., and D. M. Sedley. 1987. *The Hellenistic Philosophers: Volume 1, Translations of the Principal Sources with Philosophical Commentary*. Cambridge: Cambridge University Press.
Lorenz, Konrad. 1966. *On Aggression*. New York: Harcourt, Brace, and World.
Lurz, Robert W. 2009. *The Philosophy of Animal Minds*. Cambridge: Cambridge University Press.
Mac Cumhaill, Clare, and Rachael Wiseman. 2022. *Metaphysical Animals: How Four Women Brought Philosophy Back to Life*. New York: Doubleday.
Mace, C. A. 1949. "Mechanical and Teleological Causation". In *Readings in Philosophical Analysis*, edited by H. Fiegl and W. Sellers, 534–539. New York: Appleton, Century, and Crofts.
Machiavelli, Niccolò. 1995. *The Prince*. Edited by David Wootton. Indianapolis: Hackett Publishing.
MacIntyre, Alasdair C. 1981. *After Virtue: A Study in Moral Theory*. Notre Dame: University of Notre Dame Press.
Matthen, Mohan, and André Ariew. 2002. "Two Ways of Thinking about Fitness and Natural Selection". *Journal of Philosophy* 99(2): 55–83.
McLaughlin, Peter. 2000. *What Functions Explain: Functional Explanation and Self-Reproducing Systems*. Cambridge: Cambridge University Press.
Meehan, Courtney L., and Alyssa N. Crittenden, eds. 2016. *Childhood: Origins, Evolution, and Implications*. Santa Fe; Albuquerque: University of New Mexico Press Published in Association with School for Advanced Research Press.
Midgley, Mary. 1978. *Beast and Man*. Ithaca: Cornell University Press.

Mikhail, John. 2011. *Elements of Moral Cognition: Rawls' Linguistic Analogy and the Cognitive Science of Moral and Legal Judgment by John Mikhail*. Cambridge: Cambridge University Press.

Miller, Christian B. 2014. *Character and Moral Psychology*. Oxford: Oxford University Press.

Millgram, Elijah. 2009. "Life and Action". *Analysis* 69(3): 557–564.

Millikan, Ruth Garrett. 1984. *Language, Thought, and Other Biological Categories: New Foundations for Realism*. Cambridge: MIT Press.

Millikan, Ruth Garrett. 1990. "Truth Rules, Hoverflies, and Kripke-Wittgenstein Paradox". *Philosophical Review* 99(3): 323–353.

Mills, Susan K., and John H. Beatty. 1979. "The Propensity Interpretation of Fitness". *Philosophy of Science* 46(2): 263–286.

Moore G. E. 1903/1988. *Principia Ethica*. Buffalo: Prometheus Books.

Moosavi, Parisa. 2018. "Neo-Aristotelian Naturalism and the Evolutionary Objection: Rethinking the Relevance of Empirical Science". In *Philippa Foot on Goodness and Virtue*, edited by John Hacker-Wright. New York: Palgrave Macmillan, 277–307.

Moosavi, Parisa. 2019. "From Biological Functions to Natural Goodness". *Philosopher's Imprint* 19(51): 1–20.

Moosavi, Parisa. 2022. "Natural Goodness without Natural History". *Philosophy and Phenomenological Research* 104(1): 8–100.

Moreno, Alvaro, and Matteo Mossio. 2015. *Biological Autonomy: A Philosophical and Theoretical Enquiry*. New York: Springer.

Morton, Jennifer, and Sarah Paul. "Grit". 2019. *Ethics* 129: 175–203.

Mossio, Matteo, Cristian Saborido, and Alvaro Moreno. 2009. "An Organizational Account of Biological Functions". *British Journal for the Philosophy of Science* 60(4): 813–841.

Müller, Gerd B. 2007. "Evo-Devo: Extending the Evolutionary Synthesis". *Nature Reviews. Genetics* 8(12): 943–949.

Neander, Karen. 1991. "The Teleological Notion of 'Function.'" *Australasian Journal of Philosophy* 69(4): 454–468.

Nietzsche, Friedrich. [1895] 1954. *Thus Spoke Zarathustra*. Reprinted in *The Portable Nietzsche*, translated by Walter Kaufmann. New York: Viking Press.

Nussbaum, Martha C. 1988. "Non-Relative Virtues: An Aristotelian Approach". *Midwest Studies in Philosophy* 13(1): 32–53.

Okasha, Samir. 2006. *Evolution and the Levels of Selection*. Oxford: Oxford University Press.

Pervin, Lawrence A. 1994. "A Critical Analysis of Current Trait Theory". *Psychological Inquiry* 5(2): 103–13.

Peterson, Christopher, and Martin E. P. Seligman, 2004. *Character Strengths and Virtues: A Handbook and Classification*. Oxford: Oxford University Press.

Pigden, Charles. 2010. *Hume on Is and Ought*. New York: Palgrave Macmillan.

Plantinga, Alvin. 1993. *Warrant and Proper Function*. New York: Oxford University Press.

Plato. 1993. *Republic*. Translated by R. Waterfield. Oxford: Oxford University Press.

Popper, Karl. 1959. *The Logic of Scientific Discovery*. London: Routledge.

Prior, A. N. 1949. *Logic and the Basis of Ethics*. Oxford: Clarendon Press.

Prior, A. N. 1960. "The Autonomy of Ethics". *Australasian Journal of Philosophy* 38(3): 99–106.

Quine, W. V. O. 1953. "Two Dogmas of Empiricism". In *From a Logical Point of View*, 20–46. Cambridge, MA: Harvard University Press.

Quine, W. V. O. 1960. *Word and Object*. Cambridge, MA: MIT Press.

Quine, W. V. O. 1963. "Carnap and Logical Truth". In *The Philosophy of Rudolph Carnap*, edited by P. Schilpp, 350–374. LaSalle, IL: Open Court.

Ripley, S. Dillon. 1959. "Competition between Sunbird and Honeyeater Species in the Moluccan Islands". *American Naturalist* 93(869): 127–132.

Ripley, S. Dillon. 1961. "Aggressive Neglect as a Factor in Interspecific Competition in Birds". *The Auk* 78(3): 366–371.

Scheffler, Israel. 1958. "Thoughts on Teleology". *British Journal for the Philosophy of Science* 9(33): 265.

Schlosser, Gerhard. 1998. "Self-Re-Production and Functionality". *Synthese* 116(3): 303–354.

Schrödinger, Erwin. 1944. *What Is Life?* Cambridge: Cambridge University Press.

Scriven, Michael. 1959. "Explanation and Prediction in Evolutionary Theory". *Science* 130(3374): 477.

Seligman, M. E., and M. Csikszentmihalyi. 2000. "Positive Psychology. An Introduction". *American Psychologist* 55(1): 5–14.

Sklar, Lawrence. 1993. *Physics and Chance: Philosophical Issues in the Foundations of Statistical Mechanics*. Cambridge: Cambridge University Press.

Sober, Elliott. 2011. *Did Darwin Write the Origin Backwards? Philosophical Essays on Darwin's Theory*. Buffalo: Prometheus.

Sober, Elliott. 2013. "Trait Fitness Is Not a Propensity, but Fitness Variation Is". *Studies in History and Philosophy of Science Part C: Studies in History and Philosophy of Biological and Biomedical Sciences* 44(3): 336–341.

Sober, Elliott. 2020. "Fitness and the Twins". *Philosophy, Theory, and Practice in Biology* 12(1): 1–13. http://hdl.handle.net/2027/spo.16039257.0012.001.

Sober, Elliott, and David Sloan Wilson. 1998. *Unto Others: The Evolution and Psychology of Unselfish Behavior*. Cambridge, MA: Harvard University Press.

Sosa, Ernest. 1980. "The Raft and the Pyramid". *Midwest Studies in Philosophy* 5(1): 3–26.

Sosa, Ernest. 2007. *A Virtue Epistemology: Apt Belief and Reflective Knowledge, Volume I*. Oxford: Clarendon Press.

Spencer, Herbert. [1879–1893] 1978. *The Principles of Ethics*. Indianapolis: Liberty Classics.

Sterelny, Kim, and Ben Fraser. 2016. "Evolution and Moral Realism". *British Journal for the Philosophy of Science* 68(4): 981–1006.

Sternberg, Robert J. 1998. "A Balance Theory of Wisdom". *Review of General Psychology* 2(3): 347–365.

Stichter, Matt. 2016. "Practical Skills and Practical Wisdom in Virtue". *Australasian Journal of Philosophy* 94(3): 435–448.

Stichter, Matt. 2021. "Differentiating the Skills of Practical Wisdom". In *Practical Wisdom: Philosophical and Psychological Perspectives*, edited by M. De Caro and M. S. Vaccarezza. London: Routledge.

Street, Sharon. 2006. "A Darwinian Dilemma for Realist Theories of Value". *Philosophical Studies* 127(1): 109–166.

Stocker, Michael. 1976. "The Schizophrenia of Modern Moral Philosophy". *Journal of Philosophy* 17(14): 453–466.

Swanton, Christine. 2003. *Virtue Ethics: A Pluralistic View*. Oxford: Oxford University Press.

Swartwood, Jason D. 2013. "Wisdom as an Expert Skill". *Ethical Theory and Moral Practice* 16(3): 511–528.

Thomas, Michael J. et al. 2019. "A New Scale for Assessing Wisdom Based on Common Domains and a Neurobiological Model: The San Diego Wisdom Scale (SD-WISE)". *Journal of Psychiatric Research* 108: 40–47.

Thompson, Michael. 1995. "The Representation of Life". In *Virtues and Reasons*, edited by Rosalind Hursthouse, Gavin Lawrence, and Warren Quinn, 247–296. Oxford: Clarendon Press.

Thompson, Michael. 2012. *Life and Action*. Cambridge, MA: Harvard University Press.

Thomson, Judith Jarvis. 2007. "Normativity". In *Oxford Studies in Metaethics*, edited by Russ Shafer-Landau, 240–266. Oxford: Oxford University Press.

Tsai, Cheng-Hung. forthcoming. "Phronesis and Techne: The Skill Model of Wisdom Defended". *Australasian Journal of Philosophy*. https://doi.org/10.1080/00048 402.2019.1618352.

Vlastos, Gregory. 1968. "The Argument in the *Republic* That 'Justice Pays.'" *Journal of Philosophy* 65(21): 665–674.

Vohs, Kathleen D., and Roy F. Baumeister. 2014. *Handbook of Self-Regulation*, 2nd ed., New York: Guilford Press.

Walsh, Denis. 2008. "Teleology". In *The Oxford Handbook of Philosophy of Biology*, edited by Michael Ruse, 113–137. Oxford University Press.

Walsh, Denis. 2012. "Mechanism and Purpose: A Case for Natural Teleology". *Studies in History and Philosophy of Science Part C: Studies in History and Philosophy of Biological and Biomedical Sciences* 43(1): 173–181.

Walsh, Denis M., and André Ariew. 1996. "A Taxonomy of Functions". *Canadian Journal of Philosophy* 26(4): 493–514.

Walsh, Denis M., André Ariew, and Mohan Matthen. 2017. "Four Pillars of Statisticalism". *Philosophy, Theory, and Practice in Biology* 9(1): 1–18. http://hdl.handle.net/2027/spo.6959 004.0009.001 (April 27, 2020).

Watson, Gary. 1990. "On the Primacy of Character". In *Identity, Character, and Morality: Essays in Moral Psychology*, edited by Owen J. Flanagan and Amélie Oksenberg Rorty, 449–469. Cambridge: MIT Press.

Weber, Marcel. 2004. *Philosophy of Experimental Biology*. Cambridge: Cambridge University Press.

Wimsatt, William C. 1972. "Teleology and the Logical Structure of Function Statements". *Studies in History and Philosophy of Science Part A* 3(1): 1–80.

Wright, L. 1976. *Teleological Explanations. An Etiological Analysis of Goals and Functions*. Berkeley: University of California Press.

Wright, Larry. 1973. "Functions". *Philosophical Review* 82(2): 139–168.

CHAPTER 14

REALISM ABOUT THE GOOD FOR HUMAN BEINGS

L. NANDI THEUNISSEN

The aims of moral philosophy, and any hopes it may have of being worthy of serious attention, is bound up with the fate of Socrates' question.

—Bernard Williams

A recognizable program in metaethics is the analysis of "moral utterances." We ask about the function of bits of normative vocabulary as they figure in contrivances about torturing babies for fun. What is meant by calling such an act "morally wrong"? What is our best theory of the properties thereby invoked? How can they be known? And so on. Initiated by G. E. Moore and spurred by developments in the philosophy of language, high analytic metaethics had its "heyday" in the early part of the twentieth century.[1] For all the backlash that ensued in subsequent decades,[2] armchair semantic analysis of "ordinary normative claims" or "moral discourse" continues to be a recognizable starting point for discussions of realism, antirealism, and their kin. How, it may be asked, could it be otherwise?[3]

It is instructive to go back to the original pioneers—to the scene before metaethics as we know it was clearly defined. I think of Moore, but more immediately, the intuitive realists he inspired—H. A. Prichard and W. D. Ross. Prichard articulates his realism by engaging with Plato, Aristotle, the consequentialists, and Kant. He defines the concepts that are basic in their theories and gives an account of their relationship. One of his key proposals is that

---

[1] I take the term "heyday" from the still relevant recounting of "Fin de siècle Ethics" by Darwall, Gibbard, and Railton 1992, 116. A differently compelling, and more explicitly editorial, account of the development of metaethics is given by Foot, 2001, ch. 1.

[2] Backlash that found a target in noncognitivism in particular. See Darwall et al (121–124) on "The Great Expansion" of the 1950s.

[3] This question is (rhetorically) posed by Darwall et al. (n. 27). As I shall indicate below, I think the (nonrhetorical) answer is contained in the avenues explicitly set to one side in the *Review* article (n. 24), in particular, literate engagement with the history of ethics.

we should sharply distinguish between the concepts of right action, moral goodness, and virtue, seeing them as sui generis forms of normative concern whose claims on us are self-evident. It is no accident that Ross—crediting Prichard's (1912) "Does Moral Philosophy Rest on a Mistake?" as a primary influence (1930, v)—outlines his realism in a work that gives the right and the good eponymous place. With Prichard, Ross's realism comes into focus by thinking through foundational concepts and making a proposal about the relation between them. Of course, Ross, like the others, was deeply literate in the history of ethics; indeed, he was a celebrated scholar of ancient philosophy.

The point of this potted history is twofold. First, the distinction between "meta" and "normative" ethics, no doubt useful for certain purposes, is also artificial and potentially misleading. Before there was this division within the field, there was simply *ethics*, and it is impossible to read canonical figures in ethics—Plato, Aristotle, Hume, Kant, Mill—without seeing them as interested in metaethical questions. The so-called normative theorists of the tradition are also metaethicists. Second, this is no accident. If metaethics takes ethics as its object, it has something to say only if the object is clearly in view. How we delineate the ethical—what we identify as the primary subject; how we propose to conceptualize it; what we take as first principles—has a decisive influence on the theories we give.[4] And there is great scope for blindness and oversight just here. We do not come to "moral utterance" innocently.[5] The concepts we find ourselves invoking have a history and being in touch with that history makes us self-conscious about the fully expressive and philosophical implications of what we are saying (or indeed the possibility that we are not saying anything at all).[6] This is something Prichard and Ross were very much alive to. Their distinctive forms of realism come into view by way of a reckoning with the concepts they take to be basic in ethics.[7]

While my substantive proposal is at a considerable remove from that of the intuitive realists, I broadly follow their methodology in this chapter. That is, by thinking through the relationship between the concepts I take to be basic in ethics, I articulate a form of realism. It is a realism that aligns the prospects of our discipline with the fate of Socrates' question: the question of what it is for human beings to live well. To supply some recognizable labels, this is the project of giving ethics an objective foundation in human nature or well-being. It is the program of relational realism in ethics—of realism about the *good for* human beings. As I will put the emphasis, it is a realism that works with a unified or integrated conception of the good in which virtue and the beneficial are the key

---

[4] This is a point long and forcefully made by Iris Murdoch (1957, 33). Her essay belongs in Darwall's et al. discussion of the "Great Expansion" in moral philosophy of the 1950s (1992, 121).

[5] Compare Shelly Kagan's (1989, 12) doubts about the existence of pretheoretical intuitions.

[6] I am thinking here of Elizabeth Anscombe's (1958) polemical claim that much of what passes for ordinary moral utterance is actually nonsensical. I accept that it is often indeterminate, vague, unfocused, provisional, and in these ways, not up for assessment as straightforwardly true or false.

[7] Of course, this way of proceeding is not the exclusive province of realists. Judith Jarvis Thomson in "The Right and the Good" (1997) and Christine Korsgaard of "The Two Distinctions in Goodness" (1983) both articulate forms of antirealism by taking a stand on the character of and relationship between foundational concepts in ethics.

concepts, and in which the "moral good" is not foundationally distinctive, but explicable in terms of the good for human beings.

Section 1: Morality and Happiness

There are different ways of expressing the basic concepts and distinctions in ethics. Some draw a basic distinction between the moral and the nonmoral good, others the right and the good, or morality and prudence, and equally, virtue and the beneficial. Our choice of terminology seems to matter, and I will work up to my preferred vocabulary. But to begin I will treat these pairs of terms as broadly synonymous, and for simplicity's sake, I will use the language of morality and happiness to express a basic distinction. My immediate interest is how these terms have been defined and related to one another, and in Section 1, I work through some representative approaches in the tradition. I discuss the proposals: (i) that morality contrasts sharply with happiness or prudence as a *distinct source of normative concern*; (ii) that morality and happiness are distinct sources of normative concern with the one taking *normative priority* over the other; (iii) that morality and happiness are foundationally distinctive and in one way or another *causally* connected; (iv) that morality and happiness are not distinct but *co-extensive*. (I)–(iii) arguably lay bare commitments of Kant and his followers, while (iv) is familiar from ancient Greek discussions. I give my reasons for rejecting (i)–(iv) before making my own proposal in Section 2. As I will argue there, I think we are well-served by finer-grained distinctions, and I will make use of a threefold distinction between virtuous action, virtuous people, and the good for human beings.

1.1 Distinct Sources of Normative Concern

According to a familiar style of proposal, while we may want to distinguish right action from moral motivation, these are alike forms of moral exemplariness. Living happily, on the other hand, felicity—that is something else altogether. We have here two forms of the good—the moral and the prudential—or a deontic category that is at a remove from an evaluative one—the right and the good. Either way, these are ethical categories with distinctly different rationales.[8] The idea that there is a basic duality here finds defenders from various quarters, but the proposal owes much—mediately or immediately—to Kant.[9] For Kant, what matters morally is a person's principle of action.[10] While

---

[8] That morality and prudence are distinctly different sources of normative concern is arguably a mark of modern moral theory. Darwall (2012) gives a tremendously clear-sighted account of this and Rawls (2000, 1–14), whom Darwall also cites, makes a related set of claims.

[9] Here, and below, I draw broadly from Kant's treatment of the moral and the nonmoral good in Chapter II of the Analytic of the second *Critique* (esp. 5:58–5:63).

[10] One of Prichard's criticisms of Kant is that he does not properly distinguish between right action and moral goodness (acting from a moral motive) because he takes motivation, or the ground of action, to be all that matters morally. Prichard also urged that Kant's conception of virtue (of being a good

principles of action may concern oneself, they are not made right by advancing one's happiness. The foundation of morality is not one's own happiness, and it is not the happiness of anyone else either. Morality may concern the happiness of others, but what makes a principle of action rational and good has nothing to do with its standing to do good for anyone. Morality is independent of happiness, and happiness is understood in subjectivist terms as the satisfaction of desire or inclination.[11] In this way, morality and happiness are distinctly different sources of normative concern, and it follows that they can crosscut one another.[12] The demands of morality may strain one's happiness (or "interest"), and what is in one's interest may strain the demands of morality. Just to this extent, there is pressure to establish a normative order of priority between them. And that gives scope for connecting these distinctly different sources of practical concern by way of a relation of normative constraint.

1.2 Normative Constraint

Conceivably, a relation of normative constraint could go in either direction, but for reasons that are not hard to come by, the tradition affords readier examples of the moral constraining the prudential good. In Kant's own discussion, that which conduces to the satisfaction of a person's desire, or the realization of their end, is "good for" them in the sense that it facilitates their end. And Kant supposes that what facilitates a person's end is practically significant for them and must be seen by others as so.[13] Where it lacks full evaluative and normative significance is in its susceptibility to being outweighed or trumped by another kind of value, viz, the moral good. On one way of making sense of Kant's proposal, what conduces to the poisoner's end of poisoning her victim is good for that purpose, and it is rationally incumbent on the poisoner to seek it out. There is a bona fide rational demand here, and yet, on account of its immorality, it is not decisive.

---

person) is inadequate on the grounds that to be virtuous for Kant is no more than to be committed to moral motivation (action from duty). Prichard sees the notion of virtue as broader, and as involving distinctly different motivational states. I am sympathetic to both of Prichard's criticisms. What I am emphasizing at this juncture is Kant's commitment to a basic duality between the moral and the nonmoral good.

[11] Rawls (1999, 27; 361–365) considers qualifications to the effect that it is the strongest of our desires, or the largest number, or those that stand the best chance of being satisfied, and etc.

[12] Kant discusses this at 5:60–5:61.

[13] That what is instrumentally good for p must be recognized by others as instrumentally good for p follows from the fact that good is the kind of concept for which we share grounds and about which there is pressure to agree. In Kant's terminology, *good*—be it moral or non-moral—is a "rational concept." Moreover, Kant proposes that the good must in every reasonable person's judgment be an object of desire. So, we can all agree that such and such conduces to p's end, and we can all agree that such and such is something p (instrumentally) ought to seek out. What is "good for" some purpose or other is the evaluative analogue of the hypothetical imperative, and Kant moves freely between the idioms of the good and practical reason. See 5:58.

To take a related example from Rawls—whose dictum about normative priority is self-consciously drawn from Kant—if a person enjoys seeing others oppressed ("in positions of lesser liberty"), then though the enjoyment would be good for him, his interest will not issue in practical reasons.[14] Importantly, the claim is not that having a desire to oppress others is not properly good for the one who has it. It is that *despite* the fact that its satisfaction would be good for them, it is illicit or wrong for them to act on it.

1.3 Causal Connection

Apart from a relation of normative constraint, on a scheme according to which morality and happiness (prudence, what is "good for" oneself, what is in one's interest) are distinct sources of normative concern, there is scope to countenance a causal relation between them. A causal relation may be drawn in either or both directions. We may venture that showing up for the obligations of the day gives rise to feelings of satisfaction, and/or that when we feel good and satisfied, we tend to show up with greater alacrity for moral demands. Or perhaps we seize more readily on the negative analogues here—that bad behavior conduces to states of loneliness and misery, and/or that states of loneliness and misery set one up for being bad.[15] While these may be homely truths, it is natural to wonder about the stability of the connection between morality and happiness where the latter is treated (extraethically) as desire satisfaction, pleasure, or good feeling. Kant was interested in the scope for a causal connection between a commitment to principled action and happiness in just this extra-ethical sense, but he thought there needed to be a considerable massaging of the conditions.[16] Kant is not prepared to allow that we observe good people getting the satisfaction they deserve with anything approaching regularity. But he is prepared to postulate the existence of a benevolent being to see to it that the righteous have the commensurate gains of satisfaction in the *next* life. Rectitude does pay, or at least, as we strive to attain the highest good that is moral rectitude in conjunction with happiness, we are constrained to postulate that there is this mediated species of connection down the line. In this way Kant gives a version of the causal proposal with a (signature) twist.

Kant's treatment is interesting to think about because, having carved morality and happiness at the joints as he sees them, he takes measures to stitch them back together. Happiness is in no way the standard or foundation of morality, but Kant thinks that as practical reasoners we "cannot but" desire happiness in proportion to morality. This is not quite the thought that morality must fit with happiness if it is to have a chance of

---

[14] Rawls, 1999, 31. Here Rawls explicitly cites Chapter II of the Analytic. I set aside some much discussed complexities in Rawls's treatment of these issues.

[15] Williams (1986, 45–6) says these should be regarded as ordinary and powerful facts. But he also contends that they are some facts "in a range of" others, to adapt his examples, the nice guy who finishes last, and the tycoon who has it all.

[16] See Ch. 2 of the Dialectic of the *Critique of Practical Reason*.

being taken seriously, but it is a concession to the idea that as practical agents we cannot allow the moral life to be, quite generally, and absent tragic circumstances, a miserable life. One may find the aspiration to find some unity between morality and happiness right even as there is something disappointing about the treatment. One is interested in the bearing of ethical considerations on living happily in *this* life, and Kant kicks the can (quite far) down the road. As I will indicate later, I think there is something to be said for postulating some kind of causal relationship between doing and being as one ought and feeling "happy." But to see the truth here, I think one first needs to probe the conception of happiness—subjectivist and extraethical—that has so far been at issue. I turn to proposals that in one way or another apply pressure here.

1.4 Coextension

I began with the view that there is a foundational difference between morality and its cognates (the moral good, the right) and happiness and its cognates (prudence, what is in one's interests, what is good for one). I discussed ways of connecting these concepts through relations of normative priority and causation. I now consider a distinctly different approach, one that seeks a more radical rapprochement. I state it using the vocabulary of virtue and happiness. While the one connotes excellence or exemplariness, and the other faring well or being in a felicitous state, according to the present proposal, they actually coincide. Living as a *good person* does (virtue) is coextensive with what is *for the good of* a person (happiness).

When Kant canvasses views about how the concepts of virtue and happiness are connected, he contrasts a causal approach—some version of which he accepts—to views that in one way or another see them as equivalent.[17] He attributes the approach he rejects to the ancient Greeks and distinguishes two ways of construing the proposal depending on which, "virtue" or "happiness," is taken as fundamental. If "virtue" is treated as fundamental, then to the extent that someone is living as a virtuous person lives, she is in a felicitous state. And if "happiness" is fundamental, then to the extent that someone is in a felicitous state, she is living as a virtuous person does.[18] As I will construe the first proposal, one starts with commonsense ideas about right and wrong, and defines happiness and its cognates in terms of them. What it is for someone to be happy is fixed by whatever it is to be properly responsive to moral considerations. According to the second (or a version that is relevant to discussions of ethical naturalism), one starts with an account of what it is for human beings to fare well and what one antecedently

---

[17] "The connection between virtue and happiness can therefore be understood in one of two ways: either the endeavor to be virtuous and the rational pursuit of happiness are not two actions but quite identical [. . . .] or else that connection is found in virtue's producing happiness as something different from the consciousness of virtue, as a cause produces an effect" (5:111).

[18] "Of the ancient Greek schools there were, strictly speaking, only two which [. . .] followed one and the same method insofar as they did not let virtue and happiness hold as two different elements in the highest good and consequently sought the unity of the principle in accordance with the rule of

recognizes as ethical virtue emerges from it. Ethical virtue is whatever equips a person to fare well, where faring well is understood in prephilosophical ways. I consider these options in turn.

1.4.1 *Virtue Is Happiness*

In defining happiness and its cognates in ethical terms, the first variant of the proposal is highly revisionist. While I will urge that it revises too far, it does push us to contend with a key question about the form of happiness that is the proper object of ethical study, and indeed, whether "happiness" is quite the word for it. When we inquire about the happiness that is "humanity's good," what sense of "happy" should be at issue?[19] Happiness can connote contentment, satisfaction or pleasure—the sense that is broadly at stake in Kant's account—and on that way of saying "happy" there is no suggestion that virtue bears conceptually on it. But there are terms in the neighborhood that carry other implications. Phillipa Foot has claimed that we would not say the person who is aiding and abetting a pair of serial killers is doing what is "beneficial" for the pair (2001, 93). In a similar vein, we hesitate to say that someone who is thoroughly wicked is "living well." Or take the homely question, "How is your daughter doing"? And the reply, "She's doing great!" The "doing great" connotes a state of excellence and satisfaction both, and presumably it is relevant that we have to do with a parent's perspective on a child (since parents tend to want their children to find joy in doing what is honorable).[20] The term "wretched" seems to carry the negative analogues of badness and misery together. These are registers in which it is not preposterous to speak of an ethical *conception* of happiness (misery), or of an internal rather than causal connection between virtue and happiness (vice and unhappiness).

---

identity; but they differed, in turn, in their choice of which of the two was to be the fundamental concept. The Epicurean said: to be conscious of one's maxim leading to happiness is virtue; the Stoic said: to be conscious of one's virtue is happiness. For the first, *prudence* was equivalent to morality; for the second, who chose a higher designation for virtue, *morality* alone was true wisdom" (5:111). Kant goes on to decry both approaches for suppressing "essential and irreconcilable differences in principle by trying to change them into disputes about words and so to devise a specious unity of concept under merely different names" (5:111–5:112). There are interpretive questions that I cannot take up here. (For example, Richard Kraut has suggested that the Stoic view is not that happiness and virtue are different names for one and the same concept, but that the latter is the sole constituent of the former. Happiness is a placeholder good in the sense that one possesses it only by possessing what it consists in.) Strikingly, John McDowell (1980, 368) uses something comparable to Kant's schema for the Stoics and Epicureans to describe two ways of interpreting Aristotle. In McDowell's telling, Aristotle is committed to a biconditional: if a person is living as a virtuous person would then she is happy; and if a person is happy then she is living as a virtuous person would. But there is a question of whether the biconditional is to be read left to right or right to left. McDowell defends a "left to right" reading, while Wilkes (1980) defends what could be described as a "right to left" reading.

[19] This question is thoughtfully posed by Foot, and the formulation in the text is taken from her (2001, 85).

[20] I owe it to Michael Thompson (in conversation) and Vogt (2017b) to think of the parent's perspective.

The discussion brings out that there is philosophical work involved in isolating the form of the good for human beings that is centrally of interest in ethics. For Kant, and those following him, we are interested in what conduces to the satisfaction of desire, where desire varies from individual to individual, and is independent of ethical considerations. Where the subject is taken to be living well, the beneficial, or flourishing, we are set on a different track, and it is not out of the question to posit a nontrivial (conceptual) connection to virtue. However, to the extent that it *identifies* virtue and happiness, the present proposal seems to me to overreach. That we hesitate to say that a wicked person is living well does not mean that there are no substantive questions about how, say, being unjust is disadvantageous to the one who is so.[21] The difficult questions here cannot be dispensed with by stipulation. What is more, if what it is to be in a good state just is to be responsive to the demands of morality, then the subject of the good for human beings has lost all connection with our sensible condition—with what contributes to and promotes our life, and conversely, with what maims or deprives it. We may not share Kant's view that the form of the good for human beings which ethics properly studies is satisfaction or pleasure, but these are surely not categorically misguided proposals. Presumably Kant is also right to countenance the possibility of conflict between virtue and the good for oneself, or to put it differently, the scope for moral tragedy, something that is ruled out on the present view.[22] While I agree that we need a more sophisticated conception of happiness than Kant's, and my own eventual proposal will reflect this, these are my reasons for rejecting the view that being virtuous just is being happy.

1.4.2 *Happiness Is Virtue*

The second variant of the proposal treats responsiveness to moral concerns as a matter of "enlightened prudentiality."[23] The prudent person, the person who excels at practical reasoning, is one who deliberates well about what is advantageous to themselves. They have a well-conceived "life plan" with the right understanding of the ingredients that are necessary to live well, an appreciation of how to integrate these elements coherently, and the technical facility to bring them into form.[24] Since they are social beings who live in community, they recognize that cooperation and responsiveness to the concerns of others are among the essential elements for a successful life. Accordingly, they have developed the other-regarding virtues of justice and beneficence. They recognize that part of what living well involves is fulfilling their social roles and obligations, being fair in

---

[21] Kraut (2018, 16–17) makes this point and in doing so picks up the animating question of the *Republic*.

[22] This criticism of 1.4.1 is made by Foot (2001, 97–8) and Wiggins (1995, 226–229), whom Foot also cites (97).

[23] This is Wilkes's (1980, 356) formulation, and as she observes, while having the advantage of being blunt, the formulation will mislead if the terms are taken to carry their familiar connotations, i.e., that morality and prudence (happiness) are distinct sources of normative concern.

[24] Again, the term "life plan" is from Wilkes (41). For recent development of a comparable style of proposal, see Vogt 2017a, chs. 5 and 6.

their dealings with others, and helping where they can. Virtue just is exceling at thinking about and actualizing what is really in one's interest, and that includes the canonical virtues.

Needless to say, the proposal has countless detractors, and describing it as a form of "egoism" is usually taken to be enough to reject it out of hand.[25] Insofar as the ground of moral reasons is self-concern, the proposal is thought to miss the point of moral normativity. We are not told we *ought* to act as morality requires, the objection runs, only that we *want* to (or would want to if only we understood our own happiness in an adequate way).[26] This begs the question about the nature or ground of practical reasons, but I myself accept that we have reasons to do things independently of agent-relative considerations. As I will argue below, the reasons we have to be fair and generous with others can be quite independent of our own good. This is my principal reason for rejecting the proposal.

Even so, and even as it seems too hopeful to suppose that there is no scope for conflict between concern for others and the good for oneself, the proposal holds out the promise of an account of the good for human beings that is more adequate, let's say, to the perspective a parent takes on their child in hoping (for their sake) that they will build their life around what is decent and honorable. It tells us that ethical virtue equips human beings to live the life that is most satisfying to us because it aligns with our flourishing true and properly speaking. If this is not a piece of wishful thinking, we need an account of what is really good for us, and we need to be brought to understand how something like justice or fairness of mind is good for someone in a way that makes contact with prephilosophical ideas about this (i.e. with platitudes about what promotes or contributes to a person's well-being). I return to these issues below.

SECTION 2: VIRTUOUS ACTION, VIRTUOUS PEOPLE, AND THE GOOD FOR HUMAN BEINGS

I have been discussing familiar ways of defining and relating basic concepts in ethics. According to one family of views, there is a basic duality between the moral and the nonmoral good, or the right and the good, or morality and prudence. According to another, there is a fundamental unity between what are apparently different forms of the good: being good and being well, or virtue and happiness. As I said earlier, the terms we use for these categories seem to make a difference. For example, it makes a difference whether the form of the good for human beings that centrally concerns us in ethics is "happiness"

---

[25] To my mind Williams (1985, ch. 3) and Vogt (2017a, ch. 6) offer thoughtful responses to charges of egoism.

[26] See Prichard 1912, 23, which McDowell refers to at 1980, 368.

or "living well" and equally "benefit," for these terms set us on different tracks. I share Foot's sense that the right concept in this area is the good for human beings understood as the beneficial, and I will shift to this vocabulary for the remainder of the essay. Equally, it makes a difference whether we talk of "morality" or "virtue." Arguably the former finds its home in a dualistic framework, the latter in a unified one. Since I will defend some form of ethical monism, I will use the vocabulary of virtue, and because I think they admit of different treatments, I will distinguish between virtuous *action* and virtuous *people*.

To anticipate my positive proposal, I am setting aside the view that morality is foundationally independent of happiness, or to put it another way, that the right is foundationally independent of the good. Against proposals that are in one way or another basically dualistic, my view is that the good is the ground of practical reason, though the good that is in question is not happiness understood in subjectivist terms (desire satisfaction). The *good for human beings*, understood in terms of the *beneficial*, is the foundational notion on my view, and it is something I propose to theorize in a realist way. The concepts of *virtuous action*, and of *being a virtuous person*, importantly distinguishable dimensions of virtue to which my account also refers, make essential reference to it. I argue (a) that virtuous *actions* are such because and insofar as they successfully protect, preserve, secure, or promote the good for human beings, and (b) that being appropriately responsive to the good for human beings is (at least part of) what it is to be a virtuous *person*, where this form of responsiveness can itself be shown to be good for the one who is so. While my proposal has more in common with the monists of Section 1.4, I depart sharply from the monistic proposals considered there. I am not working with a conception of the good for human beings that is simply defined in terms of virtue, and neither am I accepting that our reasons to be virtuous are always agent-relative. I am also making room for the possibility of conflict between self- and other-concern. I begin with my approach to the good for human beings, before drawing out the connections to virtuous actions, and virtuous people. Since I offer a realist account of the good for human beings, I start with a discussion of realism.[27]

2.1. The Good for human beings.

I am making *good* understood as *good for* foundational in ethics. This is one strategy (among others) taken by moral realists who feel called to deliver realism from its

---

[27] My proposal is one way of developing a schema for the relationship between virtue and the beneficial that is defended by Philippa Foot (2001) who acknowledges Elizabeth Anscombe (1969) for the core idea. The schema is that virtues are ways of doing and being that are necessary because and insofar as some human good hangs on them. In Anscombe's example, keeping our promises is a virtue because human beings need to bind one another by word and not force in the cooperative activities that are given to us as dependent, social beings (1969, 18). In Foot's example, beneficence is a virtue because every one of us needs help in facing the losses and difficulties that are inevitable for us (108). I am not developing this schema in light of Foot's and Michael Thompson's (2008) larger apparatus of natural normativity, even as, as I will make clear, I share key points of emphasis. The proposal is also comparable to Judy Thomson's (1997) account of the right and the good in making *good for* the primary

reputation for extravagance and dogmatism. Peter Railton long ago urged that the notion of the good for a person holds out the promise of explaining how values can be objective without being "cosmic": they are a function of "nothing more transcendental" than facts about the physical and psychological constitution of human beings and their contingent circumstances in the world.[28] To reach for another idiom, according to this view, "normativity is a problem" for human beings because things can go better or worse for us, and how we live, our forms of affiliation, the activities we engage in, the choices we make, can affect this.[29] This is realism understood *relationally*: a realism about the good for human beings. So how do realists propose to deliver on their promise of objective relational value? Let's consider some contemporary-classic realist proposals.

Take the account due to Railton. Railton is concerned with what is good for a person in the sense that it puts them in a *better* state than the one they were in.[30] Importantly, Railton's target is what he calls the "*non-moral* good for a person." By the designation "non-moral" Railton means to allow, in the spirit of *normative constraint* above (cf. Section 1.2), that something could be good for a person but morally bad, and I will come back to this shortly. But the point of the designation is also to signal that Railton's sights are set on an uncontentious notion of well-being, one in which ideas of physical and psychic health are at home. And this seems natural given his relational realist aspirations. We are more sanguine about the prospects for an objective account of biological benefit and harm.[31]

Railton's substantive proposal makes use of the perspective of an ideal cognitive, imaginative, and deliberative version of a person on their ordinary self. Which considerations would a person's ideal self take into account in issuing sage advice about what would promote their good in the situation in which they find ourselves? Railton's proposal is that those facts, whatever they are, are what make it true that following the advice of their ideal self is good for them. For something, X, to be good for a person, S, is for there to be a complex, relational set of facts about X and S and their interaction in

---

notion; in conceiving of the right in terms of virtue; and in making virtuous actions metaphysically prior to virtuous people. A comparable proposal to the one articulated here is independently put forward as an interpretation of Aristotle's axiology by Sukaina Hirji (ms). Hirji emphasizes Aristotle's distinction between virtuous action and acting as a virtuous person does, arguing that the source of the value is different in each case. She defends an instrumental reading of the value of virtuous actions, and a constitutive reading of the value of acting virtuously. The notion of needs is also central to her account of the human good.

[28] Railton, 986, 201. I would not construe the point in such a way as to suggest that ethical questions are simply empirical. As the discussion in Section 1 is intended to bring out, ethical questions are also importantly conceptual. I am grateful to Richard Kraut for prompting me to make this clarification.

[29] That (and how) normativity is a problem for us are formulations due to Korsgaard 1996. Talk of "the problem of normativity" is likely to introduce the thought that there is an open question whether we have reason to care about what is good for us. I hope to present a view that makes that question seem undermotivated. But the issues require more care than I can give them here. Thanks to Sarah Buss for raising this issue.

[30] As he makes clear, we could investigate, equally, whether doing *this* would be better for the person than doing *that*, or we could investigate not merely what would on balance improve a person's state or condition, but what would be best for them overall. Railton discusses these related distinctions at 176.

[31] Cf. Whiting 1988, 40.

virtue of which S's ideal self, S+, would want X for S. Railton illustrates with the example of a person who is dehydrated and because of that in a state of malaise. Their ideal Self would be able to recommend drinking fluids of a certain kind. This is so because there are facts about the sick person's constitution and the properties of the liquid, and their interaction, as well as facts about the interaction between states of dehydration and psychic distress, that explain why the ideal Self would recommend the drink.

The account raises a number of questions and is much discussed. But what I want to draw attention to here is that Railton gives an account of the good for an *individual* person, and moreover, the good for an individual person *at some particular time*. This is striking because it is not what medical or psychological researchers take as their "primary relatum" when they study physical and psychological health.[32] The question is what is the standard relative to which we evaluate an individual's well-being. In medicine the standard is the human body (psyche) in the first place, and particular conditions, or conditions at particular times, as ways the human body (psyche) can go. Given our understanding of the human heart, we study the effects of high cholesterol, and among those with high cholesterol, we look at people who smoke a pack a day. We understand benefits and harms to individuals in light of our understanding of human biology, and it is hard to imagine a study of the one in the absence of the other. Naturally, there is variation in what is healthy for people. Some people cannot process lactose. Others cannot produce enough insulin. What counts as a healthy meal will be accordingly different for the one and for the other. There is predictable and explicable variation among us, but if someone said that drinking a gallon of diesel a day put them in optimal health, we would be rightly skeptical. The field of medicine is not reduced to particular truths about what is healthy for this individual and that one at certain times. Rather, there are truths about human health that hold within a certain range. This gives us a field of study, medicine, in which there are, to be sure, no perfectly universal truths, but stable generalities.

These considerations lead me to think that the primary relatum in accounts of the good for a person is *human beings* (and only secondarily *individuals*). It matters that the S in Railton's account is a person (and not a horse, or a God, or a frog).[33] We want to understand what is good for S in all their particularity, but supposing, with Railton, we are interested in an uncontentious notion of benefit and harm, where that at least includes biological and psychic health, we do not get far in our thinking about individuals without a theory of what is beneficial for *human beings*.[34]

---

[32] Here, and below, I am taking the term "primary relatum" from Vogt 2017a, 93. My discussion is also indebted to her account of the nature of the subject matter of ethics in which there are general truths that hold for the most part. See 2017a, ch. 5.

[33] See Vogt's (2017a, 92) discussion of Aristotle (*NE* 1141a22-28) on the good for human beings and the good for fish.

[34] More would need to be said in full defense of the view that philosophy should seek a theory of the *human* good. Why not say, with hedonists, that what is needed is a theory of the good for all conscious living beings? Why not say that the human good is too coarse grained to be of much use given differences among individuals? For discussion of related questions, see Vogt 2017a, ch. 4.

So, consider an account that makes human beings the primary relatum. Take Bernard Williams' (lesser known) discussion of "real interests."[35] Like Railton, Williams is interested in a realist account of what it is for a person to be better off as the result of a change. But unlike Railton, the account that interests Williams takes human-level well-being as primary and understands the well-being of individual people in light of it. To bring out the contrast, Railton allows that an individual could be constituted in such a way that they have heinous (or presumably bizarre or self-destructive) commitments and values which no amount of information or imaginative-cum-cognitive expansion on the part of their ideal Self would alter, meaning that what we would find unappetizing (to say the least) would count as a constituent of their good.[36] Williams, on the other hand, is supposing that human beings are set up in such a way, motivationally and otherwise, that we would not be prepared to accept that facilitating certain kinds of commitment is in a person's *real interest*. (Compare drinking the gallon of diesel.)[37]

To illustrate, Williams offers an example of a self-destructive commitment. A young person who is depressed but otherwise healthy does not wish to live. A guardian who takes measures to keep the young person alive, seeking out therapy and so on, can be thought to act in their real interest, and if the guardian is right, we can expect the young person to acknowledge this down the line. For the young person to be better off as a result of these changes, they should reasonably be expected to acknowledge that the changes have helped. But, importantly, for the acknowledgment to indicate a genuine improvement (and to be more than evidence of brainwashing, or browbeating, or whatever), it must be that what *explains* their sense that things are better now is that something was impeding their psychic health which people who are functioning well reasonably acknowledge to be important for their psychic health. As I will formulate his proposal, a person, S, is objectively better off as the result of a change, X, if X ameliorates a symptom that was impeding S's effective functioning as a human being, and S can reasonably be expected to acknowledge X as a cure for this reason.

In a clear sense, Williams is not offering a full account of what it is for someone to be in a better state than the one they were in—that is, of improvement. For we can be made better off, not just through the mitigation of symptoms that were holding us back, but, more positively, through whatever enhances or amplifies our state or condition. Can the account be extended to accommodate more positive improvements, so that human beings are made better, not merely through the mitigation of impediments to human functioning but, more positively, the excellent expression of them? That is of course to court a familiar form of perfectionism about the human good. Like Williams's own proposal, it appeals to a notion of human functioning that is arguably more contentious

---

[35] Williams 1986, ch. 3. I say discussion because Williams is engaging with Aristotelian ideas about the good for human beings that he is sympathetic to even as he expresses ambivalence and only equivocal support.

[36] Railton 1986, 177, n. 20.

[37] Sharon Street's (2009) argument that figures like the one Railton has in mind are not human beings as we know them, but alien creatures, is very much to the point here.

than the notion of improvement that it was brought in to explain. Williams was himself famously leery about the prospects of providing a full account of human functioning, and he gives the proposal only equivocal support for this reason.

But perhaps a full account of human functioning is not needed to get going. In broaching the question of what is in our real interests, Williams targets the notion of *need* in particular: the dimension of our good that is such that, when unmet, things go awry for us. And this notion, even unanalyzed, is arguably precisely the place to begin. The question of what is good for human beings is an ambitious one. It can be answered in one of several theoretical keys, and one wants a full picture. But to get going, perhaps we do well to make use of a modest notion of *starting points*. At several junctures in the *Nicomachean Ethics*, Aristotle announces that he is addressing people who are in possession of relevant starting points.[38] These are people who, through ordinary observational and inferential powers, and through the typical course of upbringing, grasp *that something is so*, and in grasping this they are prepared to understand the matter in a more theoretical way. So, consider some starting points about the good for human beings.[39] Human beings need to receive love as children; to acquire language; to grow physically; to make use of our sensory capacities.[40] The key term here is *need*, for the relevant starting points concern practices, forms of development, response, and activity that are necessary for a human life—necessary in the sense that without them things go badly for us. While some things are good and bad for people in light of their particularities as individuals—this person is allergic to nuts, that one has a pronounced aversion to crowds—these platitudes are offered as fixed points about what is good and bad for human beings as such.[41] To the extent they are offered as starting points, the suggestion is that they admit of more substantial study, including investigation of how what I am calling "fixed points" are shaped and made determinate in the life of any one of us. But the suggestion is that the starting points constrain the development of more substantive accounts. We have reason to reject a theory of the good for human beings that denies that, as dependent social beings, mutual reliance, community, and forms of intimacy are good for us.

So far, I have briefly considered some realist treatments of the good for human beings. I have made the modest suggestion that we proceed with the notion of *human needs* understood in a provisional way. Now I turn to consider how the concepts of *virtuous*

---

[38] *NE* 1095b5-1095b14; 1098b1-10.

[39] Here I am employing Aristotle's notion of a starting point, but I focus on different kinds of case. At *NE* III. 1 Aristotle clearly has in mind starting points that we would classify as moral principles, e.g., that causing needless harm is bad, or that matricide is wrong.

[40] I draw these from Richard Kraut (2007, 138). When Anscombe says that human beings need to be able to bind one another by their word she is appealing to a starting point about the beneficial. When Foot says that human beings need acts of kindness when misfortune strikes, she is making a similar appeal. The starting point is that human beings need to rely on one another, and that we need supportive forms of community.

[41] In Whiting's (1988, 36) terminology, they are unconditional rather than conditional goods for human beings. Whiting refers to discussion by Cooper 1980, 317.

action and of *being a virtuous person* bear on this way of thinking about the good for human beings. Among other things, I hope to demonstrate how even an uncontentious notion of need can be used to show that being responsive to ethical considerations is itself a constituent of the good for human beings.

2.2. Virtuous action.

In contrast to intuitive realists like H. A. Prichard, for whom that we ought to perform some action (keeping a promise, paying a debt) is an underivative fact, I am taking the position that ethically suitable or virtuous action is made suitable or virtuous by the fact that it protects, facilitates, produces, or realizes some good.[42] In this way, I am endorsing a form of value fundamentalism. I am taking the view that ethically virtuous actions are made virtuous by the independently valuable ends they realize, so that what matters is not the *motivation* of the person performing the action, but the (actual or potential) protection, honoring, acknowledgement, or realization of something of value.[43] The value in question is paradigmatically goods in the social community.[44] For beneficent action and species thereof (kindness, compassion, practical love, generosity), an action is made good by (actually or potentially) doing something that benefits another. A room is offered to stave off the night; a community garden is planted so that neighbors have independent sources of food; the distraught are comforted so that they can face what is next; the students are instructed so that they can learn to think for themselves. The goods that are appealed to here are basic human goods—they answer to human needs.

The schema for what are often referred to as the "reliance virtues" (justice, promising, paying debts) is less straightforward insofar as we think that bullies should be opposed even when no one stands to gain. Or take the person, in the stock example, who refuses the mob's offer to kill the one to save three more from being killed. Though fewer are benefited, the person is right not to kill, and in that case, we cannot say that the just action is "on balance" good for people.[45] There are a range of familiar responses here, and my own inclination is to make the familiar point that some actions are assessed in terms

---

[42] Or could have done so. The failed rescue mission is still commendable. It is commendable because there was a live possibility that it could have helped.

[43] I agree with Prichard, at least, that we need some notion of right action that is independent of motivation (hence Prichard's distinction between right action and moral goodness). Thomson takes a similar line, defending, in her terminology, an objectivist (success based) rather than subjectivist (motivation based) account of virtuous action. I fully agree with Thomson that a person's *motivation* does not settle whether they performed a virtuous *action*. But I would allow that an action that does not succeed in realizing some good, but that could have done so, as in a failed rescue mission, can still be commendable. Thomson may deny this (1997, 281). Distinguishing virtuous action and actions done virtuously is central to Hiriji's (ms) account.

[44] The form of value fundamentalism that I am defending is humanistic insofar as it looks in the first place to human life and its quality. Ultimately, I think the account should be extended to the quality of life more generally. But that is a more ambitious project, and I rest content with a more modest focus on humanity here. I am here following Raz 1986, 194.

[45] The example is Thomson's (1997, 282).

of standards that are internal to a practice, where the practice finds its point because it protects some good. A just action does not itself discretely contribute to what is on balance good, but it is a constituent of a beneficial practice. For something to constitute a practice is for us to be committed to adhering to it in a way that is not easily revocable (for what is easily revoked does not constitute a practice). The good the practice protects plausibly has a privileged status because it is a condition for the possibility of the forms of affiliation and community without which we cannot secure the goods that are essential to us. I would not construe this point in such a way that there are *no* circumstances in which a person should break a promise or tell a lie or kill someone. It is for the most part the case that we should not do these things, but given sufficiently specific features of a given case, I leave it open that doing these things could be the better choice.[46]

The proposed schema is that ethically virtuous actions are good because they honor, acknowledge, protect, facilitate, produce, or realize a good for human beings. In other words, virtuous actions are (in one way or another) *instrumentally valuable*. By the lights of some traditions, i.e., the tradition in which virtue (or better, morality) is the expression of a superlative form of worth that is independent of being good for anything, this will be a great scandal. I only have this to say in defense. Instrumental value is not here the degraded category that figures in a Kantian view on which something can be "instrumentally valuable" even when it conduces to something worthless or bad. I am taking the view that if something is instrumentally valuable then it is *valuable*: it conduces to something worthwhile. I have not said anything about the status of the goods that are brought about or secured by virtuous actions—whether they are themselves constituents or necessary conditions for other things that constitute the human good. Some may be both. Plausibly they are (at least) conditions for the pursuit of higher things. They make it possible for us to engage in projects and endeavors that are noninstrumentally good for us.[47] While it will not satisfy the Kantian, I am rejecting the idea that insofar as they are instrumentally valuable, virtuous actions are a lowly form of "mere" usefulness. By my lights, that is vastly to undervalue the very conditions for human flourishing.

2.3. Being virtuous.

A virtuous action can be performed for any reason whatever. It can be performed in ignorance, and under compulsion or constraint. It can be accompanied by sundry thoughts and feelings. What is key is that it (actually or potentially) honors,

---

[46] I am offering no more than a schema in this well-trodden domain. My approach is broadly in line with Thomson's (1997) approach (even as I am not taking her dispositionalist treatment of the reliance virtues at 282). It is also in the spirit of Williams's (1973) discussions of Jim and the protesters. Williams discredits consequentialist thinking about what we should be doing. But he leaves open whether there might be situations with features that are such that it is in fact better to kill one person in order to save several others. The approach is also in the spirit of some of Foot's points of emphasis about promising (2001, 11; 47–51). Thanks to Aaron Abma and Katja Vogt for discussion of some of these positions.

[47] I defend a valuing based account of the human good along these lines in Theunissen 2020, ch. 4.

acknowledges, protects, facilitates, or realizes the good for human beings. Matters are different with good or virtuous *people*. An ethically virtuous person certainly performs virtuous actions. But they perform them with an appropriate cognitive, affective, and motivational orientation. They choose to perform the actions willingly, and with pleasure. They also understand what they are doing and why it matters. Of the range of practically relevant, value-based considerations that bear on a given situation, they know how to select the one that is suitable. They understand which goods are important relative to the features of a situation, and how to achieve them.[48] While I will not argue for it here, I doubt that there is a way of specifying which of a range of practically relevant considerations are decisively relevant in a situation-independent way. What is central to my argument is that the virtuous person is not in some fundamental way responsive to their *own* good (contrast 1.4.2). Of course, virtuous action *may* concern the good for oneself. Prudence is a word for beneficence that is self-directed, and in some situations, it is true that what one should do is take measures to have enough to eat. Temperance is a word for prudent action where appetitive pleasure has to do, and in some situations, it is true that what is decisive is not to have so much wine that one cannot show up for work. Courage is self-directed when it serves prudence where there is fear about doing what is for one's good, and in some situations the suitable action is going through with the root canal. But the important point is that a virtuous person may be perfectly (and independently) responsive to agent-neutral concerns: to making sure *others* have enough to eat, to supporting *their* resolve to drink moderately, to accompanying *them* to the root canal.

When Prichard decried value-based explanations of right action, he said that the fact that something is good does not show that it ought to be brought about. To show this, we would need to suppose that what is good ought to be. And this, he urged, is preposterous.[49] It is interesting that Prichard does not make use of the now ubiquitous notion of a normative reason. Put in the language of reasons, Prichard's claim is that the good is not reason giving—such that it licenses, or makes appropriate, particular forms of response. On the view I am defending, this is quite false. The good is practically relevant—it gives us reasons (at least) to acknowledge, protect, secure, and promote—and the good in question may be personal or impersonal. In contrast to the proposal described in 1.4.2 above (*happiness is virtue*), I am not supposing that the good of others is action guiding on the condition that it relevantly relates to the good for oneself, something whose motivational force is guaranteed. I am suggesting that we can be directly motivated to uphold or facilitate what is good for others. There is no mystery here because, as the point has long been made, intentional action standardly involves beliefs about things as being good.[50]

I have been working with a provisional and uncontentious notion of the good for human beings, appealing to human needs in my discussion of virtuous action and virtuous people. Virtuous actions find their point in meeting human needs, and virtuous

---

[48] I am avowedly appealing to Aristotle's discussion of what being virtuous adds to virtuous action from *NE* Bk. II. 4.

[49] Prichard 1912, 24.

[50] See Nagel's (1970) seminal discussion of reasons and desire. The position is defended by many, including Raz 1999, ch. 2, and Foot (2001).

people choose to perform virtuous actions out of an appreciation of the good they protect, acknowledge, uphold, or facilitate, and why it matters. I have argued that the good to which the virtuous person is responsive may be perfectly impersonal so that the ground of other concern is not the good for oneself. While I am breaking with the classical view that all action is undertaken for the sake of the agent's own good, I also do not wish to overstate the controversy. For I find it plausible to suppose that responding appropriately to the good of others can *itself* be good for the person who does so. While the monists who contend that *virtue is happiness* reach this conclusion by stipulation (see 1.4.1 above), introducing a revisionist conception of the good for human beings (of benefit, advantage, living well, happiness, etc.), I think we can be brought to the same conclusion without revision. And this is what I now look into.

The claim that being virtuous is itself a constituent of the good for human beings is traditionally supported through a function argument. If an X *qua* X has as its function or characteristic activity to φ, then the good of an X *qua* X (its flourishing as an X) consists in φ-ing well (with excellence or virtue).[51] So if it is characteristic of human beings to engage in rational activity, and if a dimension of rationality is appropriate responsiveness to the good for human beings, then doing so is constitutively good for us. Hence, being good and being well are actually inseparable. This is a venerable form of argument, but it is also a fraught one. We need a reason to accept that human beings have a function or characteristic activity, and it would help if the reason did not depend on accepting a full-blown teleological theory. But even if it is permitted that human beings have a function, and permitted that our function involves (at least) the exercise of practical reason, we also need to rule out a rival conception of practical rationality as the advancement of one's ends whatever they may be. For on that way of thinking about practical reason, it is unclear how it aligns with the other-regarding virtues.[52] In fact, I think defenders of the function argument have a lot to say here.[53] But for my purposes, what is wanted is to bear out the argument in light of what we know of ourselves and one another. That is to say, we need to see how appropriate responsiveness to the good for others is good for us in light of *starting points* about the human good.[54] So let me offer an example. It is an example that is meant to show how the motivational and affective orientation of a person who is genuinely concerned for the good of others is itself a dimension of their good.

Think of the friend or family member who habitually gets in touch when they need something and not otherwise. Perhaps they lack support in their life and things are hard. They make routine inquiries about one's health and happiness, but one knows from the *way* they ask, or from experience over time, that the interest is insincere. They know enough about the outward form of relationships to make a show of concern, but they do

---

[51] There is, of course, more than one function argument. Plato gives one in Bk. 1 of the *Republic*; Aristotle in *NE* 1. 7. I take the present formulation of Aristotle's argument from Barney 2008, 311.

[52] See Whiting 1988, 41–43.

[53] I find Barney's treatment especially compelling. She reconstructs and motivates Aristotle's argument independently of the broader teleology.

[54] I am here following Kraut (2018, 6–11).

so, narrowly, with a view to gain. It is natural to wish that this sort of person would *really* take an interest. Why is that? Certainly, being genuinely interested in others would make them better as people. No doubt, being better in this way would make the relationship better *for us*. But my sense is that, particularly when we care about the person in question, we wish they would really take an interest because it would be better *for them*. To be without the motivations and forms of affection that mark genuine concern is to be deprived of the real pleasure of intimacy or friendship itself—its *inner* dimension. If that is right, having the underlying attitudes and feelings of a fair-minded person is good for the one who is so because it is part of what constitutes a good (friendship or intimacy) whose status as beneficial can be understood in prephilosophical ways. If the point generalizes to the other dimensions of virtue, we are brought to see how being good is itself part of the good for human beings.[55]

I spoke earlier of an ethical conception of happiness, a conception on which there is an important and trivial connection between virtue and the good for human beings. If we are to think of happiness ethically, it is no good to stipulate that being good is being well, so that the topic of the good for human beings loses its intuitive connection with what promotes our life, and with what gives rise to joy. But I hope to have shown how we can think of ethical virtue as equipping human beings to live a life that is satisfying for us because genuine forms of other concern are a constituent of things we can intuitively recognize as part of our good, namely, friendship and other forms of intimate connection. All the same, I do not wish to overstate. Being responsive to ethical concerns can itself be a constituent of our good, but it can also come at the cost of other dimensions of our good. There are difficult and tragic choices. We may be in circumstances that are such that we cannot respond adequately to the good for others without making a great and even an ultimate sacrifice.[56] In this, Kant was right to allow the possibility of conflict between being good and being well.

Conclusion

Against those who contend that there is a basic duality between the moral and the moral good, or the right and the good, I have sought to articulate a form of realism that works with a unified or integrated conception of the good in which virtue and the beneficial are the key concepts, and in which the "moral good" is not foundationally distinctive, but explicable in terms of the good for human beings. I have suggested that we make headway in thinking realistically about the human good, broaching what Bernard Williams has called a notion of "real interests," by thinking about human needs. I argued

---

[55] I draw this example from Theunissen (2023). Of course, this conclusion is supported variously by many others. Cf., for example, insightful discussion by Bloomfield 2014.

[56] In the words of Philippa Foot, "there is indeed a kind of happiness that only goodness can achieve, but [...] by one of the evil chances of life it may be out of the reach of even the best of men" (2001, 97).

(a) that virtuous *actions* are such because and insofar as they (actually or potentially) protect, acknowledge, preserve, secure, or promote the good for human beings in this sense, and (b) that being appropriately responsive to the good for human beings is (at least part of) what it is to be a virtuous *person*, where this form of responsiveness can itself be shown to be good for the one who is so.[57]

References

Anscombe, G. E. M. 1958. "Modern Moral Philosophy." *Philosophy* 33(124): 1–19.

Anscombe, G. E. M. 1969. "On Promising and Its Justice." *Critica* 3 (7–8): 61–83.

Aristotle. 2011. *Nicomachean Ethics*. Translation, introduction, and commentary by Sarah Broadie and Christopher Rowe. Oxford: Oxford University Press. [Cited by book, chapter, and Bekker number.]

Barney, Rachel. 2008. "Aristotle's Argument for a Human Function." *Oxford Studies in Ancient Philosophy* 34: 293-322.

Bloomfield, Paul. 2014. *The Virtues of Human Happiness: A Theory of the Good Life*. Oxford: Oxford University Press.

Cooper, John. 1980. "Aristotle on Friendship." In *Essays on Aristotle's Ethics*, edited by Amelie Oksenberg Rorty, 301–340. Berkeley: University of California Press.

Korsgaard, Christine. 1983. "The Two Distinctions in Goodness." *Philosophical Review* 92(2): 169–195.

Korsgaard Christine. 1996. *The Sources of Normativity*. Cambridge: Cambridge University Press.

Darwall, Stephen, Allan Gibbard, and Peter Railton. 1992. "Toward *Fin de Siecle* Ethics: Some Trends." *Philosophical Review* 101(1): 115–189.

Darwall, Stephen. 2012. "Grotius at the Creation of Modern Moral Philosophy." *Archiv für Geschichte der Philosophie* 94(3): 296–325.

Foot, Philippa. 2001. *Natural Goodness*. Oxford: Oxford University Press.

Hirji, Sukaina. Manuscript. "How Virtue Is a Means to Contemplation."

Kagan, Shelly. 1989. *The Limits of Morality*. Oxford: Clarendon Press.

Kant, Immanuel. 1900–. *Kants gesammelte Schriften*. 24 vols. Edited by Königlich Preussische Akademie der Wissenschaften zu Berlin, Deutschen Akademie der Wissenschaften zu Berlin, and Akademie der Wissenschaften zu Göttingen. Berlin: De Gruyter.

Kant, Immanuel. 1996. *The Critique of Practical Reason*. In *Practical Philosophy*, translated and edited by Mary J. Gregor. Cambridge: Cambridge University Press. [Cited by volume and page of the Akademie edition.]

Kraut, Richard. 2007. *What Is Good and Why*. Cambridge: Cambridge University Press.

Kraut, Richard. 2018. *The Quality of Life: Aristotle Revisited*. Oxford: Oxford University Press.

---

[57] I am most grateful to the editors of this volume for their helpful feedback and, above all, their patience. I have learned from conversations with Japa Pallikkathayil and Michael Thompson. I am very grateful to Aaron Abma, Robert Audi, Sarah Buss, Rajiv Hurhangee, Richard Kraut, and Katja Vogt for written comments that improved the paper and prompted clarifications including, but by no means only, in the places where they are acknowledged in the notes.

McDowell, John. 1980. "The Role of Eudaimonia in Aristotle's Ethics." In *Essays on Aristotle's Ethics*, edited by Amelie Oksenberg Rorty, 359–376. Berkeley: University of California Press.

Murdoch, Iris. 1957. "Vision and Choice in Morality." *Proceedings of the Aristotelian Society, Supplementary Volumes* 30: 14–58.

Nagel, Thomas. 1970. *The Possibility of Altruism*. Princeton: Princeton University Press.

Prichard, H. A. 1912. "Does Moral Philosophy Rest on a Mistake?" *Mind* 21(81): 21–37.

Railton, Peter. 1986. "Moral Realism." *Philosophical Review* 95(2): 163–207.

Rawls, John. 1999. *A Theory of Justice*. Rev. ed. Cambridge, MA: Harvard University Press.

Rawls, John. 2000. *Lectures on the History of Moral Philosophy*. Edited by Barbara Herman. Cambridge MA: Harvard University Press.

Raz, Joseph. 1986. *The Morality of Freedom*. Oxford: Clarendon Press.

Raz, Joseph. 1999. "Agency, Reason, and the Good." In *Engaging Reason: On the Theory of Value and Action*, 22–45. Oxford: Oxford University Press.

Ross, W. D. 1930. *The Right and the Good*. Edited by Philip Stratton-Lake. Oxford: Clarendon Press.

Street, Sharon. 2009 "In Defense of Future Tuesday Indifference: Ideally Coherent Eccentrics and the Contingency of What Matters." *Philosophical Issues* 19: 273–298.

Theunissen, L. Nandi. 2020. *The Value of Humanity*. Oxford: Oxford University Press.

Theunissen, L. Nandi. 2023. "Explaining the Value of Human Beings." In *Rethinking the Value of Humanity*, edited by Sarah Buss and Nandi Theunissen, 225–247. Oxford: Oxford University Press.

Thompson, Michael. 2008. *Life and Action: Elementary Structures of Practice and Practical Thought*. Cambridge MA: Harvard University Press.

Thomson, Judith Jarvis. 1997. "The Right and the Good." *Journal of Philosophy* 94(6): 273–298.

Vogt, Katja Maria. 2017a. *Desiring the Good: Ancient Proposals and Contemporary Theory*. Oxford: Oxford University Press.

Vogt, Katja Maria. 2017b. "The Stoics on Virtue and Happiness." In *Cambridge Companion to Ancient Ethics*, edited by Chris Bobonich, 183–199. Cambridge: Cambridge University Press.

Wiggins, David. 1995. "Eudaimonism and Realism in Aristotle's Ethics: A Reply to John McDowell." In *Aristotle and Moral Realism*, edited by Robert Heinaman, 219–231. London: UCL Press.

Wilkes, Kathleen. 1980. "The Good Man and the Good for Man." In *Essays on Aristotle's Ethics*, edited by Amelie Oksenberg Rorty, 359–376. Berkeley: University of California Press.

Williams, Bernard. 1973. "A Critique of Utilitarianism." In *Utilitarianism For and Against*, 77–150. Cambridge: Cambridge University Press.

Williams, Bernard. 1986. *Ethics and the Limits of Philosophy*. London: Fontana.

Whiting, Jennifer. 1988. "Aristotle's Function Argument: A Defense," *Ancient Philosophy* 8 (1): 33–48.

III

NON-NATURALISM

CHAPTER 15

MORAL CONCEPTUAL TRUTHS

JOHN BENGSON, TERENCE CUNEO, AND RUSS SHAFER-LANDAU

ALL versions of moral realism include a commitment to objective moral truths. Realists have offered a variety of conceptions of such truths and their truth-makers. Here we advance a relatively unexplored option for moral realism, arguing that a set of substantive moral propositions qualify as conceptual truths: their truth-makers are the essences of their constituent concepts. Although this claim is in one respect ecumenical—strictly available to both naturalists and nonnaturalists alike—we believe it is a key element in a powerful form of nonnaturalism.[1]

While a number of moral philosophers have floated the idea that some moral propositions are conceptual truths,[2] few have advanced anything like the position we'll develop. Our discussion has four distinctive features. First, whereas others have suggested that one or another abstract moral proposition is a conceptual truth, our project encompasses concrete moral claims regarding the moral status of richly intentional actions, specific character traits, and the like. Second, our defense of this position is backed by a systematic account of what it is to be a conceptual truth. Third, this account adverts to essences, rather than linguistic, semantic, psychological, or epistemic phenomena. Fourth, our defense is notable not only because it enables realism to address unanswered questions about the explanation of moral truths, but also because it supports a key premise in a new argument for moral realism.

1. THE MORAL FIXED POINTS

Our focus in this chapter is a range of moral platitudes or truisms that are central to ordinary moral life in at least two ways: for morally engaged agents, they can be invoked

---

[1] Developed more fully in Bengson, Cuneo, and Shafer-Landau (2024).
[2] Moore (1903, §89), Ewing (1939), Smith (1994, ch. 3, §9 and 185), Darwall (2006, 20, 27–8, and 94), Street (2009, 292 and 2016, 327), and Swinburne (2020).

in defense of their moral decisions in particular situations, and can inform decision-making and behavior in those situations. We call the relevant platitudes *moral fixed points* (or simply "fixed points"). Here are candidate examples of what we have in mind:

- It is (defeasibly) right to offer aid to those in deep distress.
- It is (defeasibly) right to protect one's children from lethal danger.
- It is (defeasibly) wrong to recreationally slaughter fellow persons.[3]
- Acting from prideful ignorance is bad.
- There is reason not to break a promise on which another is relying simply for convenience's sake.
- It is fitting to repay kindness with kindness.
- Justice is a virtue.

While there are important differences among these and other candidate fixed points—including the fact that they invoke a variety of moral and nonmoral considerations—let us highlight what they have in common.

First, they identify an entity's specific moral status, whether right or wrong, fitting or unfitting, virtuous or vicious, or the like. Each moral status comes with a valence, whether positive or negative. To reiterate, that status may be defeasible. For example, it may be that the fixed point is not that acting from prideful ignorance is bad, but rather that it is only defeasibly bad.[4]

Second, we'll understand fixed points to be conditional in their logical form. For instance, the logical form of the fixed point that it is required to protect one's children from lethal danger is: if an action is an instance of protecting one's children from lethal danger, then that action is required. Similarly, the logical form of the fixed point that justice is a virtue is: if a character trait is that of being just, then that trait is a virtue. And so on.

Third, fixed points are not contingent but metaphysically necessary, being true in every possible world.[5] So, while fixed points are platitudes, they are distinct from other sorts of moral maxims that might be thought of as platitudinous because they are broadly endorsed, widely relied upon, apparently obvious, or generally helpful. A claim's having features such as these is not enough to qualify it as a fixed point.

---

[3] By "right" we mean required; by "wrong" we mean prohibited. To be clear, these examples are meant to be instances of *moral* requirement, reason, virtue, etc. We omit the "moral" qualifier throughout.

[4] It is possible to qualify fixed points in other ways as well. For example, their application could be restricted in such a way that, although they are true in every possible world, they do not *apply* to certain beings in certain worlds (*cp.* Cuneo and Shafer-Landau 2014, §2). Such restrictions would protect against putative counterexamples involving bizarre scenarios. It might be alleged, for instance, that there is nothing wrong with recreational slaughter in worlds containing agents who spontaneously regenerate. We believe that in any such scenario, the action is defeasibly wrong, though we allow that there may be some cases in which its wrongness has been fully defeated. Those who disagree (or who wish to err on the side of caution) are invited to interpret the platitudes as being restricted in their application to beings like us in worlds like ours.

[5] We defend this claim in §5.1, below.

We will argue that fixed points are true fully in virtue of essence facts regarding their constituent concepts. This idea is the keystone to our view, defended below, that fixed points are conceptual truths.

2. The Essences of the Concepts in Fixed Points

We first elucidate the notion of essence before identifying two components of the idea, which we subsequently defend, that fixed points are true fully in virtue of essence facts regarding their constituent concepts.

2.1 Essence

The essence, or nature, of something is *what it is to be that thing*, or *what that thing is at its core*. Philosophers through the ages have found the notion of essence helpful, and recent theorizing in post-modal metaphysics and formal logic has shown it to be on firm footing. Essences are not spooky or ghostly auras that somehow attach to things, but are always given by reference to features (or sets of features) identified by "essential truths": true propositions that specify or state what it is to be a given entity.

There are essential truths about entities belonging to a wide variety of ontological categories (e.g., properties, material objects, mental states, concepts, numbers, and people). Possible examples of essential and nonessential truths Include:

Candidate Essential Truths	Nonessential Truths
Water is composed of hydrogen molecules.	Water is sold in plastic bottles.
Desire is directed at something.	Desire is a topic of Shakespeare's sonnets.
The concept SHELTER is satisfied by something only if it has a particular type of function.	The concept SHELTER is satisfied by some of Frank Lloyd Wright's favorite artifacts.
The property *being a triangle* is instantiated only by figures with exactly three interior angles.	The property *being a triangle* is instantiated by an image on the flag of the Bahamas.

Although none of these candidate essential truths purports to reveal the whole essence of its target, each plausibly registers at least one strand of the thing's essence. For example, what it is to be a desire is, at least in part, to be directed at something. Contrast being a topic of Shakespeare sonnets—that is not part of what it is to be a desire. As the examples above illustrate, we often have an easy time discerning essential truths and distinguishing them from nonessential ones. (We'll have more to say about the epistemology of essence in §3.)

Essential truths identify the essences of things without announcing that they are the essences of those things. There are also facts that explicitly register that the essence of some entity is such and such. An example is

[It belongs to the essence of water that it be composed of hydrogen molecules.]

Though distinguishing such 'essence facts' (as we'll call them) from their corresponding essential truths may seem overly fastidious, the difference between them proves to be philosophically significant, and will play an important role below.

Essence is distinctive in large part owing to its logical behavior. There are four logical principles that are particularly relevant for our purposes.[6]

First, essence has *modal force*: every essential truth is metaphysically necessary. That is, if it belongs to the essence of x that x is F, then, necessarily, x is F.[7]

Second, essence is *hyperintensional*: metaphysical necessity is insufficient for essentiality, which is not closed under intensional equivalence. The insufficiency clause says that it is not true that if, necessarily, x is F, then it thereby belongs to the essence of x that x is F. For example, as Aristotle observed, while it may be necessary that a human being is featherless, it is not part of the essence of a human being to be featherless: this is not what a human being is at its core. The second clause adds that even if it is essential to x that it is F, and x's being F is necessarily equivalent to x's being G, it needn't be essential to x that it is G. Developing Aristotle's example, although it may be that it is essential to a human being that it is rational, it is not essential to a human being that it is both rational and such that yellow is a color.

Third, essence is *noncontingent*: if it belongs to the essence of x that x is F, then, necessarily, it belongs to the essence of x that x is F. Put in the language of "worlds": necessarily, for any worlds w_1 and w_2, if x is essentially F at w_1, then x is essentially F at w_2. For example, if it belongs to the essence of a vase that it is a type of vessel, then a vase has that essence as a matter of necessity. It's not that a vase just happens to be, at its core, a type of vessel.

Fourth, essence is *non-transient*: necessarily, for any times t_1 and t_2, if x is essentially F at t_1, then x is essentially F at t_2. For instance, if gold essentially has atomic number 79, then gold has that essence at all times.

2.2 The Essentialist Thesis

Having explicated the category of fixed points and clarified the notion of essence, we can now state our main proposal:

---

[6] See Fine (1995) and Correia (2005, Appendix A) for further work on the logic of essence.
[7] Some may wish to add here (and perhaps in the other principles): "at every possible world where x exists." Some may also (or instead) wish to add a restriction to times.

Essentialist Thesis: Moral fixed points are essential truths with respect to the concepts that constitute their antecedents and are true fully in virtue of essence facts regarding those concepts.

We first discuss the claim that fixed points are essential truths with respect to their constituent concepts; we then turn to the additional claim that they are true fully in virtue of essence facts regarding their constituents. Our remarks in this section are not intended to offer defenses of these claims (we defend them below), but rather to clarify what they say.

Some fixed points include moral concepts in their antecedents, such as

1. <Justice is a virtue>.

As we see it, it is not an accidental feature of the concept JUSTICE that any character trait that falls under it also falls under the concept VIRTUE. Rather, it is essential to the concept JUSTICE that (when it concerns character traits) it is an aretaic concept with a positive moral valence. The idea is not that its being such a concept follows from its essence, but instead that this is part of its essence. Thus the claim is that the concept JUSTICE is essentially such that any character trait to which it applies must also fall under the concept VIRTUE. In this way 1 is like the proposition <Desire is directed at something>: they are each essential truths.

Similar claims hold for other fixed points, including those that contain only non-normative concepts in their antecedents. To illustrate, consider the fixed point

2. <It is wrong to recreationally slaughter fellow persons>.

The concept RECREATIONAL SLAUGHTER OF FELLOW PERSONS is itself non-normative; after all, this concept does not belong to any of the standard normative categories (viz., evaluative, deontic, favoring, fitting, or aretaic). At the same time, the concept RECREATIONAL SLAUGHTER OF FELLOW PERSONS is not accidentally related to the moral concept WRONG. What it is to be the concept RECREATIONAL SLAUGHTER OF FELLOW PERSONS is to be a concept that applies to an action only if that action also falls under a deontic concept with a negative moral valence.

By way of contrast, consider the claim that

3. <Leaving sharp knives unattended is wrong>.

This claim, though true in most cases, is no essential truth. The concept LEAVING SHARP KNIVES UNATTENDED is not essentially related to the moral concept WRONG, even if, as a matter of fact, we are ordinarily subject to a moral obligation to make sure that such dangerous objects are stored with care. The former concept is not essentially such as to apply to an action only if that action also falls under the latter. This marks an important difference between 3, on the one hand, and 1 and 2, on the other.

In the previous section we identified four logical principles governing essence. Our view that fixed points are essential truths fully accords with each. Take 2, for instance. On our view, this truth has modal force: necessarily, an action satisfies the former concept only if it also satisfies the latter.[8] At the same time, our view does not imply that all metaphysically necessary truths pertaining to the concept RECREATIONALLY SLAUGHTERING FELLOW PERSONS are essential truths, or that those truths can be swapped out for necessarily equivalent ones when registering the essence of this concept; accordingly, our position obeys hyperintensionality. Similarly, our position obeys intransience and non-contingency, which implies that RECREATIONALLY SLAUGHTERING FELLOW PERSONS has the essence that it does at all times and in all worlds. By respecting all four of the logical principles governing essence, the Essentialist Thesis shows itself to be highly disciplined.

So far we have focused on clarifying the claim that fixed points are essential truths with respect to the concepts in their antecedents. The Essentialist Thesis adds that they are true *fully in virtue of* essence facts regarding those concepts.

To illustrate, consider 1. We claim that it belongs to the essence of the concept JUSTICE that it is satisfied by a character trait only if that trait also falls under the concept VIRTUE. Because of this essence fact, 1 is true: that proposition is true fully in virtue of an essence fact regarding JUSTICE. Likewise for 2 and the other fixed points: they do not simply state truths regarding the essences of their constituent concepts, but are true fully in virtue of corresponding essence facts, which explicitly register the essences of those concepts. That is what the Essentialist Thesis asserts.[9]

2.3 The Theoretical Significance of the Essentialist Thesis

The Essentialist Thesis is theoretically important in several other ways as well. We will briefly mention two. First, it supports a key premise in a new style of argument for the thesis, central to moral realism, that there are moral truths. As we've seen (and will further defend in the next section), a range of non-normative concepts possess moral essences. Supposing, as is plausible, that at least some of those concepts are satisfied, it follows that the moral concepts in the essences of these non-normative concepts are satisfied as well. And so we achieve the conclusion that there are true moral propositions—just as moral realism says.[10]

Second, the Essentialist Thesis supports a key step in an explanation of a wide range of moral truths, including fixed points, that is friendly to realism, including its

---

[8] Recall our earlier caveat (from §1.1) that the relevant moral status may be defeasible. See also note 4.

[9] The *in virtue of* claim in the Essentialist Thesis may seem to follow naturally from the essentialist claim in that thesis. But we won't rely on this link when defending the *in virtue of* claim, for there is much to be learned from a different style of argument, which we develop in §5.

[10] This essence-based argument should not be confused with controversial Moorean arguments (as discussed by, e.g., McPherson 2009, Rowland 2012, Olson 2014, ch. 7, and Sampson 2023), which differ from ours in several respects: for example, Moorean arguments focus on claims that range well beyond conceptual truths, and do not concern themselves with the essences of concepts.

nonnaturalist incarnations. Realists are often perceived as skirting the question: *why* are such propositions true? The Essentialist Thesis allows a straightforward answer: *because* it belongs to the essence of the concepts in their antecedents that they are satisfied only if the moral concepts in their consequents are also satisfied. Notice, moreover, that such explanation does not advert to agential stances, social conventions, divine commands, or the like. Consequently, the Essentialist Thesis helps to make good on moral realism's commitment to the objectivity of morality.[11]

3. Pricean Reflection

Our claims about the morally-valenced essences of the concepts in fixed points can be defended by enlisting the support of the eighteenth-century British moral philosopher Richard Price, who wrote in his *Review of the Principal Questions in Morals*:

> [A]ll actions ... have a nature.... This may be, that some of them are right, others wrong. But if this is not allowed; if no actions are, *in themselves*, either right or wrong, or any thing of a moral and obligatory nature ... it follows, that, in themselves, they *are* all indifferent. This is what is essentially true of them, and this is what understandings, that perceive right must perceive them to be.... [I]t seems sufficient to overthrow any scheme that such consequences ... should arise from it: ... That there be nothing [by its nature] proper or improper, just or unjust; there is nothing *obligatory*; but all beings enjoy, from the reasons of things and the nature of actions, liberty to act as they will.[12]

Price is inviting us to reflect on the essences of actions, and asserting that at least some of those essences are morally valenced—and, moreover, that "understandings that perceive right" see this to be so. The implausibility of holding otherwise—of maintaining that all actions are, by their nature, morally indifferent—suffices to "overthrow" any theory that implies such a thing.

We find the core of this line of thought deeply congenial. Consider the act of raising one's arm. Consider the action itself, wholly apart from whatever might happen to be associated with it. If you are like us, you find the action itself indifferent at its core: no moral valence belongs to its nature. Despite being permissible in most (or even all) contexts, this is not part of *what it is* to raise one's arm. Now place before your mind a different type of action—betraying the vulnerable, say, or deliberately humiliating those who are weak and guileless. See the difference? Not all actions are created equal: While it

---

[11] This is a brief sketch of an argument that we develop at greater length in Bengson, Cuneo, and Shafer-Landau (2024, ch. 6).

[12] Price (1787/1948, §I.3, emphases in original).

may be that some are morally indifferent, not all are. Some are, by their nature, morally loaded, possessed of a moral essence that at least partly contributes to that action's being what it is.

Let us introduce the following procedure. Consider an entity, then ask if it is at its core morally indifferent: is its essence devoid of moral content? If the answer is no, then we possess at least some justification for believing that it belongs to its essence to have a moral valence (positive or negative). In some cases, a specific moral status (right, wrong, fitting, etc.) may also be apparent. Call an application of this procedure an instance of "Pricean reflection." This is a species of essentialist reflection, whereby we consider an entity, x, and ask what belongs to its essence. If the answer is that what it is to be x is to be y, then we possess at least some justification for believing that y belongs to x's essence.[13]

When applied to concepts, the procedure can be stated succinctly: consider a concept, then ask whether the target concept is, by its nature, satisfied only if whatever falls under it also satisfies some moral concept. If reflection reveals that the answer is yes, then we possess at least some justification for concluding that it belongs to its essence to be morally valenced. When the target concept constitutes the antecedent of a proposition, and a moral concept revealed through Pricean reflection constitutes its consequent, we possess at least some justification for believing that that proposition is an essential truth regarding the concept in the antecedent.

Such reflection is not wholly alien to contemporary philosophers; it, or something very much like it, has been employed in recent metaethical theorizing regarding nonnormative properties. Consider, for instance, a prominent objection to the divine command theory. Metaethicists of a wide variety of orientations have found the theory wanting because, at least in its unrestricted form, it implies that all actions (including, say, rape and torture) are morally indifferent at their core. They have no moral nature at all; a moral status is superimposed upon them only when a divine command is directed their way. But this offends against the conviction that rape and torture are not morally vacuous at their core. Their obtaining does not merely happen to come with a negative moral valence, or modally covary with such. Rather, they are *essentially* immoral. A careful consideration of what these actions are, independently of any accidental associations, reveals their moral character. Any theory that regards all actions as essentially morally indifferent is thereby starting from a false assumption. This is just what Pricean reflection teaches.

---

[13] Naturally, an adequate theory of essentialist reflection will fill in various details and qualifications. For instance, we (like Price himself) maintain that the relevant answers are those provided by intuitions, and that the relevant sort of justification is defeasible (see Bengson, Cuneo, and Shafer-Landau forthcoming). Unlike other participants in metaethical debates, we deny that justified beliefs about moral reality are mediated by linguistic or semantic theorizing (as in, e.g., Williamson this volume).

Now consider the following concepts:

OFFERING AID TO THOSE IN DEEP DISTRESS;

GRATUITOUSLY SLANDERING;

COMPASSIONATELY INTERVENING TO PROTECT THE OPPRESSED;

TORTURING FOR MERE ENTERTAINMENT.

We maintain that Pricean reflection reveals that these concepts are not essentially morally indifferent. Being morally valenced is not an accidental feature of these concepts, but pertains to what they are at their core.

These concepts differ dramatically from concepts such as:

SPONTANEOUSLY RECITING A POEM;

EARNESTLY STARING AT STRANGERS;

GRATUITOUSLY PROPOSING TO COUNT YOUR NEIGHBOR'S ROSES;

PLAYING VIDEO GAMES FOR MERE ENTERTAINMENT.

Pricean reflection yields a rather different verdict about these concepts: they are essentially morally indifferent. The non-normative concepts on the first list, unlike those on this second list, have moral essences. It belongs to their very core that anything that satisfies them must also satisfy concepts such as REQUIRED or WRONG, or instead FAVORED or DISFAVORED. The propositions that they constitute are essential truths regarding their constituent concepts.

The concepts on the first list are among the non-normative concepts that feature in the antecedents of a range of fixed points. We have just seen that Pricean reflection supports our contention that these concepts have moral essences. Further, we can easily repeat the exercise when reflecting on the concepts that appear in the antecedents of other fixed points—they, too, have moral essences.

We believe that Pricean reflection yields essentialist judgments that enjoy at least some justification. When the reflection is undertaken in favorable cognitive conditions, as it often is, the justification increases. Hurried or inattentive reflection may yield only a very slight degree of justification; by contrast, careful, attentive, and sober reflection will yield a higher degree of justification for the essentialist judgments that emerge. In the case of fixed points, the justification imparted by such reflection is far from conclusive. Nevertheless, it is nontrivial. And it is buttressed by the independent fact that fixed points fully accord with the four logical principles governing essence (as discussed in §2.2). Taken together, this fact and our efforts at Pricean reflection generate strong reason to believe that fixed points are essential truths, propositions that state the essences of their constituent concepts—just as the Essentialist Thesis asserts.

Some may balk at this conclusion, driven by an alternative conception of the logical form of fixed points. To appreciate this option, consider the fixed point

<It is wrong to recreationally slaughter fellow persons>.

When we lay bare its underlying structure, we find that it is equivalent to a simple conditional:

<If an action satisfies the concept RECREATIONAL SLAUGHTER OF FELLOW PERSONS, then it satisfies the concept WRONG>.

Others, though, might insist that the logical form be understood as a complex conditional along the following lines:

<If anything satisfies the concept WRONG, then if an action satisfies the concept RECREATIONAL SLAUGHTER OF FELLOW PERSONS, then it satisfies the concept WRONG>.[14]

Some, including error theorists, might then aver that the initial antecedent is necessarily false. While the falsity of this antecedent would render the fixed point true, it would also rob that fixed point of its capacity to subserve a defense of moral realism.

Fortunately, there is good reason to doubt that such complex conditionals give the correct logical form of fixed points. This becomes clear when we consider nonmoral essentialist truths, such as

<Gold has atomic number 79>.

Consider two renderings of its logical form:

<If something satisfies the concept GOLD, then it also satisfies the concept ATOMIC NUMBER 79>.

<If anything satisfies the concept ATOMIC NUMBER 79, then if something satisfies the concept GOLD, then it satisfies the concept ATOMIC NUMBER 79>.

While the first rendering in terms of a simple conditional seems to us a natural and correct construal of the original claim, the second, complex rendering strikes us as a patently implausible way of interpreting that claim. Absent any reason to think that

---

[14] See Evers and Streumer (2016, 3–4). They allow that a simple conditional gives the logical form of some propositions (e.g., <Bachelors are unmarried>), but only when those propositions do "not require more of the world than the satisfaction of the concept" in those propositions' antecedents do (5). But as shown by our example below involving gold, this restriction is mistaken.

essentialist truths and facts exhibit a different logical form depending on whether their content is moral or not (and we know of no such reason), we should accept that the moral fixed points have the logical form given by the first rendering—the one on which our defense of the essentialist claim in the Essentialist Thesis relies.

4. The Essentialist Conception of Conceptual Truth

We turn now to our defense of the second claim in the Essentialist Thesis: namely, that fixed points are true *fully in virtue of* essence facts regarding the concepts in their antecedents. We'll defend this claim by arguing that fixed points possess a special status: they are conceptual truths.

Since the term "conceptual truth" is open to multiple interpretations, many of which we do not wish to invoke, it is important to make clear the conception of conceptual truths to which we are committed. We call it

> **The Essentialist Conception**: <p> is a conceptual truth $=_{def}$ <p> is true fully in virtue of at least one essence fact regarding one or more of its constituent concepts.[15]

This section endeavors to clarify and defend this conception, revealing what it is and isn't committed to. We can do this by distinguishing it from other conceptions of conceptual truth on offer. That will position us to formulate an argument for the Essentialist Conception. It will also set the stage for our defense of the second claim in the Essentialist Thesis in the next section.

4.1 Alternative Conceptions

The Essentialist Conception differs from other widely held views regarding what it is for a proposition to be a conceptual truth. These include:

> **The Semantic Conception**: <p> is a conceptual truth $=_{def}$ <p> is true fully in virtue of its meaning.

> **The Conventionalist Conception**: <p> is a conceptual truth $=_{def}$ <p> is true fully in virtue of some practice or stipulation.

> **The Logical Conception**: <p> is a conceptual truth $=_{def}$ <p> is transformable into a logical truth by the substitution of synonyms for synonyms.

---

[15] *Cp*. the similar views endorsed by Fine (1994, 9-10) and Wedgwood (2017, 20-1).

The Psychological Conception: <p> is a conceptual truth =_{def} understanding <p> is sufficient to bear, or be disposed to bear, a certain attitude (such as belief) towards <p>.

The Epistemic Conception: <p> is a conceptual truth =_{def} understanding <p> is sufficient to acquire a certain positive epistemic standing (such as justification) with respect to <p>.

None of these express what we mean by "conceptual truth."[16]

In fact, the Essentialist Conception does not entail any of the other five conceptions of conceptual truth. Moreover, it is importantly different from some of the other conceptions inasmuch as it does not imply that conceptual truths are somehow empty, vacuous, trivial, insubstantial, or obvious. To the contrary, the Essentialist Conception allows that some conceptual truths are substantive and nonobvious. Plausibly, it is a conceptual truth in the essentialist sense that <Justified true belief is not knowledge> or <Any Turing-computable function is recursive>; these truths are certainly substantive and, pre-Gettier and pre-Turing, were hardly obvious.

The Essentialist Conception is distinctive in that it simultaneously:

- identifies the source or ground of a conceptual truth's status as a truth (unlike the Logical, Psychological, and Epistemic Conceptions);
- is noncommittal about meaning and logic (unlike the Semantic and Logical Conceptions);
- is compatible with some conceptual truths being substantive truths (unlike the Logical, Conventionalist, and perhaps Semantic Conceptions);
- does not make conceptual truths language- or convention-relative or somehow reliant upon our practices or acts of stipulation (unlike the Conventionalist Conception);
- allows that conceptual truths can sometimes be highly nonobvious to competent thinkers (unlike the Psychological Conception);
- leaves room for genuine disagreement between competent thinkers about conceptual truths and their applications in particular instances (unlike the Psychological Conception); and
- is neutral with respect to the epistemology of conceptual truths—including both their epistemic status and how they come to have whatever epistemic status that they do (unlike the Epistemic Conception).

---

[16] Sometimes the conceptions we've just listed are framed in the language of analyticity: for example, Boghossian (1996) calls the Semantic Conception "metaphysical analyticity," the Logical Conception "Frege-analyticity," and a specific version of the Epistemic Conception "epistemic analyticity." Eklund (2017, 90–1) endorses what he calls "semantic analyticity," which is basically the Psychological Conception shorn of a commitment to truth. Other conceptions are of course possible: see, e.g., Juhl and Loomis (2010, §6.5) on "analyticity*" and Soysal's (2018) discussion of "formal analyticity."

We do not maintain that the Essentialist Conception is the uniquely correct or adequate way of explicating the expression "conceptual truth," or that its distinctiveness in the just-mentioned respects makes it always preferable to the other conceptions. After all, there might be several, equally legitimate conceptions that can be useful for a variety of theoretical purposes. Still, some of these conceptions might be particularly interesting and theoretically fecund. We believe that the Essentialist Conception is both.

4.2 Defending the Essentialist Conception

Our defense of the legitimacy of the Essentialist Conception identifies a range of taxonomical data regarding cases of evident conceptual truths and contends that the Essentialist Conception accommodates and explains these data. To be clear, our aim is not to defend the Essentialist Conception itself, providing a good reason to believe that it is true whereas the various alternatives are false. It is rather to defend its legitimacy as a conception of conceptual truth. We do this by showing that the Essentialist Conception can accommodate and explain a range of data concerning evident conceptual truths.[17]

Our discussion focuses on evident conceptual truths for the following reason. There is bound to be a lot of disagreement about how best to think about conceptual truths. In identifying the data that should constrain inquiry regarding these truths, it will be helpful to remove ourselves from that disagreement to the extent possible, and to stick with data that are plausibly viewed as being neutral. Those data are likely to come from reflection on conceptual truths that are evident, since these are the central cases whose status is not highly contested.

We divide the data that we'll consider into two groups. The first calls attention to four nonepistemic, nonpsychological features of evident conceptual truths:

Truth: Evident conceptual truths are true.
Necessity: Evident conceptual truths are necessarily true.
Conceptuality: The truth of evident conceptual truths has something to do with the concepts that constitute them.
Paradigms: Among the evident conceptual truths, there are a range of paradigms. There are also a range of paradigms of truths that are not conceptual truths.

These data are deliberately vague. The Truth datum leaves open why conceptual truths are true. The Necessity datum does not specify which kind of necessity—logical, semantic, metaphysical, epistemic—attaches to each conceptual truth. The Conceptuality datum leaves open what it is about the constituent concepts of an evident conceptual truth that bear on its truth (or how they do so). It could be that these concepts are meanings, that

---

[17] We distinguish a defense of a *thesis* from a defense of the *legitimacy of a thesis*. Whereas the former involves providing good reason to believe a given thesis, the latter merely involves establishing that a thesis accommodates and explains relevant data.

they bear certain relations to conventions, that they are suitably related to logical truths, that they have essences of certain kinds, and so on. The Paradigms datum allows that the paradigms are sparse or abundant. While this last datum itself includes no examples to help us fix our thoughts about likely candidates, the following seem to us clear cases of such truths:

a. <Every bachelor is unmarried>.
b. <Either grass is green or it is not>.
c. <Vermilion is a color>.

Conversely, the following seem to us clear cases of truths that are not conceptual truths:

d. <Nigeria is more populous than Greece>.
e. <Necessarily, gold has atomic number 79>.
f. <If the moon is made of green cheese, then pigs fly>.

The Essentialist Conception readily accommodates and explains all four of these data. It tells us that conceptual truths are true, and that they are true fully in virtue of essence facts regarding their constituent concepts; it thus accommodates and explains both Truth and Conceptuality. It does the same for Necessity, since the Essentialist Conception sees conceptual truths as a species of essential truths, which are necessarily true.[18] Finally, the Essentialist Conception accommodates and explains the fact that certain paradigms, such as (a)–(c), are conceptual truths, while others, such as (d)–(f), are not.

We turn now to the second group of data, which spell out, at a pretheoretical level, what the evidentness of evident conceptual truths entails. In other words, these four data are not marks of the evident per se, but rather the evidentness of evident conceptual truths. The four data in this second group call attention to a series of broadly epistemic-cum-psychological dimensions of evident conceptual truths:

Reflectivity: Evident conceptual truths are such that duly positioned agents can readily come to know them just by thinking about them.
Bewilderment: An agent's sincere expression of denial of an evident conceptual truth tends to induce a response akin to bewilderment in duly positioned agents.
Comprehension: An agent's sincere expression of denial of an evident conceptual truth provides duly positioned agents with (defeasible) epistemic reason to believe that the agent has not fully grasped this proposition.
Classification: An agent's sincere expression of denial of an evident conceptual truth according to which x satisfies C provides duly positioned agents with (defeasible)

---

[18] Recall (from §2.1) the first logical principle governing essential truths and facts: if it belongs to the essence of x that x is F, then, necessarily, x is F.

epistemic reason to believe that the agent would misclassify at least some things that satisfy C in actual or possible circumstances.

All four of these data refer to *duly positioned agents*, whom we define by two traits: (i) they have at least reasonable mastery of relevant concepts and (ii) they occupy favorable cognitive conditions (e.g., of sobriety and attentiveness) that enable such agents to readily apply those concepts correctly.[19] Furthermore, as noted, each of these data identifies a mark of an evident conceptual truth; any proposition that exemplifies all four features recorded here is an excellent candidate for being such a truth.

The Essentialist Conception arguably comports with all four of these data (both individually and jointly). Keeping in mind that favorable cognitive conditions may include sustained and careful reflection, an evident proposition that is true fully in virtue of essence facts regarding one or more of its constituent concepts is compatible with its being knowable by mere reflection by a duly positioned agent (per Reflectivity). The Essentialist Conception is similarly compatible with the idea that denial of a conceptual truth will tend to induce bewilderment, puzzlement, or bafflement in a duly positioned agent who has grasped it (per Bewilderment). Such an agent would thereby gain reason to question the denier's grasp of the proposition in question (per Comprehension), as well as the denier's ability to successfully deliver relevant classifications (per Classification)—including those that involve further applications of that proposition's constituent concepts.

We've claimed that the Essentialist Conception accommodates and explains all four of the data regarding central cases of evident conceptual truths and is consonant with a range of data concerning the evidentness of such truths. These are nontrivial considerations in favor of regarding the Essentialist Conception as a legitimate conception of conceptual truth. Together, we take them to compose a strong defense of that claim.

4.3 A Further Mark

Thus far we have been working with data that are indicators or marks of evident conceptual truths, on any of the conceptions of conceptual truth we've canvassed. But there may also be conception-specific marks of conceptual truth. For example, the Conventionalist Conception calls attention to the idea that some propositions are true fully in virtue of certain conventions. On this view, that a given truth reflects various conventions is a mark of being a conceptual truth *under that conception*. Such possession is not, however, an indicator of being a conceptual truth per se.

---

[19] We'll have much more to say about the notion of concept mastery in §6, below. Bengson, Cuneo, and Shafer-Landau (forthcoming) present a fuller theory.

There may be multiple marks of being a conceptual truth according to the Essentialist Conception. Here we draw attention to an important one given our aims—that of possessing *framework status*. We'll properly explicate this notion below; for now, we can stick with the intuitive idea that having such status is a matter of being a non-negotiable element of a set of propositions of a certain kind. The basic idea is that when we want to identify a set of propositions belonging to a given category, we can look to the conceptual truths generated by the essences of the central concepts of the category in question—those propositions that are true fully in virtue of essence facts regarding those concepts—to assist us in this matter. While a proposition's having this mark is neither necessary nor sufficient for its being a conceptual truth, it is nonetheless good (albeit defeasible) evidence of a proposition's counting as such under the auspices of the Essentialist Conception, at least when the proposition also satisfies sufficiently many data regarding conceptual truths per se.

5. The Moral Fixed Points as Conceptual Truths

In the last section, we introduced and defended the Essentialist Conception of conceptual truths, identifying a number of marks pertaining to conceptual truths along the way. In this section, we defend the claim that fixed points are conceptual truths of the kind described by the Essentialist Conception. We do so by appeal to the *Conceptual Truth Argument*.

Its first premise states:

1. Fixed points are essential truths with respect to their constituent concepts.

We defended this premise in §3. Since we won't assume that all essential truths are grounded in corresponding essence facts (recall note 10), premise 1 can't be relied upon to deliver the claim that fixed points are true fully in virtue of essence facts regarding their constituent concepts. Indeed, this premise does not by itself support classifying those platitudes as conceptual truths under any conception, including the Essentialist Conception. Two further premises begin to bridge this gap:

2. Fixed points satisfy the Truth, Necessity, Conceptuality, Reflectivity, Bewilderment, Comprehension, and Classification data.
3. Fixed points do not contravene the Paradigms datum.

The conjunction of these two premises provides defeasible evidence in favor of the claim that fixed points are conceptual truths, no matter the conception of conceptual truths one is operating with. When combined with premise 1 and

4. Fixed points have framework status with respect to morality,

these premises provide strong evidence for (and arguably entail) the conclusion that

5. Fixed points are conceptual truths of the kind described by the Essentialist Conception: each is true fully in virtue of at least one essence fact regarding one or more of its constituent concepts.

In concert, then, the four premises provide good reason to believe 5.

As noted, we've had our say about premise 1. Let us turn now to a defense of the remaining premises in the argument.

5.1 Evidence of Conceptual Truth

Premise 2 identifies seven data regarding evident conceptual truths that fixed points satisfy (i.e., they possess the features that those data identify). Let's consider these data in order.

That fixed points are true (per the Truth datum) follows from their being platitudes in the sense specified in §1. Moreover, we've defended the claim that they are essential truths; this is the upshot of our Pricean reflections in §3. Now recall, from §2.1, that essential truths have modal force: if it belongs to the essence of x that x is F, then, necessarily, x is F. Thus fixed points, being essential truths, are also necessary (per the Necessity datum).[20] So we can tick the first two boxes.

Regarding the third datum, we've defended the claim that fixed points are essential truths *with respect to their constituent concepts*. If our discussion there is on target, it does not imply the conclusion we ultimately seek, namely, that fixed points are true in virtue of those concepts. But it does entail that the truth of fixed points has *something* to do with the concepts that constitute them (per the Conceptuality datum).

We've also, fourthly, defended the claim that agents can grasp the morally valenced essences of the concepts in the antecedents of fixed points, such as RECREATIONAL SLAUGHTER OF FELLOW PERSONS; this, once again, is the contribution of Pricean reflection, coupled with the observation that the fixed points fully accord with the four logical principles governing essence. In this way, agents are able to appreciate, via reflection alone, that anything satisfying the antecedent concept of a fixed point also satisfies the moral concept in its consequent. It follows that such agents can readily come to know fixed points just by thinking about them (per the Reflectivity datum).

---

[20] Recall that the platitudes may be defeasible. If so, then they are essentially so. On such a view, what is necessary is (for example) that any action that satisfies the concept RECREATIONAL SLAUGHTER defeasibly satisfies the concept WRONG.

As for the fifth and sixth data invoked by premise 2, we recognize that philosophy is replete with positions that deny highly evident claims, even platitudinous ones. But we shouldn't lose sight of the fact that the sincere denial of highly evident propositions such as <Justice is a virtue> and <Recreational slaughter of fellow persons is wrong> tends to induce a response akin to bewilderment in those who have reasonable mastery of their constituent concepts and occupy favorable cognitive conditions (per Bewilderment). We recognize the possibility of contexts in which the tendency in question will be stymied, as when others are aware that the denier possesses highly unorthodox theoretical commitments. But even so, the tendency remains.

Thus it is no surprise that we look for explanations of why an agent would sincerely deny evident truths, and we form expectations about what else they will deny or believe. Consider an agent who sincerely denies that there is anything wrong with recreational slaughter. In contexts outside the philosophy seminar room, and perhaps even within it, that provides defeasible reason to believe that his failure must be deep; it is arguably that of simply failing to grasp the proposition <It is wrong to recreationally slaughter fellow persons>. Moreover, this failure would presumably betoken a grasp of the constituents of this proposition that would lead this person to issue similar denials when it comes to other fixed points, and to issue erroneous verdicts about various actual and hypothetical cases. His error would not likely be entirely isolated or local, but would rather be indicative of a tendency to misclassify many other phenomena. It follows that fixed points also satisfy the seventh and final datum (per the Classification datum).

Having defended premise 2 of the Conceptual Truth Argument, let us now turn to premise 3. Suppose fixed points were similar to paradigmatic nonconceptual truths such as <The Uffizi houses the *Birth of Venus*>. That would be reason to believe that fixed points are not conceptual truths of any sort; they would contravene the Paradigms datum (i.e., fail to possess the feature identified by that datum). However, while fixed points are not paradigms of conceptual truths, neither are they paradigms of nonconceptual truths. This last point ensures that fixed points do not themselves contravene the Paradigms datum, as the third premise claims.

But might our principal claim—that fixed points are conceptual truths—imply or license violations of the Paradigms datum? Since some critics have charged as much, it is worth pausing to explain why the view we've developed does not illicitly recast paradigm nonconceptual truths as conceptual ones. We'll focus on three instances of these worries.

The first alleges that if fixed points are conceptual truths, then this implies that the proposition

    A. <Moral properties exist or are instantiated>

is as well.[21]

---

[21] Copp (2017, 23) raises this objection; *cp.* Copp (2007, 126–7).

The second alleges that any view according to which fixed points are conceptual truths must allow that a proposition such as

B. <God rewards the benevolent>

is a conceptual truth, which in turn implies that

C. <God exists>

is a conceptual truth.[22]

The third alleges that any view according to which fixed points are conceptual truths must allow that there could be "anti-moralist" conceptual truths, such as:

D. <Recreationally slaughtering fellow persons is required>.[23]

We agree that no satisfactory position should imply or support the claim that A–D are conceptual truths. We also see no reason to believe that our position suggests otherwise. To appreciate why, recall the logical form of the fixed point that we'll call "No Slaughter":

<If an act satisfies the concept RECREATIONAL SLAUGHTER OF FELLOW PERSONS, then it satisfies the concept WRONG>.

This conditional proposition does not imply or support A, let alone the claim that A is true fully in virtue of essence facts regarding its constituent concepts, as it must if it were a conceptual truth under the Essentialist Conception.[24]

Similarly, if B has any chance of being a conceptual truth, it would have the logical form:

B*. <If something satisfies the concept GOD, then it satisfies the concept REWARDS THE BENEVOLENT>.

But B* does not imply C, let alone offer any support to the claim that C is a conceptual truth.[25] Moreover, for B to be a conceptual truth under the Essentialist Conception, B*

---

[22] Evers and Streumer (2016, 3) raise this objection.

[23] Both Copp (2017, 18–21) and Evers and Streumer (2016, 5–6) press this objection.

[24] Copp (2017, 23) notes that Cuneo and Shafer-Landau (2014, 414n33) anticipate and reply to the objection. But he maintains that the reply is unsatisfactory, since "it does follow [from the claim that No Slaughter is a conceptual truth] that recreational slaughter is wrong" and that "recreational slaughter is wrong only if there is such a thing as wrongness." This claim, however, strikes us as failing to take into account the conditional logical form of propositions such as No Slaughter.

[25] It might be that critics assume that the logical form of B is really <If something satisfies the concept BENEVOLENT, then it satisfies the concept GOD REWARDS IT>. But this proposition also does not imply

must both state an essential truth regarding at least one of B's constituent concepts, and be true fully in virtue of an essence fact regarding that concept (or those concepts). Our position licenses neither conjunct, and it is far from evident that either conjunct is true. So our claim that fixed points such as No Slaughter are conceptual truths doesn't support or imply the idea that B is a conceptual truth.

As for putative "antimoralist" conceptual truths, our view implies that there could be none. After all, according to our position, it belongs to the *essence* of the concept RECREATIONAL SLAUGHTER OF FELLOW PERSONS that anything that satisfies it must also satisfy the concept WRONG. Given the plausible assumption that no act could at once satisfy incompatible concepts, such as REQUIRED and WRONG, it follows that D could not be true, let alone be a conceptual truth.

Of course none of this as such rules out the possibility of there being alternative normative concepts, such as REQUIRED* and WRONG*, whose application conditions diverge sharply from REQUIRED and WRONG. There are many things to say about this possibility.[26] For present purposes, let us say simply that REQUIRED* and WRONG* are philosophers' inventions, and absent a lot of additional information, it is very difficult to gain any grip on what belongs to their essences. Moreover, it is not credible to suppose that such inventiveness can make it the case that the essences of the non-normative concepts in the antecedents of fixed points make reference to one or another of these invented concepts. For example, there is no plausibility to the suggestion that we can simply *stipulate* that it belongs to the essence of RECREATIONAL SLAUGHTER OF FELLOW PERSONS that the proposition

<Recreational slaughter of fellow persons is required*>

is an essential truth regarding the concept RECREATIONAL SLAUGHTER OF FELLOW PERSONS, or that this proposition is true fully in virtue of an essence fact regarding this concept. While our powers of creation are extensive, they are not so far-reaching as to allow philosophers to craft the essences of familiar concepts of intentional actions by fiat. If that is so, then there could be no normative conceptual truths involving familiar concepts such as RECREATIONAL SLAUGHTER OF FELLOW PERSONS and unfamiliar normative concepts such as REQUIRED* and WRONG* that parallel fixed points. Our conclusion is that examples such as these provide no reason to believe that our claim that fixed

---

that C is a conceptual truth. Nor is there anything about the essence of the concept BENEVOLENT that implies something about God, let alone that God exists—or at least we know of no credible arguments to the contrary. Whether there is something about the concept GOD that implies that God exists is famously somewhat more controversial, but it is no objection to our position that it fails to have any implications regarding the issue.

[26] Both Copp and Evers and Streumer explicitly raise the possibility in the course of their criticisms (*cp.* Eklund 2017). Bengson, Cuneo, and Shafer-Landau (2024, Chapter 11, §3) address the possibility in greater detail.

points are conceptual truths has untoward implications. In particular, the examples do not support the charge that our claim contravenes the Paradigms datum.

We've now defended premises 2 and 3 of the Conceptual Truth Argument. Together, these premises provide reason to believe that fixed points are conceptual truths of some sort. The issue that remains is whether these platitudes are conceptual truths of the sort countenanced by the Essentialist Conception. The conjunction of premise 1, which we already defended, and premise 4, to which we turn next, helps to deliver this conclusion.

5.2 Framework Status

Premise 4 states that fixed points have framework status with respect to morality. We indicated earlier that such status attaches to propositions that somehow "frame" a given category, standing as non-negotiable elements of it. Otherwise put, these propositions somehow "fix the subject matter" or "hold in place" other propositions that belong to that category. It's now time to unpack these metaphors. Our aim in doing so is not to prioritize morality over other categories, but rather to defend the claim about fixed points in premise 4.

Let us call a reasonably comprehensive and consistent body of propositions a "system" of propositions, and a system of propositions with regard to a category C a "C-system." We propose that

> A nonempty set of propositions {P} has framework status with respect to C if:
> - all members of {P} are paradigmatic truths of C;
> - a system that omitted {P} would be either a radically incomplete C-system or not a C-system at all;
> - a system that included the negation of each member of {P} would be either a highly deviant C-system or not a C-system at all; and,
> - a system that included any proposition that is inconsistent with a range of members of {P} would be either a highly deviant C-system or not a C-system at all.

Satisfaction of these four conditions is sufficient for a set of propositions to be a non-negotiable element of a given category, framing that category, fixing its subject matter, holding other propositions in place, and so on.

Consider, for example, the category of love. Candidates for propositions with framework status with regard to this category might be:

> <An agent loves another only if she is concerned with the well-being of that other>.
>
> <An agent loves another only if she is disposed to seek a conscious, meaningful relationship with that other in at least some circumstances>.
>
> <An agent loves another only if she is committed to not wronging the other>.

These are good candidates for being paradigmatic truths about love. If they are such truths, then a system of propositions that failed to include these would either be radically incomplete, leaving out some of its significant elements, or not a system regarding love at all. If a system were instead to include the negation of these propositions, or other propositions that are inconsistent with a range of those like the ones just retailed, then it would at best offer a highly deviant conception of the category and, at worst, lose its claim to being a system regarding love.

We believe that fixed points satisfy the four conditions on framework status with respect to the category of the moral. They are paradigmatic moral truths—exemplary, obvious instances of the category. Further, any set of propositions that failed to include fixed points, or that included their negations or other propositions that are inconsistent with a range of them, would be either a radically incomplete moral system, a deviant one, or no moral system at all.

Sharon Street, who is no fan of moral realism, seems to concur with our verdict that certain platitudes possess framework status with respect to morality. When considering a case of wanton torture, she writes:

> For of course refraining from torture is what Caligula has most *moral* reason to do; one might think this is close to a conceptual truth about what morality consists in, since any "morality" that gave a green light to maximizing the suffering of others for fun would be hard to recognize as a system of *morality* at all.[27]

We see no bar to extending Street's insight to the set of fixed points. In our terms, they possess framework status with respect to morality, just as premise 4 says.

Our goal is to utilize this point about the framework status of fixed points in order to help us make the case that they are conceptual truths under the Essentialist Conception. When a set of propositions possesses framework status with respect to a given category and is also such that its members both are essential truths with respect to concepts belonging to that category and satisfy the seven data pertaining to evident conceptual truths, then we have a good, albeit defeasible, indicator of their being conceptual truths according to the Essentialist Conception. The defense of this claim is abductive: Why does a set of propositions—such as the fixed points—with framework status satisfy the seven data and contain only essential truths with respect to concepts belonging to that category? Because those propositions are true in virtue of essence facts regarding these propositions' constituent concepts, and so are conceptual truths under the Essentialist Conception.

This concludes our defense of the premises of the Conceptual Truth Argument. If this defense has been successful, then there is strong reason to regard fixed points as conceptual truths.

---

[27] Street (2009, 292).

6. Diagnosing Doubt and Denial

We are well aware of the skepticism that is likely to greet our claim that moral fixed points are conceptual truths. Perhaps the most important worry about our proposal is its implication—which we'll highlight in a moment—that those who reject fixed points thereby suffer from conceptual deficiencies. This section responds to these worries. Specifically, we wish to address a set of questions regarding whether, how, and to what extent rational doubt or denial of any fixed point is possible, given our claim that they are conceptual truths.

If fixed points are conceptual truths, then we allow that there is a sense in which those who doubt or deny them suffer from a *conceptual deficiency*. As we understand it, there are two main types of conceptual deficiency. After elucidating each type, we will then illustrate how they help to diagnose doubt and denial.

6.1 Two Types of Conceptual Deficiency

Let's begin with a type of conceptual deficiency we'll call "imperfect concept possession," which concerns whether and how one grasps a given concept. Such grasp may be better or worse along (at least) two dimensions. We can illustrate using the concept RAINFOREST. One *incompletely* grasps this concept when the possibility of a temperate rainforest is not yet within one's purview. One grasps this concept *incorrectly* if one's grasp conforms to the condition that RAINFOREST refers only to wooded areas near the Equator that are under threat. Both imply imperfect possession of the concept.

It is helpful to distinguish three levels of concept possession. At one extreme lies *perfect mastery* of a concept; at the opposite extreme, just short of complete lack of a concept, lies *mere possession* of it (as when a child memorizes a mathematical proposition whose constituent concepts she does not yet master in any interesting sense). In between lies *reasonable mastery*, which is the kind of competence with a concept that one possesses when one grasps its basic or paradigm applications. Exemplified in many exercises of ordinary human cognition, reasonable mastery is compatible with a host of classificatory gaps (as in the case of incomplete grasp) and mistakes (as in the case of incorrect grasp).[28] The first main type of conceptual deficiency—imperfect concept possession—is found in cases of mere possession as well as various forms of reasonable mastery.

A second main type of conceptual deficiency is what we'll call "performance error," which concerns one's exercise of one's grasp of a concept. Just as an athlete may possess

---

[28] This is not to say that correct or reliable application in belief or judgment is necessary for reasonable mastery. This is one important implication of some of the examples described by Burge (1979 and 1990), Williamson (2006), and Bealer (2008).

a skill but, due to injury or nerves, fail to exercise that skill in a range of situations, one may have reasonable or even perfect mastery of a concept but fail to exercise that mastery in various circumstances, owing to nontrivial cognitive impediments. Among these are drunkenness, nervousness, inattention to details, emotional associations, or forgetfulness. Or one may simply fail to appreciate or follow through on the basic implications of a concept or its application to a particular case—perhaps because one is convinced of a claim or set of claims that have deeply revisionist implications.

It is worth stressing three points about our treatment of conceptual deficiency. First, it does not imply that conceptually deficient agents are "abusing concepts"[29] or conceptually confused in the sense that they are disposed to apply the relevant concepts arbitrarily or indiscriminately, or would have seriously muddled thoughts involving them. Second, our treatment is compatible with the point, emphasized above, that not all conceptual truths are obviously true or evident; they can be cognitively accessible to different degrees (including: not at all). Many conceptual truths are substantive, nontautologous truths; questioning or denying them need not, therefore, be chalked up to failure to see what's before one's nose. Third, and relatedly, our treatment does not imply that beliefs based on or influenced by conceptual deficiency are always irrational or unjustified: nonevident conceptual truths may be doubted or denied for a variety of genuine or merely apparent reasons.

We realize that some will regard our treatment of conceptual deficiency as fairly capacious. But such latitude is perfectly legitimate: imperfect concept possession and performance errors each generate ways in which one might come to violate or fail to respect a conceptual truth (as understood not only by the Essentialist Conception but by several of the others we canvassed). It thus seems appropriate to regard them as types of conceptual deficiency.

6.2 The Diagnosis

We are now in a position to diagnose doubt and denial of fixed points. As noted, if they are conceptual truths, then we should say that those who doubt or deny them suffer from a conceptual deficiency. Such a deficiency would consist in either

i. *lacking* the relevant concepts;
ii. possessing the relevant concepts but having an *incomplete grasp* of some of them;
iii. possessing the relevant concepts but having an *incorrect grasp* of some of them; or
iv. possessing the relevant concepts (perhaps even having a correct and complete grasp of them) but *failing to apply them accurately* in all-things-considered judgment.

---

[29] The expression is employed by Zangwill (2000, 281).

While (ii)–(iii) identify conceptual deficiencies that fall under the rubric of imperfect concept possession, (iv) concerns a conceptual deficiency that is best classed as performance error.

Let us begin with a diagnosis of some simple cases of conceptual deficiency that may not yet implicate any actual agents. Suppose that one brings the fixed point we've labeled No Slaughter to mind but fails to carefully attend to the concept RECREATIONAL SLAUGHTER—for example, one inattentively neglects the restriction to instances of *recreational* slaughter. This might lead to a performance error that results in one doubting whether the action is wrong. Or suppose one registers this restriction but mistakenly conceives of the domain of the recreational as encompassing any physically demanding activity, regardless of whether it's undertaken simply for entertainment. Suppose, further, that one conceives of slaughter as nothing other than mass killing. If one accepts that engaging in physically demanding mass killing in self-defense is morally justified, one may be led to doubt the truth of the platitude. In such a case, one will doubt a conceptual truth because of a conceptual deficiency that is explained by an incorrect grasp of the concept RECREATIONAL and an incomplete grasp of the concept SLAUGHTER.

Turning now to a different type of case, one that might be more likely to be realized, suppose one were to wonder whether one has failed to appreciate the force of various arguments against moral realism, such as those that J. L. Mackie offers for moral error theory.[30] One might find that such worries—for instance, how could the world that science describes also include values not of our own creation?—loom large enough in one's thinking that they eclipse the evidentness of the platitude, moving one to discount its apparent obviousness, due to the judgment that the overall balance of reasons is tipped against it. Or suppose one were to wonder whether there is something deeply defective about our moral concepts, something that would render them incapable of referring to moral properties if any were to exist (say, because their application is subject to extensive disagreement).[31] Again, this worry might operate on one's thinking in such a way that it also leads one to doubt or deny the platitude. Or, to take another—and much darker—example, suppose one is like the Nazi war criminal Herman Göring, who seems to have rejected certain platitudes when ordering a genocide simply on the grounds of love of country. The evidentness of the platitudes may have been concealed by his nationalistic fervor, together perhaps with his ruinous conceptions of his leader and of those whom he ordered to be slaughtered.

Two comments on these examples. First, given the circumstances in which the agents in these cases find themselves, some of their doubt or denial might not be irrational. Indeed, whether such doubt or denial is irrational may be decidable only on a case by case basis, through a careful examination of the particularities of the doubter's or denier's overall epistemic situation.[32]

---

[30] Mackie (1977, ch. 1).

[31] See, e.g., Loeb's (2008) discussion of "moral incoherentism."

[32] Contrary to Ingram (2015). Copp (2007, ch. 4) offers three arguments for thinking that propositions such as fixed points are not conceptual truths. We addressed one of these arguments in §5.1 above. The

Second, the types of cases just described should strike most of us as familiar. Several of them exemplify a dynamic of doubt that is not uncommon when engaging in philosophy and other kinds of abstract reflection. While attending to the proposition that there are two prime numbers between 4 and 9, it is very difficult to see how there could be no numbers. But then one steps back and wonders whether Hartry Field's arguments for numerical nihilism might have bite.[33] While attending to the law of noncontradiction, one finds it impossible to see how there could be true contradictions. But then one is introduced to the Liar Paradox and becomes open to the possibility, perhaps in light of Graham Priest's arguments, that dialetheism might be correct.[34] In each of these cases, one acknowledges, as some nihilists and dialetheists do, that although a proposition seems highly evident, it might nonetheless be false.

Of course, Field and Priest go beyond these doubts to embrace genuine belief with respect to numerical nihilism and dialetheism, respectively. These philosophers may even acknowledge that the propositions they deny—<There are two prime numbers between 4 and 9> and <Contradictions cannot be true>—seem highly evident; still, they maintain that the propositions are nonetheless false. Such denials need not impugn the rationality of these thinkers. The same could be true of those who deny No Slaughter and other fixed points.

We go further. Even those who do not deny fixed points and are not tempted by the dynamic of doubt should acknowledge a sense in which these propositions *might* be false. Compare a highly reflective mathematician's avowal that (say) Fermat's Last Theorem might be false, even though it seems to her to be obviously true and she is aware that the community of mathematicians considers it to have now been proven. It is plausible to interpret her as avowing that she is uncertain that Fermat's Last Theorem is true, because she recognizes that even falsehoods can seem highly evident, and acknowledges that she cannot rule out the possibility that what has been accepted as a proof contains unnoticed errors. There is nothing incoherent or irrational about such an expression of humility, which is consonant with common sense, and which we intend as a perfect analogue of our own concession that there is a sense in which fixed points *might* be false. That a proposition might be false in this sense is not, however, a good reason to doubt, let alone deny, its status as a conceptual truth. On the contrary, we submit that the Conceptual Truth Argument provides strong reason to believe that a wide range of substantive moral propositions possess that very status.[35]

---

other two arguments hinge on the claim that it is not incoherent to deny them. Since, as we've now argued, our view does not imply that it is, these two arguments do not make contact with our position.

[33] Field (1980 and 1989).
[34] Priest (1987).
[35] We thank participants in a workshop at the Vrije Universiteit in Amsterdam, colloquia and seminars at Harvard, the University of Sydney, the University of Texas at Austin, and UW-Madison, and the editors of this volume for feedback on earlier drafts of this chapter.

REFERENCES

Bealer, George. 2008. "Intuition and Modal Error." In *Epistemology: New Essays*, edited by Quentin Smith, 189–224. Oxford: Oxford University Press.

Bengson, John, Terence Cuneo, and Russ Shafer-Landau. 2024. *The Moral Universe*. Oxford: Oxford University Press.

Bengson, John, Terence Cuneo, and Russ Shafer-Landau. Forthcoming. *Grasping Morality*. Oxford: Oxford University Press.

Boghossian, Paul. 1996. "Analyticity Reconsidered." *Nous* 30: 360–391.

Burge, Tyler. 1979. "Individualism and the Mental." *Midwest Studies in Philosophy* 4: 73–122.

Burge, Tyler. 1990. "Frege on Sense and Linguistic Meaning." In *The Analytic Tradition, Meaning, Thought and Knowledge*, edited by David Bell and Neil Cooper, 243–270. Oxford: Basil Blackwell.

Copp, David. 2007. *Morality in a Natural World*. Oxford: Oxford University Press.

Copp, David. 2017. "Are There Substantive Moral Conceptual Truths?" In *Moral Skepticism: New Essays*, edited by D. Machuca, 91–114. Cambridge: Cambridge University Press.

Correia, Fabrice. 2005. *Existential Dependence and Cognate Notions*. Berlin: Philosophia Verlag.

Cuneo, Terence, and Russ Shafer-Landau. 2014. "The Moral Fixed Points: New Directions for Moral Nonnaturalism." *Philosophical Studies* 171: 399–443.

Darwall, Stephen. 2006. *The Second-Person Standpoint: Respect, Morality, and Accountability*. Cambridge, MA: Harvard University Press.

Eklund, Matti. 2017. *Choosing Normative Concepts*. Oxford: Oxford University Press.

Evers, Daan, and Bart Streumer. 2016. "Are the Moral Fixed Points Conceptual Truths?" *Journal of Ethics and Social Philosophy* 10: 1–9.

Ewing, A. C. 1939. "A Suggested Non-Naturalistic Analysis of Good." *Mind* 48: 1–22.

Field, Hartry. 1980. *Science without Numbers*. Princeton: Princeton University Press.

Field, Hartry. 1989. *Realism, Mathematics, and Modality*. Oxford: Basil Blackwell.

Fine, Kit. 1994. "Essence and Modality." *Philosophical Perspectives* 8: 1–16.

Fine, Kit. 1995. "The Logic of Essence." *Journal of Philosophical Logic* 24: 241–273.

Ingram, Stephen. 2015. "The Moral Fixed Points: Reply to Cuneo and Shafer-Landau." *Journal of Ethics and Social Philosophy* 9: 1–5.

Juhl, Cory, and Eric Loomis. 2010. *Analyticity*. New York: Routledge.

Loeb, Don. 2008. "Moral Incoherentism: How to Pull a Metaphysical Rabbit out of a Semantic Hat." In *Moral Psychology*, vol. 2, *The Cognitive Science of Morality: Intuition and Diversity*, edited by Walter Sinnott-Armstrong, 355–386. Cambridge, MA: MIT Press.

Mackie, J. L. 1977. *Ethics: Inventing Right and Wrong*. London: Penguin Books.

McPherson, Tristram. 2009. "Moorean Arguments and Moral Revisionism." *Journal of Ethics and Social Philosophy* 3: 1–24.

Moore, G. E. 1903. *Principia Ethica*. Cambridge: Cambridge University Press.

Olson, Jonas. 2014. *Moral Error Theory*. Oxford: Oxford University Press.

Price, Richard. 1787/1948. *A Review of the Principle Questions in Morals*. Oxford: Clarendon Press.

Priest, Graham. 1987. *In Contradiction: A Study of the Transconsistent*. Leiden: Martinus Nijhoff.

Rowlands, Richard. 2012. "Moral Error Theory and the Argument from Epistemic Reasons." *Journal of Ethics and Social Philosophy* 7: 1–25.

Sampson, Eric. 2023. "Moorean Arguments against the Error Theory: A Defense." *Oxford Studies in Metaethics* 18.

Smith, Michael. 1994. *The Moral Problem*. Oxford: Blackwell.

Soysal, Zeynep. 2018. "Formal Analyticity." *Philosophical Studies* 175: 2791–2811.

Street, Sharon. 2009. "In Defense of Future Tuesday Indifference: Ideally Coherent Eccentrics and the Contingency of What Matters" *Philosophical Issues* 19: 273–298.

Street, Sharon. 2016. "Objectivity and Truth: You'd Better Rethink It." *Oxford Studies in Metaethics* 11: 293–334.

Swinburne, Richard. 2020. "How to Define 'Moral Realism.'" *Journal of Philosophical Theological Research* 22: 15–33.

Wedgwood, Ralph. 2017. *The Value of Rationality*. Oxford: Oxford University Press.

Williamson, Timothy. 2006. "Conceptual Truth." *Proceedings of the Aristotelian Society* 80: 1–41.

Zangwill, Nick. 2000. "Against Analytical Functionalism." *Ratio* 13: 275–286.

CHAPTER 16

FIVE KINDS OF EPISTEMIC ARGUMENTS AGAINST ROBUST MORAL REALISM

JOSHUA SCHECHTER

I. INTRODUCTION

THERE are many objections that have been presented against non-naturalist moral realism. The objections involve several different kinds of considerations. There are objections from metaphysics: For instance, how can non-natural moral properties fit into a general scientific picture of the world?[1] How can moral realism explain the supervenience of non-natural moral properties on natural properties?[2] There are objections from the philosophy of language and philosophy of mind: If moral properties are non-natural properties, how can our linguistic and mental representations stand for them?[3] There are objections from moral psychology: If the role of moral beliefs is to represent facts about objective moral properties, what explains the tie between moral belief and moral motivation?[4] There are also objections based on normative considerations: If moral properties are non-natural properties more akin to abstract mathematical properties than anything tied to the natural world, how can we explain the significance of morality and the place it does and should have in our lives?[5]

---

[1] This is one strand in Mackie's (1977, ch. 1) "queerness argument."
[2] Blackburn (1984, pp. 182–4).
[3] See Wedgwood (2001) for discussion of this kind of objection and a response to it.
[4] See Shafer-Landau (2003, p. 121) for a presentation of this kind of objection, which he attributes to several earlier philosophers, going back to Stevenson (1937).
[5] It is tempting to reply to this sort of objection by saying that there can't be an issue here since, of course, morality has significance—it has moral significance. But this response is too quick. If a metaethical view tells us that morality concerns such-and-such, and such-and-such looks to be

The purpose of this chapter is to examine a different group of objections to non-naturalist moral realism, objections that are epistemic or at least have an epistemic flavor. These objections involve the nature of knowledge, justification, rationality, and reliable belief. The aim of this chapter is not to answer these objections or to argue that they are successful. Rather, the goal of this chapter is to discuss several families of epistemic objections to non-naturalist moral realism and to examine which ones are more pressing and which ones may safely be dismissed. In particular, I will discuss five families of epistemic objections to non-naturalist moral realism: (i) one involving necessary conditions on knowledge, (ii) one involving the idea that the causal history of our moral beliefs reflects the significant impact of irrelevant influences, (iii) one relying on the idea that moral truths as the realist conceives of them do not play a role in explaining our moral beliefs, (iv) one involving the claim that if moral realism is true then our moral beliefs are unlikely to be reliable, and finally, (v) one involving the claim that moral realism is incompatible with there being a plausible explanation of our reliability about morality. My overall conclusion is that most of these objections are not very persuasive. The final objection, concerning the difficulty of explaining our reliability, is by far the most pressing.[6] (The third objection, concerning the apparent failure of moral truths to explain our moral beliefs, does show that moral realism should not be taken to be the default metaethical view.)

Before I discuss these families of objections, it will first be useful to briefly present a strong form of non-naturalist moral realism to serve as the target of these objections. We may call this view "robust moral realism."[7] I present this view for two reasons. First, robust moral realism is the metaethical view that I am most tempted by. Second, treating the objections as targeted against a strong form of moral realism will help us to avoid various complexities that arise when additional targets are considered. For instance, we won't have to determine the exact range of realist views that each argument is best targeted against. (That's an interesting question, but it would distract attention away from the focus of this chapter.) So that is the task to which I now turn.

II. Robust Moral Realism

Robust moral realism, as I use the term here, has seven theses. The first thesis concerns moral language and moral thought:

---

insignificant, then we have reason to worry either about the significance of morality or (more likely) the truth of the metaethical theory.

[6] This chapter is thus in agreement with Enoch (2011, ch. 7) and Schechter (2017).
[7] I borrow this term from Enoch (2011).

Cognitivism. Certain sentences and mental representations purport to represent moral facts. They are both meaningful and truth-apt (that is, capable of being true or false).

This thesis rules out views on which, for instance, the role of moral language is not to represent but rather is to express emotions or other noncognitive attitudes. It is, however, compatible with the view that moral language has multiple roles simultaneously, such as both expressing emotions and representing moral facts.

The second thesis is the denial of moral error theory:

Non-Error Theory. Some basic moral properties and relations are exemplified.

This thesis rules out error theoretic views on which basic moral properties and relations are never exemplified. Different moral views will take different moral properties and relations to be basic, but natural candidates include *being morally right*, *being morally permissible*, *having moral value*, *being a moral reason for*, and so forth.[8]

The third thesis is the claim that the moral facts are independent of our attitudes, linguistic practices, and social practices.

Independence. The fundamental moral facts do not depend on us. In particular, they do not depend on facts about our minds, language, or social practices.[9]

Of course, some moral facts do depend on our minds, language, and social practices. The fact that someone has a strong preference may be relevant to what I morally ought to do. The fact that a word has a certain meaning in my community may be relevant to what I morally ought to say. And so forth. But these are not the fundamental moral facts—the ones that (in concert with the non-normative facts) determine the rest. According to this thesis, what is independent of our minds, language, and practices are the fundamental moral facts. For example, perhaps it is a fundamental moral truth that it is wrong to cause a gratuitous harm. If so, then the thesis entails that this truth does not depend on our minds, language, or social practices. But it is compatible with the thesis that it does depend on our practices that making a particular utterance would cause a gratuitous harm, and thus be morally wrong.

---

[8] We might want to generalize this thesis to also rule out simple patterns of exemplification of basic moral properties and relations. For instance, we might want to rule out a view on which *being morally permissible* is the sole basic moral property and every action is morally permissible.

[9] The thesis is distinct from what Shafer-Landau (2003, p. 15) calls "stance independence". Stance independence is the thesis that the moral facts are not true in virtue of being ratified by some privileged stance (or privileged set of stances). That rules out a certain kind of dependence of the moral facts on our practices. By contrast, this thesis rules out any kind of dependence. The reason for the generalization is that realism is also intuitively incompatible with a view on which the moral facts fully depend on our practices but not in virtue of the acceptance of any stance.

The fourth thesis is non-naturalism about the moral:

Non-naturalism. Moral properties and relations are not identical with, reducible to, or fully grounded in natural properties and relations.

It's controversial exactly how to understand the natural/non-natural distinction. For instance, perhaps the natural properties should be understood to be the properties that play a role in the natural sciences. Alternatively, perhaps the natural properties should be understood to be the descriptive properties. We don't need to decide between these conceptions. What's important for some of the arguments considered here is a consequence of non-naturalism, namely that moral facts are not causes of natural facts. And that is plausible on any reasonable characterization of the natural/non-natural distinction.

The fifth thesis concerns the possibility of moral error:

Intelligibility of Error. It is intelligible and genuinely possible to have moral beliefs that are largely wrong.

This thesis rules out certain kinds of morally plenitudinous views. Consider a view on which there are the properties of (moral) rightness and wrongness as well as the properties of rightness* and wrongness*, the properties of rightness** and wrongness**, and so forth. Suppose that for every coherent practice of assessing actions as "right" or "wrong", there is a corresponding pair of properties that exactly fits that practice.[10] Finally, suppose that moral semantics works so that the terms "right" and "wrong" as used in a community, and the corresponding concepts of *right* and *wrong*, have their semantic values assigned so as to stand for the pair of properties that most closely fits the community's usage.[11] On such a view, it couldn't have been the case that our moral beliefs were grossly wrong.[12] Ruling out such plenitudinous views is important because they fit the prior theses but are intuitively non-realist (or, at least, non-objectivist) views. The thesis is also important because it is part

---

[10] We might also want to add that the situation is perfectly symmetric. For instance, there is no pair of properties that is somehow metaphysically privileged.

[11] This view is broadly analogous to Balaguer's (1998) full-blooded Platonism about mathematics.

[12] The Intelligibility of Error thesis should presumably be strengthened to rule out applications of what Lewis (1989, p. 132) calls "the trick of rigidifying." Consider the view that is just like the plenitudinous view with the addition that when members of a community are considering what would be the case in a counterfactual scenario, they apply their actual standards of rightness and wrongness, not their counterfactual standards. On such a view, gross moral error is possible—we can imagine a situation in which we had very different moral beliefs and correctly judge that in that situation we would get it wrong. But this sort of plenitudinous view presumably should be ruled out, too, since it is intuitively a non-realist (or non-objectivist) view.

of what generates some of the intuitive worries facing moral realism. If gross moral error were not intelligible, then (at least prima facie) it would not be puzzling how it is that we have moral knowledge, how it is our moral beliefs are reliable, and so forth.

The sixth thesis is that we are not, in fact, largely wrong about morality:

> *Reliability.* The moral claims we believe (at least upon reflection and discussion) are true considerably more often than chance alone would predict.[13]

Despite the intelligibility and possibility of gross moral error, our beliefs are reliable in the sense that a much greater proportion of them are true than would be predicted by chance alone. Notice that this thesis does not have modal force. To be reliable requires only that our actual beliefs are true more often than chance predicts. It is not also required that our beliefs tend to be true in various counterfactual scenarios.

Notice that the Reliability thesis is compatible with our moral view departing from the true moral view in important ways. Our moral view may contain a considerable number of falsehoods or omit a considerable number of truths. One way to think about the thesis is as follows: Consider the set of all possible coherent moral views (or the set of moral views that are at least as coherent as our own moral view). Our moral view is much closer to the true moral view than a random moral view chosen from the set is likely to be. That's because we're broadly on the right track about many moral matters—for instance, suffering is morally bad—and a randomly selected moral view will likely be highly off track.[14]

The seventh and final thesis is that many of our moral beliefs have a positive epistemic status:

> *Justification.* Many of the moral claims we believe (at least upon reflection and discussion) are epistemically justified.

Taken together, these seven theses describe a strong form of non-naturalist moral realism. This package of theses will serve as the official target of the epistemic arguments discussed below.

---

[13] For present purposes, we can take "the moral claims we believe" to be the general consensus of presently living people. It is plausible that the Reliability thesis is true on this understanding. But readers who are worried about this claim are welcome to take the relevant group of people to be smaller.

[14] It could be that there are some limits on how far off track a community's beliefs can be on moral matters—if they are too far off track, they are no longer thinking about morality but (at best) something else. See Cuneo and Shafer-Landau (2014) for a view in this ballpark. But even if that's true, the limits are pretty wide—a community can have moral beliefs that are widely off the mark. (Indeed, there are examples of past and present communities with that feature.) See Plunkett (2020) for relevant discussion.

III. Argument 1: A Necessary Condition on Knowledge

The first family of arguments I will consider is based on the idea that if robust moral realism is true, then our moral beliefs fail to satisfy some necessary condition on knowledge. More explicitly, arguments in this family have the following schematic form:

(i) For a belief to count as knowledge requires that it have feature F;
(ii) If robust moral realism is true, then our moral beliefs don't have feature F;
(iii) So either robust moral realism is not true or we don't have moral knowledge.

This kind of argument is sometimes extended as follows: (iv) We do have moral knowledge, and so (v) Robust moral realism is false.

Arguments in this family differ on what feature F is. The most familiar version of this argument—albeit concerning a different domain—is what is often called "the Benacerraf problem" for mathematical Platonism.[15] In Benacerraf's argument, the relevant feature F is that the believer be in some causal relation with what the belief is about. More specifically, Benacerraf claims that for a belief to count as knowledge requires the believer to stand in a causal relation with the referents of the names, predicates, and quantifiers featuring in the belief. But, if mathematical Platonism is true, mathematical entities are acausal, so the referents of mathematical terms—e.g., numbers—cannot stand in any kind of causal relation. So either mathematical Platonism is not true or we don't have mathematical knowledge. An analogous argument can be made against robust moral realism.

It is widely recognized that Benacerraf's argument fails against mathematical Platonism and that the analogous argument fails against robust moral realism. The trouble is with the claim that there is a causal constraint on knowledge. Benacerraf made this claim because it was a then-popular response to the Gettier problem for the justified true belief analysis of knowledge.[16] The idea was that the reason that subjects in Gettier cases don't count as knowing the relevant claim is that their belief failed to satisfy a causal constraint.[17] However, proponents of the causal theory, such as Goldman, explicitly exempted a priori knowledge from requiring the satisfaction of a causal constraint, since they recognized that otherwise the constraint would rule out pretty much all a priori knowledge. The causal theory is also no longer popular, and for good reason. There are Gettier-style cases in which the relevant belief satisfies the causal constraint.[18]

---

[15] Benacerraf (1973).
[16] Gettier (1963).
[17] Goldman (1967).
[18] Goldman's (1976) fake barn case is such a case. So is the following variant of Chisholm's (1966) sheep in the field case: Suppose a thinker sees something that resembles a sheep in a field in the distance and comes to believe that there is a sheep in the field. If there really is a sheep in the field, but what the

More importantly for present purposes, there are cases of knowledge where the relevant belief does not satisfy a casual constraint. These include cases of knowledge of the future: I can know that something will exist tomorrow, say tomorrow's newspaper, without my standing in a casual relation with the future existent. So there are good reasons to reject the causal constraint as playing a role in the analysis of knowledge, or even as being a necessary condition on knowledge.

More recent arguments in this family make use of different (purported) necessary conditions on knowledge. Like Benacerraf's argument, the conditions are supposed to be necessary conditions on knowledge, but not on justified true belief. For instance, arguments of this sort can be presented where feature F is that the belief in question satisfies an explanatory rather than a causal constraint—the truth of the belief is somehow explanatorily connected with the believer's believing it.[19] Or the feature F could be that the belief in question is non-accidentally true,[20] or that it satisfies a sensitivity constraint (roughly: if the proposition believed were false, the thinker would not believe it), or that it satisfies a safety constraint (roughly: the thinker could not easily have had a false belief on the matter).[21]

Given such a (purported) necessary condition on knowledge, one could try to argue that robust moral realism precludes our moral beliefs from satisfying the condition. For instance, one could argue that if robust moral realism is true, moral facts do not cause or ground our moral beliefs, so the moral facts cannot explain our moral beliefs. And if robust moral realism is true, by the mind-independence of morality, the moral facts do not depend on our moral beliefs. So there is no explanatory connection between our moral beliefs and the moral facts. Similarly, one could argue that if robust moral realism is true, the truth of our moral beliefs would have to be accidental, since there is no obvious reason why our moral beliefs would correlate with the moral facts. Or, again, one could argue that if robust moral realism is true, our moral beliefs don't satisfy a sensitivity condition because if the non-natural moral properties were differently distributed, we would not have different moral beliefs, so it is not the case that if the contents of our moral beliefs were false, we would not believe them.[22] Or, finally, one could argue that if

---

thinker saw was a sculpture modeled on the sheep in question, the thinker's belief would be a justified true belief that satisfies the causal constraint but isn't knowledge. (I don't know who first modified Chisholm's example in this way.)

[19] For an example of an argument of this sort, see Lutz (2020).

[20] For an example of an argument of this sort, see Bengson (2015).

[21] See Nozick (1981) for a sensitivity constraint on knowledge and Sosa (1999) for a safety constraint on knowledge. The "roughly" hedges are present because there are many ways to formulate such constraints. They can be formulated using counterfactual conditionals, by a direct appeal to possible worlds, or in terms of whether something could easily happen. Some formulations also add a requirement that the counterfactual belief be formed using the same belief-forming method so, for instance, a belief counts as sensitive if the following obtains: If the proposition believed were false, the thinker would not believe it using the same method.

[22] 'Assuming that basic moral truths are necessarily true, this line of thought requires that some counterfactual conditionals with necessarily false antecedents are false, contrary to the orthodox Lewis/Stalnaker semantics.

robust moral realism is true, our moral beliefs don't satisfy a safety condition, since we can easily imagine having had false moral beliefs—indeed, there are plenty of past and present groups with false moral beliefs.

What should we make of such arguments? It is important to notice that they are not dialectically very effective. This is for three main reasons, in order from least to most important. The first reason is that it is not obvious that if robust moral realism is in fact true, the constraints fail to be met. Consider an explanatory constraint. Is it obvious that robust moral realism precludes there being an explanatory connection between our moral beliefs and the moral facts? If we permit common-explanation (i.e., third factor) accounts, then there may be an explanatory connection after all. For instance, on an account suggested by Enoch, our moral beliefs—or, better, the motivational tendencies that ultimately give rise to our moral beliefs—are the products of evolution by natural selection. Evolution "aims at" survival and reproductive success. Survival is, proposes Enoch, of positive moral value. So there is a kind of explanatory connection between our moral beliefs and the moral truths.[23]

Similarly, it is not obvious that given robust moral realism, our moral beliefs fail to be sensitive or safe. If the moral truths are necessary, and if counterfactuals with necessarily false antecedents are trivially true, it will be trivially true that if the moral facts were different, the thinker would not still believe them. So the sensitivity constraint will be met. If there is a good causal evolutionary/historical/sociological explanation of how we came to have our moral beliefs, then perhaps it is not the case we could easily have had deeply mistaken moral beliefs, so many of our moral beliefs will in fact be safe. And so on for other purported constraints.

The second, and more important, reason that these arguments are not dialectically very effective is that the purported conditions on knowledge are controversial. They may not be as obviously wrong as Benacerraf's original causal constraint. But there is nevertheless strong reason to worry about each of them.

It is plausible that there is some kind of non-accidentality condition on knowledge. But the precise formulation of such a condition is a vexed matter. To give an illustration, consider the case of someone who wins a raffle whose prize is a well-known encyclopedia of birds. Suppose the thinker randomly flips to a page and reads that the average airspeed velocity of a European swallow is approximately twenty-four miles per hour, and comes to believe this. Such a belief (assuming it's true, etc.) would seem to count as knowledge even though it was highly accidental that the thinker came to believe it. So, plausibly, we have to distinguish between kinds of accidentally true belief and restrict the condition on knowledge to require that the belief not have the wrong kind of accidentality, whatever that is.[24]

There are worries that face an explanatory constraint on knowledge. For instance, to accommodate knowledge of the future, we should allow common-explanation stories

---

[23] Enoch (2011, ch. 7).
[24] Pritchard (2005) distinguishes five varieties of epistemic luck and argues that knowledge is compatible with three of them.

to count as an explanatory connection—my belief that tomorrow's newspaper will exist and the fact that tomorrow's newspaper will exist are both explained by various facts about the present and past, e.g., concerning the newspaper publisher. Even permitting such explanatory connections, there are also apparent counterexamples to an explanatory requirement. Consider, for instance, the following case: Suppose that Edgar knows that Allan has taken a fatal dose of poison and that enough time has now passed that Allan is dead. Suppose Allan is in fact dead. However, unbeknownst to Edgar, Allan died because he ran into the street after taking the poison and was promptly run over by a bus.[25] In such a case, Edgar knows that Allan is dead despite there not being an explanatory connection between Edgar's belief and Allan's death, at least not the way it actually happened.

There are also numerous purported counterexamples to sensitivity and safety constraints on knowledge. Against sensitivity, it might be pointed out that anti-skeptical beliefs are not sensitive. Take the belief that I am not a brain in a vat being fed the perceptual experiences of a normal non-envatted person. If this belief were false, I would still presumably have it. So the belief is not sensitive. But it is plausibly an instance of knowledge. There are also more mundane purported counterexamples, such as this one due to Sosa: Suppose I throw a bag of trash down the garbage chute of my apartment. A little while later I believe, and presumably know, that the trash bag is in the basement. However, the nearest world in which my belief is false is one where unbeknownst to me, the bag got stuck somewhere along the chute and in which I still believe it is in the basement.[26] Similarly, there are many purported counterexamples to safety, although to be fair, they tend to be a bit more complicated than the counterexamples to sensitivity.[27]

The third reason that these arguments are not dialectically very effective is the most important one. Namely, despite appearances, the conclusion of the argument is not very worrisome for the robust moral realist. Recall that the conclusion of the argument is that either robust moral realism is false or we do not have moral knowledge. The latter disjunct, at least initially, may sound highly unpalatable. But this is a mistake. The various purported constraints on knowledge are all intended to be constraints on knowledge rather than on justified true belief. It is compatible with the conclusion of the argument that robust moral realism is true, and that while our moral beliefs do not strictly speaking count as knowledge, they do count as justified true beliefs.[28] It seems to me that if robust moral realists are forced to endorse this view, they should not find that very concerning. Robust moral realists can still maintain that their moral beliefs are true. They can still maintain that their beliefs are well supported by the evidence or are justified in whatever way moral beliefs are justified. They can also maintain that it is perfectly rational to hold on to robust moral realism and to their moral beliefs. Insofar as what we

---

[25] This is a variant of a case in Feldman (2003, p. 85).
[26] Sosa (1999, p. 145).
[27] See Grundmann (2018) for a useful survey of purported counterexamples to safety.
[28] This response was originally made to the Benacerraf problem for mathematical Platonism in Burgess and Rosen (1997, p. 37). I think this point has been underappreciated in the literature.

do (or should) epistemically care about is to get at the truth, and perhaps also to have justified or rational doxastic states, the robust moral realist needn't feel very concerned by the conclusion of the argument.

There would be a bigger problem for the robust moral realist if the conclusion of this family of arguments could be parlayed into a claim about justification. Lutz suggests a principle of this sort. His principle says, in effect, that if a thinker learns that one of her beliefs lacks some necessary condition on knowledge, this defeats the thinker's justification for the belief.[29] For the purpose of extending the arguments, we need a principle that is stronger still, something like: If a thinker learns that, assuming some theory is true, one of her beliefs lacks some necessary condition on knowledge, this defeats the justification of the conjunction of the theory with the belief. But in what follows, for simplicity, I'll focus on the weaker principle.

There is reason to think that Lutz's principle is false. If the principle is true, presumably so is the principle that says that having strong reason to believe that one does not know a claim defeats the justification one has for the claim. (Indeed, this latter principle, if true, is plausibly what explains the truth of Lutz's principle.) But it is plausible that the latter principle is not true. Indeed, it is plausible that it is not even true that having strong reason to believe that one does not know a claim is incompatible with knowing the claim. Consider, for example, the case of someone who has strong reason to believe a false theory of knowledge. Perhaps, for instance, the thinker is a college student taking an epistemology course who rationally comes to believe, based on the say-so of their eminent (but mistaken) professor, that knowledge requires absolute certainty. Given that they are not absolutely certain of some mundane proposition (e.g., their car is parked in their driveway), they have strong reason to believe that they don't know the mundane proposition. But surely, they still count as knowing it.[30]

In response to this sort of case, Lutz might point to the fact that his principle differs in two ways from the latter principle. First, his principle is put in terms of "learning", which is factive, unlike "having strong reason to believe". Second, his principle concerns learning that a belief does not satisfy a genuine constraint on knowledge, rather than something that one justifiably takes to be a constraint on knowledge. But these two differences seem unlikely to be relevant—it is plausible that if Lutz's principle is true, so is the latter one. Lutz also might also reject the claim that the college student in the case has strong reason to think knowledge requires certainty, or that the student counts as knowing the mundane claim. But there are other kinds of cases, too, in which a thinker can know a claim while having strong evidence that they don't know.[31]

There is another problem with Lutz's principle. Suppose I'm told that I'm in a group of people (say, the people in the room I'm presently in) who have the following feature: Anyone in the group who has a justified true belief about some specific topic (e.g., the weather) is in a Gettier situation and so doesn't have knowledge on that topic. Lutz's

---

[29] See Lutz (2020, p. 293), loosely inspired by Enoch (2011, pp. 161–1).
[30] This is a variant of a case due to Barnett (2021, p. 659).
[31] One such example is Williamson's (2011) case of the unmarked clock.

principle predicts that this should defeat my justification for my beliefs about the topic. But that is not intuitively correct. Learning that if my belief on the topic is a justified true belief, then it is not knowledge, doesn't give me any reason to think that my belief is untrue or unjustified or otherwise defective. So there doesn't seem to be any rational pressure on me at all to give up the belief or to reduce my confidence in it. So, it seems, Lutz's principle is false.[32]

What this suggests is that arguments against moral realism that appeal to a necessary condition on knowledge are not dialectically effective. Even if it were to turn out that one of them can be used to show that robust moral realism is incompatible with moral knowledge, this wouldn't be very worrisome, since it could still be maintained that one has justified true moral beliefs, which seems plenty good enough.

IV. ARGUMENT 2: IRRELEVANT INFLUENCES

Let me now turn to the second kind of epistemic argument against robust moral realism. This argument is based on the idea that, assuming moral realism, our moral beliefs were formed in a way that reflected the significant impact of irrelevant factors.[33] In more detail, the argument goes something like this:

(i) If, under the assumption that some theory is true, a thinker has good reason to believe that one of her beliefs was formed in a way that reflects the significant impact of irrelevant influences, then there is rational pressure on the thinker against accepting the combination of the theory and the belief.

(ii) Under the assumption that robust moral realism is true, we have good reason to believe that our moral beliefs were formed in a way that reflects the significant impact of irrelevant influences.

(iii) So there is rational pressure against our accepting the combination of robust moral realism and our moral beliefs.

Here, an irrelevant influence is a factor in the causal history of the belief that is disconnected from the truth of the claim in question.

This kind of argument is one way of trying to make sense of "evolutionary debunking arguments" against robust moral realism, which try to show that robust moral realism is false on the grounds that our moral beliefs (or the underlying motivational tendencies that help to generate them) were shaped by evolution by natural selection, and assuming

---

[32] Why is Lutz's principle intuitively plausible to begin with? A natural diagnosis is that when a thinker learns (or acquires good reason to believe) that one of their beliefs fails to satisfy a constraint on knowledge, this usually comes along with knowledge (or good reason to believe) that the belief may not be true. And that would defeat the justification for the belief.

[33] See Vavova (2018) for a general discussion of irrelevant influence arguments.

robust moral realism, evolutionary pressures are disconnected from the moral facts.[34] On such an argument, the irrelevant influences are evolutionary (e.g., survival and reproductive) pressures. But there can also be irrelevant influence arguments against robust moral realism that appeal to different kinds of irrelevant influences—for instance, psychological, sociological, or historical processes.

There is an immediate problem with this argument.[35] Namely, the central epistemic principle featuring in it, premise (i), is false. Many if not all of our beliefs were formed in a way that reflects the significant impact of irrelevant influences, and this does not count against their justification.

For an everyday example, consider the following case: It's the first sunny day in a while, and I have a bit of free time, so I decide to go on a walk. I take a fairly randomish path, and find myself on Ives St., where I happen to notice the new vegan ice cream place. Out of curiosity, I look at its menu, and learn that in addition to vegan ice cream, it also serves knishes. I count as justified in my belief that the new vegan ice cream place serves knishes, despite the fact that my coming to have the belief reflects the significant impact of irrelevant factors—the weather, the fact I had some free time, the randomish decisions to turn right and left along my walk, my curiosity about the menu, and so forth.

In response to cases like these, it is tempting to try to restrict or otherwise modify the epistemic principle. I can think of two main strategies for doing so. The first strategy is to say that irrelevant influences are not problematic when they lead to the discovery of new evidence. In the vegan ice cream case, the various irrelevant influences led me to read the menu, which provided me with evidence about what the vegan ice cream places serves. Such evidence "screens off" the impact of the irrelevant factors. According to this line of thought, learning about the significant impact of irrelevant influences on a belief, under the assumption that a theory is true, only generates rational pressure not to accept the combination of the theory and the belief if one is justified in believing that the irrelevant influences did not act via leading one to acquire new evidence that bears on the truth of the belief. Using this refined principle, we can argue that the irrelevant influences that generate our moral beliefs did not yield evidence for our moral beliefs, at least assuming robust moral realism.

This proposal faces several difficulties. One difficulty is that it is not clearly correct to claim that the irrelevant influences (evolutionary, historical, sociological, psychological, etc.) on our moral beliefs did not lead us to acquire evidence about moral matters. One could say that some of our evidence about moral matters comes from our intuitive judgments about specific (actual and hypothetical) cases, and that the irrelevant influences had an impact in generating these intuitions. So the influences did in fact play a role in leading us to acquire evidence about moral matters. A second difficulty

---

[34] See, for example, Street (2006).
[35] Some of the points in this section overlap with points made in Schechter (2017). This chapter is, in some ways, an update of that paper.

with the proposal is that if learning about irrelevant influences can defeat the justification of a belief, it presumably can do so even if the influences led me to acquire new evidence—I might learn that the influences led me to acquire evidence in a biased way or to misevaluate my evidence. A third problem with the proposal is that learning of the significant impact of irrelevant influences can fail to defeat my justification even if the influence did not lead to me acquire new evidence—for instance, the influence might have led me to better evaluate the evidence that I already possessed. For instance, here is a case of that sort: I felt the need to relax and so took a shower, which enabled my mind to wander, which led me to figure out the crucial step in working out a practical or theoretical problem, which led me to a new belief. That I felt the need to relax had a significant impact on my belief but didn't provide any new evidence bearing on its truth. Nevertheless, learning of this causal history would not defeat my justification for the belief.

The second strategy to restrict the epistemic principle is to distinguish between irrelevant influences and distorting or pernicious influences. On this line of thought, learning about the significant impact of some causal influences on a belief only defeats the justification of the belief if the thinker is justified in believing that the influences had a distorting effect on the belief. One difficulty facing this suggestion is that in many cases, it is a mistake to think of the casual influences as distorting some pre-existing belief. Rather, there would not have been a belief about the matter at all were it not for those influences. For instance, in the case of an evolutionary debunking argument, it is not the case that were it not for the relevant evolutionary forces, we would have had undistorted moral beliefs. Rather, were it not for the relevant evolutionary forces, we would not have existed at all.

These concerns show that there are difficulties facing irrelevant influence-based arguments against robust moral realism. It is difficult to formulate a plausible version of the epistemic principle featuring in such arguments. But even if some restricted or modified version of the epistemic principle can be formulated that avoids counterexample, there is a still more significant difficulty facing the entire line of thought. There is something wrong with the strategy of pointing to specific influences on our moral beliefs and arguing that such influences led us astray. There is a deeper intuitive problem facing robust moral realism—not that our moral beliefs reflect the impact of irrelevant influences, but that they fail to reflect the impact of relevant ones. Given robust moral realism, we don't need to learn about the causal history of our moral beliefs to locate a problem. We know that, since moral facts are acausal, they cannot play a role in generating our moral beliefs. And that is a deeper and intuitively more worrisome problem.

V. Argument 3: Harman's Challenge

There is a familiar argument against moral realism based on the thought that, assuming robust moral realism, the moral facts don't play a role in generating our moral beliefs.

This argument is due to Harman and is sometimes called "Harman's challenge."[36] One way to formulate this argument is as follows:

(i) If, under the assumption that some theory is true, the truths about a domain do not play a role in the best explanation of our beliefs about the domain, then there is rational pressure against accepting the combination of the theory and our beliefs about the domain.
(ii) Assuming robust moral realism, the moral truths do not play a role in the best explanation of our moral beliefs.
(iii) So, there is rational pressure against accepting the combination of robust moral realism and our moral beliefs.

(Harman's discussion focuses on whether the moral truths play a role in explaining what he calls our "moral observations", but the change to moral beliefs is harmless. Harman also targets a wider class of metaethical theories than robust realist ones, but the challenge seems strongest when presented against robust moral realism.)

The idea behind the second premise is that if robust moral realism is true, then the moral truths are acausal, and so can't play a role in explaining our moral beliefs. What is the idea behind the first premise?

There are three very different lines of thought that could support an epistemic principle like the first premise. The first is that a belief counts as knowledge only if the relevant truth plays a role in the explanation of the belief. If there's also a principle linking necessary conditions on knowledge with justification, such as Lutz's principle, then we can derive something like the first premise. I've already discussed this kind of argument above and argued that it runs into serious problems.

The second line of thought motivating something like the first premise concerns reliability. If the truths about a domain do not play a role in explaining our beliefs about the domain, it is mysterious how it is that we believe the truths about the domain. In the absence of an explanation of our reliability, there is pressure against accepting the combination of our beliefs about the domain and the background beliefs that help to generate the mystery. (Those background beliefs include (i) Non-naturalism, which rules out an explanation on which the moral facts explain our moral beliefs and (ii) Independence, which rules out an explanation on which our moral beliefs explain the moral facts.) I think that something like this line of thought is a challenging one for the robust moral realist, and I will discuss it in detail later in this chapter.

The third line of thought seems closest to what Harman himself seems to have had in mind. The idea is that for us to have reason to believe in the existence of some objects or the exemplification of some properties or relations, then commitment to those

---

[36] See Harman (1977, pp. 3–10).

objects, properties, and relations had better do some explanatory work for us.[37] The objects, properties, or relations had better "earn their keep." This is a kind of Ockamite consideration—we shouldn't be committed to an ontology or ideology that is more expansive than necessary. Learning that (purported) objects, properties, or relations don't earn their keep defeats any justification we may have for being committed to them.

Given this methodological principle, the argument, then, goes like this: To justifiably retain a commitment to moral truths, properties, and relations, such truths, properties, and relations had better do some explanatory work for us. According to robust moral realism, moral truths, properties, and relations are not identical with, reducible to, or grounded in natural truths, properties, and relations. So our commitment to moral truths, properties, and relations cannot be defended by appealing to the explanatory roles that natural truths, properties, and relations play in our overall view of the world. The only explanatory work that moral truths, properties, and relations apparently can do is in helping to explain how it is we have our moral beliefs. But given robust moral realism, it seems that moral truths, properties, and relations cannot play a role in explaining our moral beliefs either. So there is pressure to give up our commitment to moral truths, properties, and relations, at least as the robust moral realist conceives of them.

This argument has some force. The general principle that we shouldn't be committed to an ontology or ideology that is more expansive than necessary is plausible. But Harman's challenge is less powerful than it is sometimes treated as being.

Harman's line of argument does, I think, show that we should not take robust moral realism to be the default view in metaethics. A line of argument that I've sometimes heard is that the pretheoretically most natural view is moral realism, so we should treat moral realism as the default view and only give it up if we have compelling reason to do so. What Harman's challenge, in effect, points out is that there is a cost in accepting moral truths, properties, and relations as the robust moral realist conceives of them. Once we notice that, it is hard to maintain that robust moral realism is the default position.[38] To justifiably endorse robust moral realism requires showing how moral truths, properties, and relations (as the robust moral realist conceives of them) earn their keep in our overall picture of the world.[39]

---

[37] This claim presumably should be restricted to positive properties and relations. The property of being a non-unicorn, for example, presumably doesn't need to do work for us in order for us to have reason to think it is exemplified. I'll leave this restriction implicit in what follows.

[38] Woods (2018) similarly argues that Harman's challenge should be seen as a "burden-shifting" argument.

[39] This understanding of Harman's challenge has several points of contact with Wright's discussion of Harman in Wright (1992, ch. 5.v). Wright argues that moral realism faces trouble if moral facts do not have a "wide cosmological role" in the sense that they cannot play a role in explaining anything other than our moral judgments and beliefs. There are two principal differences between this line of thought and the one I'm taking from Harman. First, Wright does not count explanations of our moral judgments and beliefs as a way that moral facts can earn their keep. Second, Wright identifies the distinction between domains in which the facts can play an explanatory role and domains in which they cannot with a distinction between realism and antirealism. (On Wright's view, there are several realism/antirealism distinctions.) By contrast, on my rendering of Harman's argument, that moral facts realistically

However, Harman's line of argument seems much too quick in concluding that if moral truths (as conceived by the robust moral realist) do not play a role in explaining our moral beliefs, then they cannot do any work for us, and so we should give up our commitment to them. There are other ways that these truths can earn their keep beyond playing a role in explaining our beliefs. Versions of this point have been made by Sayre-McCord and by Enoch.[40] Sayre-McCord considers the view that our general explanatory practices rely upon value judgments to legitimate them, value judgments that may also legitimate our moral judgments. If that view is right, Sayre-McCord argues, then we may justifiably retain our commitment to moral truths as the robust moral realist conceives of them. Enoch argues that we are entitled to accept normative truths as the robust realist conceives of them, because a commitment to such truths is needed to make sense of our deliberative practices. Deliberation only makes sense if it aims at figuring out the independent normative truths. And once we allow normative truths as the robust realist conceives of them into our worldview, it is not costly to also allow specifically moral truths into our worldview.

Sayre-McCord and Enoch are right that we can respond to Harman's challenge by showing that moral truths, properties, and relations can earn their keep in ways other than by helping to explain our moral beliefs. But the point generalizes still further than they explicitly note. The basic idea behind Harman's challenge is that we shouldn't be committed to a more expansive ontology or ideology than is needed—or better, than we have good reason to accept. One way that a commitment to objects, properties, and relations can be defended is by showing that the objects, properties, and relations do explanatory work for us, for instance in helping to explain our beliefs. But the commitment to objects, properties, and relations can be defended in other ways, too. If we have any kind of good reason whatsoever to accept the objects, properties, and relations, that shows that the objects, properties, and relations can earn their keep. So all one needs to do to answer Harman's challenge is to show that we have some kind of positive reason to accept moral truths, properties, and relations as the robust moral realist conceives of them. Any good reason will do. That's why Harman's challenge is less powerful than it may at first appear.

VI. Argument 4: The Argument from Improbability

In discussing Harman's challenge, I put off discussion of the suggestion that the problem facing robust moral realism has to do with our reliability about moral

---

construed cannot play an explanatory role provides reason to reject moral realism, which is understood as a distinct thesis.

[40] See Sayre-McCord (1988, pp. 278–80) and Enoch (2011, ch. 3).

matters. Let me turn to that suggestion now. The thought is that if robust moral realism is true, then it is mysterious how it is that our beliefs about morality are reliable, but since we are in fact reliable, we should give up moral realism. A version of this argument has recently been presented by Warren.[41] Warren's argument is not aimed against robust moral realism in particular, but against what he calls "non-causal realism" about any domain. Somewhat simplifying and reordering Warren's presentation, and focusing on the specific case of morality, we can put the argument schematically as follows:

(i) If robust moral realism is true, then our moral beliefs don't have feature F.
(ii) If our moral beliefs don't have feature F, then they are unlikely to be reliable.
(iii) Our moral beliefs are reliable.
(iv) So robust moral realism is not true.

Warren uses the safety and sensitivity of our beliefs as feature F, but similar arguments can be made for other candidate features, such as standing in a causal or explanatory relation with the relevant facts or being non-accidentally true. This family of arguments thus resembles the first family of arguments I considered, involving features that are proposed as necessary conditions on knowledge, but without the tie to knowledge. Instead, the tie is between these features and reliability. (As before, beliefs about a domain count as reliable if they are true far more often than chance alone would predict.)

Notice that this argument, as I formulated it, is not deductively valid—the second premise concerns whether our moral beliefs are likely to be reliable and the third concerns whether they are in fact reliable. This is not, by itself, a problem with the argument. Plenty of good philosophical arguments are not deductively valid but nevertheless have significant epistemic force.

However, there is a difficulty with this family of arguments. There need not be much of a clash between the claim that such-and-such is unlikely to be true and such-and-such is in fact true. For example, suppose I flip a coin twenty times and the following sequence of heads and tails results: HHTTTHTTHTTTHTHHHTT. That this specific sequence resulted is highly unlikely, at least given my understanding about how coin flips work, etc. Indeed, the probability of that specific sequence is approximately one in a million. Nevertheless, there is no epistemic pressure on me whatsoever to give up my theory of how coin flips work based on the occurrence of this unlikely sequence of flips.

Warren responds to a version of this objection.[42] He argues that in many cases of improbable events, such as the case of Lucky Larry winning the lottery, we have plenty

---

[41] Warren (2017).
[42] Warren (2017, pp. 1648–9).

of independent evidence for the occurrence of the improbable event. The difference is that in the case of our moral beliefs, we don't have independent evidence in support of their reliability. That's why the improbability of our reliability poses a problem but Luck Larry's lottery win does not.

I'm not convinced by this response. A first point is that we can think of cases in which we don't have much independent evidence of the occurrence of an improbable event. Consider a coin flip case in which I didn't flip the coin but my friend did, and he reports to me a specific sequence of heads and tails. Suppose my friend is not a very reliable testifier. The fact that what my friend reports is an unlikely occurrence isn't germane to whether or not I should believe my friend's report—I should believe it roughly as much or as little as I would believe his report of a not-unlikely occurrence, say that he had orange juice with breakfast.[43] So if there is a problem due to the lack of independent evidence, this has nothing to do with unlikelihood.

A second point is that the response misidentifies the target of the argument. Recall that Warren's argument is an argument against robust moral realism, not the reliability of our moral beliefs. So whether or not we have independent evidence of our moral reliability seems irrelevant to the argument. Indeed, consider a situation in which I have strong independent evidence for my moral reliability. Suppose, for instance, the epistemology oracle appears before me and tells me that my moral beliefs are highly reliable. Suppose the oracle is nearly always correct about what she pronounces upon (and I know this based on her excellent track record). I now have strong independent evidence of my moral reliability. But this doesn't seem to answer the intuitive problem for robust moral realism. The fact that I am reliable still seems mysterious, given robust moral realism, whether or not I have strong independent evidence in support of it.

What this suggests is that Warren's argument doesn't quite capture the problem for robust moral realism. The unlikelihood of an event isn't enough to generate an epistemic problem. The natural suggestion to make is that our reliability about morality isn't merely an unlikely fact (given robust moral realism) but is a striking fact that "calls out for explanation." The trouble for robust moral realism is that there doesn't seem to be such an explanation compatible with robust moral realism. And that is what generates the intuitive problem.

---

[43] There are two caveats to make here. First, if the reason my friend is unreliable is that he has a dodgy memory, perhaps I should be less confident in his report on the coin toss than on the orange juice, simply because a sequence of twenty tosses is harder to remember. So we should understand the case to be one in which the reason for his unreliability is different. Second, if my friend tells me a highly implausible story (a fish tale), I should have less confidence in that report than that he had orange juice at breakfast. But this is not solely due to the low probability of the story. Rather, it is due to the fact that my evidence suggests that the best explanation of my friend's recounting the story is not that the story is true but that he made it up.

VII. Argument 5: The Reliability Challenge

The fifth and final kind of argument I'll discuss is based on the idea that robust moral realism runs into difficulty because it is not compatible with there being an explanation of how it is we have reliable moral beliefs. This argument is often called "the reliability challenge" against moral realism. It is analogous to an argument made by Field against mathematical Platonism which is often called "the Benacerraf-Field problem."[44]

The argument depends on the idea that some facts are striking or "explanatorily urgent."[45] Whether a fact is striking doesn't depend only on whether it is unlikely. For instance, the fact that a coin was tossed a hundred times and resulted in a random-seeming pattern of heads and tails is not striking. The fact that a coin was tossed a hundred times and resulted in heads every time is striking. So is the fact that a coin was tossed a hundred times and resulted in the first few lines of *Hamlet* in Morse code. This is so despite the fact that every sequence of heads and tails is equally likely for a fair coin.

Given the notion of a striking fact, the reliability challenge can be put as follows:

(i) It is a cost of a theory if it is incompatible with there being a plausible explanation of some striking fact.
(ii) According to robust moral realism, our moral beliefs are reliable in the sense that they are true far more often than chance alone would predict.
(iii) Given robust moral realism, the fact that our moral beliefs are reliable is a striking fact.
(iv) Robust moral realism is incompatible with there being a plausible explanation of the fact that our moral beliefs are reliable.
(v) This is a cost to accepting robust moral realism.

The first premise is a general principle governing theory choice. It is a cost of a theory if the theory requires us to treat some striking fact as inexplicable. In other words, there is at least some epistemic pressure to not accept the theory. (This is compatible with the overall balance of considerations epistemically supporting the acceptance of the theory.)

The second premise of the argument follows from the definition of robust moral realism provided above. (If one doesn't want to include our reliability about morality as a component of moral realism, the argument could be refashioned to conclude that there

---

[44] See the Introduction and title essay in Field (1989) for the Benacerraf-Field problem for mathematical Platonism. See Enoch (2011, ch. 7) for the analogous problem for robust moral realism. See Schechter (2010) for the analogous problem for realism about logic, as well as a brief discussion of the cases of mathematics, modality, and morality.

[45] I borrow the phrase "explanatory urgency" from White (2005).

is a cost to accepting the combination of moral realism with the claim that our moral beliefs are reliable.)

In support of the third premise, it would be nice to provide a general theory of when a fact is striking. Unfortunately, I do not have such a theory to provide.[46] Nevertheless, it is plausible that the reliability of our moral beliefs, if true, is a striking fact. Part of the reason the fact is striking is that, assuming robust moral realism, it is intelligible and genuinely possible that our moral beliefs are largely false, but our moral beliefs are in fact largely true, or at least are true considerably more reliable than chance alone would predict. How striking our reliability about morality is depends on just how reliable our beliefs are—the more reliable we are, the more striking our reliability is. It also depends on who the "we" is in the statement of reliability—the bigger and more diverse the group, the more striking our reliability is.

The fourth premise depends on a particular understanding of what exactly calls out for explanation. There are different explanatory tasks one could undertake in explaining our reliability about morality. One question is: How do our belief-forming methods work so as to generate reliable moral beliefs? A second question is: How is it that we have belief-forming methods that generate reliable moral beliefs? In earlier work, I called the first question "the operational question" and the second question "the etiological question."[47]

For the purpose of formulating the reliability challenge, the second question is the relevant one. There are plausible candidate answers to the first. For example, here is one possibility: We have a cognitive mechanism for making moral judgments that involves implicit commitment to general moral principles that are more-or-less correct.[48] (One such principle could be that causing gratuitous suffering is wrong). Our mechanisms of concept application make use of these principles as well as our beliefs about the world to yield moral verdicts on actual and hypothetical cases. This is what generates some of our moral judgments. We then use our general reasoning abilities to arrive at further moral beliefs. Since the general moral principles embedded in our cognitive mechanism are more-or-less correct, this explains how it is that our belief-forming methods work so as to yield reliable moral beliefs.

My claim here is not that this explanation is correct. Rather, it is that this explanation is a plausible explanation compatible with robust moral realism. More importantly, it is a proof of concept that there are plausible explanations to be had that are compatible with robust moral realism.

---

[46] There are plausible heuristics for when a fact is striking: (i) A general fact is striking if it describes a simple pattern—e.g., "all heads"; (ii) A particular fact is striking if it violates an otherwise well-confirmed generalization—e.g., "the coin has started to float in mid-air"; (iii) A fact is striking if there is a salient (but perhaps improbable) theory that would explain it—e.g., "someone is intentionally controlling the coin with their mind".

[47] Schechter (2010).

[48] This is what Peacocke (1998) calls an "implicit conception".

Given robust moral realism, the second explanatory task is, at least prima facie, much more challenging. Suppose the above answer to the operational question is correct. How is it that we have a cognitive mechanism for making moral judgements that involves the implicit commitment to more-or-less correct moral principles? Given robust moral realism, the answer cannot be that the moral truths caused us to have these commitments—moral truths are acausal and so cannot cause anything. Given robust moral realism, the answer cannot be that our moral commitments explain the moral truths—the fundamental moral truths are mind-independent and so cannot be explained by our commitments. So it appears much more difficult to provide a plausible explanation of how it is we have a cognitive mechanism that yields reliable moral beliefs. It is this explanatory task that the reliability challenge should be understood to focus on.

Notice that the conclusion of the argument is not that robust moral realism is mistaken. Rather, it is that there is a cost to accepting robust moral realism. Even if the conclusion is correct, it could be that this cost is outweighed by the considerations supporting the theory. It could be that robust moral realism is superior to its alternatives.

What should we make of this argument? In my view, it is a serious concern facing robust moral realism. The premises are all plausible. And the argument seems to get to the heart of what is disquieting about robust moral realism, at least from an epistemic point of view. So this argument is what I take to be the central epistemic argument against robust moral realism.

There are responses in the literature to the reliability challenge that aim to show that it is not as pressing as it appears. One such response is to argue that the epistemic principle (i.e., that it is a cost of a theory if it is incompatible with there being a plausible explanation of a striking fact) is unmotivated. Relatedly, it could be argued that it is unmotivated to think there is a distinction between striking and non-striking facts at all. Baras argues for this latter conclusion by arguing, among other things, that most of the examples that have been taken to motivate the idea that some facts are striking can be accounted for using purely Bayesian reasoning, and so the notion of strikingness does no explanatory work for us.[49]

A different kind of response is to argue that the reliability challenge can be answered with a trivial kind of explanation: We first explain how we came to have the moral beliefs that we do, appealing to some combination of evolution, history, sociology, and psychology. We then explain why the moral truths are the way they are, appealing to the fundamental moral principles as well as contingent claims about the way the world actually is. (The fundamental moral principles themselves either have no explanation, are explained by the fact that they are necessary truths, or are explained by the fact that they follow from the nature of moral properties and relations.) Finally, we put both explanations together and argue that there is a causal story of why we believe

---

[49] Baras (2022).

such-and-such claims, and such-and-such claims are in fact largely true, so this explains how it is we believe moral truths.[50]

These are interesting responses. I don't have the space to adjudicate them in detail here.[51] But I do want to claim that intuitively, some facts seem to require explanation more than others. For example, flipping a coin many times and seeing a sequence of all heads requires explanation in a way that a random-seeming sequence of heads and tails does not, despite the fact that the two sequences are equiprobable (for a fair coin). And, intuitively, an "explanation" of how we have reliable moral beliefs that merely points to an explanation of how we came to believe the claims that we do and then says that these claims are largely true does not seem like a genuine explanation of our reliability. Of course, it would be nice to have a worked-out account of what it would take to explain our reliability. But this follows from a more general point: It would be nice to have a general account of explanation. Formulating such an account has proved difficult, even though there is generally broad agreement about when some purported explanation does and when it does not count as a genuine explanation.

My view is that the best response to the reliability challenge for moral realism is not to reject the challenge or to provide a trivial kind of explanation, but to respond to the argument by providing a substantive explanation of our reliability. In carrying out this task, a question arises: Is it legitimate for the contents of our moral beliefs to play a role in the explanation? Can we, for instance, appeal to the claim that causing gratuitous harm is wrong in trying to formulate an explanation of why it is we correctly believe that claim (or other moral claims)? Or would that be problematically question-begging?[52]

Given the structure of the reliability challenge, there is no problem with appealing to our substantive moral views in responding to the challenge. The challenge is an explanatory one—what is the explanation of our reliability? In general, in providing an explanation of some phenomenon, it is perfectly acceptable to make use of our views about the world.[53] The challenge tries to point to an internal tension in the moral realist's package of views. In responding to the claim that one's view has an internal tension, it is perfectly acceptable to show how the tension can be resolved using materials provided by the view.

---

[50] This is close to what Linnebo (2006) calls "the boring explanation" in the context of explaining our reliability about mathematics. Also see Lewis (1986, pp. 114–5), who considers (and rejects) the view that explanations of our reliability are needed only for contingent subject matters. Also see Clarke-Doane (2017), who argues that the only legitimate explanatory demands concerning our reliability about a domain are to show that our beliefs about the domain are safe and to show that our beliefs about the domain are sensitive. Since the fundamental moral principles are necessary truths, our beliefs in such truths are automatically sensitive. An evolutionary, historical, sociological, or psychological explanation suffices to show that our beliefs are safe.

[51] See Schechter (2010; 2018) for discussion of the latter kind of response, in the context of the reliability challenge for logic. I hope to address the first kind of response in future work.

[52] See Street (2008, pp. 216–7) for a version of this concern, aimed at responses to the "Darwinian dilemma" for moral realism.

[53] What is prohibited is to explain a phenomenon in terms of itself or in terms of anything that is itself (in part) explained by the phenomenon.

What would be objectionably question-begging is if someone argued as follows: Our moral beliefs are reliable. This is a striking fact. So there must be an explanation of our reliability. So there is no problem facing the realist. To answer the challenge, it is not enough to conclude that there is an explanation. Rather, we need to exhibit such an explanation, a sketch of such an explanation, or some kind of proof of concept that such an explanation can ultimately be provided.

What could an explanation of our reliability about morality look like, if it is to be compatible with moral realism? The most promising suggestion is to provide a third-factor explanation. The idea is that there is some factor that both causally explains our moral beliefs and metaphysically grounds the moral truths, thus ensuring some kind of match between them. There are several candidate third-factor explanations that appear in the literature.[54] While it is beyond the scope of this chapter to evaluate them, I will say that I am not satisfied with the third-factor explanations that have so far been developed. If the robust moral realist is going to directly respond to the reliability challenge, this is where they should focus their attention. If no such account is workable, then the best they can do is to argue that the reliability challenge poses a cost for robust moral realism, but it is a cost which they think they should bear.

VIII. Conclusion

Let's take stock. There are many different families of argument with an epistemic flavor that have been presented against robust moral realism. What I've claimed here is that many of these arguments are not very pressing. Arguments appealing to (purported) necessary conditions on knowledge face several difficulties, most notably that their conclusion is not very threatening. Arguments appealing to irrelevant influences face difficulty in formulating a plausible epistemic principle and also seem not to capture the intuitive epistemic problem facing robust moral realism. Harman's challenge has some force, but only ends up showing that robust moral realism is not the default metaethical position. The argument from improbability is not very threatening, since the occurrence of an improbable event, by itself, does not pose an epistemic problem for a view. What does seem to be the most challenging problem is the reliability challenge. It makes use of plausible premises. It also captures the intuitive epistemic problem with robust moral realism. (And the same is true for our beliefs about other domains, such as logic, mathematics, modality, and so forth.) So this is the problem on which robust moral realists should focus their attention.[55]

---

[54] See, for instance, Wielenberg (2010), Enoch (2011, pp. 168–74), and Sarksaune (2011).
[55] Thanks to David Christensen for helpful discussion. Thanks also to the two editors of this volume for numerous helpful suggestions.

REFERENCES

Balaguer, Mark. 1998. *Platonism and Anti-Platonism in Mathematics*. Oxford: Oxford University Press.

Baras, Dan. 2022. *Calling for Explanation*. Oxford: Oxford University Press.

Barnett, Zach. 2021. "Rational Moral Ignorance." *Philosophy and Phenomenological Research* 102: 645–664.

Benacerraf, Paul. 1973. "Mathematical Truth." *Journal of Philosophy* 70: 661–679.

Bengson, John. 2015. "Grasping the Third Realm." *Oxford Studies in Epistemology* 5: 1–38.

Blackburn, Simon. 1984. *Spreading the Word*. Oxford: Oxford University Press.

Burgess, John, and Gideon Rosen. 1997. *A Subject with No Object*. Oxford: Oxford University Press.

Chisholm, Roderick. 1966. *Theory of Knowledge*. Englewood Cliffs, NJ: Prentice-Hall.

Clarke-Doane, Justin. 2017. "What Is the Benacerraf Problem?" In *New Perspectives on the Philosophy of Paul Benacerraf: Truth, Objects, Infinity*, edited by Fabrice Pataut, 17–43. Cham: Springer.

Cuneo, Terence, and Shafer-Landau, Russ. 2014. "The Moral Fixed Points: New Directions for Moral Nonnaturalism." *Philosophical Studies* 171: 399–443.

Enoch, David. 2011. *Taking Morality Seriously*. Oxford: Oxford University Press.

Feldman, Richard. 2003. *Epistemology*. Upper Saddle River, NJ: Prentice Hall.

Field, Hartry. 1989. *Realism, Mathematics, and Modality*. New York: Blackwell Publishers.

Gettier, Edmund. 1963. "Is Justified True Belief Knowledge?" *Analysis* 23: 121–123.

Goldman, Alvin. 1967. "A Causal Theory of Knowing." *Journal of Philosophy* 64: 357–372.

Goldman, Alvin. 1976. "Discrimination and Perceptual Knowledge." *Journal of Philosophy* 73: 771–791.

Grundmann, Thomas. 2018. "Saving Safety from Counterexamples." *Synthese* 197: 5161–5185.

Harman, Gilbert. 1977. *The Nature of Morality*. Oxford: Oxford University Press.

Lewis, David. 1986. *On the Plurality of Worlds*. Oxford: Blackwell Publishers.

Lewis, David. 1989. "Dispositional Theories of Value." *Proceedings of the Aristotelian Society, Supplementary Volume* 63: 113–137.

Linnebo, Øystein. 2006. "Epistemological Challenges to Mathematical Platonism." *Philosophical Studies* 129: 545–574.

Lutz, Matt. 2020. "The Reliability Challenge in Moral Epistemology." *Oxford Studies in Metaethics* 15: 284–308.

Mackie, John. 1977. *Ethics: Inventing Right and Wrong*. Harmondsworth, UK: Penguin.

Nozick, Robert. 1981. *Philosophical Explanations*. Cambridge, MA: Harvard University Press.

Peacocke, Christopher. 1998. "Implicit Conceptions, Understanding and Rationality." *Philosophical Issues* 9: 43–88.

Plunkett, David. 2020. "Conceptual Truths, Evolution, and Reliability about Authoritative Normativity." *Jurisprudence* 11: 169–212.

Pritchard, Duncan. 2005. *Epistemic Luck*. Oxford: Oxford University Press.

Sarksaune, Knut. 2011. "Darwin and Moral Realism: Survival of the Iffiest." *Philosophical Studies* 152: 229–243.

Sayre-McCord, Geoffrey. 1988. "Moral Theory and Explanatory Impotence." In *Essays on Moral Realism*, 256–281. Ithaca: Cornell University Press.

Schechter, Joshua. 2010. "The Reliability Challenge and the Epistemology of Logic." *Philosophical Perspectives* 24: 437–464.

Schechter, Joshua. 2017. "Explanatory Challenges in Metaethics." In *The Routledge Handbook of Metaethics*, edited by Tristram McPherson and David Plunkett, 443–458. New York: Routledge.
Schechter, Joshua 2018. "Is There a Reliability Challenge for Logic?" *Philosophical Issues* 28: 325–347.
Shafer-Landau, Russ. 2003. *Moral Realism: A Defense*. Oxford: Oxford University Press.
Sosa, Ernest. 1999. "How to Defeat Opposition to Moore." *Philosophical Perspectives* 13: 141–153.
Stevenson, Charles. 1937. "The Emotive Meaning of Ethical Terms." *Mind* 46: 14–31.
Street, Sharon. 2006. "A Darwinian Dilemma for Realist Theories of Value." *Philosophical Studies* 127: 109–166.
Street, Sharon. 2008. "Reply to Copp: Naturalism, Normativity, and the Varieties of Realism Worth Worrying About." *Philosophical Issues* 18: 207–228.
Vavova, Katia. 2018. "Irrelevant Influences." *Philosophy and Phenomenological Research* 96: 134–152.
Warren, Jared. 2017. "Epistemology versus Non-Causal Realism." *Synthese* 194: 1643–1662.
Wedgwood, Ralph. 2001. "Conceptual Role Semantics for Moral Terms." *Philosophical Review* 110: 1–30.
White, Roger. 2005. "Explanation as a Guide to Induction." *Philosophers' Imprint* 5: 1–29.
Wielenberg, Erik. 2010. "On the Evolutionary Debunking of Morality." *Ethics* 120: 441–464.
Williamson, Timothy. 2011. "Improbable Knowing." In *Evidentialism and its Discontents*, edited by Trent Dougherty, 147–164. Oxford: Oxford University Press.
Woods, Jack. 2018. "Mathematics, Morality, and Self-Effacement." *Noûs* 52: 47–68.
Wright, Crispin. 1992. *Truth and Objectivity*. Cambridge, MA: Harvard University Press.

CHAPTER 17

THE EXPLANATORY ROLES OF MORAL FACTS AND THE CASE FOR MORAL REALISM

ROBERT AUDI

A major question in the metaphysics of ethics is whether there are moral facts and, if so, whether they are reducible to natural facts. On one strong version of metaphysical naturalism, natural facts are taken to be the only genuine facts; but some metaphysical realists countenance the wider view that facts earn their keep (or at least can do so) by playing certain explanatory roles. This ecumenical view allows that natural facts are not the only facts. It can countenance facts that are a priori and apparently non-natural, such as truths of (pure) mathematics. The view is maintained by a number of moral realists who also hold that some genuine moral facts are non-natural and, in this and other respects, like facts of pure mathematics.[1] This non-naturalist moral realism raises the question whether moral facts can play explanatory roles and, if so, are like mathematical facts that have roles in explaining not only facts in their own domain, but also empirical facts *outside* it. This essay considers both questions: whether moral facts can play roles in explaining other facts of their own kind and whether, like mathematical facts, they have roles in explaining *non*-moral empirical facts. In doing this, it explores explanatory roles that apparent moral facts can play. These facts include particular facts such as that one person was unjust toward another, and range to apparently a priori facts, such as that lying is (prima facie) wrong. The explanatory roles to be examined range from (1) the heuristic role of leading to discovery of explanations, to (2) the explanatorily dominating role of being what explains—an explainer of—something,

---

[1] W. D. Ross famously called the moral principles he proposed "self-evident, just as a mathematical axiom, or the validity of a form of inference, is evident. The moral order expressed in these propositions is just as much as part of the fundamental nature of the universe . . . as is the spatial or numerical structure expressed in the axioms of geometry or arithmetic." See *The Right and the Good* (Oxford: Oxford University Press, 1930), 29–30.

to (3) the subsidiary role of being essential in a fact that explains certain empirical phenomena, to (4) the auxiliary role of supplying, as does mathematics, concepts or propositions whose empirical interpretations have explanatory power, to (5) the theoretical role of providing a unifying explanatory account of a group of related phenomena. Each kind of role will be illustrated, and its bearing on moral realism will be described.

I. Intra-domain Explanation

To begin with a simple case, if anyone needed an explanation of why $7 + 5 = 12$, it could be given (informally) by indicating that, for integers, addition corresponds to a kind of counting by single steps from zero, and then showing that the resulting number (i.e. 12) is the one represented by the equation. The idea is roughly that what explains the truth of the equation just written is that counting from 0 to 7 and from 7 to 12 takes the same number of single steps as counting "straight" from 0 to 12. Mathematical explanation is also possible in geometry. One could explain diagrammatically why the Pythagorean Theorem holds for right triangles with sides of, say, 3, 4, and 5 units by drawing squares with sides equal to those of some arbitrarily sized right triangle. This would also be an informal (though valid) proof, but explanations, whether or not they constitute proofs, need not have a formal structure.

Might ethics include similar informal, intra-domain explanations? Consider how someone's resenting a well-meaning lie can be both justified and explained. One answer is that if a (hypothetical) physician inexcusably lies to a patient about the seriousness of one's illness, then, even if well-intentioned, this justifies the patient's resenting the act. Since "inexcusably lying" and "justify resentment" are broadly moral, this is a kind of moral explanation, and the arbitrary choice of a physician as exemplar parallels choosing an arbitrarily sized right triangle to explain determination of the length of the hypotenuse from that of the sides. The explanation is not, however, empirical, since (for one thing) it is hypothetical and does not presuppose anyone's existence, much less any actual lies usable in providing empirical evidence.

A different case might be a direct explanation of a kind of wrong: one person's incarcerating another for a crime that the other did not commit violates the other's right to be free, and incarceration on a false charge explains the incarceration's being wrong. If, as I assume, prima facie wrongness is intended, this explanatory statement has as good a claim to be a priori as the previous example. In both cases, moreover, although apriority is desirable for staying close to the mathematical case, it is not presupposed in simply maintaining that the two moral examples represent intra-domain explanation.

Moral realists of virtually any kind will hold that these explanations, in part because they can provide *understanding* of the propositions explained, are genuine. Providing understanding is a prima facie indication that the fact or apparent fact providing it has explanatory power. This holds at least in hypothetical situations and in part because the explanatory statements in question *interconnect* various notions important for describing aspects of human life—wronging and resentment, promising and obligation, freedom and rights, and many others. The underlying idea is perhaps that if a thing's having a property explains its having another property (or something else's having a property)—in neutral terminology, "explains why it is true that a predicate applies to some object"—this explanatory success provides some reason to regard the explained predication as ascribing a real property. If one takes it that properties are obviously real and does not want to presuppose this assumption in describing the case, one could say instead that if ascribing a predicate "F," e.g. "lying," to some act, explains the applicability of another predicate to it, say "justifies resentment," this supports the predicate's expressing a genuine property.

These considerations are not conclusive. This is in part because, such intra-domain explanations—hypothetically connecting possession of one normative property with possession of another normative property—do not show that there are any *particular* moral facts, say the contingent fact that some actual deed was inexcusable. But intra-domain explanations need not be taken in isolation. Each, like the mathematical examples given, may be associated with empirical explanations. Consider this exchange. "I don't see why Mae is justified (as you claimed) in resenting what Carson did." One answer would be, "Because she discovered that he inexcusably lied to her." These propositions, in addition to apparently ascribing moral properties, are empirical (in part because they are existential), and Mae's discovery instantiates the antecedent of the a priori generality in question, while her having a reason for disapproval instantiates its consequent.

Anti-realists will object that "Mae's discovering Carson's inexcusably lying to her" should not, without further argument, be taken to express a moral fact. Suppose we accept this. We might even grant the anti-realist that discovering something (regardless of its content) is a psychological property and that an instance of this natural cognitive property is what explains the fact in question. We can even grant that if the apparent discovery is not genuine because there *is* no lie, then Mae's *believing* Carson lied might have equal explanatory power regarding empirical facts.

In reply, realists may appeal to a distinction between explaining, in the sense of being *what explains*, a phenomenon and the weaker notion of *playing a role in explaining*. In the light of this, the revised realist claim would be that even intra-domain explanations are connected in a certain way with empirical explanations in which moral facts (or properties) play a role, and that this connection supports moral realism. The claim is not arbitrary, and there is an appropriate analogy to the mathematical case. Consider an actual piece of property, such as a corner lot, that represents a right triangle. The empirical facts about its border lengths can explain why a square lot with a side on the diagonal has the area it does. (Perhaps this area cannot be measured easily and the buyer wants to know its cost per square yard.) We measure the triangular lot's shorter sides and are satisfied that we know their lengths. We can then explain to the buyer why the area being sold has the area we say it has.

But no mathematical truth taken by itself—as opposed to an empirical numerical truth—is what explains that, and our calculations involve physical measurements that provide (approximate) physical values to the sides of the square. Suppose the south and west sides are 30 and 40 meters respectively and that we appeal to these facts to explain why we are billing for 2500 square meters (50, the calculated length of the hypotenuse, squared). We are appealing to numerical empirical propositions to explain another one, not to mathematical propositions that a priori explain another mathematical proposition, as in an ideal Euclidean area calculation. Still the property of having (e.g.) a 30-meter length is essential in an explanatory empirical proposition, as is the theorem that leads us to square the hypotenuse to determine the relevant area. The case is parallel to the one in which the moral property of being an inexcusable lie figures in explaining an empirical proposition by representing the lie as instantiating the moral principle that someone's concrete action of *telling* an inexcusable lie justifies the recipient's response of *having* resentment.

II. Hard and Soft Moral Realism

The moral realism so far defended is not reductive and hence may be considered "soft." One might think that hard moral realism would be a view that moral properties are reducible to natural ones—since these are presumably genuine properties and can be instantiated in empirical facts—and that the soft variety is non-reductive or even avowedly non-naturalistic. The terms are characterized differently, however, by Lei Zhong in a paper intended to provide a plausible conception of some important explanatory roles that facts may play and an argument to support the view that mathematical facts, but not moral facts, have an essential role in explaining facts outside their own domain.[2] His paper provides a basis for extending the defense of moral realism begun in Section I, and it also makes points important in their own right.

As Zhong describes soft moral realism, "(1) There are knowable moral facts [the realism element]; and (2) they cannot play explanatory roles in non-moral domains [the soft element, in which they appear unlike natural facts]," whereas, for hard moral realism, knowable moral facts "can play explanatory roles in non-moral domains" (555). Hard moral realism coheres with the influential metaphysical view that "any *real* entity must be capable of making a difference to the world" (555–56). Making a difference "to the world" is plausibly taken to entail exercising a causal power, and Zhong appropriately wants to leave room for a non-causal realism about mathematical entities. He thus distinguishes explanatory efficacy from causal power (557). The explanatory condition he employs in appraising soft moral realism is accordingly

---

[2] Lei Zhong, "The Hard Problem for Soft Moral Realism," *Journal of Philosophy* CXVI (2019), 555–576. (Further references to this paper are given parenthetically in the text.)

broad (as well as controversial): "We can have moral knowledge only if moral facts play explanatory roles in non-moral domains (such as the role of explaining moral beliefs)" (558).

This explanatory condition rules out the view that general moral facts—which include any true (thus factual) moral principles—satisfy the explanatory requirements for knowledge just by explaining other moral facts, thereby providing an intra-domain explanation. Consider the propositions that (1) lying to people wrongs them and (2) wronging people morally justifies resentment. These together can apparently explain why (3) if one person lies to another, the second has justification for resenting the first. This intra-domain explanation, however, lacks the kind of explanatory efficacy Zhong considers necessary for defending soft moral realism.

Although some ethical intuitionists consider intra-domain explanation strong support for moral realism, some offer further support. Zhong takes them to hold that "(Basic) moral beliefs can be justified in an *a priori* way, without the [evidential] mediation of sensory experience" (564). This claim is plausible for Ross and other leading intuitionists. But Zhong believes that, even for empirical knowledge, including some based on moral perception, intuitionists *also* reject an "explanatory inference condition on knowledge," namely that "we can have knowledge about a domain of facts F [e.g. perceptible moral facts] only if the [knowledge-constituting] beliefs about F are results of inference to the best explanation" (567). Such abductive reasoning, however, is a posteriori inference and so "cannot apply to *a priori* knowledge, such as mathematical knowledge" (568).

In this light, we might ask how mathematical facts can explain facts in other domains and whether, if so, a parallel point holds for moral facts. Zhong's offers a memorable example:

> Honeybees use hexagonal cells to build their honeycombs ... The dominant explanation among biologists is that natural selection would choose those bees that made their honeycombs in the most efficient manner with the minimal amount of wax. This explanation in fact appeals to a mathematical truth, the so-called "honeycomb theorem": A hexagonal grid is the most efficient way to divide a Euclidean plane into regions of equal area with the least total perimeter (568).

Presumably the claim that the evolutionary explanation "appeals to a mathematical truth" is intended to show that this truth plays an essential role in the explanation of the empirical fact that bees use hexagonal cells in nesting. By contrast, Zhong apparently takes moral facts—at least if a priori—to play no role in explaining any empirical fact. If that is correct, soft moral realists cannot, like Ross, appeal to an analogy between moral and mathematical explanatory power in arguing for countenancing moral facts.

The sections to follow will show how moral realists can take account of Zhong's most important sound points without accepting certain major claims he makes against robust moral realism, whether reductive or not.

III. COULD MORAL FACTS YIELD A KIND OF NON-INFERENTIAL EMPIRICAL KNOWLEDGE?

In part because recent years have seen the emergence of full-scale theories of moral perception, Zhong quite reasonably puts pressure on the claim, made by intuitionists and others, that some moral knowledge is non-inferential. His background epistemological assumption is that "There are two types of empirical knowledge: *perceptual* . . . and *abductive*" (565). He does not defend this,[3] and it seems too narrow. Surely we have much self-knowledge and much memory-based knowledge that is both empirical and non-inferential, yet not perceptual. I know that I am seated and that I turned on a light moments ago. Could one know such things by (possibly abductive) inference from perception, say kinesthetic perceptions in the first case and memorial seemings in the second? The inferentialist view that this is the only way we know them is phenomenologically implausible, but the important point here is that if phenomenology is as hospitable to apparently unconscious inferences (including abductive ones) as it would have to be to account for these cases as abductive or perceptual, then it may be equally hospitable to moral perception. The point is important because if there are moral perceptions, then perceptible moral facts do play a role in producing empirical phenomena—at least in producing the moral beliefs that constitute perceptual moral knowledge.

Consider two cases, one premised on an inferentialist notion of moral perception and the other not. Suppose I see a stabbing. On an inferentialist view, given my standing belief that stabbing others is wrong, I might subsume the act under that generality without awareness of doing so, and thereby believe one person wronged another. This belief would be tacitly inferential yet might be considered a kind of perceptual response. But might seeing wrongdoing also yield the same belief perceptually and *non*-inferentially? Perhaps to have a *moral* perception, I must in some way see the act *as* wrong. This does not entail *inferring* that it is wrong, say from the moral proposition that stabbing is wrong and the perceptually known proposition that the act is a stabbing. Note that, in ordinary (non-inferential) physical perception, a sensitivity condition could hold: that I would not have believed the stabbing wrong if it weren't wrong. Granted, this depends on whether, e.g., I *also* saw someone about to swing a baseball bat at the stabber. If I did, I might believe it excusable rather than wrong. Of course, I could be deceived in believing it (on balance) wrong—I might miss such an excusing factor. But that shows fallibility, not lack of the sensitivity to relevant facts that we expect with perceptual knowledge. It would be a mistake to claim that we cannot perceptually know a surface to be red because we would have believed it to be yellow if we had viewed it under an undetected yellow beam.

---

[3] He grants that the claim does not accommodate introspective knowledge that one is in pain, but he seems content to note that (by contrast with moral facts) "it is *pain* that helps to explain why I believe I am in pain" (567).

Suppose we assume for the sake of argument that, as some philosophers have thought, there is a kind of subliminal inference in what passes for moral perception. Must this assumption matter epistemologically? Even if perceptual knowledge is non-inferential—say my knowledge that there is a chair before me—skeptics may ask how I know this. One reply (in line with an inferentialist view of perception) is that I know there is a chair before me abductively, as what best explains how things seem to me. But why should my perceptual belief have a better claim to constitute knowledge because *inferential*, and so premise-based, than it would have if produced *directly* (and non-waywardly) by the facts that are affirmed *in* those premises? Broadly speaking, whether a belief that a proposition, p, constitutes knowledge is apparently—and in a complex way—a matter of how, and how well, it is supported by the fact that p or some fact(s) appropriately related to p. Indeed, it might be "safer" to believe that there is a chair before me directly on the basis of seeing it than on the basis of inferring its presence from premises about how things seem to me. It is a contingent matter whether we are more likely to know such facts by following nature's direct response path from external objects to belief or by following an indirect path to belief through mediating premises.[4]

If this line of thinking is correct, then inferentiality need not undermine the case for empirical moral knowledge *by perception*. If perception is in some way inferential (which I very much doubt[5]), this would at best undermine a phenomenological thesis about moral perception. The issue here is important. If we can know by perception that, e.g., A wronged B, this causal route from the apparently moral fact to a cognitive fact—a person's knowledge—favors regarding the apparently moral fact as genuine. This point holds even if the wrongness of the act—say, a fatal stabbing—is not a causal property. The most important point here is that the a priori proposition that stabbing a person to death is wrong plays an essential role in explaining why the morally sensitive observer acquires, by perception, the belief that the stabber wronged the victim. Given that moral proposition, what the person sees *is* wrong, much as, given the Pythagorean Theorem and the measurements of the triangle's sides, the area the area of the square lot *is* the square of the side constituting the hypotenuse. In each case, the a priori proposition plays an essential role in explaining why what is perceived—seen or physically measured—has the property in question. The central concern of his essay is metaphysical and epistemological; and, broadly speaking, the difference between the inferential and the non-inferential in relation to moral judgment is neutral with respect to the reality of what it attributes—say, the property of wrongness—and also to whether such

---

[4] The point here supports a related one Frances Kamm brings against Jonathan Haidt's skepticism about moral judgment on the assumption that it is initially intuitive and then rationalized afterwards (in typical cases of challenge). She says, "The intuitive judgement is no less objectively true if awareness of the factors and reasoning that justify it comes after the judgment than if the awareness comes before, contrary to what Haidt says." See "Should You Save This Child? Gibbard on Intuitions, Contractualism, and Strains of Commitment," in the commentary section of Allan Gibbard, *Reconciling Our Aims* (Oxford and NY: OUP, 2008), 121.

[5] As argued in detail in ch 6 of my *Seeing, Knowing, and Doing: A Perceptualist Account* (Oxford and NY: OUP, 2020).

judgments express justified belief or knowledge of a particular moral fact. My main points can be sustained, however, even on the view that moral beliefs and knowledge are never properly considered perceptual. This will be supported by the remaining sections.

IV. EXPLANATORY ROLES

Let us return, then, to the ontological significance of explanatory power. There is a considerable difference between a fact's simply playing an explanatory role in explaining some non-moral phenomenon and its being *what* explains that fact. Regarding the importance of explanatory roles, we may assume at least this: that if a fact is essential in a correct explanation of some other fact, then it plays a role in explaining the latter fact. This point is quite general and, whatever its significance for moral realism, holds not just for extra-domain explanations but also for intra-domain explanations, e.g. explaining why racial discrimination is wrong by appeal to the general facts that it is an injustice and that injustices are wrong.

As already suggested, if (apparent) moral facts play roles in explaining beliefs and actions, which are concrete empirical phenomena, this would support moral realism. Might they? Suppose someone asks why Janet rejects a policy. One answer might cite the facts that she believes it is discriminatory and that she is committed to avoiding discrimination. Her belief and commitment are psychological properties, but what makes them the properties they are depends on their content, which is moral. (She attributes a moral property, *being discriminatory*, to the policy.) If an apparent moral fact, e.g. that a policy is discriminatory, can be an essential element in a fact that explains an action, then it can play an explanatory role in explaining that action.

Granted, we might also be able to explain her action differently, appealing to what *grounds* her believing the policy discriminatory, say its exclusions on such bases as skin color. But this would not constitute the same explanation, and it is not clear that it would be better or, more important, that its availability invalidates the moral explanation. The point is not that the moral fact that the policy is discriminatory is *what* explains her action; it is that this fact plays an essential though auxiliary role in the constitution of an element, a belief she holds, which (in the context) *does* explain it. The point does not even require that an explanatory moral belief be *true*. (An untrue moral belief's explaining an event need not be undermined in parallel cases in which it is true.) Nor does the point require viewing moral properties as causal, or even taking such intentionalistic explanation to be causal (though many would argue that it is broadly causal).

I have been assuming for the sake of argument that the plausibility of non-reductive moral realism depends on a strong explanatory condition for moral knowledge—thus on whether moral facts (or fact-like moral phenomena) can play a role in explanations of *non*-moral phenomena. If I have been correct so far, then one explanatory role they may play—through their place in determining the character of psychological phenomena that explain behavior—seems to meet his condition. Their playing this explanatory role does not require reductive naturalism regarding moral properties and significantly counts in favor of at least non-reductive moral realism.

This point does not entail that playing an explanatory role of the kind illustrated in Janet's case *suffices* for the genuineness of a purported fact. An ethical noncognitivist might object that since moral "beliefs" lack truth-value, they cannot even be false.[6] How might such a view be maintained? It is understandable that just as there is a concept of a round square—which enables us to see the impossibility of a fact that there is one—there might be a concept of (say) wrongness but no possible fact that an act is wrong. But this version of anti-realism would allow that the *concept* of wrongness could nonetheless figure essentially in making an action-explaining belief the belief it is and thereby play a role in explaining an action. If concepts c and c^* are not equivalent, then the belief that x is c is not the same belief as that x is c^*, and different beliefs may differ in their range of possible explanatory roles. I doubt that there is any good reason to hold that there could not be genuine moral properties expressed, or in some way indicated, by moral concepts. Then distinct beliefs could, as illustrated, owe their difference to the distinct properties figuring in their content; and different beliefs may of course differ in their range of possible explanatory roles.

A noncognitivist could, to be sure, hold that sentences to the effect that an act is wrong are simply expressions of dislike in the way shouting "Boo!" is, and that therefore there could be no such case supporting realism. This crude emotivist version of noncognitivism, however, is not plausible enough to need a response here.[7] On a sophisticated noncognitivist view, however, it might be argued that moral concepts are not "descriptive" and, in contexts of moral judgment, function to guide complicated expressions of pro and con attitudes that, though not fact-stating, are not essentially emotive and may even, in some rational way, respond to reasons. This is not the place to appraise such views, though it should be pointed out that many expressive functions of, e.g., judgments of right and wrong are compatible with moral realism. What can be said here is that, minimally, the overall case for moral realism made in this essay may, on balance significantly raise the bar for making noncognitivism plausible. I assume, then,

---

[6] I am taking it as highly plausible that the kind of moral belief in question has cognitive content, but in addition to presupposing that point, the analogy I am drawing must deal with cases in which, e.g., a belief that someone has worked black magic explains anger. I see no a priori way to rule out cognitivity for "working black magic," but surely there are conditions for using "inexcusably lied" and other moral terms that would not be met by the use of "working black magic" in question or, if they would be met, might justify describing a real property that the agent in question, unlike Janet, did not instantiate. In any case, the burden is on the anti-realist to show that either the relevant moral terms lack cognitivity or the apparently satisfactory explanations fail.

[7] For one thing, it cannot explain such logical operations as emphasized in setting out the Frege-Geach problem. This problem concerns (among other things) the implausibility of holding that such moral sentences as "Lying is wrong" are merely emotive when they figure in such reasoning as "If x lied to y then x did wrong, and x did lie to y, so S did wrong". Such points have apparently been noted even by writers posing such questions after Frege and before Geach. David Phillips's suggests that Ross is one such. See Phillips' *Rossian Ethics: W. D. Ross and Contemporary Ethical Theory* (Oxford: Oxford University Press, 2019), 166–67.

that there *can* be moral facts and that some of those facts (such as what Janet asserts) can be empirically confirmed or disconfirmed. This confirmability supports positing the explanatory role just illustrated for moral facts and thereby supports moral realism. This support is neutral, however, between hard and (any kind of) soft moral realism, at least assuming that the explanatory power of a belief is neutral with respect to whether a normative property it ascribes is reducible to a natural property.

V. A Mathematical Analogy

The case of the honeybees is instructive in relation to the question whether moral facts also play roles significantly similar to explanatory roles played by mathematical facts. Let us assume that the Honeycomb Theorem of Euclidean geometry is important for explaining the efficiency and thus the evolutionary fitness value of bees' nests as (approximately) instantiating the Theorem. The theorem certainly might suggest that the nests are efficient in storage, which in turn suggests an evolutionary explanation of bees' building such nests. This heuristic role, however, does not require the truth of the theorem, which is framed in terms of idealized, widthless lines. Efficiency is a multidimensional concept in such an evolutionary case. One efficiency factor (noted by Zhong) is the thickness of the wax walls of the storage chambers. Efficient storage is also partly a matter of preservation, which could be better for a less spatially economical shape.

If it were an a priori truth that physical space is Euclidean, then one could at least infer from the theorem that, apart from the variables of the durability and thickness of the hexagons' walls, spatial storage capacity would be most efficient given hexagonal subdivisions. But this would leave open whether some other shape might better *preserve* what is to be stored long-term. Efficiency of storage might also vary with accessibility for use. Whether physical space is Euclidean is a difficult question to explicate (and would require specifying variables involving a good deal of physics); but the matter is empirical. Euclidean efficiency is ideal; evolutionary efficiency is physicochemical, diachronic, and causal. What we can hope to do here is ascertain whether there is some analogy between the explanatory role of such a priori propositions as the Honeycomb Theorem and certain apparently a priori moral propositions.

On the heuristic side, there is significant analogy. Consider the moral view that a government's treating its people unjustly entails their having a pro tanto obligation to resist. Considering this view a priori does not preclude taking it to have systematic connections with empirical phenomena. Its proponents would hold that unjust treatment is partly constituted by, and is knowable by perceiving, such things as confiscation of property without due process, arbitrary body searches, unexplained domestic travel restrictions, and police brutality. Instances of the concept of resistance are also identifiable by perceptible conditions. Given these empirical connections between perceptible indications of the properties figuring in the moral proposition, does it not indicate a number of hypotheses? For instance, sufficient conditions for injustice might be expected to predict necessary conditions for resentment of it. Arbitrary body searches might, e.g., be hypothesized to engender verbal protest, avoidance of check points, and other perceptible elements that confirm resistance. This illustrates significant value of the general (apparently a priori) moral fact in leading to hypotheses which, in turn, are testable and have empirical explanatory power. This value is not, moreover, merely power to suggest explanatory hypotheses; that power could in principle come from a purely imaginary construct. The hypotheses are discovered by reflection on instances of the properties that are systematically connected with the moral or mathematical ones figuring in a priori generalizations.

So far, I have raised no doubts about the possibility of mathematical knowledge or even about its apriority. There remains much controversy about how such knowledge is possible.[8] Here we might appropriately consider the possibility Ross adapted from Aristotle: that knowledge of at least elementary arithmetic is acquired, not by enumerative induction or even abduction but by intuitive induction.[9] Ross took this mathematical analogy as suggesting how a priori moral truths are learned. He assumed that for at least certain abstract entities, such as mathematical entities and (non-Russellian) propositions, direct non-causal apprehension is possible. To some, this will seem mysterious. But (to take a contemporary example connected with the resurgence of naïve realism) is it less mysterious that knowledge should be considered a state of mind,[10] even when much knowledge entails the existence of perceptible objects existing outside the mind? If the content of a state of mind can be intelligibly argued to be outside it and even physical, why is it less mysterious that it may be abstract and non-physical? Perhaps anyone's primitive will be someone's mystery, and philosophers who countenance anything mysterious (most of us, perhaps) must continue trying to dispel the clouds.

VI. A Neglected Dimension of Explanatory Roles

I believe there is a less speculative and more positive point to be made here concerning realism and explanation. Most criticism of moral realism focuses on what moral facts *cannot* explain, such as physical events. By contrast, it is commonly assumed, at least

---

[8] For an important and representative statement of the epistemological problem here, see Paul Benacerraf, "What Numbers Could Not Be," *Journal of Philosophy* LXVII (1970), 661–679. I have responded to this problem in detail in ch 9 of *Seeing, Knowing, and Doing*.

[9] On Ross's view, "We find by experience that this couple of matches and that couple make four matches... and by reflection on this and similar discoveries we come to see that it is of the nature of two and two to make four. In a precisely similar way, we see the *prima facie* rightness of an act which would be the fulfillment of a particular promise...." See Ross, *The Right and the Good*, 1930, 32–33.

[10] As argued by Timothy Williamson in chapter 1 of *Knowledge and Its Limits* (Oxford: Oxford University Press, 2000).

by explanationist realists, who take having an explanatory role to be a condition for countenancing the reality of facts and properties, that natural facts by their very nature *can* explain other natural facts. This turns out to be far from obvious. I want to show that and to bring out a role, so far not evident in our discussion but pertinent to moral realism, that certain kinds of facts can play in explanations of empirical phenomena.

Take the natural property, shape, i.e., *being shaped*. A vast variety of objects are shaped, being round, oval, hexagonal, heart-shaped, and so forth. But consider the fact that a stone has a shape. The shape fact conveys information, then, but what kind of explanatory role does it play? Compare the stone's being merely shaped with its being round. The latter fact would explain why it easily rolls, just as its being cubical would explain why it is stackable with stones of the same shape. Here it is not the generic fact of being shaped that explains these things, but particular facts that ground that fact, in the sense that the generic fact obtains in virtue of the particular one(s). The relation between being shaped and having a particular shape is that of determinable to determinate, and it appears that the (empirical) explanatory power of shape depends on that of its determinates.[11]

Now consider wrongness, which is an important generic moral property. How significantly like a thing's being shaped is an action's being wrong? A crucial similarity is that neither property is *brute*; both are grounded, as are the facts constituting ascriptions of them. An action cannot be brutely wrong, any more than an object can be brutely shaped. An object is shaped in virtue of being, say, round; an action is wrong[12] in virtue of being a killing, or in virtue of being a lie, and so forth for a presumably finite list of types of grounds. The point is not that wrongness is a determinable, though it is certainly generic, having many kinds of "species."[13] It is like such determinables as shape and color in being such that having it requires a certain kind of structure (or anyway constitution). Much as shapes have a perimeter or (typically) a visible surface quality of a spectral sort, in the moral case, wrongness requires being an act or act-related phenomenon of a certain person-related kind. But in the moral case, wrongness can be *multiply grounded* in, for instance, lying, harming, and promising-breaking—all instantiable by a single action—whereas a shaped object cannot simultaneously have different shapes. Nonetheless, wrongness is at least sufficiently like certain determinables to sustain a similarity in relation to explanation. The fact that a thing is shaped entails that it has some (grounding) shape property, and shape properties are such that a thing's having one can explain certain facts about it, including facts about its explanatory power. Analogously, the fact that an act is wrong entails that it has some (grounding) natural

---

[11] One thing that simply being shaped might explain is having at least one perimeter. Such an explanation would be both intra-domain and apparently a priori—an explanatory condition certain moral facts also appear to meet.

[12] The wrongness in question is a kind compatible with excuses like self-defense; one might also speak of wrong-makingness—any morally negative term should serve for the point.

[13] For a related account of goodness as a generic property see Panayot Butchvarov, *Skepticism in Ethics* (Bloomington: Indiana University Press, 1989), esp. chs. 1–4 (on his view, however, goodness is also a determinable).

property, i.e., is wrong in virtue of being, say, a killing of a person—having a negative moral shape, we might say. In both cases, the grounding facts can figure essentially in explaining empirical facts.

These points of similarity coexist with differences so various and important that one might easily overlook the similarities. The similarities do not require taking wrongness to be a determinable (which it cannot be, given that the different grounds, such as lying and harming, are compatible). But the similarities do provide room to argue that wrongness is not only a real property that can play roles in empirical explanations but also a natural property, as some intuitionists, being hard moral realists, presumably take it to be.[14]

The analogy between moral properties and certain determinable natural properties indicates a kind of explanatory role that is, in a certain way, indirect for the determinables but direct for their determinates. A thing's possessing the determinable entails having the indirect explanatory role of entailing the existence of a determinate that can—as what some would call a "realizer" of the determinable—play a direct explanatory role: being *what explains* some empirical fact. It appears, moreover, that both naturalistic determinables and generic moral properties a priori entail the presence of grounding facts that can directly explain—roughly, constitute what explains—some natural fact. There are entailments (also apparently a priori) in the other direction too: being a killing entails being (prima facie) wrong, as being round entails having a shape. Both moral facts and natural facts can have a basis in natural facts (the grounding relation required for a metaphysical basis is neutral with respect to whether the moral facts in question are reducible to natural facts). It appears, then, that wrongness is much like shape in "making a difference the world": without being a causal property but through playing roles in causal explanations in such a way that it would be a mistake to call it epiphenomenal.[15]

---

[14] Zhong cites intuitionists who are hard realists; he does not, however, note an epistemological point important here: that the moderate rationalism of some versions of intuitionism is compatible with a naturalistic account of moral properties. His note 30 (p. 564), cites Terence Cuneo and Ralph Wedgwood as intuitionists who are hard moral realists, but, though he frequently cites me as defending soft moral realism (in his sense), he does not note that I have said, in one of my works he cites, "My account [of moral perception] thus allows, though it does not require, a naturalizing of moral properties by providing a causal account of their constitution." See *Moral Perception* (Princeton: Princeton University Press, 2013), 55. To be sure, I have also suggested that certain "moral explanations" can be naturalized, but that is where they are presented in such a way that the explaining factors are natural phenomena. I nowhere suggest that moral properties play no role in empirical explanation. See, e.g., "Ethical Naturalism and the Explanatory Power of Moral Concepts," in Steven Wagner and Richard Warner, eds., *Naturalism: A Critical Appraisal* (Notre Dame: University of Notre Dame Press, 1993), 95–115, reprinted in *Moral Knowledge and Ethical Character* (Oxford: OUP, 1997).

[15] There is an analogy between my way of defending the reality of moral properties and certain ways of defending the reality of the mental. A major difference is that the latter case (at least typically) aims at showing how mental properties figure in causal explanation, whereas I am not taking moral properties to be causal properties. For an instructive case against the explanatory exclusion principle on which the physical realizers of mental properties do all the causal work mental properties may seem to do, and in support of the causal significance of mental properties, see Stephen Yablo, "Mental Causation," *Philosophical Review* 101, 2 (1992), 245–89. Using diverse examples of determinables and

What we have seen indicates how certain generic properties, including both shape and wrongness, may also play unifying roles relevant to explanation. The instantiation of these generic properties does, after all, entail that of at least some of the (natural) properties that partly constitute something's having the generic property. There may, e.g., be some generic explanation of the behavior of certain macroscopic objects that essentially employs the fact that they have some shape within a certain range. Shape might be important in calculating friction as a factor in movability. Perhaps, other things equal, the more nearly round a macroscopic object is, the less the force needed to move it across a flat surface; and perhaps, other things equal, the closer to being unjust a government is, say to imposing life-changing curfews and disabling taxes, the more likely is civil resistance. This can be tested empirically by seeing, first, whether the sufficient conditions for governmental injustice predict (independent) sufficient conditions for civil resistance and, second, whether intensification of the phenomena constituting grounds for governmental injustice make resistance more likely or more intense.

Might there also be, associated with such testable hypotheses, some generic explanation of certain types of human behavior that essentially employs the fact that certain acts, such as resistances to a government, share one or another ground of wrongness, say being responses to seizures of property? Such responses may (though they need not) be more directly produced by moral perceptions of the seizures as unjust. This essay suggests some directions in which empirical inquiry might pursue the question of how moral properties and their instances may figure in empirical explanations or unify behavioral patterns that might otherwise seem unconnected. But quite apart from how that line of inquiry might go, the points about the explanatory roles of moral facts made in sections I–V do not depend on either that or the analogy drawn between generic moral properties and shape as a generic natural property.[16]

VII. SHOULD MORAL REALISTS RESIST NATURALISTIC REDUCTION?

It should be evident that I have not implied that a reductive version of moral realism cannot explain the considerations I have brought in favor of moral realism. Presumably,

---

mental properties—properties I consider relevantly analogous to shape—he contends that "If the causally sufficient antecedent monopolizes all the influence, then the others are left with none ... rather than competing for causal honors, determinables and their determinates seem likelier to share in one another's success" (272).

[16] One response to the view suggested here is that both wrongness and shape may be viewed as epiphenomenal. If the point is that a thing's simply having a shape and an act's just being wrong are not causal explainers, I have not denied it. Being causal explainers is not necessary for being real or "factive" or indeed for playing explanatory roles, and it is significant that clearly natural facts as well as moral facts (whether natural or not) illustrate this.

it can, at least if it incorporates a priori moral truths and particular moral facts such as ascriptions of rightness or wrongness to particular actions. It might incorporate them. I have elsewhere argued that a rationalist moral epistemology does not require irreducibility of wrongness and all the other important moral properties. Why might it not be that wrongness, for instance, is a natural property so complex that we neither have a good overall grasp of it nor even an apt naturalistic name for it?[17]

If one countenances disjunctive properties (as distinct from disjunctive concepts or something like states of affairs expressed by disjunctive predicates), one might use the best normative framework one can formulate to provide a reduction, e.g. taking wrongness to be the property of being either a lie *or* a broken promise *or* a killing *or* a failure to render aid... for all the dimensions of wrongness. This project seems to me unpromising even if there are disjunctive properties.[18] Suppose, however, that in the spirit of cooperative speculation we imagine a different route to naturalization, a quasi-functionalist route to naturalization.

We might begin with the idea of the institution of morality—the framework of normative standards captured in such venerable generalities as that lying and promise-breaking are wrong, that unequal treatment on the basis of sex is unjust, and that killing innocent people who block one's route to material success is morally outrageous. These and other kinds of wrongness are in a sense "anti-social," and the point goes with the broad plausible idea that a function of the institution of morality is to conduce to human well-being—"flourishing" may be a better term, but nothing in what follows will turn on the differences. This suggests that, on the negative side, wrongness is a property of actions whose instantiation in actions tends to induce fear, reduce social coordination, and engender retaliation and, on the positive side, obligatoriness is a property with contrasting tendencies. The question immediately arises whether we can naturalize the needed descriptions of the properties we must posit to explicate moral functioning. That is a significant challenge that to my knowledge has not been met.

---

[17] Nicholas Sturgeon suggests this in "Moral Explanations Defended," in James Dreier, ed., *Contemporary Debates in Moral Theory* (New York: Routledge 2006), 241–262; and, for a recent attempt to explain the causal power of moral facts along the lines expectable from a Cornell realist perspective, see Andres Luco, "How Moral Facts Cause Moral Progress," *JAPA* 5, 4 (2019), 429–448. The basic idea in this perspective is one Luco quotes from Boyd's characterization of a causal regulation theory of reference: "A Term *t* refers to a kind ... *k* just in case there exist causal mechanisms whose tendency is to bring it about, over time, that what is predicated of the term *t* will approximately be true of *k*" (433 in Luco; 195 in Richard Boyd, "How to Be a Moral Realist," in Geoffrey Sayre-McCord, *Essays on Moral Realism* [Ithaca: Cornell UP, 1988]). The moral realism defended here does not depend on this regulation view and certainly not on the idea that causal regulation of property-ascriptions entails their having causal power.

[18] One condition for property identity is necessary equivalence, and, given the varieties and complexities of wrongness, it seems doubtful that there is a naturalistic disjunction necessarily equivalent to it. A further problem is that some of the needed disjuncts, such a *failure to render aid*, are themselves not at all clearly naturalistic in character (what is relevant, of course, is failure to render aid *when*, within certain limits, one "can").

A related point is this. It is not clear that, without appeal to such normative epistemic notions as justification and adequate evidence, we can explicate the relevant notions of, e.g., what moral agents may be *reasonably* expected to do or what it is to know or *justifiedly* confirm that moral facts have a tendency to yield certain consequences for well-being. Even apart from whether explicating moral concepts requires explicating certain epistemic concepts, then from a broad metaphysical point of view there is limited value in naturalizing the domain of practical reason if we cannot naturalize that of theoretical reason, which is at least as important a realm needing, at least from the perspective of parsimony, ontological accommodation. I doubt that we can naturalize it. Even if we can hope to naturalize the notion of knowledge, that of justification is quite recalcitrant to naturalization. If objectivity in ethics or science required naturalization of moral or epistemic properties, there would be more reason to seek to naturalize them, but there is no good reason to think that objectivity does require it. Ethical objectivity needs certain kinds of necessary conditions and certain kinds of sufficient conditions for the right and the wrong and for the morally good and the morally bad. These provide a basis for moral judgment in virtually all of the important cases. The needed objectivity does not require a set of conditions that are conceptually equivalent to, and so both necessary and sufficient for, any of these moral properties. The goal may still be a worthy one with the idea of ontological economy in view. Here, however, mathematics and the a priori come back to mind. If we must be realists about abstract entities to account for mathematical and other a priori knowledge, and if these are essential for a good understanding of the natural world, I cannot see why moral realism should not form a part of an adequate ontology.

We have considered a variety of explanatory roles that presumptive moral facts might play: the heuristic role of leading to discovery of explanations; the explanatorily central role of being what explains—an explainer—of something; the subsidiary role, illustrated by believed moral facts, of constituting a determinant of the nature of what explains certain empirical phenomena; the auxiliary role of supplying, as does mathematics, concepts or propositions whose empirical interpretations can play one of the roles just mentioned; and the theoretical role of providing a unifying explanatory account of a group of related phenomena. Moral facts are like facts of pure mathematics in a capacity to explain facts in their own domain. Mathematical facts can play a role in scientific explanations, but that kind of role in explaining empirical phenomena is not impossible for certain priori moral facts. Indeed, there are apparently natural facts, for instance at least some ascribing determinable properties such as shape or non-normative grounds of specific moral properties such as police brutality, that, in explaining empirical phenomena, play a role quite analogous to the role generic moral facts may play in explaining them. Non-reductive moral realism can account for significant explanatory powers apparently possessed by moral facts and moral properties. Moreover, it appears that the explanatory role of pure mathematical truths has some parallels in the normative realm. It is not clear, moreover, that mathematical knowledge can be accounted for without making room for knowledge of certain basic moral principles that resist interpretation as empirical propositions. As to ethical naturalism, it remains a metaphysical option even for moderate intuitionists. But moral realism does not depend on it, either as a condition for moral knowledge, whether empirical or a priori, or in accounting for the explanatory significance of moral facts. Whether from a reductive or non-reductive perspective, that there are both moral properties and particular moral facts about people who exemplify those properties seems well supported by the explanatory roles that those properties and facts can play.[19]

---

[19] For discussion of earlier drafts I think Paul Audi, Feraz Azhar, Isabel Canfield, Anjan Chakravartty, Brian Cutter, Rachel Dichter, Lucia Dikaczova, Dominic Lamantia, Kristopher McDaniel, Micahel Zhao, and, especially, Paul Bloomfield and David Copp, whose editorial commentaries were extensive and very helpful.

CHAPTER 18

DEREK PARFIT'S NON-NATURALIST COGNITIVISM

ROGER CRISP

Over the last two decades of his career, Derek Parfit, largely through objections to opposing positions, developed a wide-ranging and powerful defence of a non-naturalistic form of moral realism (as Parfit's metaphysical claims became more modest, he came to prefer the term "cognitivism"). This article will focus on elucidating, and explaining the development of, his position and the main arguments for it. Reference to various lines of further interpretation and criticism will be confined largely to footnotes.

1. Earlier Work

Several of the claims made in Parfit's first book, *Reasons and Persons* (1984), could be said to have metaethical implications, but the book contains no direct discussion of metaethics. Parfit was aware of the skeptical arguments of Mackie, and used to say that he avoided metaethics because he feared that he would be persuaded by these second-order arguments and lose interest in first-order philosophical ethics.[1] His later writings on metaethics showed that this fear was ungrounded, since Parfit came to hold a strong version of the moral or normative "objectivism" which Mackie took as his main target (1977: ch. 1).[2]

---

[1] In his later book, *On What Matters* (2011–2017), he says he postponed thinking about metaethics (presumably also) because he found it too difficult (142.109). (References to the main text of this book, where appropriate, will be by section number, and sometimes, as here, also by page. Note that the third volume, which contains a good deal of metaethical discussion, was published six years after vols. 1 and 2, and that the first section of vol. 3 is 128.)

[2] For a helpful discussion of the notion of normativity, including its use by Parfit, see Finlay 2019.

Parfit's first published work on metaethics was "Reasons and Motivation" (1997). Williams was an early and continuing influence on Parfit, and is the first to be thanked in Parfit's acknowledgements. The paper itself is a defence of externalism about reasons, largely in response to Williams's seminal "Internal and External Reasons" (1979) and some later papers. According to internalism, for me to have a reason to φ is for it to be the case that φ-ing may help to fulfil at least one of my current intrinsic or non-instrumental desires, or that, were I to know the relevant facts and to deliberate rationally, I would be motivated to φ.[3] Externalists claim that at least some reasons are not internal; according to Parfit's version, there are no internal reasons (i.e., even if these facts about motivation are true in some case, they do not give me any reason).[4]

In this early paper, Parfit draws a tripartite distinction between different types of metaethical theory which provided the background to much of his later thought (1997: 108). Consider, for example, internalism. According to an *analytically reductive* version, the claim that I have a reason to φ has the same *meaning* as the claim that φ-ing would fulfill one of my current desires or that I would be motivated to φ were I to know the relevant facts and to deliberate rationally. On the *nonanalytically reductive* view, these claims do not have the same meaning, but the fact of my having a reason to φ *is the same as*, or *consists in*, the fact about desire-fulfillment and motivation. Finally, according to the *nonreductive* view, these facts are quite different: the first is normative, while the second is psychological.

This distinction between normative and non-normative facts came to be the most significant element in Parfit's metaethics. Parfit argues that we should be not only externalists, but also nonreductive normative realists (121–7). Normative concepts form a separate category of their own, like temporal or logical concepts, such that they, and the facts which they may be used to state, cannot be explained, reductively, in non-normative or "naturalist" terms.[5] The psychological terminology used in stating internalism is non-normative:

---

[3] Parfit suggests (1997: 114n28) that we can understand motivating reasons as *psychological states*, viz. beliefs and desires, or the *contents* of those beliefs and desires. So we might explain someone's jumping from a window, for example, by saying "He believed the hotel to be on fire" or "The hotel was on fire."

[4] Parfit ends his 1999 (which is primarily a discussion of the views of Shoemaker) with the claim that "reductionism about reasons" (i.e., internalism) is not only "deeply mistaken", but such that, "if it were fully believed, its effects would be bleak". This concern with the effects of belief in certain metaethical views is a constant theme in Parfit's later work.

[5] Just how different these categories are is perhaps the most important focus of debate about Parfit's position. Parfit suggests that the claim that a normative fact consists in certain natural facts is analogous to claiming that rivers are sonnets (91.324). But, Railton points out (2016: 55–8; see also 38–43; Nuccetelli and Seay 2012a: 137), rivers do not supervene on sonnets, and there may here be an opportunity for rapprochement between the naturalist and the non-naturalist (see also Crisp 2012). Parfit (142.104–8) came to accept Railton's point about supervenience and its implications for the debate between naturalists and non-naturalists. Gibbard (2016) rejects ascription of non-natural properties entirely, preferring to start with notions of preferences and plans that can be disagreed with. But he accepts that normative concepts are non-naturalistic.

> Normativity, I believe, is very different from motivating force. Neither includes, or implies, the other. Other animals can be motivated by their desires and beliefs. Only we can understand and respond to reasons.[6] (1997: 127)

In "Rationality and Reasons" (2001), Parfit restates his view that the concept of a reason is basic or fundamental, but makes it clear his non-naturalist realism is purely normative and not evaluative (2001: 18–20). On Parfit's view, desires provide no reasons for action: reasons are based on value, and the main aim of the paper is to defend that claim. But we should not follow G. E. Moore in postulating a non-naturalist property of goodness, or being valuable. Rather we should adopt what T. M. Scanlon (1998: 95–100) calls a *buck-passing* view of goodness.[7] Consider the painfulness of some ordeal you are contemplating facing. According to Moore, this painfulness gives the ordeal the further, non-natural property of being bad, and this badness in turn gives you a reason to avoid it. On the buck-passing account, the property of being good (or bad) is not itself an independent reason-giving property, but merely the higher-order property of having some natural reason-giving property.

Parfit's metaethical project continued with "Normativity" (2006), and here we see him providing more of the background to what became his central metaethical statement in part 6 of the second volume of *On What Matters* (OWM). Throughout his metaethics, Parfit offers many ad hominem arguments against proponents of naturalism,[8] partly because of his view that disagreement with epistemic peers gives one a reason to doubt one's views. On the first page of the preface to OWM (2011–2017: xxxiii), Parfit describes Sidgwick as one of his "masters", the other being Kant. Sidgwick's influence can be seen throughout Parfit's work, and hence it is no surprise to find him quoting from *The Methods of Ethics* one of Sidgwick's main reasons for doubting one's own beliefs:

> [I]f I find any of my intuitions in direct conflict with an intuition of some other mind, there must be error somewhere: and if I have no more reason to suspect error in the other mind than in my own, reflective comparison between the two intuitions necessarily reduces me ... to a state of neutrality. (Sidgwick 1874: 321)

Parfit believed that many of the changes Sidgwick made to the *Methods of Ethics* as it went through various editions were for the worse, and this passage is perhaps an example. From the fourth edition of 1890 onward, Sidgwick substituted the word "judgement" in this passage for "intuition". Only the former is standardly used by naturalists

---

[6] For an argument that Humeans can distinguish between the normative and the purely descriptive, see Blackburn 2016: 90–91. Driver (2017) argues that Humeans should be less worried than Parfit and others think they should be by the implication of their view that moral norms are contingent on certain aspects of human nature.

[7] For discussion of Parfit's version of this thesis, see Stratton-Lake 2017.

[8] On disagreement, see further 105; also 4 (d) below. I shall refer to these ad hominem arguments only if they help in elucidating Parfit's own position. Note that in vol. 3 of OWM, Parfit responds in detail to many of the criticisms leveled at his position in Singer (ed.) 2016. See also Parfit's "Responses" (2017).

(though Sidgwick himself somewhat confusingly used it to refer both to moral judgments, however understood, and to judgments arrived at through the faculty of intuition), so Parfit's choice of edition here may be taken as evidence of his using the notion of "intuition" in Sidgwick's epistemological, "philosophical" sense (Sidgwick 1907: bk. 3, ch. 13).[9] Though Parfit's metaethics is focused primarily on metaphysics, in particular the nature of the property of being a reason, our attributing to him a broadly Sidgwickian form of intuitionism may help us to interpret some of his more elusive metaphysical claims (see below 4 (a), (b)).[10] It could be suggested, that is to say, that Parfit came to think that what really matters is whether we can know normative truths, not the metaphysical status of such truths, or of normative properties.

Consider, in light of this suggestion, some of Parfit's criticisms of Hare (1972) on "what matters" (2006: 328–30; see also OWM 103–4). According to the "objectivists" (or "realists") to whom Hare is opposed, Parfit notes, our moral beliefs, are *descriptive*, rather than merely *prescriptive*. And this, the objectivist will claim, explains why it seems that there can be genuine moral disagreements, as well as illustrating a serious problem with subjectivism. Hare accepts that the notion of objectivity does make sense in some domains, but not in morality, where it does not draw "any real distinction":

> Behind this argument lies, I think, the idea that if it is possible to say that it is right or wrong to say a certain thing, an affinity of some important kind is established between that sort of thing, and other things of which we can also say this. So, for example, if we can say of the answer to a mathematical problem that it is right, and can say the same thing of a moral judgment, this is held to show that a moral judgment is in some way like the answer to a mathematical problem, and therefore cannot be "subjective" (whatever that means).

Parfit's laconic response is: "That is what it means". Implicit in this is his commitment to the claim that, if some moral judgement is right, then its rightness is—"in some way"—like the rightness of a mathematical judgement. In what way becomes clearer in Parfit's response to the following Harean argument:

> Think of one world into whose fabric values are plainly objectively built; and think of another in which those values have been annihilated. And remember that in both worlds the people in them go on being concerned about the same things—there is no difference in the "subjective" concern which people have for things, only in their "objective" value. Now I ask, What is the difference between the states of affairs in these two worlds? Can any other answer be given except "None whatever"?

---

[9] Sidgwick sees the faculty of intuition essentially as doxastic, delivering noninferential beliefs. Philosophical intuitions are "those primary intuitions of Reason, by the scientific application of which the common moral thought of mankind may be at once systematized and corrected" (1907: 373–4).

[10] For a defense of Parfit's appeals to intuitions, see Russell 2016: 231–9.

Parfit returns to the partial analogy with mathematical necessity, and asks whether a thought experiment analogous to Hare's about morality might be used by an empiricist to show that arithmetical truths are contingent. Parfit suggests that we cannot imagine a world in which such truths are not necessary, and that the same is true of the moral world Hare asks us to imagine, in which values alone have been "annihilated". It is necessarily true, for example, that 7 + 5 = 12, so this will be true in all possible worlds. Now consider the claim that intense suffering is bad.[11] If objectivism is true, then this is a necessary truth, true in all possible worlds.[12] Likewise, if someone denies that intense suffering is bad in some world, then it is an implication of their view that this normative truth holds in no possible world. Parfit claims that nonreductive realists cannot offer much in explanation of how we understand or recognize normative truths (2006: 330). But he says enough in his critique of Hare, and elsewhere (e.g., OWM 91), to suggest that he is working in the intuitionist tradition of Samuel Clarke and others who draw analogies between mathematical and moral knowledge (see, e.g., Clarke 1728: 111–14, 121, 174–7).[13] Like Clarke, Parfit believes that we have a rational capacity to apprehend normative truths, such as the truth that we have a reason to avoid or prevent suffering. Since nonreductive realists believe that normative notions can be elucidated only with reference to other normative concepts, the best strategy for them, at this point, is attack:

> Though we cannot explain what normativity is, or what normative concepts mean, we can say what normativity is *not*, and what those concepts do not mean. It could not be true that, as naturalists claim, normative statements mean the same as, or report the same facts as, statements about natural facts. Nor could these statements, as non-cognitivists claim, have merely an emotive or prescriptive sense. For these statements to be normative, they must be capable of being, in a strong sense, true. (2006: 331–2)

It is this strategy that Parfit employs in "Normativity," in which his targets include, in addition to Hare, Williams, Korsgaard, Nagel, Nowell-Smith, Falk, Mackie,[14] Scheffler, and Railton. As we have seen, it was Williams's defense of internal reasons that seems to have drawn Parfit into metaethics. But Korsgaard receives the most attention in "Normativity," and Parfit used to joke that she had woken him from his "undogmatic slumber". By this he probably meant that he realized that his earlier arguments against Williams were insufficient, and that more work was needed. This work is what we find in OWM, and it is no surprise that Parfit remains largely on the offensive throughout.

---

[11] Parfit is probably thinking of suffering that would be considered both entirely undeserved and not a constitutive part of some overall good.

[12] Parfit may mean "all accessible possible worlds." There is no reason to think he is assuming S5 modality here.

[13] Terry Irwin has told me that Parfit mentioned to him in about 1998 that he had been reading Clarke (as well as Price, another intuitionist) with admiration.

[14] Focusing on OWM, Phillips (2014) argues that Mackie must be understood as using the same moral concepts as non-naturalist realists.

2. ANALYTICAL NATURALISM

On the very first page of OWM, Parfit reiterates the claim that the concept of a reason is, like temporal and modal concepts, indefinable, suggesting that the only way to enable someone to grasp such concepts is by encouraging them to entertain a normative thought, such as that anyone has a reason to want to avoid being in agony (1.31).[15] The following three chapters of the volume go on to discuss what Parfit calls "objective" and "subjective" theories of practical reasons. It turns out that these two views are in effect equivalent, respectively, to externalism and internalism about reasons. According to *objectivism*, Parfit states, there are certain facts that give us reasons to have desires or aims, or to act (3.45).[16] These facts are about the objects of our desires, rather than our desires themselves, and in most cases the facts make certain outcomes good or certain actions worth doing. So we can call these *value-based* reasons. According to *subjectivism*, the facts that give us reasons for action are about our current actual desires, or the desires that we would have if we considered all the relevant facts. Hence we can call these reasons *subject-given*.[17]

Parfit goes on to make it clearer than he did in his earlier work that these views about reasons are to be distinguished from metaethical theories about the nature of normative properties (15.109–10). But the best objectivist theories, he suggests, will include the claim that the fact that we have some reason is an irreducibly (*non-naturalist*) normative truth.[18] Many subjectivists base their position on *metaphysical naturalism*, according to which the only facts and properties are those investigated by the natural and social sciences.[19] But it is important to note something not emphasized here by Parfit: that non-naturalist realism can be combined with subjectivism (or internalism) about practical reasons, and naturalism can be combined with objectivism (or externalism). Parfit's view on the latter position is implicit in his comment on subjectivism: if the only facts are natural facts, then there are no normative reasons of any kind.

Parfit later returns to the question of how to characterize naturalism itself, accepting that the "scientific" criterion may plausibly be criticized as imprecise (88.305–7). He suggests a "reductive" sense of "natural", according to which a fact is natural if it could be restated by making some non-normative *and* naturalistic claim.[20] If a fact cannot be restated in non-normative terms, then we can say that it is non-natural without offering

---

[15] Against Parfit's claim, Smith (2016) offers a broadly Humean analysis of reasons.

[16] Note that this view is not to be confused with that described as "objectivism" in the previous section.

[17] A case for subjectivism is set out, in the light of Parfit's criticisms, by Markovits (2017).

[18] Hayward (2019) argues that belief in non-naturalist realism is itself immoral. Rabachou (2019) expresses doubts about its practical implications.

[19] For the claim that naturalism should be understood primarily as a methodological rather than a metaphysical position, see Railton 2016: 44–6.

[20] Parfit does not suggest that these terms must have the same meaning as those in the original statement.

a precise account of what makes a fact naturalistic.[21] Parfit goes on to consider, and reject, *wide naturalism*, according to which normative facts would be natural *even if* they were irreducibly normative because they could not be restated in non-normative terms. First, wide naturalists could not appeal to a *causal criterion* to distinguish natural properties, since some irreducibly normative facts *might* have caused certain natural facts. For example, had the actual universe in fact been the best possible universe, in that it was as good as it could be, this may have been *because* this was best.[22] Second, wide naturalists will anyway accept the non-naturalist cognitivist view that the most basic normative facts are necessary truths, which cannot be restated in non-normative terms. When Parfit uses the word "natural", then, we can take it in the reductive sense.

Part 6 of OWM, "Normativity," begins with the following table (24.263):

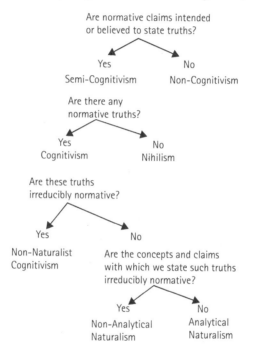

Before proceeding to his criticisms of analytical naturalism, Parfit makes some important preliminary points (2.264–9). First, his focus will be *concepts*, which are what is meant or expressed by certain words. For example, the concept *new* is expressed by "new" and "Nuevo." Second, most of the concepts he intends to discuss refer to *properties*, such as the property of being new or an act that is. Third, he will concentrate

---

[21] This of course raises the question of what "non-normativity" consists in. Parfit believes, for example, that "pleasantness" is a natural property; but if it is a necessary truth that pleasure is good, and hence always to be promoted, other things being equal, then it is not clear why it should not be described as a normative property.

[22] Parfit sometimes employs a narrower, material notion of causation (e.g., 115.503). For discussion, see Gibbard 2016: 62–4; Temkin 2016: 3–12.

on the *thin* normative concepts, such as "wrong" or "good," rather than thick concepts such as "murder," which combine normativity with naturalistic content (a murder is a wrongful killing). Fourth, we should note the important distinction between *metaphysical naturalism*, according to which all properties and facts are natural, and *normative naturalism*, the view that normative facts are natural facts. Some metaphysical naturalists are non-cognitivists, or nihilists (that is, *error theorists*, who believe all normative judgements are false), and hence not normative naturalists. By "naturalism" on its own, Parfit says, he will mean "normative naturalism," and his aim will be to show that naturalism and noncognitivism are both close to nihilism, since normativity must involve irreducible, non-natural facts.[23] Finally, Parfit distinguishes between different conceptions of normativity.[24] On the *rule-involving* conception, normativity concerns rules, such as those of grammar or etiquette, which allow or disallow certain things. On the *reason-implying* conception, a normative claim implies that someone has or might have some reason or apparent reason. Consider the eating of peas with a knife. That might be forbidden by etiquette, but it is an open question whether you have a reason not to do it. On the *motivational* conception, normativity consists in actual or possible motivating force. On the *attitudinal* conception, normativity involves certain attitudes, such as approval, to acts. Lastly, on the *imperatival* conception, normativity involves commands. One might combine these conceptions. A naturalist, for example, might seek to combine the reason-implying and motivational conceptions. Partly because he wishes to defend a self-standing version of the reason-implying conception of normativity, Parfit also notes that he will focus on (practical) reasons in general, rather than moral reasons or morality in particular, and—later—that he accepts that normative facts in any but the reason-implying sense can be natural.

Now let us consider Parfit's critique of analytical naturalism. On this view, normative words have meanings that can be analysed entirely in non-normative or natural terms. Parfit distinguishes between two forms of the view: *analytical subjectivism*, and *analytical objectivism*. The first, he suggests, is exemplified in Williams's internalism about reasons. Consider this case (83.270–1):

Early Death: Unless you take some medicine, you will later die much younger, losing many years of happy life. Though you know this fact, and you have deliberated in a procedurally rational way on this and all of the other relevant facts, you are not motivated to take this medicine.

According to Williams, you have no reason to take this medicine, whereas on Parfit's externalist view, you have a reason—an external reason—to take it, arising from the fact that doing so will give you many years of happy life.[25]

---

[23] Street (2016) argues that, since existing independently of a subject's point of view is not the only way of being "real," and that normativity depends on our taking things to matter, nihilism is not the only alternative to Parfit's view.

[24] Kiesewetter (2012) argues that Parfit's allowing for "oughts" without reasons leads to a dilemma for his non-naturalist realism.

[25] In his 2006, Finlay argues for a middle position on reasons between Williams's internalism and Parfit's externalism.

It is not clear whether Parfit is right to characterize Williams himself as an analytical subjectivist.[26] It is true, as Parfit notes (83.272), that Williams finds statements about external reasons "mysterious" and "obscure" (see 107.434). But it is plausible to think that Williams would have allowed that certain facts "count in favour" of certain actions, these facts of course consisting in facts about the agent's motivational set. What Williams may have found obscure is not the very notion of normative reasons as employed by Parfit, but the idea that facts other than motivational facts could constitute normative reasons. But the view itself can of course be considered independently of Williams's own claims, and Parfit goes on to argue that, even if we have both internal and external reasons, only external reasons matter (84.275–88).

According to *subjectivism about reasons*, (A) I have most reason to φ just when (B) φ-ing would best fulfill my present desires or is what after ideal deliberation I would choose to do. *Analytical internalists* (among whom Parfit includes Williams) claim that (A) *means* the same as (B), that is, that the phrase "I have most reason to φ" has exactly the same sense as "φ-ing would best fulfil my present desires or is what after ideal deliberation I would choose to do." But then it is misleading to express their view as if they were giving a condition for having a reason (consider someone who claims that, in saying that someone is a bachelor if they are an unmarried man, they are giving a condition for being a bachelor). Rather, they are expressing the tautology: (B) = (B), and this is not a substantive normative view.[27] Consider the following case (84.283):

> *Burning Hotel:* You are in some burning hotel, and you can save your life only by jumping into some canal. I am outside your hotel, which I know to be on fire, and I can see you at some window above the canal.

On the internalist view, if I think "You ought to jump," I am thinking that jumping would fulfill your current desires, or is what you would, after ideal deliberation, choose to do. But these two claims are not normative—the first is causal, and the second is psychological—and hence, Parfit is suggesting, they cannot mean the same as the normative claim that you ought to jump. If I knew that you have no desire to jump, and would not choose to do so after ideal deliberation, I might still reasonably believe—if your life is worth living—that you have a decisive reason to jump.

Parfit allows that an analytical internalist might express their view in terms of what the agent would do after *rational* deliberation, and hence admit non-natural normative claims. But, he suggests, these normative claims would be about not what we *ought* or have decisive reason to do, but what ideal deliberation consists in.

---

[26] Williams may be read as what Parfit calls an "*externalist subjectivist*" (85), or as using a "standard" or "thin" sense of "reason" common to both Williams and Parfit (see Street 2016: 124). See also Blackburn 2016: 93; Jackson 2016: 209–11. Darwall (2016) argues that the moral "ought" is conceptually connected with accountability and blameworthiness in such a way that this sense of ought must inherit any constraints motivational capacities impose on accountability and blame.

[27] Cf. Sidgwick 1907: 26n.

3. Nonanalytical Naturalism

Parfit's critique of the nonanalytical version of naturalism is more sustained than that of the analytical, extending over three chapters (87–98). He begins with *moral naturalism*, the view that moral properties are natural properties, and asks us to consider a simple monistic moral theory such as act utilitarianism, according to which acts are right just when they maximize happiness. If this is the case, then the two concepts *right* and *maximizing happiness* are necessarily coextensive. If we assume that happiness is itself a naturalistic notion, and claim that when two concepts are necessarily *coextensive*, they refer to the same property, then rightness would be, or would consist in, the maximization of happiness.

Parfit rejects this argument, using a mathematical analogy (87.296–7). Consider these properties of the number 2: *being the only even prime number* and *being the positive square root of 4*. These are necessarily co-extensive, since they are properties only of the number 2. And yet it seems clear that being the only prime number is not the same as being the positive square root of 4. Parfit then claims that this case is analogous to the moral one, and refers us to his later arguments that if the coextensiveness argument worked in the moral case then normative theories would be either impossible or trivial.[28]

Parfit then moves to a version of moral naturalism which is less ambitious in that it seeks to show only that moral naturalism *might* be true. According to this position, the relation between moral and natural properties might be seen as analogous to that between the property *being water* and *being H_2O* (87.297–305). In response, Parfit suggests first that the claim that some natural property is the property that *makes* acts right is not equivalent to the claim that this natural property is the property of *being* right. This claim, then, can be contrasted with the claim, for instance, that having greater molecular kinetic energy, for example, makes something hotter. Here the relation between having this greater energy and being hotter holds between the same property referred to in two different ways. This is not true, Parfit claims, of the relation of *making right*. Rather, in the case of simple utilitarianism, for example, the fact that some act would maximize happiness would make this act right by making it have the different, normative property of being right.[29] (A naturalist might take this to be mere assertion on Parfit's part, to which Parfit might respond that at this point he is close to bedrock, and can ask only that his claim be assessed carefully on its own merits.)

---

[28] In 133, Parfit claims that his earlier argument was faulty. He should have accepted that, when two concepts are necessarily coextensive, these concepts refer to "the same property" in the *necessarily coextensional* sense. Non-naturalists could then claim that these concepts would refer to different properties in the *description-fitting sense*.

[29] Parfit's argument here is intended to apply to forms of naturalism according to which, if there is only one natural property that makes things right, an act's having that natural property is the same as this act's being right, or, if there are several such natural properties, an act's rightness consists in its having one of these properties (87.300).

Parfit returns to this form of argument a little later (93), in discussing a naturalist argument that, if we consider the function in our thought of certain key indefinable normative concepts, such as that of a *normative reason*, we shall find that claims using these concepts can state facts that are both normative and natural. This argument is also often expressed using the analogy with water and H$_2$O. But, Parfit claims, what scientists discovered was that the stuff that has the properties of quenching thirst, falling as rain, etc., is the same as the stuff that has the different property of being composed of these particular molecules. This discovery was about two different properties, whereas the naturalist claim that some natural property is the same as the property of being right is about merely a single property. The scientific analogy here supports non-naturalism (with its two properties) rather than naturalism.[30]

At this point, a moral naturalist might just insist that moral rightness is, or consists in, some natural property or properties, since the concept *right* might refer to such a property or set of properties. Parfit returns to the analogy with science. The prescientific meaning of the word "heat" was something like: "the property, *whichever it is*, that can have certain effects, such as those of melting solids, or causing us to have a certain kind of sensation." This concept has, as Parfit puts it, a "gap" waiting to be filled, since the concept refers to some property without telling us what this property is. It does this by referring to that property indirectly, as having certain effects. But this, Parfit claims, is not the case with the concepts *right* or *wrong*. Consider for example wrongness understood in terms of the concept *blameworthy*.[31] This concept refers directly to the property of blameworthiness, so naturalists would have to claim that it is a natural property. But there is a clear difference between facts about, for example, what people say is blameworthy, and blameworthiness itself. Social scientists can discover facts about the former, but not, as social scientists, about the latter.

Parfit claims that if there were not this clear difference between rightness and natural properties, then he would have wasted his life, as would have other philosophers, since normativity would turn out to be an illusion.[32] Parfit believes that many people—including the noncognitivists and nihilists he has known—can respond to (objective) reasons without knowing what they are doing (because they do not use the concept of a normative—that is, an external—reason) (111.461–2). He then considers the suggestion that, because this is so, what he is discussing is of little practical importance. His response is that these noncognitivists and nihilists may have accepted certain normative truths before they developed their metaethical views. Parfit's concern is about others, who have never accepted such normative truths: "When these people are young, for example, they would be more likely to start smoking, drive dangerously, and make the lesser, non-lethal mistakes that Hume calls 'fatal errors'" (Hume 2007: bk. 3, part 2, sect.

---

[30] It has to be admitted that, since Parfit accepts that heat is the same as mean molecular kinetic energy, this analogy might be more promising for a naturalist.

[31] Parfit will claim that this term is sufficiently "thin" to allow it to serve as an elucidation of wrongness: it does not specify any particular type of act as worthy of blame.

[32] For criticism of Parfit's claim, see Gibbard 2016: 78–9; Schroeder 2016; Temkin 2016: 22–32.

7, para. 8). This concern of Parfit's contrasts strongly with the sanguine attitude of Hume himself, and his philosophical followers (see e.g. Foot 2002: 167).

Parfit returns to the scientific analogy in OWM, vol. 3 (135). He accepts that a naturalist might plausibly argue for an analogy between the following claims, on the assumption that hedonistic act utilitarianism is correct:

a) An object's having molecular kinetic energy both noncausally makes that object hot and is the same as being hot;
b) Being an act that minimizes suffering both noncausally makes an act right and is the same as being right.

Parfit claims that he now has a better objection to the use made by naturalists of this analogy. What corresponds to heat is not the property of being right, but the property that *makes* acts right. So what is relevantly similar to a) is not b) but:

c) Being an act that minimizes suffering both noncausally *makes* an act have the property that makes acts right, and is the same as *same* as the property that makes acts right.[33]

Before criticizing nonanalytical naturalism directly in OWM, vol. 2, Parfit discusses certain arguments the validity of which would challenge the fundamental distinction he is asserting between normative and natural facts.

The first is an argument that certain normative conclusions (*ought*-statements) can be derived from purely non-premises (*is*-statements) (89.310–14; see Hume 2007: bk. 3, part 1, sect. 1, para. 27). Consider the following argument:

(a) You said to me "I promise to help you."
(b) You promised to help me.
(c) You put yourself under an obligation to help me.
(d) You are under an obligation to help me.
(e) If other things are equal, you ought to help me.

According to Searle (1964), this argument is valid. Parfit points out that the inference from (b) to (c) is invalid, even if it is true that one cannot sincerely promise without believing that one is putting oneself under an obligation. The inference could coherently be denied, for example, by an act utilitarian, or indeed anyone who denies that promising in itself puts the promiser under an obligation, in the reason-implying sense.

A second naturalist argument appeals to thick concepts. Consider the following:

(a) Some woman often has sexual intercourse with strangers.
(b) This woman is unchaste.

---

[33] Parfit provides further defense of this claim about c) at 135.80–83.

(b) may appear to be a normative conclusion based on a non-normative premise. But, Parfit points out, a move analogous to that made against Searle is also available here. We can deny that chastity is a virtue, or assert that there is no reason to be chaste. The same general move can be made against other similar arguments based on thick concepts. But consider this *injustice* argument:

(a) Blue has not committed any crime.

Therefore

(b) Blue deserves not to be punished.

Therefore

(c) Blue's punishment would be retributively unjust.
(d) These facts would make Blue's punishment wrong.

Denying the wrongness of injustice is harder than denying that of unchastity. Nevertheless, a nihilist might deny the inference from (a) to (b), and some (such as Parfit himself, and act utilitarians) might claim that no punishment could ever be retributively unjust. In general, as Parfit goes on to point out in a critique of Anscombe, we cannot give *merely* linguistic or conceptual proofs of positive substantive normative truths.[34]

Parfit believes that claiming that normative facts are natural facts is analogous to claiming, for example, that the fact that galaxies rotate is a legal fact (91.324).[35] He calls this the *normativity objection* to naturalism, but realizes that many naturalists will deny it and hence offers further arguments against nonanalytical naturalism.[36]

Returning to arguments with the same general structure as those discussed above using analogies with science, Parfit first criticizes those naturalists who claim that, though normative *concepts* should be distinguished from naturalistic concepts, normative concepts can refer to natural properties, and be used to make normative claims about such properties so that, if these claims are true, they state facts that are both normative and natural (92). Consider now the phrase: "the natural property, whichever it is, that makes acts right". Parfit elucidates this as follows: "the natural property, whichever it is, that has the different, second-order property of being the natural property that makes acts right". This different property is normative.

Parfit goes on, using what he calls the *fact stating argument* (94), to clarify his suggestion by distinguishing two senses in which different claims may state the same fact (that is, we assume, the same state of affairs): in the *referential* sense, the claims refer to the same things

---

[34] For the view that normative "fixed points" are conceptual truths, see Cuneo and Shafer-Landau 2014.
[35] For some doubts, see McPherson (2018: 627).
[36] For elucidation and defense of the argument, see Howard and Laskowski 2019. Lenman (2009) and Fleming (2015) claim that it begs the question.

and ascribe the same properties to these things; in the *informational* sense, the claims give us the same information.[37] So "water is water," in the referential sense, states the same fact as "water is H$_2$O." And, if this is how we think of facts, the claim that water is H$_2$O could not have been a scientific discovery, since the fact allegedly discovered would be the same as the fact that water is water. The fact stating argument is then presented by Parfit as follows:

(1) We make some irreducibly normative claims.
(2) According to nonanalytical naturalists, when such claims are true, they state facts that are both normative and natural.
(3) If such normative facts were also natural facts, any such fact could also be stated by some other non-normative, naturalistic claim.

Therefore

(4) Any such true normative claim would state some fact that is the same as some fact that could be stated by some other, non-normative claim.
(5) If these two claims stated the same fact, they would give us the same information.
(6) This non-normative claim could not state a normative fact.[38]

Therefore
If these two claims stated the same fact, by giving us the same information, this normative claim could not state a normative fact.
Therefore
Such normative claims could not, as these naturalists believe, state facts that are both normative and natural.[39]

Parfit's central point is that, since nonanalytical naturalists must use the notion of "the same fact" in the informational sense, they must accept the fifth premise.

Parfit then turns to the *triviality objection* (95; see also 84).[40] According to utilitarian naturalists:

(a) when some act would maximize happiness, this act is what we ought to do;
and
(b) when some act would maximize happiness, this property of this act is the same as the property of being what we ought to do.

---

[37] Russell (2016: 252–3) suggests that Parfit's argument rests on the assumption that we cannot discover that two expressions with different meanings in fact refer to the same property.

[38] This premise is crucial if Parfit's argument is not to be just a reiteration of Frege's worry about the claim that the morning star is the evening star. A naturalist may object that it is mere assertion on Parfit's part; his response may again be that he has reached bedrock, and that the naturalist should consider their view in the light of Parfit's suggestions about basic conceptual categories.

[39] For discussion and defense of what they call the "two-tier" view of reasons, which distinguishes between reasons (e.g., the fact that it is cold) and the fact that some such fact is a reason, see McNaughton and Rawling 2017.

[40] For responses, and defenses of reductionist hard naturalism (see main text below) in ethics, see Jackson 2016, esp. 205–9; Schroeder 2016, esp. 218–26. For further criticism, see Lemaire 2019; Russell 2016: 253–4; also 249–52; Dowell and Sobel 2017. For exegesis and a conditional defence, see Tanyi 2006.

But if (b) were true, then (a) could not state a substantive normative fact, since this would require the postulation of a normative fact in an entirely different category from the natural fact that the act maximizes happiness. Hence, (a) would be trivial. And because (a) is not trivial, (b) cannot be true.

So-called *hard naturalists* accept the triviality of claims like (a). A *soft naturalist* might claim that, were (a) and (b) both true, (a) is not trivial, since it provides us with information about what we ought to do.[41] But these naturalists deny that the property of being what we ought to do is different from that of maximizing happiness, and so will have to find some other normative property to give (a) informational content.[42] Parfit calls this the *lost property problem*. Further, of course, such naturalists would have to give a naturalistic account of whatever property they claim to find, which leads to a reductio.

A soft naturalist might now claim that (b) itself is a normative claim. But the question remains what property a utilitarian naturalist is attributing to a happiness-maximizing action in addition to that of maximizing happiness. And whatever that property is, it will have to be normative. It might appear that the naturalist claim that being a happiness-maximizing act is the same as being what we ought to do means the same as the claim that maximizing happiness is what we ought to do. But that appearance, Parfit claims, is false, since the second claim could be true only if maximizing happiness has the different, normative property of being what we ought to do. This he calls the *single property illusion*.

Having applied the triviality objection to claims about reasons (96), Parfit goes on to state the *soft naturalist's dilemma* (97).[43] According to the soft naturalist, although all facts are natural, we have strong reasons to make some irreducibly normative claims. That leaves soft naturalists with a choice. Either they can allow for irreducibly normative claims, by becoming non-naturalists, or they accept hard naturalism, the view that we can do without irreducibly normative claims, stating all normative facts by making non-normative, naturalistic claims. What about hard naturalism (98)? Its problem should now be obvious: it rules out the making of substantive normative claims, "because irreducibly normative claims could not state natural facts" (98.377).

4. NONCOGNITIVISM

Noncognitivists are likely to be metaphysical naturalists, but they deny normative naturalism in its standard form (99). Normative properties, they believe, lie in our attitudes

---

At 136.85, 91–2, Parfit notes that the name for this argument is misleading, since if it were true that there are no irreducible normative facts, this would not be trivial: "I should have said only that, if there were no such truths, our normative beliefs could not help us to make good decisions and to act well".

[41] Laskowski (2015) argues that soft naturalists can sidestep Parfit's argument by claiming that the aim of normative thought can be understood as independent of normative properties.

[42] There is room here for a further naturalist position, according to which there are two concepts in play, but only one property, against which Parfit needs to use a different argument.

[43] For a defense of the view that, though we should allow self-standing normative concepts, normative properties are natural properties, see Copp 2017: esp. 38–49; also Copp 2009; Copp 2012 (which also contains a helpful overview and analysis of Parfit's arguments against naturalism). Parfit (2017: 195–200) argues that he and Copp are both nonrealist cognitivists.

to acts, not in the properties of those acts independent of our attitudes. The idea that our moral convictions consist in conative attitudes, Parfit calls *moral sentimentalism*. He first rejects, on the ground that it would make disagreement impossible, a cognitivist version of this view, *moral subjectivism*, according to which, when I claim that some act is wrong, I am claiming that I disapprove of this act. Another cognitivist view, *moral intersubjectivism*, suggests that when I claim that an act is wrong, I mean that most people, in ideal conditions, would disapprove of such acts. In general, Parfit suggests, *response-dependent* views (presumably whether analytic or non-analytic) may be true of secondary qualities, such as colours, but they cannot be accepted as an account of wrongness. This is not what I mean when I claim that an act is wrong, nor do I believe that acts are wrong because they would be disapproved of. Rather, Parfit claims, the relation runs in the opposite direction.

Now consider a noncognitivist version of sentimentalism:

> *Moral Expressivism*: When we claim that some act is wrong, we are not intending to say something true, but are expressing our disapproving attitude towards such acts.

According to Parfit, three main arguments have been offered for such noncognitivist positions. (1) According to the *Humean argument*, since moral convictions necessarily motivate us, they must constitute some motivating state, such as desires, rather than beliefs. But, as Parfit points out, it could be that a moral belief itself causes us to have a new desire. Further, there might well be cases in which someone knows that some act is wrong, but is not motivated at all to avoid acting in this way. We might say that their moral belief is insincere, but that is another matter. And in fact it seems that there can be sincere normative beliefs without motivation. Consider a severely depressed person who recognizes that they have a reason, say, to prevent some serious future harm to themselves, but who lacks any motivation.

(2) According to *naturalist arguments for nihilism or noncognitivism*, moral claims could not state facts, since moral claims, if true, would state facts that were not natural but irreducibly normative, and all facts are natural. According to nihilists, moral claims are intended to state facts, and so are false, while according to noncognitivists, moral claims are not intended to state facts, but can justifiably be made.

Parfit focuses on relatively recent and more sophisticated versions of expressivism, in particular those of Gibbard and Blackburn, partly with a view to articulating problems for all forms of noncognitivism. His first point (100) is that noncognitivists cannot allow for genuine disagreement, since such disagreement is not merely a conflict of two attitudes, such as desires or commitments to some plan, but between two contradictory beliefs. Nor can they explain how normative mistakes are possible (101). If you and I adopt different plans, or have two desires that cannot both be fulfilled, that does not show that at least one of these plans or desires must be mistaken. Or consider

Blackburn's Humean suggestion that I can make sense of the possibility that I myself may be mistaken by accepting that there may be some "improved standpoint" from which I would see my current attitude as "inept" (1993: 20). Parfit cannot see what could be meant by an "improved standpoint" other than a standpoint from which I am less likely to be mistaken. Nor does it help to *internalize* moral questions. If Blackburn were to claim that cruelty is wrong, we might object that cruelty's being wrong has nothing to do with his attitudes toward it. Blackburn might agree that what makes cruelty wrong is the suffering it causes, making clear that his attitude toward cruelty is based on his attitude to suffering. But if we ask the non-cognitivist what it is, in general, for any moral judgement to be true or false, the internalizing answer is not available, since it is appropriate only for particular moral judgements, such as that cruelty is wrong. Blackburn claims that quasi-realism is aiming to show us how to "earn our right to talk of moral truth" (1984: 197), but at least in certain passages, Parfit, suggests, it seems that his view involves merely asserting this right: "The only answer we should recognize to the question 'what is it for happiness to be good?' is happiness being good" (2009: 207).

And if he were to earn it, he could do so only by allowing that attitudes can be genuinely correct or mistaken, that is, by becoming a cognitivist.[44]

Parfit goes on to note (103.409–10) that it is also important to remember, as many non-cognitivists do not, that non-cognitivism cannot easily be restricted to practical reason, and so will apply also to epistemic reasons, reasons to believe. If there could not be facts about what it is rational to believe, then it could not be rational to believe anything. As Parfit says: "This bleak view is close to Nihilism".

(3) Returning to his earlier discussion of Hare and other writers (2006), Parfit outlines the *normativity argument for noncognitivism*, according to which, were moral judgements truth-apt, they could not also be action-guiding (104). The heart of Parfit's response, which depends on his view that normative truths are independent of willing, is captured in his comments on Korsgaard:

> If there are answers to normative questions, these answers would have to be truths. If there were no truths about what we have reasons to care about, or to do, we could not make better or worse decisions. We might as well act on impulse, toss coins, or do nothing. But there *are*, I believe, such truths. No disagreement could be deeper. . . . Normativity is not created by our will. (104.419, 424)

---

[44] The quasi-realist is likely to object that Parfit's arguments depend on an unnecessarily robust account of truth. For a response, using a deflationary Ramseyan account, see Blackburn 2016: 81–8. A similar response might be made to Parfit's suggestion about epistemic reasons (see following paragraph in main text). At 150.179, Parfit suggests that if quasi-realists earn their right to move beyond pure expressivism and become expressivist cognitivists, they would be able to claim that they had retained what is most distinctive in their metaethical position.

5. Four Objections

(a) Metaphysics

Parfit's various assertions of the significance of irreducible normative truths lead him into four chapters discussing different areas in which objections are raised to the very idea of such truths. The first is metaphysics (112–13).[45]

Parfit begins his discussion of metaphysical objections to irreducibly normative truths with a reference to Mackie's *argument from queerness* (Mackie 1977: ch. 1, sect. 9), according to which such truths are too strange for it to be reasonable to believe in

---

[45] It might help at this point to note Parfit's revision of his tree-diagram of positions in OWM, vol. 3 (130.56):

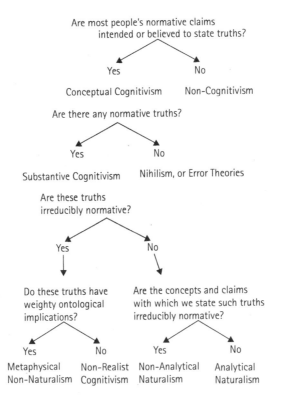

Note the new layer of disjuncts second from the bottom, as a response to critics including Gibbard and Railton, and the distinction between metaphysical non-naturalism and non-realist cognitivism. According to nonrealist cognitivism (Parfit's own view), irreducible moral truths are not made true by describing, or corresponding to, some part of reality (131.59). For doubts on whether nonrealist cognitivism can provide substantive accounts of the truth conditions for normative statements, see Copp 2018; Gasser 2018: 564–5; Suikkanen 2017. Veluwenkamp (2017) argues that Parfit's view is best understood as alethic pluralism, and that it is inconsistent with realist intuitions. For further doubt about Parfit's pluralism, see Olson 2018: 261–5.

them.⁴⁶ He then goes on first to reject views that rule out the existence of composite objects, such as rocks. He then rejects *actualism*, according to which to exist is to be actual, in favour of *possibilism*, which allows that there are things which are never actual, but merely possible. Actualism, he claims, is inconsistent with very many of our beliefs, such as, for example, my belief that I am sometimes able to choose between different possible acts. Nor is it enough for actualists to restate their views without reference to such acts (claiming, for example, that it might either be true that I shall choose to act in a certain way, or be true that I shall choose to act in some other way), since such restatements themselves imply that there are different possible acts.

Just as he distinguishes between different senses of "reason," so Parfit advocates what he calls the *plural senses view* about existence.⁴⁷ There is one wide, general sense, in which we can claim that things exist, but also narrower senses, such as the "narrow actualist" sense, in which we mean that the items in question actually exist as "concrete parts of the spatio-temporal world" (112.469; see also app. J). Parfit particularly wishes to object to physicalist versions of actualism, according to which, for example, there are no facts, meanings, symphonies, or logical truths. We might allow that certain physical objects are fundamental, in that they are the ultimate components of certain larger objects. But our metaphysics should be capacious rather than restrictive, focusing, as Aristotle put it (1963: 1076a36–7), on *how* things exist, not *whether* they do.⁴⁸ For example, we can note that certain things are subject-dependent, concrete, or mind-dependent, but recognize that these categories do not have sharp boundaries. It is a mistake, for example, to claim that abstract entities do not exist in space and time: consider the Equator, which is spatially located, or the Eroica Symphony, which began to exist at a certain time.

Truly normative properties are mind-independent and abstract, Parfit believes, and he returns to the analogy with mathematics, discussing the debate about the existence of numbers. He raises various issues concerning the dispute between platonists and nominalists, advocating the *no clear question view*, according to which numbers are not one of those entities about which it is a clear enough question whether, in some ontological sense (see below), they exist, though they are not in space and time. He then defines *cognitivism* about any kind of claim as the view that such claims can be (in a "strong sense") true. Many such claims have metaphysical or ontological implications—consider a claim about a rock, for example. If we believe that such claims can be in a strong sense true, we are *metaphysical cognitivists*. According to *nonmetaphysical cognitivism*, however, there are some claims which are in a strong sense true, but which have no positive ontological implications, and "when such claims assert that there are certain things, or that these things exist, these claims do not imply that these things exist in some ontological sense" (113.479).⁴⁹ In effect making a metametaphysical rather than metaphysical point, Parfit gives as his example mathematical

---

⁴⁶ See also Gibbard 2016: 61, 72, 77.
⁴⁷ For some doubts, see Gasser 2018: 565–6.
⁴⁸ Aristotle's point concerns the structure of his own argument concerning mathematical objects.
⁴⁹ Parfit drops the term "realism" in favour of "cognitivism" because he takes the former to be associated with "positive ontological claims" (OWM, vol. 2: index, s.vv. "realism, normative"). Orsi

truths, such as that 2 is greater than 1. For such claims to be true, there must be a sense in which there are numbers, but deciding which mathematical claims are true does not require an answer to the question whether numbers really exist "in an ontological sense". Parfit then goes on to make a significantly stronger claim: that numbers exist not only in the wide sense, but in a *non-ontological* sense, in that they are not either actual or possible, nor either real or unreal.[50] Not only do we not need to answer ontological questions about them, but such questions themselves are out of place because they have no answer.

To understand Parfit's claim here we might return to the no clear question view (see 113.482, 484). It is not as if Parfit is working with some clear distinctions between actuality and possibility, or between reality and unreality, and then denying that numbers cannot be placed on either side of these dichotomies. Rather, there is no "*relevant*" sense of any of these notions in play.[51] The nonontological sense of "existence", then, may well be "distinctive" (113.480), but it is essentially negative in character. To form true beliefs about numbers, we need not answer questions about their actuality or possibility, or their reality or unreality, and any conception of such notions which someone might attempt to apply to numbers would be irrelevant to mathematical concerns.

Parfit then returns to the argument from queerness, proposing a non-metaphysical cognitivist view of irreducible normative truths, according to which, for there to be such truths, it need not be the case that reason-involving properties exist either as natural properties in the spatiotemporal world, or in some nonspatiotemporal part of reality. These properties, then, are not natural, and hence

---

(2018: 582n1) distinguishes Parfit's position from a "quietist" view such as Dworkin's. According to Wodak (2017), Parfit is a quietist, and hence his view is to be rejected, since quietism allows reasons to be created "out of thin air"; see also Enoch 2011: 121–8. Böddeling (2019) argues that Parfit's quietism faces a dilemma: either it is equivalent to quasi-realism, or it is not quiet. For further criticisms of Parfit's ontological position and its motivation, including the claim that Parfit's metaphysical commitments are more substantial than he realizes, see Akhlaghi 2022; Constantinescu 2014; Cowie 2014; Fischer 2019; Mintz-Woo 2018; Niederbacher 2018.

[50] Railton (2016: 46–54) suggests that "soft" naturalists can also accept non-natural properties in a nonontological (viz. nominal or linguistic) sense. Parfit believes that this results in agreement between him and Railton (141). In his commentary (143), Railton accepts that there are non-natural facts, but prefers to call them "non-objectual" rather than "non-ontological": "What is a non-objectual fact? It need be no more than what is stated by some true positive claim, which is some true proposition. There can be non-natural non-objectual facts if there are true, positive claims or propositions essentially involving a non-natural concept, such as the concept of a normative reason". There may be little significance in this difference of terminologies. Parfit and Railton might perhaps agree that these facts are, in a sense, actual and real, but this is to say no more than that there are these facts (see 3.151.183; also Gibbard's commentary at 155.218–19 and Parfit's response at 156.228). Any further metaphysical enquiry into them, using more substantive conceptions of actuality and reality, would therefore be pointless. For some trenchant questions about Parfit's "pleonastic" conception of properties, see Gibbard's commentary (155.213–15).

[51] Fitzpatrick (2018: 539–41) argues plausibly that this is a purely methodological point, with no metaphysical implications.

Parfit calls his view *non-metaphysical non-naturalist normative rationalism* (the last word being chosen instead of "cognitivism" merely because his main claims are about reasons). The notion of "non-naturalness," then, also turns out to be essentially negative, involving merely the denial of naturalness, and not implying any particular "non-natural" realm.

(b) Epistemology

Parfit then turns to naturalist objections that suggest we could not have any reason to *believe* that there are irreducible normative truths (114–16). The first is the *causal objection*, according to which, since non-natural normative properties or truths could have no effects, we could have no way of coming to know about them.[52] Parfit notes first, again appealing to an analogy between normative and mathematical truths, that those who defend normative truths—*rationalists*—do not need to postulate any epistemic faculty like sense perception. To discover the contingent truth that the moon has craters requires us to look. But necessary truths can often be discovered merely by thinking about them, and normative truths are necessary: in any possible world, for example, pain would be bad.[53] Nor is that proposition analytic, and hence potentially empty. This view, as Parfit notes, is close to Sidgwick's intuitionist view that normative propositions are "self-evident."

This position also enables Parfit to respond to a variation of the causal argument, the *massive coincidence* argument, according to which, since we have no causal interaction with the alleged domains of mathematical and normative truths, any match between the beliefs we have and these truths would be highly unlikely. Not only, Parfit suggests, can we form such beliefs without such causal interaction, but we can explain how we came to possess this general epistemic capacity to grasp certain a priori truths: through the evolutionary advantage it brought (he calls this the *Darwinian* answer). Nor should we accept that this capacity's having an evolutionary origin throws any doubt on what it delivers.

Further, this argument can be run in the opposite direction (the *reverse coincidence* argument). We can form many true beliefs which are not based on sense perception, such as beliefs about possibilities. We have that capacity because we can respond to epistemic reasons. If we were not responding to such reasons, any match between our beliefs and those reasons would itself be a massive coincidence. Parfit goes on to develop the *validity* argument against any purely naturalistic attempt to explain our mathematical capacities, and hence against metaphysical naturalism itself. Consider computers which can perform correct mathematical calculations. Their ability to do this can be

---

[52] For a recent statement of this objection with reference to Parfit, see Zhong 2019.

[53] By "pain", here, Parfit means a kind of sensation that is *disliked* (see n. to 6.54 at OWM, vol. 2, pp. 455–6).

explained not by the laws of physics alone, but only by appealing to the validity of their reasoning. The same goes for us. We can form true mathematical beliefs only because our reasoning is valid, and since we can have no causal interaction with validity then our response must be noncausal. And a similar sets of claims can be made about normativity.[54] Parfit concludes his discussion by running arguments about epistemic normativity analogous to those used against naturalists about practical normativity, defending the view, for example, that when we know that certain facts have the (non-normative) property of implying that P is true, that makes these facts have the different, normative property of giving us a decisive reason to believe P.

(c) Rationalism

Having sought to show that we are able to respond to reasons, Parfit goes on to argue that we can justifiably believe that there are normative reason-involving epistemic truths (117–19).

He begins with the *naturalist argument for normative skepticism*, according to which, because normative beliefs are evolutionarily advantageous, our having them cannot be explained by their truth and, hence, we cannot justifiably believe them to be true. Parfit claims first that it is seldom the case that normative beliefs themselves would be advantageous. If one of our ancestors had believed that the next tiger they met was likely to be carnivorous, that might well have had survival value. But they would not have needed the further belief that the likelihood of their belief's being true gave them a reason to have this belief about tigers. Further, even if natural selection was *a* distorting influence on the formation of normative beliefs, there are noncausal ways in which we can respond to certain epistemic properties and truths.

Parfit then turns to practical reasons, and develops a structurally similar argument to that concerning epistemic reasons. It was certainly true, for example, that it was advantageous for early humans to be motivated to act in ways that would lead them to promote their own and their children's survival. But it does not follow that there was any evolutionary advantage in their believing that they had reasons to act in these ways. Parfit notes, however, that the claim that the ability to respond to reasons has survival value applies only to epistemic and not to practical reasons. Many nonhuman animals promote their own survival and that of their offspring without responding to reasons in the way that we do. The same point can be made about agony. Remembering what it is like is sufficient to motivate me to avoid it in future. How, then, should we explain my belief that I have a practical reason to want to avoid agony? Because it is obviously true. This explains why it is not a massive coincidence that this normative belief is true, even if part of the explanation of my having it involves natural selection.

---

[54] Against this extension from mathematical to practical normativity, see Gibbard 2016: 62–6.

Finally, Parfit turns to the suggestion that, since the content of our normative beliefs has been shaped by evolutionary forces, we cannot plausibly claim that these beliefs correspond to any independent normative truths.[55] But, Parfit points out, if our normative beliefs are primarily the result of evolutionary forces, we might expect that people would have beliefs that were reproductively advantageous, such as the belief that we have strong reasons to have as many children as possible and that it is wrong not to do so. But of course very few people have either of these beliefs. Or consider the fact that the earliest societies accepted something like the "golden rule," which requires one to treat others as one would be willing to be treated in their position, even if those others are unlikely to reciprocate (and so provide potential evolutionary advantage). Further, it may be that evolutionary explanations can be found for beliefs such as that we should care for our aged parents. But we can often find plausible evolutionary explanations of two conflicting normative beliefs, so that the probative force of each explanation is cancelled.

Parfit has been focusing primarily on reproductive advantage. But what about the social or cultural advantage that comes from, say, the widely held belief that it is wrong to lie? Such beliefs are often not open to debunking arguments, because they have clearly not been mostly produced by evolutionary forces of any kind. Consider, for example, the belief that all have equal rights. It may be true that our earliest normative beliefs were distorted by evolutionary forces, but it can plausibly be claimed that these distortions have to some extent been overcome. Parfit closes his discussion with a reiteration of his intuitionism:

> When we ask whether we can have practical and moral reasons, nothing is relevant except our normative intuitions. If it seems to us to be clearly true that we can have such reasons, and we seem to have no strong reason to believe that we can't have such reasons, we can justifiably believe that we can have such reasons. (33.542)

(d) Agreement

The influence of Sidgwick on Parfit emerges not only in his intuitionism, but in his concern for the epistemological implications of disagreement (120–122; see Sidgwick 1907: 342). Sidgwick focuses on actual disagreement, Parfit on ideal disagreement. According to the *argument from disagreement*, since we would in fact disagree about normative questions even in ideal conditions, we cannot justifiably believe that any of our normative beliefs are, or even might be, true. Against this, Parfit defends the *Convergence Claim* (CC), according to which, if everyone knew all of the relevant non-normative

---

[55] For a response, see Street 2016: 143–7. Chappell (2016) questions the significance Parfit attaches to the distinction between evolutionary and other causes, and suggests that a realist should claim that causal origins are never in themselves epistemically undermining. De Lazari-Radek and Singer (2016) develop an argument along Parfitian lines, claiming that it resolves Sidgwick's "dualism of practical reason" (see Sidgwick 1907: index, s.v.).

facts, used the same normative concepts, understood and carefully reflected on the relevant arguments, and was not subject to any distorting influence, nearly all of us would have sufficiently similar normative beliefs.[56] Parfit allows that the question of which conditions are ideal is normative; but, he suggests, CC itself is empirical.

Parfit asserts that what are under discussion are not conceptual claims, but substantive claims such as that, if we know that there is a 99 percent chance of some belief's being true, this fact gives us a strong epistemic reason to have this belief, or that the nature of agony gives us a reason to want to avoid future agony. We can reasonably believe CC to hold of moral beliefs also, since there are various ways to account for widespread existing moral disagreement. Such disagreements often rest on nonmoral disagreements, or ignorance of relevant nonmoral facts. Moral beliefs are often affected by distorting influences, such as self-interest. Moral disagreements often concern the implications of some more ultimate principle, on which there is agreement. People may disagree because they are using words such as "ought" in different senses. Disagreement may be at the level of explanatory moral theory only, with agreement at the substantive level on which acts are wrong. Some disagreements are about borderline cases only (e.g., about whether a fertilized embryo is or is not a human being). Others rest on the mistaken ideas that wrongness is all-or-nothing, when it is often a matter of degree, or that normative truths must be precise or determinate. When we consider most actual moral disagreements, Parfit suggests, these do not count strongly against CC. Further, there is much agreement on certain normative beliefs, such as the belief that it is bad to suffer, or that it is bad when people suffer undeservedly. And powerful arguments can be made against philosophers who have denied this, such as Nietzsche (123–5).[57]

Parfit believed that his continuing debate with Railton and Gibbard led to a significant degree of convergence. Because Railton is prepared to accept, for example, that there are some non-ontological properties and truths, he can avoid Parfit's objections to normative naturalism (OWM, vol. 3, "Summary": 10). And because Parfit explicitly denies any ontologically weighty non-natural properties or entities, his view comes much closer to Gibbard's (OWM, vol. 3, "Summary": 14). Parfit was greatly encouraged by this convergence (see, e.g., OWM, vol. 3, "Preface": xiii).[58] It came about partly through his distancing himself from metaphysical non-naturalism in putting more weight on a "thinner" conception of normative fact, and the recognition on both sides of the significance of the distinction between concepts and properties. But of course Parfit's non-naturalist cognitivism has itself become the focus of objections from many quarters, and doubtless that will remain the case for a long time. His contribution to metaethics should be measured, then, not primarily in terms of convergence, but by the brilliance, clarity, and power of his own arguments.[59]

---

[56] For some doubts, see Laskowski 2018.

[57] For a defense of Nietzsche against Parfit, and in particular of the claim that it is unlikely that in ideal conditions he and Parfit would agree, see Huddleston 2016.

[58] For discussion of the limits of this convergence, see Bykvist and Olson 2019.

[59] For comments on, discussion of, and assistance with previous drafts, I am deeply grateful to the editors, as well as to John Broome, Jonathan Dancy, Terry Irwin, and Theron Pummer.

References

Akhlaghi, F. 2022. "Non-Realist Cognitivism, Truthmaking, and Ontological Cheating." *Ethics* 132: 291–321.

Aristotle 1963. *Metaphysica*. Edited by W. Jaeger. Oxford: Clarendon Press.

Blackburn, S. 1984. *Spreading the Word: Groundings in the Philosophy of Language*. Oxford: Clarendon Press.

Blackburn, S. 1993. *Essays in Quasi-Realism*. New York: Oxford University Press.

Blackburn, S. 2009. "Truth and *a priori* Possibility: Egan's Charge against Quasi-realism." *Australasian Journal of Philosophy* 87: 201–213.

Blackburn, S. 2016. "All Souls' Night." In *Does Anything Really Matter?*, edited by P. Singer, 81–98. Oxford: Oxford University Press.

Böddeling, A. 2020. "Cognitivism and Metaphysical Weight: A Dilemma for Relaxed Realism." *Australasian Journal of Philosophy* 98: 546–559.

Bykvist, K., and J. Olson. 2019. "What Matters in Metaethics." *Analysis* 79: 341–349.

Chappell, R. Y. 2016. "Knowing What Matters." In *Does Anything Really Matter?*, edited by P. Singer, 149–167. Oxford: Oxford University Press.

Clarke, S. 1728. *A Discourse concerning the Being and Attributes of God, the Obligations of Natural Religion, and the Truth and Certainty of the Christian Revelation*. 7th ed. London: J. and J. Knapton.

Constantinescu, C. 2014. "Moral Vagueness: A Dilemma for Non-naturalism." In *Oxford Studies in Metaethics*, vol. 9., edited by R. Shafer-Landau, 152–185. Oxford: Oxford University Press.

Copp, D. 2009. "Towards a Pluralist and Teleological Theory of Normativity." *Philosophical Issues* 19: 21–37.

Copp, D. 2012. "Normativity and Reasons: Five Arguments from Parfit against Normative Naturalism." In *Ethical Naturalism: Current Debates*, edited by S. Nuccetelli and G. Seay, 24–57. Cambridge: Cambridge University Press.

Copp, D. 2017. "Normative Naturalism and Normative Nihilism: Parfit's Dilemma for Naturalism." In *Reading Parfit: On What Matters*, edited by S. Kirchin, 28–53. Abingdon and New York: Routledge.

Copp, D. 2018. "A Semantic Challenge to Non-Realist Cognitivism." *Canadian Journal of Philosophy* 48: 569–591.

Cowie, C. 2014. "A New Explanatory Challenge for Nonnaturalists." *Res Philosophica* 91: 661–679.

Crisp, R. 2012. "Naturalism: Feel the Width." In *Ethical Naturalism: Current Debates*, edited by S. Nuccetelli and G. Seay, 58–69. Cambridge: Cambridge University Press.

Cuneo, T., and R. Shafer-Landau 2014. "The Moral Fixed Points: New Directions for Moral Nonnaturalism." *Philosophical Studies* 171: 399–443.

Darwall, S. 2016. "Morality, Blame and Internal Reasons." In *Does Anything Really Matter?*, edited by P. Singer, 259–278. Oxford: Oxford University Press.

de Lazari-Radek, K., and P. Singer 2016. "Parfit on Objectivity and the "Profoundest Problem of Ethics"." In *Does Anything Really Matter?*, edited by P. Singer, 279–296. Oxford: Oxford University Press.

Dowell, J. L., and D. Sobel. 2017. "Advice for Non-Analytical Naturalists." In *Reading Parfit: On What Matters*, edited by S. Kirchin, 153–171. Abingdon and New York: Routledge.

Driver, J. 2017. "Contingency and Constructivism." In *Reading Parfit: On What Matters*, edited by S. Kirchin, 172–188. Abingdon and New York: Routledge.

Enoch, D. 2011. *Taking Morality Seriously: A Defense of Robust Realism*. New York: Oxford University Press.

Finlay, S. 2006. "The Reasons That Matter." *Australasian Journal of Philosophy* 84: 1–20.

Finlay, S. 2019. "Defining Normativity." In *Dimensions of Normativity: New Essays on Metaethics and Jurisprudence*, edited by D. Plunkett, S. Shapiro, and K. Toh, 187–220. New York: Oxford University Press.

Fischer, S. 2019. "Still a Misty Mountain: Assessing Parfit's Non-Realist Cognitivism." *Zeitschrift Für Ethik Und Moralphilosophie* 2(2): 213–230.

Fitzpatrick, W. 2018. "Ontology for an Uncompromising Ethical Realism." *Topoi* 37: 537–47.

Fleming, P. 2015. "The Normativity Objection to Normative Reduction." *Acta Analytica* 30: 419–427.

Foot, P. 2002. "Morality as a System of Hypothetical Imperatives." Repr. in *Virtues and Vices and Other Essays in Moral Philosophy*, 157–173. Oxford: Clarendon Press.

Gasser, G. 2018. "Normative Objectivity without Ontological Commitments." *Topoi* 37: 561–570.

Gibbard, A. 2016. "Parfit on Normative Concepts and Disagreement." In *Does Anything Really Matter?*, edited by P. Singer, 61–79. Oxford: Oxford University Press.

Hare, R. M. 1972. "Nothing Matters." In *Applications of Moral Philosophy*. London: Macmillan, 32–47.

Hayward, M. 2019. "Immoral Realism." *Philosophical Studies* 176: 897–914.

Howard, N. and N. Laskowski 2021. "The World is not Enough." *Nous* 55: 86–101.

Huddleston, A. 2016. "Nietzsche and the Hope of Normative Convergence." In *Does Anything Really Matter?*, edited by P. Singer, 171–194. Oxford: Oxford University Press.

Hume, D. 2007. *A Treatise of Human Nature*. Edited by D. F. Norton and M. J. Norton. Oxford: Clarendon Press.

Jackson, F. 2016. "In Defence of Reductionism in Ethics." In *Does Anything Really Matter?*, edited by P. Singer, 195–211. Oxford: Oxford University Press.

Kiesewetter, B. 2012. "A Dilemma for Parfit's Conception of Normativity." *Analysis* 72: 466–474.

Kirchin, S., ed. 2017. *Reading Parfit: On What Matters*. Abingdon and New York: Routledge.

Laskowski, N. 2015. "Non-Analytical Naturalism and the Nature of Normative Thought: A Reply to Parfit." *Journal of Ethics and Social Philosophy* 9: 1–6.

Laskowski, N. 2018. "Epistemic Modesty in Ethics." *Philosophical Studies* 175: 1577–1596.

Lemaire, S. 2019. "Contre Parfit: Une défense du naturalism." *Klēsis Revue Philosophique* 43: 59–95.

Lenman, J. 2009. "Naturalism without Tears." *Ratio* 22: 1–18. Repr. in *Essays on Derek Parfit's On What Matters*, edited by J. Suikkanen and J. Cottingham, 21–38. Chichester, UK; Malden, MA: Wiley-Blackwell.

Mackie, J. L. 1977. *Ethics: Inventing Right and Wrong*. Harmondsworth, UK: Penguin.

Markovits, J. 2017. "On What It Is to Matter." In *Reading Parfit: On What Matters*, edited by S. Kirchin, 54–81. Abingdon and New York: Routledge.

McNaughton, D., and P. Rawling 2017. "Normativity, Reasons and Wrongness: How to Be a Two-Tier Theorist." In *Reading Parfit: On What Matters*, edited by S. Kirchin, 96–122. Abingdon and New York: Routledge.

McPherson, T. 2018. "Explaining Practical Normativity." *Topoi* 37: 621–630.

Mintz-Woo, K. 2018. "On Parfit's Ontology." *Canadian Journal of Philosophy* 48: 707–725.

Niederbacher, B. 2018. "An Ontological Sketch for Robust Non-Reductive Realists." *Topoi* 37: 549–559.

Nuccetelli, S., and G. Seay. 2012a. "Does Analytical Moral Naturalism Rest on a Mistake?" In *Ethical Naturalism: Current Debates*, edited by S. Nuccetelli and G. Seay, 131–143. Cambridge: Cambridge University Press.

Nuccetelli, S., and G. Seay, eds. 2012b. *Ethical Naturalism: Current Debates.* Cambridge: Cambridge University Press.

Olson, J. 2018. "The Metaphysics of Reasons." In *Oxford Handbook of Reasons and Normativity*, edited by D. Star, 255–274. New York: Oxford University Press.

Orsi, F. 2018. "Ethical Non-Naturalism and the Guise of the Good." *Topoi* 37: 581–590.

Parfit, D. 1984. *Reasons and Persons.* Oxford: Clarendon Press.

Parfit, D. 1997. "Reasons and Motivation." *Proceedings of the Aristotelian Society*, suppl. vol. 71: 99–146.

Parfit, D. 1999. "Experiences, Subjects, and Conceptual Schemes." *Philosophical Topics* 26: 217–270.

Parfit, D. 2011–17. *On What Matters* [OWM]. 3 vols. Oxford: Oxford University Press.

Parfit, D. 2017. "Responses." In *Reading Parfit: On What Matters*, edited by S. Kirchin, 189–236. Abingdon and New York: Routledge.

Phillips, D. 2014. "Sympathy for the Error Theorist: Parfit and Mackie." *Ethical Theory and Moral Practice* 17: 559–666.

Rabachou, J. 2019. "Parfit ou le Renoncement à la Métaphysique?" *Revue de Métaphysique et de Morale* 102: 9–22.

Railton, P. 2016. "Two Sides of the Metaethical Mountain?" In *Does Anything Really Matter?*, edited by P. Singer, 35–59. Oxford: Oxford University Press.

Russell, B. 2016. "A Defense of Moral Intuitionism." In *Does Anything Really Matter?*, edited by P. Singer, 231–258. Oxford: Oxford University Press.

Scanlon, T. M. 1998. *What We Owe to Each Other.* Cambridge, MA: Belknap Press.

Schroeder, M. 2016. "What Matters about Meta-Ethics?" In *Does Anything Really Matter?*, edited by P. Singer, 213–230. Oxford: Oxford University Press.

Searle, J. 1964. "How to Derive 'Ought' from 'Is.'" *Philosophical Review* 73: 43–58.

Sidgwick, H. 1874. *The Methods of Ethics.* London: Macmillan.

Sidgwick, H. 1907. *The Methods of Ethics.* 7th ed. London: Macmillan.

Singer, P., ed. 2016. *Does Anything Really Matter?* Oxford: Oxford University Press.

Smith, M. 2016. "Parfit's Mistaken Meta-Ethics." In *Does Anything Really Matter?*, edited by P. Singer, 99–119. Oxford: Oxford University Press.

Stratton-Lake, P. 2017. "The Buck-Passing Account of Value: Assessing the Negative Thesis." In *Reading Parfit: On What Matters*, edited by S. Kirchin, 82–95. Abingdon and New York: Routledge.

Street, S. 2016. "Nothing "Really" Matters, but That's Not What Matters." In *Does Anything Really Matter?*, edited by P. Singer, 121–148. Oxford: Oxford University Press.

Suikkanen, J. 2017. "Non-Realist Cognitivism, Objectivity and Truth." *Acta Analytica* 32: 193–212.

Tanyi, A. 2006. "Naturalism and Triviality." *Philosophical Writings* 32: 12–31.

Temkin, T. 2016. "Has Parfit's Life Been Wasted?" In *Does Anything Really Matter?*, edited by P. Singer, 1–34. Oxford: Oxford University Press.

Veluwenkamp, H. 2017. "Parfit's and Scanlon's Non-Metaphysical Moral Realism as Alethic Pluralism." *Ethical Theory and Moral Practice* 20: 751–761.

Williams, B. 1979. "Internal and External Reasons." In *Rational Action*, edited by R. Harrison, 101–113. Cambridge: Cambridge University Press.

Wodak, D. 2017. "Why Realists Must Reject Normative Quietism." *Philosophical Studies* 174: 2795–2817.

Zhong, L. 2019. "The Hard Problem for Soft Moral Realism." *Journal of Philosophy* 116: 555–576.

CHAPTER 19

ARDENT MORAL REALISM AND THE VALUE-LADEN WORLD

WILLIAM J. FITZPATRICK

THIS chapter explores an ambitious form of moral realism we will call "ardent moral realism," which aims to capture the idea that "reality itself favors certain ways of valuing and acting," where this favoring involves categorical moral normativity.[1] That robustly realist idea is driven by a set of convictions about both metaethics and ethics: namely, the sense (i) that metaethics should begin by taking seriously the appearances yielded by our core experience as engaged and committed moral agents, keeping these in view as we seek to make metaethical sense of moral discourse and practice; (ii) that these appearances, taken at face value, remain more compelling in the end than arguments for discounting them or regarding them as erroneous; (iii) that the moral appearances carry rich implications concerning moral objectivity and categorical moral normativity; and (iv) that these implications cannot be adequately accounted for within a nonrealist framework (such as metaethical constructivism or expressivism)—or even within less robust realist frameworks.

Each of these claims is, of course, controversial. Some metaethicists may instead approach the subject more like philosophically oriented anthropologists, setting aside any special role for their experience as engaged moral agents and seeking parsimonious metaethical accounts based on impartial observation of moral discourse and practice. Relatedly, some might find their confidence in the appearances from their own moral experience readily overcome by various skeptical or deflationary arguments or

---

[1] The expression "ardent realism" along with the above initial characterization of it comes from Matti Eklund, though his own concern is with ardent *normative* realism generally, not specifically with *moral* realism, and he does not himself endorse the view (Eklund 2017, 1). I understand ardent moral realism to combine ardent normative realism with a moral realism that takes moral requirements to have the kind of objective normative authority embraced by the ardent normative realist, as will become clear below.

interpretations. And others might argue that these appearances don't carry such rich purport after all, or that insofar as they do it can all be accounted for in some nonrealist manner.[2] It is not my aim here to try to defend the convictions underlying ardent moral realism against such alternatives, or to show that ardent moral realism is in fact true (though it is the view I find most attractive).[3]

My primary aim is instead to shed light on what is ultimately at stake in debates over moral realism by exploring an important recent challenge to the very coherence of ardent moral realism and then offering a solution. While this is not intended to establish the truth of the view, I do hope to illuminate the central motivation for it—especially in contrast with certain naturalistic forms of moral realism—and to clarify its central commitments. In particular, by bringing out what drives the move to (what is typically considered) "non-naturalism," we will see that what is doing the crucial work is not some abstract metaphysical commitment to an obscure non-naturalistic realm, but simply an appeal to the *irreducibly evaluative or normative nature* of certain elements of the one familiar world we inhabit. This suggests that the focus of debates over different forms of moral realism should shift from metaphysical concerns over non-naturalism in the abstract to questions specifically about irreducibly evaluative or normative properties and facts. Perhaps what really matters to ardent realists might ultimately fit within a broader, nonscientistically conceived naturalism after all, as long as it accommodates such irreducible value or normativity. Indeed, this possibility is suggested by an intriguing parallel in the philosophy of mind, where a broadly conceived physicalism might satisfy those who are typically considered "nonphysicalists" about consciousness by incorporating irreducibly phenomenal properties and facts within the scope of the physical. We'll return to that idea.

1. Ardent Moral Realism: Initial Characterization and a Challenge

In keeping with the ardent moral realist's approach to metaethics as inquiry originating in reflection on first-personal ethical experience, let's begin with a typical moral judgment we're likely to take seriously as engaged moral agents:

> M: It is morally wrong for people in the midst of a pandemic to refuse to wear a mask in public or to follow distancing guidelines, out of mere dislike for the inconvenience

---

[2] Terry Horgan and Mark Timmons (2008 and 2018) grant that moral phenomenology includes the appearance of categorical authoritativeness but deny that this includes any ontological objective purport, maintaining that it can be fully accommodated by their nonrealist cognitivist expressivism. I argue that this accommodation project falls short in FitzPatrick (2021).

[3] In FitzPatrick (2022) I discuss the complex argumentative strategy plausibly required to support such a view and take some steps in that direction.

to themselves, prioritizing their personal freedom to do as they please over public health protocols.

Suppose we sincerely endorse M. How does this present itself to us upon reflection? The ardent moral realist (henceforth just "ardent realist") will begin by noting that we seem to be embracing something both true and robustly important. We don't follow our assertion of M with disclaimers such as "but that's just me," or "though such refusals might be fine in another culture with different values," as we might do with matters of mere taste or etiquette. Consider the features of the behavior that we think *make* the antimasking behavior wrong (thus making M true): the self-indulgent recklessness and callous disrespect involved in posing serious risks to a broad range of people simply in order to avoid inconveniences to oneself. These features seem to make the behavior wrong in a way that is far more objective than is suggested by such disclaimers.

Nor are we content to suppose that although M might technically be true given the meaning our linguistic community has given to the expression "morally wrong," the normative significance of a behavior's counting as morally wrong depends on the desires and interests of the agent in question. That is, the normative force of M does not strike us as something a person might escape simply by shrugging and claiming either not to care about such moral concepts and strictures or to care more about being free to do as one pleases. The appearance from within the engaged moral perspective (or so we are here granting the ardent realist) is instead that such people are making an important practical mistake. Their mistake is not merely a semantic one (if they deny that their behavior counts as "morally wrong" given the way we use those words); and it is not merely that they are making a practical choice we don't like and to which we attach a negative label ("morally wrong"), which they might then just acknowledge and shrug off without error. They are doing something, it seems, that there is—as an objective matter—genuine and unqualified normative reason for them not to be doing, full stop. They seem to be flouting normative reality—going against the normative grain of the world (in a sense to be explicated and developed later).

This appearance of "objective prescriptivity" (as Mackie 1977 put it) associated with judgments such as M is in any case a familiar one, and it is what animates ardent realists. They take it to be veridical and to be what justifies our being prepared, in connection with claims such as M, to argue forcefully for them, to press criticisms and demand changes in behavior even in the face of indifference, and to resent (not merely dislike) failures to comply with them. We wouldn't be inclined to take these stances if we thought we were using moral terms merely to slap an additional label on behavior with certain empirical features we happen to care about (in the way we might use a term like "unfriendly" to label social behavior with certain practically salient features). There seems to be more going on with moral evaluation. It's not, for example, simply a matter of our having strong feelings or commitments concerning behavior with certain empirical features, but seems to go the other way around: we feel strongly about such things *because* of the negative moral status actions have by virtue of having those empirical features; and this negative moral status seems to carry with it normative implications for any agent concerning what there is genuine, unqualified reason for them to do (such as masking during a pandemic) regardless of what they happen to care about.

To be sure, not everyone takes their moral commitments to carry such implications, especially if they have independent philosophical qualms about such things as unqualified, all-things-considered, authoritative "oughts" or reasons to begin with (Copp 2007; Conee 2016). But many of us do find our moral experience to be characterized by such appearances of robust normativity associated with our moral judgments.[4] And for ardent realists this is both a starting point and something they continue to find compelling as they proceed with metaethical inquiry. Moreover, as realists they take these appearances to be an accurate reflection of *objective moral reality*—part of the way the world is.

Now one basic question about such a position is what exactly we would need to posit in the world in order to accommodate it, and whether this is tenable. We will return to this. A prior and more fundamental question, however, arises from a recent challenge posed by Matti Eklund (2017), focused on apparent contingencies in the language and concepts we employ in the moral domain. Suppose it is granted to the realist up front that "right" does in fact pick out a real property, rightness, and that there are thus facts about how it is right or wrong to live, expressed by true statements such as M. Let's even grant that rightness is an objective property—such as the property of being happiness maximizing. This may seem like a substantial victory for the realist: positive statements about rightness express truth-assessable propositions, some of which are literally true, and in a stance-independent way! In fact, however, it hasn't gotten us very far toward ardent realism at all.

To see this, suppose it also turns out that other linguistic communities have analogous but different concepts that play similar normative roles in their practical deliberation and social guidance and criticism, but that pick out different, equally real and objective properties of actions. Instead of our concept of what is right, they employ a concept of what is right* or right**, etc., with different referents. For example, rightness* (the property picked out by "right*") might be the property of maximally promoting the cohesion and strength of one's broad social group, while rightness** is the property of maximally promoting the happiness of one's kin, and so on for other possibilities. In that case, while it is true that there are indeed ways it's right to live, it is equally true that there are (other) ways it's right* to live, ways it's right** to live, and so on. Different communities might thus adopt different concepts and organize their lives around them,

---

[4] It is not just ardent realists who construe morality as having such rich purport: even error-theoretic antirealists such as Mackie (1977) and Joyce (2001) agree that moral judgment has these implications; the difference is just that they're skeptical that anything in the world answers to this idea of objective prescriptivity or categorical normativity. And expressivists typically accept much of the moral phenomenology that drives ardent realists but attempt to accommodate it within a nonrealist, expressivist metaethics (Blackburn 1993, 1998; Gibbard 2003, 2006; and especially Horgan and Timmons 2008 and 2018). I will not explore such expressivist projects here, though elsewhere I've tried to show that they fail to capture what matters to ardent realists, due to an analogue of the parity problem explored below (FitzPatrick 2011 and 2021).

one endorsing and seeking what is right, another what is right*, etc., each championing a different but equally real property in the world. This then raises the question: how should one decide which concept, property and way of life to care about and pursue? And is there an objectively correct way to make that decision? What would that even *mean* here?

It will be disconcerting—and obviously problematic for the ardent realist—if this imagined conceptual pluralism just bottoms out in *parity*, as it may seem to, with nothing to decide among the different possibilities except, of course, trivially insofar as each way of life can be endorsed using the concept corresponding to the property targeted by that way of life. We could naturally point out that rightness is a real and objective property and our prescribed way of life is in fact *right* (while theirs is not!), and we would be perfectly correct in saying this. But while this might sound impressive, it is a hollow victory: for they can of course equally say with as much truth on their side that rightness* is a real, objective property and their way of life is *right** (while ours is not!), feeling themselves similarly vindicated. This kind of parity, bottoming out in the idea that each community is just talking about a different property, with nothing to choose objectively between them, is clearly anathema to ardent realist ambitions. Nor would it help here to introduce the metaphysical idea that rightness is in some sense "non-natural." Suppose the happiness to be maximized were a mystical, non-natural phenomenon: this would do nothing at all to help make sense of the idea that the choice of one concept/property/life package would be objectively correct while the others would not.

What this shows is that merely positing a real, objective property of rightness (with whatever metaphysical status we like) is not enough to get us what we were after for ardent realism (Eklund 2017, and cf. Horgan and Timmons 1991). Or at least this is true *if* the assumptions underlying the abstract thought experiment above, about how reference works for evaluative or normative concepts and what evaluative or normative properties would be like, are correct (which I will argue in the next section they are not).

Perhaps, one might think, we can remedy the situation by appealing to *reasons*: what sets rightness apart from rightness* and other variants is that rightness is intimately connected to reasons for acting (which might be denied for rightness* and the like). But alas, this won't help either, at least if we remain within the same metasemantic framework. For suppose we grant the claim about reasons. Even so, perhaps rightness* is similarly associated with some variant of reasons that plays a similar normative role: reasons*. Once again (so the challenge goes), we can imagine rival communities, one defending rightness by appeal to its connection to reasons (where reasons are understood as considerations in light of which an action would promote happiness maximization, say), the other defending rightness* by appeal to its connection to reasons* (understood as considerations in light of which an action would promote group cohesion and strength). We are thus right back to the parity problem: one way of life is right and is supported by reasons, while another is right* and is supported by reasons*, and so on. What is to choose objectively between the alternative conceptual and lifestyle packages, in a way that would satisfy the ardent realist? What could the *objective privileging* of one of these over the others even amount to, given that we've already granted that the empirical properties picked out by the rival normative concepts are *equally real* ones? It's unclear so far whether ardent realists can even articulate what it is they are claiming about objective normativity without running back into this same problem. This raises worries, then, about whether ardent realism is even a coherent position (Eklund 2017).

2. A Solution to the Challenge

Ardent realists wish to capture the idea that "reality itself favors certain ways of valuing and acting" (Eklund 2017, 1), but it seems impossible even to give a clear sense to this idea on the above picture. If reality merely yields a multitude of properties of the sort we've considered, which serve as referents of various practically employed concepts one could adopt, none privileged over the others in its ontological credentials and each merely favored trivially in terms of its corresponding concept, then it is hard to see how reality itself could possibly favor certain ways of valuing and acting over others. This puzzle arises, however, only due to a misguided conception of how evaluative or normative concepts work in the first place.

The core problem lies in erroneously construing evaluative judgment, i.e., the judgment involved in evaluation, on the model of ordinary property ascription, as in the sciences, with the addition of some practical roles. A simple form of ethical naturalism, for example, might propose that in judging an act to be right we're using the term "right" to ascribe an empirically specifiable property to it, like being happiness maximizing—just as in a scientific judgment we might use "magnetic" to ascribe to a piece of metal the property of being magnetic—while also giving the concept of rightness certain practical roles. Similarly, a structurally parallel form of moral non-naturalism would just add that the property we're ascribing is instead a non-natural one, on the model of ascribing an occult healing power to a crystal.[5] If we approach evaluation using such a model, then we run headlong into the earlier problem. Different groups might simply use different moral concepts to ascribe different properties they care about, one using the concept *right* to pick out the property of being happiness maximizing while the other uses *right** to pick out the property of maximally promoting group cohesion and strength, each giving their concept and property a similar practical role in social guidance of action. This leaves us, first of all, with familiar Moral Twin Earth problems: we have, it seems, precluded the possibility of even addressing a common subject matter and having genuine disagreement across such communities.[6] More to the present point, however, it also leaves us with the *parity problem* raised by the earlier challenge: how is one such concept

---

[5] Allan Gibbard (2003, 16) imagines the non-naturalist to be operating on this sort of model, ascribing to acts some obscure, simple non-natural property he labels "exnat" (a non-normatively characterized, empty placeholder for whatever property it might turn out to be).

[6] See Horgan and Timmons (1991). For a naturalist attempt to avoid such problems see Brink (2001).

or property objectively privileged over the others, and what could such privileging even amount to? The ardent realist clearly needs something very different here.

What is needed is a different realist model of how reference works in the context of evaluation or normative judgment—a different metasemantics for such judgment—and a different understanding of the sort of property an evaluative property like rightness, attributed in evaluation, would be.[7] There is, of course, a trivial sense in which on any realist view, at least, we must be "ascribing a property" to something in judging it to be right or good—namely, the evaluative property of rightness or goodness. But the appropriate model here is not the simple one for ordinary property ascription (as with ascribing to something the property of being magnetic), but something more complex. This is true even for mundane nonmoral evaluation, so it's worth starting there.

Consider the evaluation of an artifact, again assuming here a realist framework in which evaluation consists in attributing an evaluative property to something (since alternative frameworks, such as an expressivist one, will not be suited to the ardent realist's aims). In evaluating a knife as a good one, attributing goodness to it as a knife, we're not simply ascribing to it a property like being sharp, using "good" merely to pick out or talk about a property like sharpness. Someone can attribute sharpness to a knife without evaluating it at all: perhaps she mistakes the knife for a bookmark, or she's ignorant that a knife's function is to cut, or she fails to understand that sharpness makes things well-disposed toward cutting, and so doesn't even see it as good-making here. We evaluate a knife when we judge that it's a good knife, for example, and this attribution of an evaluative property to it is clearly something more than ascribing sharpness or any other prosaic property of that sort to it.

A property like sharpness may be a good-*making* feature, as it is in a knife—or, for that matter, it could be a bad-making feature, as it is in a bookmark—which means that we can cite it in support of our evaluations. But the evaluation—attributing an evaluative property—is more than just saying that something is sharp or not. And this matters because the property appropriately identified as the evaluative property should of course be *the property whose ascription can constitute evaluation*, which would be goodness here, not something like sharpness or any other property the ascription of which fails to constitute evaluation. What, then, is the knife's goodness? It is a complex property: namely, the resultant positive evaluative status the knife has by virtue of having resultance-base properties (like sharpness) that are good-*making* insofar as they make it satisfy relevant or appropriate *standards of excellence* for knives.[8]

We thus need to avoid conflating evaluative concepts and properties, such as the concept or property of goodness, with nonevaluative concepts or properties, such as the concept or property of sharpness: sharpness may be a good-making property in a knife but it is not the property of goodness itself here. Though we cite prosaic good-making

---

[7] The next few paragraphs draw on work developed in FitzPatrick (2008, 2014, 2018b,c).

[8] On the *resultance* relation between resultant properties and resultance-base properties, and the distinctness of the property attributed in evaluative judgment from the base properties by virtue of which it is attributed, see Dancy (2004, 2006) and Parfit (2011).

properties in the course of evaluation, the evaluation is not just the ascribing of those properties as such, but the citing of them *as* good-making insofar as they make the thing in question satisfy appropriate evaluative standards—such as functional standards involving cutting in the case of a knife. And this means that in evaluation we're making implicit reference to relevant evaluative standards, ascribing to the thing a resultant evaluative status due to the relation between the thing's base properties and the standards—for example, the fact that the knife's sharpness makes it good at cutting, thus satisfying the relevant or appropriate standards of excellence for a knife and thereby making it count as a *good* knife.

This complex structure is precisely what fixes a common subject for evaluative discourse, making disagreement possible even where people agree about all the prosaic base properties: they may just have different views of the appropriate standards, and so of how the base properties make the thing "stack up." For example, two people may disagree over whether someone's performance constitutes good singing, despite agreeing on all its nonevaluative features. This wouldn't be possible if they were each using "good" simply to ascribe such base properties to the singing. But that is not what they're doing. They are instead both using "good" in a common, *formal* way, i.e., a way that abstracts from any specification of particular base properties or of the standards, to refer simply to the positive resultant evaluative status something has when its base properties make it satisfy the relevant standards of excellence for such things. And they are having a genuine evaluative disagreement because one is attributing that status to the performance and the other is denying it.[9]

Their disagreement here comes down to different conceptions or specifications of the relevant or appropriate standards, such that for one the base properties satisfy those standards and result in the singing's having the positive evaluative status of being good singing, whereas for the other they don't. (Perhaps on the latter's understanding of the standards the degree of vibrato and belting in the performance is excessive, disqualifying it from being good.) Of course, if we think that what constitutes good singing comes down largely to a matter of taste—i.e., the standards are not ultimately provided by reality itself—then we won't be ardent realists about good singing! So the above structural points about evaluation obviously don't themselves get us to ardent realism. But they are a first step in avoiding the confusions that make ardent realism seem incoherent.

Turning to the moral domain, the same structural points apply. Saying that an experience is pleasant or that an act is happiness maximizing (whether in these terms or using other terms to which we give special practical roles) is no more in itself to evaluate the experience as good or the act as right than saying that something is sharp is to evaluate it as good. We might cite an act's being happiness maximizing in the course of evaluating it

---

[9] I will typically speak of "the standards" (plural) or "the set of standards" relevant to evaluating something, rather than "the standard," simply to indicate that the set of criteria in question may be complex, addressing a variety of features (as with good singing), rather than articulable as a single rule. The point is that evaluation involves implicit reference to some particular set of standards (or conception of the standards) one is employing and taking to be appropriate.

as right, but the evaluation is not just the ascription of that property as such: it is (at least in a realist framework) the citing of that property as right-making, thus supporting the evaluation, which latter is the distinct attribution of rightness to the act—where rightness is a more complex, resultant property implicating claims about appropriate evaluative standards and the relations of base properties to those standards.[10]

It is this sort of role in the practice of evaluation that gives clear sense to talk of "evaluative concepts and properties" in a realist model. It explains why the concepts of goodness or rightness are evaluative ones while the concepts of sharpness or of being pleasant or happiness maximizing are not; and it explains why the complex properties of goodness or rightness, attributed using the concepts of goodness or rightness in evaluative judgment, are evaluative ones, while properties like sharpness or being pleasant or happiness maximizing are not. This is also what makes it possible to be talking about the same thing and disagreeing about it. And it is ultimately what allows us to articulate the ardent realist's claim and to see what the world would have to be like in order for it to be true (as described in the next section).

Let's illustrate this by returning to our example of moral evaluation:

> M: It is morally wrong for people in the midst of a pandemic to refuse to wear a mask in public or to follow distancing guidelines.

As noted earlier, we have reasons for why we believe M to be true, which amount to what we take to be the wrong-making features of the behavior in question, namely:

> F: refusal to wear a mask and to physically distance in public during a pandemic poses a serious risk to others and contributes to the potentially catastrophic spread of disease.

What we have now added is that the moral thought that the features described in F constitute wrong-making features of the behavior reflects certain background assumptions about the content of the *appropriate set of moral standards* for evaluating human behavior. While that content is obviously a complex matter, it will involve some conception of relevant values and their interactions and relative weightings. In the present case,

---

[10] The recognition of the role of standards within the structure of evaluative judgment is a virtue of David Copp's (1995) society-centered, standard-based version of moral naturalism, which avoids the structural problems of certain other forms of naturalism (FitzPatrick 2008, 2011, 2014). Note that on the above account evaluation involves implicit reference to a set of standards taken to be *relevant* or *appropriate* to assessing the thing in question. This explains why in evaluating something we are also plausibly expressing endorsement of a certain set of standards (cf. Copp 2007, chap. 5): that expression of endorsement is due to the normative content built into the judgment involved in evaluation (it is not, as on expressivist views, some distinct noncognitive element). Again, this is important for the ardent realist, who will ultimately need to posit objective truths corresponding to that normative content about the appropriateness or correctness of a certain set of standards, given the ambition to capture objective moral prescriptivity, as discussed below.

the underlying thought behind endorsing M-based-on-F is roughly that the importance of life, health and happiness vastly outweighs the importance of avoiding minor inconveniences to oneself. This means that we are conceiving of the appropriate set of moral standards as requiring us, as part of their content, to prioritize the protection of life, health and happiness over avoiding minor inconveniences to ourselves. If the standards are articulated in virtue-theoretic terms, for example, this might be incorporated as part of the specification of the requirements of justice and respect for persons. The anti-masking behavior then violates those standards by having the features described in F—features that make the behavior selfish, callously disrespectful and reckless, in violation of the set of moral standards in question, leading us to M.

Our judgment M is thus not merely another way of stating the empirical facts in F (facts that even those who reject M might grant).[11] To evaluate the behavior as morally wrong is not merely to attribute to it such empirical features as being dangerous or harmful (the resultance-base properties): it is instead to attribute to the behavior the resultant evaluative property of being morally wrong by virtue of having such resultance-base empirical features (given in F) and thereby violating relevant moral standards. This is why two people can genuinely disagree about M even if they agree about F: they can both be talking about the same thing at a formal level—a single, resultant evaluative property of wrongness—but disagreeing about whether it is in fact manifested by the behavior, because they disagree about the content of the proper moral standards by which to judge human character and regulate social life. On one conception of those standards, F makes antimasking behavior run afoul of the standards and thus count as wrong; on another conception of the standards it is instead compatible with acting rightly to opt not to wear a mask, despite F, so that F does not ground any resultant wrongness. Genuine disagreement is thus possible here, which also means that there is a common subject matter about which there could in principle be an objective fact of the matter.

To return, then, to the moral appearances animating ardent realism: when we sincerely endorse a judgment such as M it appears to us that M is objectively true in a way that implies the objective correctness of the underlying set of moral standards supporting it (and the objective incorrectness of the incompatible set of standards employed by the antimasker), for purposes of morally evaluating human action. It is this idea (in part) that the ardent realist is trying to capture: the idea of an objectively correct set of moral standards, which we will say more about in the next section (along with the idea of the categorical normative force of the moral truths yielded by such standards, discussed just below).[12]

Similar points apply to talk of *reasons*, such as the claim that in light of M there is genuine *reason* for each person to wear a mask (so that M has robust normative force). Such talk could not do the work we want it to do if saying that there is reason to do something were just another way of saying that so acting will promote some specific end built

---

[11] Again, this point is emphasized by Dancy (2004, 2006) and Parfit (2011).

[12] We have illustrated the motivation for this idea using a conviction about M, assuming its correctness for the sake of argument, but obviously nothing depends on this particular example.

into the meaning of "reason," such as maximizing happiness. If that's all we were saying then someone else could similarly use "reason*," with a parallel but different meaning incorporating some other specific end such as maximizing personal freedom, to say that there is genuine reason* for them *not* to wear a mask. As before, this would land us back in the parity problem: there may be reason to abide by M and the standards underlying it, but there might equally be reason* for our opponent to shrug off M and the significance of the standards underlying it, and to live amorally instead. Such a situation would prevent claims about reasons from helping to establish in any meaningful sense the genuine normative force of moral claims like M. Fortunately, however, talk of reasons does not operate on such a model.

As with talk of rightness or wrongness, talk of reasons is again *formal* and *normative* in a way that allows us to address something in common and then potentially disagree about it. Claims about reasons are claims about *which considerations should guide and settle practical deliberation, forming the appropriate basis of action.* This is a common and essentially normative subject matter that can be addressed by all parties, salient for us as rational agents occupying a reflective and critical deliberative perspective. This formal notion of reasons for acting is itself a basic constituent of that perspective, figuring in the competent exercise of practical reason, just as a theoretical analogue of this notion (reasons for believing) comes essentially into theoretical reasoning and rationality. It is not something for which different communities or individuals will have different contingent concepts with specific contents (as we earlier imagined with reason*, etc.).

The ardent realist claims not only that there is an objectively correct set of standards yielding moral truths such as M, but that these truths have implications for what there is genuine reason for people to do. In the above terms, then, this comes down to the claim that moral truths (backed by objectively correct moral standards) bear directly on the determination of which considerations should guide and settle practical deliberation as such. This is a substantive normative claim that, if true, rules out competing claims about what properly determines which considerations should guide and settle practical deliberation—such as the claim that what matters for this are simply facts about an individual's desires and interests. There is no parity problem here but instead a common, normative subject matter about which there can be disagreement—and therefore also, in principle, an objective fact of the matter one way or the other.

3. Filling Out Ardent Moral Realism

With all this in place, we can now fill out the ardent realist's claims more fully. According to ardent realism, some moral judgments are objectively true and normatively authoritative because they are grounded in a set of moral standards that (i) is objectively correct or appropriate for evaluating human action and character, and (ii) is such that there is genuine reason to take its verdicts seriously in our deliberations, as directly informing conclusions about reasons for acting and thus appropriately guiding our lives. The ardent realist I have in mind seeks to capture this by proposing that the world has certain inherently evaluative or normative aspects, and so objectively favors whatever set of moral standards—call it "S"—accurately reflects those aspects *through prescribing action that is inherently fitting to them.*

We can illustrate this idea with familiar examples. Many of us think that suffering is an element of the world that is intrinsically bad, such that there are inherently fitting or unfitting ways of responding or otherwise relating to it. Given the nature of suffering, it is inherently fitting, all else being equal, to seek to avoid causing suffering or to mitigate it when we encounter it, while it is unfitting to cause it, exacerbate it, or treat it with indifference.[13] If that is right, then it implies that the correct set of moral standards (S) will include requirements of beneficence and nonmaleficence among the standards for right action, articulating how we need to live in order to respond in fitting ways to the badness of suffering. Similarly, many think that rational nature is an element of the world that inherently confers on its possessor a special kind of worth or dignity, grounding a distinctive moral status for the being in question with familiar implications (often put in terms of basic moral rights). The idea here is that it is inherently fitting, all else being equal, to treat persons with certain forms of respect and unfitting to engage in acts of deception or harm or callous indifference to their flourishing, for example. If this is right, then it implies that S will also include requirements of justice and respect among the standards for right action, articulating how we need to live in order to respond in fitting ways to human dignity.[14]

The idea, then, is that there is among the various possible sets of moral standards one special set—what we are calling "S"—that properly reflects such inherently evaluative or normative features of the world insofar as these standards prescribe action that is fitting to those features: that is what it is for S to be the objectively correct set of standards. This will naturally be complicated, taking into account all the interaction and balancing considerations that come into any comprehensive conception of what it is to live well as we navigate the complex combinations of values we encounter in various circumstances. And there may be limits to the extent to which this set of standards is codifiable, given that complexity. It may be that they are best captured in virtue-theoretic terms, with only rough and open-ended articulations of virtues such as beneficence, justice, respect, etc., and how they interact. One might need practical wisdom to discern what it is to act well overall when confronting a complex situation where suffering can be mitigated for

---

[13] This is not to deny the instrumental value of pain that protects against exacerbating injury, or the fact that given the loss of a loved one it is appropriate to suffer grief—indeed, better than not doing so. The point is just that all else being equal and setting aside instrumental benefits, it is inherently better not to be in pain or otherwise suffering (e.g., better to be enjoying a loved one than suffering their loss).

[14] In FitzPatrick (2008), I propose capturing realist facts about the intrinsic badness of suffering and the inherent worth of persons using a *dual-aspect theory*—where certain elements of the world have both empirical, scientifically investigable aspects and irreducibly evaluative or normative aspects. The notion of inherently fitting or unfitting responses figures prominently in the account of moral phenomenology Horgan and Timmons (2008) adopt from Mandelbaum, though they deny the ardent realist claim that fittingness or unfittingness are real properties or relations instantiated in the world.

one person only at the cost of infringing the rights of another, for example. The point is just that given a value-laden world there will be a set of moral standards, S, that will be "favored by reality itself" in the sense that it is grounded precisely in the evaluative or normative profile of the world, thus setting it apart from rival sets of standards (such as one that would permit cavalier behavior during a pandemic) that lack such grounding. We thus have a way of escaping the earlier parity problem, providing a sense for at least part of the central ardent realist idea and showing how it could at least in principle be true.[15]

The reason for the qualification here is that there is still work to be done in capturing the overall ardent realist aim. Recall that the full idea is that there is a set of moral standards favored by reality itself not only as the appropriate one for evaluating human action and character as such, but also as appropriately playing a central role in governing practical deliberation, bearing on what we have genuine reason to do, full stop. We must capture and motivate the idea that this proper set of moral standards also possesses *real and categorical normative authority*, thus addressing the familiar question: "why be moral?" And this requires linking the above picture to a related conception of practical reason, to explain why we should care about living in ways that are fitting to the value we confront in the world.

One way to do this, which will be our focus here, begins with a broadly Aristotelian conception of practical reason.[16] Human practical reason is a faculty capable of comprehensive, all-things-considered, critical deliberation about what to do: it is capable not merely of addressing specific questions about what will satisfy one's desires or maximally promote one's self-interest, for example, but of addressing the open-ended, formal, evaluative question "what would it be all-things-considered good to do, given my circumstances?" or "what would constitute acting well here and now, all told, and without qualification?" This is a question that comprehends each of the more specific questions but takes in much more besides, being the broadest and most fundamental question that can be asked from the practical perspective. For present purposes, let us assume (with the ardent realist) that this question is intelligible and that there exist corresponding facts about what would or would not constitute acting well all-things-considered and without qualification (Aristotle's *eupraxia*), in various circumstances.

---

[15] We may here set aside familiar complications about legitimate variation in moral standards reflecting relevant differences in cultural circumstances and choices. I am focusing on core elements of S that are plausibly invariant, as in our example, without denying that there is room for variation in how S can legitimately be filled out across different settings (i.e., limited moral pluralism but not full relativism). The same point applies to plausible variation in the details of appropriate standards for possible extraterrestrial rational species: different structures of needs and interests will make for plausible differences in standards related to mutual care, for example. It is also important to note that any developed ardent realist view will also have to provide some epistemic account of how we come to know these various fittingness facts—something I have not taken up here.

[16] I have begun to explore this idea, initially inspired by ideas from Gavin Lawrence in connection with Aristotle, in FitzPatrick (2004, 2014, and 2022), though it requires further development and can only be sketched here.

Next, we can ask: what standards for successful functioning would it be appropriate to apply to a deliberative faculty with this profile? Presumably the standards appropriate to a faculty are those that are fitting to its nature and capacities. But it would not be fitting to our faculty of practical reason, given its comprehensive deliberative capacity, to hold it only to lower standards that would be appropriate to a more limited faculty that can only handle more limited practical questions about what will satisfy one's desires, for example—just as it would not be fitting to hold adults only to standards of behavior appropriate to children. This, at any rate, is something the ardent realist will take to be axiomatic—an intuitively plausible and fundamental normative claim. It follows, then, that the appropriate standards of good practical reasoning for this sophisticated faculty of practical reason will be standards that are similarly comprehensive and critical. Such standards will articulate conditions for success in practical reasoning construed in a way appropriate to the nature of practical reason and the functioning of which it is capable. Success here will be construed not merely in relation to parochial aims such as satisfying one's desires or maximizing self-interest, but in the broadest terms, characterized by the formal aim of deliberating soundly to action that constitutes *acting well*, period.

The ardent realist can now build on this Aristotelian framework as follows.[17] Acting well in this fundamental sense plausibly comes down to acting in a way that is ultimately fitting to the character of the reality we encounter and shape through our action—responding fittingly to the evaluative aspects of the world as we navigate through it. Relevant elements of the world will include our own needs, desires, experiential states, flourishing, etc., but they also include other people and animals and their mental states and flourishing, all of which have evaluative aspects that need to be respected as well. The idea, then, is that the proper aim of practical reason (i.e., the aim deliberating agents will have insofar as they are exercising practical reason appropriately) is to deliberate and act in a way that responds fittingly to all of that, such that practical reasoning issues in action that constitutes acting well all-things-considered. In other words, this sets the standard for success in the realm of practical reason, against which considerations are ultimately determined to be genuine reasons for acting or not (rather than appealing to narrower aims like desire-satisfaction or self-interest maximization).

This is the same idea of fittingness used to explain the notion of acting in accordance with the correct moral standards S, except that the scope of practical reasons is broader. One might have good reason to go get lunch or to read a novel, for example, which stems from certain values but not from specifically moral values and standards. Still, the moral standards are concerned with constraining action in a way that is similarly fitting to a certain range of operative values. And, crucially, moral standards yield verdictive or all-things-considered requirements only after giving a comprehensive and fair hearing to *all* values that are in play. For example, in requiring you to wear a mask

---

[17] Let me emphasize that I am not claiming to have shown so easily that this Aristotelian framework is correct, but only to be unpacking the sort of picture that would satisfy the demands of ardent moral realism. As noted earlier, some reject the idea of unqualified normative authority or all-things-considered "oughts," and this would have to be addressed in defending the account.

during a pandemic, the moral standards don't simply ignore your own personal desires and interests: they take them into account too but find that values of public safety outweigh them, such that acting well requires wearing the mask, period.[18]

This brings us to the central point. Since the moral standards S bear in this way on *the same thing* that practical reason is also properly concerned with more generally—that is, acting well all-things-considered—S will have a proper and central place in governing deliberation, bearing on what is or is not a good, or sufficient, or decisive reason for acting. It is precisely because of this connection between the grounds of correct moral standards and the grounds of the appropriate standards governing practical reason that moral verdicts can have the robust kind of normative authority that claims such as M seem to have. The connection is the common grounding in *fittingness to a value-laden world*.

We can therefore summarize the overall view and its commitments as follows:

Ardent Realism: Certain elements of the world (1) have an inherently evaluative or normative character such that (2) there are inherently fitting or unfitting ways of responding or otherwise relating to them given that character—these facts being what is captured and articulated by S, making it the objectively appropriate or correct set of moral standards, where (3) this normative fact about fittingness/unfittingness is also itself inherently relevant to practical reason, directly affecting what there is unqualified, all-things-considered reason to do, thus linking S to genuine reasons for acting.[19]

4. Analysis and Implications

What exactly allowed us to escape the problems raised in the challenge and to give a clear sense to the ardent realist claim? The first step was resisting a misconstrual of evaluative discourse and replacing it with a model that brings out the complex structure of

---

[18] This idea figures importantly into Seana Shiffrin's (1999) account of moral overridingness, which is relevant to the issue of the special normative force of all-things-considered moral requirements.

[19] Suppose someone grants that mask wearing in a pandemic is required by moral standards that are fitting to real worldly values, but still demands to know *why they should care* about that. Obviously philosophy cannot force them to care, but this does not reveal any philosophical gap in the account. Their question amounts to asking for *a reason* for something (i.e., for caring about conforming their behavior to what is fitting to relevant worldly values), and we have already provided an account of reasons—through the above account of practical reason and its proper aim—that answers this question. Someone can certainly question whether that account itself is sound, which will lead to further philosophical debate about it. But if it *is* sound then there is no further room for a demand for reasons to care about the fittingness facts at the heart of it, as if one had an independent purchase on the notion of reasons. Nor is there any intelligible further demand to be told *why we should care about reasons*, i.e., to be given a reason for caring about reasons.

evaluative or normative properties and related facts about standards and relations to base properties. This enabled us to see that there is in fact a single, common set of basic evaluative or normative concepts relevant to rational agency itself, allowing disputing parties to address a common evaluative or normative subject matter rather than talking past each other. We could then understand the ardent realist to be claiming that there is such a thing as *getting it right* when we make judgments employing these concepts, where this is cashed out in terms of fitting responses to inherently evaluative or normative features of reality itself.

This involves a theoretical commitment to certain *irreducibly evaluative or normative properties and facts*, namely:

(1) There is a set of moral standards, S, that is objectively correct or appropriate insofar as it is fitting to relevant evaluative or normative characteristics of the world, by prescribing action that is inherently fitting to them;
(2) Those standards and the moral facts to which they give rise also appropriately bear directly on the determination of which considerations should guide and settle practical deliberation—i.e., which considerations are genuine reasons for acting, because:
(3) Practical reason has as its proper aim nothing less than acting in a way that is overall fitting to the inherently evaluative or normative characteristics of the circumstances we encounter in the world.

If these facts obtain then there is no parity worry. But again, such facts seem to be irreducibly evaluative or normative ones, incapable of being adequately characterized and accounted for in non-normative terms without losing precisely what the ardent realist is after.

For example, suppose we try cashing out the claim that S is the correct set of standards by claiming that S reflects natural teleological facts rooted in evolution, or that S will (if widely adhered to) maximize happiness or flourishing or social stability as construed according to some psychological or biological or sociological theory. This may avoid any appeal to irreducibly evaluative or normative properties or facts, but at the same time it loses any grip on ardent realist aims. For even if we grant such non-normative facts about S, we so far lack any sense for the idea that we should all care about such teleological facts, or this psychological or biological conception of happiness or flourishing, or the sort of social stability being assumed as an end—in particular, any sense that would avoid the parity problem raised in the earlier challenge.[20] For example, if one simply uses "should" in a specific way that ties it to such psychological or biological or sociological facts, while someone else uses "should*" in an alternative way tied to other

---

[20] For a developed critique along these lines, including use of a revised, limited form of Open Question Argument against such views, see FitzPatrick (2014 and 2018c). In FitzPatrick (2000) I argue for both the objectivity of biological teleological norms of proper functioning and their irrelevance either to morality or to practical reason.

such facts, then we again land back in the earlier difficulties: why adopt one over the others, or use any of those concepts at all? What objective and nontrivial practical mistake would one be making if one disregarded them? This may not be a pressing worry for "less ardent" forms of moral realism, concerned primarily with just securing literal, objective reference for moral terms and saving moral truths in a way that avoids error theory, subjectivism and expressivism. But it won't do for the ardent realist, who instead needs the claims to bottom out in irreducibly evaluative or normative facts in order to capture the intuitive idea that the world itself favors certain ways of valuing and acting.

The difference here actually matters a great deal. To see just how much daylight there is between ardent realism and "less ardent" views, consider this: even Mackie's (1977) radically antirealist error-theoretic position on morality allowed for the existence of genuine evaluative truths: these are easy to come by when we have evaluative judgments linked to given standards and ends, as in judging pies or pigs at the county fair, or judging the health of maple trees at the nursery. Mackie was not concerned to deny that there might be something like moral truths *relative to certain given standards*, whether rooted in some biological, psychological or sociological theory or in conventionally adopted ends. As another antirealist, Sharon Street (2008), puts it: varieties of moral realism trading only in such moral truths are not the ones "worth worrying about" in the realism/antirealism debate. What is worth taking issue with, for both Mackie and Street, are forms of realism that include "objective prescriptivity," by positing standards S that have objective normative authority in governing our practical reasoning, legitimately demanding our attention and concern. That is the heart of ardent moral realism.

Notice, however, that we have said nothing at all yet about non-naturalist metaphysics. The ardent realist has made no bizarre, unmotivated appeals to spooky or mystical properties and facts about which we cannot say anything illuminating (recall Gibbard's caricature with "exnat"). What we have seen instead is the ardent realist appealing to properties and facts characterized in entirely familiar terms, claiming simply that their evaluative or normative nature is irreducible. There is no mysticism here: just the idea that the intrinsic badness of suffering or the intrinsic worth and dignity of persons is an irreducibly evaluative or normative feature of the world, grounding moral standards and reasons for acting in a way that supports an ardent realist interpretation of moral experience.

If the ardent realist's claims take us into non-naturalist territory it is only because our conception of the natural excludes irreducibly evaluative or normative properties and facts. Perhaps we conceive of the natural world as consisting of the objects, properties and facts that are scientifically discoverable or at least constructible from and exhaustively constituted by those that are. If so, then while this may accommodate moral properties and facts of the sort posited by "Cornell Realism" (Brink 1989, Boyd 1997, Sturgeon 2006), it will exclude the ardent realist's irreducibly evaluative or normative properties and facts: as we have seen, the latter do not seem even in principle to be discoverable through scientific methods or constructible simply out of properties and facts that are, which always seem to leave out precisely what the ardent realist is after (FitzPatrick 2014, 2018c, 2022). Ardent realists would thus be labeled "non-naturalist" realists, positing not only irreducibly normative *concepts* (as both nonreductive naturalists and expressivists also do) but irreducibly normative worldly properties and facts themselves. But this would count as "non-naturalist" only because of the commitment to irreducibly evaluative or normative reality, given a scientistic conception of what can fit into the "natural" world.

The notion of what is natural could, however, be broadened. Instead of requiring of all natural properties that they enter into the same kinds of objective causal relations that scientifically investigable properties like magnetism do, we could formulate a broader conception of the natural world as the one reality we encounter and in which we live, leaving open what exactly it might contain and how we acquire knowledge of various parts of it. The natural world may be a single reality that reveals different aspects of itself to us in different ways, both through objective scientific inquiry and through subjective experience. Just as some physicalists have a broad conception of "the physical" that includes irreducibly phenomenal reality known to us only through first-personal conscious experience, so too we might have a broad conception of "the natural" that includes irreducibly evaluative or normative reality (such as the badness of suffering) known to us only through moral experience and reflection.[21]

What really matters for ardent moral realism is therefore not non-naturalism per se, but just irreducibly evaluative or normative aspects of reality. Whether that involves one in non-naturalism depends on further questions about how best to draw such metaphysical distinctions. In any case, if someone wishes to deny that the world contains irreducibly evaluative or normative elements, it will not do simply to dismiss them as "spooky": for there is nothing spooky in the idea that suffering has an inherently evaluative or normative character of badness that there is reason to avoid. This character is not scientifically discoverable, but it is not thereby rendered "bizarre," any more than *qualia* are, except to a metaphysical sensibility already distorted by scientific bias. From an engaged moral perspective the reason-giving badness of suffering presents as something close to common sense. It could, of course, still turn out to be an illusion in the end—a trick of moral phenomenology. But that deflationary claim is not the obvious default, especially for those of us who continue to find the moral appearances more compelling than arguments for discounting them.

My purpose here has been to explore the motivation behind ardent moral realism, to clarify its claims, to show how it escapes a challenging objection to its very coherence, and to unpack its core theoretical commitments to show what the world would have to be like in order for it to be true. Depending on how we understand metaphysical

---

[21] Speaking of mental phenomena in a nondeflationary way, as manifesting "experiential being" not reducible to the merely structural reality physics describes, Galen Strawson (2015, 162–3) maintains that "we have no good reason to think that we know anything about the physical that gives us any reason to find any problem in the idea that mental phenomena are physical phenomena." That is, mental phenomena may simply be intrinsic aspects of relevant parts of physical reality that are not transparent to physics but are nonetheless plain to us in experience. Noam Chomsky (2016, chap. 4) has emphasized the same point, finding it prefigured in Locke, Priestley, Russell, and Eddington.

naturalism, ardent moral realism may turn out to be a non-naturalist view or an expansively naturalist view. The real question is whether we ultimately have good reason to deny that the world has any irreducibly evaluative or normative features. If so, then we would have to settle for a "less ardent" form of realism or some form of antirealism. If not, then like the ardent realist we can reasonably use our reflective moral experience to expand our conception of what the world is like.[22]

References

Blackburn, Simon. 1993. *Essays in Quasi-Realism*. Oxford: Oxford University Press.
Blackburn, Simon. 1998. *Ruling Passions*. Oxford: Oxford University Press.
Brink, David. 1989. *Moral Realism and the Foundations of Ethics*. Cambridge: Cambridge University Press.
Brink, David. 2001. "Realism, Naturalism and Moral Semantics." *Social Philosophy and Policy* 18(2): 154–176.
Boyd, Richard. 1997. "How to Be a Moral Realist." In *Moral Discourse and Practice*, edited by S. Darwall, A. Gibbard, and P. Railton, 105–136. Oxford: Oxford University Press.
Chomsky, Noam. 2016. *What Kind of Creatures Are We?* New York: Columbia University Press.
Conee, Earl. "A Mysterious Case of Missing Value." *Philosophic Exchange* 45(1), 1–21.
Copp, David. 1995. *Morality, Normativity and Society*. Oxford: Oxford University Press.
Copp, David. 2007. *Morality in a Natural World*. Cambridge: Cambridge University Press.
Dancy, Jonathan. 2004. "On the Importance of Making Things Right." *Ratio* 17: 229–237.
Dancy, Jonathan. 2006. "Nonnaturalism." In *The Oxford Handbook of Ethical Theory*, edited by David Copp, 122–145. Oxford: Oxford University Press.
Eklund, Matti. 2017. *Choosing Normative Concepts*. Oxford: Oxford University Press.
FitzPatrick, William. 2000. *Teleology and the Norms of Nature*. New York: Garland.
FitzPatrick, William. 2004. "Reasons, Value, and Particular Agents: Normative Relevance without Motivational Internalism." *Mind* 113(450): 285–318.
FitzPatrick, William. 2008. "Robust Ethical Realism, Non-Naturalism and Normativity." In *Oxford Studies in Metaethics*, vol. 3, edited by Russ Shafer-Landau, 159–205. Oxford: Oxford University Press.
FitzPatrick, William. 2011. "Ethical Non-Naturalism and Normative Properties." In *New Waves in Metaethics*, edited by Michael Brady, 7–35. New York: Palgrave Macmillan.
FitzPatrick, William. 2014. "Skepticism about Naturalizing Normativity: In Defense of Ethical Non-Naturalism." *Res Philosophica* 91(4): 559–588.
FitzPatrick, William. 2018a. "Ontology for an Uncompromising Ethical Realism." *Topoi* 37(4): 537–547.
FitzPatrick, William 2018b. "Representing Ethical Reality." *Canadian Journal of Philosophy* 48 (3–4): 548–568.
FitzPatrick, William. 2018c. "Open Question Arguments and the Irreducibility of Ethical Normativity." In *The Naturalistic Fallacy*, edited by Neil Sinclair, 138–161. Cambridge: Cambridge University Press.

---

[22] Thanks to Paul Bloomfield and David Copp for helpful comments on an earlier draft.

FitzPatrick, William. 2021. "Moral Phenomenology and the Value-Laden World." *Ethical Theory and Moral Practice*. https://doi-org.libproxy.viko.lt/10.1007/s10677-021-10213-4
FitzPatrick, William. 2022. *Ethical Realism*. Cambridge: Cambridge University Press.
Gibbard, Allan. 2003. *Thinking How to Live*. Cambridge, MA: Harvard University Press.
Gibbard, Allan. 2006. "Normative Properties." In *Metaethics after Moore*, edited by Terence Horgan and Mark Timmons, 319–338. Oxford: Oxford University Press.
Horgan, Terry, and Mark Timmons. 2008. "What Can Moral Phenomenology Tell Us about Moral Objectivity?" *Social Philosophy and Policy* 25: 267–300.
Horgan, Terry, and Mark Timmons. 1991. "New Wave Moral Realism Meets Moral Twin Earth." *Journal of Philosophical Research* 16: 447–465.
Horgan, Terry, and Mark Timmons. 2018. "The Phenomenology of Moral Authority." In D. Machuca ed., *Moral Skepticism: New Essays*, 115–140. New York: Routledge.
Jackson, Frank. 1998. *From Metaphysics to Ethics*. Oxford: Oxford University Press.
Joyce, Richard. 2001. *The Myth of Morality*. Cambridge: Cambridge University Press.
Joyce, Richard. 2006. *The Evolution of Morality*. Cambridge, MA: MIT Press.
Mackie, J. L. 1977. *Ethics: Inventing Right and Wrong*. Harmondsworth: Penguin.
Parfit, D. 2011. *On What Matters*. Vol. 2. Oxford: Oxford University Press.
Shiffrin, Seana. 1999. "Moral Overridingness and Moral Subjectivism." *Ethics* 109: 772–794.
Strawson, Galen. 2015. "Real Materialism (with New Postscript)." In *Consciousness in the Physical World: Perspectives on Russellian Monism*, edited by T. Alter and Y. Nagasawa, 161–208. Oxford: Oxford University Press.
Street, Sharon. 2006. "A Darwinian Dilemma for Realist Theories of Value." *Philosophical Studies* 127, 109–166.
Street, Sharon. 2008. "Reply to Copp: Naturalism, Normativity, and the Varieties of Realism Worth Worrying About." *Philosophical Issues* 18: 207–228.
Sturgeon, Nicholas. 2006. "Ethical Naturalism." In *The Oxford Handbook of Ethical Theory*, edited by David Copp, 91–121. Oxford: Oxford University Press.

CHAPTER 20

OH, ALL THE WRONGS I COULD HAVE PERFORMED!

Or: Why Care about Morality, Robustly Realistically Understood

DAVID ENOCH AND
ITAMAR WEINSHTOCK SAADON[*]

SUPPOSE that someone is brought up as an orthodox Jew, and so only eats kosher, is very conservative sexually, etc. Suppose they then come to believe that this Judaism stuff—at least in its orthodox, literal reading—is just all a big mistake, perhaps because there is no God. If they then regret all the fun they could have had, all the shrimp they could have eaten, all the sex they could have had!—well, if they regret all this now, this makes perfect sense.

Now suppose that someone is brought up as a moralist,[1] and so they restrict their pursuit of their own self-interest and other things they care about by the interests of others, their rights, and perhaps other morally important considerations. They then come to view morality in the same way the lapsed theist from the previous paragraph views religion—they think that it is all grounded in some error, perhaps, that there are no moral truths. Perhaps they come to adopt some kind of moral nihilism, or something

---

[*] The authors contributed equally to section 2. The rest of the chapter was primarily written by DE.

For relevant correspondence, conversations, and comments we thank Dani Attas, Dan Baras, Paul Bloomfield, Richard Yetter Chappell, David Copp, Sharon Krishek, Jed Lewinsohn, Ofra Magidor, Aaron Segal, Levi Spectre, and Preston Werner. This chapter was presented "at" the University of Lorraine, Sheffield, and McMaster philosophy departments (by Zoom), and we thank the participants for the discussion, and Paul Clavier, Paul Rezkalla, and Anna C. Zielinska also for written follow-ups.

[1] We mean this term to be the analogue of "theist": The "moralist," as we'll be using this term, is someone who takes morality seriously, who—even if not quite a robust metaethical realist—still rejects nihilism and error theory. So we do not intend any of the bad, perhaps moralistic overtones this term has come to have in some circles.

like Mackie's (1977) error theory.[2] And they now regret all the fun they could have had, how much more they could have promoted their self-interest, all the money they could have made, if they were only willing to hurt people's feelings, and so on. This doesn't seem to make sense. Even if it does, there's a fairly strong disanalogy between the moral and the religious case: As experienced by the lapsed orthodox Jew, "All the sex I could have had"-regrets, and maybe even "all the sins[3] I could have performed"-regrets, make perfect sense. But "all the wrongs[4] I could have performed"-regrets from the now (purportedly) disillusioned moralist are at least suspicious, and so are—though to a lesser degree—"all the money I could have made"-regrets. (Below we'll call these all-the-sins-regrets and all-the-wrongs-regrets, respectively.) At the very least, we wouldn't be surprised if such regrets were not there for the lapsed moralist, as we would be surprised if they were absent for the lapsed orthodox Jew. The details of the religious-moral asymmetry here may not (yet) be entirely clear, but it's hard to deny that there is such an asymmetry.

This asymmetry calls for explanation. What is it about the nature of moral commitments that makes all-the-wrongs-regrets suspicious, and what is it about them that makes them different from religious ones in the ways that this little thought experiment makes salient? In morality, it seems, moral beliefs and motivations are to an extent immune to changes in one's beliefs *about* then, one's metaethical beliefs[5], in a way which does not seem to be the case in the religious case. What explains this? Now, perhaps some metaethical views—views that tie moral judgments and facts very closely to motivation—can explain these phenomena rather easily: Your gustatory preferences, it seems safe to assume, are immune to your philosophical views about such preferences, and are nothing like the religious person's religious commitments. So it's not surprising that a change of philosophical mind here—say, coming to believe an error theory about gustatory judgments—will not lead to your regretting having missed on all the

---

[2] We are not invested, of course, in Mackie exegesis. Some parts of his text lend themselves more easily than others to this (orthodox) reading. For (unorthodox) discussion, see Ridge (2020).

[3] Having turned atheist, our protagonist no longer believes anything *is* a sin. So the use of "sin" in the sentence in the text should be understood in an inverted-commas way, referring to (roughly) what the religious people around here think of as sins.

[4] Having turned error theorist or a nihilist, our protagonist no longer believes anything *is* a wrong. So the use of "wrong" in the sentence in the text should be understood in an inverted-commas way, referring to (roughly) what the moralists around here think of as wrongs.

[5] In what follows we think of the explanatory challenge as primarily a challenge for robust realism. But we don't think of the protagonist in our opening example as a robust realist. He or she are—at least as a first pass—a naïve moralist, without highly refined metaethical beliefs (though, of course, perhaps with implicit metaethical commitments that us theorists may want to flesh out and render explicit). The point in the text here is that with regard to such moralists, their moral judgments and motivations are to an extent immune to second-order revisions. This is the phenomenon to be explained (alongside the asymmetry with the religious case). Coming up with such an explanation is a task for theorists, and we focus here on discharging this theoretical task from a robust realist perspective.

We remain neutral here on whether other ways of coping with this challenge are available to naturalist realists.

We thank David Copp and Paul Bloomfield for pressing us on this and related issues.

opportunities to have guava juice (if you didn't like it then, you probably don't like it now). So metaethical views that understand moral judgment as more closely resembling gustatory preferences can explain why all-the-wrongs-regrets are suspicious, in a way that distinguishes between them and all-the-sins-regrets. But the explanatory challenge is harder for moral realists, and perhaps even more so for robust moral realists, according to whom moral judgments have the kind of objectivity and force that on some theological views religious ones do.[6] In this chapter, we address this challenge as a challenge to robust moral realism.

Thinking about this explanatory challenge also throws interesting light on several related discussions: the question whether the virtuous are motivated by de re or de dicto moral motivation (or both), the why-be-moral challenge, and worries that robust realism makes it mysterious why we should care about the moral facts and properties (all the way out there in Plato's heaven, as it were).

The solution we will be suggesting is that there is an important difference between the way in which it is plausible to think of the moralist's moral commitments (not to act wrongly) as conditional on his or her moralism and the way in which it is plausible to think of the theist's religious commitments (not to sin) as dependent on his or her theism. The conditionals capturing these commitments should be seen as junk-knowledge in the former case, but not in at least many instances of the latter.

Not everyone, we've come to see, is immediately struck by the asymmetry we are out to explain. If you're not, don't despair on this chapter just yet. Questions often get clarified during the attempts to answer them. That a phenomenon calls for explanation is sometimes more clearly seen after some attempts at explaining it fail. By the end of this chapter, we believe, thinking about our initial challenge will end up being productive in ways many of which are available to you even if you are not immediately struck by the strength of the phenomenon we want explained.

After making some preliminary clarifications (in Section 1), we proceed in Section 2 to discuss the distinction between de re and de dicto moral motivation as well as a common suspicion against the latter, concluding that those alone do not offer a sufficient explanation for the moral-religious asymmetry in the thought experiment we started with. Then, in Section 3, we discuss the relation between our puzzle and the why-be-moral challenge (mostly in Dreier's recent version). In Section 4 we discuss the related worry that it's not clear why moral properties—robustly realistically understood—are ones we should care about (mostly in Dasgupta's recent version). Finally, in Section 5, we

---

[6] At least one of us *is* a robust realist (see Enoch (2011)), and has been accused in the past (at least in conversations with Hartry Field) of adhering to the robust realism religion.

We're not sure to what extent what we say in this chapter—both the explanatory challenge, and the attempts at addressing it—applies to other, naturalist forms of moral realism. We suspect that the challenge arises, but that different explanations are available, at different costs, to robust realists and to (different kinds of) naturalist realists. Be that as it may, in this chapter we discuss things only from a robust realist perspective.

tell our preferred story of why all-the-wrongs-regrets do not make sense, noting under what conditions this story will also explain the religious-moral asymmetry.

1. Clarifying the Challenge

We want to make three clarifications about our explanatory challenge: about the relevant kind of mistake or change of mind; about different examples; and about the point of view of the observer or theorist.

1.1 Different Kinds of Mistakes

There are mistakes, and then there are mistakes. The mistake that our thought experiment focuses on is of a global, perhaps meta- kind. We want to distinguish it from two other kinds of mistake.

The first is a local moral mistake. Suppose that I put a lot of time and thought into advising graduate students. And there are opportunity costs, as it were, in terms of time for research, for watching sports, and so on. A part of my reason for doing so (though see the next section for worries about this way of putting things) is that I think it's morally important to do so. But I may be mistaken about this. Suppose that someone convinces me that putting all this work into advising graduate students is really just a way of giving them an unfair advantage over those graduate students whose advisors are less conscientious. The job market is ridiculously competitive, after all, and I'm just helping my students jump the queue. When I change my mind about the moral importance of being a conscientious graduate student advisor—because I find out about relevant nonmoral facts I hadn't thought of, or because I appreciate differently the weight of some moral considerations—I may very well regret spending all that time on helping my students jump the queue. All that snooker I could have watched! There's nothing mysterious about such a regret-response to a local moral change of mind. This kind of mistake is analogous to an orthodox Jew finding out that, say, there's no halachic rule against eating some delicacy that he had thought was nonkosher. In both these cases, regret makes perfect sense. These are not the kind of cases we want to focus on (though they will be significant again in the next section).

The second kind of mistake—or a change of mind—that we want to distinguish from the one we'll be focusing on is the one analogous to an orthodox Jew coming to believe that actually, the One True Religion is not orthodox Judaism, but some other religion. In morality, the analogue of that would be (we think) that of a Kantian who converts to utilitarianism, or the other way around. This kind of change of mind is, of course, much more global than the one in the previous paragraph, but it remains within the moral or religious domain. In the religious case, if the orthodox Jew converts to a religion that is much more liberal on sex (or on food), "All the sex I could have had"-thoughts again seem to make perfect sense. In the moral case, though, we are less confident: Think of a Kantian who takes care not to treat people as a mere means, but then converts to utilitarianism, and comes to regret all the ways he could have instrumentalized people to maximize overall wellbeing. This kind of regret doesn't seem entirely unproblematic, but nor is it clear to us that it's objectionable—certainly not as clear as it is in the case we started with. Let us put such cases to one side for now (they will return).

The change of mind about morality that we are interested in is analogous specifically to that of the committed religious person who *turns atheist*, who has come to accept a metareligion error theory. With regard to morality, this is not the person who has come to believe that the things that matter morally are different from those he had thought mattered morally, but rather the person who, perhaps roughly, has come to believe that *nothing matters morally*. It is the disanalogy on this level that we want to insist on—the relevant regrets make perfect sense in the religious case, but not (or less) in many moral cases. It is this asymmetry that we want explained.

One final clarification: Our lapsed moralist is not a *global* nihilist, she or he does not now believe that *nothing matters*, only that *nothing morally matters*. This is important, because it's not clear how even to make sense of regret given this more global nihilism—in order to feel regret, it seems, one must *care*.[7] In this way too we keep the case of the lapsed moralist analogous to that of the lapsed orthodox Jew, whose newly accepted error theory is just about the religious, not about all things normative.

1.2 Examples Matter

You may think that there's something about our choice of examples that illegitimately skews the evidence, and artificially strengthens the disanalogy with the religious case. Regretting all those cases in which I refrained from hurting people—certainly under this description—seems sadistic. Who *would* regret that, independently of whatever they thought about morality? In the moral case we started with, in other words, there were victims. In the religious case, not so (who is hurt if an orthodox Jew stops keeping kosher, or is being more sexually liberal?). The presence of a victim, though, seems to matter significantly. So in introducing the contrast between the religious and the moral cases, we weren't sufficiently careful to keep all other things equal. What we need are religious cases with victims, and also moral cases without them.

There *is*, we agree, a problem with the examples, but it's not clear that it can be fixed. We can think of religious commandments whose violations hurt some people, but the paradigmatic cases—not to murder, not to humiliate others, perhaps even to love thy neighbor—will arguably overlap with moral duties, and so will not do for fleshing out intuitions that may distinguish between the two (this, of course, is why we focused on

---

[7] For some discussion of the likely causal effects of believing in such global nihilism, and of the relevant philosophical upshots, see Kahane (2017).

victimless sins;[8] it goes without saying that there are many purported sins that also constitute wrongs). And it is doubtful that there *are* entirely victimless wrongs.[9] In other words, the distinction between offenses with victims and those without them is in our context *very* close to the distinction between morality and (the relevant parts of) religion, and so assuming it away may be dangerously close to assuming the explanandum away rather than to help zeroing in on the explanans. We suggest, then, proceeding with the examples we started with, but with caution, remaining open to the possibility that the presence of a victim makes an important difference here (as elsewhere). Indeed, that the presence of victims may make an important difference may motivate an attempt to explain the disanalogy in terms of the distinction between de re and de dicto moral motivation, an attempt that we discuss in Section 2, below.

1.3 The Observer's Point of View

Another attempt at explaining away the moral-religious asymmetry emphasizes the intuitive difference that the observer's normative perspective probably makes here. Perhaps you agreed about the intuitive difference between the religious and the moral case because you are an atheist and a moralist. That is, you believe that the religious Jew converted from falsehood to truth, and the moralist converted from truth to falsehood. Then, when asked whether the relevant regrets make sense, you replaced your own beliefs for the protagonists': Perhaps you agreed that all-the-sins-regrets make sense, because sex is good, and severe religious restrictions on it are misplaced. And perhaps you agreed that all-the-wrongs-regrets don't make sense because one shouldn't act wrongly, one shouldn't hurt people. If so, what explains the initial intuitive appeal of the asymmetry (and explains away the asymmetry itself) is not something about the nature of religious and moral commitments, but rather something about the substantive, normative commitments of the likely reader of this text.[10]

There is something to this thought, we are sure. But still, enough of an asymmetry survives. Even an orthodox Jew can appreciate, it seems to us, that there is a way in which all-the-sins-regrets—from the point of view of a lapsed orthodox Jew—make perfect

---

[8] There are going to be classificatory controversies. For instance, the nature of sexual sins in orthodox Judaism would be classified as sins against another (and so not victimless) by some, but as sins against God (and so victimless) by others, Maimonides chief among them. We thank Jed Lewinsohn for this point.

[9] By "entirely victimless wrongs" we mean to refer to moral wrongs, if there are any, where no victim is involved *in any way*—no one is harmed, no one is likely to be harmed, no one is intended to be harmed, and so on.

[10] Related to this point is also the literature on imaginative resistance (e.g., Szabó Gendler 2000)—for it may be hard for us to imagine things other than the ones we value being of value. We thank Preston Werner for this point.

sense.[11] It is this, internal, "from the perspective of" kind of sense-making that we want to focus on, and that we claim is not there in the case of the past-moralist.

2. DE RE AND DE DICTO MORAL MOTIVATION

Michael Smith (1994; 1997)—and following him, everyone else—famously distinguishes between de re and de dicto moral motivation. Suppose that in the circumstances I find myself, the right thing to do would be to read carefully my graduate student's work, and give her detailed feedback. And suppose, furthermore, that I am indeed motivated to do so. If I am so motivated *because* it is the right thing to do, if I don't care much about her and her interests, or anyway this is not what motivates me in this case, but what motivates me is something like a respect for rightness or for the moral law, if I'd be motivated differently had different actions been right—then I am motivated to act morally *de dicto*, under this (moral) description. If, however, I am motivated by a deep concern for my student and her interests, or by the unfairness she would suffer if deprived of reasonably good supervision—certainly, if explicitly moral questions about what's right here don't even cross my mind—then my motivation to act morally is *de re*—I am motivated to act in a way that is in fact morally called for, but not under that description, not *because* it is the right thing to do. Smith argued that the virtuous are motivated by the moral de re—by suffering, humiliation, justice, fairness, wellbeing, the substantive things that make a moral difference, rather than by the *fact that* they make a moral difference, or by the moral de dicto.

Everything here is controversial, and we'll get to some complications shortly. For now, though, this initial gloss of the distinction and its significance suffices to show how it can do relevant explanatory work. For the virtuous[12] moralist, on this picture, is motivated to act in ways that are respectful of others and their interests, that are helpful, that are compassionate, that are considerate (and so on), not *because that's what morality requires*. It's not as if he or she arrives on the morally loaded scene with the single motivation to act rightly, then looking around for ways of acting that amount, in the circumstances, to acting rightly. This would be precisely the moral fetishism Smith warned about, and a person with such motivation may perhaps be a moralist, but is certainly not virtuous. The virtuous moralist will care about those things that matter morally de re, about the

---

[11] We're not sure what we want to say about the analogous case—namely, whether even an error-theorist should be able to recognize the sense in which all-the-wrongs-regrets do *not* make sense. But seeing that this chapter addresses the challenge from the point of view of the moral realist, we don't have to decide this interesting issue. We get back to the error theorist's point of view on this in the final section.

[12] This is rather crude on what virtue consists in (as Paul Bloomfield noted). We acknowledge that there's room here for doing serious virtue theory, and seeing where it gets us regarding Smith's distinction. For our purposes, though, we don't need more details and accuracy here.

interests of those involved, about the suffering that can be alleviated (and also the suffering that cannot), about what is fair, and so on. And this explains why all-the-wrongs-regrets do not seem to make sense: Upon coming to accept Mackie, our lapsed moralist is no longer committed to the moral judgments they used to be committed to. In particular, perhaps, they no longer believe that it's morally important not to hurt others' interests in all sorts of ways. But this change in moral beliefs need not express itself in a motivational change—after all, explicitly moral beliefs did not play a significant role in our protagonist's motivational structure. They are motivated by morality de re, not de dicto. And in de re terms, nothing has changed. If our protagonist was motivated by someone else's need, then that need is still there, as is our protagonist's relevant motivation. True, our protagonist no longer believes that this need matters morally, but this change of mind is divorced from his or her de re moral motivation. Assuming, as seems very likely, that regret is much more closely associated with motivation than with cold, motivationally detached beliefs, we have an explanation for why it is that all-the-wrongs-regrets do not make sense, at least not for our virtuous lapsed moralist.

The analogous explanation does not seem to apply to the religious case, so we may have here an explanation of the moral-religious asymmetry as well. Now, we should be very cautious here, because the thought that anything of substance and relevance can be said about religion and the religious in general is ludicrous—these phenomena are extremely wide and diverse, of course. But it is safe to say[13] that at least in many cases, at least within the major Western religions, the pious are expected to be motivated by the religious de dicto.[14] Indeed, in many cases such a motive has a special positive religious status—the religious are expected to do as God commands precisely because God commands as He does. This does not necessarily mean that the religious are expected to *only* be motivated by the religious de dicto. There may be nothing wrong with motivational overdetermination. But—rather minimally, and crucially for our purposes here—on many occasions there need be nothing religiously problematic or objectionable about having a de dicto religious motivation. Thus, it makes perfect sense, within a Jewish orthodox context, to avoid eating shrimp precisely because shrimp is not kosher, or to avoid certain sexual practices precisely because they are contrary to religious laws. Indeed, it is sometimes emphasized that there is no religious violation involved in

---

[13] For a subtle discussion in the Jewish context that vindicates the point in the text (though possibly just with regard to a subset of Jewish commandments), see Lewinsohn (2016) and Weinshtock Saadon (2022). We thank Aaron Segal for relevant discussion.

[14] Smith (1994, 81) uses—when introducing the distinction between de re and de dicto moral motivation—a disanalogy with the *legal* case. The legal case may more closely resemble the religious than the moral, but even with regard to the legal case things are not all that simple. At least with regard to the criminal law in reasonably just states, it does seem that the morally virtuous will not need the criminal law in order to avoid doing the bad things it prohibits doing. As for the *legally* virtuous—well, it's not clear who those are. It's true that the law sees no flaw in someone who avoids crimes because they are crimes (that is, who is motivated by the legal de dicto). But we doubt that much can be learned from this, because much more generally the criminal law, by and large, cares about avoiding crimes, not about why it is that one avoids committing a crime.

being drawn to forbidden sexual practices, only in *acting* on such impulses or desires.[15] If so, when one deserts one's religious commitments and the de dicto religious motivation is lost, regretting not having eaten shrimp and not having engaged in those sexual practices seems to make perfect sense.

Here is another way of putting what is essentially the same point. There need be nothing wrong with someone who is deeply religiously committed, and who experiences at least some religious commandments as a *constraint* on what he would otherwise have done. But, if the morally virtuous are motivated by morality only de re, then *there is* something wrong with someone who experiences morality as a constraint on what she would otherwise have done. It's not as if the morally virtuous are tempted to act in all these immoral ways, except that they are strong enough to resist such temptation, because of their respect for the moral law (understood de dicto). The virtuous—at least the perfectly virtuous—have no need for such respect for the law,[16] as they are motivated directly by the things that matter morally. So: If (some) religious commitments may very well serve a constraining role in the motivation of the pious, there's no wonder that when such constraints are (thought to be) lifted (because the person loses his or her faith, say), regret about the lost options makes sense. And if the moral commitments of the morally virtuous do *not* play a similarly constraining role, then there's no room for the analogous regrets in the moral case. The distinction between de re and de dicto moral motivation seems to do a good job of explaining the moral-religious asymmetry.

Now, as already noted, Smith's claims about the distinction between de re and de dicto moral motivation are controversial. Many think that at least sometimes, at least for the nonideally virtuous, de-dicto moral motivation also has an important role to play.[17] So

---

[15] This is a common thing one hears in some orthodox circles—but, we think, not in others—about homosexual urges and acting on them.

For a Maimonides-inspired discussion of whether there's a flaw in desiring the religiously forbidden, again see Lewinsohn (2016, 244–5), and the references there. Maimonides contrasts the wholehearted, who is not drawn to the bad, with the continent, who is, but who overcomes temptation—and contrasts "the philosophers" who prefer the former with the Jewish "sages" who are more impressed by the latter. Lewinsohn shows that (Maimonides shows that) even if "the philosophers" are right about some commandments—perhaps those that are "between man and his fellow," and so the closest religious thing to moral obligations—still the sages may be right about others—perhaps those that are "between man and God".

The details are not that important for our purposes here, but the point in the text stands—at least in Judaism, at least in an important subset of cases, religious motivation de dicto is seen positively.

[16] The Kantian overtones are intended, of course, but no serious scholarly commitments here are. It's not clear how exactly to understand the Kantian idea of a respect for the moral law, and we don't have a view on that. And there's also more than one way to understand the (perhaps Aristotelian) idea that the perfectly virtuous are best not at overcoming temptation, but rather in their constitution, so that they are not tempted in the first place. For our purposes in the text, we don't need the virtuous to be immune to any temptation whatsoever. We just need them to be immune to temptation that cannot be overcome without something like moral motivation understood de dicto.

[17] See, for instance, Svavarsdottir (1999), Sliwa (2016), Aboodi (2017), Johnson King (2020). And in the context of a challenge specifically for Robust Realism, there is special reason not to rely too closely on Smith's rejection of moral motivation de dicto, as robust realists have other reasons—independently of

it's important to see how minimal the claim needed here is, and how plausible it is, even if the stronger claims made by Smith cannot withstand criticism. First, with regard to the moral-religious asymmetry, all that's needed for an explanation in terms of the de-re-de-dicto distinction to succeed is that the significance of this distinction plays out in different ways in the moral and the religious contexts. And this seems true *even if moral motivation de dicto is often virtuous*. After all, even if this is so—if, for instance, moral motivation de dicto has an important role to play in cases of moral uncertainty, or if motivational overdetermination is often virtuous—still it's clear that moral motivation de re has some kind of priority, that being motivated *only* by moral motivation de dicto at least falls short of the ideal. But this is precisely not the case when it comes to the religious case, where—so we've argued—at least in many cases motivation de dicto *is* the ideal, and motivation de re is either neutral or even to be frowned upon. So even if Smith is too quick to dismiss de re moral motivation, the distinction between de re and de dicto motivation can explain, at least partly, the asymmetry between the regret of the lapsed theist and that of the lapsed moralist. And for similar reasons, the de-re-de-dicto distinction can explain, at least to an extent, the awkwardness of all-the-wrongs-regrets, even if de dicto moral motivation is sometimes perfectly acceptable. It can do that because regretting all the wrongs one could have performed indicates an absence of moral motivation de re, and even if moral motivation de dicto is sometimes virtuous, still moral motivation de re has privileged status. So its absence is, at the very least, often problematic. Perhaps, if smith is wrong and de dicto moral motivation is not always and necessarily fetishistic, the force of the explanation in terms of the de-re-de-dicto motivation loses some of its force, then. But it does not collapse entirely.

Despite its advantages, though, we don't think that the explanation in terms of the distinction between de re and de dicto moral motivation gives the full picture of the moral-religious asymmetry we started with.[18] The problem is that it doesn't have the required scope. Recall local moral mistakes and changes of mind, and the regret that may follow them, such as my regretting having spent so much time giving my graduate students detailed feedback (because I thought—falsely, as I've later come to think—this was morally required) instead of watching snooker. Such regrets, we noted in the previous section, make perfect sense, and are in this way (and perhaps in others too) crucially different from the suspicious regret of the lapsed moralist. So an adequate explanation of the suspiciousness of the latter must not include in its scope also the former. But the explanation in terms of the de-re-de-dicto distinction seems to fail this test. The

---

the explanatory challenge discussed in this chapter—to reject this claim. For discussion, see Enoch (2011, Chapter 9), and the references there.

[18] Also, notice that our intuitive starting point doesn't sit well with Smith's insistence—in the same context in which he puts forward his claims about de dicto moral motivation and fetishism—that when the virtuous change their mind about some moral matters, their motivation reliably changes accordingly. At least in the case of the lapsed moralist, we're relying on the intuition that there is something suspicious about their motivations changing "accordingly." This is not the kind of case Smith seems to have had in mind, perhaps because this is a change first in a *meta*ethical opinion, and only derivatively in one's moral judgments. It's not clear to us whether this is a problem for Smith.

de re motivations, after all, are supposedly insensitive to changes in even local moral beliefs[19]. So an explanation of what's suspicious about all-the-wrongs-regrets that relies heavily on the distinction between de re and de dicto moral motivation classifies local moral regrets together with all-the-wrongs-regrets, and deems them equally suspicious. This is unacceptable.

More can be said, of course. Perhaps some further apparatus can be added in order to distinguish between the status of (suspicious) all-the-wrongs-regrets and (legitimate) local regrets. But at this point we think that enough has been said to at least cast doubt about the de-re-de-dicto explanation of our phenomenon. And as you will see, the explanation we end up endorsing—in Section 5—will not have a similar shortcoming (and will be related to the de-re-de-dicto explanation).

3. WHY BE MORAL?

One natural thought to have about why it is that all-the-wrongs-regrets don't seem to make sense is that this is so simply because morality (understood in a de-dicto-ish way) doesn't matter. And this natural thought shows how the traditional why-be-moral challenge (for instance, but not only) to moral realism is relevant here.

It is not entirely clear how to understand the why-be-moral challenge. It is often put normatively—roughly, as asking for a reason to be moral, or indeed for a reason to do what one has reason to do, or some such—but when it is thus put, robust realists are quick to point out that it is based on a confusion—or perhaps on several different confusions.[20] Recently, though, Jamie Dreier (2015a; 2015b) has presented what we believe is a better version of the challenge, one that is free from such confusions.[21] On Dreier's suggestion, the challenge is not normative—asking for a reason to do what morality or rationality requires—but rather *explanatory*. Using a notion of rationality that is not meant to capture reason-responsiveness in a general, objective sense, but something more closely related to internal coherence (2015a, 174–5), Dreier presents the challenge, which he calls the New Normative Question, thus: "Why is it irrational to fail to be motivated to do what one believes one ought to do?" (177).

We want to acknowledge, right off the bat, that this is a legitimate challenge to robust realists (and perhaps to others as well): It does seem that often, and perhaps always and necessarily, if one believes that one ought to do something, but is nevertheless

---

[19] Smith, of course, thinks that moral beliefs are themselves much more intimately connected to motivations than robust realists take them to be. But we've restricted our discussion here to the robust realist perspective.

[20] See the references in Dreier (2015a) to Parfit. See also Enoch (2011, 242–247).

[21] There may be other ways of understanding "the" why-be-moral challenge, of course. We focus on this one, partly because it seems an especially clear challenge that avoids the confusions characteristic of some other statements of the challenge, and partly because it is interesting. But we are not committed to all other understandings of it being confused, of course.

not motivated at all—not even a little bit[22]—to do that thing, some internal tension is involved. Here's an even weaker claim, that captures, we think, the Dreier point, and is even harder to resist, partly because it can be put in a way that clearly avoids any judgment-internalist assumptions:[23] When someone believes he or she ought to do something, but is nonetheless not at all motivated to do it, this at the very least calls for explanation. The thing to expect is that they *would* be so motivated. If they aren't, this calls for explanation, at least in the following minimal sense: A theory that can offer an explanation of this fact is pro tanto better, for this reason, than theories that cannot, it gains plausibility points compared to those that cannot offer such an explanation.

We don't share the suspicion that realists cannot supply the needed explanation,[24] and we'll have more to say about this below. But it's easy to see why realists should at least be worried, for on some alternative views such an explanation is more clearly and readily available. Any metaethical view, for instance, on which there's a very close connection between accepting a moral judgment and motivation (perhaps expressivist views, and some subjectivist or contextualist views or naturalist reductive views that tie the nature of moral facts to something about us and our desires, say) should be able to solve "the New Normative Question" with relative ease. If, however, moral judgments express beliefs, and true moral judgments depict facts all the way out there in Plato's heaven, it becomes harder to explain why one can't have such a belief, and without any internal tension lack the relevant motivation. We could, of course, accept such a connection as brute, but that would hardly be ideal—at the very least, going brute will have its cost in plausibility points.

What we want to focus on here, though, is the relation between Dreier's New Normative Question and the explanatory challenge we started with—namely, the need to explain why it is that all-the-wrongs-regrets do not make sense for the lapsed moralist, at least not nearly as much as all-the-sins-regrets do for the lapsed orthodox Jew. For there is a certain tension here that you may find surprising.

The intuitive datum—that there's something off about all-the-wrongs-regrets—restricts the scope of Dreier's explanandum, or at least a natural extension thereof. Dreier's explanandum, to repeat, is that it's irrational to fail to be motivated to do what one believes one ought to do, and if you accept that it *is* irrational, you may expect that more generally one's motivations will track changes in one's moral beliefs. But our intuitive datum, once coupled with a plausible assumption about a tight connection between regret and motivation, draws attention to a way in which it's *not* rational to change what one cares about when one changes one's moral beliefs (because of one's metaethical ones). When the moralist comes to accept the error theory, and so presumably to desert all of her first-order moral judgments,[25] she does *not* seem to be irrational in any way

---

[22] As in discussions of judgment-internalism, the condition in the text can be met even if the relevant motivation is on some occasions defeated by other motivations.

[23] Dreier is a judgment-internalist, but it's not clear that this challenge of his presupposes such internalism. Be that as it may, the formulation that follows clearly avoids such a presupposition.

[24] See Dreier's (2015a, 178) comment on Parfit.

[25] But see section 5.

when she still cares about the moral de re, when she still cares about not harming others' interests or dignity, say.

The contrast with the religious case is again telling: We can ask analogues of why-be-moral questions: Why adhere to the Commandments, for instance? Here too we may have a normative challenge in mind, but we may also have an explanatory one, à la Dreier: At least for an Orthodox Jew, it seems that there's something irrational in coming to believe that one is religiously required to act in a certain way, and not be at all motivated to act in that way. In the religious case, though, it seems easy to come up with explanations (without going noncognitivist about religious commitment): Something about the divine source of religious commandments, say, or about reward and punishment, can easily explain why it would be irrational (for the believer) not to be motivated in a way that's sensitive to his beliefs about his religious obligations. And arguably, this is a part of the reason why all-the-sins-regrets make sense. The lapsed Orthodox Jew no longer believes in the divine source of the relevant commandments, he no longer believes in the reward and punishment mechanism he used to believe in, and this is why he no longer accepts a reason to abide by the relevant religious obligations. Meanwhile, the reasons to eat shrimp and to engage in all those sexual practices are still very much in place (as they always have been). Hence the regret.

But the stories that make such a regret sensible in the religious case do not extend to the moral case. And the fact that they don't seems to be a part of what distinguishes between all-the-sins-regrets and all-the-wrongs-regrets. Whatever explanation there is of the irrationality of not being motivated to do something when one believes one ought to—whatever answer there is to Dreier's New Normative Question—it doesn't seem to extend to the case of the lapsed moralist. Hence the restriction on Dreier's explanandum.

We don't think this is a problem for Dreier. Indeed, on the explanation of the religious-moral asymmetry that we present below (in Section 5), the lapsed moralist does not after all desert her or his first-order moral convictions, so even the appearance of the need to restrict Dreier's explanandum will disappear. And the notion of rationality he is working with may—we're really not sure—allow him to say that there *is* something irrational about our lapsed moralist, if he remains motivated by his old moral beliefs.[26] What the discussion in this section shows, though, is that a solution to our puzzle—why all-the-wrongs-regrets are suspicious in a way in which all-the-sins-regrets are not—is unlikely to fall out of a general response to the why-be-moral challenge, at least not in Dreier's version.

---

[26] Recall that Dreier works with an internal-coherence notion of rationality. It is not implausible to think that before the conversion to error theory, the mental life of our moralist (who has a bunch of moral beliefs, and is motivated accordingly) exemplifies a certain kind of internal coherence that, after conversion (with the same motivations, so without all-the-wrongs-regrets, but also with a belief in the error theory) lacks. Indeed, Dreier may argue that the appearance that there is something irrational about changing one's motivations (and regretting all those missed opportunities) stems from an implicit shift to a more substantive notion of rationality.

Dreier's New Normative Question remains a challenge, then. It will be easier to address it together with Dasgupta's related recent challenge, to which we now turn.

4. WHY CARE ABOUT THESE NON-NATURAL PROPERTIES?

The fact that the lapsed orthodox Jew's all-the-sins-regrets make perfect sense can be seen as evidence that—at least in the eyes of the religiously committed—religious obligations matter. The religiously committed only avoided some of these sexual practices precisely because he took them to be religiously forbidden, and he used to care deeply about that. If so, perhaps the fact that it doesn't make sense for the lapsed moralist to have all-the-wrongs-regrets may serve as some evidence for the claim that moral realists lack the resources to vindicate caring about morality.

Here's an oft-quoted passage from Nowell-Smith:

> If there are sui generis properties of rightness and wrongness, then learning about them might well be as exciting as learning about spiral nebulae or watersprouts. But what if I am not interested? Why should I *do* anything about these newly-revealed objects? Some things, I have now learnt, are right and others wrong; but why should I do what is right and eschew what is wrong? (Nowell-Smith 1954, 41; quoted in Dasgupta 2017, 298)

Despite the rhetorical strength of this way of putting things, it is not very helpful. For one thing, the challenge is here put in normative terms (what I *should* do about these interesting things). But if the question is normative, it invites a normative answer, and then the robust realist seems perfectly entitled to insist that the challenge doesn't make much more sense than asking why we should do what we should do; hardly the devastating challenge it is intended to be.

Recently, however, Shamik Dasgupta (2017) has given a new shape to this fairly old thought. Like Dreier, Dasgupta is happy to leave this intra-normative challenge (the "internal" one) behind, and focus on an explanatory challenge instead. Here is how he puts the challenge at one point: "More generally, the external objection asks what makes the nonnaturalist's sui generis property fit to play whatever role she believes it to play in normative theory." (303) Dasgupta uses an analogy to Divine Command Theory (DCT) in order to press his objection. Even if DCT is true, it owes us an answer to the question "What is it that makes the orders of this being fit to play the role of generating obligations?". And the DCT-ist is happy to step up to the explanatory plate—after all, there *is* something very special about the apparatus the DCT-ist uses here—God is special in what seems like relevant ways, and His commands are special (partly because they are commands, and partly because they are His). So it's not mysterious, on DCT, why it is that those supernatural properties (and not others, for instance) are the ones fit to play the relevant role in normative theory. By comparison, the robust realist[27]—argues Dasgupta—has much less to offer, perhaps nothing. Why is it, Dasgupta asks the realist, that those non-natural properties—rather than other non-natural properties, or no properties at all—are fit to play the normative role they play in your theory? And the robust realist seems to have nothing to say.

Dasgupta emphasizes that the somewhat dismissive responses realists have been giving[28]—perhaps because of problems with common ways of putting the challenge (like Nowell-Smith's above, or Korsgaard's (1997, 240))—will not work. Robust realists can't respond "Why, these *are* the normative properties, so of course they are fit to play the role those play in normative theory," any more than the DCT-ist can respond with "Why, these *are* the supernatural facts that constitute rightness, so of course they are fit to play the rightness-role." The difference, though, is that the DCT-ist acknowledges the explanatory need, and responds to it, whereas the realist shuts his eyes and pretends that there's no explanatory problem to begin with. So says Dasgupta.

We shamelessly respond, on behalf of the robust realist, in the way that Dasgupta anticipates:[29] We say that there's nothing wrong, or almost nothing wrong, with accepting that nothing explains why it is that some non-natural properties are fit to play the relevant roles in normative theory. Let's use Dasgupta's (305) example: So focus on the property *goodness*, and assume that its role is to be action-guiding. Now suppose that the robust realist argues that her favorite non-natural property P *just is* goodness. Dasgupta insists that there must be an explanation why it is that P is fit to serve the action-guiding role.[30] We say: No, there mustn't. That P is fit to play the action-guiding role is a brute fact about P. Sometimes, there may be such explanation—if P, say, is not a basic normative property (in a fairly intuitive sense of "basic"), an explanation in more fundamental normative terms may be available. But if P is a basic normative property, then this is where such explanations come to an end. Insisting that there must be more really amounts to a refusal to take seriously robust realism as a view about the metaphysics of morals.

Interestingly, it is here that the analogy with DCT breaks down. If someone offers an account of rightness or obligations in terms of some expressions by some creature,

---

[27] Divine Command Theorists (DCT-ists) are voluntarists, and so are not robust realists in the sense we're using this term (and Dasgupta too contrasts DCT-ists with robust realists). If this way of putting things makes you uncomfortable, feel free to add "who is not a DCT-ist" to "robust realist" in the text.

[28] This includes Enoch (2011, 242–247).

[29] "Admittedly, there is nothing incoherent about [the response we are about to give]. In fact, I think this is the non-naturalist's only refuge, and I have no decisive argument against it. Still, once exposed for what it is, it seems to me a clearly unattractive position" (307). We return below to the question of how unattractive it is.

[30] Dasgupta emphasizes that the robust realist cannot get this "for free," by insisting that P *is* goodness, and that goodness is action-guiding. Rather, Dasgupta insists plausibly enough, the robust realist must *first* be willing to attribute to P the action-guiding role, and only *later on*, as it were, should she be willing to identify P and goodness. Otherwise, the realist is not "playing fair," in the sense Dasgupta (301) takes from Lewis (1994).

without offering any explanation why it's *this* creature, and *those* expressions of hers, that constitute obligations, this is sufficient ground for rejecting the theory. But this is because on such a theory, the rightness-facts and properties are not metaphysically fundamental, they are metaphysically grounded in some creature's will. So it's crucial to say which creature, and to explain why (and as we saw, the DCT-ist has a story to tell). The robust realist, by contrast, thinks of the most fundamental moral facts and properties as fundamental, entirely ungrounded.[31] This is why the robust realist is entitled to claim bruteness where the DCT-ist is not.

So we are going to insist that rejecting the call to explain how it is that the relevant non-natural properties play the relevant normative role is not a deal-breaker, it is not a severe flaw that renders robust realism unacceptable. Is it a flaw at all, though? Does robust realism lose any plausibility points because of its refusal to offer an explanation here? We're not entirely sure. On the one hand, we are inclined to say that it does lose *some* plausibility points, simply because it's almost always the case that as between two (otherwise equally good) competing theories, a theory that classifies a phenomenon as brute is less good as a theory than the one that offers an informative explanation of that phenomenon.[32] On the other hand, though, we don't feel the force of this consideration: Us robust realists have told you from the get-go, as it were, that we take the basic moral (or normative) facts to be entirely fundamental, that there's nothing in virtue of which these facts obtain.[33] You may have been skeptical of this all along. Fair enough.[34] But we don't see that any additional reason for skepticism is given by Dasgupta's challenge.

This concludes, then, our response to Dasgupta's version of the why-care-about-these-non-natural-properties challenge. This response does not aspire to positively showing a robust-realist-friendly reason to care about morality—it merely aims to reject the thought that something about robust realism somehow makes caring about morality less sensible, but this suffices to disarm this objection to robust realism. Much more can be said here—perhaps especially because Dasgupta's metaethical challenge is *very* closely related to a much more general metaphysical challenge, which Dasgupta discusses in another paper (2018). But here we have to return to our main order of

---

[31] Though some intricate grounding-related issues arise. See Enoch (2019).
For closely related points see Kramer (2009, throughout) and Chappell (2019, 128).

[32] Though this may have to be qualified to something like initially surprising or striking phenomena, those that intuitively seem to call for explanation. And there are complications down that route: There are going to be controversies over what calls for explanation (the basic physical constants, for instance? That there's something rather than nothing?); and it's anything but clear how precisely to understanding the property of strikingness. For some (skeptical) discussion, see Baras (2022).
One way of understanding the next point in the text is as claiming that the phenomenon Dasgupta accuses realists of failing to explain does not in fact call for explanation.

[33] Preston Werner insisted that this is not so—that robust realists more often put things in terms of the *irreducibility* rather than the *ungroundability* of moral or normative facts. He's right, but this may be due to the sociology of the field. Grounding talk was not that big in 2011 (Parfit 2011; Enoch 2011) and certainly not in 2005 (Huemer 2005) or 2003 (Shafer-Landau 2003). We think that a robust realism worth its name will also go for ungroundability. For some relevant discussion, see Enoch (2019) and Wygoda Cohen (2021).

[34] Though see the discussion of "sheer queerness" in Enoch (2011, 134–136).

business—tying what has been said back to Dreier's challenge, and then to the religious-moral asymmetry we're trying to explain throughout this chapter. (Nevertheless, we comment on the more general metaphysical context of Dasgupta's challenge in a long footnote.[35])

Even though Dreier puts things differently, and even though Dasgupta reads Dreier as engaging the "internal" objection to realism (and himself to be addressing a different, "external" one), there are close connections between the two discussions. Dasgupta asks for an explanation of what it is about the relevant non-natural properties that makes them fit to play the relevant normative role. Dreier asks for an explanation of the irrationality of having a normative belief without having the relevant motivation. These are different explananda, but if we plug in some plausible auxiliary premises—say, about the normative role of those non-natural properties having something to do with motivation (or action-guiding, say), and perhaps about the relation between fitness and rationality—they become very similar.[36] And our response to Dreier will be very close to our response to Dasgupta.

What explains the internal tension (designated by Dreier's use of "irrationality") that is present when someone believes that something is good but is not motivated accordingly is *the nature of goodness*. It lies in the nature of goodness that good things are to be desired.[37] And nothing explains *that*. That it makes sense to desire the good (or

---

[35] Dasgupta (2018) puts forward an argument against metaphysical realism that is similar in structure to his argument against robust metaethical realism. Using the predicate "elite" to designate the special properties that our scientific inquiries should focus on, Dasgupta says (288):

"My objection to realism therefore rests on three familiar premises:

1. Eliteness is theory-guiding.
2. If naturalness is theory-guiding, there must be some explanation of why naturalness is theory-guiding.
3. There is no explanation of why naturalness would be theory-guiding."

In the metaethical case, we rejected the analogue of premise (2). In the metaphysical case, though, we want to accept premise (2), and reject premise (3), *relying on robust metanormative realism*. That is, once we are entitled to help ourselves to fundamental, ungrounded normative facts (because, well, robust metanormative realism is true) we can use them in order to explain why we should guide our theory by naturalness (or some such). In other words, we only need to go for bruteness once—once we've done that for the metanormative argument, we have enough explanatory resources to take care of the metaphysical challenge as well. In a way that metaethicists of all stripes should find satisfying, when metaphysics seems in trouble, it's metaethics (or more precisely, metanormativity) that comes to the rescue. (In personal correspondence, Dasgupta agreed that the way to save metaphysics from his challenge may depend on defending robust metanormative realism from his metaethical challenge).

Of course, this is very quick and underdeveloped. But if this is a promising line to take, this adds quite a few plausibility points to robust realism, because, as Lewis (1986, vii) notes, the fact that systematic philosophy goes more easily if we may presuppose a hypothesis is a reason to believe it.

[36] The similarity is perhaps clearest when Dreier (2015a, 161) asks what makes Scanlon's relation R special, compared to some other (non-natural) relation Q.

[37] Dreier's explanandum is put in terms of beliefs about what one ought to do, not about the good. So in order to complete the response to Dreier, either a similar story must be told about *ought*, or a fairly strong connection must be defended between the good and what one ought to do, or both.

something close to this) is a fundamental, ungrounded normative truth. This doesn't guarantee, of course, that everyone desires the good. And we're not sure it guarantees the irrationality of failing to desire what one takes to be good. Then again, we're not sure that failing to desire what one believes to be good is always and necessarily irrational (even in Dreier's sense). Recall, though, the weaker, more plausible explanandum we mention above, in Section 3: If someone takes something to be good, but is not motivated accordingly, this is surprising, it calls for explanation. If this is what needs explaining, the point above suffices: Goodness, by its nature, is to be desired. So if you believe that something is good but you don't want to pursue or promote or engage with it, this is surprising. Perhaps this reply to Dreier's New Normative Question doesn't give you all you wanted. If so, we're inclined to repeat the discussion above, about whether Dasgupta's challenge costs the robust realist plausibility points, and if so, how many. We are in the same situation vis-à-vis Dreier as we were vis-à-vis Dasgupta.

But now it's time to get back to the moral-religious asymmetry. The initial suspicion was that perhaps what explains it is that while it's clear why, on the religious orthodox view, one should care about religious obligations, it is not clear why, on the moral realist view, one should care about moral obligations. Of course, had this been true, this would have explained the asymmetry, but at a very high price for the realist—it's very little comfort for the realist, after all, if he can explain this asymmetry by accepting the claim that there's no reason to care about morality, or that Nowell-Smith is right to suggest that indifference toward the realist's favorite non-natural properties is unproblematic. What we've been arguing, though, is that the realist has a reply to Dasgupta, and Dreier, and related worries. While this (if true) is good news, it means that we still need an explanation for the moral-religious asymmetry.

5. Junk Knowledge and Regret

The thought-experiment we started with is about regret *after* changing one's mind (about God, or about morality). But now think of things *before* the conversion to atheism and to error theory. What conditionals should the orthodox Jew, who also accepts a straightforwardly realist interpretation to theist discourse, believe with the antecedent "If there is no God, . . ."?[38] And what conditionals should the moralist—who also accepts a straightforwardly realist interpretation of moral discourse[39]—believe that start with "If there are no moral facts, . . ."? It seems plausible, we think,

---

[38] Again see Lewinsohn (2016), and the rabbinic sources there cited.
[39] We here tie these two together, not because they are equivalent or some such, but because of the constraints of our project here—we are trying to offer an account of the moralist and the lapsed moralist from a robust realist perspective. We're not assuming that all moralists are robust realists—just that the story we are after should be consistent with robust realism.

that this orthodox Jew should believe conditionals like "If there is no God (or if orthodox Judaism is false, or some such), then there's no reason not to eat shrimp or engage in much more liberal sexual practices." And the moral realist should believe conditionals like "If there are no (non-natural) moral facts, then there's no (moral) reason not to hurt people's feelings."[40] So far, then, symmetry is retained. But, we want to suggest in this final section, this is where the symmetry ends, because our two protagonists should treat these conditionals very differently. In particular, the orthodox Jew should be willing to use such conditionals in modus-ponens inferences, should he or she come to believe their respective antecedents. (But we qualify this statement toward the end of this section). The moral realist, however, should not—he or she should think of this conditional as an instance of "junk knowledge." That is, knowledge that cannot play the more standard role such conditionals play in reasoning.

To see this, it will be helpful to consider another recent objection to robust realism—the suggestion that there is something *morally* objectionable about moral realism.[41] This objection—recently put forward, with different details and nuances, by Melis Erdur, Matt Bedke, and Max Hayward[42]—claims that moral realism commits one to objectionable moral views, or (at least) that moral realists, if they are rational, will have morally objectionable dispositions.

The different versions of the objection vary in details, but they all develop a similar suspicion, that starts with conditionals robust realists are committed to. Robust realists[43] believe, for instance, that moral facts are non-natural facts that do not constitutively depend on us and our perspectives in any way. But this belief commits them to the conditional

(C1) If there are no non-natural facts, then nothing is wrong.

Also, realists seem to be committed to more specific conditionals. For instance, you may initially think that pain is intrinsically bad, whether it occurs in humans or in dogs. But if you're a robust realist, you're also committed to the conditional:

---

[40] This does not mean, of course, that (the realist should believe that) expressivists, say, don't have reasons not to hurt people. There are non-natural moral facts, the robust realist believes, and those apply to the expressivist as they do to everyone else.

[41] The discussion that follows draws on Enoch (2022).

[42] Erdur (2016), Bedke (2019), Hayward (2019).

[43] At the outset we noted that while the explanatory challenge this chapter addresses arises in an especially troubling way to robust realists, the protagonist in the example need not be a robust realist—any kind of metaethically naïve moral realist or moralist will do. Still, here we proceed to talk as if the protagonist too must be a robust realist—simply because this is how the people to whom we respond here put their objections. Both the objections and our reply can be rephrased in ways that avoid the commitment (for the protagonists) to robust realism.

(C2) If human pain and dog pain have no non-natural property in common, then (seeing that human pain is intrinsically bad, and that intrinsic badness according to robust realism is a non-natural property), dog pain is not intrinsically bad.

This already seems bad enough. But things get even worse. How should realists respond to metaphysical evidence about the existence and distribution of non-natural properties, say, a fully reliable oracle that testifies that the universe is natural (so that the antecedent of (C1) is true), or that human pain and dog pain share no non-natural properties (so that the antecedent of (C2) is true)? The most natural response seems to be to adopt the consequents of these conditionals. If there are no non-natural properties, then the realist—who is committed to something like the thought that non-natural mattering is the only way things *could* matter—should conclude that nothing matters.[44] And if dog pain and human pain share no non-natural properties (and if the realist believes, or even knows, as much), then the antecedent of (C2) is true, and given her commitment to (C2), the realist should now endorse its consequent. This, however, seems morally repugnant—surely, dog pain *is* intrinsically bad, and while it's perhaps not inconceivable that we should come across evidence that will convince us otherwise, surely the oracle's metaphysical proclamations are not evidence of this kind. The only alternative for the realist seems to be to resist a modus-ponens inference whose premises she accepts—a clearly irrational move. So realists are either irrational or immoral.[45]

To see how we can respond, suppose that I believe—based on both empirical evidence and philosophical analysis—that having a brain is a necessary condition for having thoughts. So I believe, for any creature or object, that if it doesn't have a brain, it doesn't have thoughts. And because I know my first-year logic, I accept the following conditional, which is entailed by this view:

(C3) If I don't have a brain, I don't have thoughts.

Furthermore, I believe (C3) rather firmly and confidently, because it obviously follows from the generalization which I believe firmly and confidently—namely, that having a brain is necessary for having thoughts.

---

[44] This is very close to Hayward's (2019, 2) way of putting things. Hayward's main target is Parfit, who endorses conditionals like (C1) explicitly—Hayward calls them Parfit-conditionals. We do not intend to defend Parfit, who may be vulnerable to Hayward's objection. We merely claim that robust realism is not similarly vulnerable.

[45] This dilemma is Bedke's way of putting things. For more details regarding Hayward's and Bedke's objections, again see Enoch (2022).

Erdur's version is different from both—she emphasizes the implausibility of the thought that what grounds the wrongness of pain (say) is non-natural stuff in Plato's heaven, rather than the very worldly fact that *it hurts*. We think that the way out of Erdur's challenge proceeds via a distinction between normative and metaphysical grounding (see, for instance, Enoch 2019 and the references there), so that the realist is only committed to the non-natural stuff metaphysically (but not normatively) grounding moral facts. For a similar response (in different terms), see Blanchard (2019).

Suppose I then receive evidence—from an oracle, perhaps, or from a reliable scan-technician—that in fact my skull is empty, and I do not have a brain. Am I supposed to draw the modus-ponens inference, and conclude that I don't have any thoughts? Of course not. Rather, I should take back my commitment to the conditional (C3). Clearly, I have thoughts. If I don't have a brain, this is conclusive reason to reject the theory according to which having a brain is necessary for having thoughts.[46]

A natural way of thinking about my belief in—perhaps knowledge of—(C3) is as "junk knowledge." That is, a known proposition that can nevertheless not play the knowledge-extending role more commonly played by similarly known propositions.[47] I may very well know (C3), but I can't use it in the canonical inferential way, namely, as a premise in a modus-ponens inference. There need be nothing mysterious about this, of course: In this specific case, the reason for this is probably that my way of knowing that the consequent is false neither depends on nor is undercut by evidence either for the antecedent or for the conditional as a whole. This fact, perhaps together with the fact that I am (justifiably) so much more confident in the denial of the consequent than in the conditional, is why conclusive evidence for the antecedent is guaranteed to be evidence against the conditional rather than evidence for the consequent. And this is why while I may very well know (C3), I cannot use it in the standard modus-ponens kind of way.

As we're sure you've already realized, we want to say something very similar about (C1) and (C2).[48] If I am a robust realist, then seeing that these conditionals (perhaps more precisely put, or slightly massaged) follow from robust realism, I believe them as well. But this doesn't commit me in any way to responding to the oracle's metaphysical proclamations by drawing the relevant modus-ponens inferences. Rather, given the evidence about the truth of the antecedents, the thing to do is to reevaluate one's commitment to the conditionals (and to robust realism), and reject them on the combined strength of the plausibility of the negation of their consequents, and the evidence for their antecedents.

William Fitzpatrick (2018, 558), in responding to an earlier version of Bedke's argument (2014), makes what is essentially this point, though he does not refer to the more general phenomenon of junk knowledge.[49] And both Bedke and Hayward respond. But once we put things in the broader epistemological context—the phenomenon of junk knowledge—their responses can be seen to fail. Consider Hayward first.

Hayward compares conditionals like (C1) and (C2) with what he calls (7) "Ivan's Conditional": "If God is dead, then everything is permitted." But this comparison is

---

[46] I (DE) heard this example many, many years ago, from Stephen Schiffer in a conversation whose context I don't now remember (but it was not in metaethics).

This example works very well for our purposes here, but is nevertheless not without shortcomings: One may believe (C3) not because it follows from the general theory as in the text, but simply because its consequent is absurd. So let us stipulate that this is not the case here—perhaps (C3) hadn't occurred to me until it was pointed out to me that it follows from a general theory that I believe.

[47] Sorensen (1988).

[48] Chappell (2019) pursues a *very* similar line.

[49] He also makes some other points, with some of which we are not sure that we agree.

misleading. When Dostoyevsky's Ivan puts forward this conditional, presumably he has *precisely* the modus-ponens inference in mind. Indeed, licensing that inference is presumably the very *point*, for Ivan, of accepting and asserting the conditional. So if that conditional turns out to be an instance of junk knowledge, the very point of accepting it is defeated. But when robust realists accept conditionals like (C1) and (C2), we don't do so in order to use them in modus-ponens inferences. Rather, we accept them because they follow from our theory, a theory that presumably has other theoretical advantages. So if our (purported) knowledge of (C1) and (C2) ends up being junk knowledge, this is not a problem at all—our reasons for endorsing them are not in any way undercut by them being junk knowledge. In this respect too, the situation is precisely analogous to that with (C3). We accept (C3)—that if I don't have a brain I don't have thoughts—not out of anticipation of using it in a modus-ponens inference, but because it follows from a more general theory that we have sufficient reason to believe. If it ends up being junk knowledge, that's no problem at all.

Hayward also seems to think that if the realist is willing to give up on (C1) and (C2) in the face of conclusive evidence for their antecedents, this creates a coherence problem for the realist: "If moral claims could be "true" and authoritative even in a world without non-natural facts, why posit facts of this kind?" (16). But this trades on the ambiguity of "could". The realist who thinks that realism is metaphysically necessary agrees, of course, that moral claims metaphysically-could be true only in a world with non-natural facts. But that is consistent with the *epistemic* possibility to the contrary: So long as the realist concedes, as any reasonable realist should, that he or she is fallible in her commitment to realism, they must concede that it's epistemically possible that their metaethics is false, and then, it's epistemically possible that the relevant moral judgments are true in a naturalist world.[50] And as can be seen from the example of (C3), again there's nothing special or ad hoc about this claim of the realist. Someone can believe not just that (C3) is true, but also that it's metaphysically necessary, without committing herself to modus-ponensing her way to (C3)'s consequent upon coming to believe its antecedent.

---

[50] In this paragraph in the text we are using "epistemic possibility" somewhat loosely. On some understandings, a proposition p is epistemically possible for a believer B iff the evidence available to B together with ideal reasoning do not suffice to rule out p. (See, for instance, Kment (2017, section 1), and the many references there.) On such an understanding, it's not clear that what we say in the text is true. The sense of epistemic possibility we're after is the sense in which it's true to say such things as "For all we know, Goldbach's Conjecture may be false," even if Goldbach's Conjecture—as we will find out at some point in the future—is true, metaphysically and perhaps conceptually necessary, and knowable a priori. When Hayward and Bedke ask us realists to imagine a case in which highly surprising evidence comes in, evidence that may give us conclusive reasons to change our minds about metaphysically necessary claims, this is the relevant sense. For comparison, consider: What would you believe if all the mathematicians suddenly agreed that some new genius found a flaw in the proof of Fermat's Last Theorem, and that some computer program came up with a counterexample? Well, you would believe that Fermat's Theorem is false. This counterfactual in no way shows that you don't really believe that it's true, as a matter of a fairly strong necessity, nor does it show that there's any incoherence in your belief (that it's true and necessary) and your disposition (to give up on that belief in the relevant, highly surprising, counterfactual scenario).

Bedke too recognizes the possibility of rejecting the conditionals rather than accepting their consequents. And a central thought for Bedke here is that if this is the line the realist takes, this shows that his commitment to realism is "maximally fragile," and indeed perhaps unintelligible (11, 15). But this is plainly false, as can be seen from the (C3) example. The fact that we're not willing to take evidence for (C3)'s antecedent as reason to believe its consequent doesn't show in any way that we don't really believe (C3), or that we believe it only in some minimal sense, or that it's "maximally fragile." It may be quite robust—depending on how strongly (C3) is embedded in a more general theory about minds and brains, and on how strong the evidence is for that theory. Note also that the fact that (C1) and (C2) are instances of junk knowledge in no way shows that *robust realism* is. Robust realism may have other important implications, may be knowledge-extending in other ways and in other contexts, indeed may entail other conditionals that can perfectly well play their standard role in modus-ponens inferences. So pursuing the junk knowledge line in no way compromises the strength of the realist's commitment to robust realism, nor does it reduce its significance.[51]

More should be said in response to Bedke. In particular, we should distinguish between highly idealized, hypothetical, oracle-style scenarios—where the junk-knowledge line suffices as a response—and less heavily idealized cases, where what we have is not a perfectly reliable oracle, but the messy kind of evidence we usually have, both for normative claims and for metaethical ones. In the latter case, the junk knowledge line may need some help from the observation that in some such messy scenarios, it makes perfect sense to reduce one's confidence in some normative claims based on evidence for or against relevant metaphysical claims (like the distribution of non-natural properties). But for our purposes here, giving more details will not be necessary.[52] Instead, let's get back to the attempt to explain the religious-moral asymmetry, and why it is that all-the-wrongs-regrets do not make sense.

If the junk-knowledge line on conditionals like (C1) works, this means that a well-informed robust realist knows that should he or she come to believe that robust realism is false (or something to that extent), they will not (and should not) infer the conditional's consequent. Rather, they will (as they should) re-evaluate their commitment to the conditional, and come to reject it. If so, the rational thing for a lapsed moral realist to do is, of course, to maintain his commitment to any number of moral judgments, and come to reject the thought that moral realism (or the existence of non-natural properties) is a necessary condition for their truth. If so, *of course* he shouldn't now regret all the wrongs he could have performed—he still thinks they are wrong, and so in the relevant

---

[51] In correspondence, Bedke explained that he's thinking of "maximal fragility" as restricted in the way suggested in the text—that is, the belief in robust realism is guaranteed to be defeated by evidence for the relevant normative judgment (such as the antecedents of (C1) and (C2). Thus understood, he's right that the belief in realism is "maximally fragile," but his choice of terminology is misleading. "Maximal fragility" in this sense is consistent with robustness vis-à-vis many kinds of evidence. In other words, the claim that his belief in realism is "maximally fragile" in this stipulated sense is no embarrassment at all for the realist.

[52] Again, see Enoch (2022).

respects, really nothing has changed. Put differently, upon coming to believe the antecedent of (C1), the lapsed robust realist wouldn't (and shouldn't) infer the conditional's consequent, which results in endorsing an extreme error theory. Rather, he would (and should) reject the conditional, thereby rejecting robust realism but accepting some other (perhaps not fully explicit or determinate) metaethical view that still allows belief in the negation of the consequent.

The case of the lapsed moralist who is also a rather extreme error-theorist is a bit harder, because believing the error theory may be inconsistent with still adhering to the relevant first-order judgments.[53] So let us say the following: Either one can continue to adhere to moral judgments consistently with endorsing an error theory, or one cannot. If one can, then the discussion above applies. If not, then adherents of the error theory either continue to adhere—inconsistently—to some moral judgments, or else they desert them. If they remain faithful to their moral judgments, then the fact that they now do so in a way that is inconsistent with something else they believe (the error theory) doesn't matter for the purposes of explaining why they won't regret all the wrongs they could have performed—they still believe they are wrong, after all. So the only remaining problematic case is that of the error-theory-convert who has abandoned, because of their new commitment to the error theory, their moral beliefs. We doubt that there are many people who fit this description.[54] And this is important. For what we are after is not necessarily an explanation of why it is that all-the-wrongs-regrets are always and necessarily irrational. Rather, what we are after is an explanation for why there is something off about such regrets, and in particular, why they make much less sense than their religious analogues. And we now have such an explanation at hand: For most people, in most cases, conditionals with fancy meta-ethical or metaphysical antecedents and moral consequents are junk knowledge; so upon coming to change their minds about the former, they don't really change their minds about the latter (nor should they);[55] so as far as the intelligibility of regret is concerned, nothing has changed.

---

[53] Kramer (2017) makes similar points about the error theory.
Mackie (1977) famously thought otherwise, and in the second half of that book it sure seems as if he's doing normative ethics with the rest of us. But it's not clear how to reconcile all of this with his error theory (it may even give some reason not to read him as a straightforward error theorist).

[54] At least one error theorist is famous for claiming not to believe his own error theory. See Streumer (2017). And see Bedke (2014) for arguments for the conclusion that error theorists tend to retain their first-order moral judgments.

[55] This raises a much wider question (for which we are thankful to Paul Bloomfield): How often should we change (other) beliefs upon coming to believe a fancy new philosophical theory, say, in metaphysics? In the opposite direction, how often should we treat conditionals with a philosophical antecedent and more down-to-earth consequent as junk knowledge? Bloomfield indicated that he thought in many, perhaps most cases of this kind such conditionals are junk knowledge. We agree that this is sometimes the case, but are not sure—and obviously, can't further discuss this—how often this is so.

Think, for instance (as Paul Bloomfield encouraged us to think) of mathematical Platonists, who believe that mathematical discourse is committed to the existence of abstract objects. They accept such conditionals as "If $2 + 3 = 5$, then there are abstract objects," which is logically equivalent to "If abstract objects do not exist, it's not the case that $2 + 3 = 5$." Do they accept this conditional as junk knowledge? If

Actually, it is an interesting—and unobvious—question what to say here of the religious case. The shrimp case, to repeat, is easy: The reasonable thing for an orthodox Jew to think about this is that *if Jewish orthodoxy is false* (perhaps because there is no God), *then there's no obligation to refrain from eating shrimp*. Furthermore, we're sure (and one of us can testify) that for many orthodox Jews this is not a junk-knowledge conditional, nor should it be.[56] So if they come to believe its antecedent, they should be happy to infer its consequent, and then regrets over the lost opportunities for eating shrimp make sense. But how about other cases? Think of an orthodox Jew who is also a Divine Command Theorist of sorts, so she believes that the "source" of all moral obligations is God's commands. She also believes that we (morally) ought not to humiliate people. So she seems committed to the following conditional: "*If God doesn't exist, it's not the case that we ought not to humiliate people*." What will she do if she comes to believe the antecedent? What *should* she do? One possible answer treats this case precisely as it does the shrimp case. But this seems to miss something important: She may very well treat the conditional as junk knowledge, and upon coming to believe its antecedent remain faithful to the denial of its consequent, and come to reject the conditional. As a psychological matter, different religious people (and different Divine Command Theorists) probably differ in their responses to such scenarios. As a normative matter, we think that the junk-knowledge line is the more promising one here (but not, of course, in the shrimp case), but this may be because, well, humiliating people is morally wrong, and eating shrimp (arguably) is not. If this is so, what we get is that it makes sense, for the lapsed orthodox Jew, to regret all the shrimp he could have eaten, and perhaps also all the sex he could have had, but not all the ways he could have acted that would have humiliated others (and similarly for other religious obligations that are also, independently, moral ones). This seems like a plausible result.

Notice that the conditionals from the previous paragraph are particular instances of Hayward's "Ivan's Conditional" from a few pages back. And the discussion here shows, first, that not all instances of Ivan's Conditional are relevantly alike; and second, that such conditionals may play a different inferential role for different people. For some, a specific conditional of this kind may amount to junk knowledge (if, say, they have and acknowledge an independent reason to reject its consequent), and for others this may not be so. If so, it becomes an interesting question to pose to believers—and to theological views, and to Divine Command Theorists—how they view different instances of Ivan's Conditional.

Recall our objection to the explanation in terms of the de-re-de-dicto distinction in Section 2. There, we argued that such a story implausibly classifies regrets over missed opportunities after a local change in moral beliefs ("all the snooker I could have watched!") together with all-the-wrongs-regrets. So it's important to see that the

---

the oracle tells them that there are no abstract objects, will they be disposed to give up the belief that 2 + 3 = 5? We suspect that they won't, and we don't think that they should be. But more may be said here.

[56] This, for instance, is Maimonides's view as presented by Lewinsohn (2016).

problem does not arise for our explanation in this section. After all, even the conscientious thesis advisor may believe the following conditional:

(C4) If giving my graduate students detailed feedback is not morally required, then there's nothing wrong with watching more snooker instead.

And there's no reason to think that (C4), for the conscientious thesis advisor, amounts to junk knowledge. Upon coming to believe its antecedent, he or she can unproblematically infer to its consequent. This is why the regret over those missed snooker hours makes sense.

Let us finish with the following three related observations. First, note that our explanation of the asymmetry in terms of junk knowledge can serve not merely as a response to the challenge for robust realists, but also to gain insight on the relations between first- and second-order moral and religious commitments more generally. In the moral case one's first-order commitments are typically much more resilient than the metaethical ones. Hence, upon realizing that one's metaethical commitments—robust realist or otherwise—cannot stand, one would (and should) retain one's first-order moral commitments, and settle for a less committed metaethics. In the religious case, by contrast, it seems that one's first-order religious commitments are typically much more sensitive to the second-order ones. So upon realizing that God doesn't exist, for example, the religious person would not feel the pressure to retain many of her or his first-order religious commitments, and thus to embrace a less committed view of religious discourse (as not committed, say, to the existence of God after all). Rather, she or he would abandon their first-order religious commitments altogether.

Second, in the religious case, even if one cares about the religious obligations de dicto, this doesn't mean that more de re thoughts (and more de re motivation) are irrelevant. At the very least, they may serve an *epistemic* role. The fact that humiliation is wrong may serve as evidence that God indeed frowns upon such humiliation.[57] And something similar can be said, it seems to us, about moral motivation de re and de dicto, thus showing yet another way in which the two are more closely related than some seem to assume. De re moral thoughts and motivation may play an epistemic role in helping us come up with the right moral theory or moral principles, about which we should care also de dicto.

Third, this last point extends to more purely moral cases as well in a way that takes us back to one of the two kinds of mistake (or change of mind) that we put to one side in Section 1 above. Recall that we distinguished the lapsed moralist (who converted, as it were, to the error theory) from the person who undergoes an intramoral conversion, say from Kantianism to Utilitarianism. As we noted there, our intuitions about the appropriateness of regret are less clear in that case—should the lapsed Kantian now regret all the

---

[57] On some theological views, the *metaphysical* priority goes the other way. But this doesn't preclude an *epistemic* priority as in the text here.

good he could have promoted, if only he had been willing to treat people as mere means, or to ignore the separateness of persons? We still don't have an answer to this question, but we think that our discussion allows us to better understand it. Suppose, for simplicity, that some version of Kantianism and some version of Utilitarianism are the only two moral theories. Our protagonist, while still a Kantian, presumably accepted the following conditional: "If Kantianism is false, there's no specific moral objection to treating people as mere means." Now, she has come to accept this conditional's antecedent. Should she infer its consequent? Or should she now come to reject the conditional, on the combined strength of her evidence for its antecedent and against its conclusion? The question may depend on why it is that she initially found the consequent so implausible. If this was just because its negation followed from her then-believed moral theory, we get one answer. If she found the rejection of the consequent plausible on independent grounds, we get another. Thinking about such conditionals may thus help you better understand the role of moral theory in your own moral commitments.

6. CONCLUSION

This has been long, and the discussion was not entirely linear, so it may be helpful to draw all the threads together.

Our main order of business has been to explain why there's something suspicious about all-the-wrongs-regrets, and in particular, why they are more suspicious then all-the-sins-regrets. After rejecting three possible explanations—one that fully relies on the de-re-de-dicto distinction, one that connects the challenge to the traditional why-be-moral challenge, and one that connects it to the why-care-about-these-non-natural-entities challenge—we presented an explanation that utilizes the idea that the robust realist's commitment to relevant conditionals amounts to seeing them as junk-knowledge.

You may think that this last point (from Section 5) weakens the extent to which Sections 3 and 4 succeed in responding to Dreier's and Dasgupta's challenges. At the end of the day, on the emerging picture, should we or shouldn't we care about morality, robustly realistically understood? We answer in the positive, of course. We should care about morality, often de re, but perhaps also sometimes de dicto. Nothing about robust realism makes these intuitively plausible claims any less available. It's just that—as is evidenced by the junk knowledge line—this commitment often takes priority over our meta*ethical* commitments.[58] This result, it seems to us, is as it should be.

---

[58] Nor does this mean that we shouldn't care about metaethics. Metaethics is interesting, and this may be enough. And metaethics may have, in other contexts, first-order, normative implications that do not constitute junk-knowledge.

References

Aboodi, Ron. 2017. "One Thought Too Few: Where De Dicto Moral Motivation Is Necessary." *Ethical Theory and Moral Practice* 20: 223–237.

Baras, Dan. 2022. *Calling for Explanation*. Oxford: Oxford University Press.

Bedke, Matthew S. 2014. "A Menagerie of Duties? Normative Judgments Are Not Beliefs about Non-Natural Properties." *American Philosophical Quarterly* 51(3): 189–201.

Bedke, Matthew S. 2019. "A Dilemma for Non-Naturalists: Irrationality or Immorality?" *Philosophical Studies* 177: 1027–1042.

Blanchard, Joshua. 2019. "Melis Erdur's Moral Argument against Moral Realism." *Ethical Theory and Moral Practice* 22: 371–377.

Chappell, Richard Yetter. 2019. "Why Care about Non-Natural Reasons." *American Philosophical Quarterly* 5: 125–134.

Dasgupta, Shamik. 2017. "Normative Non-Naturalism and the Problem of Authority." *Proceedings of the Aristotelian Society* 117: 297–319.

Dasgupta, Shamik. 2018. "Realism and the Absence of Value." *Philosophical Review* 127(3): 279–322.

Dreier, Jamie. 2015a. "Can Reason Fundamentalism Answer the Normative Question?" In *Motivational Internalism*, edited by Gunnar Björnsson, Caj Strandberg, Ragnar Francén Olinder, John Eriksson, and Fredrik Björklund, 167–181. Oxford: Oxford University Press.

Dreier, Jamie. 2015b. "Another World: The Metaethics and Metametaethics of Reasons Fundamentalism." In *Passions and Projections: Themes from the Philosophy of Simon Blackburn*, edited by Robert N. Johnston and Michael Smith, 155–171. Oxford: Oxford University Press.

Enoch, David. 2011. *Taking Morality Seriously*. Oxford: Oxford University Press.

Enoch, David. 2019. "How Principles Ground." *Oxford Studies in Metaethics* 14: 1–22.

Enoch, David. 2022. "Thanks, We're Good: Why Moral Realism Is Not Morally Objectionable." *Philosophical Studies* 178: 1689–1699.

Erdur, Melis. 2016. "A Moral Argument against Moral Realism." *Ethical Theory and Moral Practice* 19: 591–602.

FitzPatrick, William J. 2018. "Representing Ethical Reality: A Guide for Worldly Non-Naturalists." *Canadian Journal of Philosophy* 48: 548–568.

Hayward, Max Khan. 2019. "Immoral Realism." *Philosophical Studies* 176: 897–914.

Huemer, Michael 2005. *Ethical Intuitionism*. New York: Palgrave Macmillan.

Johnson King, Zoe. 2020. "Praiseworthy Motivations." *Nous* 54: 408–430.

Kahane, Guy. 2017. "If Nothing Matters." *Nous* 51: 327–353.

Kment, Boris. 2017. "Varieties of Modality." *Stanford Encyclopedia of Philosophy*. https://plato.stanford.edu/entries/modality-varieties/.

Korsgaard, Christine M. 1997. "The Normativity of Instrumental Reason." In *Ethics and Practical Reason*, edited by Garrett Cullity and Berys Gaut, 215–254. Oxford: Oxford University Press.

Kramer, Matthew H. 2009. *Moral Realism as a Moral Doctrine*. Oxford: Wiley-Blackwell.

Kramer, Matthew H. 2017. "There's Nothing Quasi about Quasi-Realism: Moral Realism as a Moral Doctrine." *Journal of Ethics* 21: 185–212.

Lewinsohn, Jed. 2016. "Reasons for Keeping the Commandments: Maimonides and the Motive of Obedience." In *Jewish Philosophy Past and Present*, edited by Daniel Frank and Aaron Segal, 243–255. London; New York: Routledge.

Lewis, David. 1986. *On the Plurality of Worlds*. Blackwell: Oxford.
Lewis, David. 1994. "Humean Supervenience Debugged." *Mind* 103: 473–490.
Mackie, John L. 1977. *Ethics: Inventing Right and Wrong*. Harmondsworth: Penguin Books.
Nowell-Smith, Patrick H. 1954. *Ethics*. Harmondsworth: Penguin Books.
Parfit, Derek. 2011. *On What Matters*. Vols. 1–2. Oxford: Oxford University Press.
Ridge, Michael. 2020. "Reinventing *Ethics: Inventing Right and Wrong*." *Journal of the History of Analytical Philosophy* 8: 1–20.
Shafer-Landau, Russ. 2003. *Moral Realism: A Defense*. Oxford: Oxford University Press.
Sliwa, Paulina. 2016. "Moral Worth and Moral Knowledge." *Philosophy and Phenomenological Research* 93: 393–418.
Smith, Michael. 1994. *The Moral Problem*. Oxford: Blackwell Publishers.
Smith, Michael. 1997. "In Defense of the Moral Problem: A Reply to Brink, Copp, and Sayre-McCord," *Ethics* 108: 84–119.
Sorensen, Roy. 1988. "Dogmatism, Junk Knowledge, and Conditionals." *Philosophical Quarterly* 38: 433–454.
Streumer, Bart. 2017. *Unbelievable Errors: An Error Theory about All Normative Judgements*. Oxford: Oxford University Press.
Svavarsdóttir, Sigrun. 1999. "Moral Cognitivism and Motivation." *Philosophical Review* 108: 161–219.
Szabó Gendler, Tamar. 2000. "The Puzzle of Imaginative Resistance." *Journal of Philosophy* 97: 55–81.
Weinshtock Saadon, Itamar. 2022. "A Dilemma for De Dicto Halakhic Motivation: Why Mitzvot Don't Require Intention." *Journal of Analytic Theology* 10: 76–97.
Wygoda Cohen, Shlomit. 2021. "Mind Independence Versus Mind Nongroundedness: Two Kinds of Objectivism." *Ethics* 132: 180–203.

IV

NEITHER NATURALISM NOR NON-NATURALISM

CHAPTER 21

RESPONSE-DEPENDENT REALISM

MARK LEBAR

WRITERS on metaethics divide over two conceptions of what moral realism comes to. The first of these—what I will refer to as the "Modest" conception—commits to the truth-aptness or "cognitivity" of moral (or more generally normative[1]) judgments. The second—I will refer to this as the "Robust" conception—commits to the mind- or stance- or response-dependence[2] of such judgments. In this chapter I take up the relationship of response-dependent (RD) moral theories to these conceptions of realism. Some proponents of RD views see themselves as opponents of realism. In the case of Modest realism, I shall argue that they are not. But the ways they can respond to the challenges of Robust realism are worth considering. A capably mounted form of RD, responsive to the motivations for Robust as opposed to Modest realism, puts pressure on the resources Robust realism has for resisting response-dependence. If that is right, the theoretical distance between RD views and Robust realist views may be narrower than one might suppose.

My plan is as follows. I begin in §1 with a characterization of Modest and Robust conceptions of realism. In §2 I set out what "response-dependent" views are for present purposes, and how they stand relative to these two conceptions. In §3 I take up the variety of responses that RD views are built upon, and some of the motivations for them. In §4 I consider what this variety offers by way of responses to the challenges posed by Robust realism. I conclude in §5 with the claim that the challenge of response-dependence to Robust realism may not be dismissed easily, and that Robust realists have work to do in explaining just what RD views are missing.

---

[1] Our concern is *moral* realism and irrealism, but moral normativity is not a special case: the issues concern normativity, period. So I will move back and forth between these: various views take the relevant concerns sometimes to be about values, sometimes about reasons, sometimes properties.

[2] Though these are sometimes treated as interchangeable, as will become apparent these are not the same thing. The differences among them bear on what I explore in what follows.

§1. Competing Conceptions of Realism

Two distinct conceptions of the debate between realists and their opponents have been at work in recent decades. The one with earlier provenance focuses on a distinction between views that do, and do not, take moral judgments to lay claim to facts. This I refer to as the Modest conception. Modest realists believe that such judgments do lay such claims, and that some of them succeed. The second focuses primarily on a distinction between views that do, and do not, afford the responses of subjects to moral claims a role in fixing those moral facts. This I refer to as the Robust conception. Robust realists deny such a role to such responses.

One way to understand the motivation for the Modest conception is to look back to Hume, who can be understood as challenging the idea that our moral judgments actually *represent* anything, indeed, that they are operations of reason at all. Famously he argues that "moral distinctions . . . are not the offspring of reason," but the passions (Hume, [1739] 1978, §III.III.i, 458). Why? Because the production of action is not reason's job, and moral judgments concern what we *do*, consequently with how we are motivated to act. Reason's job is to discover truth or falsehood. It can "have an influence on our conduct" only through exciting a passion (459). But passions themselves lack representational content, and are "original facts and realities, compleat in themselves, . . ." (458).

> A passion is an original existence, or, if you will, modification of existence, *and contains not any representative quality,* which renders it a copy of any other existence or modification. (§III,II.iii, 415, emphasis added)

In effect, we have our choice of *either* motivation *or* representation in our attitudes; we do not get both. Now it is not clear that Hume himself cleaved consistently to this sharp division of labor.[3] Still, this reading has inspired at least one form of challenge to moral realism, from Simon Blackburn:

> Hume replaces Plato's rationalistic picture with the view that our courses are set by our passions or concerns. Reason can inform us of the facts of the case, features of the situations in which we have to act. And it can inform us which actions are likely to cause which upshots. But beyond that, it is silent. (Blackburn 1998, 239)

On Blackburn's view, like Hume's, we are "gilding and staining all natural objects with the colors, borrowed from internal sentiment" (Hume, [1777] 1975, 294). We are not *tracking* (or perhaps representing) those colors. The thought that in making moral judgments we track states of the world or report facts is a mistake.

---

[3] Hume interpretation is vexed and contentious. Dale Dorsey, for example, argues that Hume's aesthetics offer, in effect, a strategic retreat, conceding that at least our aesthetic sentiments are tracking qualities in the objects of those sentiments (Dorsey 2018, 582).

Modest realism, then, stands opposed to this picture of moral reality. It asserts that there *is* something which moral judgments attempt to track, and that true ones succeed in doing so. Consider, for example, Geoffrey Sayre McCord's characterization of realism:

> Moral realists are those who think that . . . moral claims do purport to report facts and are true if they get the facts right. Moreover, they hold, at least some moral claims actually are true. (Sayre-McCord 2020)

Michael Smith frames the Modest realist position along similar lines. As Smith has it, moral realists "believe that the sentences we use when we make moral claims . . . are capable of being true or false, and, second, they believe that some such sentences really are true" (Smith 2000, 15). The point for Smith is that the relevant sense of truth and falsehood here is one tracking *truth-aptness*, where that is a matter of belief-formation (successful or not) in response to our engagement with the world, as an upshot of acquiring information about it.[4]

That is not the issue that is of crucial interest to Robust realists. Russ Shafer-Landau focuses on the *objectivity* of moral claims: "Moral realism is the theory that moral judgments enjoy a special sort of objectivity: such judgments, when true, are so independently of what any human being, anywhere, in any circumstance whatever, thinks of them" (Shafer-Landau 2003, 2). The relevant form of independence Shafer-Landau refers to as "stance-independence":

> Realists believe that there are moral truths that obtain independently of any preferred perspective, in the sense that the moral standards that fix the moral facts are not made true by virtue of their ratification from within any given actual or hypothetical perspective. (Shafer-Landau 2003, 15)

The focus on independence from "ratification" allows such a realist to accept as real the facts that are the subject of psychology and other social sciences, even if they are not (obviously) independent of *minds*. In a similar vein, Sharon Street says, "The defining claim of realism about value . . . is that there are at least some evaluative facts or truths that hold independently of all our evaluative attitudes" (Street 2006, 110).[5] Shafer-Landau and Street represent proponents of opposite sides of the Robust realist divide, agreeing

---

[4] In what follows, I assume that Smith aims to capture some sort of truth predicate at work in the claims of realists beyond what "minimalism" (or disquotationalism) about truth would allow; cf. §2 below. I take all parties to the debates rehearsed here to agree on that, though even characterizing what is at stake in that way is challenging.

[5] She adds, in a footnote to this definition: "Realism about value may be understood as the view that there are *mind-independent evaluative* facts or truths. I focus on independence from our *evaluative attitudes* because it is independence from this type of mental state that is the main point of contention between realist and antirealists about value" (2006, 156; original emphasis).

For other characterizations of Robust realism in a similar vein, see Brink 1989, 7; Joyce 2015, §1; Brock and Mares 2014, 2.

nevertheless on what the divide is about: a form of objectivity that is constituted by independence from our perspective and attitudes.

A similar characterization of Robust realism arises from opposition to it by Kantian constructivists. In John Rawls's work, "Kantian constructivism" contrasts with "rational intuitionism" on an ontological point: the intuitionist affirms, and the constructivist denies, that moral reasons are "fixed by a moral order that is prior to and independent of our conception of the person and the social role of morality" (Rawls 1980, 557). Rawls's concern is with a public conception of justice in particular, but the ontological contrast he offers here may more broadly be associated with constructivism in ethics generally.[6] Christine Korsgaard follows him in opposing her conception constructivism to realism:

> By moral realism, I do not mean the view that propositions employing moral concepts may have truth values. That . . . is a point on which realists and constructivists can agree. Moral realism, rather is a view about *why* propositions employing moral concepts may have truth values. (Korsgaard 2003, 100)[7]

Korsgaard's target is a "perceptual model" of moral intuition that she ascribes to realism, and from which she wishes to distance her own view (along with Aristotle's and Kant's).[8] Though the endorsement of perception as an epistemic model, and the emphasis on objectivity as a matter of attitude- or perspective-independence, are not quite the same issue, they align naturally with one another. However, the antiperceptual concern is one driven by Robust realism's opponents, so it is perhaps more appropriate to take the objectivity issue, voiced so consistently by its proponents, as being the more fundamental point for Robust realism.

That is the background. Let us now turn to the idea of response-dependence, which we aspire to locate somewhere relative to these competing taxonomies.

---

[6] We might of course cite Rawls himself as the most famous Kantian constructivist of all, except that he is clear that he is *not* a constructivist about normativity overall, only about the domain of justice (Rawls 1980; Rawls 1993, 104).

[7] In her well-known 1996 work, Korsgaard identifies with a "procedural" realism as opposed to a "substantive" one. It is not obvious how to map that distinction onto the conceptions of realism we are concerned with here.

[8] Similarly, Onora O'Neill distances her version of Kantian constructivism from "metaphysical realism," by which she means the sort that posits moral facts "prior to and independent of" our processes of discovering them. If there are other conceptions of realism, they serve little purpose: "once metaphysical realism is set aside, the use of the term *realism* becomes so promiscuous that I can see little advantage either in laying claim to it or in hoping to refute its appropriation for other positions" (O'Neill 1996, 39). Derek Parfit takes this point even further: he says of "normative realism" that it is "belief in normative truths that are not response-dependent, mind-dependent, or constructivist; often assumed to make positive ontological claims; the word 'realism' not used by me for this reason" (Parfit 2011, 823).

§2. Response-Dependence

Our interest in response-dependence is a matter of understanding moral properties as response-dependent (RD). Response-dependence is often characterized as a quality of *concepts*.[9] One does not grasp the concept of the *nauseating* except that it is, essentially, a concept of a property of substances with physical properties in virtue of which we react to them with nausea. So that concept is of a property, the nature of which we cannot grasp except by way of reference to some response from some responder. Thus, to say that some property is RD is to say that its instantiation is contingent on some response, by some responding subject or subjects. To say that *moral* properties are RD is to say they are contingent upon some response, by some responding moral subject or subjects. The range of RD responses can be quite broad, as can the range of subjects having such responses, so the possible range of moral RD views is quite broad. For example, an ideal observer theory counts as a form of RD insofar as it characterizes *rightness* (say) as constituted by a stipulated reaction of an observer idealized in stipulated ways.[10] Simple subjectivism maintains that moral rightness is somehow contingent on the attitudes of the agent (or subject) under consideration. Kantian constructivism maintains that moral value is ontologically dependent on practical reason exercised by moral agents in a specified way. And so on. Each of these has the structure of an RD view of moral properties.

As I construe the notion of *properties* in RD conceptions, RD views are not *minimalists* about properties. Jamie Dreier formulates property-minimalism this way: the schema

x has the property of being F iff *x* is F

provides all there is to know about F. As he observes, the sort of ontological deflationism at stake in property minimalism, like deflationism about truth, threatens to undermine the distinction between irrealism and realism on the Modest conception (Dreier 2004, 26). RD views resist this sort of deflation and in so doing join the ranks of Modest realists; part of the *point* of Modest realism is to affirm that moral properties are instantiated in some more-than-minimalist sort of way. To do so, one essential task for RD accounts will be to characterize the nature of the responses that are to realize or instantiate these properties in the world.

However, by the same token, part of the *point* of Robust realism is to insist that moral properties are instantiated in some sort of way that is *not* dependent on the responses of

---

[9] See, for example, Pettit 1991.

[10] I am inclined to read Roderick Firth's ideal observer theory (1952, esp. pp. 329, 343) this way, though there is certainly room for dispute on this point. Perhaps a clearer example may be found in Peter Railton's account of the nature of the nonmoral good in Railton 1986 (esp. §III), though Railton characterizes his view as "stark, raving moral realism" (Railton 1986, 165).

agents in the way that RD views insist they are. A time-honored formulation of what is at stake here comes from Plato, who has Socrates challenge Euthyphro as to his understanding of the nature of the property of *piety*. It has something to do with being loved by the gods, Euthyphro is certain, but the question is whether what is pious is pious because it is loved by the gods, or whether it is loved by the gods because it is pious (*Euthyphro*, esp. 10d*ff*). We could translate Socrates' question into our metier: is piety an RD property, in that to be pious *just is* to be the object of a god's attitude of love? Is that property a *product* of the gods' attitudes? Or should we be Robustly realist about piety, taking the love of the gods to be the appropriate attitude toward things possessing the property of piety entirely independently of their attitudes—possessing it *objectively*, as it were? This is a question of the ontological priority of the attitudes and normative properties that are their objects.

The quest for "objectivity," as Robust realists conceive it, is an aspiration to answer that question in a way that gains some sort of distance from the various subjective reactions that human moral agents may have to the world and events in it. So, it seems, RD views will count as Modest forms of realism, but not as Robust forms of realism.

It is striking, however, that this oppositional commitment of Robust realism is framed in as many different ways as it is. Robust realists are averse to dependence of normative properties and facts on *something*, but cannot quite agree on what. So, in addition to response-independence (Enoch 2011, 95; Lenman 2010, 179), we get insistence upon stance-independence (Shafer-Landau 2003, 15), mind-independence (Brink 1989, 14-15; Street 2011, 2016; De Maagt 2019), evidence- and theory-independence (Brink 1989, 7, 16, 31), attitude-independence (Lenman 2010, 179; Street 2012, 2016; Driver 2017, 174), belief-independence (Nagel 1986, 139; Brink 1989, 15), thought-, judgment-, and knowledge-independence (Bloomfield 2001, 14). These forms of independence importantly do not seem to amount to the same thing. What should we make of that fact?

Consider that some RD properties are ontologically unproblematic, as the mundane products of causal interactions in the world. The RD nature of the *nauseating*, for example, should be something Robust realists (and everyone else) can accept, and we can generalize. RD properties can feature in the relationships that nonhuman creatures have with their environments. Consider, for example, the phenomenon of *affordances* in ecological psychology. Affordances are the relations between organisms and features of their environments that meet the organism's needs in ways the organisms are adapted to be able to take advantage of (Chemero 2003). When the weaverbird calibrates its movements in nest-building to the materials and their arrangements available in its environment, those materials have the RD property of suitability for weaverbird nests (Ingold 2000, 359). So not just any response of any subject is problematic for the Robust realist; to narrow the scope of objectionable RD properties we need more focus. *Attitude*-dependence is the term of choice for some Humean opponents of Robust realism, and it isn't the attitudes of the weaverbird that make some materials nest-suitable and some not. So we can provisionally take the responses of concern to Robust realists as "attitudes" in a broad sense: they do not want moral properties to be contingent on our attitudes *about* those properties.

Still, the precise nature of the *objectivity* that Robust realists seek is in important ways elusive. Strikingly, this murkiness also characterizes the nature of the attitudes that RD theorists feature in *their* views, and the nature of those attitudes is crucial to their differentiation from Modest *irrealism*. The attitudes in question, and what sort of objectivity they might be capable of, bear closer scrutiny.

§3. Attitude-Dependent Response-Dependence

Moral response-dependent views maintain, we have said, that the instantiation of moral properties metaphysically depends on the attitudes of some agents. Those views fill a big tent, displaying a wide variety in their characterizations of the attitudes that do the fixing of moral facts. We have views as diverse as simple subjectivism, some forms of ideal observer theory, desire-based dispositional theories, quasi-Aristotelian secondary-quality theories, and various forms of constructivism, just to pick some obvious ones. This diversity is not innocuous. There is controversy among these various views that, on the one hand, is consistent with realism on the Modest realist model, while reflecting, on the other hand, the struggle against Robust realism to be clear about just what sort of response-dependence is objectionable, and why. To bring out the controversy, in this section I survey some of that diversity on this point.

David Lewis's dispositional theory of value is a good place to start. Saying that value is dispositional means, simply, that "values are what we are disposed to value" (Lewis 1989, 113). And since valuing is a favorable attitude, it cannot be belief (Lewis thinks), because there is no guarantee that what we believe is favorable. However, there is no guarantee that what we *desire* will be favorable either (consider the unfortunate addict). So we must rule out the unfortunate who desires to value differently than he actually values. What does this is adverting to second-order desires. Lewis concludes that "valuing is just desiring to desire" (Lewis 1989, 116). On this form of response-dependence, values (and thus moral facts) are brought into being as matters of objects of our *conative* attitudes.

In something of a development of this line of thought, recently there have been several versions of "constructivism" taking their inspiration from Hume. James Lenman offers a version of a "metaethics which is anti-realist in spirit" (Lenman 2010, 178). Though he does not explain exactly what sense he ascribes to "antirealism," he suggests that our moral thought is not constrained by response-independent moral features of the cosmos but by each other—by features of the social world (177). That leaves room for his view to be a version of RD. But this story Lenman wants to tell in a resolutely noncognitivist way—that is, a way that stands in opposition to Modest realism.[11] Passions, he claims,

---

[11] As well, of course, as Robust realism; Lenman 2010, 182. Lenman identifies himself as an expressivist (184); but the language of "constraint" and "structure" fits best with a model involving (nonminimalist) *properties*, as on RD models, as a form of constructivism.

"are what our talk of reasons fundamentally express" (186). By *passions* here, Lenman (like Lewis) is thinking (inter alia) of desires, but rather than just ascending in order as Lewis does, Lenman wants to insist on the *structures* that desires realize. "I inhabit a highly structured desiderative landscape characterized by a considerable degree of patterned stability and commonality. The right sort of structure is no less essential than the desire to get normativity off the ground" (186).

Now, the Modest realist may push back a bit here. The management of structure does seem, after all, to be a function of cognition, not passion. The structure in question is one needed to support inferences; it requires representation, and insofar as it does, it represents a move away from a simple Humean division of attitudinal labor.[12] We will return to this point; for now it suffices to observe that the attitudinal plot has begun to thicken.

It thickens more with Sharon Street's version of Humean constructivism. In her earlier work, Street is at pains to develop an evolutionary challenge to Robust realism (Street 2006). In consequence, she presents her own view as having a kind of evolutionary credibility, and develops it in light of a kind of phylogenetic continuity with evaluative attitudes in other species, chimpanzees for example (Street 2006, 117; see also Street 2008, 241n.). While she holds that valuing involves a "counting in favor of" even in these cases, she says that in the primitive and unreflective, nonlinguistic cases this might involve merely a "motivational 'push' or pull' in the direction of a certain behavior" (Street 2006, 146). Now, it is not clear such a conative state really can instance a "counting in favor of" in the creature that is experiencing it. Without linguistic capacities, the kind of metacognition necessary to "step back" from one's attitudes and think about what might count for and against an overall verdict as to what to do, would not seem to be available.

However, for whatever reason in later work that aspect of her view of valuing attitudes is de-emphasized, in favor of something much more like the "structuring" account provided by Lenman. Now she insists on the *difference* between valuing and mere desiring. Valuing, she says, has a discipline, a "structural complexity," that desiring lacks (Street 2012, 43-4).

This latter move inherits the same sorts of questions Lenman's view faces. Moreover, in Street's case, it is not clear whether she thinks this is continuous with her first pass at identifying value-fixing attitudes, or is a revision of them, or what exactly. So it is uncertain just what attitudes Street thinks values are dependent upon.[13]

---

[12] Lenman resists an earlier argument to this effect by Elijah Millgram, with what success it is not clear.

[13] The same might be said of the appeal, in Dale Dorsey's "perfectionist Humean constructivism," of the details of "humanity's evaluative nature" that are essential to his account (Dorsey 2018, 587–588), and of Julia Driver's appeal to "corrected attitudes" (Driver 2017, 177). Michael Smith investigates some of the complications in RD (or "dispositional") theories that build on desire as the operative attitude—in particular how to understand moral or practical *deliberation* on such an account, in Smith 1989, 2002.

Valerie Tiberius' "wise-judgment constructivism" puts *judgments* front and center as the operative attitude generating all-in practical reasons (Tiberius 2012). However, in later work she picks up the Humean focus on "valuing," providing a clearer—but not simple—conception of what that attitude comes to (Tiberius 2018). "Valuing," she says, "has an affective, a conative, and a cognitive dimension—it involves our emotions, our desires, and our judgement—and values are the objects of these valuing attitudes" (35). At this point in our roster of relevant attitudes, the sharp Humean division of attitudinal labor between representation and motivation is no longer in sight.

Let us move from the Humean end of the spectrum to the Kantian. Onora O'Neill and Christine Korsgaard both represent themselves as Kantian constructivists and—although they do not represent themselves likewise as response-dependence theorists, and even represent themselves as anti-realists, accepting as they do the Robust conception of what realism involves—the point of their projects is that moral facts are fixed by the judgments of moral agents. And in being Kantian, they follow in the train of Kant's clear insistence on representational content in the attitudes that fix moral values: "Rational beings alone have the capacity to act *in accordance with the representation* of laws—that is, according to principles" (Kant [1785] 2005, Ak. 412).[14] In Onora O'Neill's Kantian account, this representational content is reflected (as in the account of Kant himself) in the *maxims*—the subjective principles of action—whose consistency when universalized constitutes the basis for the moral value of the good will (O'Neill 1989, 87). So here the relevant intentional attitudes are something much more like *intentions* than the desires or conations that are focal on the Humean accounts.

In Korsgaard's best-known variant of the Kantian approach, on the other hand, those representations are not so much embedded in attitudes as they are in *identities*: representations of ourselves under descriptions we see as reason-giving (Korsgaard 1996, Lecture 3). It is clearer *that* these identities involve both representation and motivation, and that on Korsgaard's account they fix moral facts—in particular obligation—than it is *how* they do so.

However, Korsgaard also has a later, more carefully worked-out account of "acting on a reason." She suggests that the attitude that fixes normative facts amounts to a "consciousness of the appropriateness of your own motivation," which she takes to be tantamount to the test Kant is thinking of as applicable to our maxims, for suitability as universal laws of nature (Korsgaard 2008, 214). And here she explains that she is trying to split the difference between "empiricist" and "rationalist" ways of thinking about the explanations of action:

> Empiricists tend to think that reasons are provided by our mental states, especially our desires; that the relevant facts concern the desirability of the goals to be achieved through action; and that the relation between reasons and actions is causal.

---

[14] There is some dispute among Kantians whether Kant himself should be thought of as constructivist. Since that obviously cannot be settled here, I assume with his constructivist heirs that there is at least a strong interpretive case for doing so.

> Rationalists tend to think that reasons are provided by the facts in virtue of which the action is good, that these facts need not be limited to the desirability of the goals that are achieved through action, but may concern intrinsic properties of the action itself; and that the action is caused not by the reason, but rather by the agent's response to the reason. To some extent, this essay follows the familiar Kantian strategy of making a case by showing how the debate between rationalists and empiricists leads to an impasse. (Korsgaard 2008, 208 (n1))

Korsgaard's proposal is that the way to avoid the impasse is to focus on the act of judgment in which one takes one's maxim—the taking of certain considerations to count in favor of certain acts and being motivated accordingly—to be good or appropriate.[15] Our taxonomy of relevant attitudinal responses is growing still more complex.

While not operating within a self-identified constructivist framework, Mark Johnston also adverts to judgment in characterizing the relevant responses for moral (or, strictly speaking, value) fact-fixing: "judging something valuable." This focus is one he shares with Tiberius's and Korsgaard's views, but here it is without the Humean or Kantian overtones. Johnston maintains this is a "qualified" or "response-dependent" realist account of value, so he counts his own view as *realism* of the Minimal form in our taxonomy (Johnston 1989, 148). It is response-dependent in that there is no escaping the role of our judgments, in particular the deliverances of "substantive practical reasoning," in realizing the instantiations of value (155).

John McDowell is better known for the argument that value properties are analogous to secondary qualities than for any account of what our responses to those qualities are. McDowell speaks of "value experience" and "virtue" and the like, but not of the specific kinds of attitudes that might underwrite these responses. He is clear that he thinks of these as a form of subjectivity,[16] but he is equally clear that this subjectivity is one (i) thought to be shared, or intersubjective (McDowell 1981, 149), and (ii) to be opposed to the kind of "objectivity" typically thought to obtain with respect to, say, one conception of primary qualities, in contrast to qualities that cannot be conceived of independently of our experience of them (McDowell 1997, 203).[17] In fact, McDowell's most signal contribution to this particular inquiry—that is, what are the responses that fix moral facts—apart from the secondary-quality analogy for which is best known, would be his resistance to the Humean bifurcation that we have increasingly left behind. This is perhaps clearest in "Are Moral Requirements Hypothetical Imperatives?," where he pushes back on the idea that "states of will and cognitive states are distinct existences" (McDowell 1978, 19).

---

[15] Herman's Kantian constructivist account of moral judgment takes a similar line (Herman 1993, ch. 10).

[16] This is true also of David Wiggins's seminal treatments of "subjectivism," by which he means, effectively, response-dependence. See his "Truth, Invention, and the Meaning of Life," and "A Sensible Subjectivism," in Wiggins 1987.

[17] In this sense McDowell's view counts as squarely response-dependent. Cf. LeBar 2013, §IX.2.

The querulous reader may wonder why Simon Blackburn has not reappeared as a member of this round-up. The simple answer is that he has insisted repeatedly that his quasi-realism is not a variety of response dependence.[18] Over the years he has offered a variety of objections to response dependence ((Blackburn 1984, 218; 1993, 9–10, 160, 172–73), but he does concede the central point of this section, that it is difficult to corral response-dependent views into one target of objection, given the array of possible responses to draw upon:

> But of course a response-dependent theorist can introduce other responses: desires or attitudes understood in other ways, or even taken as primitive for the purpose of understanding values. . . . The response-dependence theorist is able to plug in the best available account of the response, in terms of attitudes, dispositions, emotions, or desires. (Blackburn 1998, 108)

Just so. We have seen that RD theorists marshal a wide variety of attitudes to provide response-dependent accounts of moral facts. That profusion suggests, I believe, that RD theorists are tacitly sensitive to the very features of moral judgments that motivate the Robust conception of realism, as opposed to its Modest counterpart. What are these features? And to what degree can RD views hope to explain them?

§4. The Crux of Realism

We have seen that realists contend over what is essential in identifying a domain or discourse as real. Modest realists take the crucial point to be one of something like responsiveness to facts in the world, resisting the Humean insistence that moral judgments are matters of sentiment, "original existences" without relation to anything else. Robust realists accept that commitment in moral judgments, but insist further that the facts to which we respond in true moral judgments are independent of the attitudes of moral subjects. What drives this insistence? Prima facie, there are two candidates, perhaps not always crisply distinguished. One we have already seen to be *objectivity*, the other we can call *categoricality*. Let us consider this latter point before returning to objectivity.

The intuitive idea behind categoricality is that moral requirements apply to us whether we like them or not, independent of (in particular) our desires. The Kantian origin of this thought opposes categorical imperatives to *hypothetical* ones—imperatives that ground the normativity of a demand on their service to something further, in particular some object of inclination or desire (Kant [1785] 2005, Ak pp. 414*ff*). Categorical

---

[18] It is worth noting that Sharon Street has argued that Blackburn's (and for that matter Allan Gibbard's) would-be mind-*in*dependence is an awkward companion for his avowed naturalism; in effect, Blackburn and Gibbard would be better off joining the others in the response-dependence tent (Street 2011, 29).

imperatives necessitate unconditionally, "even in opposition to inclination" (Ak. 416). The thought, then, would be that RD views, in particular if grounded in responses that count in the relevant sense as inclinations, would undermine this categorical nature of moral requirements.

But even for the most "inclination-grounded" RD view we have considered, this is not quite so. To see why, take a thought experiment offered by Sharon Street. We are to imagine an idealized Caligula, who sees himself as having reason to torture others for fun (Street 2010, 371). Street uses this example to argue that the canons for assessing the rightness of Caligula's judgments are confined to Caligula's own "practical point of view." In particular, the sort of universal canons espoused by Kantian constructivists have no place; only consistency among his own attitudes matters for their correctness. Now, suppose we have a fully specified formal structure for the sort of coherence that Street's version of constructivism requires (call it F), and that Caligula's set of desires satisfies F. Now Caligula acquires a new desire which fails to satisfy the requirements of F; it fails to cohere in the way her accounts specifies with the F-satisfying structure. On Street's view, the requirement that Caligula abandon the new desire will be in the relevant way categorical.[19] In no way does it arise from Caligula's desires; in fact, just the opposite.

Although this is a form of categoricality, it will not satisfy the Robust realist in search of a grounding of the categorical nature of moral demands. But neither is it the most that a RD theory can offer in terms of categoricality. Both the Kantian and the Aristotelian forms of constructivism offer more. The Kantian one, obviously, takes the notion of the Categorical Imperative to be central to its notion of duty and moral worth. And while the Aristotelian form gives a central place to desire, any normative purchase desire might have occurs only when regulated by practical reason (cf. LeBar 2013, ch. 4; Korsgaard 1986). Is more required? Perhaps, but not in the abstract: we need an argument for why we need an understanding of the categorical nature of morality that RD accounts cannot provide, and that only a Robust realist account can.

We face a similar situation with objectivity, though here perhaps the intuitive force of the demand is greater. Consider, for a moment, the form of response-dependence we might call Simple Subjectivism. On this view, individual determinations about what is right fix what is right—not generally, let alone universally, but for the person whose determinations they are. It is a challenge to render this position intelligible, but that does not prevent it from being widely espoused by undergraduate students and (sadly) others who should know better. It represents the worst of what can happen once we begin to recognize human attitudes as contributing in some essential way to the making of moral facts.

One notable feature of this view is that on it, it appears impossible to be mistaken about our moral judgments; nor is moral improvement possible. This follows trivially from the fact that the standard of correctness for one's judgments is constituted by

---

[19] This is a version of the point that even the hypothetical imperative applies categorically; cf. Korsgaard 1997.

those very judgments themselves. Whatever else the aspiration for objectivity in moral truthmakers might include, solving that problem is surely among the first. In order for an account to be, plausibly, of moral judgments, there must be a *standard of correctness* for such judgments, independent of them, and to which are in some way responsible, so that the possibilities of error and of improvement are sustained.

Is the problem here *relativism*? We might call it that, but it is an unhelpful label. Consider that, if we accept the supervenience of the normative on the normative, then all normative facts and properties are relative to something.[20] What matters, it would seem, is what that something is. Whatever we take it to be, it must at a minimum allow us to get moral judgments wrong. But beyond that, I think this way of coming at the problem offers little illumination.

Better, perhaps, is to consider the Robust realist's objection to RD theories in their commitment to the "constructive" or "creative" side of the Euthyphronic contrast, as opposed to the "discovery" (as Robust realists have it) of moral facts. Why? One explanation would be that we begin a slide that cannot be stopped until we reach something as critically bankrupt as Simple Subjectivism. The Robust realist's insistence on *objectivity* is a product of the determination to resist this slide.

Most of the response-dependent theorists we have surveyed believe, it is safe to say, that this slide may be arrested, though how far short of Simple Subjectivism may be an open question. I want now to take up the strategies for resisting such a slide—for laying claim to as many benefits as possible of the "objectivity" that Robust realists insist upon—available under the response-dependent umbrella. Doing so will focus on the controversies over the attitudes that, on various RD views, contribute to the establishment of moral facts and properties. But within that survey I also want to bring out the work that is being done—tacitly or explicitly—by a commitment to something very like Modest realism.

Disputes about correctness conditions are common among the various constructivist approaches, so that will be my focus. I believe we can see three broad strategies for providing this form of objectivity in the three camps. Constructivists of a Humean bent focus on formal criteria for correctness; these produce substantive constraints, but only *within* a given practical point of view. Kantian constructivists argue that substantive constraints—constraints that apply universally—follow from or are implied by formal constraints. And Aristotelian constructivists add substantive constraints on correct moral judgments. Let us see how these play out schematically.

The clearest example of the first is Street's Humean constructivism. Some of the first ways she sought to develop this form of constructivism emphasized exactly this feature of the view, that it could offer standards of correctness, but held that these are set by "our own normative judgments" in ways rejected by Robust realism (Street 2008, 207). Though she does not herself use the language of objectivity, or take that up as an issue, it

---

[20] Compare LeBar 2013, §X.5.

is clear that she sees this standard-setting work as at the heart of Robust realist concerns, and meriting address.

I said above that the Humean strategy is to see these standards as fixed formally, and that too is a theme Street emphasizes. What does she have in mind? Recall her hypothetical Caligula. Now, we might think that this Caligula is making a normative mistake: he has no such reasons, and is in error in supposing that he does. This Street denies, because there is no standard of correctness beyond the coherence of Caligula's own attitudes. He might, of course, hold inconsistent attitudes, and be mistaken in that way, but that is the extent of substantive mistake. "Normative truth does not outrun entailments from within the practical point of view," Caligula's in this case being the relevant practical point of view (Street 2008, 207). Entailments within a particular point of view provide a standard of correctness for that point of view, but that is the only standard there is.

Street presents her view in contrast to Kantian constructivist positions. As Street claims, we can think of the Kantian idea here being that there are standards of correctness that are not only formal, but universally substantive, and in fact the substantive standards emerge from proper response to the formal standards (Street, 2010, 369). This idea is reflected in Kant's argument that the Categorical Imperative, in particular the Formula of Universal Law, can be criterial for the moral worth of subjective principles of action, or maxims (Kant [1785] 2005, Ak. pp. 421*ff*). We are to apply a formal standard to these maxims: we see whether they can be willed to be universal law without contradiction. From that formal test, we get substantive results as to the universal requirements of duty and the moral law.[21]

The idea appears in different forms in two important threads in Christine Korsgaard's work. In early work on reasons, Korsgaard defends what she calls "intersubjective" agent-neutral reasons, as against "objective" agent-neutral reasons (of the sort a Robust realist might defend) and "agent-relative" reasons, of the sort (perhaps) that Street has in mind. Here Korsgaard rejects the idea that deontological reasons—say, the reasons Caligula might have for forbearing from torturing others—are merely agent-relative, merely the property (as it were) of Caligula or his victims. Instead, such reasons are by their very nature shared (Korsgaard, 1993, §V). The very formal nature of reasons secures the result that the reasons his victims might have for wanting not to be tortured must be shared by Caligula as well. So from the formal properties of reasons, substantive and universal moral results follow.

A similar effect is produced in her later work, *Sources of Normativity*. Here, instead of formal properties of reasons doing the work, it is the formal nature of agency itself. Our reasons for acting, Korsgaard argues, are grounded in our practical identities: our conceptions of ourselves under which we value ourselves (Korsgaard 1996, 101).[22] And she has two arguments that get us from that point to moral obligation. One is a new version of the argument just rehearsed, that reasons, in virtue of their very nature,

---

[21] Barbara Herman argues that all three formulas of the CI are necessary for these results (Herman 1993, ch. 10).

[22] See Herman 1993, ch. 10 for a similar strategy.

must be shared or "public" (Korsgaard 1996, §4.2). The other is an argument that, for any of our practical identities to succeed in giving us reasons, it must be the case that they are grounded in a deeper moral identity—an identity as a "reflective animal who needs reasons to act and live" (Korsgaard 1996, 121). We must, she argues, set value on that identity, but in doing so all of us are implicitly committed to similarly valuing the identities of others as sharing that same moral identity, or humanity. And thus what they value is reason-giving for us as well. Again, she has argued for universal substantive moral conclusions on the basis of formal properties, of agency and of reasons.

Aristotelian constructivists, among others, are skeptical that these arguments to produce universal substantive standards of correctness in attitudes will succeed. On the other hand, the Humean view of substantive standards is not adequate either. That places Aristotelian constructivists in a dicey spot. An obvious out is to accept substantive constraints as part of an Objective Moral Reality, as it were, and sign on to Robust realism. Whatever other problems such views have, they hold out promise for meeting this challenge, and that is a considerable part of the appeal of Robust realism. But Aristotelian constructivists resist that allure, and want to improve on the meager criterial results that the Humean approach can produce, without hoping to extract substance from form as the Kantian aspires to do. What strategy is left?

My own defense of Aristotelian constructivism meets this challenge by positing two critical normative concepts—eudaimonia (the good human life) and phronesis (practical wisdom)—and supposing that these critical concepts have their content progressively determined in interaction with each other (LeBar 2013).[23] At a first cut, the standard for action is determined by virtue, as on Aristotle's account, and the traits that count as virtues are those that are congruent with living well as the kind of being we are. But the standard in particular cases is as phronesis determines it. There are no facts about either what counts as a good human life or what counts as wisdom apart from the judgments of people with wisdom and the moral virtues. But these judgments are substantive, not formal, and particular, not universal. They are the products of, and vindicated by, wide reflective equilibrium, taking into account any reasons that may be pertinent.[24] This is obviously only a very abbreviated nutshell account of complicated story, but it gives some idea of how it attempts to meet the need for a standard of correctness in moral judgment and action, without appealing to response-independent moral facts, or attempting to extract them from purely formal procedures.

All these forms of response-dependent theory, in other words, afford some sort of standard of correctness for moral judgment. Whether or not any or all are adequate is another question, of course. But one striking result here is that in virtue of this feature, each of these views counts as Modestly realist. We can see each as specifying conditions

---

[23] Though I take my account to be largely Aristotelian in spirit and letter, I do not claim it as an interpretation of Aristotle. For a reading of Aristotle as explicitly constructivist, see Berryman 2019.

[24] The notion of "wide reflective equilibrium" is somewhat indeterminate. What I take to be a sharper model, congruent with the account I give, is of Hegelian "re-cognition," as adumbrated in Brandom 2019, ch. 10.X.

under which something like *rightness* is instantiated in a RD way, and in a way which it is possible to get wrong. In each case our judgments are thought to bear scrutiny as to their fidelity to a standard, varying though the conception of that standard may be. Whether Caligula's judgments are internally coherent is a fact about them, and a normative one as well. Whether Brian's practical identity as a father excludes a form of thoughtless cruelty to his child is another fact. Whether it is practically wise for Susan to give over a promising career as a microbiologist to take up puppetry is another matter about which there is a fact. In each of these cases there is a moral judgment that is at least aspirationally informed not only by everyday, non-normative facts about the world, but by normative facts as well. I take this to be true of most (at least) forms of response-dependent moral theory. Even those (like Street and Korsgaard) who brandish the antirealist label seem to be realists in this sense.

But the very ease of securing this point may energize the doubt that Modest realism is the form of realism that matters. Surely there is something more at stake, whether some other form of objectivity, or some other basis for caring about response-independence. But what?

§5. Conclusion: A Residue of Robustness?

I have argued that at least some forms of RD theory can lay claim to significant elements of moral realism. They can and should lay claim to Modest realism, and at least some versions offer their own take on the requirements of categoricality and objectivity that are the hallmarks of Robust realism. I do not suppose that most Robust realists will be satisfied with these elements as they appear in RD accounts, but then addressing such concerns in the abstract is difficult. To assess where things lie, we need not only a more careful specification of the desiderata the Robust realist demands, but also a more careful rehearsal of available strategies among the varieties of RD accounts to supply them. Both go far beyond what can be done here.

Absent such a specification, there remains the thought that what underlies Robust realism is the sheer insistence on independence from the responses of moral subjects in order to count as real. But without motivation for this insistence, it has little going for it.

Recall that response-dependence is not merely an anthropocentric property. It is germane to our understanding of, e.g., weaverbirds in their environment, and we are not tempted to discount the realism of what is suitable for their nests. If we do not, why qualify the realism of the response-dependent nature of what is suitable for us? As Gideon Rosen has argued, it is an odd notion of objectivity that marks off a special case for the human as opposed to other members of the animal community (Rosen 1994, 293).[25] Having attitudes is what we do naturally, and it is not obvious why they should be

---

[25] I thank Sigrún Svavarsdóttir for pointing me to Rosen's work.

singled out as sources of the unreal. Nor is it clear why, given that in our case (unlike the weaverbirds') the response in question is one of *minds* or more generally *attitudes*, that amounts to a departure from the real. Jerry Fodor has made this point succinctly; he too is puzzled by the suggestion that somehow the upshot of being "constituted of human minds" is supposed to contrast with the real. After arguing that the facts about Tuesdays are real, despite being products of conventions, he observes the following:

> . . . there are many properties that are untendentiously mind-dependent though *not* conventional; *being red* or *being audible* for one kind of example; or *being a convincing argument*, for another kind; or *being an aspirated consonant*, for a third kind; or *being a doorknob*, if I am right about what doorknobs are. . . . Doorknobs are constituted by their effects on our minds, and *our minds are in the world*. Where on earth else could they be? (Fodor 1998, 149)

Similarly, on RD views, moral properties are matters of relations between our minds and their attitudes, and the elements of our natural and social environments, all which are in the world. Where else could they be?

This is not an argument that there are no worthwhile challenges to Fodor's position. My point here is that some such challenge is needed to show why we need Robust realism, given the fact that *some* RD properties are clearly real in even a Robust sense, and *some* RD accounts of moral properties offer explanations of the objectivity and categorically necessitating demands of moral requirements. And they do so without the ontological and epistemological freight that Robust realism must manage. There is a hefty dose of realism to at least some RD theories, and that is something both friends and foes of response-dependence should acknowledge.[26]

REFERENCES

Berryman, Sylvia. 2019. *Aristotle on the Sources of the Ethical Life*. Oxford: Oxford University Press.
Blackburn, Simon. 1984. *Spreading the Word*. Oxford: Oxford University Press.
Blackburn, Simon. 1993. *Essays in Quasi-Realism*. Oxford: Oxford University Press.
Blackburn, Simon. 1998. *Ruling Passions*. Oxford: Oxford University Press.
Bloomfield, Paul. 2001. *Moral Reality*. Oxford: Oxford University Press.
Brandom, Robert. 2019. *A Spirit of Trust*. Cambridge, MA: Harvard University Press.
Brink, David. 1989. *Moral Realism and the Foundation of Ethics*. Cambridge: Cambridge University Press.
Brock, Stuart, and Edwin Mares. 2014. *Realism and Anti-Realism*. Utrecht: Acumen Publishers.
Chemero, Anthony. 2003. "An Outline of a Theory of Affordances." *Ecological Psychology* 15: 181–915.

---

[26] My thanks to Michael Bukoski, Matthew Jernberg, Marc Kaufman, Daehyun Kim, Jacob Koval, and Sigrún Svavarsdóttir for comments on earlier versions of this chapter.

De Maagt, Sem. 2019. "Why Humean constructivists should become Kantian constructivists." *Philosophical Explorations* 22: 280-93.

Dorsey, Dale. 2018. "A Perfectionist Humean Constructivism." *Ethics* 128: 574-602.

Dreier, James. 2004. "Creeping Minimalism." *Philosophical Perspectives* 18: 23-44.

Driver, Julia. 2017. "Contingency and Constructivism." In *Reading Parfit: On What Matters*, edited by Kirchin. Abingdon, UK: Routledge Publishers.

Enoch, David. 2011, *Taking Morality Seriously*. Oxford: Oxford University Press.

Firth, Roderick. 1952. "Ethical Absolutism and the Ideal Observer." *Philosophy and Phenomenological Research* 12: 317-45.

Fodor, Jerry. 1998. *Concepts: Where Cognitive Science Went Wrong*. Oxford: Oxford University Press.

Herman, Barbara. 1993. *The Practice of Moral Judgment*. Cambridge, MA: Harvard University Press.

Hume, David. [1739] 1978. *A Treatise of Human Nature*. Edited by Selbe-Bigge. Oxford: Clarendon Press.

Hume, David. [1777] 1975. *Enquiries concerning Human Understanding and concerning the Principles of Morals*. Edited by P. H. Nidditch. Cambridge, MA: Harvard University Press.

Ingold, Tim. 2000. *The Perception of the Environment*. Abingdon, UK: Routledge Publishers.

Johnston, Mark. 1989. "Dispositional Theories of Value." *Proceedings of the Aristotelian Society*, Suppl. Vol. 63: 139-174.

Joyce, Richard. 2015. "Moral Anti-Realism." In *Stanford Encyclopedia of Philosophy*, revised Winter 2016, edited by Edward N. Zalta. https://plato.stanford.edu/archives/win2016/entries/moral-anti-realism/.

Kant, Immanuel. [1785] 2005. *Groundwork for the Metaphysics of Morals*. Translated by Thomas K. Abbott, edited by Lara Denis. Petersborough, ON: Broadview Press.

Korsgaard, Christine. 1986. "Aristotle on Function and Virtue." *History of Philosophy Quarterly* 3: 259-279.

Korsgaard, Christine. 1993. "The Reasons We Can Share." *Social Philosophy and Policy* 10: 24-51.

Korsgaard, Christine. 1996. *The Sources of Normativity*. Cambridge: Cambridge University Press.

Korsgaard, Christine. 1997. "The Normativity of Instrumental Reason." In *Ethics and Practical Reason*, edited by Garrett Cullity and Beryl Gaut, 215-254. Oxford: Clarendon Press.

Korsgaard, Christine. 2003. "Realism and Constructivism in 20th Century Moral Philosophy." *Philosophy in America at the Turn of the Century*. Charlottesville, VA: Philosophy Documentation Center: 99-122.

Korsgaard, Christine. 2008. "Acting for a Reason." In *The Constitution of Agency*, 207. Oxford: Oxford University Press.

LeBar, Mark. 2013. *The Value of Living Well*. New York: Oxford University Press.

Lenman, James. 2010. "Humean Constructivism in Moral Theory." *Oxford Studies in Metaethics* 5: 175-193.

Lewis, David. 1989. "Dispositional Theories of Value." *Proceedings of the Aristotelian Society*, Supplemental Volume 63: 113-137.

McDowell, John. 1978. "Are Moral Requirements Hypothetical Imperatives?" *Proceedings of the Aristotelian Society*, Suppl. Vol. 52: 13-29.

McDowell, John. 1981. "Non-Cognitivism and Rule-Following." In *Wittgenstein: To Follow a Rule*, edited by Holtzman and Leich, 141-187. Abingdon, UK: Routledge & Kegan Paul.

McDowell, John. 1997. "Values and Secondary Qualities." *Moral Discourse and Practice*, edited by Stephen Darwall, Allan Gibbard, and Peter Railton, 201–213. Oxford: Oxford University Press.

Nagel, Thomas. 1986. *The View from Nowhere*. Oxford: Oxford University Press.

O'Neill, Onora. 1989. *Constructions of Reason*. Cambridge: Cambridge University Press

O'Neill, Onora. 1996. *Towards Justice and virtue*. Cambridge: Cambridge University Press.

Parfit, Derek. 2011. *On What Matters*. Vol. 2. Oxford: Oxford University Press.

Pettit, Philip. 1991. "Realism and Response-Dependence." in *Response-Dependent Concepts*, edited by Peter Menzies, 4–45. Canberra: Australian National University.

Railton, Peter. 1986. "Moral Realism." *Philosophical Review* 95: 163–207.

Rawls, John. 1980. "Kantian Constructivism in Moral Theory." *Journal of Philosophy* 77: 515–572.

Rawls, John. 1993. *Political Liberalism*. New York: Columbia University Press.

Rosen, Gideon. 1994. "Objectivity and Modern Idealism: What Is the Question?" In *Philosophy in Mind*, edited by Michael and O'Leary-Hawthorne, 277–319. Alphen aan der Rijn, Netherlands: Kluwer Publishing.

Sayre-McCord, Geoffrey. 2020." Moral Realism." *The Stanford Encyclopedia of Philosophy*, Winter 2020, Edited by Edward N. Zalta. https://plato.stanford.edu/archives/win2020/entries/moral-realism/.

Shafer-Landau, Russ. *Moral Realism*. Oxford: Oxford University Press.

Smith, Michael. 1989. "Dispositional Theories of Value." *Proceedings of the Aristotelian Society*, Suppl. Vol. 63: 89–111.

Smith, Michael. 2000. "Moral Realism." In *Blackwell Guide to Ethical Theory*, 15–37. Blackwell Publishing.

Smith, Michael. 2002. "Exploring the Implications of the Dispositional Theory of Value." *Philosophical Issues* 12: 329–347.

Street, Sharon. 2006. "A Darwinian Dilemma for Realist Theories of Value." *Philosophical Studies* 127: 109–166.

Street, Sharon. 2008. "Constructivism about Reason." *Oxford Studies in Metaethics* 3: 207–245.

Street, Sharon. 2010. "What Is Constructivism in Ethics and Metaethics?" *Philosophy Compass* 5: 363–384.

Street, Sharon. 2011. "Mind-Independence without the Mystery: Why Quasi-Realists Can't Have It Both Ways." *Oxford Studies in Metaethics* 6: 1–32.

Street, Sharon. 2012. "Coming to Terms with Contingency: Humean Constructivism about Practical Reason." In *Constructivism in Practical Philosophy*, edited by Lenman and Shemmer, 40–59. Oxford: Oxford University Press.

Street, Sharon. 2016. "Objectivity and Truth: You'd Better Rethink It." *Oxford Studies in Metaethics* 11: 293–334.

Tiberius, Valerie. 2012. "Constructivism and Wise Judgment." in *Constructivism in Practical Philosophy*, edited by Lenman and Shemmer, 195–212. Oxford: Oxford University Press.

Tiberius, Valerie. 2018. *Well-Being as Value Fulfillment*. Oxford: Oxford University Press.

Wiggins, David. 1987. *Needs, Values, and Truth*. Oxford: Clarendon Press.

CHAPTER 22

DEFLATIONARY METAETHICS

PAUL HORWICH

Ethics so far as it springs from the desire to say something about the ultimate meaning of life, the absolute good, the absolute valuable, can be no science. What it says does not add to our knowledge in any sense. But it is a document of a tendency in the human mind which I personally cannot help respecting deeply and I would not for my life ridicule it.

Wittgenstein, A Lecture on Ethics (1929)

SYNOPSIS

THIS chapter will sympathetically explore a Wittgenstein-inspired view of _morality_—one that combines recognition of the non-natural character of basic moral concepts (such as OUGHT), the existence of moral facts, and the dim prospects for moral knowledge. This perspective will derive from applying, to ethical (= moral) discourse, his deflationism about TRUTH and FACT, his conception of meaning as "use," his conservative, antitheoretical, "quietist" metaphilosophy, his pragmatist view of language as a useful multipurpose instrument, and his pluralistic appreciation of the variety of functions, types of concept, and norms of belief that this instrument needs to encompass.

I will attempt to show how those commitments support a common-sense metaethics according to which:

(1) We have *absolute* moral beliefs—e.g., most of us hold *that lying is <u>wrong</u>* (and not merely <u>*wrong relative to some moral outlooks but not others*</u>). Such beliefs consist in our acceptance (—our holding true—) of moral sentences, which express moral propositions —also taken to be true. And facts are nothing but true propositions. So we are committed to the existence of absolute moral facts.

(2) The skeptical views of certain philosophers—*that no such facts exist*—couldn't be coherently accepted by anyone who has any genuine moral beliefs,[1] and are based on theoretical assumptions that are easily resisted.
(3) The moral facts can be neither naturalized nor neatly systematized.
(4) There's a tendency for those who are *certain* they *ought* (morally speaking) to do a certain thing, to be *inclined* to do it. And, conversely, there's a tendency for those who feel *repelled* by a certain way of treating people to believe that they *ought no*t to treat people in that way.
(5) The distinctive character of *moral* concepts comes from such facts about them:—that the basic (hence concept-constituting) regularities in our deployment of any such concept include, not merely its usage in relation to other moral concepts, and not only, in addition, the bearing on our use of it of our purely *empirical* commitments, but also in there being a correlation between our simple applications of that concept to something and our having a characteristic positive or negative desire-like attitude toward that thing.
(6) However, a person's states of moral belief are not *reducible* to her possession of such attitudes.
(7) Another fact about their deployment that's constitutive of moral concepts (= of the meanings of moral terms) is that moral principles are taken to apply equally to everyone. So, if a person believes that *s/he* ought to do A in circumstances, C (where C in includes **all** the relevant circumstances) then s/he tends to believes that *any*one ought to do A in C.
(8) And, in addition, it's constitutive of what we mean by "ought" that we accept "S <u>ought</u> to have done A on a given occasion only if it was *possible* for S to do A on that occasion."[2]
(9) Moreover, general principles of logical deduction apply to *moral* propositions, exactly as they do elsewhere.
(10) Moral thinking and discourse (including the having of moral beliefs) is *pragmatically* justified by the benefits of the social coordination and cohesion that it promotes.
(11) And certain moral beliefs can be *morally* justified.—One is morally justified in having a certain *fundamental* moral belief just in case it's true.
(12) Although it may well be *an inexplicable coincidence* for a high proportion of our moral beliefs to be true, that would *not* a be good reason for concluding that they are unlikely to be true, hence *epistemologically* unjustifiable.
(13) Nonetheless, our moral beliefs cannot be *objectively epistemologically* justified.
(14) For that reason, moral knowledge is impossible. But this doesn't matter; for it doesn't really matter which moral beliefs are <u>true</u>. All that really matters is which of them *people actually have*.

---

[1] I'm supposing that to believe merely (e.g.) *that lying is wrong <u>relative to certain <u>moral frameworks but not others</u></u>* is to believe a trivial logical truth that's devoid of moral significance.

[2] I owe this point to David Copp and Paul Bloomfield.

1. Wittgenstein

My aim in this chapter is to devise a plausible metaethics in light of the principal tenets of Wittgenstein's mature philosophy (which are most clearly articulated in his *Philosophical Investigations*). These tenets don't themselves include statements about ethics. And the works in which Wittgenstein *does* engage in metaethical philosophizing are his *Tractatus Logico-Philosophicus* (1921) and his *Lecture on Ethics* (1929), which preceded the development of his mature philosophy. So they are unlikely to have more than a slight bearing on the present project.

More relevant perhaps are the occasional remarks on ethics that he jotted down in his diaries (from which selected entries have been published as *Culture and Value*).[3] But these observations are few and far between, and characteristically cryptic; so don't provide the guidance that's needed.

Rather, the task of identifying a satisfying, later-Wittgensteinian metaethics must begin with an appreciation of the general philosophical (and metaphilosophical) commitments of his *Investigations*—which he himself regarded as his masterwork. We can then try to carve out a plausible collection of metaethical ideas (encompassing language, metaphysics, justification, and knowledge) that cohere with those commitments.

However, I must emphasize that the *primary* aim here is not to identify precisely what Wittgenstein himself really thought about the meanings of ethical terms, the reality of ethical facts, the nature of ethical beliefs, their justification, and the possibility of ethical knowledge. I suspect that we'll never be rationally sure about that. My project is the *hermeneutically less* ambitious one—but *philosophically more* ambitious—of presenting and defending a collection of plausible answers to these questions—answers that *may well* have been his, since they respect his deepest philosophical commitments.

I think we need especially to bear in mind the following three of those broad commitments.

First: Wittgenstein's militantly *antitheoretical metaphilosophy*—according to which philosophizing, if it is to have any distinctive value, can't be *scientistic*. We must beware of the mainstream view that, although *a priori* philosophy is obviously not an empirical science, it should nonetheless be *modeled* on science: first, with respect to its aspirations, which are to discover profound, potentially radical, explanatory theories (of free-will, of consciousness, of morality, etc.); and second with respect to its methodology, whereby theoretical conjectures are to be justified by inference to the best explanation of the relevant data (which—when we're doing philosophy rather than science—will have to be a priori *intuitions* rather than *empirical observations*). This approach to our subject—although standard—has been notorious unsuccessful. Progress

---

[3] *Culture and Value*, revised 2nd edition, Blackwell, 1998. Equally fascinating, yet quite opaque and of doubtful reliability, are the notes of his students, published as *Lectures and Conversations on Aesthetics, Psychology and Religious Belief*, Blackwell, 1966.

in philosophical theorizing is embarrassingly absent And I'd suggest that's because the methodology responsible for spectacular success in the sciences can't work in philosophy. Specifically (and in a nutshell) the strategy of causally explaining the properties of material systems in terms of the properties of their parts and how the those parts are spatially arranged—which is the key to achieving *simplicity*, hence *plausibility*, and hence *progress* in scientific investigations of naturalistic phenomena—is unavailable in the a priori, non-naturalistic domains of philosophy. So, the most important work for philosophers to do is the challenging *therapeutic* job of achieving demystification by exposing and expunging the confused presuppositions in the questions and puzzles that can seem to call for such projects of *a priori* theory-construction.[4]

A second commitment of his that shouldn't be overlooked is Wittgenstein's pragmatic *linguistic pluralism*:—according to which language is a multipurpose instrument, and our overall discourse divides into domains (such as history, chemistry, morality, psychotherapy, aesthetics, the law, religion, etc.) whose functions (i.e., ways of being useful to us) can vary considerably from one area to another—often requiring substantial variations in the norms of belief and assertion that enable those distinctive functions to be performed.

And a third core view of the later Wittgenstein is his *use-conception of meaning*—according to which the *fundamental* kind of meaning possessed by a word-type in a given communal language *isn't* the word's *referent*—i.e., what it stands for "out in the world." Nor is it an image, or any other sort of mental entity, invariably accompanying the word's deployment. Rather it consists in *how the word is used* within the linguistic community—that is, in the *basic use-regularities* (or implicitly followed *basic <u>rules of use</u>*) that govern, and help explain, the word's <u>*overall*</u> use.[5]

I take this third idea to be justified by the following pair of considerations.

---

[4] For details, see my "Wittgenstein's Global Deflationism," in H. Cappelen, T. Szabó Gendler, and J. Hawthorne (eds.), *The Oxford Handbook of Philosophical Methodology*, Oxford University Press, 2016, pp. 130–6.

[5] In PI 43 he writes:

"For a large class of cases—though not for all—in which we employ the word 'meaning' it can be defined thus: the meaning of a word is its use in the language. And the meaning of a name is sometimes explained by pointing to its bearer."

This is standardly read (but mistakenly, I think) as maintaining that only in the case of *some* words, but not *all*, can their meanings be identified with how they are used. But what he's really saying—what coheres much more smoothly with the rest of his book—is that the term, "meaning," is *ambiguous*: that, no matter which particular word, w, is under consideration, only in the case of *some employments of the term "meaning"* can that term be taken to refer to w's use in the language. And, as for his concluding sentence, Wittgenstein is <u>*not*</u> telling us (as suggested by the standard reading of PI 43) that *the class of words whose meanings <u>aren't</u> a matter of how they're used includes <u>names</u>, since their meanings are simply their <u>bearers</u>*. Rather, he's merely observing that in order to help someone to grasp the meaning of a name—i.e., to get across *how to use it*—it is sometimes effective to point at whatever it is that the word names.

(I) When we internally accept (and sometimes proceed to assertively utter) a specific sentence containing the word, w, one of the factors that helps explain *why* we do so is *how we understand that sentence*—which includes *what we mean by its constituent word, w*. Therefore, a hypothesis of the form, <w's meaning is constituted by w's possession of underlying property K>, can be plausible only if w's possession of K contributes to explaining why we accept the w-sentences that we do. And the property most likely to satisfy that condition will itself be a *use*-property:—a basic tendency to accept certain specified sentences containing the word in certain specified circumstances. For example, it's pretty clear that the explanatorily basic (hence meaning-constituting) use of our word "true" is our tendency to accept any instance of "<p> is true if and only if p." And, in the case of "red," it's arguably our tendency to accept "That's red" while looking at red things.

(II) Moreover, this proposal is merely an application of the *general* methodology for determining when a given naturalistic property, N, is constituted by (= reducible to) a certain underlying property, U. The condition for U to constitute N is that the various causal *symptoms* of a thing's possession of N (that is, the observable consequences of possessing it, on the basis of which we attribute that property) are explained by the thing's possession of U. (For example, a reason for concluding that *being a sample of water* is constituted by *being a liquid sample of H_2O molecules* is that this conjecture enables us to explain why water is transparent, has low viscosity, boils at 100 degrees centigrade, etc.). But the symptoms of word w's meaning what it does—the data on the basis of which we judge what a person means by it—are its characteristic ways of being used. More specifically, they are facts of the form, <the sentence "p" (containing word w) was accepted by person S at time t>. And this vindicates the idea that w's meaning what it does is constituted by its *explanatorily basic* use-property (i.e., the one that contributes (along with many other factors) to explaining w's *overall* use.

2. Moral Language: The Meaning of "Ought"

Ethics is a <u>normative</u> domain alongside various others, such as decision theory, epistemology, aesthetics, and everyday appraisals of quality (e.g., "That's a good penknife"). In other words, it's a domain of discourse whose simple categorical utterances are used to *evaluate*, to *proscribe* or *recommend*, to *praise* or *blame*, and to convey *approval* or *disapproval*. And it does these things by means of a characteristic vocabulary, including "ought", "good", "bad", "reason", "right", "wrong", "correct", and "obligation".

Arguably, the term "ought" (in its *subjective* sense[6]) is the most important of these: first, because it's deployed in *every* area of normative discourse; and second, because, although some of the other normative terms (e.g., "good") also enjoy that broad use, "ought" appears to be the *fundamental* one.[7] We might define "x is good" along the lines of "x ought to be admired, or desired, or promoted, or pursued, or brought about." But proposed explicit definitions of the word "ought" strike me as relatively artificial.[8]

It's not even clear which *logical category* is the one to which "ought" belongs. Consider, "Sam ought to visit his mother." One possibility is that the "ought" be regarded as a predicate of propositions. So the logical form of the sentence would be, "<u>*That Sam will visit his mother*</u> ought-to-be." Less contrived perhaps, it's a two-place *relational* predicate. Granted, in that case, the expression, "to visit his mother," would have to be counted as a singular referring term, which at first sight it does not seem to be! Still we might well decide that it really is one—that it refers to the property of acting in a certain specified way (or, more broadly, to the property of *doing* a certain kind of thing). So, perhaps, the logical form of "S ought to φ" is "Ought[S, φ-ing]"—where "S" is replaceable by a name or description of some person or group, and "φ" is replaceable by the specification of some "<u>*doing*</u>," broadly conceived: for example, "visit their mother," "keep their promises," or "have concern for the welfare of others."

A further complication comes from the above-mentioned fact that the same word, "ought", is used in *various* areas of normative discourse. We might on different occasions say, "He ought to keep his promises", "We ought to believe in global warming given our evidence", and "She ought to find a job she'll enjoy". But do we mean the same thing by "ought" in all these cases? Or is the word systematically ambiguous?

The latter view is suggested by the fact that a single action by S might, on the one hand, be *dictated* by the norms of *practical rationality* (in light of S's desires and his beliefs about what will lead to their satisfaction), and yet, on the other hand, be *morally prohibited*. Thus, it would seem that "S ought to φ" always calls for further clarification—that one should always follow the "ought" with either "morally", or "prudentially", or "epistemologically", or .... In other words, the various normative domains of discourse

---

[6] This is the notion of ought that's linked to what one has conscious <u>reason</u> to do, in contrast with the <u>objective</u> "ought" which concerns what it will <u>*in fact*</u> be best to do, regardless of whether one is aware of that being so.

[7] Following A. C. Ewing ("A Suggested Non-Naturalistic Analysis of Good", *Mind*, 48, 1939, 1–22), Allan Gibbard convincingly advocates this position in his *Meaning and Normativity* (2012: 14–5)

[8] Instead of defining "good" in terms of "ought" along the lines just suggested, one might be tempted to go in the opposite direction, and define "S ought to φ" as "For S to φ would be better (= more good) than anything else S could do instead." In which case "good" would be taken to be the fundamental moral term. But although this might be an adequate way of defining the *objective* OUGHT (see footnote 6), it's hard to see how that could be converted into a definition of the *subjective* OUGHT. Alternatively, one might think that "S ought^{sub} to φ" can be defined as "S has reasons to φ that are stronger than S's reasons not to φ." But arguably the relevant notions of REASON and STRONGER are considerably less familiar and considerably more contrived and obscure than the everyday subjective concept of OUGHT. So I'll continue to treat that as the fundamental normative concept.

in which "ought" is deployed do indeed seem to involve somewhat different senses of that word.

And if that's right, we should be able to specify what those different senses (= meanings) are. Of course, one can't hope to identify them by means of a series of <u>explicit definitions</u>; i.e., rearticulation of their meanings in more fundamental terms; i.e., complex expressions for which the "ought"-terms are abbreviations (in the style of "bachelor" means "unmarried man"). But extremely few words—perhaps not even "bachelor" (n.b., the Pope!)—can be defined in this way. So it's only to be expected that in none of its senses will "ought" be one of those few.

But perhaps each sense of "ought" has an *implicit* definition? More specifically, we have learned from Russell, Carnap, Ramsey, and Lewis that the meaning of a theoretical term of physics (e.g., "neutrino") is implicitly fixed by its role within the theory formulation in which the word fundamentally occurs. So can we not suppose, similarly, that what we mean by "ought" in the moral domain is implicitly fixed by the ethical principles to which we subscribe—and that, for each other normative domain, the sense of "ought" deployed in it is engendered the particular normative principles that are accepted there?

No! That's not at all plausible. A decisive objection to this application of the Russell *et al* strategy is that, unlike in science, where there's often a fair degree of consensus on what the correct theory is, there's notoriously widespread and deep disagreement as to how people ought (and ought not) behave with respect to others. So, on the view in question, we'd have to say that there's no <u>English</u> meaning of the moral word, "ought"— and that different English speakers (whose ethical opinions are not the same) thereby mean different things by it. And this is not only implausible in itself, but has the highly counterintuitive implication that the apparent conflict between someone who accepts, for example, "People ought to help others" and someone who accepts "People ought not to help others" is an illusion, deriving from equivocation.

The approach I would advocate (on behalf of Wittgenstein) involves identifying considerably *deeper* and *less idiosyncratic* regularities in how the "ought"-terms are used in different domains—regularities that help explain (in conjunction with features that vary from person to person) why different people end up with the different normative convictions they do; therefore, regularities that deserve to be regarded as meaning-constituting.

To flesh this out, let's begin by considering what the factors are that distinguish the various normative domains from one another. One obviously important factor is *the kind of thing that is assessed*.—A defining feature of the domain of epistemic normativity is that the objects of assessment are *a person's beliefs*. Whereas in the case of moral norms, the primary objects of assessment are *actions*. OK—but <u>the kind of thing that is assessed</u> won't always suffice to identify a domain of normativity. For example, the entities assessed with *prudential* norms are also actions.

So another distinguishing factor is needed.—Specifically, I'd suggest that it's *the kind of consideration regarded as relevant to the assessment*. For example: it's distinctive of *prudential* norms that the circumstances relevant to their assessment of an action are restricted to the agent's desires, $D_1, D_2, \ldots, D_k, \ldots$ (<u>including the strength of each one of</u>

them) and to her degrees of confidence, concerning each of the alternative actions that are open to her : $O_1, O_2, \ldots O_j, \ldots$, and concerning each of the agents desires..., that the action will result in the desire's satisfaction. In other words, the circumstances relevant to prudential assessment are restricted to the agent's desires and to her confidence, for each instance of k and j, that $O_j \rightarrow D_k$. In contrast, it's constitutive of *moral* norms that the circumstances of *primary* relevance to the assessment of an agent's action are restricted to its intended and expected and actual impact *on other people*.[9]

Suppose (optimistically!) that we have managed to distinguish the OUGHT-notion deployed in moral discourse from those deployed in other normative domains. That still leaves the question of what that notion is.—What does "ought" mean when it's used in that sense?

From our Wittgensteinian point of view, that amounts to the question of *how the word is used*. And part of the answer is surely given by the pair of just-mentioned factors which, taken together, are peculiar to moral discourse. But a further determinant of the meaning of "ought" (in its moral sense), is its association with desire-like states. More specifically (but still very roughly) the idea is that each person's moral beliefs are constrained by his/her disinterested desires for how people will act with regard to one another. If someone is sickened at a certain way of treating others s/he will tend to believe that this way of treating others is wrong, bad, and ought not be practiced. And if s/he is made disinterestedly happy by certain ways of acting toward others, s/he will tend to believe that those actions ought to be performed (and are morally right and good). Thus a person's strong feelings—strong likes and dislikes—are expressions of (i.e., manifestations of) his basic moral convictions (aka "ethical intuitions"). In other words, a fundamental (hence meaning constituting) regularity in our use of the *moral* "ought-to-be-done" is that simple predication of it to things tend to be accepted by a people as a direct causal consequence of their disinterested desire for it to be done.

Given such a basis of 'intuitive' convictions, a person will typically arrive at further moral beliefs, either by abductive reasoning from them, or by bringing to bear empirical beliefs, or both. For example, if one has the desire-engendered intuitions: (i) that, given the opportunity to save six threatened people by sacrificing two that aren't threatened, one should take it, and (ii) that given the opportunity to save three threatened people by sacrificing one that isn't threatened, one should take it; and similarly for lots of other cases where the number of threatened people is greater than the number that would have to be sacrificed to save them, then one will tend to believe the natural generalization, and proceed to deduce further instances of it. And, given the *empirical* belief that performing a certain action will in fact bring it about that one will be sacrificing two people and thereby saving five threatened people, one will come to belief that one ought to perform that action.

---

[9] I say "*primary* relevance" in order to allow (i) that an agent's <u>own</u> desires and well-being are sometimes relevant to *moral* assessments of what he does; and (ii) that the action's impact on <u>*non*</u>-human <u>animals</u> can also be relevant sometimes.

In sum, I'm suggesting on behalf of Wittgenstein that the meaning of the moral "ought" is partly constituted by the tendency of those who are *certain* they *ought* do a certain thing, to be *inclined* to do it: and conversely, by the tendency of those who feel repelled by a certain way of treating people, to believe that they *ought not* to treat people in that way. And, more generally, the distinctive meanings of *moral* terms (= the distinctive characters of moral concepts) come, in part, from such facts about them:—that the explanatorily basic (hence concept-constituting) regularities in our deployment of any such concept include, not merely its usage in relation to other moral concepts, and its usage in relation to purely empirical commitments, but also in there being a correlation between our simply applying that concept to something and our having a characteristic positive or negative desire-like attitude toward that thing.

A further use-fact that's constitutive of moral concepts is that moral principles are taken to apply equally to *everyone*. So that if a person believes that <u>s/he</u> ought to do A in circumstances, C (where C includes **all** the relevant circumstances) then s/he tends to believe that *anyone* ought to do A in C. And, in addition, it's constitutive of what we mean by "ought" that we accept "S *ought* to have done A on a given occasion only if it was *possible* for S to do A on that occasion."

The position that I've just sketched has obvious affinities with the notorious *logical positivist* view, "emotivism," according to which a person's moral pronouncements—despite their syntactic form (which suggests that they are categorical, proposition-expressing, assertive sentences)—are really nothing but outbursts of feeling; and so it's a mistake think naively that there any moral propositions, moral beliefs, moral inferences, moral truths, moral falsehoods, or moral facts!

But my Wittgensteinian-inspired picture is much less revisionary than emotivism, hence considerably more plausible. It does retain the positivists' insight that the most distinctive feature of moral terms is their association (in certain contexts) with desire-like attitudes. But it shows how this idea can perfectly well be reconciled with obvious common sense regarding the existence of moral beliefs, propositions, deductions, truths, and facts[10]

---

[10] The well-known attempts by Simon Blackburn. Allan Gibbard, and others to develop improved versions of emotivism were aimed, in the first instance, to rescue that perspective from Peter Geach's observation (in "Ascriptivism," *Philosophical Review* 69, 1960, pp. 221–5) that normative terms often appear in contexts where they **don't** express feelings. (For example: "If Jane ought not to tell lies, she ought not to get her little brother to tell lies"). The Blackburn/Gibbard responses—known as forms of "expressivism"—were to try (each in his own way) to devise a compositional theory that would assign, to every sentence containing any moral terms, the complex desire-like state that would be expressed by accepting it. (For example, Blackburn's proposal for Geach's above-mentioned example was that it expresses *disapproval of the combination of approval of Jane telling lies with disapproval of Jane getting her little brother to lie.*).

And this was wonderfully ingenious, but clearly problematic. For in the first place, it was (and is) not at all obvious that a Blackburn-style account can be devised that really will cover *every* sentential construction involving "ought"—that will cover, not merely those complex "ought"-sentences that issue from the classical logical operators ("or," "not," etc.), but also, for example, constructions involving counterfactual implication, belief attributions, conditional probability, etc. And, in the second place,

3. Metaphysics: The Existence of Moral Facts

So let's turn now to the questions of whether there really are any absolute ethical facts, and if so, what their underlying nature might be.

I have been arguing against the *emotivist* objection to their existence: namely, that there aren't any absolute ethical beliefs or propositions—hence no ethical truths or facts. But it's a further question whether, even assuming that such beliefs and propositions *do* exist, any of them are true.[11]

So let me first assess the main reasons that have been given for concluding that *none* of them could be true, and then go on to consider whether there are positive reasons for concluding that, on the contrary, some of them *are* true.

One fairly popular line of thought that's skeptical of ethical facts goes as follows: (i) Such facts couldn't have causal consequences—although S's *believing* she ought to φ might well cause things (including her act of φ-ing), the normative fact itself (*that S ought to φ*) can have no such consequences. (ii) But in that case such facts would not be

---

Blackburn's improvement remained implausibly skeptical. Surely we have *real* ethical *beliefs* (and not merely the desire-like states, which he was pleased to call "quasi-beliefs"). Surely there are genuine ethical propositions. Surely some of them are *true*. So surely there are ethical facts.

Allan Gibbard's attempt (in his *Wise Choices, Apt Feelings*, Harvard University Press, 1990, and in his *Thinking How to Live*, Harvard University Press, 2008) at a better version of emotivism resembled Blackburn's. But there were some significant differences between them. First, unlike Blackburn, who held that "ought"-sentences don't express beliefs but merely express more-or-less complex *conative* states, Gibbard *identified* genuine moral believings with such conative states. So he didn't deny that we really have moral beliefs. Nor did he deny that these are genuinely true or false:—trivially, the belief *that S ought to φ* is true if and only if S ought to φ. For these reasons Gibbard's metaethics could seem to be less revisionary than Blackburn's, hence more palatable. However, the price to be paid for retaining moral *belief* (as opposed to Blackburn's moral *quasi-belief*) was to accept that these so-called "genuine beliefs" are in fact complex desire-like states! And this was and is rather hard to swallow. Not only does it seem obvious that *believing* and *desiring* are very different propositional attitudes. But we'd have to abandon the compelling Fodorian idea that, quite generally, believing *that p* is simply a matter of internally accepting a sentence whose meaning is *that p*. In addition, of course, the difficulties of devising a systematic theory that will determine for each OUGHT-belief which conative state it's to be identified with, is no less severe—indeed are just as likely to be insuperable—as those that confronted Blackburn's parallel theoretical project.

For their more recent work in this area—which goes to some extent in the direction of the neo-Wittgensteinian perspective that's developed here—see, for example, Blackburn's "Truth, Beauty and Goodness," (in Russ Shafer-Landau (ed.), *Oxford Studies in Metaethics, Volume 5*, Oxford University Press, 2010) and Gibbard's *How Much Realism? Evolved Thinkers and Normative Concepts*. (in Russ Shafer-Landau (ed.), *Oxford Studies in Metaethics, Volume 6*, Oxford University Press, 2011).

[11] Anyone who believes the moral proposition *that p* is committed to <p> being true and—since facts are simply true propositions—committed to the existence of moral truths, hence to moral facts. But this doesn't provide the slightest reason to think that such commitments are *correct*, i.e., that such truths (= facts) *do* exist.

naturalistic. (iii) However, alleged non-natural phenomena are surely too *weird* to exist. (iv) Therefore, there are no absolute ethical facts.

I myself am happy to concede the first and second steps of this argument. But—following Wittgenstein—I'd say that the third step is a dangerous scientific overgeneralization. Obviously, lots of things *are* naturalistic. But quite a few are not: for example, numbers, values, and unactualized possibilities. And these things may well be described as "unusual" (each in its own way). But to apply the words "spooky" or "weird" or "bizarre" to them—thereby assimilating them to conceivable naturalistic phenomena such as ghosts, witches, and goblins in the garden: phenomena for whose nonexistence we have overwhelming empirical evidence—is simply irrational. We should recognize that our languages, plus the worldly things to which our terms refer, are vastly more complex and varied than can be captured by the simplistic theories that the prevailing scientific methodology of philosophy pushes us toward accepting.

A second source of suspicion about absolute ethical OUGHT-facts derives from another respect in which they would be unusual. As we have observed, a person's *becoming convinced that she ought to* ϕ tends to be highly correlated with her *being inclined to* ϕ. So the worry is this.—How could there be such a fact—a fact which is such that your becoming aware of it would tend to coincide with your having an inclination to ϕ?[12]

Well I've already suggested that the highly unusual character of an alleged component of reality doesn't imply that its existence would be weird or spooky, and shouldn't be considered the slightest reason for thinking that its existence is unlikely. But a further response worth making is that the supposedly *bizarre* feature of ethical facts trivially derives from the intrinsic motivational nature of ethical *belief*. So anyone persuaded by Mackie's argument against ethical facts might equally well have argued that there can be no ethical *propositions*. For any such proposition would have to possess the "bizarre" feature that believing it would automatically goes hand-in-hand with a *desire*. And isn't that unheard of?! So surely there can be no such propositions; hence, no such true propositions; hence no such facts.

Against this way of putting the skeptical argument, we can observe, not only that this feature (which distinguishes *ethical* believings from others) gives no reason to doubt their existence, but—more strongly—that we have excellent reason to think that there *are* such beliefs (despite their unusual characteristics). And we have been given no decent reason for thinking that none of the propositions believed could be true. Therefore, since we can and should identify facts with true propositions, we have been given no reason to think that there are no ethical facts.

But we should consider a third influential basis for skepticism about such facts:—the objection that ethical opinions vary widely and sharply from one culture to another, and even within cultures, from one person to another. And these disagreements very often appear to be irresolvable. There would seem to be no methodology (as there is science,

---

[12] See John Mackie's *Ethics: Inventing Right and Wrong*, New York, Viking Press, 1977.

for example) providing a way of objectively adjudicating between conflicting opinions. In a nutshell: ethical claims can't be verified.

Again, I can see nothing wrong with this argument, *as far as it goes*. What's wrong is the next step—the move from "not verifiable" to "not true." Granted, that step was embraced by the logical positivists. They claimed, even more extremely, that unverifiable claims are <u>meaningless</u>. But that perspective has rightly fallen out of favor. The view that truth is some sort of epistemological property—perhaps, "what nearly everyone believes," or "what will be believed in the limit of inquiry," or "what would be the conclusion of a perfectly rational investigation"—is subject to compelling counterexamples. And this is because an uncontroversial constraint on any decent analysis of truth—whether or not it's given in epistemological terms—is that it cohere with the equivalence schema, "<p> is true ↔ p". Indeed, it's assumed by Wittgenstein, and by many contemporary deflationists, that our understanding of "true" consists in nothing more than our disposition to accept any instance of that schema—and <u>not</u> in our endorsing any of the traditionally proposed explicit definitions. And there's nothing in the equivalence schema to suggest that an unverifiable proposition cannot be true.[13]

A fourth argument against accepting the existence of moral facts—one based on Occam's Razor—has more recently been pressed by Jonas Olson.[14] He would shave off from our ontology anything that doesn't earn its keep by providing explanations of phenomena that couldn't otherwise be explained. And, he supposes (with considerable plausibility) that nothing requiring explanation is best explained by the postulation of moral facts. So we shouldn't believe that any such facts exist.

The trouble with this argument is its reliance upon a gratuitously *inflated* version of Occam's Razor—one according to which, *no matter what sort of entity is at issue*, entities of that sort should not be believed to exist unless their existence is needed in good explanations (or is logically presupposed by them). But this doctrine is implausible for a couple of reasons. In the first place, although "inference-to-the-best-explanation" may well be an impeccable form of reasoning within <u>naturalistic</u> domains (e.g., physics, psychology, and history)—these being domains of discourse that essentially involve the giving of explanations—it's not at all compelling when extended to domains that refer, for example, to imaginary numbers, or that refer to un-actualized possibilities, or that contain 1st person sensation reports, or that invoke basic moral intuitions and facts. On the contrary, such extensions appear to be yet further illustrations of the tendency of

---

[13] Gilbert Harman argues (in his *Moral Relativism*, 1996) that the pervasiveness and intractability of disagreement over moral matters would be explained by the *nonexistence* of absolute ethical facts, but not by their *existence*—so we can reasonably reach the antiabsolutist conclusion via *inference to the best explanation*. But it's hard to see how sociological, naturalistic facts about the frequency (and the common irresolubility) of ethical disagreement could be causal consequences of either the existence, or the nonexistence, of absolute ethical facts—since the truth of neither of these philosophical theories could bring about *any* naturalistic phenomena at all. What <u>would</u> appear to be needed in order to help explain the phenomena of moral disagreement is that nearly everyone be *committed* (rightly or wrongly) to absolute ethical facts!

[14] Jonas Olson, *Debunking Moral Belief*, Oxford University Press, 2014 (pp. 142–8).

scientistic philosophy to insistently overgeneralize (which Wittgenstein deplored for being the root-cause of philosophical confusion and paradox).

And in the second place, Olson's beefed up version of Occam's Razor leads quickly to incoherence. For if our commitment to the existence of things of type F is justified by its enabling us to explain phenomena of type G, it would presumably have to be the case that we're *already* justified in maintaining the *existence* of the G-phenomena. But if that justification can be achieved only via inference-to-the-best-explanation, there would have to be some third phenomenon, H, whose existence is explained by G. But then what about H, ... and so on?! We're confronted by a vicious regress! And the obvious escape from it is to admit that there are things in whose existence we legitimately believe, but *not* via inference to the best explanation.—For example: that I'm having a headache, that i = the square root of minus 1, and that it's logically possible for our sun to have had fifteen planets. So why not: *that torturing children for fun is wrong*?

Even if, as I've been insinuating, the philosophical literature to date contains no compelling demonstration that OUGHT-facts don't exist, a skeptic can reply that the burden of proof in borne by those who maintain that some such facts *do* exist. So something of a reason for believing that they don't exist is provided merely by the absence of any reason to think that they do.

In fact, it's far from clear that in a dispute between S, who believes that there *are* things that exemplify a certain property, and T who believes that there *aren't* any such things, the burden of proof is invariably with S. (Suppose the property is that of *being a chair*). But let us grant this dubious assumption for the sake of argument, and consider what might be said in favor of the existence of OUGHT-facts. After all, the obvious alternative (and more plausible) "burden of proof" position is to suppose that each of the disagreeing parties is epistemically obliged to provide some reason for taking the view s/he does. And, in that case, those of us who do have moral beliefs (and thereby countenance moral facts) really should do more to support our position than merely criticizing the arguments of those who have been led to divest themselves of moral convictions.

Here's a *superficially* plausible attempt to do more. Consider a dispute between S, who believes that torture is always morally impermissible, and T, who denies this, believing that it's occasionally permissible. Surely one of them must be right. So either the proposition that S believes is true (and is therefore a fact) or the proposition that T believes is true (and is therefore as a fact). So, one way or the other, there's an ethical fact. And parallel arguments show that there are *many* ethical facts.

What's wrong with this reasoning is that, although S's belief and T's belief are incompatible with one another, it doesn't follow that one of them must be true. They might both be untrue (as in the case of "Superman can fly" and "Superman cannot fly"). And that will be so if, just as there's no Superman, there are no absolute moral facts. For, in that case, nothing is permissible, and nothing impermissible either.

A better response to the demand for some reason to think that there do exist moral facts—or so it seems to me—derives from the pragmatic entitlement each of us has to participate in moral discourse.

Moral discourse—including moral assertion, moral disagreement, and moral debate—has considerable utility within a community. That's why no society does without it. So the existence of moral discourse is pragmatically justified. But moral discourse requires that there be people with moral beliefs. So the advisability of moral discourse entails the legitimacy of our maintaining that certain moral propositions are true; hence the legitimacy of recognizing the existence of moral facts.

As indicated before, I myself am not persuaded that in the dispute between those who do and those who don't countenance moral facts, the burden of proof is with the former. Nor am I fully convinced by the alternative position: that it's incumbent on each side to give some reason in favor of adopting its opinion. For one might well think, on the contrary (with Neurath, Wittgenstein, and Quine), that, in issues of belief-justification, there's a powerful norm of *conservatism* such that only those people who would advocate a revision of what's almost universally accepted need provide a reason for the change. But I've tried to suggest that even if this conservativeness-norm is *not* part of our epistemic practice, there is something positive to be said in favor of believing in the existence of moral facts.

Okay. But it remains for me to substantiate what I have so far merely asserted: that moral discourse has considerable pragmatic value. Of course, the mere fact that all societies engage in it is itself evidence in favor of that view. But this observation should and can be fortified by a plausible specification of what the function *is* of moral discourse, and of how societies and their members benefit from its existence.

I would suggest that (unsurprisingly) the answer to this question goes hand-in-hand with what I've proposed concerning the *meaning* of moral terms, including "ought":— that our understanding of these terms is constituted (in part) by the fact that our epistemologically basic moral beliefs are determined by (and express) our desires.

It seems to me that the function (utility) of moral concepts—which derives of course from the function (utility) of deploying words in accordance with regularities of use that constitute their expressing those concepts—is twofold. In the first place, a person's *desires* regarding how people or groups will treat others, will be much easier to keep under rational control when organized via the moral beliefs with which those desires are correlated—since believed propositions can be constrained and adjusted in light of familiar logical and epistemological principles. And in the second, place, social cohesion depends upon shared desires, so we can expect mechanisms for such coordination to have been developed. Moreover, beliefs are *contagious*, in that we have a natural tendency to believe what we are told. Putting these things together, we can see why it's good for there to be a form of belief that's linked to desire. "You ought not to hit your sister," in purporting to characterize a *fact*, carries a certain authority and so is much more effective than, "I'd prefer you not to hit your sister."

Anyway, given that moral discourse is pragmatically valuable (perhaps for the just-mentioned reasons), we should continue to engage in it, therefore continue to have moral beliefs, therefore continue to regard certain propositions as true, and therefore continue to maintain that certain moral facts exist. So, even if the burden of proof *does* rest on those who countenance absolute ethical facts, we can supply some sort of justification for that position.

Granted, this has a whiff of sophistry about it—perhaps more than a whiff! For, when the issue is what to *believe*, the normal demand is for a justification that's *epistemological*, not *pragmatic*. But it's perfectly plausible that, in fact, the burden of proof is with the skeptics who advocate an extremely radical revision of the common sense view—almost universally accepted, hence (arguably) <u>*default epistemologically justified*</u>—that, despite all the disagreements, and the difficulty of ascertaining who has latched onto the moral truth, still, there surely does exist at least one case of a subject, S, an action, ϕ, and a circumstance, C, such that, *given C, S ought to* ϕ. And if S ought to ϕ in C, then it's a fact <u>*that S ought to ϕ in C*</u>.

3. Epistemology: The Prospects for Moral Knowledge

This naturally brings us to the *epistemological* questions provoked by <u>*specific*</u> ethical judgments.—Not the general issue, just discussed, of whether it's reasonable to think there are any ethical facts at all; but rather, questions that concern particular ethical opinions about how one should and shouldn't behave, morally speaking, given the details of one's circumstances. Can a person's particular ethical convictions be justified? If so, how? And do some such beliefs amount to ethical knowledge?

To begin with, it's pretty clear that no belief of the form, <S ought to ϕ>, can be justified solely on the basis of *empirical data*. Certainly, *some* evidence of that sort may *sometimes* be needed. For an ethical belief may have been acquired via deduction from another ethical belief in conjunction with an obviously *empirical belief*. For example, someone might arrive at her belief *that Tom ought to help his neighbor* by inferring it from her ethical belief *that people ought to do what they promised to do* and her empirical belief *that Tom promised to help his neighbor*. But empirical evidence by itself can never be enough by itself, and will often be irrelevant.

So, what other sources of justification might be available? One tempting and widely accepted view (—one that I've already endorsed—) is that each of us has *ethical intuitions*.—We have attitudes of repugnance or admiration toward different ways in which people sometimes conduct themselves with respect to others. And such positive or negative feelings go hand-in-hand with ethical beliefs—as sketched in Section 2 above. Those beliefs have something like the status of observational beliefs of science.— They qualify as fundamentally justified, and can serve as justifiers (or alternatively as *disconfirmers*) for more general and theoretical moral views (e.g., that one's choices ought to be aimed solely at maximizing the world's happiness).

But a glaring objection to this science-like picture of ethics is that, whereas different people in similar circumstances tend to agree on, for example, whether a certain liquid is red, on whether the needle on the dial of an instrument is pointing at "2," etc.—thus observed data provide a shared objective basis with which scientists confirm or disconfirm more general and more theoretical conjectures—that is notoriously *not* the case when it comes to basic ethical intuitions. From one society to another—and even from one individual person to another within the same society—we find substantial disagreement, and no neutral methodology for determining whose intuitions are correct. And, since it's not surprising that desires concerning how to treat others will vary considerably from one person to another, then—given the fairly tight connection between a person's desires of that kind and his moral beliefs—the latter variation should also be quite unsurprising.

Of course, we might conceivably decide to bite the bullet and maintain, nonetheless, that all the disagreeing parties are justified in their conflicting beliefs—just as long as each beliefs of each person is either one of his basic intuitions or else inferred by good abductive reasoning from his intuitions. But we may well be left with the uncomfortable feeling that such so-called justifications are too easy to acquire and aren't worth very much. It would seem to be a major defect of the methodology-of-justification under present consideration that it isn't strong enough to settle most of the most important ethical disagreements.

Perhaps we can articulate the upshot of these considerations as follows.—The ethical beliefs of an individual can be *subjectively* justified, insofar as they cohere with one another and with his or her conative states (in the context of his nonethical beliefs). But the individual's ethical beliefs cannot be *objectively* justified. In contrast with science, one cannot speak *impersonally* of what *should* be believed. There's no such thing as data that any properly placed person would acquire. So there's no such thing as the body of ethical principles that are objectively rationalized by the data. Nor is there any such thing as an ethical *expert* from whose testimony the rest of us can acquire justified ethical views about what people ought (or ought not) to do to others.

A final idea worth considering about how a moral belief might be justified derives from the recognition that when we are convinced that a certain sort of behavior is morally appalling, and if that conviction does not at all rest on any *empirical* assumptions, then we tend also to be inclined to think that failing to appreciate the appalling character of that behavior is also morally appalling. So it would seem that if, independently of any empirical facts, S ought to φ in circumstances C, then S ought to *believe* that S ought to φ in C—where the OUGHT deployed here must be the *moral* OUGHT. In other words, we can say that one is morally obliged to believe all the *fundamental* moral truths (i.e., all the moral truths that are not dependent on empirical truths).[15]

I've been suggesting that moral belief might conceivably be assessed by means of three different brands of OUGHT. In the first place, our engaging in moral discourse—which

---

[15] David Copp observes that if we knew that terrible consequences would issue from believing Utilitarianism, then—contrary to my claim—if this fundamental moral theory is true, we would *not* be justified in believing it. On the contrary, we'd be *prohibited* from believing it. A very nice point!!! But my inclination is to regard it as one more nail in the coffin of Utilitarianism.

inevitably involves having moral beliefs—is *pragmatically* justified. Second, specific moral beliefs of specific people at specific times may be epistemically justified (but merely *subjectively*—and not *objectively*, as is fairly normal in science). And third, a moral belief is *morally* justified if it's a fundamental moral truth.

But how do these results, if correct, bear on the prospects for moral <u>knowledge</u>? For the sake of simplicity, let's ignore Gettier considerations, and assume that (to a first approximation) knowledge is simply *justified, true belief.* Having argued that we should not buy into the emotivist thesis that there aren't any moral beliefs. And having also argued that, if we are to adopt the radically revisionary view that no such belief is true, we'd need to do so on the basis of very good reasons (which in fact we don't possess)—it remains to settle which of the three brands of justification is the one needed for moral knowledge, and whether justifications of the needed sort can ever be obtained.

To begin with, how about *moral* justification? Would we take a person to possess moral knowledge if (i) she *believes* that a given thing is morally required, and (ii) it's a *fundamental* ethical *truth* that the thing is morally required, so (iii) she's *morally justified* in thinking it is? I'd say no. For as we've seen, S's *moral* justification would trivially derive from the fundamental truth of her belief. So the sufficient condition for S's knowledge would turn out to be nothing more than her belief's being fundamentally true. But we surely need a way of <u>*finding out*</u> what's true in this area. And all we have to go on is that S believes it is (when lots of people don't!). And that seems too little. We would say that it's S who knows, rather than his opponent, only if we can be satisfied that S has arrived at his opinion via some reliable method.

Turning to epistemological justification: since, in other domains of discourse, this kind of support is what's taken to be required, it's natural to think that the same goes for ethics. But, if this is right, I think we have to conclude that moral knowledge is impossible, since it would presumably be the *objective* form of epistemic justification that we'd need. But that's the form we can't get!

So how about pragmatic justification? On the face of it—and as already suggested—that won't do. On the face of it, any consideration of the beneficial effects that are likely to derive from believing a certain thing are irrelevant to the thing's plausibility, and so are irrelevant to the question of whether the thing, even if true, is *known* to be true. A notorious illustration of this is Pascal's Wager—his idea that everyone ought to believe in God in order to avoid the eternal damnation that would be the fate—if God exists—of anyone who doesn't believe He does (and given that one loses next to nothing by believing He exists, even if He doesn't).

But I say, "on the face of it," since it might be argued that although the norm requiring *that beliefs not be merely <u>pragmatically</u> advantageous* surely applies in science and in other naturalistic domains, it does not so obviously apply in other kinds of domain—including ethics. Moreover, I've already argued that there's a *pragmatic* rationale for the members of a society to engage in moral discourse—which will, of course, involve them having moral beliefs. So it's not much of a stretch to suppose that the sharing of *specific* moral beliefs within a society might be pragmatically justified.

I've been suggesting that's moral beliefs cannot be epistemologically justified and so cannot amount to knowledge.[16] But it seems to me that these results are by no means as radical as they sound. For although there are many areas in which knowledge is valuable and important—subjects such as history, engineering, physics, and weather forecasting—we must beware against over-generalizing and taking for granted that knowledge is important in *all* areas, including ethics.

In many domains, such as those just listed, it's important that our beliefs be *true*—so it's important for us to have a way of finding out what's true and what isn't. That's primarily because our beliefs of the form, <If I do A then X will occur>, are deployed in means-ends deliberations whose outcomes are successful when (and usually *only* when) the operative beliefs are true. For, given that belief, if in addition we want X to occur, then we'll do A. And, if the belief is true, then that desire will certainly be satisfied—whereas if it *isn't* true, probably not. So it's important that such "directly action guiding beliefs" be true. Moreover, such beliefs are derived from other naturalistic beliefs of ours, via reasoning that we take to be truth-preserving. Therefore, it's important to each of us that a good proportion (if not all) of our beliefs within naturalistic domains be true.

However, this reasoning doesn't apply to a person's *ethical* beliefs. For they don't have any role in means-ends reasoning. They don't, when true (and in conjunction with a person's desires) engender actions that will enhance the likelihood of the desires being satisfied. This is not at all to deny that it matters a great deal which ethical beliefs people possess.—For those beliefs, *all by themselves*, can motivate corresponding actions. But these immediate consequences (and their effects) are completely independent of whether or not the beliefs engendering them are true. Thus, <u>knowledge</u> of ethical facts (as opposed to mere <u>beliefs</u> about what those facts are) has no relevance to anything of compelling importance! So we shouldn't be disturbed if it can't be obtained. On the contrary, given the pointlessness of moral knowledge, one can hardly be surprised that no methodology for acquiring it can be discerned.[17]

---

[16] Let me emphasize that the reasons I've given for concluding that moral beliefs cannot be epistemologically justified have nothing to do with the widely discussed "evolutionary debunking argument" (developed and advocated by Sharon Street, and others). According to that argument: (i) assuming that moral facts are not naturalistic, they are incapable of playing any role in explaining (either via evolution, or in any other way) why anyone has acquired the particular moral beliefs that s/he has acquired; (ii) therefore, if nonetheless nearly all of a person's moral beliefs are true, this would have to be nothing but a massive coincidence; (ii) but massive coincidences are highly improbable; (iii) so we should recognize that most of our moral beliefs are almost certainly not true, and that it's irrational for us to retain them.

It seems to me that this reasoning goes wrong in assuming that *any* massive coincidence is highly improbable. Granted, uncaused high correlations between *naturalistic phenomena* are vanishingly rare. That's an extremely well-confirmed empirical generalization, and has a physical explanation (in terms of *randomness* features within the Big Bang). But there are no grounds whatsoever for extending this generalization to *non*-naturalistic domains. There's no empirical evidence (nor evidence of any other kind) for regarding it as incredibly unlikely that there exists an inexplicably high correlation between *being an ethical proposition **that we believe*** and being *an ethical proposition **that's true***.

[17] Since it matters what people's moral beliefs are, it matters what moral propositions people <u>take</u> to be true. However that's consistent with its not mattering which of those propositions actually <u>are</u> true.

4. Postscript: On Realism versus Antirealism

It's standard for philosophers who propound metaethical views to label themselves either as "realists" or as "antirealists" about morality. And one might be tempted to wonder in which of these categories in the one in which we should place the Wittgensteinian perspective developed in this chapter.

But I'd like to suggest that we shouldn't take this question seriously. For attributions of "realism" or "antirealism" convey no information. And that's because "philosopherese" hasn't settled on a definite meaning for "I am a realist about domain D," or (equivalently) for "Realism is the correct perspective on domain D"—where D might be arithmetic, or aesthetics, or physics, or history, or morality, or . . . On the contrary, a bewildering variety of candidate meanings are commonly deployed (—at least a dozen!—) and it's far from uncommon for different philosophers to have different meanings in mind, and to be arguing at cross-purposes, when they take themselves to be disagreeing with one another over whether one should be "realists" about a given area of discourse.

Thus a good case can be made for thinking that unless and until this chaotic, confusion-breeding situation is rectified, anyone caught using those words should be drummed out of the APA (bad joke!)! I have no doubt that the later Wittgenstein would be in full agreement with such a policy. Certainly, he himself never used those terms—whether in relation to ethics or anything else.

In order to provide substance to the complaint that I'm airing, let me list some of the prominent proposals for being the defining characteristic of a "realist" domain:—

- Some of its atomic sentences are *true*
- Some of its atomic sentences are *absolutely* true (and not merely true relative to a framework)
- Some of its atomic sentences are absolutely *true*, in the sense of "corresponding to facts," and not merely in some *deflationary* sense, or in some *epistemic* sense

---

But (as Paul Bloomfield and David Copp have suggested to me) isn't there a violation of Wittgenstein's quietism in my supposing that it doesn't matter whether our moral beliefs are true? I'm not quite convinced that there is. After all, what's the evidence that we do make considerable efforts trying to ensure that our moral beliefs are true? Granted, we (or many of us) each try to ensure their coherence with one another (and with other convictions). But can't there be a striving for coherence that isn't in the service of a striving for truth?

Also, it's worth noting that people say many things whose truth or falsity nobody cares about, and rightly so (e.g., in performing a play, or in singing "For he's a jolly good fellow" at someone's birthday party). Obviously, truth is irrelevant in such cases. Similarly (but more controversially) religious pronouncements (expressing religious beliefs) might well be regarded in this way. Arguably their function is to provide comfort, and fulfillment of that function is independent of the truth or falsity of those beliefs. For further discussion, see my "Wittgenstein on Religion." forthcoming in D. Pritchard and N. Venturinho (eds.) *Wittgenstein and the Epistemology of Religion*, Oxford University Press.

- The meanings of its sentences consist in their *truth* conditions, not their *assertibility* conditions
- The facts articulated by its true sentences are not constructed from what people *believe* the facts to be
- Its sentences obey the law of excluded middle ("p or not-p")
- Its declarative sentences obey the principle of bivalence (each one is either true or false)
- The relations between its terms and their referents is *causal*
- There will be eventual epistemological convergence on its truths
- Amongst nondefective inquirers who possess the same evidence, there will be consensus on which of its sentences are true
- Its propositions are such that a person's *believing that p* can be justified only if her having that belief is explained by *the fact that p*
- Its sentences include in-principle-undiscoverable truths
- It exhibits a fair number of the above features

It's surely wrong to regard these alternative proposals for what counts as a "realist domain" as competing with one another with respect to *correctness*—i.e., with respect to which one of them articulates *what realism really is*. Rather, each criterion highlights a specific feature that some domains of discourse possess and others don't, and comes with the stipulation that possession by a given domain of that specific feature be what defines it as a "realist" domain (in *one* sense of that word)—all other domains qualifying, again by definition, as anti"realist" (in that same sense).

Thus, with respect to any domain (including moral discourse) the only cogent questions that can be raised with regard to whether realism is the correct perspective to have on it are those of the form: "Does realism apply in the sense articulated by criterion C?"—where one of the above listed proposals (or perhaps some further definition of "realism") is substituted for C.

And, in that case, one might well wonder if it wouldn't be best to simply drop that contentious term, given (i) that we could investigate and discover which domains satisfy any instance of C, without reformulating our conclusion with the word "realism"; (ii) that the continued use of that word by philosophers perpetuates the confused view that there's single realism/antirealism distinction, and (iii) also fosters another massive misconception—namely, that realist domains are somehow (and nontrivially) "*more real*" than antirealist domains, and so are of greater metaphysical importance.

Adopting this "drop the term" policy, it's still perhaps worth observing how—according to the above-sketched Wittgensteinian metaethics.—

(a) Fundamental moral predicates, such as "wrong:" are absolutely true of certain things, but not in a "correspondence" sense of "true." (b) The meanings of moral terms consist, *not* in their referents, but in the basic regularities governing their use. (c) The meaning of a moral sentence consists, *not* in its truth condition, but in the basic use-regularities of its words and the syntactic structure in which those words are embedded. (d) The moral facts aren't constructed from our beliefs about what they are.

(e) Declarative moral sentences obey both the law of excluded middle and the principle of bivalence. (f) The relation between moral predicates and their referents is not causal, but merely deflationary. (g) We have no reason to expect either eventual convergence of moral opinions, or agreement among nondefective inquirers who are in possession of the same evidence. (h) In order for a person to be justified in *believing* (for example) *that torture is wrong*, it's *not* required that this mental state of his be explained by the fact that torture is wrong. And (i) there may well be undiscoverable moral truths; in fact, a case can (and has!) been made that there's no moral knowledge—so moral truths are never literally discovered.

If these conclusions are correct, they may be of some value in providing a partial description of the distinctive character of our *moral* domain of discourse. It's hard to think of any gain that would derive from re-articulating them in the heavily ambiguous language of "realism" and "antirealism" (or even "quasi-realism"). But it's easy to think of very good reasons *not* to do so. Both here, and elsewhere in philosophy, "realism/antirealism" talk tends merely to muddy the waters.[18]

---

[18] I am profoundly grateful to Paul Bloomfield and David Copp for their extraordinarily astute, detailed, generous, and helpful comments on my woefully deficient initial draft of this paper.

CHAPTER 23

ON THE PROPERTIES OF QUIETISM AND ROBUSTNESS

MATTHEW H. KRAMER

This chapter appears in a section that initially carried the rubric of "Quietism," yet the term "quietism" is rejected by most moral philosophers to whose work it is applied. In the first half of this chapter, after a terse introductory section, I shall expand on why the term "quietism" is so objectionable. In lieu of that term, the phrase "Moral Realism as a Moral Doctrine" is the best designation for the moral-realist theory which I have expounded in some of my previous writings. (Other designations that are acceptable alternatives to "quietism"—and to the equally pejorative phrase "relaxed realism"—are "noninflationary moral realism" and "minimalist moral realism.") As will be argued in the first half of this chapter, quietism is a chimerical property insofar as it is predicated of Moral Realism as a Moral Doctrine.[1]

In the second half of the chapter, the focus shifts to the property of robustness. Naturalistic moral realists typically ascribe robustness to their accounts of morality, as they contend that moral properties are equivalent or reducible to properties that are causally efficacious. However, Moral Realism as a Moral Doctrine is a non-naturalistic variety of moral realism; like other non-naturalistic moral realists, the proponents of Moral Realism as a Moral Doctrine deny that moral properties are equivalent or reducible to causally efficacious properties. Nevertheless, supposedly what separates most of the other varieties of non-naturalistic moral realism from Moral Realism as a Moral Doctrine is that the former varieties are robust. Such is the contention of numerous opponents of Moral Realism as a Moral Doctrine, who are clearly appealing to a conception of robustness that differs from the naturalistic conception. Yet when the property

---

[1] The present chapter uses the terms "moral" and "ethical" (and "morality" and "ethics") interchangeably, but only because the difference between those terms does not matter for my arguments herein. In contexts where that difference does matter, "ethical" is a more capacious term than "moral"; all moral propositions are ethical, whereas not all ethical propositions are moral. For an explication of that distinction, see Kramer 2009, 2–3.

of robustness is invoked to distinguish between Moral Realism as a Moral Doctrine and other non-naturalistic varieties of moral realism—rather than to advert to something which they have in common—it turns out to be illusive. As will be argued in the second half of this chapter, every dimension of objectivity attributed to morality by robust non-naturalistic realists is also attributed to morality by proponents of Moral Realism as a Moral Doctrine. Hence, philosophers err both when they affirm that Moral Realism as a Moral Doctrine is a species of quietism and when they deny that Moral Realism as a Moral Doctrine is non-naturalistically robust.[2]

1. A Sketch of Moral Realism as a Moral Doctrine

Before this chapter embarks on its critiques, it should lay the groundwork for those critiques by outlining what Moral Realism as a Moral Doctrine is. That doctrine, which I have elaborated and defended elsewhere at length,[3] comprises two principal multifaceted theses. First is the Objectivity Proposition, which proclaims that morality is objective in seven major dimensions: (1) basic moral principles and many derivative moral principles are strongly mind-independent in more than one sense;[4] (2) there are determinately correct answers to countless moral questions; (3) moral principles are uniformly applicable to moral agents, in a number of respects; (4) all basic moral principles and many derivative moral principles are invariant across times and places; (5) individuals can and do converge in their moral views on any number of matters while diverging from one another in their moral views on any number of additional matters; (6) a distinctively moral stance of impartiality can be suitably specified and often achieved; and (7) countless moral judgments are truth-apt,[5] and many of them are true. Second is the Reconception of Metaethics Proposition, which declares that

---

[2] This chapter does not say anything further about naturalistic moral realism, for the second half of the chapter is focused instead on the non-naturalistic moral realists who commend their theories as robust. Elsewhere, I have assailed naturalistic versions of moral realism; see Kramer 2009, 190–212, 247–9.

[3] My two most sustained treatments of the topic heretofore are Kramer 2009 and 2017. See also Kramer 2013 and 2019. The present chapter does not recapitulate the lines of reasoning through which I have endeavored to vindicate Moral Realism as a Moral Doctrine in those earlier writings. Instead, I here seek to explain why Moral Realism as a Moral Doctrine is not accurately classifiable as quietist and why it is accurately classifiable as robust (in a non-naturalistic sense).

[4] The strong mind-independence of basic moral principles is both existential and observational. An entity partakes of strong existential mind-independence if and only if the entity's continued existence is not dependent on the mental functioning of any members of any group individually or collectively. An entity partakes of strong observational mind-independence if and only if the nature of the entity is not dependent on what it is thought to be by any members of any group individually or collectively. See Kramer 2009, 23–6.

[5] A judgment or statement is truth-apt if and only if it is evaluable as true or false.

the objectivity of morality is itself a moral matter—as the sundry propositions which expound that objectivity are grounded on ethical considerations and are endowed with ethical implications, albeit mainly at very high levels of abstraction. Whereas the Objectivity Proposition with its multiple conjuncts is unmistakably a doctrine of moral realism, the Reconception of Metaethics Proposition affirms that such a doctrine—along with every other metaethical theory—is a substantive ethical position. Anyone inclined to apply the label of "quietism" to Moral Realism as a Moral Doctrine is almost certainly not concentrating on the Objectivity Proposition, to which that label is so patently inapplicable. Rather, anyone so inclined is almost certainly concentrating instead on the Reconception of Metaethics Proposition.

Now, insofar as any other philosophers commonly pigeonholed as quietists would concur with the two theses that have just been distilled here, this chapter is defending them as well as myself. However, I disagree with nearly every one of those philosophers on some other points,[6] and they disagree among themselves. I will not herein be exploring those divergences (partly because I have mulled over a number of them in the past, and partly because I shall be addressing some more of them in future work). Hence, this chapter is most safely construed as an effort to vindicate my own account of Moral Realism as a Moral Doctrine; it is not an effort to vindicate "quietist" versions of moral realism more generally, though it might have the effect of doing so.

2. Why the Label of "Quietism" Is Inapposite

Having previously taken exception quite briefly to labels such as "quietist" and "relaxed" (Kramer 2017, 208–10), I will here contemplate the matter at greater length. A discussion of the inappositeness of such labels can help to avert or rectify some common misapprehensions about Moral Realism as a Moral Doctrine. Hence, although the present section of this chapter is partly defensive in its purpose and tone, it is primarily an exercise in clarification.

2.1. The Continuation of Metaethical Enquiry

One of the misapprehensions just mentioned is the notion that the proponents of Moral Realism as a Moral Doctrine are calling for the discontinuation of metaethical

---

[6] For some of my objections to Ronald Dworkin's work on matters of moral philosophy, see Kramer 2009, 107–26; 2013, 120–2; 2017, 199, 205–6, 208–9. For one of my main points of disagreement with Thomas Scanlon, see Kramer 2009, 67–9. For one of my main points of disagreement with Bernard Williams, see Kramer 2014, 14–16.

theorizing. A parallel notion has often been voiced in response to Ronald Dworkin's anti-Archimedean perspective on moral philosophy, which resembles Moral Realism as a Moral Doctrine in some salient respects. Commenting on a draft of Dworkin's 2011 book *Justice for Hedgehogs*—a book in which Dworkin brought to bear his anti-Archimedeanism on moral, political, and legal philosophy—Russ Shafer-Landau has expressed a worry along these lines. Shafer-Landau writes (2010, 479):

> I found the first few chapters of Ronald Dworkin's *Justice for Hedgehogs* very disconcerting.... [T]wo distinct sources of worry kept pressing. My initial unease grew steadily to something approaching panic as I assimilated the underlying message of these chapters—metaethics is largely a sham; its central question—that of the status of ethical and moral views—is a pseudo-question. This was bad enough, surely, for someone who has spent the last dozen years devoted to trying to make progress on that question.

Reactions of this kind, brimming with consternation, are probably due to the superciliousness and overheatedness of Dworkin's prose as much as to the substance of his arguments. At any rate, whatever the pertinence of such a reaction in a confrontation with Dworkin's anti-Archimedean sardonicism, it is not pertinent at all in response to Moral Realism as a Moral Doctrine.

As has been emphasized in my past writings on this matter, a proponent of Moral Realism as a Moral Doctrine is aiming for a reorientation of metaethical ruminations rather than for the cessation of them. In the Objectivity Proposition—the first of the two main theses of Moral Realism as a Moral Doctrine, which affirms the objectivity of morality in multiple respects—we encounter most if not all of the issues that have long preoccupied metaethical theorists. As Shafer-Landau observes in the quoted excerpt, where he rightly asserts that "the status of ethical and moral views" is the "central question" of metaethics, the objectivity of ethical matters has always been the paramount concern of philosophers in the domain of metaethics. It has been paramount both for the philosophers who affirm that objectivity and for the philosophers who deny it. Accordingly, the Objectivity Proposition is patently an array of metaethical claims. Its affirmation of the objectivity of morality on sundry fronts is a set of positions in the debates that are waged by metaethicists. Far from contending that those debates are a sham, anyone who champions Moral Realism as a Moral Doctrine is engaging squarely in them; and far from dismissing the question of ethical objectivity as a pseudo-question, anyone who champions Moral Realism as a Moral Doctrine is advancing a wide-rangingly positive answer to that question.

2.2. Metaethical Debates as Moral Disputation are Metaethical Debates

At the same time, as has been remarked, a proponent of Moral Realism as a Moral Doctrine is advocating a reorientation of metaethical debates. Here we come to the

Reconception of Metaethics Proposition, the second main thesis of Moral Realism as a Moral Doctrine: the thesis that any questions about the objectivity of morality are substantive ethical questions, albeit usually at high levels of abstraction. Whereas all or nearly all moral realists endorse the gist of the Objectivity Proposition, quite a few of them—and many of their opponents—balk at the Reconception of Metaethics Proposition. Let us ponder here some of the misconceptions that underlie such wariness.

First, as will become evident in §2.3 below, the term "metaethics" in the Reconception of Metaethics Proposition is being employed more narrowly than it is often employed in some other contexts. As is indicated in my one-sentence formulation of the Reconception of Metaethics Proposition in §1 above, the domain of metaethics covered by that proposition is concerned with the objectivity of morality. Although that domain comprises all of the seven dimensions that are addressed by the Objectivity Proposition, it does not encompass some other matters that are foci of enquiries which many philosophers would classify as "metaethical." We shall explore this point in my next subsection, where we shall see that my limitation of the domain of metaethics to matters of ethical objectivity is grounded in a distinction that has always been central to Moral Realism as a Moral Doctrine.

Second, virtually any general metaethical position is neutral among a multitude of relatively concrete moral judgments such as "Lying is morally wrong." Correctly observing as much, someone might incorrectly infer that general metaethical positions are not moral theses and are instead purely philosophical theses. Such an inference would fail to take account of a fact which I have noted already in this chapter and which I have elsewhere emphasized (Kramer 2009, 3–5 *et passim*): namely, the fact that metaethical theses are typically pitched at very high levels of abstraction and are therefore typically neutral among wide arrays of relatively concrete moral judgments. In that respect, metaethical theses are like other highly abstract moral doctrines.

For example, the error theory of morality propounded originally by John Mackie—and subsequently by others such as Jonas Olson and Charles Pigden—is neutral among all moral judgments that ascribe obligatoriness or forbiddenness to any modes of conduct. Branding every such judgment as false, the error theory does not single out any ascription of obligatoriness or forbiddenness as better than any other such ascription. However, as I have argued at length elsewhere (2017, 186–96), the error theory saddles its proponents *malgré eux* with the conclusion that every ascription of moral permissibility to any mode of conduct is true. In other words, that theory is not neutral between ascriptions of obligatoriness or forbiddenness on the one hand and ascriptions of permissibility on the other hand. Hence, notwithstanding that the abstractness of the error theory leaves it neutral among the vast throng of obligatoriness-ascribing and forbiddenness-ascribing moral judgments, it is a moral position with some far-reaching moral implications.

A third misapprehension that has led many philosophers to resist the Reconception of Metaethics Proposition is their assumption that the status of metaethical tenets as substantive ethical theses is somehow inconsistent with the status of such tenets as metaphysical or epistemological or semantic theses. That is, the proponents of Moral Realism as a Moral Doctrine are often taken to be denying that the enquiries and argumentation undertaken by metaethicists are metaphysical or epistemological or semantic in their orientation. However, any such understanding of the Reconception of Metaethics Proposition is a misunderstanding. Proponents of Moral Realism as a Moral Doctrine are overtly engaged in the enterprise of marshaling metaphysical and epistemological and semantic arguments about moral principles and properties. A defense of the objectivity of ethics—a defense of the Objectivity Proposition—has to involve such arguments, which are pitted against any metaphysical or epistemological or semantic arguments that impugn the objectivity of ethics.

Indeed, as I have emphasized in my previous writings on these matters, Moral Realism as a Moral Doctrine is replete with existential commitments. Basic moral principles and many derivative moral principles such as "Torturing babies for pleasure is morally wrong" have always existed and will always exist. They are binding always and everywhere in all possible worlds; they would have existed even if no human beings or other rational moral agents had ever existed (Kramer 2009, 26–48, 154–61). These existential commitments are fully consistent with my claim that moral realism as an affirmation of the objectivity of morality is a moral doctrine, for all of the foregoing commitments are to be construed minimalistically.[7] When I declare that the principle "Torturing babies for pleasure is morally wrong" has always existed and will always exist, I am declaring that torturing babies for pleasure always has been morally wrong and always will be morally wrong. Such existential commitments are moral theses that have to be substantiated (or contested) on moral grounds—but their status as moral theses is entirely consistent with their status as metaphysical claims. They are claims about what is morally correct, and *pari passu* they are claims about what ultimately exists. They are opposed to any contrary claims about what ultimately exists.

Cognate points are applicable here to the epistemic and semantic dimensions of the defense of moral objectivity that is mounted by the proponents of Moral Realism as a Moral Doctrine. Any vindication of the epistemic dimensions of moral objectivity is both an epistemological position and an ethical position, and any vindication of the semantic dimensions of moral objectivity is both a semantic position and an ethical position. At high levels of abstraction, the argumentation that supports and constitutes a vindication of either type just mentioned is epistemological or semantic. It is also of course ethical (at high levels of abstraction), in that it carries certain ethical implications and is grounded on certain ethical considerations. Still, a defense of the epistemic dimensions of moral objectivity is a set of claims about what can be known, and is at odds with any contrary claims about the limits of knowability; and a defense of the

---

[7] On the importance of minimalism for Moral Realism as a Moral Doctrine, see Kramer 2009, 200–7, 261–88; 2017, 206–8.

semantic dimensions of moral objectivity is a set of claims about the relationships between moral assertions and the world, and is at odds with any contrary claims about those relationships.

2.3. The Domain of Metaethics

Near the outset of my book *Moral Realism as a Moral Doctrine* (2009, 12–14), I distinguish between two main ways in which the notion of morality or ethics can be understood. On the one hand, that notion can be construed as referring to what I there designate as "morality or ethics *tout court*": namely, "the whole array of correct ethical/moral standards that truly determine the ethical/moral consequences of people's conduct, and . . . the diverse categories and properties associated with those standards." On the other hand, the notion of morality or ethics can be construed as referring to "the contents of the ethical/moral convictions that generally prevail among the members of some society (or of some set of societies)" and to "the observable practices of ethical/moral deliberation and judgment that actually give expression to those prevailing convictions" (2009, 12).

This distinction, which partly resembles the familiar distinction between transcendent or objective morality and conventional or positive morality, is what underlies my demarcation of the domain of metaethics in the manner briefly suggested in §2.2 above. As has been stated there, I take the domain of metaethics to be concerned with the objectivity of morality and thus to be concerned with morality *tout court* rather than with morality as an observable array of convictions and practices. However, what is not adequately highlighted in my 2009 book—in contrast with the emphasis in a more recent article of mine (2017, 199–203, 206 n18)—is that such a demarcation of the metaethical domain is narrower than the demarcation that has been taken for granted by quite a few other philosophers. As a consequence, the Reconception of Metaethics Proposition may have encountered resistance that would not have been directed against it if the circumscribed scope of its conception of metaethics had been more clearly signaled.

2.3.1. *Expressivism as a Doctrine of Pragmatics*

In the aforementioned article (2017, 199–203), I have discussed at some length the expressivist account of moral discourse propounded by Simon Blackburn. Expressivists in moral philosophy highlight the role of conative attitudes in moral judgments and deliberations. For many decades, and to some degree even in the present day, expressivism has been presented as an account of the semantics of moral discourse. Proponents of expressivism in this form (including Blackburn in his early writings) have treated the semantics of moral statements as relevantly similar to the semantics of interjections or volitives or imperatives or other truth-inapt utterances. When expressivism is elaborated in this form, it is squarely opposed to the semantic dimension of the Objectivity Proposition.[8] Consequently, it is straightforwardly classifiable as a metaethical doctrine that is covered as such by the Reconception of Metaethics Proposition. As a metaethical doctrine, it is a moral doctrine.

In recent times, however, expressivism has come to be re-elaborated—especially by Blackburn but also by some others[9]—as an account of the pragmatics of moral discourse rather than of the semantics thereof. This transfiguration of expressivism could have turned it into a social-scientific theory whose proponents conduct empirical investigations of the patterns of behavior associated with the invocation of moral concepts and the exchanging of moral judgments in various societies. Valuable though such investigations can be, they are not the sorts of enquiries in which philosophers such as Blackburn have engaged. Rather, prescinding from the specificities of any particular societies, Blackburn has proceeded at a philosophical level of abstraction as he seeks to recount what people achieve at practical levels by suffusing their interactions with moral judgments and by articulating many of those judgments as propositional assertions. That is, he has endeavored to shed light on the important social functions that are performed by the inclusion of moral judgments in human intercourse. Such a project, conducted on a philosophical tier of abstraction, is philosophical rather than social-scientific.

Even more important in the present context is that Blackburn's expressivist account of the pragmatics of moral discourse is not a moral theory. Instead of being both philosophical and ethical, it is philosophical rather than ethical. In this very respect, it is fundamentally different from expressivism as an account of the semantics of moral discourse. Now, many philosophers may be inclined at this point to conclude that the Reconception of Metaethics Proposition is false. After all, as I have just readily allowed, Blackburn's expressivist account of the pragmatics of moral discourse is not a moral theory—yet, in the eyes of many philosophers, Blackburn's account is paradigmatically a theory within the domain of metaethics. Those philosophers will therefore be disposed to view Blackburn's expressivism as a falsifying counterexample to the Reconception of Metaethics Proposition.

However, given the understanding of the domain of metaethics that informs the Reconception of Metaethics Proposition, Blackburn's expressivism as an account of the pragmatics of moral discourse is definitely not a metaethical theory. It is not about the objectivity of moral principles or properties or judgments or categories; it is not about morality *tout court*. Rather, it is about the practical import of the activities in which human beings engage by forming and communicating and controverting moral judgments. Of course, Blackburn is scrutinizing those activities from a philosophical

---

[8] Here the difference between objectivity qua determinate correctness and objectivity qua truth-aptitude is of great importance. Philosophers who propound expressivist accounts of the semantics of moral discourse can argue in favor of the former type of objectivity—as Allan Gibbard (1990, 153–250) does at length, for example—but not in favor of the latter type.

[9] Stoljar 1993 was an important contribution to this development, as I have noted in Kramer 2017, 200 n10. The key text by Blackburn which contributes to that development is Blackburn 1998.

level of abstraction rather than as a social-scientific gatherer of data. Still, his explication of the pragmatics of moral discourse is about morality in the second sense which I have delineated in the opening paragraph of §2.3 above. Accordingly, that explication is not within the domain of metaethics, as far as the Reconception of Metaethics Proposition is concerned.

As has been mentioned, Blackburn early in his career developed a version of expressivism that was focused predominantly on the semantics of moral discourse. At that juncture, then, his expressivism was opposed to the Objectivity Proposition and was a metaethical doctrine—and thus a moral doctrine—by the reckoning of the Reconception of Metaethics Proposition. However, when Blackburn later moved away from that traditional version of expressivism and refashioned it into a philosophical account of the pragmatics of moral discourse, his expressivism became consistent with the Objectivity Proposition. It ceased to be within the domain of metaethics by the reckoning of the Reconception of Metaethics Proposition, and it instead came to be situated within the domain of the philosophy of action (and the domain of the philosophy of language, where it had always been). Accordingly, the Reconception of Metaethics Proposition is entirely unscathed by the fact that Blackburn's expressivist approach to the pragmatics of moral deliberations is not a moral theory; that proposition is unscathed because its claim about the substantive moral character of every metaethical doctrine is inapplicable to an approach that is not a metaethical doctrine. Blackburn's expressivism in his later work is fully consistent with Moral Realism as a Moral Doctrine.

2.3.2. *Metasemantics versus Semantics*

Like accounts of the pragmatics of moral discourse and unlike accounts of the semantics of moral discourse, accounts of the metasemantics of moral discourse are not correctly classifiable as metaethical doctrines by the reckoning of the Reconception of Metaethics Proposition.[10] Metasemantic theories in themselves neither affirm nor deny the objectivity of the semantics of moral discourse. Rather, at a philosophical level of abstraction, they seek to distill the conditions that are sufficient (or necessary and sufficient) to constitute the occurrence of sundry discourses with the semantic relationships that are characteristic of those discourses. At very high levels of abstraction, they endeavor to delineate the factors through which the phrasing in those discourses is vested with whatever meanings it possesses. For example, such a theory might advert to the characteristic circumstances in which sentences and sub-sentential units are used, whatever those circumstances might be; or it might advert to the attitudes which the sentences and sub-sentential units characteristically express, whether the attitudes be

---

[10] My thinking about the topic of the present subsection has been sharpened through my perusal of the first draft of Tiefensee 2022. I should note that the designation "metasemantics" is employed in various ways by various philosophers. There is no canonical pattern of usage. Some philosophers employ that designation to cover parts of what I would classify as semantics (along with what I would classify as metasemantics). Other philosophers, including me, instead use that designation to cover only theories that delineate the fundamental factors which account for the presence of meanings as such. Such theories prescind from all the specifics of semantics.

propositional or conative; or it might advert to the inferences which the employment of sentences and sub-sentential units would characteristically warrant; and so forth. Instead of expounding the nature of morality *tout court* in any of its dimensions, these theories are expounding a major aspect of morality as an array of practices of deliberation and judgment—that is, morality in the second sense which I have specified at the outset of §2.3 above.

A metasemantic exposition of this kind is relevantly similar to the account of the operations of a legal system elaborated by H.L.A. Hart and other legal philosophers who have been influenced by Hart.[11] Hart maintained, at a philosophical level of abstraction, that those operations are constituted by various beliefs and conative attitudes and behavioral patterns on the part of legal-governmental officials (and, to a lesser degree, on the part of private citizens). Philosophers who espouse such an account of the workings of a legal system are not committed by it to any specific positions on the semantics of legal statements.[12] Nor are they committed by it to any positions on the morality of legal systems; their account of the conditions that constitute the operations of a legal system is a philosophical theory rather than a moral theory.

Similarly, a metasemantic account of the conditions that constitute the meaningfulness of sentences and sub-sentential units in moral discourse and other types of discourse does not commit its proponents to any specific account of the semantics of moral statements. Nor does it commit them to any other specific moral positions. It is a philosophical theory rather than a moral doctrine. This point is fully consistent with the Reconception of Metaethics Proposition, since the philosophical theory in question is not within the domain of metaethics—given how that domain is understood in Moral Realism as a Moral Doctrine. A metasemantic theory does not provide an account of any aspect of morality *tout court*, but instead provides an account of one main aspect of morality as an array of observable practices of meaningful deliberation and assessment.

Some of the criticisms that have been directed against so-called quietism are pretty clearly based on the premise that metasemantic theorizing is a component of the quietist project. At least in relation to Moral Realism as a Moral Doctrine, however, any such premise is a misapprehension. Let us consider here the following assertion by Ralph Wedgwood: "According to [a] quietist approach, nothing more can be said about the meaning of statements of the form '*A* ought to φ' except things of the following forms: that this statement means *that A ought to φ*, that it can be used to state that *A* ought to φ, and to express the belief that *A* ought to φ, and so on" (Wedgwood 2007, 18, italics in original). At first glance, Wedgwood appears here to be recounting a quietist approach to the semantics of moral utterances. Insofar as he is ascribing a semantic view to the

---

[11] For Hart's account, see especially Hart 1994, 79–123. For some germane reflections on Hart's model of a legal system, see Kramer 2018, 23–31, 60–109.

[12] Indeed, the substance of Hart's own position on the semantics of legal statements is a matter of dispute among legal philosophers who all endorse his account of the conditions that constitute the operations of a legal system. See Kramer 2018, 180–203.

proponents of Moral Realism as a Moral Doctrine, his assertion here is overstated but is partly accurate. It is overstated because the basic concepts of ethics are interrelated in ways that enable translations among them at a fundamental level. Nonetheless, what is correct in Wedgwood's assertion—when it is construed as an ascription of a semantic view—is that the proponents of Moral Realism as a Moral Doctrine take the semantics of ethics to be irreducibly normative and deontic.

However, there is an ambiguity in Wedgwood's wording. Specifically, there is an ambiguity in the phrase "nothing more can be said about the meaning of statements." I have just interpreted those words as the opening portion of a claim in which Wedgwood asserts that quietists adhere to a certain position on the semantics of moral utterances. However, that interpretation is probably incorrect, in light of what he goes on to say. Instead of signaling the attribution of a semantic view to the quietists, the words in question are probably suggesting that the quietists have declined to furnish any metasemantic account of the meaningfulness of moral discourse and other discourses. We can arrive at such an interpretation of Wedgwood's phrasing when we look at his mordant riposte to the quietists (2007, 19, emphasis in original): "[I]t should be clear that [the quietist approach] is hardly obviously true. Indeed, it would seem to me incredible that it could be an absolutely unanalysable feature of a particular thought or statement that it is about one thing rather than another. . . . It is obviously incredible to suppose that the name 'Socrates' refers to a particular individual purely by *magic*, as it were." Though Wedgwood could be construed here as inveighing against the quietists for their not having supplied a causal-aetiological account of the emergence of meanings, he is most plausibly construed as inveighing against them for their not having supplied a metasemantic account of the existence of those meanings. Or, rather, he is inveighing against them for supposedly presuming that the metasemantic status of those meanings is brutely unanalyzable.

Insofar as any such retort by Wedgwood is aimed against Moral Realism as a Moral Doctrine, it is misconceived. On the one hand, he is correct in thinking that Moral Realism as a Moral Doctrine does not include any metasemantic account of the meaningfulness of moral discourse. On the other hand, he errs in thinking that the absence of such an account is a shortcoming of Moral Realism as a Moral Doctrine, and he likewise errs in thinking that the proponents of Moral Realism as a Moral Doctrine somehow believe that the metasemantic basis for the patterns of meanings which are operative in moral discourse is brutely unanalyzable. As has been emphasized throughout this chapter, Moral Realism as a Moral Doctrine is a theory of morality *tout court*. Neither at a social-scientific level nor at a philosophical level is it a theory of morality as an array of deliberative and evaluative practices. Consequently, its omission of any metasemantic theorizing is not a display of quietism at all. That omission is not an oversight, and it is not indicative of any assumption that such theorizing will be futile. Instead, it stems from the fact that the questions addressed by the proponents of Moral Realism as a Moral Doctrine—questions about the objectivity of morality *tout court* in its several dimensions—are not the same as the questions addressed by Wedgwood when he is engaging in metasemantic ruminations. Those ruminations are distinct from the lines of reasoning involved in upholding or assailing the Objectivity Proposition and the Reconception of Metaethics Proposition.[13]

2.3.3. *What Is the Upshot?*

Naturally, many philosophers will continue to insist that Blackburn's account of the pragmatics of moral discourse and Wedgwood's account of the metasemantics of moral discourse—and any homologous theories or rival theories—are within the domain of metaethics. They will insist that that domain pertains not only to morality *tout court* but also—at a philosophical level of abstraction—to morality in the second sense which I have delineated at the outset of §2.3 above. In the presence of such inclinations, this chapter is certainly not issuing any terminological or taxonomical ukases. As I have stated elsewhere (2017, 206 n18), the expansive understanding of the domain of metaethics is unexceptionable, provided that the philosophers who adhere to it are aware that a narrower understanding of that domain is operative among some of their fellow philosophers. Of particular interest in this chapter, of course, is that the narrower understanding is operative in the Reconception of Metaethics Proposition.

What should be emphasized, at the close of this section, is that the narrower understanding of the domain of metaethics is very wide-ranging indeed. It includes every expressivist account of the semantics of moral statements, and every version of the error theory of morality, and every version of moral realism, and every version of moral skepticism, and every version of moral fictionalism, and every exposition of the supervenience of ethical properties on empirical properties, and every version of moral relativism that is a theory of morality *tout court* rather than a social-scientific theory about cross-cultural differences in prevalent moral convictions. It also comprises most of the other topics and theories that are comprehended within the more expansive understanding of the metaethical domain. Indeed, it even encompasses a couple of doctrines in the pragmatics and metasemantics of moral discourse; as I have discussed elsewhere (Kramer 2022, 442–5), those doctrines are unlike other matters of pragmatics and metasemantics in that they do have a bearing on the objectivity of morality. In short, taking as a point of departure the key distinction that is drawn at the outset of §2.3 above,

---

[13] As is evident from what has been said in this subsection, Wedgwood pursues semantic enquiries as well as metasemantic enquiries in his 2007 book, and they are often interwoven. Similarly, David Enoch in his book *Taking Morality Seriously* devotes several pages to what he describes as "a problem of . . . metasemantics rather than semantics" (2011, 177), yet the matters which he explores in those pages are only partly metasemantic and are in fact predominantly semantic; he draws on metasemantics to help him in framing a semantic problem which he needs to address. (My own approach to the semantic problem which Enoch needs to address—a problem of accounting for the success of normative discourse in referring to strongly mind-independent normative principles—is to adopt an externalist theory of reference and to cash out the metaphysical commitments of such a theory minimalistically.) At any rate, notwithstanding the frequent conjunction of metasemantic theses and semantic theses, and notwithstanding the occasional difficulties of differentiating between them, the distinction between them is crucial for one's understanding of Moral Realism as a Moral Doctrine.

the delimitation of the domain of metaethics that is operative in the Reconception of Metaethics Proposition is not a peculiarly cabined understanding of that domain.

3. THE ROBUSTNESS OF MORAL REALISM AS A MORAL DOCTRINE

Quietism, then, is not a property that can accurately be predicated of Moral Realism as a Moral Doctrine. We should now consider whether Moral Realism as a Moral Doctrine can be differentiated from other non-naturalistic varieties of moral realism on the ground that it lacks robustness. What is the property of robustness which Moral Realism as a Moral Doctrine is often said to lack and which those other non-naturalistic varieties of moral realism are said to possess?

In pursuit of an answer to this question, the second half of this chapter will grapple with the version of moral realism propounded by David Enoch in his powerful 2011 book *Taking Morality Seriously*. The subtitle of Enoch's book is *A Defense of Robust Realism*. Hence, if an answer to the foregoing question is to be found, we should be able to locate it in the pages of his chapters. As will become apparent, however, any answer is elusive at best.

One reason for the elusiveness of such an answer is that Enoch and I agree on so many metaethical issues. On a welter of such issues—ranging from idealization in response-dependent accounts of morality to the doctrine of motivational internalism—his arguments in *Taking Morality Seriously* are closely similar to my arguments in *Moral Realism as a Moral Doctrine* or are incisively complementary to them. What is most important, those two books concur in maintaining that the basic principles of morality and many derivative principles of morality are strongly mind-independent. Indeed, everything said by Enoch in the opening paragraph of his book to summarize his robust-realist account of morality is equally applicable to Moral Realism as a Moral Doctrine. He writes as follows (2011, 1):

> [T]here are irreducibly normative truths and facts, facts such that we should care about our future well-being, that we should not humiliate other people, that we should not reason and form beliefs in ways we know to be unreliable. These are, of course, just examples: even if I am wrong about them, I believe there must be *some* examples of this sort, examples of normative (and indeed moral) truths that are irreducibly normative, truths that are perfectly objective, universal, absolute. They are independent of us, our desires and our (or anyone else's) will. And our thinking and talking about them amounts not just to an expression of any practical attitudes, but to a representation of these normative truths and facts. These normative truths are truths that, when successful in our normative inquiries, we discover rather than create or construct. They are, in other words, just as respectable as empirical or mathematical truths (at least, that is, according to scientific and mathematical realists).

Enoch here distills most of the dimensions of ethical objectivity which are championed by *Moral Realism as a Moral Doctrine* and which are summarized near the outset of this chapter. Immediately after the quoted passage, he declares that " 'Robust Realism' is my name for the view just sketched" (2011, 1). He could just as aptly have invoked the designation "Moral Realism as a Moral Doctrine."

Similarly, when Enoch proceeds in his opening chapter to delineate further the substance of his robust moral realism, his statements serve to encapsulate some of the chief tenets of Moral Realism as a Moral Doctrine: "Robust Realism is, then, an objectivist, non-error-theoretical, cognitivist, or factualist position, it states that some normative judgments are objectively non-vacuously true. But Robust Realism goes further than that. It asserts that some normative truths are *irreducibly* normative" (2011, 4, emphasis in original, footnote omitted). Everything said in this quotation about robust moral realism is also true of Moral Realism as a Moral Doctrine.

Nevertheless, despite the major and abundant affinities between Enoch's robust moral realism and my Moral Realism as a Moral Doctrine, there are some points in his 2011 book from which I dissent. Most of those are on matters of detail or of exegesis that are inconsequential for the present chapter, and even some of the relatively important points do not straightforwardly bear on the question whether my version of moral realism is similar to his in its robustness. However, a few of those points do have such a bearing, and they will be the foci of the rest of this chapter.

3.1. Enoch's Critiques of Quietism

Though Enoch acknowledges that the pejorative term "quietist" is rejected by the philosophers to whom he applies it, he persists in using that label. Among the philosophers whom he thus designates, the main target is Thomas Scanlon. However, my Moral Realism as a Moral Doctrine is also a target of some if not all of Enoch's animadversions on quietism. Hence, although the present chapter will not mull over the pertinence of those animadversions as objections to Scanlon's ideas, it will explore whether they have any force against Moral Realism as a Moral Doctrine.

Enoch glancingly engages with the so-called quietists in the opening chapter of his book, where he asserts that they "think that a fairly robust metaethical and indeed metanormative realism can nevertheless be metaphysically light, ontologically uncommitted.... I have no such illusions. My Robust Realism wears its ontological commitment on its sleeve." He declares that "[t]he thing for us realists to do, I believe, is not to disavow ontological commitment.... Rather, we must step up to the plate, and defend the rather heavy commitments of our realism" (2011, 7). The heavy ontological commitments to which Enoch here adverts are those which he adumbrates in the opening paragraph of his book, from which I have already quoted. He there affirms the existence of moral principles that are irreducible and strongly mind-independent and timeless and universal. In *Moral Realism as a Moral Doctrine* and in many of my subsequent writings, I have argued at length for the existence of just such moral principles.

Hence, insofar as Enoch in his opening salvo against quietism is seeking to specify a difference between his robust moral realism and my Moral Realism as a Moral Doctrine, he misfires.

Enoch marshals his main set of ripostes to quietism in the fifth chapter of his book (2011, 121–33). In the first of those ripostes, which is directed almost entirely against Scanlon, Enoch takes aim at the proposition that the answers to questions about the existence of various moral principles and properties are internal to the moral domain (2011, 122–7). He assumes that the moral domain in question is a practice or a set of practices. Perhaps that assumption about the nature of the relevant moral domain is warranted in an interpretation of Scanlon's ideas, but it is mistaken in any engagement with Moral Realism as a Moral Doctrine. Though I too contend that the answers to questions about the existence of various moral principles and properties are internal to the moral domain, I am invoking the notion of the moral domain not with reference to practices or discourses but instead with reference to morality *tout court*. That is, to quote again the phrasing from *Moral Realism as a Moral Doctrine*, I take the moral domain to be "the whole array of correct ethical/moral standards that truly determine the ethical/moral consequences of people's conduct, and . . . the diverse categories and properties associated with those standards" (2009, 12). In *Moral Realism as a Moral Doctrine*, the moral domain as morality *tout court* is explicitly distinguished from people's moral practices and discourses rather than equated with them. Hence, the proposition about internality to the moral domain is accurately construable as the claim that the correct answers to questions about the existence of various moral principles and properties are always grounded at least partly on correct moral precepts.[14] No correct answers to such questions can ever be grounded entirely on considerations that do not include any correct moral precepts. Once the proposition about internality to the moral domain is aptly construed in this fashion—as it would be construed by any proponent of Moral Realism as a Moral Doctrine—all of Enoch's worries about that proposition fall away.[15]

In his next two rejoinders to the so-called quietists (2011, 127–9), Enoch suggests that they regard metaethical questions as either unintelligible or undecidable. His paramount target in this portion of his discussion is Dworkin. Yet I have elsewhere emphatically differentiated Moral Realism as a Moral Doctrine from Dworkin's anti-Archimedeanism on this very point as well as on some other points.[16] Whereas Dworkin did appear to believe that many metaethical disputes are unintelligible, no such notion is operative in Moral Realism as a Moral Doctrine. On the contrary, Moral Realism as a Moral Doctrine is itself a multifaceted metaethical position that engages with sundry

---

[14] Any proponent of Moral Realism as a Moral Doctrine will of course maintain that the correctness of moral precepts is a strongly mind-independent matter.

[15] Enoch contends that the view which he ascribes to Scanlon is largely indistinguishable from some versions of moral fictionalism. I am inclined to contend instead that that view is largely indistinguishable from some versions of moral relativism.

[16] See, for example, Kramer 2017, 208–9. See also Kramer 2009, 22.

metaethical debates. It affirms rather than denies the intelligibility and distinctiveness of metaethical issues. Its point is simply to establish that all such issues are substantive ethical matters (mostly at very high levels of abstraction) and that they cannot be resolved except on the basis of ethical considerations. "Properly attuned to the ethical bearings of those issues, meta-ethical philosophers can and should pursue their characteristic foci of enquiry" (Kramer 2009, 22). Thus, even if Enoch has managed to specify a genuine dissimilarity between his robust moral realism and Dworkin's anti-Archimedeanism, he has again failed to adduce anything that would distinguish his own position from Moral Realism as a Moral Doctrine.

In his final main rejoinder to the quietists, Enoch submits that their real concern is to maintain that all metaethical matters are substantive ethical matters (2011, 129–32). Although his suggestion along these lines is much closer to a veritable engagement with Moral Realism as a Moral Doctrine than are any of his previous suggestions about quietism, his framing of the matter is tendentious: "Perhaps what is crucial here [from the perspective of quietists] is that *apparently* metanormative arguments are really normative themselves. What is *apparently* a detached, normatively neutral metadiscourse is thus folded back into the normative discourse itself. And such claims are supported mostly, I think, by examples of *supposedly* metanormative issues that can be shown to be normative" (2011, 129, emphases added, footnote omitted). With the three adverbs that I have italicized in this quotation, Enoch runs together two theses. A thesis embraced by the proponents of Moral Realism as a Moral Doctrine is conflated by him with a thesis which they reject. On the one hand, such proponents do maintain that metaethical discourse is always ethically engaged—usually at very high levels of abstraction—rather than ethically disengaged and "normatively neutral." Any appearance of ethical neutrality is only an appearance. Thus, the second instance of "apparently" in the sentences just quoted is apposite. However, the other two italicized adverbs in those sentences are inapposite. With them, Enoch conveys the impression that the proponents of Moral Realism as a Moral Doctrine are denying the genuineness or distinctiveness or intelligibility of metaethical matters. As I have just reaffirmed, any such impression is unfounded.

Enoch's conveyance of that impression is exacerbated by the heading of the subsection in which his discussion of the matter occurs: "It's all first-order after all" (2011, 129). As I have sought to emphasize elsewhere (Kramer 2017, 206), the distinction between first-order inquiries and second-order or higher-order inquiries is a hindrance to one's understanding of Moral Realism as a Moral Doctrine. Any proponents of Moral Realism as a Moral Doctrine will readily accept that all metaethical matters are second-order or higher-order. Instead of relying on the first-order/second-order dichotomy, those proponents rely on the internal/external dichotomy. That is, they hold that all metaethical matters are internal to the domain of morality *tout court*. Positions on such matters are grounded in ethical considerations, and each such position carries ethical implications. In other words, any factors that are sufficient to render a metaethical thesis true are ethical considerations—or include ethical considerations—and any metaethical thesis is inconsistent with some substantive ethical conclusions.

When pondering why the advocates of Moral Realism as a Moral Doctrine insist that metaethical theses are internal to the domain of ethics, Enoch again presents an ungenerous account of his target (2011, 131, footnotes omitted):

> Suppose some metaphysical or epistemological—apparently metaethical—considerations seem to undermine morality altogether, supporting either a nihilist or a skeptical conclusion. Then, it seems, all it takes to refute them is the strength of our convictions that wanton cruelty is wrong, and that we know as much. If metanormative considerations were of a very different type from normative ones, perhaps such a move would be objectionable, because of its conflation of two distinct, perhaps even independent, levels of discourse. But given the quietist observations, this worry can be set aside.

In the first place, no moral realist would accept that the strength of our convictions about the moral status of some mode of behavior is properly invocable as a consideration that can refute moral nihilism or skepticism. Furthermore, although the objective moral status of such a mode of behavior is properly invocable in support of a refutation of moral nihilism or skepticism, any proponent of Moral Realism as a Moral Doctrine will recognize that typically a successful refutation has to involve far more. For example, although my critique of Mackie's error theory of morality does invoke the moral bearings of some fairly concrete modes of behavior, it also advances a number of lines of much more abstract argumentation (2017, 186–96). Much the same is true of my critiques of moral relativism and moral skepticism (2009, 30–46, 87–106). Those critiques do not furnish any support for Enoch's suggestion that philosophers who espouse Moral Realism as a Moral Doctrine somehow think that "all it takes" to refute certain rival doctrines is the invocation of the moral status of some fairly concrete mode of conduct.

At the end of his cogitations on quietism, Enoch returns to claiming that the targeted philosophers have endeavored to "show that the realist, even the robust realist, can get what she wants without any heavy metaphysical commitments," and he retorts that "there are no metaphysically light ways of getting the robust realist what he wants" (2011, 132, 133). Like the other metaphors that saturate the writings in which philosophers express their hostility toward quietism—metaphors such as relaxedness versus serious-mindedness, or laziness versus earnestness, or indeed quietism versus robustness (Kramer 2017, 210 n21)—Enoch's metaphors of heaviness and lightness are misdirected. When Enoch writes about heavy metaphysical commitments, he is referring to the strong mind-independence and irreducibility and universality and timelessness of moral principles. What should be emphasized here yet again, then, is that the proponents of Moral Realism as a Moral Doctrine robustly ascribe all those "heavy" properties to basic moral principles and to many derivative moral principles.

In sum, throughout his critique of quietism, Enoch fails to specify any points of dissimilarity between his own robust moral realism and my Moral Realism as a Moral Doctrine. We should now move on to consider a genuine dissimilarity between the two.

As will be argued, that dissimilarity does not militate in favor of the notion that Enoch's moral realism is more robust than Moral Realism as a Moral Doctrine.

3.2. Unknowability and Realism

In the opening chapter of his book, Enoch indicates that his robust moral realism is compatible with extreme skepticism about the knowability of moral truths (2011, 4–5, footnote omitted):

> Robust Realism as characterized above is prima facie neutral on the epistemology of the normative, and is thus compatible with even the most thoroughgoing epistemological skepticism about the normative. This, I think, is as it should be: at least since Descartes' realist skepticism about the external world and Berkeley's idealist (and, we would say, antirealist) reply to this skepticism, skeptical positions have been motivated by realist intuitions (and antirealist retorts have been motivated by anti-skeptical convictions). It would thus be a mistake to use the term "realism" so as to make realism incompatible with skepticism. Arguing for Robust Realism and defeating the normative skeptic—*this* normative skeptic, at least, the one claiming that no moral belief is justified, or amounts to knowledge—are thus two different, though related, tasks: different, because Robust Realism is compatible with skepticism; related, because if the apparatus needed for a rejection of normative skepticism is unavailable to the robust realist, and if normative skepticism is highly implausible, this may count as a reason to reject Robust Realism after all.

Whereas Enoch's broadsides against quietism do not broach anything that differentiates robust moral realism from Moral Realism as a Moral Doctrine, this passage on epistemic skepticism does signal a divergence between them. Let us first ponder what that divergence is, before we consider how it pertains to the matter of robustness.

Though Enoch believes that robust moral realism is noncommittal on the question whether radical epistemic skepticism is correct, he himself is far from noncommittal on that question. Just as I devote many pages of *Moral Realism as a Moral Doctrine* to rebutting such skepticism (2009, 233–57), he devotes many pages of *Taking Morality Seriously* to the same enterprise (2011, 151–77). Nor do Enoch and I disagree at all over the fact that the strong mind-independence and irreducibility of moral principles are logically consistent with the unknowability of such principles. Given that he takes moral realism to consist solely in an insistence on that strong mind-independence and that irreducibility, he is correct in asserting that the substance of moral realism as he understands it is noncommittal on the matter of radical epistemic skepticism.

What is at issue, then, is his understanding of moral realism. Proponents of Moral Realism as a Moral Doctrine take moral realism to consist in a wide-ranging insistence on the objectivity of morality in several major ontological and epistemic and semantic dimensions. Among the chief aspects of the objectivity of the moral domain is the knowability of moral principles; my arguments against epistemic skepticism, which

I have mentioned above, are integral to my defense of moral realism rather than separate therefrom. Despite Enoch's curious suggestion to the contrary in the passage quoted above, my position on this matter has nothing to do with any thesis about the way in which the term "realism" should be used. Rather, it stems from the fact that my affirmations of the several dimensions of moral objectivity are mutually supporting and are to some degree mutually reliant.

As has already been remarked, Enoch is plainly correct in maintaining that the strong mind-independence and irreducibility of basic moral principles are logically consistent with the unknowability of those principles. However, he is on a much shakier footing when he presumes that an *affirmation* of the mind-independence and irreducibility of basic moral principles can intelligibly be conjoined with an *affirmation* of the unknowability of those principles (or with a noncommittal stance on their unknowability). On the one hand, he allows that an affirmation of the former kind would lose much of its plausibility if it were combined with an affirmation of the latter kind or with a noncommittal stance on skepticism. On the other hand, he underestimates the self-condemning bizarreness of such a combination. He asserts that, if a proponent of robust moral realism were to conclude that skeptics are right about the unknowability of robust normative principles, "the realist can then maintain her commitment to realism only at the price of a rather thoroughgoing skepticism about the normative. And while this is a possible position to have, stakes have certainly been raised" (2011, 162, footnote omitted). He adds that, "if the only way to be a realist is to deny epistemic justification for any normative belief, then Robust Realism loses significant plausibility points" (2011, 162). Several pages later he declares that, if he fails in his attempt to parry the epistemological challenges posed by skeptics, "Robust Realism may be committed to skepticism" (2011, 171).

What makes Enoch's position here so problematic is that one's commitment to moral realism is itself an array of normative beliefs and indeed an array of moral beliefs. Both in his robust moral realism and in my Moral Realism as a Moral Doctrine, the considerations that underpin one's insistence on strongly mind-independent and irreducible moral principles are sundry normative theses which also partake of strong mind-independence and irreducibility. Hence, if a philosopher feels obliged to accept that thoroughgoing skeptics are correct about the unknowability of robust normative truths, then she will lack any basis for maintaining her commitment to robust moral realism. She at best will have to suspend all judgment on the matter. She will be enmeshed either in a variant of Moore's paradox or in Moore's paradox itself. If the extreme epistemological skepticism which she embraces is an attack on the possibility of any justification or warrant for one's credence in the existence of robust normative principles, then her affirmation of that skepticism in combination with her affirmation of robust moral realism will amount to asserting "p, and I do not and cannot have any basis for believing that p." If the skepticism which she endorses is instead an attack on the possibility of any genuine credence in the existence of robust normative principles, then her affirmation of that skepticism in combination with her affirmation of robust moral realism will amount to asserting "p, and I do not believe that p." Both in the variant of

Moore's paradox and in Moore's paradox itself, far more than an impairment of plausibility is involved. In each case there is no formal contradiction between the asserted conjuncts, but in each case the conjunction of a theorist's assertions of those conjuncts is weirdly self-condemning. For this reason, rather than because of any strange lexicographical stipulation focused on the meaning of the word "realism," we should recognize that an endeavor to rebut skeptical doubts about the knowability of robust moral principles is indispensable as an element of one's espousal of moral realism. It is not a separate though related project.

4. A Pithy Conclusion

My aim in the second half of this chapter has scarcely been to deny that the moral principles envisaged by robust moral realism are genuinely robust (in a non-naturalistic sense). On the contrary, the point has been to underscore the fact that the robustness of all basic moral principles and of many derivative moral principles is proclaimed not only in Enoch's robust moral realism but also in Moral Realism as a Moral Doctrine. Both in robust moral realism and in Moral Realism as a Moral Doctrine, such moral principles are presented as strongly mind-independent and irreducible and universal and timeless. Hence, insofar as robustness is supposed to be a property that distinguishes Enoch's moral realism from Moral Realism as a Moral Doctrine, it is elusive and indeed illusive.

Even more problematic is the notion that Moral Realism as a Moral Doctrine can appropriately be classified as "quietist." A doctrine which holds that morality is objective in several major dimensions, and which argues for the objectivity of morality on moral grounds, is fully engaged rather than quietistically diffident or detached. Precisely because philosophers go astray if they invoke the property of robustness to differentiate between Moral Realism as a Moral Doctrine and Enoch's version of moral realism, they equally go astray if they apply the label "quietist" to Moral Realism as a Moral Doctrine.[17]

References

Blackburn, S. 1998. *Ruling Passions*. Oxford: Oxford University Press.
Enoch, D. 2011. *Taking Morality Seriously*. Oxford: Oxford University Press.
Gibbard, A. 1990. *Wise Choices, Apt Feelings*. Oxford: Oxford University Press.
Hart, H. 1994. *The Concept of Law*. 2nd ed. Oxford: Oxford University Press.
Kramer, M. 2009. *Moral Realism as a Moral Doctrine*. Oxford: Wiley-Blackwell.
Kramer, M. 2013. "Working on the Inside: Ronald Dworkin's Moral Philosophy." *Analysis* 73: 118–129.

---

[17] I am very grateful to Paul Bloomfield, David Copp, David Enoch, and Christine Tiefensee for their valuable comments on earlier drafts of this chapter. The usual disclaimers apply.

Kramer, M. 2014. *Torture and Moral Integrity*. Oxford: Oxford University Press.

Kramer, M. 2017. "There's Nothing Quasi about Quasi-Realism: Moral Realism as a Moral Doctrine." *Journal of Ethics* 21: 185–212.

Kramer, M. 2018. *H.L.A. Hart: The Nature of Law*. Cambridge: Polity Press.

Kramer, M. 2019. "Shakespeare, Moral Judgments, and Moral Realism." In *Routledge Companion to Shakespeare and Philosophy*, edited by C. Bourne and E. Bourne, 234–245. London: Routledge.

Kramer, M. (2022). "Looking Back and Looking Ahead: Replies to the Contributors." In *Without Trimmings: The Legal, Political, and Moral Philosophy of Matthew Kramer*, edited by V. Kurki and M. McBride, 363–552. Oxford: Oxford University Press.

Shafer-Landau, R. 2010. "The Possibility of Metaethics." *Boston University Law Review* 90: 479–496.

Stoljar, D. 1993. "Emotivism and Truth Conditions." *Philosophical Studies* 70: 81–101.

Tiefensee, C. 2022. "Metasemantics, Moral Realism, and Moral Doctrines." In *Without Trimmings: The Legal, Political, and Moral Philosophy of Matthew Kramer*, edited by V. Kurki and M. McBride, 189–204. Oxford: Oxford University Press.

Wedgwood, R. 2007. *The Nature of Normativity*. Oxford: Oxford University Press.

CHAPTER 24

PROSPECTS FOR A QUIETIST MORAL REALISM

MARK D. WARREN AND AMIE L. THOMASSON

To some, moral realism has seemed obvious: *Of course* there are moral facts (that torturing babies is wrong), moral obligations (to keep one's promises), and so on. To others, it has seemed mystifying. For what *could* these special "moral entities" be, how could they relate to ordinary physical properties such as weighing 200 pounds or being made of steel, how could we come to know them, and how could such things motivate us to act?

The Quietist Moral Realist aims to address both of these reactions: agreeing with the realist that of course there are moral facts, obligations, etc. (that is the realism), while finding a way to shed the metaphysical worries that have traditionally been thrown at moral realists (that is the quietism).

But what is quietism?

Taken in its original sense, quietism reaches back to the Pyrrhonian skeptics, who sought "imperturbability, quietude or tranquility of mind (*ataraxia*) through suspension of judgment (*epoché*) and refused assent (*synkatathesis*) to any philosophical thesis" (Virvidakis and Kindi, 2013). This characterization, however, leaves a great deal open: which philosophical theses are we refusing assent to? And why should we withhold judgment about them?[1]

A common answer to the first question is to say: we are withholding judgment on any *metaphysical* question. So, for example, having aptly noted that quietism may be held *about certain topics*, David Macarthur goes on to say "Arguably, the most interesting and

---

[1] Philip Pettit treats quietism as the view that "much philosophizing leaves no impact on ordinary experience or behavior. Philosophy has no place in practice" (2004, 304). We will leave this meaning of "quietism" to the side here, and we certainly do not mean here to endorse the view that any of these metaethical issues have no impact on practice. As Eric Campbell has argued forcefully (2014), even if there are no *metaphysical* problems that require us to revise our ethical practices, there may be other philosophical grounds for revision.

important form of quietism is quietism about metaphysics" (2008, 198). This, however, (as Macarthur mentions) just pushes back the question to: what do, or should, we mean by "metaphysics" here?[2]

In one standard sense of the word, "metaphysics" refers to attempts to answer questions about the existence and natures of things of various sorts. But we can't mean that quietists in metaethics are silent on the question of whether moral properties, facts, norms, or reasons exist.[3] For all of those theorists commonly labeled "quietists" insist that there *are* such things. As a result, it has become common in the metaethics literature to refer to the relevant position not simply as "quietism", but rather as "Quietist Moral Realism."[4]

There is, however, another sense of "metaphysics" in which the term is taken to refer to an *explanatory* enterprise: one on which certain entities are not just said to exist, but rather are *posited* in an effort to *explain* certain observations. The form of metaphysics the quietist realist rejects seems to be along these lines. Tristram McPherson, for example, describes the "quietist realist" view as characterized by two claims: "On the one hand it is a form of realism, accepting that there are normative facts and properties. On the other, it suggests that accepting the existence of such facts and properties does not lead to [certain] explanatory burdens" (2011, 224) such as explaining how moral facts could fit in with our broader metaphysical commitments, how we could come to know them, and how they could have a distinctive authority in our deliberations.

So, better understood, Quietist Moral Realists aim to accept that there *are* moral facts and properties, while avoiding many of the *explanatory burdens* thought to fall on traditional moral realists. The trick is to do the latter without appearing to simply dogmatically refuse to engage with metaphysical questions, and without giving responses that simply introduce further metaphysical difficulties.

In this chapter, we begin by examining the forms that Quietist Moral Realism has taken and the challenges they have faced, with a view to better assessing the prospects for a view along these lines. In Section 1 we give a brief overview of the history of Quietist Moral Realism, showing how quietists use an "internalizing maneuver" to treat the troubling explanatory demands of metaethics as answerable from *within* the

---

[2] Macarthur understands metaphysics as, "An attempt to explain phenomena or the appearances of things in terms of some conception of what is *really* basic, fundamental or real", which often involves asking "what is X?", looking for an essence. But, he goes on to say, metaphysics often involves claims beyond these, that are neither confirmed nor disconfirmed empirically, that are supposed to hold once and for all. (2008, 198–9).

[3] There is, we should note, a slight exegetical awkwardness here. Shall we frame the debate in terms of views about moral facts, of reasons, or of normativity in general? Some quietists, like Parfit and Scanlon, speak primarily of reasons, and offer substantive accounts of morality in terms of reasons to act—and then go on to give a quietist treatment of reasons themselves. Others, like Kramer, Dworkin, and Blackburn, offer straightforwardly quietist treatments of morality itself. In our view, little hinges on whether we express the particular problems at issue here in terms of the traditional problems regarding moral talk, truths, etc., or broader problems regarding normative talk, reasons, etc. So, we shall shift back and forth as context (and works cited) require.

[4] Tristram McPherson, for example, refers to it simply as "quietist realism" (2011, 224).

domain of moral discourse, which has its own standards for justification. Quietist Moral Realism has taken two main forms: a "relaxed realist" version, and a "pragmatist" version. In Section 2, we examine the relaxed realist version of the approach and how it aims to avoid the traditional metaphysical and epistemological problems of metaethics by treating these questions as to be settled via the "internal" standards of a distinct "moral domain." As we will see, however, even if we allow that the traditional explanatory burdens are thereby avoided, difficult new questions pop up in their place. Namely, how can we distinguish different domains? How can we justify adopting different justificatory standards in different domains, or justify claims that beliefs about some, but not other, domains may be motivating? We then turn in Section 3 to elucidate the pragmatist version of the approach, which aims to address these new questions by appealing to the different *functions* of diverse areas of discourse.

But how can we identify the functions of moral discourse? We turn in Section 4 to work in Systemic Functional Linguistics as the basis for a clearer view of the functions moral discourse serves, the rules it follows, and ways in which these differ from the functions and rules governing everyday empirical discourse. Once this is in place, as we will argue in Section 5, we can see our way to a stronger form of quietism that (while still affirming realism) does not simply remain *quiet* about the explanatory demands of metaethics, but rather is able to *diagnose* where they go wrong, and to *justify* the characteristic internalizing maneuver. The pragmatist roots of this approach might lead some to doubt that this form of *quietism* still counts as a form of moral *realism*. But as we will argue, that would be a mistake. For a functional discourse analysis also gives us reason to accept an "easy" approach to ontology (see Thomasson 2015). And given that "easy" approach we are clearly entitled to say that there *are* moral facts and properties, in the only sense that has sense—clearly affirming realism.[5]

The moral of the story will be that by combining a neo-pragmatic analysis of the discourse with an easy approach to ontology, we can get a form of Quietist Moral Realism that is far stronger than critics of quietism have appreciated. With that on the table, we argue, the prospects for a form of Quietist Moral Realism are good, and the quietist approach should get a serious hearing in debates in metaethics.

1. Two Forms of Quietist Moral Realism

Philosophers as diverse as Simon Blackburn, Tim Scanlon, Ronald Dworkin, and Derek Parfit have all been labeled "quietists."[6] If you were a metaethicist who just stepped out

---

[5] This is a position one of us has elsewhere called "simple" (as contrasted with "explanatory") realism (Thomasson 2015, Chapter 3).

[6] Applications of the label are often disputed, however. Matthew Kramer (this volume) rejects the label altogether. Price considers Blackburn's quasi-realism as motivating a local metaphysical

of a time machine from the twentieth century, you might be rather surprised to see a quasi-realist like Blackburn, on one hand, and non-naturalists like Dworkin, Scanlon, and Parfit, on the other, put in the same bucket. The ancestry of the two approaches could hardly be more different. Blackburn's expressivism can be traced back to A. J. Ayer's emotivism: a view that has no sympathies with traditional moral realism, that is deeply concerned with presenting a naturalistically plausible conception of ethical discourse, and is mobilized by skepticism about the cognitive nature of morality. The relaxed realist's approach, by contrast, traces to the non-naturalist ethics of G. E. Moore: a resolutely realist and cognitivist view about ethics, rejecting the demands of a naturalistic metaphysics.

Meta-ethicists in the twenty-first century have gotten used to it. Blackburn's quasi-realism has become more and more distanced from its antirealist ancestors. Indeed, his quasi-realism is motivated by the goal of making sense of some of the standard tenets of realism: cognitivism, objectivity, and so on. As quasi-realism makes these concessions to the philosophical "right," non-naturalists have moved closer to the "left," attenuating the denial of naturalism and insisting that positing non-natural facts doesn't commit them to strange Platonic entities to which moral truths correspond, because such a correspondence isn't required. Parfit, for his part, is happy to accept quasi-realism as a species of his non-realist cognitivism.[7]

The optimist might even suppose that the fact that two such different starting places have been tunnelling towards the same territory gives hope that there is an attractive and workable metaethical position to be found there. Our project here is to dig it out.

As mentioned above, the Quietist Moral Realist accepts that there *are* moral facts or properties, and yet aims to reject the "explanatory burdens" that have beset traditional moral realists. These "explanatory burdens" are generally placed in three categories:[8]

---

quietism about the relevant domains (2011, 12); McPherson, however, distinguishes quasi-realists from those he considers quietist realists (2011, 224–5)—including Scanlon, Parfit, and Dworkin. Enoch and McPherson label Dworkin, Kramer, and Parfit quietists (2017, 821). Cowie classifies Parfit, Skorupski, Dworkin, and Scanlon together as holding that normative entities exist in a "non-metaphysical sense" (2014, 661).

[7] As Jamie Dreier has emphasized (2004 and 2015b), we have arrived at a landscape where it has become difficult to properly differentiate between (at least some parts of) the two camps.

[8] Ridge (2019, 149–50) and McPherson (2011, 224) both raise versions of these three explanatory demands. Copp (2018) raises an additional challenge: how the relaxed realist can give a semantics for moral statements that explains the meanings of moral terms and the truth-conditions of moral claims. For, inasmuch as relaxed realists understand moral facts, properties, and the like to have no robust ontological implications—and opt instead for a minimalist treatment of these entities—then these cannot be marshalled in any *explanatory* account of the meanings of moral terms, nor can such things be explanatory truth-makers of our moral claims (compare Thomasson 2015, Chapter 3). We think this is exactly right. While we do not have space to address the semantic challenge directly here, it is worth noting that the pragmatist view we aim to develop would give an entirely different sort of account of the meanings of moral terms (pursuing a version of what Copp calls the 'Wide Non-Realist Strategy" (2018, 587)). One promising approach (following Williams 2011) is to give an account of meanings in terms of the rules of use for the relevant terms (rules that enable these terms to serve their characteristic function). For a development of this approach, see Warren (2015).

1. **Metaphysical questions:** Are there *really* normative facts, moral properties, obligations, etc.?[9] If so, how can such things "fit with our broader metaphysical commitments?" (McPherson 2011, 224). How are they related to "natural" facts, properties, etc.?[10] If they are, as some relaxed realists claim, in some sense not "ontologically weighty" (Parfit 2017, 60), what does that mean, and what is the difference between ontologically "robust" facts and properties, and those that are not?[11]
2. **Epistemological questions:** If there are moral or (more broadly) normative truths, how could we possibly come to *know* them? This problem is thought to be exacerbated if we deny (in each case) that they are truths about *natural* facts. For how can we come into the relevant kind of causal or perceptual contact with non-natural facts?
3. **Motivational questions:** How could mere beliefs or judgments about moral or normative facts or properties motivate us to act? (Scanlon 2014, 57)

One thing quietists have in common is a desire to avoid, or perhaps reconceptualize, the above "explanatory burdens" in a way that does not require serious metaphysical investigations. Quietists also share a strategy for avoiding these traditional explanatory burdens. That strategy is to deny the common metaethical assumption "that the most fundamental questions about morality are not themselves moral, but rather metaphysical, questions" (Dworkin 2011, 25). That is, they refuse to think of these issues as *external to* the moral enterprise, insisting that seemingly metaphysical questions can only be addressed by appealing to standards that are in some sense *internal* to ethical discourse. As McPherson puts it, the quietist strategy is "to suggest that the relevant explanatory burdens are best understood as falling on, and being met by, substantive normative theories rather than metanormative theories", so that in interpreting our first-order normative claims, there is "much less to explain" than others have thought. (2011, 227).

This internalizing maneuver is at the heart of Blackburn's frequent appeals to minimalism about truth.[12] If the claim that "It is true that X is wrong" means no more than "X is wrong," our understanding of the former should not attempt to outstrip our basis for the latter. How do we know that lying is wrong? Not by appealing to a moral property of wrongness (natural or otherwise) that is instantiated in all and only wrong acts, but instead by looking at how we know lying is wrong—its harmful effects on the party lied to, the way it undermines trust, and so on. If we want to understand the truth (or the error) of a moral assertion, we must recognize that it "is imputed from within the practice,

---

[9] Jamie Dreier presses the metaphysical question this way: "The idea that [normative truths] do constitute a distinct realm, another world, but need no metaphysical reality, is somewhat puzzling" (2015b, 158).

[10] The last way of presenting the metaphysical explanatory demand is a version of what Huw Price (2011, 186) has called the "placement problem", building on what Frank Jackson originally called "the location problem" (1998, 3).

[11] For discussion of this last point, see Copp 2018, 571.

[12] See also Kramer (2009, 271–3) for an account of the relationship between minimalism and this strategy.

from an immersion in the business of making, criticizing, accepting or withdrawing the verdicts whose impact is essentially practical" (Blackburn 2009, 210).

Ronald Dworkin echoes Blackburn's sentiment, arguing that there is no way to sensibly ask about the truth of moral propositions without presupposing some moral values:

> Morality and other departments of value are philosophically independent. Answers to large questions about moral truth and knowledge must be sought within those departments, not outside them. (2011, 24)

Dworkin sees moral concepts as belonging among many types of *interpretive* concepts, each with their own respective *genres*: history, poetry, religion, and law are all genres that we must interpret. Crucially, questions about the nature of moral, historical, and legal truth are fundamentally interpretive questions which cannot be answered from the outside; the answers to metaethical questions—even very abstract moral questions about, e.g., whether moral facts are objective, or whether they apply universally—are best understood as fundamentally moral questions:

> The claim that abortion is objectively wrong seems equivalent in ordinary discourse to [the further claim]: that abortion would still be wrong even if no one thought it was. That further claim, read most naturally, is just another way of emphasizing the content of the original moral claim, of emphasizing, once again, that I mean that abortion is just plain wrong, not wrong only if or because people think it is. (2011, 54)

Likewise, the claim that abortion is universally wrong makes it plain "that in my view abortion is wrong for everyone, no matter in what circumstance or culture or of what disposition or from what ethical or religious background" (2011, 54).

There is a surprising affinity between Blackburn and Dworkin here. Both encourage us to understand these further claims as moral, rather than metaphysical, assertions—indeed, they both insist that there is no other way to understand them. This has implications for potential skeptics. Dworkin argues that they cannot "stand outside a whole body of belief, and . . . judge it whole from premises or attitudes that owe nothing to it" (1996, 88)—and so they have no place from which to apply an Archimedean lever. Blackburn uses the metaphor of Neurath's boat (1993, 79; 2009, 201), which on an open sea can only be rebuilt plank by plank. Even the committed skeptic must "stand on one part of the (Neurathian) boat and inspect the other parts" (2001, 318). Both thereby suggest that metaethical issues can only be dealt with *internally*, using the same well-worn tools we use when engaged in ethical discourse.

Internalizing moral questions in this way gives the quietist an initial response to the three explanatory burdens described above. But how can we justify this maneuver? What is it that entitles us to address these explanatory burdens from *within* moral discourse—rather than treating them as "deep" questions for traditional metaphysics or epistemology? It is in addressing that question that the two forms of quietism come apart.

As noted above, despite all they have in common, those labeled as metaethical "quietists" derive from two very different origins. Broadly speaking, growing out of these distinct ancestries are two importantly different camps of contemporary quietists, which we will call the "relaxed realist" camp and the "pragmatist" camp. The "relaxed realist" camp is generally thought to be represented by Scanlon, Parfit, Dworkin, and Kramer[13] (cf. McGrath 2014, 186–87), and generally defends the internalizing maneuver by[14] insisting that the interesting and important metaphysical questions are "domain-specific—questions about the metaphysics *of* some particular domain or domains" (Scanlon 2014, 25).[15] Questions about the existence of moral facts, our knowledge of them or motivation by them are, on this view, to be addressed from within a moral standpoint, because these questions concern a distinctive "moral domain." The pragmatist camp, on the other hand, is generally thought to be occupied by such figures as Price, Blackburn, Gibbard, Brandom, and Rorty.[16] Rather than appealing to different *domains*, pragmatists typically aim to diagnose the metaphysical problems as arising from mistakes about the category or function of a relevant area of *discourse*.

We will next, in Section 2, discuss the relaxed realist approach, the problems that have been raised for it, and remaining questions it leaves us with. Thereafter, in Section 3 we will return to examine the pragmatist approach, showing the ways pragmatist quietists appeal to differences in the *functions* of the relevant areas of discourse to justify the internalizing maneuver and to undermine the thought that any legitimate explanatory demands remain.

---

[13] Matthew Kramer is grouped with the other relaxed realists by Ingram (2017), Enoch and McPherson (2017), and Tiefensee (2019)—though Tiefensee's characterization of relaxed realism is broad enough to include pragmatists like Blackburn—but we disagree with this categorization. Kramer is happy to make use of the internalizing maneuver; his (2009) is an extended exploration of this technique. But he also emphasizes the compatibility of this maneuver with a pragmatic account of moral discourse (2017).

[14] Copp (2018, 570) refers to these "relaxed realist" views as forms of "avant-garde nonnaturalism" or (following Parfit) "nonrealist cognitivism."

[15] Relaxed Realists typically aim to distance themselves from the pragmatist quasi-realism of Blackburn and Gibbard, since they take it to be tied to noncognitivism. Scanlon insists on a cognitivist interpretation of judgments about reasons for action, taking these as *beliefs about reasons* (not as decisions, imperatives, or attitudes), which he argues is "more in accord with the common-sense understanding of normative judgments than expressivist interpretations are" (2014, 61). Parfit complains that because they are noncognitivists, quasi-realists have an unconvincing model of moral disagreement (2011, 387–9) and so cannot account for the concept of moral mistakes or moral improvement (2011, 394–7). Finally, Dworkin is skeptical that the pragmatic approach has the resources available to sufficiently distinguish itself from more traditional nonquietist accounts (1996, 110–112). See also Dworkin (2011, 35–7).

[16] Though interestingly, Macarthur also places Scanlon in this camp (2008, 196).

2. Relaxed Realism and Its Challenges

Relaxed realism is a species of metaethical non-naturalism. Non-naturalists hold that moral properties are not reducible or otherwise identical to natural properties, but that nevertheless our moral assertions straightforwardly express beliefs which can be true or false. The three explanatory burdens we saw in Section 1 seem especially burdensome here. It's hard enough for a naturalistic metaethics to account for the metaphysics and epistemology of moral properties—or to explain how they come to motivate us. If moral properties aren't even natural properties, though, how are we going to have any hope of making sense of these features?

The relaxed realist offers a two-part answer: First, they distinguish the moral domain or "genre" from the domain of the natural sciences. They note that these domains operate according to their own particular rules or standards. Second, they argue that the standards suitable for some domains, like the natural sciences, are not those suitable for moral inquiry—and we can rely on the internal standards for moral inquiry to address the explanatory burdens.

This two-step process helps us make sense of why, within the moral domain, relaxed realists like Scanlon and Parfit argue that moral truths "need no natural or special metaphysical reality in order to have the significance that we commonly grant them" (Scanlon 2014, 52), because they are, "in the strongest sense, true, but these truths have no positive ontological implications" (Parfit, Vol II, 479). In the scientific domain, it's plausible to hold that facts require some kind of metaphysical grounding. The fact that water expands when it freezes is explained by "deeper" natural facts about the molecular structure of water, and how those molecules interact when they have lower average kinetic energy. But it would be a mistake to look for the same kind of explanation in the moral domain, to make what Blackburn (this volume) calls the "constitutive demand"—a demand for an account of what something being right or wrong *consists in*.

The appeal to different domains is supposed to relieve us of the metaphysical challenge about whether there "really" are such things as moral facts or properties. For we can, from an internal standpoint, make sense of moral facts (e.g., that it's wrong to torture kittens), and there is no external standpoint from which we can persist in asking if there *really* are such moral facts. Similarly, we can avoid metaphysical questions about whether "positing" such things could really *explain* anything. For the demand for this kind of *explanation* only makes sense within certain domains—such as that of empirical science (Cf. Scanlon 2014, 26–27, and Kramer 2009, 199–207).

The same two steps alleviate the epistemological explanatory burdens. We can make sense of moral knowledge as arising from a kind of competence with the rules and norms internal to moral discourse. The demand that moral knowledge requires some kind of plausible causal connection between belief and fact arises from a conflation of the standards of the moral and scientific domains:

> We cannot be, in any causal way, "in touch" with moral truth. But we can nevertheless think well or badly about moral issues. What is good and bad thinking is itself a moral question, of course: a moral epistemology is part of substantive moral theory. (Dworkin 12)

The internalizing maneuver, then, gives relaxed realists a way to sidestep concerns about how we could come to have epistemic access to strange moral entities, just as it gives them a way to dispel concerns about moral ontology. "The reality and knowability of moral properties are not starkly ontological or epistemological matters; they are fundamentally moral matters" (Kramer 2009, 200). Questions of moral epistemology only make sense when posed within the moral domain. Their answers do not require us to do any metaphysics.

Finally, the question of how an irreducible non-natural fact could have any kind of motivational import for a natural creature like a human doesn't seem so mysterious, when seen from *within* that discourse. A child asks why it's wrong to lie. You explain that it's wrong because lying hurts people's feelings; it's not the sort of thing you'd like others to do to you; it undermines trust in a community; it treats people as mere means to an end. And you don't want to do that, do you? Inasmuch as the child has become a competent moral agent—that is, inasmuch as she understands these points from within the discourse—these reasons should weigh on her decisions about lying. If she responds instead with a blank, uncomprehending stare, this is evidence that she has not yet fully developed as a moral agent (cf. Ridge 2019, 149). The relaxed realist appeals to the fact that moral judgments have a certain content that marks them out as belonging to the moral domain—a content that connects them to motivational significance (cf. Dworkin 1996, 116). Judgments in other domains (those of "ordinary matters of fact") lack this connection. The third explanatory burden, then, is also addressed by appealing to differences of domains (cf. Scanlon 2014, Chapter 3).

The idea that there are different domains, then, does crucial work for relaxed realist versions of quietist moral realism. Questions about the existence of moral facts and about how we can know them, or whether they may be action-guiding, are to be settled by the standards *internal* to the moral domain—not by invoking "external" standards of deep metaphysical or epistemological inquiry.

But the appeal to different domains raises new questions. First, what distinguishes the different domains? How can we determine where we have different domains? David Enoch and Tristram McPherson (2017) press this question, asking what domains are and how they are individuated. As they put it, we "need at least the sketch of a non–ad hoc way of explaining which (and how many) domains there are. Absent such an explanation, it is unclear whether the notion can do any work" (2017, 824). Without a clear response, they suggest, just about *anything* could be counted as a domain.

Second, what justifies the standards appropriate to acquiring knowledge within each domain? As Michael Ridge puts it, "One might worry that without some general *ex ante* constraint on what makes a domain legitimate the theory will make it too easy to have justified beliefs about esoteric domains" (2019, 152). Surely not just any standards will do. Scanlon considers and responds to this worry, writing:

> There are mathematical standards for answering mathematical questions, scientific standards for answering empirical questions about the physical world, and forms of practical reasoning for answering questions about what we have reason to do. These standards typically consist, in part, of substantive principles about the domain, such as mathematical axioms, moral principles, and scientific generalizations. (2014, 20)

This seems apt, but so far no more than trivial: to say that there are mathematical standards for answering mathematical questions does not yet tell us what these standards are, or why (other than sharing a name) they are appropriate.

Third, why should beliefs *about a domain of morality*—unlike beliefs about other sorts of things—motivate us to act? The relaxed realist can make sense of why these sorts of beliefs (unlike others) have motivational import, given what they're *about*. Explaining motivation in terms of features of the entities represented, however, would undermine the quietist's denial that metaphysical questions should take priority. It also seems to fall short as an "explanation": for if moral facts are just a special kind of non-natural thing in the world, how can we explain why we are *required to respond to these things?* (See Dreier 2015a, 177–80; 2015b, 166–8)[17].

In sum, relaxed realists aim to avoid the classic metaphysical, epistemological, and motivational explanatory puzzles by appealing to the differences that arise in different *domains* or *genres*—where the standards across domains may vary for claiming that certain things (peacocks, reasons, numbers) exist; for claiming to have knowledge of the relevant sorts of facts; and regarding whether or not beliefs with those contents motivate action. But as we have seen, this response raises new questions: How can we understand the relevant "domains," and what distinguishes them? *Why* is it appropriate to have the relevant standards in each domain? And why should these domain differences make a difference to whether or not the relevant beliefs are motivational?

As we see it, there are three options available in response to these questions:[18]

---

[17] Here we again see the awkward wrinkle we noted in fn. 3 above. Dreier's critiques of Parfit and Scanlon here are specifically levelled at the motivational implications of their "Reasons Fundamentalism"—which combines "non-naturalist realism about fundamental normative properties... with the claim that the property of being a reason is the fundamental normative property"—it is, in short, a kind of relaxed realism about reasons (2015b, 155). But the points Dreier raises apply just as aptly here for morality as they do for reasons.

[18] Huw Price (2019, 8) similarly observes that relaxed realists face a trilemma: to go metaphysical, to be extreme quietists and simply fail to engage with the questions, or to turn to a version of expressivism (broadly construed). See also Annika Böddeling (2020), who argues that relaxed realists face a dilemma: they must either account for their cognitivism in minimalist terms, in which case they fail to adequately distinguish their view from quasi-realism, or they must give a substantive account of moral truth and belief, in which case they seem to abandon the attractively quietist features of the view.

1. **Representationalism:** We can explain the differences in domains and the appropriateness of standards in terms of the facts or properties which they help us accurately represent or come to know.
2. **Extreme quietism:** We can remain quiet in the face of the question—or simply make these distinctions in trivial terms.
3. **Pragmatism:** We can address these questions in pragmatic, functional terms.

We need a way to justify the claim that there may be perfectly legitimate variations in the *standards for claiming that there are* things of certain kinds (peacocks, reasons, numbers, possibilities . . .), and also in the *methods for acquiring knowledge* of different kinds (everyday empirical, moral, mathematical, modal . . .). The thought that these concern different "domains" is okay as a starting place. But this way of putting things may encourage a metaphysics-first approach if it suggests that it is the different *natures of the objects concerned* that explain or justify the different standards. While this strategy may be tempting to heavyweight metaphysicians, it should not be on the table for quietists, who hoped to evade traditional (domain-external) metaphysical questions about the existence or natures of the entities in question.

The second approach—an extreme quietism that simply refuses to engage with these questions—however, leaves something important and interesting unexplained. Relaxed realists aptly identify different areas (domains, or genres) of discourse—the empirical, the mathematical, the modal, the moral—and urge that each is to be recognized as having its own standards. That seems right.

But *why* should we have such different areas of discourse (or, if you prefer, sorts of concepts)? Why *should* they follow different rules? What purposes in human life does it serve to have these different forms of discourse? Without addressing questions like these, this form of quietism seems rather too quiet.

3. The Pragmatist Approach

The most promising way of developing quietism seems to us to be option 3: a pragmatist approach. For such an approach offers an appealing alternative to both the representationalist's ways of dealing with the questions, and to an unsatisfying refusal to engage. As David Macarthur puts it, "One of the common misconceptions about quietism is that the quietist simply turns his back on metaphysical problems, an attitude that strikes many metaphysicians as dogmatic and dismissive" (2008, 199). Instead, as Macarthur makes clear, at its best, the pragmatist quietist aims to "earn the right not to have to answer the metaphysical problem in question" (2008, 199)—by both *diagnosing* the mistake(s) behind the original metaphysical problem and showing how we should *reconceptualize* the relevant issue.

So how can a pragmatist approach give us a more satisfying response to questions about *how* we can distinguish different domains, *why* the relevant standards are appropriate, and why some (but not other) beliefs or judgments should be motivating? The key is to begin by addressing questions about the functions of different areas of language. This is an approach that:

> begins with linguistic explananda rather than material explananda; with phenomena concerning the use of certain terms and concepts, rather than with things or properties of a non-linguistic nature. It begins with linguistic behavior, and asks broadly anthropological questions: How are we to understand the roles and functions of the behavior in question, in the lives of the creatures concerned? What is its practical significance? Whence its genealogy? (Price 2011, 231)

Approaching questions about domains in terms of differences in "linguistic frameworks" may bring to mind Carnap, who insisted that we may introduce new linguistic frameworks without first answering ontological questions "concerning the existence or reality of the total system of new entities" (1950/1956, 214). In introducing a new linguistic framework, we introduce "new ways of speaking, subject to new rules" (1950/1956, 206)—that may then *entitle* us to introduce new singular terms and variables quantifying over them—in what we may *then*, if we like, call a "domain."[19]

A related approach can be seen in Gilbert Ryle's (1949) idea that certain explanatory demands in philosophy ("how is the mind related to the body?" "how can we come to have knowledge of other minds?") arose from *category mistakes*. For as Ryle insisted, category differences must be understood first and foremost not in terms of the *category of object referred to* (in terms of the differences between minds and bodies), but in terms of *linguistic categories*, or better still, in terms of *what we are doing* when we say someone has a false belief versus when we say they have a new coffee table. Huw Price suggests understanding Ryle's category distinctions in explicitly functional terms, writing, "Ryle's functional orientation ... will ... lead us to focus on the difference between the *functions* of talk of beliefs and talk of tables; on the issue of what the two kinds of talk are *for*, rather than that of what they are *about*" (2009, 331).

In metaethics, the pragmatist approach has been most closely associated with the work of Blackburn and Gibbard. Both begin from an alternative functional view of moral discourse—seeing it as fundamentally *not* in the business of tracking and reporting on worldly facts, but rather as providing ways to express our attitudes (Blackburn) or planning states (Gibbard). But despite the alternative functional story, Blackburn and Gibbard take pains to show how, from that beginning, we could come to make moral statements which are capable of being true or false. Moreover, we could assert that there are moral facts and properties, not in some "pretending" or "as if" way, but in the ordinary English sense. While this point may be obscured by the term "*quasi-realism*" (introduced to form a contrast with traditional forms of realism, but which might suggest that something is "held back"), it is clear in Blackburn's work that that

---

[19] Scanlon distances himself from Carnap's talk of "linguistic rules" (2014, 19n.3), though it is not clear to us exactly why.

would be a misreading. As he puts it straightforwardly, "... if the words retain an uncorrupted, English, sense, then ... the quasi-realist, holds not just that we talk and think as if there are ... [moral or modal properties etc.], but that there are" (Blackburn 1993, 57). Thus we get not just pragmatism, but a form of pragmatist *moral realism*. Yet it is clearly a *quietist* form of moral realism. For the pragmatist appeals to claims about the different *functions* of the relevant areas of discourse to both diagnose the mistakes behind the alleged metaphysical problems, and to reconceptualize the relevant problems in the area: as problems not about what moral properties (say) *are* (or how they could be *known*, or how they could be *motivating*), but rather as problems about how the relevant areas of discourse function and what rules they follow (cf. Macarthur 2008, 200–204).

Broadly speaking, the pragmatist argues that the apparent metaphysical problems regarding, say, moral language, rely on misconceptions about the *functions* the relevant language serves. If this pragmatic approach requires distinguishing functions, however, this makes it crucial to say how we can identify and justify claims about the functions that different areas of discourse serve.[20] Traditional realists are often suspicious of this very enterprise, suspecting expressivists of just "making it up," and responding that we can simply give a uniform functional view: that the function of all forms of indicative discourse is *to state truths about the world*.

We can do better in responding to such skeptics, and in buttressing a pragmatist version of Quietist Moral Realism, if we can answer functional questions in empirical terms. Price makes this clear: "the verdict on the Carnap-Ryle view must await excavations—first-order scientific inquiries into the underlying functions of language in human life" (2009, 335).

We needn't wait for long. For, to make good on the pragmatist's idea that forms of language serve many different functions, we can turn to the inquiries conducted by Systemic Functional Linguistics. We will turn next to some exposition of results in Systemic Functional Linguistics, before returning in Section 5 to show the ways in which this work can enable the quietist to discharge the explanatory burdens and provide a deeper more resilient form of quietist moral realism.

4. Systemic Functional Linguistics and the Functions of Moral Language

Systemic Functional Linguistics begins from the idea that "language has evolved in the service of certain functions" (Halliday 1973, 14) and that the "nature of language is closely related to ... the functions it has to serve" (1970, 141). It involves taking a

---

[20] Blackburn addresses this question in general terms, suggesting that "For a given local area, the answer is plain: we garner evidence from its surroundings, or in other words from other things we think, for example about description, explanation, and representation of the world" (1993, 7).

"descriptive-ethnographic view" of language, on which "linguistics is part of anthropology, and grammar is part of culture" (Halliday 1977, 36–7).

Michael Halliday's inquiries in Systemic Functional Linguistics begin with language development in children. What is distinctive about the language of early childhood is that uses of language wear their functions on their sleeve—each utterance serving a single function. As Halliday puts it, in early childhood language, the internal form of the utterance "reflects rather directly the function that it is being used to serve" (1973, 19). Halliday identifies six standard functions served, including the instrumental (to request goods or services: "milk!"); the regulatory (to control the behavior of others: "Mama, come!"); the interactional (greetings, callings: "bye bye"); personal (for self-expression of feelings); heuristic (questioning, demanding explanation), and imaginative ("let's pretend"). There is also, as a relatively late development, the informative or representational function, on which language is used as a means of communicating information to someone the speaker assumes doesn't know it (1973, 27). Although this is a late development for the child, the representational function comes to dominate the adult's "conception of the use of language" (1973, 27). It has come to dominate philosophical thinking about language as well, as can be seen in the dominance of what Price calls the Representationalist proto-theory of language (2011, 4–5).

These functions of early childhood language, Halliday suggests, persist in mature language. But their expression becomes more complex. For we learn to use grammatical structures that give us options for serving these functions in various ways, and that enable us to simultaneously serve different functions (1973, 26–7; 1975, 42).[21]

Moral discourse seems to develop out of a need to serve the regulatory function—of regulating the behavior of others, and perhaps also (ultimately) of ourselves. But there are (grammatically) many ways to do this. The child aims to regulate the behavior of others through imperatives. But this would not suffice to serve all the functions of a mature moral language. In mature speech, moral requirements are characteristically expressed not (just) through imperatives ("Don't kill") but through modal terms ("You must not kill"). Ryle (1950) already noted one useful function of shifting to modals: while imperatives enable us only to impose *requirements*, modal terms also enable us to express *permissions* ("You *may* lie if needed to save a life"). Modal terms in general, as systemic functional linguistics has it, provide ways in which "a language user can intrude on her message, expressing attitudes and judgments of various kinds" (Eggins 2004, 172). Modal terms such as "should" and "must" enable us to express meanings of obligation, in *degrees ranging* from the strict (you *must* . . .) to less strict (you *should* . . .) (Eggins 2004, 179–181).

Of course simple modal statements are not our only form of regulatory language in adult speech. Even in nonmoral language, we can shift from a modal expression ("You

---

[21] Systemic Functional Linguistics identifies three categories of functions, or 'metafunctions', including ideational, interpersonal, and textual. Grammatical structure enables most clauses uttered by a mature speaker to serve all three metafunctions at once (See Eggins 2004, 11–12, and Halliday 2009, 99–104).

must all read Kant") to the use of "objective" modality ("It is required that all students read Kant"). The shift to the impersonal modal has the effect of covering the speaker; "it is a covert attempt to get people to do things without having to take responsibility for issuing the command" (Eggins 2004, 186). In the case of morality, this grammatical shift enables us to present moral language as not merely issuing commands or requirements from some individual or authority ("Give to charity"), but rather to present it as *what must be done* ("It is a moral requirement that one give to charity"), without appealing to any commands. As a result, such expressions are able to serve a regulatory function without being properly subject to challenges such as "but I don't want to," "who says I should?," and the like.[22]

From impersonal modals (like "It is required that students read Kant"), we can go on to nominalize and speak of requirements, e.g., "A requirement of the course is reading Kant." This then enables us to refer back to, enumerate, and quantify requirements, e.g., "the five requirements for this course are . . . ." We can then also qualify requirements and compare them: "The requirements of this course are very onerous," "The requirements of this course are more onerous than those for the course I took last term." Such nominalizations again play a central role in properly *moral* discourse, enabling us to say things such as: "the moral requirements incumbent on any rational being are . . . ," "our moral obligations are independent of our desires," and so on.

We began from the relaxed realist's idea that a moral "domain" should be distinguished from other domains (such as that of everyday empirical knowledge or science), and should be acknowledged as following its own standards for knowledge. We then suggested that talk of "domains" should *not* be understood in terms of differences in *objects* of the domain, but rather traced to differences in the *functions* of the discourse in question. While the crucial differences we have uncovered underlie the ways in which different "domains" have been distinguished, these are at bottom differences in the *functions* of the discourse, not in the "*natures*" of the "*objects*."

We turned to systemic functional linguistics for help in addressing questions about what the functions of moral discourse are. We have raised the hypothesis that the ur-function, out of which moral language develops, is regulatory—a function of guiding and controlling behavior. But this is certainly not all that a fully developed moral language—complete with reference to moral obligations, reasons for action, and the like—enables us to do. As we have seen, mature moral language introduces new forms of speech, including not just commands and prohibitions (such as could perform the original regulatory functions), but also modal formulations, depersonalized expressions, nominalized appeals to moral requirements or obligations, and so on. These new forms of speech, which form part of any fully developed system of moral language, are essential for a full moral system to do its work. What do they do for us? Let us summarize:

---

[22] Does this characteristic impersonal form of moral language also enable it to "cover its tracks" in ways that may be systematically deceptive, as Nietzsche would have suggested? We will leave that open here. For interesting discussion, see Campbell (2014).

- **Imperatives** serve a function of regulating behavior.
- Adding **modal expressions** enables us to not merely *command* but also to *permit* various forms of behavior, and to do so with varying *degrees* of stringency.
- **Impersonal modals** enable the commands (and permissions) to be made in a way that does not avert to the authority of the speaker to impose commands.
- **Nominalizations from modals** enable us to speak of requirements as "things," in ways that enable us to demand and give *justifications* for thinking that there are such requirements, to qualify, quantify, and compare requirements, and so on.

These more highly developed forms of moral language augment the ur-function of regulation along several dimensions. They enable a discourse wherein shared requirements and permissions can be given, presented in an *authority-independent* way, *publicly justified*, and made *open to reason, comparative evaluation, and debate*.

This suggests the beginnings of a functional account of the domain of moral discourse. Without these shared features, one may be able to have a top-down system of behavioral control (such as Hobbes imagined coming from the commands of the sovereign), but not what we would regard as a fully developed *moral* system. Taken together, we can see how these various forms of speech enable moral discourse to serve as a tool in coordinating our behavior, in public and reasoned ways. This account of the functions of a mature system of moral language fits well with other accounts of the function of a moral system. As Richard Joyce put it:

> By providing a framework within which both one's own actions and others' actions may be evaluated, moral judgments can act as a kind of "common currency" for collective negotiation and decision-making. Moral judgment thus can function as a kind of social glue, bonding individuals together in a shared justificatory structure and providing a tool for solving many group coordination problems. (2006, 117)[23]

A common response from traditional moral realists at this stage is to say: Sure, we can *all* accept views like these about the functions moral discourse serves. But (they will say) "that doesn't undermine the view that there *are* moral facts and properties, obligations and reasons, and that we can speak truths about them." So true. We will come back to these points below in clarifying why the resulting view *is* a form of moral realism.

"So why" (the critic may go on to ask), "does it make a difference—why bother with this long-winded functional story?" That is the key point, and the answer is this: the functional story does not come as a mere add-on linguistic/anthropological curiosity. These differences in function come with differences in the rules such terms follow and the methods by which they enter language. And fully grasping those differences enables us to show why many of the "explanatory burdens" placed on traditional moral realists are mistakes that grow out of a failure to acknowledge these crucial differences. We will

---

[23] Cf. Warren (2015, 269–71; 2018, 477) and Timmons (1999, 157).

next discuss these differences in introduction rules, and then turn to show how this enables us, first, to affirm realism, and second, to shed the alleged explanatory burdens.

5. How to Develop a Quietist Moral Realism

The work in Systemic Functional Linguistics enables us to see functional differences between talk of obligations versus talk of dogs and apples. But it does more than just that. It also enables us to see that the key noun terms used in moral discourse enter into language through entirely different routes, and with entirely different introduction rules, than more basic nouns like "dog" and "apple." Consider nominative terms for moral requirements, duties, or obligations, as contrasted with nouns like "dog" and "apple." In early stages of language development, semantics and grammar are "congruent": processes are represented by verbs, entities by nouns, and so on (Halliday 2009, 117–21; Hopper and Thompson 1985, 155–6). Nouns such as "dog" and "apple" are congruent: they name a single, visible, tangible object (Hopper and Thompson 1985, 155–6; Halliday 2009, 116). Children acquire such congruent nouns first, typically ostensively, in investigating their environment.[24] Such terms are initially used in serving the heuristic function—enabling the child to label and go on to acquire more information about the objects: "At this very early stage, in its most elementary form, the heuristic use of language is the demand for a name, which is the child's way of categorizing the objects of the physical world" (Halliday 1975, 20).

By contrast, the terms for duties, obligations, and requirements are not congruent. They enter language at a relatively late phase, as what Halliday calls "grammatical metaphors" (2009, 116–38). Grammatical metaphors arise when language develops such that "a meaning that was originally construed by one kind of wording comes instead to be construed by another"—including terms from another grammatical category (Halliday 2009, 117). For example, one may move from saying "wash the car" to speaking of "a carwash" or "taking the car in for a wash" (117).

The noun terms for duties, obligations, and requirements are derived through nominalizations from modal statements. There are, thus, characteristic differences not only in the *functions* of the relevant discourse (physical object discourse versus discourse about duties, or obligations), but also in the *rules and methods* by means of which the relevant noun terms are introduced into the language. It is these differences that

---

[24] These congruent nouns then would apparently fulfill the demands of what Price calls an "e-representational" view of language: one that "gives priority to the idea that the job of a representation is to *co-vary* with something else—typically some external factor or environmental condition" (2011, 20). Price emphasizes that it is a mistake to think that the "prime function" of all representations is to do this job (2011, 20–21).

account for the sense that such things as requirements, duties, and obligations belong to a different "category" or "domain" from ordinary objects such as dogs and apples. As Halliday emphasizes (2009, 131), when grammatical metaphors (which include such noun terms as "requirement" and "duty") are introduced, that brings with it the potential for absurdities and internal contradictions:[25] the hallmarks of what Ryle identified as "category mistakes" (1949, 16–18).

Some think that taking a pragmatist approach to analyzing moral discourse would take the "realism" out of quietist moral realism. But the opposite is true. For properly understanding these entry rules gives us justification for accepting so-called easy arguments for the existence of moral properties, duties, and obligations (see Thomasson 2015). Easy arguments arise where we can make inferences from uncontested truths (say, "The barn is red") via a conceptual truth ("If the barn is red, then the barn has the property of redness") to come to an apparently metaphysical conclusion ("There are properties"). Parallel easy arguments can be given for moral properties, requirements, etc. For we can move from "One shouldn't torture babies" to "There is a moral requirement to refrain from torturing babies" to "There are moral requirements." Such easy arguments are valid because the linking conceptual truth just gives an object-language version of the introduction rule for the relevant terminology.

So understood, a functional analysis of the discourse gives us reason to accept that these easy arguments are perfectly valid, and so that (barring further objections)[26] we should accept that there *are* moral properties, moral facts, requirements, and obligations—and so to accept moral realism. The quietist form of realism that results thus is what one of us has elsewhere called "simple realism" (Thomasson 2015, Chapter 3), as contrasted with "explanatory realism". The "simple realist" asserts that there *are* moral facts, properties, etc. *in the only sense that has sense* (the sense given by the rules of use governing the terms). Yet in adopting "simple realism", we do not treat these moral facts, properties, etc. as "metaphysical posits" that are supposed to do *explanatory work*.[27]

Where does this leave the quietist with respect to the three classic "explanatory burdens" with which we opened our discussion? We saw at the end of Section 2 that relaxed realists have a plausible initial response to these burdens: They insist that questions about the existence of moral facts, our knowledge of them, or motivation by them should be addressed from *within* a moral standpoint, because these questions concern a distinctive "moral domain." But the relaxed realist's reliance on domains

---

[25] Halliday's example here is "The fifth day saw them at the summit", which introduces absurdities since, of course, days cannot see (2009, 131).

[26] Of course a number of objections have been raised to such easy arguments. There is not space to address these here, but for responses to the most common objections, see (Thomasson 2015).

[27] Not even to "explain" why we should act in some ways and not others. For if talk of moral requirements arises via hypostatizations out of more basic claims about what we *should* do, then it would give only a dormitive virtue explanation to appeal to the requirements in order to *explain* why we should act in this way. (For general discussion of the relevance of dormitive virtue arguments to such claims of explanation, see Thomasson 2015, 156–7.)

raises questions about how to distinguish the different domains and what justifies their differing epistemic standards and relations to motivation.

The current approach takes a different route, insisting that it is the differences in function and introduction rules that play the crucial role here—it is not a matter of detecting differences in the natures of "objects" of distinct "domains of things." Nor are we forced to answer detailed questions about the individuation of domains—questions such as whether aesthetic properties are part of the same domain as moral properties. For we mustn't think of "domains" as if they are baskets of different sorts of objects (oranges in one, apples in another). Instead, talk of different domains is a harmless but potentially misleading objectualizing way of getting at differences that trace back to differences in the functions and rules governing the various forms of discourse.

The original "explanatory burdens" can be diagnosed and reconceptualized more clearly if we appeal not to differences in "domains" or in the "status of the objects," but instead to an analysis in terms of the functions and rules of the discourse. Let us treat the burdens in turn.

5.1. Metaphysical Questions: Are there *really* moral properties, moral facts, reasons, obligations, etc.? If so, how can such things "fit with our broader metaphysical commitments?" (McPherson 2011, 224). How are they related to nonmoral or "natural" properties, facts, etc.?

As we have seen, quietists in both camps have argued that these apparently "metaphysical" questions are best understood as moral questions, to which moral answers must be given. With a clearer view in place about the functions and rules governing moral language, we can show why this approach is justified. For talk of moral properties, moral facts, and obligations is not introduced by observing or "tracking" things in the world (as talk of dogs and apples is). Instead, it is introduced via nominalizations out of more basic forms of moralizing. So, if we can say that lying is wrong, we can trivially infer that lying has the property of being morally wrong; and if we ought to look after our children, we can infer that we have an *obligation to* look after our children. It is because the relevant noun terms (for "entities" in the moral "domain") are introduced in this way that the "internalizing move" to answer apparently metaphysical questions via first-order moral claims is legitimate. As we have argued above, this gives us a direct answer to the first of these questions. For we can use easy ontological arguments to conclude that: yes, there are moral facts, moral properties, and obligations (gaining a form of simple realism). But this method of addressing questions about whether moral properties exist (by means of trivial inferences from uncontested moral truths), is very different from the ways we must go about answering questions about whether vampire bats exist.[28]

---

[28] Unless, of course, one already knows (for example) that there are particles arranged vampire-bat-wise. (But of course, that is not the normal sense of the question "do vampire bats exist"). For, as one of

Enoch and McPherson argue, however, that if we interpret Scanlon as offering an easy ontological approach to internal questions with a pragmatic approach to external questions, his view will be "hard to distinguish from an unattractively global hermeneutic fictionalism" (2017, 829). Christopher Cowie similarly worries that "domain relative truth is not truth: a statement can be true relative to a specified domain without actually being true (e.g. that Sherlock Holmes lives at Baker Street)" (2014, 673). If we think of domains as like stories, we can see how this objection might arise.

But if, instead, we see the fundamental distinctions as lying in the different functions of different areas of discourse, and the rules they follow, then we can see that the fictionalism objection is misguided. For the rules that entitle us to introduce talk of moral properties, obligations, and the like, are the rules that *give these terms the only meaning they have.* As a result, it is simply *true* (not true in some fictional sense that could be contrasted with full-blown truth) that there are reasons, obligations, and so on.[29] That is why it is perfectly apt to say that quietism, so understood, *is* a form of moral realism.

Similarly, we can see that the quietist need not claim that obligations, moral properties, and the like are "not ontologically robust" (whatever that would mean) in some sense in which other things (such as dogs and apples) are. Instead, we should simply allow that are such things *in the only sense that has sense* (cf. Thomasson 2015, Chapter 3). Simon Blackburn makes much the same point in his response to David Lewis's claim that quasi-realism is a form of fictionalism. As Blackburn writes:

> What then is the mistake in describing such a philosophy as holding that 'we talk as if there are necessities when really *there are none*'? It is the failure to notice that the quasi-realist need allow no sense to what follows the 'as if' *except* one in which it is true. (1993, 57)

As Matthew Kramer aptly describes Blackburn's view, "There is nothing quasi about quasi-realism" (2017, 20). The apparent differences here are not traced to some obscure claim of a different "metaphysical status" or "robustness," but rather to differences in the *functions* of these areas of discourse, and the different *rules* that permit the introduction of these different noun terms.

But it is not enough to just make sense of the existence of moral obligations and properties. To secure a realism as "robust" as traditional moral realists want, we also need an argument that these obligations, properties, etc. aren't contingent on the

---

us has argued elsewhere (Thomasson 2015, Chapter 3), one can make a trivial inference from "there are particles arranged vampire-bat-wise" to "there are vampire bats," as well as across other "ontologically alternative" forms of expression. For discussion of ontologically alternative forms of expression, see Thomasson (2019, 255–7).

[29] For discussion of this point, and of why, if we can genuinely make easy arguments for existence, we are not subject to charges of fictionalism, see Thomasson (2015, Chapter 5). For a clarifying distinction between quasi-realism and fictionalism, see Blackburn (2005).

opinions or values of any particular individual or group, but that they are in an important sense mind-independent. That is, we need an argument that relativism and subjectivism are false, that moral properties are objective.

Quietists of either camp can make strides toward this goal with the internalizing maneuver. Kramer, for example, has argued that:

> Moral subjectivism and moral relativism are to be repudiated chiefly for moral reasons. That is, they are to be repudiated chiefly because they are moral doctrines that yield morally unacceptable conclusions. (2009, 31)

A commitment to moral relativism would leave us, for example, incapable of condemning the Taliban's policy of barring girls from education, since, after all, this policy is a consequence of the moral convictions of the Taliban (Blackburn 1999). It would likewise commit us to the position that "if one day people in general, or in the stipulated community, ceased to react [opprobriously] to genocide, genocide would cease to be wicked" (Dworkin 1996, 102). The wrongness of such commitments isn't a metaphysical matter; it's a moral matter. Moral objectivity, then, is a moral stance.

This is all well and good, and should be familiar by now. The Quietist Moral Realist can justify moral objectivity by making use of the standards of the moral domain itself. But as we saw in Section 2, this still leaves us with the question: Where do these domain-specific standards come from? The analysis we considered from Systemic Functional Linguistics gives us a plausible way to respond.

If moral discourse functions to regulate our social lives, to guide us into cooperative behavior, it should be no surprise that this function necessitates some kind of moral objectivity:

> The sort of inconsistency involved with ethical beliefs can be understood in terms of possibility of action: inconsistent ethical beliefs cannot coherently guide our behavior. And, in failing to guide our behavior, they frustrate one of our main practical goals: effective action in the world. (Timmons 1999, 173)

We use moral discourse to coordinate our behavior, to decide what *we* should do. But we can't serve this central function of moral discourse if we treat the opinions and values of any particular person or group as the last word on moral truth.[30]

What of further metaphysical questions, such as "how are these moral properties or facts related to nonmoral or "natural" properties, facts, etc.?" Such questions arise when we think of talk of "moral properties," normative facts, and the like *on analogy with* talk using congruent, observationally introduced terms such as "bats" or "fungus." "What is

---

[30] Cf. Blackburn (1984, 195). See Price (2003) for a generalized pragmatist account of the role that the norms surrounding truth-assessment play in engendering useful convergences in a community. See Warren (manuscript) for an exploration of how these norms could plausibly make sense of objectivity in moral, modal, and mathematical discourse.

a bracket fungus, and how is it related to the tree on which it grows?," is a perfectly good question—to be addressed by empirical investigation. But that doesn't tell us that the parallel questions for moral properties and facts are legitimate and sensible questions.

The best response here is not to say that such questions are misguided because the objects being represented by moral discourse are *non-natural* objects. (Why should that matter? And what would it even mean?) Instead, they are misguided because they treat nominalized moral terms on the model of congruent nouns observationally introduced—rather than recognizing these nominalizations as crucial parts of moral language that can enable us to impose requirements and issue permissions, in a speaker-neutral way, and in a way that enables us to compare and publicly justify these regulations. Once we see how and why these terms are introduced, the sense that there are "deep" questions about what relations these referents stand in to natural facts and properties should fade away.

5.2. Epistemological Questions: If there are moral facts, how could we possibly come to know them?

The appeal to functions can similarly help us respond to the epistemological questions: If there are moral or (more broadly) normative truths, how could we possibly come to *know* them?

The relaxed realist is inclined here to also respond by distinguishing different domains, insisting that, while causal or empirical methods of acquiring knowledge are suitable for acquiring knowledge of the natural world, different methods are appropriate for coming to know about the mathematical domain, or facts in the domain of reasons. But this appeal to domains leads to further questions: what makes the standards we use for acquiring knowledge in each domain appropriate?

A pragmatist approach can do better by noting the differences in function, and rules governing, talk of moral facts, requirements, obligations, etc., versus those governing talk of bats and fungus. For it can lead us to reevaluate the assumptions behind the alleged epistemological problems. Where terms are introduced ostensively, with a central function of tracking environmental features (which we can then go on to empirically investigate), it makes sense to worry that if we could not be in causal or perceptual contact with these objects or properties, we could not come to know anything about them. But again, the sense that these are legitimate worries for coming to know about the referents of our nominalized *moral* terms should begin to crumble once we attend to the differences in the functions and rules governing these terms.[31]

---

[31] A full pragmatist account would appeal not only to the function of moral discourse, but also to the function of *epistemic* discourse. It serves our purposes well to be able to distinguish cases in which we, or others, do or do not have moral knowledge. Like moral claims, knowledge claims play a regulative role: helping us to monitor and keep track of who can be trusted on different issues, what sources are reliable, and what puts them in a position to be reliable. Cf. Chrisman (2007), and Craig (1990) as cited in

Once we give up the assumption that talk of reasons or of moral facts is (because it uses noun terms) parallel to talk of bats, we can also give up the assumption that knowledge of these things should be achievable through some sort of causal commerce with the relevant entities. And we can see the route to a different story about how we *can* acquire moral knowledge. Talk of moral facts, for example, just involves useful hypostatization out of talk of what we may, should, or must do. So, to figure out what the "moral facts" are, we naturally go via first-order moral inquiries into what we ought to do. The internalizing maneuver again turns out to be perfectly reasonable—and now we can see why.

But how do we come to figure out what we should do? We can at least get a start if we return to our functional account of moral discourse. We have suggested that moral discourse functions to regulate social behavior, in ways that are publicly justifiable, impersonal, and not dependent on the commands of any particular individual or group. When we investigate the epistemic status of moral beliefs, we appropriately check to see if they are robust or just the product of our temperament or enculturation—and so if they are properly *impersonal*. We give reasons for them in ways that aim to be *publicly justifiable* as ways of regulating social behavior. We scrutinize our reasons for trusting the ethical judgments of others, and aim to ensure we are not just taking them on authority. Once again, we can see that different procedures are appropriate for acquiring knowledge of moral facts than of facts about fungus—though these differences are better accounted for in terms of the different rules and functions governing the different forms of discourse than in terms of differences in the "natures" of the objects in different "domains."

5.3. Motivational Questions: If there are moral facts, how could they possibly be authoritative or action-guiding for us?

We see the same pattern when we think about the motivational question. Here again, the kind of internalized explanation offered by the relaxed realist is a decent start. But it doesn't go far enough. If we take the motivational question to be, "Why is it that *I* should act in accordance with my judgment that, e.g., lying is wrong?," then the best answer we can hope for will be a moral answer. But if we instead take the question to be, "How . . . could our judgments of what we ought to do motivate us to do things, when they do?" (Dreier 2015a, 177) we don't seem to get a very informative answer. "The problem isn't that what the [relaxed realist] has to say [about motivation] is false, or that nobody else would want to say it; the problem is that it offers nothing in the way of explanation" (Dreier 2015a, 178).

Blackburn (2019). It also helps us decide when one is "in the kind of position that renders further inquiry otiose: having the status to call the case closed" (Blackburn 2019, 56).

And this is precisely where adding a pragmatic analysis to a quietist account helps. For when we look to the functional import of moral discourse, we can find a more informative answer. Moral language, on this analysis, originates from discourse that overtly has the function of regulating behavior—and so of being action-guiding. The nominalizations that enable us to talk of (and compare, and justify claims about) moral facts, obligations, and so on come later. But introducing this language is *not* done by discovering some new kind of thing in the world that we can refer to, and asking how beliefs about a thing *of this kind* could be motivational.

Instead, as we have seen, the language that enables us to speak of moral facts, obligations, and so on is introduced by grammatical metaphor on top of overtly action-guiding language. In sophisticated moral language, the overtly action-guiding language is simply transformed grammatically (so that we can better enumerate, compare, and reason about the topic), without losing the original action-guiding function. A better question than to ask how beliefs about how these queer objects could be motivational, is instead to ask how motivating discourse arises, and gets transformed into nominalized terms—which are supposed to motivate us to act in certain ways regardless of our desires or of the desires or commands of others. It is a function of the discourse to bring us into socially coordinated behavior, and that function can't be fulfilled unless the discourse has this feature—that it motivates, and does so impersonally, without the authority of a commander.

As we saw above, the relaxed realist form of quietism has faced daunting criticism, and risks being too quiet in failing to respond to questions that remain about how we can distinguish different domains, and why they should come with different epistemic standards and motivational import. We have aimed to show that taking a pragmatist approach may provide a promising way around these criticisms by moving us from simple talk of different domains, to talk of linguistic functions, and the rules that underlie them. By combining a broadly pragmatist approach with this work in Systemic Functional Linguistics, we open up the route to a response that is not simply quiet in the face of the "explanatory burdens" pressed in metaethics, but instead has something to say about them. For once we have the beginnings of a pragmatic story on the table about the *functions of* and *rules governing* the more puzzling forms of moral language, we can see why some prominent explanatory demands are misguided, and why the questions that remain *can* legitimately be addressed via the "internalizing maneuver" so typical of quietism.

We offer this as a natural development of the pragmatist approach to such problems—when fleshed out with some of the empirical linguistic work that pragmatists insist is needed, and when combined with an "easy" approach to ontological questions that is itself supported by the same kind of pragmatic discourse analysis. We also offer this development of a quietist position as an option to relaxed realists, as a development that (we think) is consistent with their central commitments, and yet is no longer open to the criticisms standardly raised against approaches that bottom out in talk of different "domains". If relaxed realists hesitate to accept this offering, perhaps it will at least

6. Conclusion

We began by observing that there have been two sorts of reactions to moral realism: some find it *obviously* true; others find it metaphysically mystifying. A quietist approach speaks to both sorts of reactions. With the first, Quietist Moral Realism, properly understood, says *yes: of course* there are moral facts, moral obligations, and moral properties. In fact, we can get the claims that there *are* by means of trivial inferences from claims we can all agree on (e.g. "we shouldn't torture babies"). To those who claim to find the realist position metaphysically mystifying, the quietist can now also offer a more satisfying response: these questions seem pressing and worrying, *if* we tacitly think of these moral terms as working analogously to terms for bats or fungi. But once we get a fuller understanding of crucial differences in the ways these moral terms are introduced and the functions they serve, we can see that these concerns arise from false analogies. In this way, the quietist can keep the realism, and yet dissolve the sense of mystery. This hope, in our view, makes a pragmatist version of Quietist Moral Realism an appealing way to go, well worth further development and investigation.

Further challenges, of course, remain to be met, including investigating concerns that the very functions served by moral discourse involve a kind of deception (presenting there as being commands without a commander),[32] showing how one can build a suitable account of moral knowledge from this basis,[33] and a suitable account of moral objectivity,[34] and explaining how (if we see moral claims as expressions of attitudes) we can allow that moral claims may retain their meaning even when embedded in force-stripping contexts,[35] and so on. The work here certainly isn't complete. Nonetheless, we hope to have shown where one might look to unearth a form of Quietist Moral Realism that is deeper and more resilient than its critics have appreciated, and that may provide a plausible and interesting response to some central problems of metaethics.

---

[32] On this score, see Eric Campbell (2014).
[33] See Blackburn (2019).
[34] See Blackburn (1999).
[35] This is of course the notorious "Frege-Geach problem." For a helpful overview, see Schroeder (2008). See Geach (1965) and Searle (1962) for the original formulations of the problem. See Hare (1970), Blackburn (1984, 192–210; 1988), and Gibbard (1990, 83–102) for proposed solutions. There has been a great deal of discussion of this issue, which we do not have space to review here. We will point out only that the crucial part of this view is not one about *meanings*, but about *functions*, and that these two views may be separated. See Thomasson (2020, Chapters 2 and 3) for these distinctions drawn for the case of *modal* discourse. See Warren (2015) for a proposed solution in metaethics that rejects expressivist accounts of meaning, but still fits well within the pragmatist tradition. See also Michael Williams (2011) for a metatheoretical account of how the distinction between meaning and function can clarify use-theoretic accounts of meaning.

References

Blackburn, Simon. 1984. *Spreading the Word*. New York: Oxford University Press.
Blackburn, Simon. 1988. "Attitudes and Contents." *Ethics* 98 (3): 501–517.
Blackburn, Simon. 1993. *Essays in Quasi-Realism*. New York: Oxford University Press.
Blackburn, Simon. 1999. "Is Objective Moral Justification Possible on a Quasi-Realist Foundation?" *Inquiry* 41: 213–228.
Blackburn, Simon. 2001. *Ruling Passions: A Theory of Practical Reasoning*. New ed. New York: Oxford University Press.
Blackburn, Simon. 2005. "Quasi-Realism No Fictionalism." In *Fictionalism in Metaphysics*, edited by Eli Kalderon. Oxford: Clarendon: 322–338.
Blackburn, Simon. 2009. "Truth and A Priori Possibility: Egan's Charge against Quasi-Realism." *Australasian Journal of Philosophy* 87 (2): 201–213.
Blackburn, Simon. 2019. "Moral Epistemology for Sentimentalists." In *Ethical Sentimentalism: New Perspectives*, edited by R. Debes & and K. Stueber. Eds., 32–51. Cambridge: Cambridge University Press.
Böddeling, Annika. 2020. "Cognitivism and Metaphysical Weight: A Dilemma for Relaxed Realism." *Australasian Journal of Philosophy* 98 (3):546–559.
Campbell, Eric. 2014. "Breakdown of Moral Judgment." *Ethics* 124 (3): 447–480.
Carnap, Rudolf. [1950] 1956. "Empiricism, Semantics and Ontology." In *Meaning and Necessity*, 2nd ed. Chicago: University of Chicago Press: 205–221.
Chrisman, Matthew. 2007. "From Epistemic Contextualism to Epistemic Expressivism." *Philosophical Studies* 135: 225–254.
Copp, David. 2018. "A Semantic Challenge to Non-Realist Cognitivism." *Canadian Journal of Philosophy* 48 (3–4): 569–591.
Cowie, Christopher. 2014. "A New Explanatory Challenge for Non-Naturalists." *Res Philosophica* 91 (4): 661–679.
Craig, E. 1990 *Knowledge and the State of Nature: An Essay in Conceptual Synthesis*. Oxford: Oxford University Press.
Dreier, J. 2004. "Meta-Ethics and the Problem of Creeping Minimalism." *Philosophical Perspectives* 18: 23–44.
Dreier, Jamie. 2015a. "Can Reasons Fundamentalism Answer the Normative Question?" In *Motivational Internalism*, edited by G. Björnsson, C. Strandberg, R. Francén Olinder, and J. Eriksson, 167–181. Oxford: Oxford University Press.
Dreier, Jamie. 2015b. "Another World." In *Passions and Projections Themes from the Philosophy of Simon Blackburn*, edited by Robert Johnson and Michael Smith, 155–171. Oxford: Oxford University Press.
Dworkin, Ronald. 1996. "Objectivity and Truth: You Better Believe It." *Philosophy and Public Affairs* 25 (2): 87–139.
Dworkin, Ronald. 2011. *Justice for Hedgehogs*. Cambridge, MA: Harvard University Press.
Eggins, Suzanne. 2004. *An Introduction to Systemic Functional Linguistics*. 2nd ed. New York: Continuum.
Enoch, David, and Tristram McPherson. 2017. "What Do You Mean 'This Isn't the Question'?" *Canadian Journal of Philosophy* 47 (6): 820–840.
Geach, P. T. 1965. "Assertion." *Philosophical Review* 74: 449–465.
Gibbard, Allan. 1990. *Wise Choices, Apt Feelings*. Cambridge, MA: Harvard University Press.

Halliday, M. A. K. 1970. "Language Structure and Language Function." In *New Horizons in Linguistics*, edited by J. Lyons. 140–165. Harmondsworth, UK: Penguin

Halliday, M. A. K. 1973. *Explorations in the Function of Language*. New York: Elsevier.

Halliday, M. A. K. 1975. *Learning How to Mean*. New York: Elsevier.

Halliday, M. A. K. 1977. "Ideas about Language." In *Aims and Perspectives in Linguistics*. Applied Linguistics Association of Australia: Occasional Papers Number 1, Queensland, Australia, 20–38.

Halliday, M. A. K. 2009. *The Essential Halliday*. Edited by Jonathan J. Webster. New York: Continuum.

Hare, R.M. 1970. "Meaning and Speech Acts." *Philosophical Review* 79 (1): 3–24.

Hopper, Paul J., and Sandra A. Thompson. 1985. "The Iconicity of the Universal Categories 'Noun' and 'Verb.'" In *Iconicity in Syntax*, edited by John Haiman, 151–183. Amsterdam: Benjamins.

Ingram, Stephen. 2017. "I can't relax! You're driving me quasi!" *Pacific Philosophical Quarterly* 98: 490–510.

Joyce, R. 2006. *The Evolution of Morality*. Cambridge, MA: MIT Press.

Kramer, Matthew. 2009. *Moral Realism as a Moral Doctrine*. Chichester: Wiley-Blackwell.

Kramer, Matthew. 2017. "There's Nothing Quasi about Quasi-Realism: Moral Realism as a Moral Doctrine." *Journal of Ethics* 21: 185–212.

Macarthur, David. 2008. "Pragmatism, Metaphysical Quietism, and the Problem of Normativity." *Philosophical Topics* 36 (1): 193–209.

McGrath, Sarah. 2014. "Relax! Don't Do It! Why Moral Realism Won't Come Cheap." *Oxford Studies in Metaethics* 9: 186–214.

McPherson, Tristram. 2011. "Against Quietist Normative Realism." *Philosophical Studies* 153: 223–240.

Parfit, Derek. 2011 *On What Matters*. Vol. 2. Oxford: Oxford University Press.

Parfit, Derek. 2017 *On What Matters*. Vol. 3. Oxford: Oxford University Press.

Pettit, Philip. 2004. "Existentialism, Quietism, and the Role of Philosophy." In *The Future of Philosophy*, edited by Brian Leiter, 304–327. Oxford: Clarendon.

Price, Huw. 2003. "Truth as Convenient Friction." *Journal of Philosophy* 100: 167–190.

Price, Huw. 2011. *Naturalism without Mirrors*. Oxford: Oxford University Press.

Price, Huw. 2019. "Global Expressivism by the Method of Differences." *Royal Institute of Philosophy Supplements* 86: 133–154.

Ridge, Michael. 2019. "Relaxing Realism or Deferring Debate?" *Journal of Philosophy* 116: 149–173.

Ryle, Gilbert. 1949. *The Concept of Mind*. Chicago: University of Chicago Press.

Ryle, Gilbert. 1950. "'If', 'So', and 'Because.'" In *Philosophical Analysis*, vol. 2, edited by M. Black, 234–249. Ithaca: Cornell University Press.

Scanlon, T. M. 2014. *Being Realistic about Reasons*. Oxford: Oxford University Press.

Schroeder, M. 2008. "What Is the Frege-Geach problem?" *Philosophy Compass* 3(4): 703–720.

Searle, John. 1962. "Meaning and Speech Acts." *Philosophical Review* 71: 423–432.

Thomasson, Amie L. 2015. *Ontology Made Easy*. Oxford: Oxford University Press.

Thomasson, Amie L. 2019. "What Can Global Pragmatists Say about Ordinary Objects?" In *The Nature of Ordinary Objects*, edited by Javier Cumpa and Bill Brewer, 235–259. Cambridge: Cambridge University Press.

Thomasson, Amie L. 2020. *Norms and Necessity*. Oxford: Oxford University Press.

Tiefensee, Christine. 2019. "Relaxing about Moral Truths." *Ergo: An Open Access Journal of Philosophy* 6 (31): 869–890.

Timmons, M. 1999. *Morality without Foundations: A Defense of Ethical Contextualism*. New York: Oxford University Press.

Virvidakis, Stelios, and Vasso Kindi. 2013. "Quietism." Oxford Bibliographies Online in Philosophy. DOI: 10.1093/OBO/9780195396577-0184.

Warren, Mark. 2015. "Moral Inferentialism and the Frege-Geach Problem." *Philosophical Studies* 172 (11): 2859–2885.

Warren, Mark. 2018. "Building Bridges with Words: An Inferential Account of Ethical Univocity." *Canadian Journal of Philosophy* 48 (3–4): 468–488.

Warren, Mark. "Objectivity for Deflationists." Unpublished manuscript. N.p., n.d.

Williams, Michael. 2011. "Pragmatism, Minimalism, Expressivism." *International Journal of Philosophical Studies* 18 (3): 317–330.

CHAPTER 25

MORAL ANTI-EXCEPTIONALISM

TIMOTHY WILLIAMSON

WHEN the editors of this volume invited me to contribute a chapter, I hesitated. Although I have occasionally dabbled in metaethics and metanormativity, I have certainly never claimed to *be* a metaethicist.[1] Not that I lack metaethical views or instincts: I have long had an outsider's impression that objections to moral realism are much weaker than they are usually taken to be. That impression comes not from any special attachment to morality, but from an attachment to rigor in logic and semantics.

Correspondingly, I have long had some methodological views about metanormativity: in particular, that the philosophy of normative language is best done as part of general philosophy of language, that the epistemology of normative knowledge is best done as part of general epistemology, and that the metaphysics of normativity is best done as part of general metaphysics. In each case, the application to normativity should be up to date with recent theoretical developments in the more general field, and meet similar standards of rigor, systematicity, and explicitness.

Naturally, an outsider to a subdiscipline who barges into one of its debates can expect to be accused by insiders of attacking a straw man. To avoid that danger, I asked the editors to nominate some self-standing pieces embodying objections to moral realism at their best, both substantively and methodologically, so that I could engage closely with them at less risk—though certainly not *no* risk—of being told that the *real* objection to moral realism is somewhere else. The editors kindly complied. They nominated Sharon Street's article "A Darwinian Dilemma for Realist Theories of Value" (2006) and two chapters of Jonas Olson's book *Moral Error Theory* (2014). I respond to their arguments just as they stand.

Notoriously, the word "realism" can mean many things; adding the qualification "moral" does little to reduce the number. Just what I am defending will emerge more

---

[1] For previous dabbling, see Williamson 2000: 238–259, 2001, 2018, 2019, 2020b, Forthcoming.

clearly below, but it includes at least this: in normative discourse, we often express mind-independent truths, many of which we know. However, I will not discuss epistemological issues in this chapter, since Olson and Street do not focus on them. Instead, I follow them in focusing on mind-independent truth.

Before I discuss Street and Olson, Section 1 explains in more detail my starting-point and general framework. That is needed to explain why developments in philosophical logic may have quite devastating consequences for contemporary metanormative debates.

1. The Null Hypothesis and an Intensional Framework

I assume that we start with some capacity to distinguish normative from non-normative language when we see it. Typical normative terms are "right" and "wrong," "good" and "bad," "better" and "worse," "kind" and "cruel," "permissible" and "impermissible," "polite" and "rude," "beautiful" and "ugly," "dainty" and "dumpy." Such terms are often used to praise or criticize. Some but not all of them concern morality; others concern aesthetics, etiquette, the law, ... I avoid the culturally specific assumption that moral norms are more "serious" than nonmoral norms. Nor do I assume that normative terms form a uniform kind in any deep way, though trivially they are all normative. The word "normative" is vague; my purposes do not require it to be made precise. As I use the word, it applies to the usual paradigms; how much further it extends matters little, for reasons about to emerge.

The null hypothesis about the normative is that it is unexceptional. On the anti-exceptionalist view, a general semantic theory which works for non-normative language will also work for normative language; a general epistemological theory which works for non-normative knowledge and belief will also work for normative knowledge and belief; a general metaphysical theory which works for non-normatively expressed states of affairs, properties, and relations will also work for normatively expressed states of affairs, properties, and relations. This is not at all to assume that the non-normative is uniform in any of those respects, just that *if* such a nongerrymandered generalization covers the non-normative, it will cover the normative too.

There is no suggestion that normative anti-exceptionalism is obviously correct. Rather, it is the null hypothesis in the modest methodological sense that it is the *default* view: the burden of proof is on its opponents. If a semantic, epistemological, or metaphysical hypothesis has withstood the worst the non-normative in all its variety could throw at it, we should not abandon it for the normative without good reason to do so. For now, the possibility remains open that such good reason will prove easy to find.

In the case of semantics, however, the null hypothesis receives significant confirmation from the *unity* of natural languages. To a first approximation, any two words of a given natural language can occur together in a well-formed sentence of that language; likewise for complex expressions of corresponding grammatical categories. For example, the mathematical term "four," the normative term "good," and the descriptive term "nurse" are combined in the sentence "Four good nurses helped." Similarly, any two declarative sentences can be combined into a third declarative sentence by means of logical particles such as "and," "or," and "if." Thus, despite widespread preconceptions to the contrary, the expressions of a natural language cannot be partitioned naturally into disjoint classes dedicated to different types of "discourse." Any such restriction would compromise the functionality of language. The semantics of natural languages must reflect that unity. For well-known reasons, the semantics has to be broadly compositional, so the semantic value of a complex expression can be derived from the semantic values of its simpler constituents and how they are combined. Thus the semantic values of diverse expressions must mesh with each other, to permit such derivations. For example, simply giving a referentialist semantics for natural kind terms and an inferentialist semantics for logical particles is a nonstarter, since the two kinds of semantics do not combine properly to permit the derivation of the semantics of a sentence containing both natural kind terms and logical particles. Similarly, a semantic account of normative expressions must be fully integrated with a semantic account of non-normative expressions in the overall framework of a semantic theory for the whole language. This, of course, is the big picture in the background of the rightly famous Frege-Geach objection to expressivist accounts of normative sentences which do not properly generalize to their occurrences embedded under negation or in the antecedent of a conditional. From the perspective of semantics, hand-waving responses to the Frege-Geach point which fail to integrate their expressivist treatment of normative terms into a clearly specified compositional semantic framework for the whole language look hopelessly amateurish. Of expressivist accounts, only those with a worked-out response to the compositional challenge have intellectual credibility. Thus theoretical considerations tend to favor anti-exceptionalism about the semantics of normative language.

In practice, anti-exceptionalism about the semantics of normative words is confirmed by standard semantic accounts of modals such as "ought," "should," "must," and "may" on their deontic readings, which apply the same overall framework to them as to epistemic and alethic ("circumstantial," "dynamic") modals (e.g., Portner 2009, Kratzer 2012). Similar comments apply to evaluative adjectives, such as "good" and "bad," which fit nicely into the standard semantic frameworks for nonevaluative adjectives (e.g., McNally and Kennedy 2008, Kamp 2013). Although semanticists do not completely ignore the distinction between the normative and the non-normative, its role in their taxonomies is secondary to deeper, more structural semantic distinctions.

Less directly, such theoretical considerations about semantics also give some support to anti-exceptionalism about both the epistemology of normative knowledge and belief and the metaphysics of normatively expressed states of affairs, properties, and relations. For had the normative differed deeply enough to need exceptional treatment in semantics, it would have been more likely to differ deeply enough to need exceptional treatment in epistemology and metaphysics too. The failure of exceptionalism in semantics rules out one salient route to exceptionalism in epistemology and metaphysics.

In itself, anti-exceptionalism is neutral between realism and antirealism. To put the point at its crudest, one might be a realist about both the normative and the non-normative, but one might equally be an antirealist about both. However, by far the best-developed frameworks for systematic compositional semantics come from the tradition of truth-conditional semantics, especially intensional semantics, whatever further twists they add. On such a semantics, to a first approximation, the intension of an expression is a function taking each circumstance of evaluation to the extension of that expression at that circumstance, where a circumstance of evaluation is a possible world and perhaps a time (and even other parameters).[2] The extension of an n-place predicate at a circumstance is the set of n-tuples of objects to which it applies at that circumstance; the extension of a declarative sentence at a circumstance is simply its truth-value at that circumstance. This central role for truth and falsity in the semantics encourages realism over antirealism, by implying that any normative expression can occur in a true declarative sentence: if not the sentence you first thought of, then its negation. Of course, one must not read *too* much into the point. In particular, nothing in the semantic framework requires the truth-value to be mind-independent or to involve a metaphysically heavyweight correspondence theory of truth. Nevertheless, the semantics works more or less as realists hoped it would, whereas antirealists might have hoped that it would avoid all talk of truth and falsity.

The intensional framework also models the metaphysics of states of affairs (or propositions), properties, and relations. For simplicity, we equate the circumstance of evaluation with a possible world, ignoring any time parameter (restoring it makes little difference for present purposes). Thus the intension of a declarative sentence is just a function from possible worlds to truth-values; it models the state of affairs obtaining in just those worlds the intension maps to the true. Similarly, the intension of a one-place predicate models the property an object has in just those worlds the intension maps to a set containing the object, and the intension of a two-place predicate models the relation one object has to a second object in just those worlds the intension maps to a set containing the ordered pair of the first object and the second.

We can abstract away from the clunky set-theoretic apparatus and formalize the resultant theory of states of affairs, properties, and relations more elegantly by quantifying directly into sentence and predicate position in a second-order language, as below. For convenience and familiarity, we still use nouns such as "state," "property," and "relation" when loosely paraphrasing formulas into English.[3] The result is a very powerful and general theory of states of affairs, properties, and relations, arguably better adapted to the

---

[2] The terminology follows Kaplan 1989. For simplicity, we omit mention of the context of utterance, needed to handle context-sensitive expressions. The considerations in the text generalize to a wide variety of intensional frameworks.

[3] For a detailed defence of such a form of higher-order modal logic as a metaphysical theory see Williamson 2013.

needs of semantics, mathematics, and other sciences than any available alternative. We note some of its most distinctive consequences.

First, the theory is *plenitudinous*. It does not require states of affairs, properties, and relations to be perfectly or at all natural or joint-carving, or causally efficacious, or nondisjunctive, or to have any other special metaphysical privilege (Olson endorses such a liberal view of properties at 2014: 12n17). For the semantics applies to all declarative sentences, however complex, and assigns each of them an intension. More formally, the schema Comprehension$_0$ holds, where "P" stands for a variable taking sentence position and "A" for any declarative sentence, however complex; the (metaphysical) necessity operator captures the generality over possible worlds in the semantics:[4]

Comprehension$_0$ $\Box \exists P \Box (P \leftrightarrow A)$

Rough paraphrase: necessarily, any sentence (A) modally corresponds to a state of affairs (P). In particular, we can substitute sentences containing normative terms for "A," since the semantics works for them too. Thus any *normative* sentence modally corresponds to a state of affairs. For instance, some state of affairs is necessary and sufficient for eating meat to be wrong.

Similarly, the semantics applies to all predicates, however complex, and assigns each of them an intension. More formally, the schema Comprehension$_1$ holds, where "Q" stands for a variable taking one-place predicate position, "x" for a variable taking name position, and "$B(x)$" for any declarative sentence, however complex:

Comprehension$_1$ $\Box \exists Q \Box \forall x (Qx \leftrightarrow B(x))$

Rough paraphrase: necessarily, any one-place predicate (abstracted from $B(x)$) modally corresponds to a property (Q). In particular, we can substitute open sentences containing normative terms for "$B(x)$." Thus any one-place *normative* predicate modally corresponds to a property. For instance, some property is necessary and sufficient for being in the wrong. The schema Comprehension$_2$ also holds, where "R" stands for a variable taking two-place predicate position, and "$C(x,y)$" for any declarative sentence, however complex:

Comprehension$_2$ $\Box \exists R \Box \forall x \forall y (Rxy \leftrightarrow C(x,y))$

Rough paraphrase: necessarily, any two-place predicate (abstracted from $C(x,y)$) modally corresponds to a relation (R). In particular, we can substitute open sentences containing normative terms for "$C(x,y)$." Thus any two-place *normative* predicate

---

[4] P must not occur free in A; $\leftrightarrow$ is the material biconditional. Similar glosses are to be understood for the other formulas. See Williamson 2013 for more discussion of logical and semantic issues about such schemata.

modally corresponds to a relation. For instance, some relation is necessary and sufficient for wronging.

The plenitudinous consequences of the theory have the abductive virtues of simplicity and strength, as well as fitting the needs of semantics. They also fit the needs of science, for mathematics in effect makes some of the most systematic applications of second-order logic in science. For example, arithmetic depends on the axiom of mathematical induction: if 0 has a property P, and $n + 1$ has P whenever n has P, then every natural number has P. In set theory, the separation axiom says that every set has a subset containing those of its members with a given property; the more powerful replacement axiom in effect generalizes over relations.[5] If the background theory of properties and relations imposed any special metaphysical requirement on them, it would trip up standard proofs in mathematics, which never dream of checking whether such requirements are satisfied.

Another aspect of the theory is that intensions are *coarse-grained*. Although distinct intensions may coincide extensionally, intensions which *necessarily* coincide extensionally are identical. This follows from the standard mathematical individuation of the functions serving as intensions in the semantics, but is also a simple, strong, and precise account in its own right of identity conditions for states of affairs, properties, and relations respectively, providing a satisfying answer to the charge of obscurity. It is explicit in these schemata:

Intensionality$_0$ $\quad \Box \forall P \forall P^* (P = P^* \leftrightarrow \Box(P \leftrightarrow P^*))$

Intensionality$_1$ $\quad \Box \forall Q \forall Q^* (Q = Q^* \leftrightarrow \Box \forall x(Qx \leftrightarrow Q^*x))$

Intensionality$_2$ $\quad \Box \forall R \forall R^* (R = R^* \leftrightarrow \Box \forall x \forall y(Rxy \leftrightarrow R^*xy))$

The identity sign "=" here symbolizes the second-order analogues of identity: in effect, sharing all higher-order properties. Since they satisfy corresponding versions of the indiscernibility of identicals, the logical analogy is perfect.

The effects of Intensionality$_0$ may seem drastic. For example, the state of affairs of Fermat's Last Theorem holding just *is* the state of affairs of all cats being cats, since they are necessarily equivalent, both being necessary. Uncontroversially, the *sentences* "Fermat's Last Theorem holds" and "All cats are cats" are cognitively quite different. But that does not imply that they express distinct states of affairs. Analogously, although "furze" and "gorse" are synonymous terms for the same natural kind, a speaker can learn them at different times of year and understand both by normal standards without appreciating their co-reference. Thus the sentences "Furze is furze" and "Furze is gorse" can play distinct cognitive roles while still picking out the same state of affairs. On the

---

[5] Shapiro 1991 explains why the first-order schemata derived from the second-order axioms are inadequate substitutes for characterizing the intended mathematical structures. For the extension to second-order modal logic, see Williamson 2013.

intensional approach, such cognitive differences play no role in the individuation of states of affairs, which is purely metaphysical.

Similarly, by Intensionality$_1$, since necessarily all and only trilaterals are triangles, trilaterality just *is* triangularity, even though the sides themselves are not the angles. Thus the semantic constituent structure of the *expressions* "three-sided" and "three-angled" does not mirror any metaphysical constituent structure of the *properties* of three-sidedness and three-angledness, even though the former pick out the latter. One benefit of the intensional conception is that it blocks the naïve tendency to project the structure of our language onto the nonlinguistic world. Of course, the *words* "trilateral" and "triangle" play different cognitive roles: for instance, substituting one for the other can make an explanation better or worse (more perspicuous or less). But that does not imply that they pick out different properties: after all, substituting "furze" for "gorse" can make an explanation better or worse (more perspicuous or less). On the intensional approach, such cognitive differences play no role in the individuation of properties and relations, which is purely metaphysical.

Perhaps the terms "states of affairs," "properties," and "relations" are sometimes used for items individuated along cognitive or linguistic lines, rather than purely metaphysically. If so, those are not the items under discussion in this chapter.

Like comprehension, intensionality has the abductive virtues of simplicity and strength, clarity and elegance. Intensionality also sharpens the effect of comprehension, for it adds uniqueness. Given Intensionality$_0$, Comprehension$_0$ entails that any sentence modally corresponds to a *unique* state of affairs. Thus, since just one state of affairs is necessary and sufficient for eating meat to be wrong, it is *the* state of affairs of eating meat being wrong (the proposition that eating meat is wrong). Similarly, given Intensionality$_1$, Comprehension$_1$ entails that any one-place predicate modally corresponds to a *unique* property. Thus, since just one property is necessary and sufficient for being in the wrong, it is *the* property of being in the wrong. Again, given Intensionality$_2$, Comprehension$_2$ entails that any two-place predicate modally corresponds to a *unique* relation. Thus, since just one relation is necessary and sufficient for wronging, it is *the* relation of wronging.

The intensional approach has significant consequences for the metaphysics of normativity. It is tempting to regard the state of affairs of eating meat being wrong, the property of being in the wrong, and the relation of wronging as themselves normative, since they were expressed with the normative word "wrong." But that is a trap. For intensionality allows that a state of affairs, property, or relation expressed in normative terms may equally be expressed in non-normative terms. This is most obvious for states of affairs. Suppose, for example, that torturing for fun is necessarily wrong. Then the necessary state of affairs of torturing for fun being wrong necessarily coincides with the equally necessary state of affairs of 7 being prime. Thus, by Intensionality$_0$, the supposedly normative state of affairs of torturing for fun being wrong just *is* the supposedly non-normative state of affairs of 7 being prime—strange, but true. Similarly, the property of wrongly torturing children for fun necessarily coincides with the property of torturing children for fun. Thus, by Intensionality$_1$, the supposedly normative property of wrongly torturing children for fun just *is* the supposedly non-normative property of torturing children for fun. Again, the relation of wrongly torturing for fun necessarily coincides with the relation of torturing for fun. Thus, by Intensionality$_2$, the supposedly normative relation of wrongly torturing for fun just *is* the supposedly non-normative relation of torturing for fun. Such examples show that we must beware of projecting features of linguistic expressions—here, normativity and non-normativity—onto the states of affairs, properties, and relations they express.[6] The difference between the normative and the non-normative is cognitive rather than metaphysical.

Such identifications may sound like *reductions* of the normative to the non-normative, or of the non-natural to the natural. But to describe them so is to fall into the very trap just warned against, of confusing states of affairs, properties, and relations with their linguistic expressions. If a sentence or predicate involving a normative or non-naturalistic term picks out the same state of affairs, property, or relation as a sentence or predicate involving no normative or non-naturalistic term, that no more shows the worldly entity to be *really* non-normative or naturalistic than it shows it to be *really* normative or non-naturalistic. Nothing in the semantics suggests that one linguistic expression is somehow more perspicuous than the other. Rather, the proper conclusion to draw is that the distinction between the normative and the non-normative inextricably involves the use of language, not just the nonlinguistic reality spoken about. That in no way impugns the reality of what we speak about in using normative language: the property of wrongly torturing children for fun is just as real as the property of torturing children for fun, since they are identical.

On independent grounds, some philosophers may regard non-normative or naturalistic words as somehow metaphysically more joint-carving than normative or non-naturalistic words, but the intensional framework itself is simply neutral towards such metaphysically charged versions of naturalism. Correspondingly, this chapter takes no stance on whether the property of being torture is more joint-carving than the property of being wrong. But if the property of torturing children for fun just is the property of wrongly torturing children for fun, they are equally joint-carving.

Of course, various alternatives are available to such an intensional account. In particular, there are also hyperintensional accounts of states of affairs, properties, and relations. For example, even though being Socrates is necessary and sufficient for belonging to {Socrates}, the properties may be held distinct on the grounds that the latter but not the former "involves" the set {Socrates}. Similarly, even though torturing children for fun is necessary and sufficient for wrongly torturing children for fun, the properties may be held distinct on the grounds that the latter but not the former "involves" wrongness. Such theories are currently fashionable, and quite compatible with realism about the normative.

---

[6] Note that the identities are not derived from any general thesis of the supervenience of the normative on the non-normative or of the non-natural on the natural; no such thesis is implicit in the intensional framework. Instead, they are derived from specific necessitated normative theses.

So far, however, the hyperintensional approach remains far less well-developed than the intensional alternative. Extant hyperintensional theories postulate vastly more complicated structures for very meagre explanatory gains. Indeed, the "data" they are designed to explain are themselves suspect: they feel like projections of discourse features such as *aboutness* and *relevance* onto nonlinguistic reality. Moreover, it is far from clear that hyperintensional semantics can emulate anything like the wide range of successes already achieved by intensional semantics. Methodologically, a notorious pitfall in scientific modelling is to give oneself too many degrees of freedom, allowing one to model almost any phenomenon by setting the parameters to suit, but as a consequence adding scant explanatory value. In brief, hyperintensionalism looks like bad science.

In the present state of logic and semantics, the hyperintensional alternative is murkier and less controlled than the intensional approach. What cannot reasonably be demanded is an approach neutral between all "substantive" metanormative views. It is not the job of logic to be neutral (Williamson 2013). If metanormative theorists make logical errors, that is their problem; it does not mean that logic should be loosened. I will use the simpler, more perspicuous, and more constrained intensional theory, with its much better track record of independent confirmation.[7] In doing so, I will not merely treat the theory operationally, as somehow *useful*, irrespective of its truth-value. Rather, I will work on the (controversial) hypothesis that the intensional theory is *true*. However, even if the intensional theory turns out to be only a good *approximation* to the truth, the objections below to antirealist arguments are still likely to work, since the gaps they reveal are so large.

The next section applies the intensional approach to Jonas Olson's argument against moral facts.

2. Olson's Argument for Moral Error Theory

Olson proposes a rational reconstruction of John Mackie's quaintly phrased "argument from queerness". He first considers three other interpretations of the argument, one targeting moral supervenience, another moral knowledge, and the third moral motivation, but argues that all three fail (116).[8] He then presents his preferred alternative.

---

[7] Some authors simulate hyperintensionality within a superficially intensional framework by permitting impossible worlds where laws of classical logic break down. This approach violates semantic compositionality and loses much of the explanatory value of the classical intensional approach, for reasons explained in Williamson 2020. It is not helpful for issues about normative realism. For more detailed discussion of the coarse-grained aspect of intensionalism with respect to epistemology and metaphysics, see Williamson 2021 and 2022, respectively.

[8] All page references in this section are to Olson 2014.

In Olson's summary, his argument has two stages. The first moves from the premises (P12) and (P13) to the intermediate conclusion (C5) (123–4, his labels):

(P12) Moral facts entail that there are facts that favour certain courses of behaviour, where the favouring relation is irreducibly normative.
(P13) Irreducibly normative favouring relations are queer.
(C5)   Moral facts entail queer relations.

The second stage moves from the intermediate conclusion (C5) and the further premise (P4') to the conclusion (C2"):

(P4') If moral facts entail queer relations, moral facts are queer.
(C2") Moral facts are queer.

Of course, the intended destination is not that there are moral facts, which are queer. One can regiment the argument as then invoking a tacit extra premise: no facts are queer. Combined with (C2"), it yields the final conclusion that there are no moral facts. Olson does not regard such an extra premise as indisputable, but it must have some plausibility for the argument to (C2") to serve his overall case against moral facts.

In light of Section 1, the talk of "moral facts" should already have rung alarm bells. For within the intensional framework, the obvious candidates for facts are obtaining states of affairs; thus moral facts are obtaining moral states of affairs. But moral realists should not expect the distinction between true moral sentences and true nonmoral sentences to project onto any corresponding distinction between moral and nonmoral facts, for a true moral sentence may express the same obtaining state of affairs as a true nonmoral sentence. However, in charity to Olson, we can take a "moral fact" to be a state of affairs expressed by a true moral sentence, irrespective of whether it is also expressed by a true nonmoral sentence. Given the intensional framework, moral realists acknowledge moral facts in that sense, since they acknowledge true moral sentences. Contrapositively, if there are no moral facts, then there are no true moral sentences—presumably, because moral predicates somehow fail.

The intended semantic underpinnings of Olson's argument are unclear. Within the intensional framework, a predicate can "fail" in two main ways. Either it has *no* intension, or it has an *empty* intension—extensionally empty (nothing has the property), and perhaps also intensionally empty (nothing *could* have the property). The difference emerges dramatically under negation. If a predicate has no intension, its negation also has no intension (semantically, there is nothing to negate). By contrast, if a predicate has an extensionally empty intension, its negation has an extensionally full intension (everything has that property). If a predicate has an intensionally empty intension, its negation has an intensionally full intension (necessarily everything has that property). Even predicates whose application to anything entails a wildly false theory have full negations: "It is not haunted" is true of any house, and "She is not bewitched" is true of any woman. For a predicate with no intension, one needs something more like pure gibberish: "He is not fghkl" is not true of anyone.

Error theorists sometimes compare moral terms to empty proper names and mass nouns such as "Vulcan" and "phlogiston." The comparison is inappropriate, because proper names and mass nouns lack natural negations. If moral adjectives such as "good" and "bad" or "right" and "wrong" are to be compared with terms complicit in a wildly false theory, a more appropriate comparison is with other terms of the same grammatical category, such as "haunted" and "bewitched." On that analogy, moral predicates should have empty intensions, and their negations full intensions. But that result is problematic for moral error theories. Since the negation of a moral predicate is itself a moral predicate, not all moral predicates have empty intensions.

Error theorists might claim that although moral predicates have intensions, ascribing a moral predicate shares a false presupposition or implicature with ascribing its negation. Of course, they would need to meet the normal evidential standards in linguistics for postulating presuppositions or implicatures. But, in any case, such discourse effects sit on top of the intensional semantics, rather than working inside it. They leave untouched the dilemma in the previous paragraph. Analogously, even if ascribing the predicate "haunted" and ascribing its negation "not haunted" share a false presupposition, and "haunted" has an empty extension, "not haunted" still has a full extension.

The problem applies to Olson's conclusion (C2"). Assume (for reductio) that moral terms have intensions. Consider a sample moral claim, with "impermissible" read in a fully moral sense:

(i) Torturing for fun is always impermissible.

Suppose that (i) is true. Then it states a moral fact (in the relevant broad sense). But by (C2") such a fact is queer, so by the implicit premise there is no such fact. Thus the supposition (i) is not true after all, so by the semantics its negation (ii) is true instead (moving the negation into the predicate makes no relevant logical difference):

(ii) Torturing for fun is not always impermissible.

Given that (ii) is logically equivalent to (iii), (iii) is also true:

(iii) Torturing for fun is sometimes permissible.

But (iii) is just as much a moral sentence as (i) is. Since (iii) is true, it states a moral fact. But by (C2") such a fact is queer, so by the implicit premise there is no such fact. Thus (iii) is not true after all. That is a contradiction.

Olson himself would deny the equivalence of (ii) and (iii), treating the implication from "not impermissible" to "permissible" as a mere conversational implicature (14). That is just the deontic version of treating the implication from "not impossible" to "possible" as a mere conversational implicature, and no more plausible. His rejection of basic principles of deontic modal logic is a heavy cost of his view. Similarly, if "permissible" and "obligatory" are duals, just like "possible" and "necessary" ($\lozenge$ is equivalent to $\neg\square\neg$ and $\square$ to $\neg\lozenge\neg$ in normal modal logic), then (i) entails "Not torturing for fun is always obligatory," and so is not just vacuously true.

Thus, on standard logical and semantic assumptions, the error theory is committed to the extreme conclusion that moral terms lack intensions, and so are closer to "fghkl" than to "haunted" and "bewitched."

One might try denying that (iii) is a moral claim in the sense at issue, since permissibility is compatible with moral indifference, so the alleged truth of (iii) would not entail any irreducibly normative favoring. However, Olson says the opposite: "Some moral facts are or entail facts that make actions permissible, where the "permissibility-making" relation is irreducibly normative" (118n12). Both permissibility and impermissibility here are moral matters.

Nor is the role of "true" in the argument problematic, for it can easily be eliminated; it was used only for convenience. Instead of supposing that (i) is true, one supposes directly that torturing for fun is always impermissible, and proceeds accordingly. As for the role of "fact," it would be pointless for an error theorist to invoke a metaphysically heavyweight sense of "fact" on which (i) does not entail (iv):

(iv) It is a moral fact that torturing for fun is always impermissible.

For, within the intensional framework, moral realism requires moral facts only in the sense of the obtaining states of affairs expressed by true moral sentences, and in that sense the move from (i) to (iv) is unproblematic.

Thus, within the intensional framework, Olson faces a dilemma: either his error theory is inconsistent on standard logical principles, or it collapses into a crass dismissal of moral discourse as mere gibberish.

One might instead object that Olson is not obliged to accept the intensional framework. That is true, but it misses the dialectical point. For the question is not whether *Olson* accepts the intensional framework but whether his opponent, the moral realist, does. If Olson wants to make trouble for a moral realist who accepts the intensional framework, he had better tailor his argument for the error theory to that opponent's background logic and semantics, unless he hopes to refute the intensional framework itself—a severe challenge for which nothing in his text offers resources or preparation.

How does Olson's argument for (C5) fare within the intensional framework? On his premise (P12), moral facts entail that there are irreducibly normative favoring relations. Some moral realists grant (P12), so Olson is entitled to use it against them. In an intensional framework, however, (P12) is problematic. This chapter defends moral realism within such a framework.

What is an irreducibly normative favoring relation? One might take it to be a relation which can be expressed in normative-favoring terms and cannot be expressed in other terms. But moral realism is not committed to irreducibly favoring relations in that sense. For example, consider a moral realist who accepts the intensional framework and holds that torturing for fun is necessarily wrong. Thus, on her view, there is a moral fact (in the broad sense), the obtaining state of affairs expressed by the true moral sentence "Torturing for fun is necessarily wrong." There is also a normative (dis)favoring relation (in a correspondingly loose sense), expressed by the normative predicate "wrongly tortures for fun." But the relation is not *irreducibly* normative in the proposed sense, since it can also be expressed by the necessarily equivalent non-normative predicate "tortures for fun." Similarly, the moral fact is not *irreducibly* moral in the analogous sense, since it can also be expressed by the necessarily equivalent nonmoral sentence "7 is prime." Reducibility in *that* sense does not compromise moral realism. Thus Olson is not entitled to premise (P12) in arguing against my sort of moral realist, for whom moral facts need not entail irreducibly normative favoring relations.

In defence of (P12), Olson invokes what he calls "*the conceptual claim*": "that moral facts are or entail irreducibly normative reasons (and correspondingly that moral claims are or entail claims about irreducibly normative reasons)" (124). This suggests some sort of "conceptual connection" between "moral" and "irreducibly normative reasons." But, as just seen, there is no such connection.

Might Olson mean something else by "irreducibly"? Perhaps he understands "irreducibly normative" as something more like "normative in a way not relativized to ends" (131). On this reading, within the intensional framework, an irreducibly normative relation is a relation which *can* be expressed by a normative predicate in a way not relativized to ends, irrespective of whether it can also be expressed by a predicate of another kind. For brevity, we may substitute "relative" and "nonrelative" for "reducible" and "irreducible" in this sense. How does his argument fare when read in this alternative way?

The problem is now with premise (P13) rather than (P12). When Olson tries to explain why nonrelatively normative relations are objectionably "queer" in a way relatively normative relations are not (his examples are rules of grammar and etiquette), what he emphasizes is that the former are "metaphysically mysterious" while the latter are not (136). What is this appeal to metaphysics supposed to achieve? Presumably, if it means anything, it enjoins us to concentrate on the putative relation itself, and abstract from the words which express it. Thus, on the hypothesis that the predicates "torturing for fun" and "wrongly torturing for fun" are necessarily equivalent and so express the same relation, it should make no difference which predicate we start with, because by taking the metaphysical perspective we abstract away the difference. But that spells disaster for Olson, for if we start with the non-normative predicate we are not supposed to encounter metaphysical mystery. Within the intensional framework, what is nonrelatively normative about the relation is just that it can be expressed by a nonrelatively normative predicate; any mystery must involve the predicate, not just the relation. Thus, by moving the discussion into metaphysics, implicitly excluding semantics, Olson chooses to fight on ground where he is doomed to lose.

Stepping back from specific readings of "irreducibly" and the intensional framework, we can state a more general problem for Olson's argument: if there is a distinctively *metaphysical* mystery about irreducibly normative relations, it should depend in some way on the metaphysics of relations. At the very least, getting more specific and precise about the metaphysics of relations should provide Olson with a welcome opportunity to get more specific and precise about what the mystery is supposed to be. But although he insists "the issue here is at the bedrock metaphysical level" (136), he says nothing whatsoever at the bedrock metaphysical level about the nature of relations (or about the nature of reduction). Yet metaphysical theories of relations differ drastically from each other on several obviously relevant dimensions: they may be nominalist, conceptualist, Aristotelian-realist, or Platonist-realist; they may treat relations as sparse or plenitudinous, and as extensional, intensional, or hyperintensional. A metaphysical mystery about relations can hardly take the same form irrespective of those radical differences. But if the nature of all relations is left metaphysically mysterious, why be surprised that the nature of "irreducibly normative" relations in particular remains metaphysically mysterious? When we got more specific and precise about the metaphysics of relations, by fixing on the well-known, well-developed and simple intensional framework, it did not make the metaphysical mystery more specific and precise. Instead, it suggested that the alleged mystery is a mere artefact of confusion between two levels: the level of relations themselves and the level of the predicates by which we express them. The invocation of metaphysics is a bluff. In brief, Olson's master argument provides my sort of moral realist with no mystery to clear up, no case to answer.

3. Street's Evolutionary Argument against Realist Theories of Value

Unlike Olson, Sharon Street argues that realism about value is utterly implausible in light of evolutionary theory. She defines her target thus (110):[9]

> The defining claim of realism about value, as I will be understanding it, is that there are at least some evaluative facts or truths that hold independently of all our evaluative attitudes.

She adds in a footnote (156):

> More broadly, realism about value may be understood as the view that there are *mind-independent* evaluative facts or truths. I focus on independence from our *evaluative attitudes* because it is independence from this type of mental state that is the main point of contention between realists and antirealists about the value.

Full-blooded moral realism entails realism about value in Street's sense.

---

[9] All page references in this section are to Street 2006.

Some initial clarification of the phrase "mind-independent" will prove helpful. Consider a paradigm of a mind-independent truth, such as "$E = mc^2$." Obviously, we could come to use the numeral "2" to mean what we now mean by "3" (and *vice versa*). If we did so, keeping the other elements of the equation fixed in meaning, the formula would express something false. What we mean by the numeral "2" is in some sense a mind-dependent matter. Humans could in principle collectively choose to make that change, and succeed in doing so, even if no single one of us has that power. This sort of mind-dependence is uncontroversial, almost trivial, and irrelevant to the issue of realism about value, just as it does not make laws of physics mind-dependent in any interesting sense. The question is not how a given sentence could have expressed a false proposition, but how the proposition it now expresses could have been false.[10] Street's use of the phrase "facts or truths" in effect acknowledges this point.

Propositions correspond to states of affairs in the intensional framework, and facts to obtaining states of affairs. Street's talk in the quoted passages of "evaluative facts or truths" must be handled with care, for the same state may be expressed by both evaluative and nonevaluative sentences, as already seen. To make best sense of her text, we count a state of affairs as "evaluative" if and only if it *can* be expressed by an evaluative sentence.

Suppose that some evaluative sentence expresses the necessary state of affairs. Then the necessary state of affairs counts as evaluative: in Street's phrase, it is an evaluative fact or truth. But the necessary state of affairs holds "independently of all our evaluative attitudes," indeed independently of *all* our attitudes. After all, the necessary state of affairs is just the state of affairs of 7 being prime, and that state of affairs holds independently of all our attitudes. Thus an evaluative fact or truth holds independently of all our evaluative attitudes, which means that realism about value in Street's sense is true, contrary to her evolutionary argument.

But *does* any evaluative sentence express the necessary state of affairs? One candidate is an ordinary logical truth using evaluative terms, such as "All good actions are good actions." That seems a rather cheap way of establishing realism about value.

We could rule out such examples by stipulating that a sentence counts as evaluative if and only if it is logically equivalent to no sentence containing only nonevaluative terms, for "All good actions are good actions" is logically equivalent to "All whales are whales." But that stipulation does not deal with sentences such as "Either all whales are mammals or torture is wrong," which states a necessary truth because its first disjunct does; the disjunction counts as evaluative because it is *logically* equivalent to no sentence containing only nonevaluative terms.

We could rule out such disjunctive examples by stipulating that a sentence counts as evaluative if and only if it is *necessarily* equivalent to no sentence containing only nonevaluative terms, for "Either all whales are mammals or torture is wrong" is necessarily equivalent to "All whales are mammals." But that stipulation implies that if

---

[10] For these purposes, linguistic expressions are assumed to be individuated nonsemantically.

torturing for fun is necessarily wrong, then "Torturing for fun is wrong" is not evaluative, because it is necessarily equivalent to "All whales are whales" (since both are necessary). But that is cheating against realism about value. If it is a necessary fact that torturing for fun is wrong, that fact is a perfectly good verifier for realism about value.

The problem here is not with Street's understanding of "realism" in terms of mind-independent truth, but with how she demarcates the "evaluative" as the target of her antirealism. She faces a tricky challenge within the intensional framework: to define which facts or truths are "evaluative" without either giving realism about value an easy victory or cheating against it. Evolutionary theory provides no obvious help in meeting that challenge.

As with Olson, someone might object that Street is not obliged to accept the intensional framework. Again, that is true, but it misses the dialectical point. For the question is not whether *Street* accepts the intensional framework but whether her opponent, the realist about value, does. If Street wants to make trouble for a realist about value who accepts the intensional framework, she had better tailor her argument against such realism to that opponent's background logic and semantics, unless she hopes to refute the intensional framework itself—a severe challenge for which nothing in her text offers resources or preparation. We may therefore continue to test Street's argument within the intensional framework.

At one point in her paper, Street addresses a related challenge. She considers a "rigidifying" move discussed by Stephen Darwall, Allan Gibbard, and Peter Railton (1992). The proposal is that the evaluative attitudes of a community determine which natural properties or relations its evaluative terms designate; they could have designated other properties or relations, had the community's evaluative attitudes been different. However, the evaluative terms are rigid designators, so as used in a given context they designate the natural properties or relations determined by the evaluative attitudes prevalent in that context even with respect to counterfactual circumstances of evaluation. For example, suppose that in our context C, evaluative attitudes E prevail and make the word "good" designate the natural property N, whereas in another context C*, different evaluative attitudes E* prevail and make the word "good" designate the different natural property N*. Since "good" is a rigid designator, the sentence "good = N" expresses a necessarily true proposition as uttered in our context C but a necessarily false proposition as uttered in C*, while the sentence "good = N*"' expresses a necessarily false proposition as uttered in C but a necessarily true proposition as uttered in C* (let "N," "N*," "E," and "E*" all stand for context-insensitive rigid designators). Thus speakers in C can truly say "Even if attitudes E* prevailed, N would still be the good," while speakers in C* can truly say "Even if attitudes E prevailed, N* would still be the good."

Here is Street's response to the rigidifying move (138, with "N*" in place of her "M"):

> Such a view is not genuinely realist in my taxonomy, however, for on such a view, there is no robust sense in which other creatures (including other possible versions of ourselves) would be making a *mistake* or *missing anything* if their evaluative attitudes tracked natural facts N*, say, instead of natural facts N. [. . .] when we say "The good

is identical to N" and they say "The good is identical to N*," we will not be *disagreeing* with each other, with one of us correct and the other incorrect about which natural facts the good is identical to, but rather simply talking past each other

Again (138–9):

there is, on such a view, no standard independent of all of our and their evaluative attitudes determining whose sense of the word "good" is right or better; neither of us can properly accuse the other of having made a mistake.

Most of what Street says in these passages about the upshot of the rigidifying move is correct, though she goes somewhat beyond what it strictly commits its proponents to. For instance, it does not require N and N* to be *equally* natural or joint-carving; they only need to be natural or joint-carving *enough* to be picked out by the evaluative attitudes prevailing in the respective contexts. The two groups may still disagree over whose distinction is the more natural or joint-carving. However, Street is right that the rigidifying move is *consistent* with the more complete symmetry she imagines.

A more pressing question: how is the lack of disagreement in Street's scenario supposed to show that the two groups are not both expressing mind-independent evaluative truths? For Street defined realism about value at the beginning of her article; presumably, she does not mean to be moving the goalposts midway through. A more charitable interpretation is that she takes herself to be refining her explanation of the relevant sort of mind-independence, by setting a standard which the rigidifying move fails to meet.

The trouble is that the higher standard for mind-independence which Street seems to be setting involves going back on the distinction rehearsed at the start of this section between harmless mind-dependence in whether a sentence expresses a true proposition and harmful mind-dependence in whether the proposition it now expresses is true—a contrast which is really just an instance of the good old use-mention distinction. If we lose sight of that distinction, we risk classifying even "$E = mc^2$" as a mind-dependent truth. For Street's complaint is that although "good = N" expresses a necessarily true proposition in C, it expresses a (necessarily) false proposition in C*.

To reinforce the point, recall some of the cases in the literature for which the rigidifying move was first introduced, involving natural kind terms. Suppose that on Earth the word "water" is used as a rigid designator for the transparent, colorless, tasteless liquid prevalent on Earth, which happens to be H_2O, while on Twin-Earth the word "water" is used as a rigid designator for the transparent, colourless, tasteless liquid prevalent on Twin-Earth, which happens to be XYZ, with a completely different chemical structure from H_2O. Thus the sentence "water = H_2O" expresses a necessarily true proposition as uttered on Earth but a necessarily false proposition as uttered on Twin-Earth, while the sentence "water = XYZ" expresses a necessarily false proposition as uttered on Earth but a necessarily true proposition as uttered on Twin-Earth. All of Street's complaints apply, with respect to variation in the environment rather than variation in evaluative attitudes:

On such a view, there is no robust sense in which other creatures (including other possible versions of ourselves) would be making a *mistake* or *missing anything* if they were on Twin-Earth instead of Earth. When we say "Water is identical to H$_2$O" and they say "Water is identical to XYZ," we will not be *disagreeing* with each other, with one of us correct and the other incorrect about which natural kind water is identical to, but rather simply talking past each other. There is, on such a view, no standard independent of our and their environments determining whose sense of the word "water" is right or better; neither of us can properly accuse the other of having made a mistake.

None of this undermines a fully realist view of "water = H$_2$O" as uttered on Earth or Twin-Earth. The fact which we use it to state on Earth is not itself environment-dependent in the relevant sense; its obtaining is not somehow limited to planets like Earth. The same goes for the fact which Twin-Earthers use "water = XYZ" to state on Twin-Earth. Indeed, on the intensional view, it is the very same fact as the one stated in C, the necessary state of affairs.

For structurally parallel reasons, none of Street's points about the lack of disagreement and the rest undermines a fully realist view of "good = N" as uttered in our context C. The fact which we use it to state in C is not itself mind-dependent in the relevant sense; its obtaining is not somehow limited to contexts like C. The same goes for the fact which others use "good = N*" to state in C*. Indeed, on the intensional view, it is the very same fact as the one stated in C, the necessary state of affairs.

One might still worry that there is something *parochial* about the envisaged use of "good" in a fully fledged version of Street's scenario. In our context C, we use "good" to designate the property N; N plays a major role in our lives. But N is of no interest to creatures in C*; it plays no role in their lives. Conversely, in their context C*, they use "good" to designate the property N*; N* plays a major role in their lives. But N* is of no interest to us; it plays no role in our lives. In both C and C*, "good" designates something of merely local interest.

Equally, there is something parochial about the use of "water" in a fully fledged version of the Twin-Earth scenario. On Earth, we use "water" to designate H$_2$O; H$_2$O plays a major role in our lives. But H$_2$O is of no interest to Twin-Earthers; it plays no role in their lives. Conversely, on Twin-Earth, they use "water" to designate XYZ; XYZ plays a major role in their lives. But XYZ is of no interest to us; it plays no role in our lives. On both Earth and Twin-Earth, "water" designates something of merely local interest.

One contrast between "good" and "water" is that creatures with no use for an analogue of "water" seem more easily possible than creatures with no use for an analogue of "good." In that respect, the word "human" is closer than "water" to "good," since creatures of any kind will have a use for a term designating the kind to which they themselves belong. The human species is of merely parochial interest too. Even if we are the only moral agents on our own planet, that is an accident of evolution, and for all we know many other species of moral agent are scattered over the universe on other planets.

Parochialism does not entail relativism. "Water = H_2O" is absolutely true as uttered by Earthers and absolutely false as uttered by Twin-Earthers; "water = XYZ" is absolutely true as uttered by Twin-Earthers and absolutely false as uttered by Earthers. Similarly, "good = N" is absolutely true as uttered in context C and absolutely false as uttered in C*; "good = N*" is absolutely true as uttered in C* and absolutely false as uttered in C. There is no room here for that will-o'-the-wisp, faultless disagreement. There is simply no disagreement between the two communities, at least on these points: just an illusion of disagreement for the unwary.

As officially defined by Street, realism about value imposes no ban on parochialism. It says simply that "there are at least some evaluative facts or truths that hold independently of all our evaluative attitudes." She explains the phrase "evaluative facts or truths" thus (110):

> *Evaluative facts or truths* I understand as facts or truths of the form that X is a normative reason to Y, that one should or ought to X, that X is good, valuable, or worthwhile, that X is morally right or wrong, and so on.

This liberal account says nothing to exclude parochial categories of evaluation. Thus, if we standardly use "good" or any other evaluative term to designate a property of merely parochial interest, but some evaluative facts or truths about that property hold independently of all our evaluative attitudes in the relevant sense, then realism about value is still vindicated. Given how Street has set up the issues, she is wrong to dismiss the rigidifying account as not genuinely realist in her defined sense.

Of course, many metaethicists will deny that "good" and "bad," "right" and "wrong," and other central members of our evaluative lexicon *are* parochial. On their view, if such terms play the same general regulative role in the lives of other creatures as they play in ours, then the terms designate the same properties and relations in their mouths as they do in ours. Thus if we apply "good" to X while the others deny "good" of X, the disagreement is genuine. In that way, morality is supposed to be *universal*: supposedly, all responsible agents take an implicit interest in central moral properties and relations, however much they disagree about their extensions. Alternatively, some metaethicists may just take the *aspiration* to universality to be so deeply built into morality that, if it fails, moral terms simply fail to designate, rather than designating something parochial. On such grounds, some may deny that, on the Darwall-Gibbard-Railton scenario, "good" functions as a strictly *moral* term in contexts C and C*, given the lack of universality.[11] But not all evaluative terms are moral terms; terms of aesthetic evaluation are

---

[11] See Horgan and Timmons 1991 and the ensuing debate. The putative failure of universality cannot be understood as a failure of supervenience because (i) the contexts C and C* differ as supervenience bases (just as Earth and Twin-Earth do) and (ii) "good" in C and "good" in C* may each satisfy reasonable supervenience constraints on evaluative terms. The complaint that the difference between C and C* does not justify the difference in evaluative attention is downstream from the demand for universality.

not. The parochialism of "good" in those contexts need not prevent it from functioning there as a nonmorally evaluative term. Are Street's evolutionary considerations more relevant to specifically moral realism than they are to general evaluative realism?

The proto-evaluative attitudes which Street emphasizes in nonhuman animals are not all proto-moral. When a leopard is chasing down an impala, the leopard takes a positive evaluative attitude to the state of affairs of the leopard catching the impala, while the impala takes a negative attitude to the same state of affairs, but their evaluative attitudes do not seem proto-moral. There is no aspiration or claim to universality. Things may not be so different when a human hunter is chasing down a prey, for food. Of course, the human hunter *might* judge that the morally best outcome would be for him to catch the prey, but that seems like a rather pompous and pretentious rationalization of something more primitive—perhaps he moonlights as a moral philosopher.

Consider a hunting case in more detail. Let CATCH be the state of affairs of the predator catching the prey. The predator and prey take positive and negative evaluative attitudes respectively to CATCH. Without too much of a stretch, we can interpret the predator and prey as making evaluative *judgments* about CATCH, which may figure in their practical reasoning.[12] To put their judgments into words, the predator judges "CATCH is good" and the prey judges "CATCH is bad." But although the predator and prey have blatantly conflicting interests, they are not exactly *disagreeing*, faultlessly or otherwise. Neither is *mistaken*, or views the other as mistaken. Both judgments are clearly correct. CATCH has both the property the predator is attributing to it and the property the prey is attributing to it; the two properties are compatible. Thus, when we use "good" and "bad" to articulate their evaluative attitudes, we do not attribute universality, or even the aspiration to it. We are content to use the words parochially: although "good" and "bad" designate mutually incompatible properties as both put into the predator's mouth, and mutually incompatible properties as both put into the prey's mouth, the property "good" designates as put into the predator's mouth is compatible with the property "bad" designates as put into the prey's mouth, and the property "bad" designates as put into the predator's mouth is compatible with the property "good" designates as put into the prey's mouth. These properties are all parochial, of merely local interest.

That a property is parochial does not mean that it is mind-dependent. More plausibly, those in CATCH concern the animal's needs and well-being. Which things will nourish an animal and which will poison it are mind-independent matters. Nor are the properties "relative" in any useful sense. They are just ordinary properties which some things have and others lack. Evaluative realism in Street's sense holds for such parochial properties.

---

[12] Taking a propositional attitude does not imply the ability to articulate it in words. Good explanations of the behavior of nonhuman animals often attribute to them propositional knowledge of the present state of their environment and preferences as to its future state. The coarse-grained nature of the intensional framework facilitates such ascriptions.

The case does not change radically when we consider a pack of predators hunting a herd of prey. Within each group, there are social relations and social attitudes, with some shared expectation that individual interests will be subordinated to those of the group, social rewards for conforming and sanctions for not doing so, and thus perhaps some sort of proto-morality. Nevertheless, if CATCH+ is the state of affairs of the predators catching some of the prey, we have in effect the predators judging "CATCH+ is good" and the prey judging "CATCH+ is bad," where neither group is mistaken; both judgments are clearly correct. Thus both judgments are still parochial, although at the social rather than individual level. In these circumstances, what is good for the predators is bad for the prey, and what is bad for the predators is good for the prey. All these properties are parochial too: they are of merely local interest. Typically, they are also mind-independent.

Even when we consider conflict between two human groups, the case may still not be altogether different. Each group may be content to evaluate potential outcomes as "good" or "bad" in a parochial way. For example, in a battle, each side evaluates victory as "good" and defeat as "bad." They are fully aware that what they judge "good" is what the other side judges "bad," and *vice versa*. But that need not make them see each other as *mistaken*. They may simply see the others as *other* and *the enemy*. Of course, there is also a human tendency to moralize conflict, to see the other side as evil and mistaken, in moral, religious, or legal error. Such an attitude may have motivational advantages. But it is not needed for conflict when there is competition for scarce resources. Each side may see the conflict as symmetrical: it's them or us.

All this is compatible with the propriety by universalist standards of universalist evaluation, in cases of human conflict and elsewhere: judgments in moral terms about properties or relations in which all responsible agents should take an interest. Perhaps, in universalist mode, we can make judgments about such properties or relations, even if those judgments are still distorted by parochial bias—just as our judgments about physical laws may be distorted by parochial features of our species' cognitive equipment. The point is just that we should not assume that all evaluation is universalist, even when universalist evaluation seems quite natural.

If the universalist aspiration is essential to morality, then moral evaluation may play a smaller role in human life than many philosophers, especially moral philosophers and metaethicists, assume. We are often content to make our decisions on parochial grounds. The aspiration to complete universality may be a product of reflective proto-theorizing rather than a normal component of human decision-making. Such a process of reflection may be compared, doubtless more in aspiration than in achievement, to the process of trying to strip out the more parochial aspects from our picture of physical matters in order to get at something more scientific, most notably with universal laws of physics. Similarly, many moral theorists try to strip out from our picture of normative matters the more parochial aspects, favoring oneself, or one's family and friends, or one's own race or nation, or one's own species. In both cases, the starting-point involves various forms of bias and limitation, but that does not mean that it is incapable of self-improvement. With science, that process has gone much further than we had any right to expect. How far it can go with morality is an open question, but generic evolutionary considerations impose no particular upper bound.

In brief, Street's evolutionary argument fails for broadly logical reasons against realist theories of parochial value. But, once a realist theory of parochial value is in place, her argument also fails to block the move from it to a realist theory of nonparochial value, through forms of reflective antiparochial theorizing which have been successful in other cases.

4. Conclusion

Facts, truths, propositions, states of affairs, properties, relations: all are freely and frequently invoked in contemporary metaethics. But one is rarely told what theory of them, if any, is being assumed in the background. Perhaps the assumption is that the choice of background logicosemantic theory makes no relevant difference. That assumption is not obviously correct. Once the intensional theory is made systematically explicit, the problems with some of the most influential recent work in the area stand out clearly. Both Olson's argument for an error theory of irreducible normativity and Street's argument against realist theories of value turn out to fail. Thus, *if* the choice of background logicosemantic theory makes no relevant difference, those arguments fail under every such choice. Of course, Olson and Street may accept that the background logicosemantic theory is relevant, and prefer another. Then they should tell us which it is and how it makes a crucial difference to their arguments. But that would not take them very far, since proponents of moral and evaluative realism can still adopt intensionalism, leaving Olson and Street with the task of either finding arguments that work within that framework or refuting the framework itself.

One test of a philosophical idea is whether it looks better or worse once formulated in a precise, systematic logical and semantic framework. Moral, evaluative, and normative realism pass that test.[13]

References

Darwall, Stephen, Allan Gibbard, and Peter Railton. 1992. "Toward *fin de siècle* Ethics: Some Trends." *Philosophical Review* 101: 115–189.
Horgan, Terence, and Mark Timmons. 1991 "New Wave Moral Realism Meets Moral Twin Earth." *Journal of Philosophical Research* 16: 447–465.

---

[13] This chapter has benefited from detailed comments by Jonas Olson, Paul Bloomfield, David Copp, Farbod Akhlaghi, and Daniel Kodsi on earlier drafts, and from discussion when I presented the material at Yale.

Kamp, Hans. 2013. "Two Theories about Adjectives." In his *Meaning and the Dynamics of Interpretation*, 225–261. Leiden: Brill.

Kaplan, David. 1989. "Demonstratives: An Essay on the Semantics, Logic, Metaphysics, And Epistemology of Demonstratives and Other Indexicals." In *Themes from Kaplan*, edited by Joseph Almog, John Perry, and Howard Wettstein, 481–564. New York: Oxford University Press.

Kratzer, Angelika. 2012. *Modals and Conditionals*. Oxford: Oxford University Press.

McNally, Louise, and Chris Kennedy, eds.. 2008: *Adjectives and Adverbs: Syntax, Semantics and Discourse*. Oxford: Oxford University Press.

Olson, Jonas. 2014. *Moral Error Theory: History, Critique, Defence*. Oxford: Oxford University Press.

Portner, Paul. 2009. *Modality*. Oxford: Oxford University Press.

Shapiro, Stewart. 1991. *Foundations without Foundationalism: A Case for Second-Order Logic*. Oxford: Oxford University Press.

Street, Sharon. 2006. "A Darwinian Dilemma for Realist Theories of Value." *Philosophical Studies* 127: 109–166.

Williamson, Timothy. 2000. *Knowledge and Its Limits*. Oxford: Oxford University Press.

Williamson, Timothy. 2001. "Ethics, Supervenience and Ramsey Sentences." *Philosophy and Phenomenological Research* 62: 625–630.

Williamson, Timothy. 2013. *Modal Logic as Metaphysics*. Oxford: Oxford University Press.

Williamson, Timothy. 2018. "Gibbard on Meaning and Normativity." *Inquiry* 61: 731–741.

Williamson, Timothy. 2019. "Morally Loaded Cases in Philosophy." *Proceedings and Addresses of the American Philosophical Association* 93: 159–172.

Williamson, Timothy. 2020a. *Suppose and Tell: The Semantics and Heuristics of Conditionals*. Oxford: Oxford University Press.

Williamson, Timothy. 2020b. "Non-Modal Normativity and Norms of Belief." *Acta Philosophica Fennica* 96: 101–125.

Williamson, Timothy. 2021. "Epistemological Consequences of Frege Puzzles." *Philosophical Topics* 49: 287–319.

Williamson, Timothy. 2022. "'Metametaphysics and Semantics." *Metaphilosophy* 53: 162-175.

Williamson, Timothy. Forthcoming. "Justifications, Excuses, and Skeptical Scenarios." In *The New Evil Demon*, edited by Julien Dutant and Fabien Dorsch. Oxford: Oxford University Press.

Index

Aeschylus, 276
agency, 99–101
Alexander, S., 256–57
Andreou, Chrisoula, 280
Anscombe, G.E.M., 267, 399
Aquinas, Thomas, 143, 193, 276
argument from queerness, 60, 404–5, 562–67
Aristotle, 142–43, 154, 193, 264, 275–77, 283, 293–94, 306, 320, 380, 405, 426, 468, 479
Armstrong, David, 177
attitude, 51
Austin, J.L., 183
Ayer, A.J., 14, 68, 166, 197, 529

Bader, Ralph, 123
Baltes, Paul, 278
Baras, Dan, 365
Beatty, John, 265
Bedke, Matt, 452, 454, 456
belief:
    expression of, xvi, 84–5
    moral, xvi, 80
    nature of, 226
Benacerraf, Paul, 213, 350–51
Bentham, Jeremy, 4, 51–3, 193
Berkeley, George, 157, 173, 522
Berker, Selim, 237
Blackburn, Simon, xv, xviii, 14, 158, 180, 197, 202, 402–3, 466, 475, 511–13, 516, 528–33, 537, 545
blame, 88
Bloomfield, Paul, 270
Boyd, Richard, 73, 75, 196–97, 199, 211, 264
Bradley, F.H., 156–57, 170
Brandom, Robert, 182, 532

Burge, Tyler, 270, 273
Butler, Joseph, 193

Carey, Susan, 213
Carnap, Rudolf, 249, 490, 537–38
Carroll, Lewis, 212
Chalmers, David, 32–3, 195
Charlow, Nate, 14
Chomsky, Noam, 214–15
Churchland, Paul, 159, 161
Clarke, Samuel, 391
cognitivism, 14–15, 66, 85, 199, 260–61, 347, 405
coherentism, 73–4
common ground, 5–6, 8, 12
concept, 46, 226
constitutivism, 99–103
Cooper, Anthony Ashley. See Shaftesbury, third Earl of
Copp, David, 216, 280, 283–85
Cornell realism, 177, 199, 212, 216, 430
courage, 276, 309
Cowie, Christopher, 545

Dahaene, Stanislas, 213
Dancy, Jonathan, 193, 201–2, 204, 208
Darwall, Stephen, 569, 572
Darwin, Charles, 145, 273
Dasgupta, Shamik, 436, 447–51, 460
Davidson, Donald, 149
Dawkins, Richard, 267
de Finetti, Bruno, 178
deflationism about truth. See minimalism about truth
Demosthenes, 276
Descartes, René, 160, 522
Dewey, John, 184–85, 193
disagreement, xii, 3, 6, 409–10, 421, 498–99

divine command theory, xvii, 5, 324, 447–49
Douglass, Frederick, 282–83
Dreier, Jamie, 179–80, 436, 444–47, 450–51, 460, 469
dualism, 195
Dworkin, Ronald, 76, 140, 179, 186, 188, 508, 519–20, 528–29, 531–32, 534

Eibl-Eibesfeldt, Irenäus, 282
Eklund, Matti, 225, 417
emotivism, 13–14, 493
Enoch, David, xiii–xiv, xvi–xviii, 7–8, 10, 117–18, 193, 201, 204–8, 239–40, 270, 280, 352, 360, 517–23, 534, 545
Epicurus, 275
Erdur, Melis, 452
error theory, 85, 179, 234, 347, 562–67
essence, 36–7, 40, 121–25, 226, 319–20, 323–24
eudaimonia, 265, 273–75, 300–301, 479
evil, 93
evolutionary debunking argument, 355–57, 409, 567–75
explanation, 363–67, 371–73, 377–83
expressivism, xv, 176, 187–88, 402, 511–13

fact:
  in general, 222
  mathematical, 370–71
  moral, xi, xiii–xiv, xvii, 6, 22, 77, 222
  natural, xvii, 37, 67, 211
Falk, W.D., 391
Feldman, Richard, 75
Field, Hartry, 169, 342, 363
Fine, Kit, 123–24
Finlay, Stephen, 10–11
Firth, Roderick, xvii
fit, 425–27
fitness, 265, 271–73
Fitzpatrick, William, 193, 201–2, 204–5, 207–8, 454
flourishing. *See* eudaimonia
Fodor, Jerry, 195, 481
Foot, Philippa, 207, 267–68, 272–73, 280, 285, 299, 302
foundationalism, 74–5
Fraser, Ben, 264
Frege, Gottlob, 178

Frege-Geach problem, 182–83, 556
function, 199, 265, 269, 271, 273–74, 305–6, 427
fundamentality, 25–6

Galilei, Galileo, 144
garbage in, garbage out objection, 77–8
Garner, Richard, 160–62
Gelman, Rochel, 213
Gettier, Edmund, 350, 500
Gibbard, Allan, 14, 197, 402, 410, 430, 532, 537, 569, 572
Goldman, Alvin, 350
Goodman, Nelson, 72
Graham, Peter J., 270
Greco, John, 270
grounding, 36–8

Habermas, Jurgen, 181
Halliday, Michael, 539, 542–43
happiness, 295–301
Hare, R.M., 14, 197, 390–91, 403
Harman, Gilbert, 70–2, 90–3, 98, 103, 160, 280, 357–60, 367
Hart, H.L.A., 514
Hayward, Max, 452, 454–55, 458
Hegel, G.W.F., 160
Hellman, Geoffrey, 213
Hempel, Carl, 194
Hobbes, Thomas, 193, 541
Horgan, Terry, 280
Hrdy, Sarah, 280–81
Hubin, Donald, 229
Hume, David, 124, 176, 181–82, 193, 212, 270, 280, 294, 397–98, 466, 471
Hursthouse, Rosalind, 267, 280
Hutcheson, Francis, 193

instrumental value, 308
intuitionism, 68
irreducible metafacts objection, 202, 208–10
Irwin, Terrence, 276

Jackson, Frank, 125
James, William, 173
Jefferson, Thomas, 283–84
Johnston, Mark, 45–8, 52, 474
Jones, Karen, 86

Joyce, Richard, 161, 167–68, 187–88, 197, 541
judgment:
    considered, 77, 80
    moral, xi, 90, 93
just too different objection, xi, 39, 106, 117–20, 126, 138, 203–8, 270
justice, 277, 280–81, 285

Kalderon, Mark Eli, 168–69
Kant, Immanuel, 293–300, 311, 389, 468, 478, 540
King, Jeff, 237
Korsgaard, Christine, xiii, 391, 403, 448, 468, 473 74, 478, 480
Kramer, Matthew, 532, 545–46
Kripke, Saul, 196

Leary, Stephanie, 120–22
Leavis, F.R., 176
Lenman, James, 471–72
Levine, Joseph, 195
Lewis, David, 5, 147, 205, 249, 471–72, 490, 545
Lewy, Casimir, 176–77
Locke, John, 254
Lutz, Matt, 354–55, 358
Lycan, William, 159
Lynch, Michael, 166

Macarthur, David, 526–27, 536
Machiavelli, Niccolò, 285
MacIntyre, Alastair, 270
Mackie, J.L., 9–10, 60–2, 67, 70–1, 85, 158, 160–61, 180, 187–88, 197, 261–62, 341, 387, 391, 404, 416, 430, 435, 441, 494, 509, 521, 562
Martin, C.B., 177
mathematical structuralism, 213–14
McDowell, John, 474
McNaughton, David, 193, 201–2, 204, 208
McPherson, Tristram, 109, 116, 127, 135, 141, 162–64, 201, 207–8, 527, 530, 534, 545
McTaggart, J.M.E., 156–59, 170
Mikhail, John, 214–16
Milikan, Ruth, 150, 270
Mill, John Stuart, 67–8, 193, 294
Miller, Christian, 275
Millgram, Elijah, 280, 282, 285

Mills, Susan, 265
mind-dependence, xvi, 66, 84
mind-independence, xvi, 84, 174, 347
minimalism about truth, 178–79, 495, 530
Moore, G.E., 26–7, 67–8, 76, 109, 113, 124, 139, 156–64, 168, 170, 173–77, 183, 209, 264, 266, 280, 293, 389, 523–24, 529
moral concept, 61–4
moral epistemological antiexceptionalism, 81
moral error, xii–xiii
moral language:
    evolution of, 257–60
    purpose of, xv, 248, 256–60, 497, 538–42, 549
    semantics of, xv–xvi, 10, 246, 248, 250–56, 348
moral realism:
    ardent, 415–19, 424–28
    basic form of, xiv–xvi, 46, 197, 465, 502–3
    mind-independent, xvi, 79
    as a moral doctrine, 506–7, 517–24
    relaxed, 533–36
    robust, 346–49, 465, 517–24
moral Twin Earth, 280, 419, 570–72
morality:
    as action guiding, 50–1
    as categorical, 227–28, 414
    contrasted with prudence, 295–96
    in the narrow sense, 98–99
    not subject to negotiation, xiii, 91
    taken seriously, xiii, xiv
motivation, de dicto and de re, 440–44
motivational internalism, 50, 224–25
Murdoch, Iris, 181

Nagel, Thomas 4, 391
natural kind, 196
naturalism
    analytical, 392–95
    in general, 26–33, 37, 85, 94, 194–97, 220–21, 392–94
    nonanalytical, 396–401
    non-reductive, 115
    reductive, 31, 34, 40, 114–15, 136–37, 146–48, 150–51, 194–96, 237–38, 250, 266, 383–85
neo-pragmatism. See pragmatism
Neurath, Otto, 497, 531

Nietzsche, Friedrich, 180, 182, 193, 285, 410
noncognitivism, 14–15, 68–9, 378, 401–3
non-naturalism, 38–40, 85, 138–39, 238, 348
normativity, 223–29, 394
normativity objection, 200–01, 220–23, 230, 235–36, 239–40, 399
Nowell-Smith, P.H., 391, 447–48, 451
Nussbaum, Martha, 275, 278

objectivity, 44, 47, 49, 52–3, 66, 416–17, 506–7
Occam's razor, 495–96
Ogden, C.K., 14
Olson, Jonas, 164–65, 495–96, 509, 554–55, 562–67, 569, 575
O'Neill, Onora, 473
open question argument, 68–9, 174–5, 183, 195
Oppenheim, Paul, 194

Parfit, Derek, 4, 186, 188, 193, 201, 203–8, 229, 235, 387–410, 528–29, 532–33
parity thesis, xi–xii
Pascal, Blaise, 500
Peacocke, Christopher, 212
Perl, Caleb, 10
Pettit, Phillip, 125
physicalism, 32–3
Pigden, Charles, 509
Pindar, 276
Plantinga, Alvin, 270
Plato, 141–43, 175, 177, 264, 275–76, 280, 285, 293–94, 466, 469
Plutarch, 277
Pollyanna objection, 280–83
Popper, Karl, 271
pragmatism, 181, 183, 185, 536–38
predicate, 47
Price, Huw, 181, 184–86, 532, 537–39
Price, Richard, 323
Prichard, H.A., 293–94, 307, 309
Priest, Graham, 342
Prior, A.N., 270–71
property:
　commonality view, xv
　definition of, 46
　elite, 108, 118
　identity of, 113

　mental 32–3, 147, 149
　moral, xi, xv, 6–7, 22, 24, 28, 132–33, 222–23
　natural, 28–30, 34, 134–36, 431
　neutral, 109–10
　nominalism about, 8, 23
　physical, 22
　social, 147
Putnam, Hilary, 194–96, 213, 251

quasi-realism, xv, 178, 180, 403, 529
quietism, 507–22, 526–50
Quine, W.V.O., 178, 194–96, 266, 497

Railton, Peter 111, 199, 302–5, 391, 410, 569, 572
Ramsey, Frank, 176, 178, 181, 183, 186, 249, 490
Rawling, Piers, 193, 201–2, 204, 208
Rawls, John, 71–2, 79–80, 214, 297, 468
Rea, Michael, 6, 9–10
realism. See moral realism
reason:
　distinguishing types of, 392
　Humean view of, 90–92, 94–5
　as relational fact, 95–6, 133, 225–26, 238–40
reasons fundamentalism, 225, 238–39
Reck, Erich, 213
reduction. See reductive naturalism
reflective equilibrium, 67, 69, 71–3, 76–8
Resnick, Michael, 213
response dependence, 45–9, 469–475
Richards, I.A., 14
Ridge, Michael, 14, 534–35
Rorty, Richard, 184–85, 532
Rosati, Connie, 209
Rosen, Gideon, 45, 47–50, 52–4, 57, 123–25, 237, 480
Ross, W.D., 293–94, 374, 380
Russell, Bertrand, 490
Russell, Luke, 93
Ryle, Gilbert, 176, 181, 537–39, 543

Sainsbury, R.M., 167
Sayre-McCord, Geoffrey, xiv, 84–6, 91, 103, 198, 360, 467
Scanlon, Thomas, 71–2, 81, 95–9, 102–3, 119, 239, 389, 518–19, 528–29, 532–33, 535, 545
Scheffler, Samuel, 391

Schiemer, Georg, 213
Schroeder, Mark, 10
Schroeter, François, 7, 10–11, 86
Schroeter, Laura, 7, 10–11
scientism, 193
Scriven, Michael, 271
Searle, John, 398
Sellars, Wilfrid, 181–83
semantics, xv–xvi, 11, 132, 183–86, 487–88, 513–16, 556–62
sentiment, 59
sentimentalism, 176, 402
Shafer-Landau, Russ, 111, 467, 508
Shaftesbury, third Earl of, 193
Shapiro, Stewart, 213
Sidgwick, Henry, 389–90, 407, 409
Sinhababu, Neil, 115
skepticism, 66, 498–501, 522–24
Smith, Adam, 193
Smith, Michael, xvii, xviii, 72, 111, 440, 442–43, 467
Smullyan, Raymond, 169
Sobel, David, 280, 283–85
Sober, Elliott, 271
Socrates, 275–76, 285–86, 294, 469
Sosa, Ernest, 270, 353
Spencer, Herbert, 264
Spinoza, Baruch, 134
Stalnaker, Robert, 5
Staudinger, Ursala, 278
Sterelny, Kim, 264
Sternberg, Robert, 278
Stevenson, C.L., 14, 69, 197
Street, Sharon, 165, 187–88, 280, 338, 430, 467, 472, 476–77, 480, 554–55, 567–75
structuralism. *See* mathematical structuralism
Sturgeon, Nicholas, 73, 75, 80, 108, 119, 138, 199

subjectivism, xvi–xvii, 198, 402, 476
supervenience, 249–250
Swanton, Christine, 276

teleology, 142, 150, 267
temperance, 276–77, 309
Thompson, Michael, 267, 280
Thomson, Judith Jarvis, 99, 103
Tiberius, Valerie, 473–74
Tiffany, Evan, 229
Timmons, Mark, 280, 546
the trolley problem, 215–16
truth:
    conceptual, 327–32
    in general, xiv–xv, 11, 14–15, 20–1
truthmaker, 20–1, 34
Twin Earth. *See* moral Twin Earth

utilitarianism, 247–48

virtue, 275–79, 298–301

Warren, Jared, 361–62
Watson, Gary, 280, 285
Wedgwood, Ralph, 31, 514–16
Williams, Bernard, 145, 188, 293, 305–6, 311, 388, 391, 394–95
Williams, Michael, 183
Williamson, Timothy, xviii
wisdom, 277–78
Wittgenstein, Ludwig, 178, 181, 183–85, 484, 486–87, 490, 492, 494–97, 502

Xenophon, 276

Yablo, Stephen, 169

Zeno of Citium, 277
Zhong, Lei, 373–75, 379